Age of Gold

H. W. Brands is the author of *The First American: The Life and Times of Benjamin Franklin*, a *New York Times* bestseller short-listed for the Pulitzer Prize and the *Los Angeles Times* Book Award. He is the Dickson, Allen, Anderson Centennial Professor at the University of Texas.

Also by H. W. Brands

The First American
T.R.
The Reckless Decade

H. W. BRANDS

THE AGE OF GOLD

arrow books

Published by Arrow Books, 2006

1 3 5 7 9 10 8 6 4 2

First published in the United Kingdom by William Heinemann, 2005

Arrow Books
The Random House Group Limited
20 Vauxhall Bridge Road, London SW1V 2SA

Random House Australia (Pty) Limited
20 Alfred Street, Milsons Point, Sydney
New South Wales 2061, Australia

Random House New Zealand Limited
18 Poland Road, Glenfield
Auckland 10, New Zealand

Random House (Pty) Limited
Isle of Houghton, Corner of Boundary Road & Carse O'Gowrie,
Houghton 2198, South Africa

The Random House Group Limited Reg. No. 954009

www.randomhouse.co.uk

A CIP catalogue record for this book
is available from the British Library

Papers used by Random House
are natural, recyclable products made from wood grown in sustainable forests. The manufacturing processes conform to the environmental regulations of the country of origin

ISBN 0 09 947656 8

Printed and bound in Great Britain by
Cox & Wyman Ltd, Reading, Berkshire

Contents

THE AGE OF GOLD

Prologue

The Baron and the Carpenter

(Coloma: January 1848)

In the wilderness a man made do. Given any choice in the matter, James Marshall wouldn't have retained Jennie Wimmer as cook and housekeeper for his construction gang. She was stubborn, surly, belligerently unimaginative in the kitchen—and fully aware she couldn't be replaced. She cooked what she wanted, when she wanted. She served the best portions to her husband, Peter, and their seven children. The hired hands, who bunked in the opposite end of the double log cabin that sheltered the Wimmers, were left with the toughest beef, the stringiest mutton, the stalest peas, the driest biscuits, and without the pumpkin and apple pies that varied, ever so slightly, the monotonous diet. Meals were served at Jennie's whim, yet she grew furious if the men weren't seated and ready when she deigned to deliver the food.

The men chafed under her arbitrary rule during the late autumn of 1847; their annoyance reached rebellion on Christmas Day, when Marshall happened to be down the river at Sutter's Fort. Most of the men were Mormons, devout Christians after their Latter-day fashion, and they desired to savor their holiday and honor their Lord's birth by grooming themselves more fastidiously than the normal work schedule allowed. But Jennie Wimmer would brook no change from her routine. She rang the bell, and when they didn't appear at once, she vowed they could feed themselves.

Henry Bigler was an elder of the Mormon Church and a military veteran; he had survived the anti-Mormon pogroms in Missouri and Illinois, and fought Mexicans in the war not quite officially ended. He had suffered Jennie Wimmer—till now. "On Christmas morning just at daylight we was called to breakfast," he recorded. "We was washing our faces. We was called the second time before we was ready to obey. She told us plainly that she was Boss and that we must come at the first call, which we had always had done before. . . . This we did not like, and we revolted from under her government."

Marshall returned from the fort to discover the rebellion. As insurrections went, it wasn't much. The Mormons simply insisted they could no longer abide Jennie Wimmer's arbitrary rule. They must be allowed to build their own living quarters, where they would cook their own meals.

Marshall was reluctant to grant the demand, for every hour devoted to building the new cabin would be an hour stolen from building the sawmill, which was the reason they were all wintering at this remote site, forty miles from Sutter's settlement and many times that distance from anything that could be called civilization. But the Mormons were as irreplaceable as Jennie Wimmer. They intended to stay only till spring, when they would trek east across the mountains to join their fellow Saints on the shores of the Great Salt Lake.

Marshall could see no alternative. The Mormons must have their own cabin. He set aside the materials; they provided the labor—while Jennie Wimmer looked on with a mixture of disgust and good-riddance. After a week's hard work the cabin was ready. Nineteen-year-old Azariah Smith, one of Bigler's fellow insurgents, noted with satisfaction in his diary: "Last Sunday we moved into it in order to get rid of the brawling, partial mistress, and cook for ourselves."

JOHN SUTTER, MARSHALL'S PARTNER, felt much the same way about Marshall that Marshall felt about Jennie Wimmer. In Sutter's homeland of Switzerland, where tapping the power of falling water was an ancient art, Marshall never would have qualified as a millwright. He had built no mills nor apprenticed to anyone who had. His training, such as it was, was in carpentry, which was not irrelevant to the construction of the shed and platform that would house and support the millworks, but lacked the elements of smithing—of fabricating iron gears and levers and steel saw-blades—that distinguished the craft of genuine millwrights from the make-do approximations of amateurs.

Marshall inspired even less confidence as a business partner. He had the uncertain, backward-glancing air of a man who had been haunted by misfortune and was reasonably sure it was still on his trail. His business acumen was demonstrably deficient, his most recent failure being the loss of a ranch in the Sacramento Valley not far from Sutter's own.

But Sutter needed a sawmill and couldn't build it himself. New Helvetia was thriving a decade after Sutter had persuaded the governor of California to award him a tract of land on the northern frontier of that Mexican province as a way of forestalling settlement by encroaching Americans—whose proximity was already reflected in the name of a principal tributary to the Sacramento: Río de los Americanos. Sutter selected a site at the confluence of the two streams, on the east bank of the Sacramento and the south bank of the American. The site was fifty river miles from the nearest arm of the San Francisco Bay, and two hundred miles by river, bay, and ocean from Monterey, the provincial capital.

Sutter hired Indians, including some whose families had first gathered around the Catholic missions in the days of the Spanish. Although the natives required stern guidance, supplied by soldiers Sutter employed, they worked cheaply—which was why they required such stern guidance. In time they dug irrigation ditches and planted fields, vineyards, and orchards. New Helvetia didn't look much like its namesake, for beyond the reach of Sutter's acequias, the broad flanks of the Sacramento Valley were parched and brown through summers unthinkably hot by Alpine standards. But it was his, and for a man whose career had taken him from Baden and Bern to New York, Missouri, New Mexico, Oregon, Hawaii, and Alaska before he finally reached California in 1839, it felt increasingly like home.

The sawmill was part of the latest stage of Sutter's expansion, a stage that also included construction of a gristmill. The latter would be located in the valley, near the fort and its fields of grain. Employing the power of gravity, as delivered by the waters of the American River, it would grind

Sutter's wheat for his own use and for sale down the Sacramento; for a fee, it would grind the wheat of Sutter's neighbors. The sawmill would be located up the American River, near the trees that would supply the timber the mill would saw into beams and boards. The cut lumber would be carted west to the fort for use there; what Sutter didn't need he would raft down the Sacramento to the village of Yerba Buena—or San Francisco, as some of the inhabitants had lately started calling it—on a sheltered cove on the inland side of the peninsula south of the entrance to San Francisco Bay.

Sutter was a soldier by training, albeit less training than he let on. He said he had reached the rank of captain in the Swiss army. This wasn't true; he never got further than first under-lieutenant of reserves. But he looked the soldier's part. He carried himself erect, in the military manner. His blond hair curled above his ears and across the crest of his broad forehead, giving him the appearance of a Teutonic Napoleon. He kept his side-whiskers and mustache neatly trimmed, imperial-fashion. His eyebrows arched quizzically above his clear blue eyes, as if to inquire whether an order had been carried out with sufficient alacrity.

The pose worked. The governor of California commissioned Sutter a captain of militia, to guard against the Americans and other foreigners. Sutter was also appointed alcalde, thereby receiving powers akin to those of an American mayor and sheriff combined. He liked the authority and the titles; when the more obsequious of those requesting his favor called him "General," he didn't correct them. For a man who had fled Switzerland just ahead of the debt-police, leaving behind a wife and children, he could congratulate himself on doing well, remarkably well. Looking out from his headquarters in the fort he named for himself, he was lord of all he surveyed.

Yet the lord slept uneasily some nights. His fitfulness traced to the March day in 1844 when an American military officer unexpectedly appeared from out of the snowdrifts of the Sierras at the head of a mounted column. Sutter knew enough about Americans to know they collectively possessed an annoying self-confidence, a smug certitude that God smiled more brightly on them than on any other portion of humanity; but he had never met anyone as infuriatingly self-assured as John Frémont. The American captain had conquered the mountains to reach California—no mean midwinter's feat, Sutter had to admit—and he acted as if he could conquer anything or anyone in the valley below. On that 1844 visit Frémont had contented himself with registering disdain for Mexican authority, parading about the province as he pleased, leaving only when he saw fit. But he returned in December 1845, and his second coming heralded the war that even now seemed likely to wrest California from Mexico and deliver it to the United States, in apparent fulfillment of the plan the Americans ascribed to Providence.

Against Frémont's arms, and those of the larger American force that followed him, Sutter had no answer. He was compelled to endure Frémont's scorn, and he prepared to accommodate himself to the new American regime as he had adjusted himself to the old Mexican one.

James Marshall was part of his strategy of accommodation. Whichever country wound up owning California would need the cattle Sutter's pastures fed, the grain his gristmill ground, the lumber his sawmill on the American River cut. In Switzerland, Sutter would have insisted on better than Marshall. But California wasn't Switzerland, as he had to keep reminding himself. "Made a contract and entered in partnership with Marshall for a sawmill to be built on the American fork," he recorded in his journal for August 27, 1847. The terms of the partnership were straightforward. Sutter would furnish materials for construction, and expenses and wages for the men; Marshall would supervise construction and manage operation of the mill. The two would split the profits from the sale of the lumber.

MARSHALL WAS COUNTING on the partnership. For most of his life, it seemed, his only partner had been bad luck. His father died when Marshall was in his early twenties, leaving the young man nothing but debts, and with little alternative—as he saw it—to heading west on the tide of the times. He drifted through Ohio, Indiana, and Illinois, stumbling into Missouri during the land rush to the Platte Purchase on the Missouri River. Briefly it appeared that his luck had changed, for he staked out a homestead and planted corn and fenceposts and the beginning of roots. And he fell in love with a young woman of Platte City, aptly named Missouri Green. But fortune fooled him. He contracted an illness his contemporaries called "fever and ague"—later generations would identify it as malaria—which sapped his strength, blurred his vision and judgment, and left him shivering and shaking in the hottest weather. Although the etiology of malaria was unknown (including the role of mosquitoes in spreading the disease), the epidemiology was plain enough, and when a local doctor advised him he would never get well till he left the bottomlands of the Missouri, he couldn't argue. Whether this doctor was the same physician for whom Miss Missouri Green rejected Marshall is unclear. But reject him she did, and for the sake of both his health and his self-respect he moved on.

In the early 1840s the Missouri Valley was a highway to Oregon, a land extolled for its fertile soil and salubrious climate. Marshall joined an emigrant train and in the spring of 1845 arrived in the Willamette Valley. But that spring was as drizzly as most Oregon springs, and in early June, having hardly seen the sun, Marshall headed south. With a small party he crossed the curiously chaotic Siskiyou Mountains (which refused to follow the north-south axis of nearly all other American ranges), and in mid-July found himself at the gate of Sutter's Fort. Sutter, looking over the new arrivals, remarked their "decent appearance" and allowed, in light of the shortage of even marginally skilled labor in the area, that some might be "very useful." He welcomed them on behalf of the Mexican government and issued them visas.

He offered Marshall work around the fort, and when the American proved handy with small tools, Sutter helped him arrange a mortgage to purchase two leagues of land on a tributary of the Sacramento. Marshall took some of his wages from Sutter in cattle, which he used to stock his new ranch.

Yet trouble was still on Marshall's trail. He had scarcely started ranching when the war broke out between the United States and Mexico. Along with nearly all the Americans in California, Marshall sided with the land of his birth against the country of his current residence. He enlisted under

Captain Frémont and marched south to San Pasqual, then to San Diego. After a great deal of walking and relatively little fighting, he was mustered out at San Diego in March 1847. Another long walk brought him back to the Sacramento Valley, where he learned that in his absence his cattle had strayed or been stolen. This was a grievous blow, for the cattle were more valuable than the land. Without the cattle he couldn't make the payments on his mortgage. He lost the land, and once again turned to Sutter for work.

Sutter spoke of a sawmill, for which Marshall began scouting. "In May 1847, with my rifle, blanket, and a few crackers to eat with my venison (for the deer were then awful plenty)," he recounted later, "I ascended the American River according to Mr. Sutter's wish, as he wanted to find a good site for a sawmill, where we could have plenty of timber, and where wagons would be able to ascend and descend the river hills." The two elements—timber and accessibility via wagon—were crucial, and not often encountered together. "Many places would suit very well for the erection of the mill, with plenty of timber everywhere, but then nothing but a mule could climb the hills; and when I would find a spot where the hills were not steep, there was no timber to be had."

Marshall assumed a certain knowledge in his listener in this account. For one thing, the mill had to be on or very near the river. Marshall and Sutter relied on falling water to drive the blade that would saw the wood, and lacking much money and many men they had to take the water where they found it. Minor modification of stream flow was feasible; major diversion was not.

For another thing, not just any timber would do. Cottonwoods grew along the lower reaches of the river, but cottonwood, being neither strong nor durable, made poor lumber. Spreading oaks were scattered in parklike stands across the hillsides of the Sacramento Valley, including the lower American River valley; close-grained from slow growth, the oak wood was both durable and strong. But it was also hard and heavy. For certain uses—fine furniture, the keels and ribs of ships—oak was ideal, but for the mundane barns and fence rails, houses and storefronts Sutter had in mind, oak was more trouble than it was worth. It would break the axes of the fallers, the backs of the haulers, the blades of the sawyers.

The best wood for lumber was pine. Light, straight-grained, comparatively knot-free, soft enough to work but sturdy enough to last, available in straight lengths as long as any builder could desire, pine was the wood of choice for commercial lumbermen. Yet for pine trees Marshall had to go many miles upriver from Sutter's Fort, to the higher elevations where the air was cooler, the rainfall greater, and the soil better-drained. If he went clear to the Sierras themselves, he could find whole forests of pine (which gave way to fir at still higher elevations); in the foothills he could discover stands of pines mixed with oaks, madrones, and other trees.

Marshall knew not to go farther upstream than necessary, for accessibility by wagon had to be combined with reasonable proximity to Sutter's Fort. Each mile from the fort was a mile the lumber would have to be hauled. Needless to say, it was cheaper to haul cut lumber than raw logs, as the bark and other wastage was a dead loss. But hauling even the finished product—by wagon, pulled by oxen—was expensive.

It was Marshall's job to discover a site that balanced availability of wood and water with accessibility and proximity. He found a likely spot about forty miles upstream from the fort, in a valley the local Indians called Coloma. The American River entered the valley from a defile at the southeast; it exited through a gap at the northwest. The ridge above the east bank separated this branch of the American River—the south fork—from the middle fork beyond. Access to the valley was from the south, via an Indian trail that crossed a pass leading west to the fort.

The bottom of the valley was essentially flat, with sandy soil covered by grass, low shrubs, and some late-spring flowers. The sides of the valley were dissected by ravines that ran full in rainy weather but soon drained dry. Oaks were scattered about the lower slopes, with madrones and cypresses interspersed. Higher up the ridges, pines predominated.

The gradient—that is, steepness—of the riverbed in the valley was such that the stream tripped along at a brisk pace. Though less than fifty yards wide in most spots, it made an insistent sound that unobtrusively filled the valley. In some wider places it was shallow enough for men and horses to wade across. Elsewhere it ran deeper and slower, but more powerfully.

A peculiarity of the riverbed in this valley made it especially appealing to Marshall. While the river ran generally from southeast to northwest across the valley, about midway it made a bend of nearly ninety degrees to the left, over a distance of several hundred yards. At the head of the bend was one of the shallow stretches, and in the middle of this shallow stretch was a low gravel island, which bisected the stream. Along the bend, the left bank consisted of a low line of gravel. Marshall had seen enough of the work of rivers to realize that they tended to exaggerate their curvature over time, as the faster flow along the outside of a bend ate away the outer bank and deposited the scourings in the calmer water along the inner shore, until some catastrophic flood breached the neck of the bend and straightened the stream overnight.

Marshall decided to anticipate nature, to create his own catastrophe. He would breach the line of gravel on the left bank of the river and allow the stream, or a substantial portion of it, to flow straight from the head of the bend to the foot. By shortening the horizontal distance traversed by the water, this diversion would increase the gradient of the stream and hence the velocity of the water: from a man's swift walk to a run. More to the point, it would increase the applicable force of the current, from that which in normal, nonflood times carried sand and other light particles gently along the stream bottom, to a force that would drive the waterwheel that would power the reciprocating saw blade that would tear the pine trees into boards. Marshall envisioned a dam at the head of the bend, which would compel the river to seek a new outlet, the millrace. Nature had done part of the damming work by depositing the gravel island, but much remained.

There was nothing elaborate or complicated about this. It required only digging and lifting: moving dirt and gravel and rocks from where Marshall didn't want them (the millrace) to where he did (the dam). Unskilled labor would certainly suffice.

MARSHALL REPORTED BACK to Sutter, described Coloma, and explained his plan. At the time, he probably intended to rely on Indian labor, although he—and Sutter too—must have had some reservations. The indigenous Nisenan and their neighbors were not especially warlike, but neither were they notably friendly to interlopers. When the interlopers stuck together—as near Sutter's Fort, which was a fort for a reason—the Indians left them alone. But Coloma was two days from the fort, and, at the least, the livestock and other provisions brought from the fort to the construction site would be prey to pilfering. Marshall and Sutter might ask Indians in their employ to guard and defend Sutter's property, but the partners would be foolish to count on the Indians to endanger themselves for the white men.

Luckily, not long after Sutter satisfied himself that Marshall's plan was feasible, and the two exchanged signatures on a contract, the labor problem solved itself, temporarily at any rate. Four months after Marshall was mustered out of the military, the army released the members of the Mormon Battalion, one of the more remarkable contingents in the long history of American military voluntarism. The war with Mexico began at just the moment when the Mormons, having been driven sequentially from Ohio, Missouri, and Illinois, were planning their hegira to the wilderness beyond the boundaries of the United States. Precisely where the hegira would end hadn't been established, but Mormon leader Brigham Young and his fellow elders could tell that the trek would be difficult and expensive. Any assistance, from almost any source, would be appreciated. When the call came from Washington for volunteers against Mexico, Young recognized the possibilities it presented. Uncle Sam was offering to transport west as many men as the Mormons could supply, and pay them for the journey. Of course, their time, and their lives, would not be their own for the duration of the fighting, but at war's end they would be closer to the Mormons' new home, wherever that proved to be, and would have pockets full of cash, which would help build the new colony. So the Mormon Council of Twelve issued its own call for volunteers on Washington's behalf, and the Mormon Battalion was born.

Like Marshall's, the Mormons' war included far more marching—in their case, across some of the most forbidding stretches of the Great Basin—than shooting, as well as the soldier's usual share of sitting around.

Consequently it was a tough, bored, but otherwise healthy crew that left the employ of the U.S. Army in July 1847 at the quiet town of Los Angeles, eager to rejoin the families and friends from whom they had parted the previous year.

Confusingly, however, they didn't know where to go. They had last heard from the church leaders almost a year earlier and had only the vaguest idea where their fellow Saints' flight into the wilderness had ended. All the same, with no means of supporting themselves at Los Angeles, they headed north, toward the more populated regions of California. There they hoped to encounter word from the new Mormon colony and receive further marching orders, this time from their own people.

Some 150 set out from Los Angeles in late July, and after a hot, wearing journey along the same route Marshall had followed the previous spring, they reached the Sacramento. There they learned that the Council of Twelve had planted the church in the valley of the Great Salt Lake. With rising hearts they marched on to Sutter's Fort, where they purchased provisions for the last leg of their journey, east over the mountains and desert to their new home.

They ascended the western slope of the Sierras, crossing the divide by the same pass—although in the opposite direction—as the ill-fated Donner party, which several months earlier had succumbed to starvation and cannibalism amid the snows of winter. Evidence of the disaster was still visible. "Their bones were lying scattered over the ground," recorded one of the Mormons. Many of the Saints were family men, and couldn't help feeling pity for the children who died. But all were veterans of the wilderness, and like many of similar experience after such disasters, they couldn't help thinking that the tragedy was at least as much the result of bad decisions as bad luck—which made it all the more tragic. Sutter, below at his fort, shared this view, and added to it a certain annoyance. He had gone to some pains and no little expense to send a relief party to rescue the Donner group, and was miffed at the way things turned out. "The provisions not satisfying the starving sufferers," he afterward complained, "they killed and ate, first, the mules, then the horses, and, finally, they killed and ate my good Indians."

The Mormons saw snow themselves, although September had barely started. Azariah Smith, traveling with his father, Albert, wrote on September 7, "We crossed the divide, which was very high and snow in places on top." That evening brought no new snow, but rather messengers with fresh word from home. "There was a letter read from the Twelve to the Battalion, which gave us much joy. I and Father received a letter from Mother, which gave us much more."

The joy was greater for some than for others. The message from the Twelve directed those veterans without dependent wives and children in Utah to return to the Sacramento. As things were, the colony at Salt Lake was already hungry; it needed no new mouths to feed, especially with winter coming on. The veterans without dependents should spend the winter in California, earning such wages as they could, saving their money, and preparing to join the rest of the Saints in the spring.

So Azariah Smith, with a heavy but obedient heart, said good-bye to his father, who had younger children in Utah, and joined about half the company in retracing their steps west across the Donner Pass. On September 15 they arrived again at Sutter's Fort and applied for work.

Sutter was delighted to see them. With the two mill projects under way, he needed all the strong arms and backs he could get. He offered to pay the newcomers either by the month ($25) or by the cubic yard of earth and rock displaced (12½ cents). Hale, confident, and zealous in their desire to help the church, they opted for the piece rate.

Sutter was impressed with their energy and ambition, and shortly he sent them to Coloma, where Marshall had just begun work. "We was three days a going there, as we had an ox team, which was very slow," wrote Azariah Smith. The Mormons discovered an unanticipated perquisite of the Coloma job, or what they initially took to be a perquisite. Referring to Jennie Wimmer, Smith noted, "We have a woman cook, which is something we have not had for a long time."

Digging ditches and piling rocks was harder than the newcomers had anticipated. "Three days this week I have worked," Smith wrote at the end of the first week, "but my back was so lame yesterday that I did not work." Although his back recovered, he fell ill. His malady seemed mild at first, but it kept recurring, so that from early October through mid-November he worked hardly at all. "By Thursday I thought I had got well," he wrote on Monday, October 11, "and, anxious to procure means to take me back home [to Utah], in the morning I went to work, and worked lightly till noon, when after dinner I had a chill, and have had one every day since." At the end of that week he wrote, "Through the goodness of the Lord my chills have left me, but I have been very weak. One night before the chills left I was very sick, and I felt bad, the thought running in my mind that likely I never should see home again, which was a perfect torment to my mind." Three weeks later he managed to resume some light work, but as late as December 12, he wrote, "Last Thursday I had a chill and fever."

Smith wasn't the only one who got sick. Others became so ill they had to be sent to Sutter's Fort to recuperate. Marshall fretted at the delay. He knew the Mormons would depart in the spring, leaving him to finish the sawmill with the Indians. He could probably do so if he had to, but it wasn't a prospect he relished.

AS WORRISOME AS the health of the men was the state of the weather. Autumn always came sooner to the mountains than to the foothills around Coloma, and sooner to the foothills than to the valley near the fort. The clouds off the Pacific typically overflew the valley before colliding with the mountains and releasing their load of moisture. In the autumn this fell as rain, which ran off the steep slopes and raised the rivers in the lower elevations weeks before those lower elevations themselves received much precipitation. As the season progressed, the moisture in the mountains fell as snow, which stuck to the slopes; by then, though, rain was falling in the foothills and the valley, greening the hillsides but making the roads difficult for men and horses, and nearly impassable for wheeled vehicles. Any provisions and equipment that didn't get to Coloma by about the first of December probably wouldn't get there till spring.

In 1847 the initial autumn rains reached Coloma in early November. "We have had a good deal of rain," Azariah Smith wrote, summarizing the week preceding November 10. Sutter accordingly accelerated his supply schedule. "Started 5 wagons with provisions," he jotted in his journal at the fort on Tuesday, November 16. The following Sunday, Smith at Coloma noted, "Yesterday there came five wagon loads of provisions, as the provision for the winter has to be brought before the rainy season commences." December saw showers, succeeded, after the first of the year, by a drenching Pacific storm. "Sunday it began raining, and rained all day and night, and has rained off and on ever since," Smith wrote on Tuesday, January 11.

The rains did more than disrupt transport; they threatened the construction of the sawmill, now at a critical stage. Most of the dam was completed, and the millrace had been etched across the peninsula on the inside of the river's bend. The foundation of the mill had been laid, and the timbers of the lower portion were in place. But the dam hadn't withstood winter's high water, and Marshall wasn't sure it could. As things happened, the storm caught him at the fort, where he was supervising Sutter's blacksmiths in the fabrication of the machinery for the mill. In Marshall's absence, the men at Coloma watched the water rise and wondered if the flood would undo all their work of the previous months. Smith wrote of the storm's effect on a crucial part of the construction: "It raised the river very high, and we expected to see the water go around the abutment almost every minute."

Marshall and Sutter worried about the danger upstream, but, realizing there was nothing they could do till the water fell, they decided Marshall should stay by the forge to see the ironwork finished. On January 14 he loaded the irons into a wagon, hitched up three yoke of oxen and, with the assistance of two Indian boys, set out for Coloma. The journey went slowly along the muddy road. After forty-eight hours they were only halfway there. But en route they encountered a party returning from a previous delivery; these men brought the welcome news that the dam had held. At Coloma, Henry Bigler recorded, "Clear as a bell and the water is a-falling and the mill safe."

BUT WINTER WAS JUST starting, and more storms would follow. Marshall was impatient to complete the work. His impatience increased, on reaching Coloma, at learning of the revolt against Jennie Wimmer and at having to grant the rebels' demand of time to build their separate quarters. Meanwhile he examined what the crew had accomplished in his absence. The headrace—the portion of the race above the mill—met his approval, but the tailrace—below the mill—was too shallow and narrow to accommodate the volume of water necessary to drive the saw. It must be enlarged.

Marshall decided to enlist the force that had nearly destroyed the project. The excavation of the headrace had had to be done more or less precisely; if the water overflowed the banks of the headrace it would erode the foundations of the mill. But once past the mill, the water's specific course mattered little. The only essential was that the water return to the river without backing up under the mill. Marshall decided to let the water cut its own course beyond the mill.

The mill's design included an undershot wheel, with the water rushing beneath the loading platform. Until the construction was complete, Marshall couldn't let the water flow while the men were at work, crawling around and underneath the mill. But at night, when the work was suspended, he could open the gates at the head of the race and let the water pour through. While the men slept, the water would carve out the tailrace. The process shouldn't take long; within a few weeks, barring an act of God or other disruption, the mill would be ready for its first logs.

Marshall supervised the work of nature as closely as he supervised the work of the men. Each morning he closed the gate and cut off the water through the race, and walked the channel below the mill to see what the flow had accomplished overnight. One morning not long after his return from Sutter's Fort—the date generally given is January 24, although Marshall's memory wavered on this point—about half past seven, he stepped along the race toward its confluence with the river. The night had been cold, and a rime of ice covered the rocks where the water had splashed. This, and the water still in the bed of the channel, gave a gleam to the pebbles and sand in the morning light. A few particular sparkles caught his eye, but at first he thought these were merely pieces of shiny quartz. Near the lower end of the race, however, just above its junction with the river, some two hundred yards from the mill, where about six inches of water pooled in the bed of the tailrace, he decided to investigate further.

"I picked up one or two pieces," he recalled, "and examined them attentively; and having some general knowledge of minerals, I could not call to mind more than two which in any way resembled this—sulphuret of iron, very bright and brittle; and gold, bright yet malleable. I then tried it between two rocks, and found that it could be beaten into a different shape, but not broken. I then collected four or five more pieces."

A more devious, or even more thoughtful, man than Marshall might have pocketed the gold and kept the discovery to himself. But a more devious or more thoughtful man might not have found himself digging ditches that January morning in a gravel bar so far from home and kin and civilization. As it was, he hastened to the mill and shared his surprising intelligence with the men there. William Scott was at the carpenter's bench, working on the mill wheel.

"I have found it," Marshall said. At least this was what he remembered saying; the words have an odd ring. The phrasing sounds as though Marshall was looking for gold, and perhaps that Scott knew he was doing so. Yet when some question arose as to Marshall's primacy in discovery, when it would have served his purpose to say he had gone looking for the precious metal, he claimed nothing of the sort. Quite possibly, in remembering things as he did, Marshall unthinkingly translated the mania of the aftermath of his discovery—when "it" was on everyone's mind—to the very moment when the new age dawned.

On the other hand, maybe he said just what he later remembered. According to that memory, Scott replied, "What is it?"

"Gold," answered Marshall.

"Oh, no!" said Scott in disbelief. "That can't be."

"I know it to be nothing else."

Scott's skepticism erased any residual inclination in Marshall to keep the discovery quiet. Several of the other men working in the vicinity were called over to examine the specimens and render judgment. Charles Bennett, at Marshall's direction, took a hammer and pounded one of the flakes into a thin sheet—strong evidence that this was the genuine article. Peter

Wimmer carried a flake to the cabin where his wife was making soap; she threw it into the boiling lye solution, and it emerged shinier than ever. A similar result followed an assay by saleratus (baking powder). Although less telling than the malleability test, these experiments added weight to the gold hypothesis.

Had anyone at Coloma known what everyone in the world knew later, Marshall's men would have dropped their tools at once and gone looking for more of what he had found. But at the time it appeared a curiosity, a fluke. After all, they had moved thousands of cubic yards of dirt and sand and gravel in that same location during the previous several months, and this was the first sign that those thousands of yards contained anything but dirt and sand and gravel. Marshall reminded them that they had come to Coloma to build a sawmill. If they didn't work on the mill, they wouldn't get paid. Perhaps he did not remind them—although they doubtless realized—that *he* wouldn't start getting paid until the mill started sawing wood.

Yet, bowing to reality, Marshall told the men that if they continued to work on the mill during regular hours, they might search for gold during "odd spells and Sundays" (as Azariah Smith recorded). At some point either then or later they agreed, in exchange for this privilege, to split their findings with Marshall.

The fact that Marshall was more concerned with lumber than with gold was underscored by the fact that he waited four days after his remarkable discovery to travel to Sutter's Fort. Perhaps he failed to appreciate how that discovery changed everything. Perhaps he *did* appreciate it, and affected nonchalance for the benefit of the men.

SUTTER WAS CONCERNED with lumber, too, but with larger issues as well. In January 1848 the United States and Mexico remained formally at war, yet the shape of the American victory was evident. The United States would acquire California, among other spoils of the conflict. While Marshall and most Americans in California cheered the change of sovereignty, Sutter shuddered. As an official of the Mexican government, he had lately been an enemy of the region's new rulers; more unnerving, everything he had built and achieved at New Helvetia—the fort, the farms, the herds, the authority he wielded, the respect he commanded—were based on his good relations with Mexico. Mexico's defeat canceled all that. Perhaps he could make himself as valuable to the Americans as he had been to the Mexicans; flexibility and the capacity to ingratiate had long been his stock-in-trade. But the process would take time—a luxury he wasn't sure he would be allowed.

Such was Sutter's thinking when, to his surprise, Marshall arrived back from Coloma. Because Marshall had left the fort only two weeks earlier, with the intention of finishing the construction, Sutter assumed something was amiss. Marshall's demeanor added to this impression. "From the unusual agitation in his manner I imagined that something serious had occurred," Sutter said afterward. He added, "As we involuntarily do in this part of the world, I at once glanced to see if my rifle was in its proper place."

When Marshall explained the cause of his excitement, the two men retired to Sutter's office on the second floor of the building at the center of the fort. They consulted Sutter's *Encyclopaedia Americana*, which had a long article describing the properties of gold. The apothecary shop at the fort possessed some aqua fortis—nitric acid—which Sutter sent a servant to fetch. Marshall's samples withstood the acid—a strong indication of gold. To determine the density of the metal, they reproduced Archimedes' famous experiment. They placed in one pan of a scales a quantity of Marshall's sample sufficient to balance three silver dollars in the other pan; then they immersed the scales in water, whereupon the pan with the sample sank, revealing the greater density of the sample—again, as expected of gold.

Sutter concluded what Marshall already had. "I declared this to be gold," he remembered. He told Marshall that it was "of the finest quality, of at least 23 carats."

Marshall thought the two of them should leave for Coloma at once. Sutter was reluctant. He cited the lateness of the afternoon and the inclemency of the weather—it had begun raining again, hard.

Sutter had another reason for delay. He needed time to think. A sleepless night got him started. By his own testimony, he "thought a great deal during the night about the consequences which might follow such a discovery." He considered himself as resourceful as the next man; his whole career, culminating in New Helvetia, was evidence of his ability to adapt to changing circumstances. But he had never encountered anything like this.

PART ONE

The Gathering of Peoples

(From the World to California: 1848–1849)

As when some carcass, hidden in sequestered nook, draws from every near and distant point myriads of discordant vultures, so drew these little flakes of gold the voracious sons of men. The strongest human appetite was aroused—the sum of appetites—this yellow dirt embodying the means for gratifying love, hate, lust, and domination. This little scratch upon the earth to make a backwoods mill-race touched the cerebral nerve that quickened humanity, and sent a thrill throughout the system. It tingled in the ear and at the finger-ends; it buzzed about the brain and tickled in the stomach; it warmed the blood and swelled the heart; new fires were kindled on the hearth-stones, new castles builded in the air. If Satan from Diablo's peak had sounded the knell of time; if a heavenly angel from the Sierras' height had heralded the millennial day; if the blessed Christ himself had risen from that ditch and proclaimed to all mankind amnesty—their greedy hearts had never half so thrilled.

—Hubert Howe Bancroft, gold-hunter and historian

James Marshall's discovery of gold at Coloma turned out to be a seminal event in history, one of those rare moments that divide human existence into before and after. When news of the discovery floated down the Sacramento to the more populated regions of California, it sucked nearly every free hand and available arm to the gold mines, leaving children to ask where their fathers had gone and wives wondering when their husbands would return. As the golden news spread beyond California to the outside world, it triggered the most astonishing mass movement of peoples since the Crusades. From all over the planet they came—from Mexico and Peru and Chile and Argentina, from Oregon and Hawaii and Australia and New Zealand and China, from the American North and the American South, from Britain and France and Germany and Italy and Greece and Russia. They came by the tens and hundreds and thousands, then by the tens of thousands and hundreds of thousands. They came by sailing ship and steamship, by horse and mule and ox and wagon and foot. They came in companies and alone, with money and without, knowing and naïve. They tore themselves from warm hearths and good homes, promising to return; they fled from cold hearts and bad debts, vowing never to return. They were farmers and merchants and sailors and slaves and abolitionists and soldiers of fortune and ladies of the night. They jumped bail to start their journey, and jumped ship at journey's end. They were pillars of their communities, and their communities' dregs.

Their journey, taken collectively, was the epic of the age, a saga of world history, an adventure on the largest scale. But their collective enterprise was the sum of hundreds of thousands of individual journeys, hundreds of thousands of small stories that changed the world by changing the lives of the men and women who traveled to California in pursuit of their common dream. For nearly all of them, the journey was the most difficult thing they had ever done, and far more difficult than they imagined on setting out. Not all survived the journey; those who did would never forget the trials they endured, the challenges they met, the companions they lost. They would tell the story of the journey to their children and their children's children.

None of those who traveled to California in search of gold had any inkling, before January 24, 1848, of what was in store for them. Their lives, about to become threads in a grand—a golden—tapestry, were still distinct, wound on spindles separated by oceans and continents and gulfs of culture and mountain ranges of history. And they would have remained distinct, in nearly all cases, if not for James Marshall's discovery. But starting on that day, a powerful engine—the engine of fate, or perhaps merely of human nature—began winding them all in.

1

In the Footsteps of Father Serra

A less likely terminus of all these journeys could scarcely have been conceived. A principal attraction of California in the period before Coloma was that it was so far off the beaten track. John Sutter could hide there from his wife and creditors; James Marshall could hope to shake the failure that had dogged his steps since Missouri. At a time when long-distance travel averaged little faster than a man could walk—railroads were appearing in the most advanced countries, and promised to revolutionize transport, but for now they were primarily local or regional affairs—California was about as far from the centers of Western civilization as a land could be. The sea voyage around South America from New York or Liverpool or Le Havre required five or six months, depending on conditions off Cape Horn, which could terrify the most hardened unbeliever to prayer. Recently, intrepid and lightly laden travelers had begun to attempt the Central American isthmus, but the justifiably dreaded Chagres fever and the uncertain connections to vessels on the Pacific side deterred many who otherwise would have employed this shortcut. For those setting out from the American East, travel by foot or wagon was feasible, but hardly attractive. Since the early 1840s emigrants had been crossing the plains and mountains to Oregon; the journey required half a year and all the fortitude and stamina ordinary folks could muster. And it was essentially one-way: when people left for Oregon, they might as well have dropped off the face of the earth for all their relatives were unlikely to see them again. The trail to California was much less traveled, and far less certain, than that to Oregon.

In the time before Coloma, those few outsiders who did visit California fell into a small number of discrete categories. European explorers arrived in the sixteenth century. Spain's Juan Cabrillo in 1542 sighted the coast of Alta California—as distinct from peninsular Baja California—but promptly sailed away. The English sea dog Francis Drake scouted California in 1579, landing at some bay never since clearly identified, but probably Drake's Bay, below Point Reyes, and burying a plaque never since found, but staking England's claim to the region. Subsequently Russian ship captains, seeking provisions for their country's Bering Sea fur hunters, began appearing in the neighborhood north of San Francisco Bay.

The English and Russians eventually awoke the Spanish, who already controlled most of the territory from Tierra del Fuego to Mexico, to the wisdom of colonizing California. The Spanish monarchy in the late eighteenth century enlisted the padres of the Franciscan order, who set out to secure California for the king of Spain even as they secured the souls of California's inhabitants for the King of Heaven.

Junipero Serra, the Majorca-born missionary who headed the effort, and his small band of Franciscan followers built a chain of missions from San Diego in the south to San Rafael in the north. The missions were located a day's walk apart, typically near the mouths of the short rivers that ran from the coastal mountains to the sea. Each mission centered on a chapel, usually built of adobe but occasionally of stone. Adjacent to the chapel was the home of the resident priests (typically two per mission) and assorted other structures. Surrounding the mission proper was a large tract of land, a hundred square miles or more. In time the mission lands supported great herds of cattle and horses and flocks of sheep. Grain fields, vegetable gardens, and fruit orchards rounded out the farms.

Besides the missions, which were controlled by the Franciscans, were four presidios, at San Diego, Santa Barbara, Monterey, and San Francisco. These forts barracked soldiers of the Spanish army, who were assigned to protect the missions and inspire awe in the local Indians. The Indians were encouraged by this means to seek refuge in the vineyards of the Lord and the fields of the friars.

Separate from the missions and the presidios were a handful of pueblos, or independent towns. Los Angeles was the most important of the pueblos; during the early nineteenth century it surpassed in size and economic activity all but a few of the missions.

In its heyday, the Spanish system in California constituted a pastoral empire of impressive proportions. Several of the missions boasted herds and flocks that numbered in the scores of thousands, barns bursting with grain and other produce, and the equivalent of tens of thousands of dollars in specie or precious plate. Indian "neophytes"—natives attached to the missions religiously and economically—totaled perhaps twenty thousand. They would have numbered far more if not for the introduced European diseases that ravaged the native populations even as they lent credence to the friars' assertion that repentance was in order because the end was near.

But the mission system was no stronger than the Spanish authority on which it rested, and when Mexico threw off Spanish control in the early 1820s, the California missions quickly declined. The new government of independent Mexico was republican and anticlerical; neither the power of the mission priests nor the subjection of the mission Indians sat well with those who now ruled California.

More precisely, the new regime *claimed* to rule California; in fact Mexican independence inaugurated an era of turbulence in California affairs. The friars preferred sabotage to secularization of the missions; they began to liquidate the herds and run down the farms. The Spanish-descended elites in California often disdained the mixed-blood mestizos of Mexico. The inhabitants of Monterey and the northern part of California fell out with the Los Angelenos of southern California. The small but growing contingent of foreigners, especially Americans, contributed a further element of restiveness and uncertainty.

OF ALL THIS, the large majority of Americans knew next to nothing until 1840, when Richard Dana published *Two Years Before the Mast*. Dana was heir to a tradition of distinguished Boston lawyers; his father had signed the Articles of Confederation and served fifteen years as chief justice of Massachusetts. The younger Dana was preparing for a legal career of his own when he contracted a bad case of measles. The illness especially afflicted his eyes, precluding an early return to his studies. Doctors suggested a sea voyage, perhaps a cruise to India. But the strapping young man, now returned to all but visual health, chafed at the thought of months in a deck chair; instead he chose to ship before the mast, on the brig *Pilgrim*, bound for the coast of California via Cape Horn.

The vessel left Boston in August 1834. After five months it reached Santa Barbara. Dana's first impression of California was decidedly unfavorable. "The hills have no large trees upon them, they having been all burnt by a great fire which swept them off about a dozen years ago, and they had not yet grown again," he wrote. "The fire was described to me by a inhabitant, as having been a very terrible and magnificent sight. The air of the whole valley was so heated that the people were obliged to leave the town and take up their quarters for several days upon the beach."

Dana's opinion of California gradually improved. He came to appreciate the climate and soil and scenery, and was fascinated by the polyglot mix of souls frequenting the coast: Polynesians, Russians, Italians, French, English. Yet he never learned to like the Californians themselves. They were "an idle, thriftless people," he said, unwilling or unable to make anything of the land they inhabited. A passenger who traveled aboard the *Pilgrim* from Monterey to Santa Barbara epitomized the type. Don Juan Bandini was descended from aristocrats, his family priding itself on the purity of its Spanish blood and its continuing importance in Mexico. Don Juan's father had been governor of California, and had sent his son to Mexico City for school and an introduction to the first circle of Mexican society. But misfortune and extravagance eroded the family estate, and the young Don Juan was now returning to California—"accomplished, poor, and proud, and without any office or occupation, to lead the life of most young men of the better families: dissipated and extravagant when the means are at hand; ambitious at heart, and impotent in act; often pinched for bread;

keeping up an appearance of style, when their poverty is known to each half-naked Indian boy in the street, and standing in dread of every small trader and shopkeeper in the place."

Señor Bandini made a fine show. "He had a slight and elegant figure, moved gracefully, danced and waltzed beautifully, spoke good Castilian, with a pleasant and refined voice and accent, and had, throughout, the bearing of a man of birth and figure. Yet here he was, with his passage given him (as I afterward learned), for he had not the means of paying for it, and living upon the charity of our agent." He was polite to one and all, from the captain to the lowliest sailor. He tipped the steward four *reals*—"I dare-say the last he had in his pocket." The sight was rather touching. "I could not but feel a pity for him, especially when I saw him by the side of his fellow-passenger and townsman, a fat, coarse, vulgar, pretentious fellow of a Yankee trader, who had made money in San Diego, and was eating out the vitals of the Bandinis, fattening upon their extravagance, grinding them in their poverty; having mortgages on their lands, forestalling their cattle, and already making an inroad upon their jewels, which were their last hope."

The decadent pride of the Bandinis, as Dana interpreted it, appeared more broadly in the Californians at large. "The men are thriftless, proud, extravagant, and very much given to gaming; and the women have but little education, and a good deal of beauty, and their morality, of course, is none of the best." The Californians would hazard everything on small points of honor and were given to murderous feuds. Meanwhile they were careless of the natural wealth around them, and were apparently impervious to any notion of progress. The contrast Dana perceived between the character of the Californians and the character of California struck him with a kind of moral force. "Such are the people who inhabit a country embracing four or five hundred miles of sea-coast, with several good harbors; with fine forests in the north; the waters filled with fish, and the plains covered with thousands of herds of cattle; blessed with a climate than which there can be no better in the world; free from all manner of diseases, whether epidemic or endemic; and with a soil in which corn yields from seventy to eighty fold. In the hands of an enterprising people, what a country this might be!"

DANA'S ACCOUNT APPEARED in the year America's sixth census showed the population of the United States to be just under 17 million people. To a later generation this number would seem minuscule, but to many of Dana's contemporaries it occasioned claustrophobia. America in 1840 was a land of farmers, and farmers—and their children and grandchildren—always needed more land. Since 1803, when Thomas Jefferson purchased the Louisiana territory from France, the only appreciable addition to the American patrimony had been Florida—swampy, disease-ridden Florida. The country was filling up; where would all the people live? What fields would they farm?

Adding to the worries was the dismal condition of the American economy. The previous decade had begun with the "bank war" between Nicholas Biddle, the powerful, prideful director of the Bank of the United States, and Andrew Jackson, the determined, prideful president. Jackson won the war by killing the Bank, but in doing so gravely wounded the economy. The Panic of 1837 bankrupted farmers, who saw the price of their crops fall 50 percent or more, and cast tens of thousands of laborers out on the streets and highways of America. Many headed west, as Americans had always done in times of trouble, hoping to make a new life where land was cheaper and opportunity more abundant. Yet land in 1840 wasn't as cheap as it had been when there weren't so many people trying to buy it, and opportunity was accordingly less abundant. As the economic depression continued into the new decade, it intensified demands for more land.

The demands acquired evangelical overtones. During the first half of the nineteenth century, American Protestantism—which was to say, the religion of nearly all Americans—bubbled and boiled with one reform movement after another. The "second Great Awakening" (the first having occurred during the previous century) saw people speaking in tongues and thrashing about wildly. One man jerked so violently—resisting grace, the pious said—that he broke his own neck. Camp meetings lasted weeks or months and spun off temperance crusades, abolitionist rallies, and missionary voyages. The religious ferment fostered an outlook that had no difficulty interpreting the pressure for territorial expansion in providential terms. If God had smiled on the United States of America—and almost none doubted that He had—wouldn't He want America to grow? Wouldn't He want Americans to spread their blessings into neighboring lands? And wouldn't He want this all the more, considering that the inhabitants of those neighboring lands were heathen Indians and papist Mexicans?

Of course He would—or so concluded the publicists of what came to be called Manifest Destiny, the ideology of expansion in the 1840s. This ideology was seductive, stroking the conscience of America even as it flattered America's vanity and served America's self-interest. It appealed most powerfully to the religiously minded majority of Americans, but the secular, too, could sign on, as advocates of the export of democracy. The popularity of Manifest Destiny naturally caught the attention of politicians, especially those in the Democratic party, who were hungry to regain the presidency after a surprising defeat in 1840. In 1844 the Democrats nominated James K. Polk of Tennessee on a platform promising the vigorous extension of America's frontiers westward. Looking southwest, Polk vowed to bring Texas into the Union. Looking northwest, he pledged to take all of Oregon.

Polk won the presidency and proceeded to act on his promises. As it happened, he didn't get all of Oregon (which at that time stretched to the southern border of Alaska), but, in negotiations with Britain, he got the largest and best part. Nor did *he* take Texas, which was annexed after Polk's election victory but before President John Tyler vacated the White House.

That didn't end the Texas story, however. Nor did it satisfy the aggressive appetite of Manifest Destiny. Although Texas had claimed independence from Mexico in 1836, the Mexican government rejected the claim and sent troops to suppress the rebellion. The Texans lost at the Alamo, but won at San Jacinto and forced the Mexicans to withdraw. Even so, Mexico refused to make peace or recognize the independence of the Texas republic. Consequently, when the United States annexed Texas in 1845, Mexico protested vehemently.

James Polk, inheriting the dispute, might have ignored the Mexican protests, except for one thing. Polk had read Richard Dana's book, and he became convinced that California—that marvelous land so neglected by its feckless people—should be brought into the Union. He offered to buy California from Mexico. When the Mexican government refused, he insisted. When the Mexicans refused again, Polk determined to take California by force.

The dispute with Texas provided the pretext. The president ordered General Zachary Taylor to assume a provocative position on the border between Texas and Mexico, intending for Taylor to be attacked. The attack was slow in coming, and the frustrated Polk began drafting a war message without it. But at the last minute the welcome news arrived that hostilities had commenced. Eleven Americans had been killed—on American soil, Polk explained to Congress. War was necessary and justified. Congress agreed, and in June 1846, Manifest Destiny went to war.

THE DECLARATION OF WAR came none too soon for John Frémont, who was in California anxiously awaiting the belligerent word. Frémont's anxiety reflected both his personal ambition and his uneasy conscience. His ambition drove him to dream of conquering California for the United States; his conscience nagged him for having started the war already, without authorization from Washington.

Frémont was one of the great enigmas of his generation. For ten years during the 1840s and 1850s he was as famous as anyone in America, a celebrity-hero whose star rose like a rocket in the West and flashed brilliantly from coast to coast. Young men idolized his physical courage and political audacity; young women swooned over his sad eyes, his black curls, and olive complexion, and the catlike grace with which he walked. In an era entranced by exploration, Frémont was the explorer par excellence, the "Pathfinder of the West." Thousands followed the trail he blazed toward Oregon; thousands more read the reports he published on the vast region that stretched from the Great Plains to the Pacific.

Yet though the whole country knew Frémont, almost no one knew him well. His origins were shrouded in mystery and scandal. His father was an itinerant French adventurer, an émigré from the French Revolution with a trail of transatlantic amours who seduced Frémont's mother and cuckolded the man to whom she was married. Consumed by her desire, she ran off with her lover and lived with him in common-law bigamy. From this illicit union sprang John Charles Frémont, who inherited his father's handsome face and dangerous habits, and his mother's passionate impulsiveness. But he inherited little else, certainly nothing on which a man could build a career.

Where he got his burning ambition was another mystery. Neither parent displayed anything comparable. Perhaps it had skipped a generation or two; perhaps it came from having to live down his illegitimate birth. In any event, it caused him to join the army, that historic institution of elevation for the ambitious but badly born. It provoked him to risk his own life and those of his men on daring crossings of the Rockies, the Great Basin, and the Sierras. And it drove him, in the spring of 1846, to dream of liberating California from Mexico and to grossly exceed his military orders.

Frémont had reached California some months earlier, on his second visit to the province. Amid the bellicose clamor of Manifest Destiny, his presence, with that of his wilderness-toughened band of cavalrymen, made John Sutter and other Mexican officials nervous. The commandant of California, José Castro, ordered Frémont to leave the province. He obliged, but slowly and with a studied insolence intended to elicit a violent response. He came close to getting it when Castro issued a proclamation calling on Californians to take arms against the "band of robbers commanded by a captain of the United States army, J. C. Frémont." Frémont claimed injury and vowed, "If we are unjustly attacked we will fight to extremity and refuse quarter, trusting to our country to avenge our death. . . . If we are hemmed in and assaulted here, we will die, every man of us, under the flag of our country." But the tense moment passed, and Frémont reluctantly headed north toward Oregon. On the way he heard rumors that Castro was encouraging local Indians to attack American settlers; still hoping to start something, Frémont launched a raid on an Indian village. Scores of Indians—as many as 175 by one count—were killed.

Yet the tinder refused to light, and Frémont continued north to the vicinity of Oregon's Klamath Lake, where he waited impatiently for an excuse to return. In May 1846 a secret messenger arrived from Washington. Precisely what this messenger said has been lost to history, for he destroyed his orders before crossing Mexican territory. But whatever he said prompted Frémont to move south at once.

Back in California, he resumed his campaign against the Indians. He led a mounted sweep of several Indian villages on the west bank of the Sacramento River; an indeterminable number of Indians were killed and hundreds were rendered homeless.

But *still* the war wouldn't start. By now Frémont was beginning to wonder if it ever would—and, if it didn't, whether he would be held accountable for the Indian war he had been waging, unauthorized, on Mexican soil.

Frémont's predicament only deepened when some of the American settlers raised the flag of rebellion against the Mexican government. These rebels modeled their "Bear Flag revolt" on the American Revolution, and just as the patriots of 1776 had appealed to France for help, so the patriots of 1846 appealed to the French-descended Frémont. Frémont obliged, and in fact took effective control of the rebellion. He seized Sutter's Fort—thereby confirming Sutter's long-standing suspicions of his malign intentions—and arrested nearby officials of the Mexican government.

These actions elevated his liability to a new level. Thus far his aggressions had been directed against Indians, who though living under Mexican jurisdiction lived somewhat outside Mexican law. But now Frémont was taking on the Mexican government itself. If war didn't break out, he would be at the center of a major international incident.

Frémont raised the stakes still further by ordering the killing of some Californians. Shortly after the start of the Bear Flag rebellion, Frémont's soldiers spied a small boat of Californians crossing San Pablo Bay. Frémont sent Kit Carson, the famous scout and Indian fighter who was Frémont's frequent partner in exploration, and some other men to intercept the boat. According to an eyewitness, Carson asked Frémont, "Captain, shall I take those men prisoner?" According to this same witness, Frémont answered, with a wave of the hand, "I have no room for prisoners." Carson and the others rode to where the boat had landed and shot three of the Californians dead. (A fourth escaped.) Frémont defended his action as punishment for the murder of two Americans, apparently by some Californians. But there was no evidence that the three men killed on Frémont's order had any connection to the murder of the Americans, and the incident created the distinct probability that Frémont would be charged with murder if no war followed.

Finally, to Frémont's relief, the news of Washington's war declaration arrived. This effectively ended the Bear Flag revolt, which was swept up in the larger contest against Mexico, and it lifted the cloud that hung over Frémont. Technically, of course, he was still guilty of having illegally waged war in a foreign country. And there was the moral matter of the blood of the Indians and Californians on his hands. But in the age of Manifest Destiny, it didn't seem likely that anyone in Washington would fault him for arriving at the same conclusion the United States government did, only sooner; and as for the deaths of the Indians and Mexican Californians, no one ever said the West was an easy or safe place to live. Americans applied different rules beyond the plains and mountains, especially to Indians and Mexicans. Frémont was confident that if the war made him a military hero—if he showed the same success in battle he had shown in the wilderness—all would be forgiven.

So he flung himself into the fighting. He raised a regiment of Americans (including James Marshall), whom he led to Monterey. By the time he got there, however, the provincial capital had already surrendered to an American naval squadron. Frustrated again, and more eager for action than ever, Frémont sailed to San Diego, where he joined the force of Commodore Robert Stockton. With Stockton he marched against Los Angeles and took part in the defeat of the Mexican garrison there. As this seemed to end the war in California, Frémont returned north to recruit a larger force for an invasion of Mexico proper. But in his absence, fighting resumed at Los Angeles. He raced back into the breach, and when the uprising was suppressed, he received the honor of accepting the Mexican capitulation. This really did terminate the fighting in California, and though Frémont couldn't claim sole credit for liberating the province, he could take satisfaction from having accomplished more toward that goal than anyone else.

His reward was appointment by Stockton as governor of California. For two months he exercised the authority of his office, which was by far the highest he had ever held. But then things began to go wrong. He fell afoul of a conflict between Stockton and Stephen Kearny, the senior army general in California, who had come overland after conquering New Mexico. Frémont assumed, with nearly everyone else in the vicinity, that Stockton outranked Kearny. Kearny differed, and after hot fighting in Washington between the War and Navy Departments, and attendant confusion and unrest in California, Kearny's view prevailed. Kearny resented Frémont's defection from army solidarity and ordered him arrested on charges of mutiny and insubordination. Frémont briefly considered resisting the arrest but thought better of it. He allowed himself to be taken ignominiously east, a prisoner, to stand trial before a court-martial.

At the trial, Frémont conducted his own defense. The charges were mutiny, disobedience to a lawful command of a superior officer, and conduct prejudicial to good order and discipline. Frémont indignantly denied all charges, contending that he had always conducted himself as an officer and a gentleman, that he had never disobeyed an order he knew to be lawful, and that mutiny was the farthest thing from his mind. In closing he pleaded the honorable work he had done during his governorship. "My acts in California have been all with motives and a desire for the public service," he declared. "I offer California, during my administration, for comparison with the most tranquil portion of the United States; I offer it in contrast to the condition of New Mexico at the same time. I prevented civil war against Governor Stockton, by refusing to join General Kearny against him; I arrested civil war against myself by consenting to be deposed."

To the surprise of no one familiar with military justice, the court returned a verdict of guilty on all counts. Frémont was sentenced to dismissal from military service. Yet several members of the court recommended clemency, citing the prisoner's valor and the confused conditions in California.

President Polk accepted the recommendation, after a fashion. He said he believed Frémont guilty of the two lesser charges but innocent of mutiny. Therefore he commuted the prisoner's punishment. "Lieutenant-Colonel Frémont will accordingly be released from arrest, will resume his sword, and report for duty," the commander in chief declared.

But Frémont would *not* report for duty. Outraged at being incompletely exonerated, he interpreted Polk's offer as an insult and resigned his commission. The army had impugned his honor; he would find other outlets for his ambition.

WILLIAM SHERMAN SHED no tears for Frémont. A graduate of West Point and an officer in the American contingent that occupied California after the fighting with Mexico ended, Sherman joined most of the regular army officers in condemning Frémont for insubordination. Kearny was Frémont's army superior; that fact alone should have settled the matter. The army was better off without the turbulent lieutenant colonel.

Besides, Sherman couldn't stand Frémont personally. As individuals they could hardly have been more different. Where Frémont was flamboyant, Sherman was steady. Where Frémont took chances, Sherman took care. Where Frémont broke rules, Sherman enforced them. Where Frémont's charisma drew people to him, Sherman's reserve put people off. Where Frémont was fire, Sherman was ice.

The ice in Sherman often took those who met him by surprise. His red hair and beard gave a first impression of a hotter temperament. Perhaps because of that, and to correct it, he kept the hair and beard clipped brusquely short. The eyes were the giveaway: blue, not like some warm southern ocean but like a glacier's heart. Gazing out from beneath a high, broad brow, the eyes assessed the world, and the people in it, with cool deliberation.

That was how they assessed Frémont, whom Sherman encountered in California. Sherman arrived at Monterey in January 1847 after a long voyage around Cape Horn. The tedium of the voyage was relieved, imperfectly, by a copy of Richard Dana's book and by the prospect of joining the fight against Mexico. With other West Pointers, Sherman saw the war as a career opportunity, one lately lacking for professional soldiers, and he anticipated bloodying his lance in battle. On the last leg of the voyage, up the California coast, he and his shipmates heard reports of the hostilities around Los Angeles. "Being unfamiliar with the great distances," he wrote, "we imagined that we should have to debark and begin fighting at once. Swords were brought out, guns oiled and made ready, and every thing was in a bustle when the old *Lexington* dropped her anchor."

To their disappointment, they learned that the action was four hundred miles away, and over. From all Sherman could see at Monterey, the war might have missed California completely. "Every thing on shore looked bright and beautiful, the hills covered with grass and flowers, the live-oaks so serene and homelike; and the low adobe houses, with red-tiled roofs and whitened walls, contrasted well with the dark pine-trees behind, making a decidedly good impression upon us who had come so far to spy out the land. Nothing could be more peaceful in its looks than Monterey in January 1847."

Deprived of a chance for distinction in battle, Sherman commenced the mundane task of quartermastering the occupation. Fortunately he came prepared. His ship carried six months' provisions for the troops it transported, the equipment for a sawmill and a gristmill, and assorted other supplies for an army headquarters. For such items as he needed to purchase, Sherman had $28,000 in cash. This seemed sufficient for a long stay, as prices were low. Horses ranged from four to sixteen dollars apiece; beef cost two cents a pound.

The occupation began uneventfully. Sherman spent days hunting in the mountains behind Monterey or watching the Californians exhibit their remarkable skills on horseback. "The young fellows took great delight in showing off their horsemanship," he wrote, "and would dash along, picking up a half-dollar from the ground, stop their horses in full career and turn about on the space of a bullock's hide." The Californians were equally adept with the lasso. "At full speed they could cast their lasso about the horns of a bull, or so throw it as to catch any particular foot." Sherman and the other American soldiers joined the locals at the weekly *baile*, where the young ladies displayed grace in dancing that matched the men's skills on horseback.

Sherman attempted the indigenous cuisine. One afternoon he and a companion rode into the countryside, reaching an isolated farmhouse at dusk. The owner, a Señor Gomez, was about to sit down to supper and wasn't pleased at having to share his meal with two of the American occupiers. But he understood he had no choice. "We were officers and *caballeros* and could not be ignored." Yet Gomez had his revenge. "I was helped to a dish of rabbit, with what I thought to be an abundant sauce of tomato. Taking a good mouthful, I felt as though I had taken liquid fire; the tomato was *chile colorado*, or red pepper, of the purest kind. It nearly killed me, and I saw Gomez's eyes twinkle."

Sherman met Frémont not long before the latter went east to face his court-martial. Sherman was curious to size up the famous explorer and so rode out to Frémont's camp. Frémont sat in his tent—a tepee, in fact—with a fellow veteran of the mountains and desert, a Captain Owens. Sherman spent an hour with Frémont, who served him tea and chatted about nothing important. Sherman had expected more, and left "without being much impressed." On the contrary, he concluded that personal pride and ambition, rather than the misunderstandings Frémont claimed, had provoked the fight with Kearny. Frémont's departure, under Kearny's arrest, was good riddance. "With him departed all cause of confusion and disorder in the country."

OR SO SHERMAN HOPED. With the political squabbling over—or transferred east at any rate, to Frémont's trial—Sherman anticipated a return to the quiet occupation. He settled into his assignment as adjutant to Colonel (and Governor) Richard Mason, expecting paperwork, more hunting and *bailes*, and perhaps another attempt at those infernal *chiles*.

A visit from some strangers in the spring of 1848 altered his plans. "Two men, Americans, came into the office and inquired for the Governor," Sherman recalled. "I asked their business, and one answered that they had just come down from Captain Sutter on special business, and wanted to see Governor Mason *in person*." Sherman knew of Sutter, although he had never met the man; naturally he wondered what this special business was.

> I took them in to the colonel, and left them together. After some time the colonel came to his door and called to me. I went in, and my attention was directed to a series of papers unfolded on his table, in which lay about half an ounce of placer-gold. Mason said to me, "What is that?"
>
> I touched it and examined one or two of the larger pieces, and asked, "Is it gold?"
>
> Mason asked me if I had ever seen native gold. I answered that, in 1844, I was in Upper Georgia, and there saw some native gold, but it was much finer than this, and that it was in phials, or in transparent quills; but I said that, if this were gold, it could be easily tested, first, by its malleability, and next by acids.
>
> I took a piece in my teeth, and the metallic lustre was perfect. I then called to the clerk, Baden, to bring an axe and hatchet from the backyard. When these were brought, I took the largest piece and beat it out flat, and beyond doubt it was metal, and a pure metal. Still, we attached little importance to the fact, for gold was known to exist at San Fernando, at the south, and yet was not considered of much value.

John Sutter apparently thought differently. The two visitors carried a letter from Sutter requesting preemption rights to the quarter-section of land on which the Coloma sawmill and millrace were located. Mason instructed Sherman to prepare an answer to Sutter's request.

Sherman explained that with the Mexican War not officially ended, California remained a Mexican province. American forces occupied the territory, but neither Governor Mason nor any other American official could convey land rights. Moreover, even after transfer of sovereignty, assuming such did occur, titles to land would await a public survey of the territory acquired. Captain Sutter would have to be patient.

Yet Sherman, not wishing to seem entirely unhelpful, remarked that the neighborhood in question contained no settlements and hardly any inhabitants. There needn't be any hurry about land titles, nor was Sutter's mill likely to be disturbed by trespassers. Mason read the letter, signed it, and handed it to the two messengers from New Helvetia, who departed north.

EVENTS SOON EXPLODED Sherman's complacency. Sutter and James Marshall, by discovering the gold, had prepared the explosive charge, but it was Sam Brannan who put the match to the powder.

Like Sherman, Brannan arrived in California from New York during the fighting against Mexico. Like Sherman, Brannan hoped to see some of that fighting. Like Sherman, Brannan was disappointed—but not so disappointed as Sherman, for, *un*like Sherman, Brannan was no soldier. Instead, he was a churchman, or professed to be. In reality, he was an opportunist, of a characteristically American—specifically, Yankee—stripe. Born in Maine in 1819 (which made him a year older than Sherman and six years younger than Frémont), Brannan bounced around several states as a journalist and speculator before landing in New York as an elder in the Mormon Church. In that capacity he sailed in early 1846 with a ship of Saints, bound for California, where the group intended to scout possibilities for a colony beyond the reach of the persecution that had dogged their sect in the United States. Brannan's vessel, the *Brooklyn*, landed first at Honolulu, where a resident American found the Mormons' naïve hopes of a new life in California touchingly funny: "The Mormon Co. talk as tho' they had nothing to do but go on to California, take such lands as they please, and No One to say boo!!!!"

Before they left Hawaii, Brannan and the others learned of the war between the United States and Mexico. Commodore Stockton, en route to California, encouraged Brannan to purchase weapons for the adult males on the *Brooklyn* and to drill the men in their use. Soon the Saints were marching to and fro, with Brannan at the command.

The *Brooklyn* entered San Francisco Bay at the end of July and anchored in the cove of Yerba Buena. Behind the beach, on a staff above the Mexican customshouse at the corner of the main plaza, Brannan and the others could see the American flag snapping in the summer breeze. "Damn that flag!" he reportedly said. As an elder of a sect ill-used under the Stars and Stripes, Brannan might have been forgiven for registering frustration at discovering that the foreign refuge for which he and the others had embarked was not foreign after all, and therefore likely not a refuge. On the other hand, he may simply have been disappointed at missing the chance to lead his troops into battle.

After getting the company settled, Brannan headed east to find Brigham Young and the rest of the Mormons. Having seen the attractions of California, he hoped to persuade Young and the others to join him there. It certainly occurred to him that as the leader of the California wing of the church, he would be well placed to benefit from general recognition of his foresight. Brannan's Sierra crossing, undertaken in the early spring of 1847, was difficult. "We traveled on foot and drove our animals before us, the snow from twenty to one hundred feet deep," he recalled, with forgivable exaggeration. "When we arrived [on the eastern slope of the mountains] not one of us could stand on our feet." Several weeks later, Brannan and his fellow travelers intercepted Young and the other Mormons on the banks of the Green River.

Brannan described to Young the wonders of California: the gentle climate, the fertile soil, the navigable rivers, the beckoning bay of San Francisco. It was just the spot for the new Zion, he explained. Yet Young resisted Brannan's arguments. Indeed, as Brannan gradually realized, the very arguments that seemed to Brannan to make California perfect seemed to Young to damn the place. If California was as desirable as Brannan contended—and Young didn't doubt that it was—it would soon be overrun by gentiles. Better to remain in the wastes of the Great Basin, where the Saints could build their colony in peace. Brannan continued to argue, to the point of insubordination. He thought Young was being willfully obstinate, and said so. Young took his as a further sign of the evil influence of California and the wider world, and chastised Brannan for consorting with mammon. After six weeks of similarly futile arguments, Brannan left the valley of the Great Salt Lake in disgust, bound again for California.

He arrived at Sutter's Fort just as James Marshall was heading up the American River to build the sawmill. With inspired timing, Brannan opened a general store at the fort. Consequently he was one of the first to know when Marshall's news leaked out of Sutter's study. Brannan briefly pondered what to do with the news. Part of him wanted to keep it quiet, in hopes of carving his own claim to the goldfields before everyone arrived. Another part wanted to publicize the discovery and thereby enlarge the clientele for his budding business.

Fatefully, Brannan—in the first manifestation of the insight that would be responsible for the most durable fortunes of the Gold Rush era—guessed that as much money might be made from the miners as from the mines, and he opted for publicity. He purchased enough gold dust to fill a jar and traveled to San Francisco, as Yerba Buena was now generally called. He paraded conspicuously about the town, waving his hat and shouting, "Gold! Gold! Gold from the American River!"

The rumors had preceded him, but this material evidence made the rumors suddenly credible. Others echoed Brannan's cry. An erstwhile skeptic found himself almost literally carried away.

> I looked on for a moment; a frenzy seized my soul; unbidden my legs performed some entirely new movements of polka steps—I took several. Houses were too small for me to stay in; I was soon in the street in search of necessary outfits. Piles of gold rose up before me at every step; castles of marble, dazzling the eye with their rich appliances; thousands of slaves bowing to my beck and call; myriads of fair virgins contending with each other for my love—were among the fancies of my fevered imagination. The Rothschilds, Girards, and Astors appeared to me but poor people. In short, I had a very violent attack of the gold fever.

So did hundreds of others. The small population of San Francisco nearly vanished overnight in the direction of Sutter's mill. The fever spread south to Monterey and Los Angeles; those towns were similarly depopulated. "The whole country from San Francisco to Los Angeles, and from the seashore to the base of the Sierra Nevada, resounds to the sordid cry of *gold*! GOLD!! **GOLD**!!!" observed a local paper, the *Alta California*, "while the field is left half planted, the house half built, and everything neglected but the manufacture of shovels and pickaxes, and the means of transportation to the spot where one man obtained $128 of the real stuff in one day's washing, and the average for all concerned is $20 per diem." With this statement, the paper announced that it was suspending publication; its entire staff was going to the goldfields.

"I OF COURSE COULD not escape the infection," said William Sherman, "and at last convinced Colonel Mason that it was our duty to go up and see with our own eyes, that we might report the truth to our Government." From Monterey, Sherman and Mason traveled overland to San Francisco, then across the bay to Sausalito, then again by land to San Rafael, Sonoma, and Sutter's Fort. Sherman described the fort and its setting, in a letter to his brother:

> The Sacramento, where we crossed it at Sutter's Fort, is a broad stream, with a current of two or three miles an hour; the banks are low, so that, when the rainy season sets in, the vast plain on the east side is one sheet of water, but at ordinary seasons the stream is confined within its banks of about three hundred yards wide. . . . Sutter's Fort stands about three miles back from the river, and about a mile from the American Fork, which also is a respectable stream. The fort encloses a space of about two hundred yards by eighty; the walls are built of adobe or sun-dried brick. All the houses are of one story, save one, which stands in the middle, which is two stories. This is the magazine, officers' mess-room, etc. It was in this that in former times Sutter held his state and issued orders amongst the tribes of Indians as peremptory and final as those of an emperor.

As it happened, the American officers arrived just in time for the first celebration of the Fourth of July in the (so far brief) American history of California. Sherman depicted host Sutter, at this time the most prominent man in California:

> His personal appearance is striking, about forty or fifty years of age, slightly bald, about five feet six inches in height, open, frank face, and strongly foreign in his manner, appearance, and address. He speaks many languages fluently, including that of all Indians, and has more control over the tribes of the Sacramento than any man living. . . . Sutter presided at the head of the table, Governor Mason on his right and I on his left. About fifty sat down to the table, mostly Americans, some foreigners, and one or two Californians. The usual toasts, songs, speeches, etc., passed off, and a liberal quantity of liquor disposed of, champagne, Madeira, sherry, etc.; upon the whole a dinner that would have done credit in any frontier town.

From Sutter's Fort, Sherman and Mason proceeded up the American River. At twenty-five miles they reached Mormon Island, so called from the three hundred Mormons—some from Marshall's company at Coloma, the rest other veterans of the Mormon Battalion—who were digging for gold in the sand and gravel of the streambed. Here Sherman met Sam Brannan, "on hand as the high-priest, collecting the tithes," Sherman recorded. Obviously the diggers were finding gold, which was making Brannan rich—which in turn was annoying some of the Mormons. One of them approached Colonel Mason. "Governor, what business has Sam Brannan to collect the tithes here?" he asked. Mason replied, "Brannan has a perfect right to collect the tax, if you Mormons are fools enough to pay it." By now the Treaty of Guadalupe Hidalgo had been ratified and California formally annexed to the United States; Mason added, "This is public land, and the gold is the property of the United States. All of you here are trespassers, but, as the Government is benefited by your getting out the gold, I do not intend to interfere."

Far from interfering, Mason—via the hand of Sherman—accelerated the search for gold. On their return to Monterey, Mason had Sherman draft a letter to Washington confirming the reports of the gold discovery. "The most moderate estimate I could obtain from men acquainted with the subject was, that upward of four thousand men were working in the gold district, of whom more than half were Indians, and that from $30,000 to $50,000 worth of gold, if not more, was daily obtained," Sherman wrote.

> The discovery of these vast deposits of gold has entirely changed the character of Upper California. Its people, before engaged in cultivating their small patches of ground and guarding their herds of cattle and horses, have all gone to the mines, or are on their way thither; laborers of every trade have left their work benches, and tradesmen their shops; sailors desert their ships as fast as they arrive on the coast. . . . I have no hesitation now in saying that there is more gold in the country drained by the Sacramento and San Joaquin rivers than will pay the cost of the present war with Mexico a hundred times over. No capital is required to obtain this gold, as the laboring man wants nothing but his pick, shovel, and tin pan, with which to dig and wash the gravel; and many frequently pick gold out of the crevices of rock with their butcher knives in pieces from one to six ounces.

To corroborate this testimony, Sherman suggested to Mason that they send some gold along with the letter. Mason agreed, and Sherman bought enough dust—over 200 ounces—to fill a small oyster-can (or tea caddy, as others interpreted the squarish metal container). The letter and the oyster-can left Monterey at the end of August, in the keeping of a special courier, a Lieutenant Loeser, whose orders were to get to Washington as quickly as possible.

2

Across the Pacific

But travel was slow. Lieutenant Loeser caught a ship bound south past Mexico and Central America for Peru. He waited in Peru for a second ship, bound back north to Panama, which he crossed by mule. A third craft carried him to Jamaica, and a fourth to New Orleans. From there he telegraphed ahead to Washington, saying he had arrived and was bearing an important message. But he didn't reach the capital himself—with the letter and the load of gold—till late November.

Loeser's arrival prompted an announcement by President Polk of the momentous discovery in California, an announcement that is often interpreted as the starting pistol for the Gold Rush. In a narrowly American sense it was, for in the months that followed Polk's announcement, a flood of American adventurers headed west, determined to fill their pockets with gold and their lives with the miracles sudden wealth would bring.

But in fact the rush to California had already begun. In terms of the most common means of long-distance transport—that is, by sea—every country that bordered the Pacific Ocean was closer to California than were the states of the American union. New York was sixteen thousand nautical miles from San Francisco, compared to two thousand for Acapulco and Honolulu, four thousand for Callao, six thousand for Valparaiso, and seven thousand for Sydney and Canton. While Lieutenant Loeser was struggling east, the word of James Marshall's discovery rippled out the Golden Gate (previously named with fortuitous aptness by John Frémont) and spread north, south, and west across the greatest of the world's oceans. In every port that heard the news, it set hearts racing. People dropped what they were doing, bought passage for the golden coast, and headed out upon the waves. They didn't all get there before the rush from America hit, but they did ensure the international character of the invading force.

THE NEWS REACHED South America almost before Loeser left Monterey. In May 1848 the supercargo of a Chilean ship at San Francisco heard the stories of gold on the American River and immediately offered $12 per ounce for as much dust as anyone would bring him. This commercial officer knew his business, for his price was substantially above the $8 to $10 local merchants were paying for gold (Sherman paid $10 per ounce to fill the oyster-can), yet comfortably below the $17 gold sellers were getting in Valparaiso, where his ship was headed.

The ship was the brig *J.R.S.*, owned by (and initialed for) José Ramón Sánchez of Valparaiso; its regular trade was hides and tallow, which heretofore were California's principal exports. (Richard Dana's *Pilgrim* was similarly engaged in the hide-and-tallow trade.) How much gold the supercargo acquired is unknown; if he ran short of cash to make good his promise, owner Sánchez had sufficient credit in San Francisco to supply the shortfall. The *J.R.S.* weighed anchor on June 14, cleared the Golden Gate, and reached Valparaiso on August 19.

Within hours the news that it carried California gold traversed the Vale of Paradise for which the town was named, and flew to Santiago, a hundred miles inland. Within days merchants were consigning cargoes for California; gold seekers were purchasing passage north. Two dozen hopefuls filled the berths of the *Virjinia*, which got away first. By chance another ship arrived from San Francisco just as the *Virjinia* was casting off; the additional gold it carried confirmed the earlier evidence of California's riches and further inflamed the dreams of the *Virjinia*'s argonauts.

"The gold nuggets were the authorized ambassadors of those riches," wrote Vicente Pérez Rosales, in line for one of the next boats north. "Their fame acquired the proportions of the calumny of the *Barber of Seville*, and aroused in the minds of the tranquil Chileans an explosion of such feverish activity that, ignoring the voices of prudence, led thousands of adventurers to the rich honeycomb where so many hopes perished. For those who gave credence to the existence of California gold, the only imprudent ones were those who did not rush off."

Pérez Rosales was too old for such stay-at-home imprudence. Forty-one when the news arrived from California, he was descended from parents who were patricians under the Spanish and rebels under José San Martín and Bernardo O'Higgins. During the Chilean war for independence they sent young Vicente to France to school; he returned to pursue what he thought would be a life of genteel, if perhaps radical, letters. But family bankruptcy overturned his plans, and he was cast upon his own practical talents. These proved more varied than most of those who knew the sheltered young man would have guessed. He dug gold in the Chilean Andes and rustled cattle, crossing into Argentina to round up the animals, then driving them back to Chile by precipitous paths only he and his fellow outlaws knew. After increased settlement brought too many witnesses to the backcountry, he abandoned the mountains for the cafes of Valparaiso, where aspiring but impoverished intellectuals like himself could talk for hours over a single cup of coffee. They read Rousseau and argued Locke, and printed their opinions on a press fitted with type purchased from the heirs of Benjamin Franklin. Upon hearing of the gold in California, Pérez reflected that however much the intellectual life nourished the soul, it left the body—at least *his* body—hungry, and he decided to join the adventurers heading north.

"Four brothers, a brother-in-law and two trusted servants constituted the personnel of our expedition to California," he recorded.

> The common capital of our escapade was: six sacks of toasted flour; six of beans; four quintals of rice; a barrel of sugar; two of Concepción wine; a small assortment of shovels, axes and picks; an iron kettle; powder, and lead for bullets; 250 pesos cash, and 612

> for the cost of passage. The private equipment of each one, apart from the linen which was abandoned over there because no one could be bothered to wash dirty underwear, only to wash gold, consisted of: military boots, a wool shirt that at the same time served as a jacket; thick woolen trousers; a leather belt; a dagger; a brace of pistols; a rifle; and lastly a canvas hat that had to serve as both a hat and a pillow. Completing our individual furnishings were: a small leather pouch for toasted flour, a tin pitcher or bowl capable of withstanding the heat of a fire; a hunter's gear; and a fire-flint.

Their ship was a French bark, the *Stanguéli*, which was so crowded that Pérez and his companions had to leave their common equipment for the next vessel. The departure evoked equal measures of anxiety and anticipation. "California for the Chileans was an unknown country, nearly a desert, full of dangers and infested besides by epidemics of disease," Pérez wrote. "There we had no friends or relatives to lend a hand; personal safety could be found only at the barrel of a pistol or the point of a dagger; and nevertheless, the risk of robbery, violence, sickness, death itself, were secondary considerations before the dazzling promise of gold."

The passengers were ninety men, two women (including a prostitute named Rosario Améstica, a favorite among the men), four cows, eight pigs, and three dogs (besides the seventeen sailors and the captain and pilot). Most seemed ordinary enough, but two attracted the special attention of Pérez Rosales. One was a gentleman named Álvarez, a Chilean by birth, eccentric to the point of paranoia. Though rich and able to afford the first cabin, he refused it, saying the Frenchmen operating the boat were all thieves and would not feed him as well as he could feed himself with the food he brought aboard. The other noteworthy passenger was "a Frenchman of such massive hips that, to enter the passageway through the narrow door that communicated with the cabin, he always had to turn sideways. For this we gave him the mischievous name *Culatus* [Big Butt]."

The ship set sail just after the solstice of the Southern Hemisphere summer, and for the first month the passengers and crew sweltered north toward the equator. On January 18, 1849, Pérez Rosales entered in his diary: "Until today our only torment has been the exasperating monotony and the suffocating heat." Amid the torpor the ship crossed the equator; none could rouse themselves to celebrate.

Yet before the mast, the steerage passengers were restive. "Álvarez is at the heart of the matter," Pérez wrote, "for it seems that his provisions, poorly distributed, will not last until the end of the voyage. We fear a mutiny on board."

Next day the ship sighted another vessel, which upon approach proved to be an American whaler. The Yankee captain dropped a boat, which rowed over to the *Stanguéli*. The captain was friendly and modest; the sailors who accompanied him were eager for faces and voices other than their own. The sailors grew more than eager upon perceiving one face—and form—in particular; they "nearly fainted with envy to see among us the charming Rosarito."

The captain told how he and his men had been thirty-nine months at sea without once touching land. (Either the Yankee captain, in the telling, or Pérez Rosales, in the retelling, may have been exaggerating; whalers often went long without landing, but rarely that long.) He savored the luncheon set before him: the soft bread and fresh meat, which he had almost forgotten after three years of hardtack and salt pork. The Chileans were lucky, he said, and doubly so to be off for the goldfields to win their fortunes. But he added, with the sigh of the homesick, "I do not envy your luck, for I am on my way to embrace my children."

The Americans continued south toward Valparaiso, carrying the Chileans' good wishes and their hastily scrawled letters; the *Stanguéli* proceeded slowly north. The restiveness in steerage persisted, until on the last day of January, when Pérez Rosales and the other cabin passengers were dining with the officers, a seaman burst into the saloon and frantically whispered a message to the captain. The captain turned to his messmates and declared, in a voice of alarm, "We have a revolution on board! Álvarez is leading it, and if you don't help me, we are lost!"

Pérez and the others literally leaped into action. While the others hurried to their cabins to retrieve weapons, Pérez hastened to deck to summon some additional passengers. Together they managed to subdue Álvarez before the mutiny spread. "This is no small luck!" Pérez remarked, pondering what the insurrection might have become. The prisoner was chained and kept under close guard.

The monotony resumed. On February 13, Pérez wrote: "Today makes 47 days of the voyage. The state of health, perfect; we have delivered to the sea but one poor dead sailor. According to what the captain says, in about four more days we shall arrive at the country of hope or deception. The wind is fresh; we are traveling at a rate of eight miles per hour. If this continues, the four days will turn into two. Dense clouds surround us on all sides. The captain has been lamenting all day the absence of the sun."

Pérez thought the captain simply disliked the gloom; in fact it was the danger the fog enshrouded that worried him. That danger became apparent shortly. "Only an hour ago we should have perished, shattered against the shores of the Farallones, which rise up just five leagues from the entrance to the port of San Francisco," Pérez recorded on February 15. In the fog the captain had shortened sail and readied anchors; this pleased the passengers, who assumed it meant they were about to land. But rather it was a precaution against striking unseen rocks. The captain, in order to keep the passengers from retiring but not wishing to frighten them by hinting at imminent wreck, proposed a game of whist.

> Great satisfaction filled the saloon. Some were playing, others were taking tea, all were talking at the same time, all boasting about what they intended to do. The good Culatus, who liked to sleep more than anything else, had placed his corpulent self upon the first step of the stairway that led from the cabin to the deck, tranquilly taking the air there, when the captain, suddenly throwing down his cards, rushed to the deck. An instant later, and when least expected, terrified shouts—"Rocks ahead! A bar to windward! Unfurl all sails!"—hit us like a thunderbolt.

Those still in the saloon couldn't flee fast enough. They scattered cards, broke china, overturned chairs, and splintered tables in their haste toward the exit. "As this was blocked by the fat Culatus, who in his fright had forgotten that he had to turn sideways to pass, the combined momentum of all of us blew out this devilish obstruction in our path to the deck like the wadding of a cannon, and we clambered over him."

Fortunately the captain's alertness rescued the ship and all aboard. Pérez was left to look over the rail at "the white and booming surf that marked the base of the black rocks where, without the swift action of the captain, we should have lost not only our dreams of riches but our very lives!"

The immediate danger past, the captain dropped anchor in forty fathoms. That day and the next, the fog persisted. A distant storm sent heavy seas that combined with the recent near-disaster to keep everyone uncomfortable. The sea lions and seabirds that inhabited the Farallones contributed to the discomfort with an incessant cacophony.

On the third day a heavy rain sheeted out of the fog. A rising wind convinced the captain to leave this dangerous zone; in doing so he almost collided with a brig that appeared ghostlike from the mist. Disaster was averted by an even narrower margin than before, as the brig scraped the stern beneath Pérez Rosales's feet. "What a hazardous position!" he scribbled.

Finally, at dawn on February 18, after a fitful night during which all slept in their clothes, expecting to have to swim for their lives at any moment, they awoke to glorious relief. "We beheld the most beautiful panorama that could have unfolded before our eyes at such a distressing moment. We described to the south the black Farallones, which had held such danger; and to the east, to which we were steering under a clear sky and with a fresh wind, the mouth of the Golden Gate, which inspired awe but at the same time smiled, seeming to open wide to receive us."

WHILE PÉREZ ROSALES and his Chilean shipmates were creeping north toward the equator, far across the Pacific in Australia an ambivalent Tom Archer pondered the startling news from America. Archer had come to Australia in his teens after his Scottish parents, transplanted to Norway, feared he would grow irretrievably Scandinavian and accepted the offer of an uncle to take the lad down under. Tommy wasn't consulted, being just then at death's door from typhus. By the time he recovered, the decision had been made, and the fourteen-year-old boy, after a brief visit to England, arrived at Sydney in company with two hundred Irish emigrants, at midnight on December 31, 1837, following a passage from Plymouth of 120 days.

During the next dozen years Tom Archer grew up with the country. Most of his time was spent in the outback herding sheep and some cattle, fending off larcenous and occasionally murderous "bushrangers," intimidating certain aboriginal "blacks" and employing others, and generally learning to survive in some of the most unforgiving country on earth. Years later he would summarize his lessons: "Morals—don't make shortcuts through the bush without food, matches, or tinder; don't attempt the impossible feat of rubbing a fire with a dry branch on a big log; don't imagine you have slept for hours when you have only slept for minutes; and finally, don't forget to be thankful for the exquisite luxury of sleeping on a sheepskin beside a roaring fire, having consumed a pot of delicious hot tea, with the usual accompaniment of damper and mutton." Archer regularly spent months at a stretch far from anything that passed for civilization, and longer than that from various accoutrements of domestic life. He remembered distinctly a day when he went to a creek to bathe. "I caught sight of the reflection of a tall broad-shouldered young man, who, on closer inspection, turned out to be myself." The Australian Narcissus gazed in wonder at his own figure. "For the first time, it occurred to me that I was verging upon eighteen, and nearly grown up. The knowledge of this inspired me with much veneration for myself." He added wryly, "But I was unable to perceive any approach to that feeling in anyone else."

Outback life was rigorous in other ways. A mate developed a severe toothache and begged the local doctor to pull the offending grinder. The doctor explained that he lacked the requisite tools. The patient moaned that the tooth must be removed or he'd die. A helpful bystander suggested that in the absence of pliers a bullet-mold (hinged and handled to accept the hot lead) might do. The doctor was game and the patient imploring, so into the mouth the instrument went. Much larger than pliers, it nearly choked the patient, who made awful noises as the doctor grappled for the tooth. Finally, after a mighty yank, the doctor triumphantly displayed the bloody molar. The patient, by now in shock, discharged a mouthful of gore before telling the doctor that what he had been trying to say—while the doctor was apparently trying to kill him—was that he had the wrong tooth. The doctor's face fell, and the patient fled as if from a torturer. But soon he was back, determined to have done with his malady or his life. The second operation succeeded.

The early summer—that is, December—of 1848 found Tom Archer sheep-rich but bored, and when he heard the news of gold in California he naturally took notice. But the news, at least as circulated in the Sydney papers, was puzzling. The editors couldn't decide whether the gold strike was a good thing or bad. As Archer himself appreciated, the Australian market for wool was slumping sadly; California offered a fresh and—if the reports of its sudden riches were true—lucrative outlet. And not just for wool. Australia was the closest English-speaking country to California, and therefore was well positioned to supply the miners with all manner of provisions. As the Sydney *Herald*, which broke the gold story in Australia, put it, "We believe several persons are going to send provisions to California, and if they arrive there before shipments from the United States, immense profits will be made."

Yet even as the papers applauded the transport of goods to California, they did their best to discourage the transport of *people*. Archer wasn't surprised, as preserving the population of Australia—in particular, that part of the Australian population that hadn't been ordered to the penal colony by British magistrates—was a regular theme with local editors. Even before the news from California, people had been edging toward docks to escape the economic slump. Now many of those same people were willing to bet ten pounds—the price of steerage to San Francisco—that they'd do better hunting gold in California than hunting jobs in Australia. And the Australian papers were trying to keep them from going. The *Herald* made a habit of deriding life in the "diggins" and depicting Californians as sharps. The "Mormons," the paper explained to readers wondering about these strange people involved in the gold discovery, "were originally of the sect known as 'Latter-day Saints,' which sect flourishes wherever Anglo-Saxon gulls are found in sufficient numbers to swallow the egregious nonsense of fanatic humbugs who fatten upon their credulity." The paper relayed satirical advice to aspiring gold-seekers:

> *What class ought to go to the Diggins?* Persons who have nothing to lose but their lives.
>
> *Things you should not take with you to the Diggins.* A love of comforts, a taste for civilization, a respect for other people's throats, and a value for your own.
>
> *Things you will find useful at the Diggins.* A revolving pistol, some knowledge of treating gun-shot wounds, a toleration of strange bedfellows.
>
> *The sort of society you will meet with at the Diggins.* Those for whom the United States are not big enough; those for whom England is too hot; those who came to clean out the gold, and those who came to clean out the gold finders.
>
> *What is the best thing to do when you get to the Diggins?* Go back home.
>
> *How gold may be best extracted.* By supplying, at exorbitant prices, the wants of those who gather it.
>
> *What will be the ultimate effect of the discovery of the Diggins?* To raise prices, to ruin fools, to demoralize a new country first, and settle it afterwards.

The discouragement was lost on Tom Archer. He guessed that conditions in California couldn't be any harder than conditions in the outback, and as for the alleged dangers from thieves and cutthroats, they might be just the thing to spice up a young man's life. With a friend named Ned Hawkins, he prepared to head east. Settling affairs—to wit, selling his sheep in a slow market—required several weeks; had Archer been of a less phlegmatic temper he would have grown impatient, for gold-hunters were embarking from Sydney's Circular Wharf by the thousands. Nor did he and Hawkins deny themselves a suitable leave-taking for their great adventure.

Friends in Sydney joined the celebration, and for days and nights the pubs of the city did a lively business by them.

With a light heart and a heavy head, Archer left Sydney on July 17, 1849. His vessel was the bark *Elizabeth Archer* of Liverpool, commanded by Charles Cobb and named, evidently, for no relation of Tom (at least he didn't comment on the coincidence of names). Archer's party consisted of himself, Hawkins, two other friends, and five servants: "my two Durandur black boys, Jackey Small and Davey . . . another black boy of Hawkins', and two Chinamen, also his." Besides Archer's group, the ship carried more than a hundred argonauts, including one Edward Hargraves, whom none particularly noticed but who would become his country's hero in just a few years.

After an easy run eastward for a week and a day, the ship sighted the islands called the Three Kings, off the northern tip of New Zealand's North Island. Captain Cobb kept the bearing east, to win as much seaway as possible before turning north into the trade winds that would push them back west. A single squall upset the smooth sailing, tilting the ship almost on beam ends in the middle of the night and leaving the passengers to survey a chaotic deck the next morning. On his earlier voyage out from England, Archer had discovered in himself a spryness about the rigging; twelve years later he astonished the *Elizabeth Archer*'s crew with his ability to scamper aloft with the best of the tars. He amazed even himself one dark night when the crew began reefing the main topsail while he was perched on the main topsail yard. Suddenly his seat swung away beneath him, leaving him dangling one-handed from the topsail stay. He managed to grasp a shroud with his other hand, and slid down the rigging, alighting with a bounce beside Captain Cobb, who was nearly as surprised as Archer himself had been two seconds before.

Several days after this, the captain proposed landing at Pitcairn Island, where the passengers might purchase fresh fruit and vegetables to complement their biscuit and mutton. Archer appreciated the shrewdness in the offer. In asking the passengers to pay for what he should have been supplying, Cobb calculated that few aboard would want to miss this singular opportunity to visit one of the most storied landfalls in the entire Pacific. As all knew, Pitcairn had been the last refuge of the mutineers of the HMS *Bounty*, seized in 1789 from its commander, Lieutenant William Bligh. Every English lad could recite the strangely stirring tale of how the brutal Bligh and eighteen loyalists had been cast adrift by Fletcher Christian and his fellow mutineers; how Bligh and the others had managed to steer their open boat four thousand miles to Timor, where Dutch colonists arranged their return to England; how Christian and the mutineers had sailed to Tahiti, where several were eventually captured by the Royal Navy and taken to England for trial and execution; how Christian and a handful of the other leaders of the mutiny, along with a number of Tahitians, had secretly sailed to the once-discovered but since-forgotten island of Pitcairn; how one by one the Pitcairn colonists had murdered one another till a single mutineer, a dozen Tahitians, and assorted offspring of the mutineers and Tahitians remained; how the long arm of British law had finally tracked down this last rebel but took pity on him and let him live out his days as the doddering patriarch of his sorry tribe.

Captain Cobb's invitation to visit the mutineers' redoubt elicited enthusiastic approval. Archer was one of the first into the boat lowered over the side; after a strenuous bit of rowing (the height of the cliff that dominated the shore had caused Cobb to underestimate the ship's distance from the island) and with the help of a whaleboat sent out to greet them, the visitors made their way through the treacherous surf to the beach.

It was obvious to Archer that conditions had improved since the colony's nadir.

> At least a score of people of both sexes and all ages now rushed upon us, seized our hands, and, shaking them most cordially, bade us welcome in excellent English. A comely, well-built set of folks they were, many of the men and nearly all the young women and children having tolerably fair, rosy complexions, with black or dark brown hair, the women's neatly gathered on the top of their heads, and fastened there in graceful, wavy ringlets. The men were all dressed in light European clothes, and the women wore a loose jacket of light striped stuff, reaching below the waist, and a long

strip of the same kind of stuff wound round and fastened to the waist.

(Edward Hargraves rendered a similar judgment of the Pitcairners. "A more happy or a more virtuous people it is scarcely possible to imagine the existence of," he wrote in his account of the voyage.)

The islanders led the visitors up the cliff to their village. Archer had never seen such a charming place. Rustic cottages provided the little shelter the inhabitants required; each cottage was surrounded by a large cultivated plot teeming with banana, plantain, and breadfruit trees, sugarcane, yams, sweet potatoes, and numerous tropical fruits and vegetables for which Archer had no names. (It was breadfruit, which the British hoped to transplant to their colonies elsewhere in the tropics, that had brought Bligh to the South Pacific on his fateful voyage.) Behind the village rose the slopes of a volcano, upon the peak of which, the islanders said, Fletcher Christian used to sit, awaiting the man-of-war that would come to take him away.

The islanders were most hospitable, throwing a banquet for their guests and providing overnight accommodations in their homes. The visitors filled their bellies with all the luscious produce they could eat and their bags with all they could buy. Archer's favorable impression of the islanders was diminished only slightly upon departure the next day. His was the last boat off the island; just as he and Hawkins were boarding, the islander in charge of accounts said that his people had been paid ten dollars too little for some of the supplies. Hawkins, who possessed a trusting heart, and Archer, who had literally given the shirt off his back to his Pitcairn host (European clothes being hard to come by in the South Pacific), assumed that the fault lay with their shipmates, especially after the Pitcairn accountant explained, with much anguish and hand-wringing, that he was a poor man with a large family, and his fellow islanders would hold him responsible for any discrepancy. "This was too touching for us to resist, and we each contributed one half of the sum required to render full justice." Only after they reached the *Elizabeth Archer* and told their story did they discover that the justice they had rendered was more than full, by ten dollars. Their shipmates got a laugh from the affair, and Archer and Hawkins a lesson in guile in Eden.

The remainder of the voyage was less eventful. East of Pitcairn the *Elizabeth Archer* encountered the southeast trades, which carried them into the tropics and the doldrums. A ten-day drift ended when they met the northeast trades, which drove them back west of Hawaii. Eventually they entered the belt of North Pacific westerlies, and proceeded before the wind toward California.

A few hundred miles from land they raised an American vessel. Archer had never met any Americans, and as he was going to their country he was curious to see what they were like. He got his wish when several came aboard. "A very queer-looking lot I thought them, dressed as they were in long blue woollen coats and brown or grey billy-cock hats, and looking more like farmers than sailors," he wrote. "With true republican freedom, they all accompanied the captain into the cabin, and were regaled with copious supplies of 'Bass's Bitter,' which they seemed to enjoy very much. The talk was animated and plentifully garnished with 'Do tell,' 'Waal, waal,' 'I reckon,' 'I guess,' and other Americanisms which I had never heard before, and thought rather expressive and amusing."

As interesting to Archer as the Yankees themselves was their vessel, christened the *Mount Vernon*. Her clean lines and aggressive rigging made her much faster in the water than the *Elizabeth Archer*. Archer thought this to be characteristic of the difference between the English and American approaches to sailing. The English built safe, boxy ships that were hard to sink but impossible to sail fast; the Americans sacrificed safety for swiftness, and left the English behind—as the *Mount Vernon* soon left the *Elizabeth Archer* behind.

Several days later Archer, scouring the eastern horizon from the crosstrees, spied what seemed a long, low bank of white clouds. When the clouds didn't move during the course of hours, Archer realized they weren't clouds but the snow-covered Sierra Nevada, at least 150 miles distant. Closer to shore the ship encountered pods of whales. The mighty mammals sported and breached, sometimes springing clear out of the water and landing with an awesome splash. Archer wondered how the animals had survived the depredations of American whalers, whose exploits were legendary and the source of international envy. (He later learned that these gray whales lacked the oil that made other species—especially sperm whales—attractive to the hunters.)

On October 5, under an azure sky and on a favorable breeze, the *Elizabeth Archer* entered the Golden Gate. The breeze expired and a strong ebb tide set in before the ship reached the cove of San Francisco, compelling Captain Cobb to anchor for the night. But the next morning the vessel reached the harbor, eighty-one days out of Sydney. Archer recorded little about the arrival, leaving Edward Hargraves to fill in the details:

> As we entered the harbour, about 500 sail of shipping came in view, presenting a complete forest of masts—a sight well calculated to inspire us with hope, and remove the feelings of doubt and dejection, which, in the course of a long voyage, are apt to take the place of the first eagerness for novelty and adventure. Boats from the shore and from ships that we had spoken on our voyage soon boarded us to welcome our arrival. "There is gold—plenty of gold—for all those who will work for it," was the answer to our numerous inquiries.

The *Elizabeth Archer* soon joined the armada of the abandoned. "The whole crew deserted on the night after our arrival in port," Hargraves wrote, "excepting one officer and the apprentice boys, four in number."

LEAVING CHINA WAS considerably harder than leaving Chile or Australia. Traditional Chinese revered their ancestors to a degree unheard-of elsewhere; a primary obligation of family life was to tend the shrine of the family dead. This duty wasn't simply familial; the respect for authority on which it was based simultaneously served as a prop to the power of the state. And it tended to tie people to the place of their birth—that is, the place of their ancestors' death. Emigration, especially across a wide ocean, prevented one from fulfilling this essential duty; it also challenged the legitimacy of the state. Consequently it was frowned upon both privately and politically and was undertaken only under the most compelling circumstances.

As things happened, circumstances were quite compelling during the late 1840s and 1850s. For centuries China's population had been growing, but with minor exceptions the land available to that population had not. By 1840 the Chinese numbered more than 400 million; where they all would live was a perennial problem. Recent developments both evinced and aggravated the problem. Since the White Lotus rebellion of the late eighteenth century, China had experienced a series of insurrections. The leadership of the rebellions often came from the educated classes, but the foot soldiers were typically peasants displaced by famine, flood, and other manifestations of the relentless population pressure. The greatest insurgency of all—the Taiping Rebellion, which touched off the most devastating war anywhere on earth during the nineteenth century, a conflict that ravaged a region the size of Western Europe and killed tens of millions—erupted at the century's midpoint, almost simultaneous with the discovery of gold in California.

Adding to the internal turbulence was the humiliation China suffered at the hands of Western imperialists. For centuries European merchants had sought some item to sell to the Chinese to balance the tea and silk the West was buying from China. The British found a solution in opium from India, which they sent to China in growing quantity. Chinese authorities, alarmed at the havoc the opium wreaked on Chinese life, outlawed the drug. British merchants, alarmed at the havoc the ban would wreak on their profits, appealed to their government. Though not yet convinced of the virtues of free trade in such insidious substances as American wheat, the British government nonetheless considered free trade in opium a cause worth fighting for, and did just that. The Opium War of 1839–42 forced open China's doors not simply to addictive drugs but to the West generally. The war-ending Treaty of Nanking guaranteed privileges to British traders at Canton, Shanghai, and other ports; additional Western countries, including the United States, soon received similar privileges (partly as a result of China's desire not to be at the mercy of Britain alone). The whole affair seriously undermined the authority of the Chinese government, and consequently encouraged the rebellions brewing in the countryside.

It was to Canton and the other treaty ports that the word of the California gold discovery came in 1848. Ship brokers quickly spread the news throughout the region around Canton. One broker based in Hong Kong, with offices in Canton, circulated a pamphlet printed in Cantonese and illustrated for the benefit of the nonreaders in his audience.

> Americans are very rich people. They want the Chinese to come and will make him welcome. There will be big pay, large houses, and food and clothing of the finest description. You can write your friends or send them money at any time, and we will be responsible for the safe delivery. It is a nice country, without mandarins or soldiers. All alike: big man no larger than little man. There are a great many Chinese there now, and it will not be a strange country. The Chinese god is there, and the agents of this house. Never fear, and you will be lucky. Come to Hong Kong, or to the sign of this house in Canton, and we will instruct you. Money is in great plenty and to spare in America. Such as wish to have wages and labor guaranteed can obtain the security by application at this office.

Whether the Chinese god traveled to California was debatable, but many Chinese certainly did. Prior to the gold discovery there were almost no Chinese in California. By contemporary accounts, one of the few, a man identified as "Chum Ming," heard the gold stories drifting down the Sacramento River in the spring of 1848 and traveled to the mountains to verify them. Satisfied that they were true, he wrote to a friend in Canton who spread the news before shipping out for California himself. Especially among illiterate peasants, such word-of-mouth reports greatly magnified the effect of the printed flackery, and before long the lure of *Gum Shan*—"Gold Mountain"—was defeating the traditional aversion to emigration. A handful of ships sailed for San Francisco in 1849; two score weighed anchor in 1850.

Yee Ah Tye was one of the emigrants. Like the great majority of Chinese gold-seekers, he left to historians no written records; the tale of his removal from China to California survives only in the memory of his descendants and their friends. The date of his birth is vague—but not the location, a fact of fundamental importance to traditional Chinese. The Yees had been living in the Sunwui District of Kwantung Province for eight hundred years. At one time they counted prominent government officials among their number, but for the last few centuries they had been farmers and fishermen. Yet Yee Ah Tye had love for neither crops nor catch. He moved from the village of his birth, Chang-wan, to Hong Kong after the British wrested that colony from China as part of the Opium War settlement; in Hong Kong he learned to speak English, evidently with an eye toward lifting himself from manual labor to commerce. He heard the news from California and read the notices of the departing vessels. He watched other Chinese leave for the land of gold and determined to follow. The longtime nurse of his eventual widow heard this part of the story from her: "Yee Ah Tye came to America in a junk. He was about twenty years old. The voyage started with twenty-two young Chinese men and ended with twenty."

Whether this rate of attrition was typical of ships sailing from China to California is hard to tell; passengers weren't counted carefully at either end of the voyage. Yet enough arrived at San Francisco—Dai Fow, or Big City—that by the end of 1851 there were perhaps 25,000 Chinese in California. Already they were a familiar, and simultaneously exotic, sight. A San Francisco parade included a contingent of Chinese; the *Alta California* reported that the "Celestials" (as the Chinese were often called, after a traditional name—"Celestial Kingdom"—for China) carried "a banner of crimson satin, on which were some Chinese characters and the inscription, 'China Boys.' "

3

The Peaks of Darien

Miss Jessie, although extremely intelligent, lacks the docility of a model student. Moreover, she has the objectionable manner of seeming to take our orders and assignments under consideration, to be accepted or disregarded by some standard of her own."

The young lady in question was Jessie Ann Benton; this letter from her teachers was addressed to her father, Thomas Hart Benton. The two were the talk of Washington and St. Louis during the 1830s and 1840s. Thomas Benton was a senator from Missouri, a bruising frontiersman who had once tussled, nearly fatally, with Andrew Jackson. Jackson had agreed to second a friend in a duel with Jesse Benton, Thomas Benton's brother. Thomas arrived at the City Hotel in Nashville late but angry, and a general melee of knives, clubs, and pistols ensued. Thomas Benton was thrown headlong down a flight of stairs while Jackson's shoulder stopped a Benton bullet. The wound would have killed many a lesser man; as it was, Jackson's blood soaked through two mattresses before being stanched, and the bullet remained in Old Hickory's flesh for years. (In a coincidence that astonished the principals when they eventually discovered it, another Benton bullet ripped a hole through the wall of an adjoining guest room, in which slumbered a nine-month-old baby named John Charles Frémont, visiting Nashville with his parents.)

The scrape with Jackson didn't cure Benton of his violent streak; he subsequently killed a man in a duel. In the East this might have disqualified him from public office, but in Missouri it simply made him more popular, and he was elected senator upon that state's admission to the Union in 1820.

Midway through his first term (of six), Benton became the father of a feisty girl who inherited his uncompromising spirit. Jessie afterward commented on "that instinctive sympathy which made us one"; in her youth, friends and neighbors commented on how impossible both were, and how much the father spoiled the daughter. When her teachers would no longer have her, he tutored her at home. When the world, including Jessie's mother, chastised the girl, he took her part. One Saturday evening Jessie stole off to the house of a French Catholic playmate, with pajamas and other spurious evidence of permission to spend the night. She returned home next day to a stern lecture from her mother, who concluded by inquiring why the young lady had missed Sunday school. "Because I planned to go to mass," Jessie replied saucily, "to learn more about a church that doesn't confine your Sunday reading to one good book. Besides, I hate the Presbyterian church—no flowers, no candle light, no pictures." After Jessie had been sent to her room, her sister inquired what their father's reaction had been. "He scolded me for disrespect to mother, but not to the Presbyterians," she said.

Jessie blossomed into a dark-eyed, raven-haired beauty, which simply made her father more protective. He tried to steer her affections toward young men of family and prospects. But Jessie had different ideas. One day a dashing lieutenant named Frémont visited the Benton home to see the senator about support for an exploratory expedition to the West. Jessie was smitten before Benton could warn her about the young man's checkered past. Sensing trouble, Benton forbade Jessie to see Frémont and made sure the explorer got the money for his journey far away from Washington.

Yet Jessie, all of sixteen years old, refused to accept the paternal veto. She smuggled letters to Frémont, and upon his return the two eloped. When Benton learned of the marriage, he ordered Frémont out of the house and told him never to return. Jessie, he said, would stay.

But Jessie would *not* stay. If her husband was banished from the family house, she declared, so was she.

Benton had never been so angry, and he held out for weeks. Yet, as he always did with Jessie, he finally gave in. Daughter and son-in-law were permitted back home. Benton once more, but now with no ulterior motives, sponsored Frémont's exploratory career.

Jessie did, too. She became her husband's collaborator and ghostwriter. When he returned from the expedition that scouted the Oregon Trail, and sat down to write the report required by Congress, he discovered that all the courage and ambition that had carried him over the mountains and deserts couldn't get him past his first paragraph. A severe case of writer's block induced headaches and nosebleeds. Jessie suggested that the man of action wasn't necessarily the one best-suited to putting action to paper. As she explained afterward, "The horseback life, the sleep in the open air, had unfitted Mr. Frémont for the indoor work of writing." (Jessie's recollections almost always make her sound more demure than she really was. As with many memoirists, so especially with her: one has to read between the lines.) The two agreed that he would tell the story to her, and she would round it into literary form. The resulting report was a popular and political triumph. Congress ordered a thousand extra copies; newspapers reprinted it and reprinted again. Emigrants to Oregon packed the authorized versions and bootlegged copies in the tops of their trunks for ready reference. With Benton's encouragement, the legislature ordered a second Frémont expedition, better funded and manned than the first.

This expedition also proved to be better armed than the first: Frémont included a twelve-pound howitzer in his kit. When news of his armament reached Washington, officials at the War Department objected. Frémont would be entering territory in dispute with Britain and Spain; any hint of an armed invasion might provoke a diplomatic crisis. Frémont's superiors dispatched an urgent message ordering him to leave his artillery at home or return to Washington to explain himself.

Jessie intercepted the message at St. Louis. Acting as her husband's secretary, she opened his mail in his absence; reading this letter, she concluded that jealous bureaucrats intended to subvert the Frémont expedition. "I felt the whole situation in a flash," she recalled. "I had been too much a part of the whole plan for the expeditions to put them in peril now—and I alone could act." She added, with hindsight, "It was in the blessed day before telegraphs; and character counted for something then, and I was only eighteen, an age when one takes risks, willingly." She hazarded the censure of the federal government by refusing to forward the letter to Frémont, instead dispatching a swift emissary with a message of her own: "*Only trust me and Go.*"

Frémont went, leaving before a copy of the letter, sent straight from Washington to his camp on the Missouri River arrived. The ensuing expedition, made possible by Jessie's brazenness, was the one that first took him to California, and when he returned east and Jessie wrote up the report, he became more famous than ever. Congress ordered ten thousand copies, which magnified the Manifest Destinarianism that elected James Polk and triggered the Mexican War.

THE IGNOMINIOUS WAY the war ended for Frémont—culminating in his court-martial and resignation—was what prompted his and Jessie's move to California. Their thinking was that in California he might restore his sullied reputation and she create a family home, which, on account of his frequent absences, they had never really had. She was pregnant, for the second time. A daughter, Elizabeth, had been born in 1842; now a son, Benton, followed. The four would make a new life in the new territory.

Before leaving California as Kearny's prisoner, John had entrusted $3,000 to Thomas Larkin, the American consul at Monterey, with the understanding that Larkin would purchase a ranch Frémont had identified in the hills behind San Francisco. The property had various charms, including an ocean view; Frémont supposed it would be both a pleasant place to live and a good investment. But through some combination of accident and shady dealing, Larkin instead purchased a property in the Sierra foothills. The Mariposa tract, as it was called, was much larger than the San Francisco ranch, but was far removed from civilization, was occupied by fiercely possessive Indians, and, for that reason, was inhabitable by outsiders such as the Frémont family only at great peril. Frémont learned of the misdealing and vowed to make it right. He demanded an explanation from Larkin, saying he wanted either his money back or the ranch he originally selected. And he was coming to California to ensure that his demands were met.

Jessie would follow, with the children. The plan she and John devised called for him to travel overland, at the head of another expedition, this one privately funded and designed to test the feasibility of a railroad route to California. Jessie, Elizabeth (whom the family called Lily), and baby Benton would travel by steamer from New York to the isthmus of Panama, cross the isthmus by riverboat and mule, and take a second ship up the coast to Monterey, where they would meet John.

Because the overland expedition would require longer than the Central American journey, and because Jessie had seen so little of John during the last several years, she accompanied him to his jumping-off point on the Missouri River. They traveled by train to St. Louis, then by steamboat up the Missouri to Westport. En route little Benton, who had never been strong during the several weeks of his young life, fell ill and died. Doctors attributed the death vaguely to a defective heart, and attempted to console the mother and father by explaining that the child couldn't have lived long in any case.

John carried his grief into the wilderness, bidding Jessie and Lily farewell in late October 1848. Jessie sadly returned down the Missouri to St. Louis. There she received a message that General Kearny, in the city and sick with yellow fever, wished to see her—to ask forgiveness for his treatment of John, she inferred. She rejected the invitation. Not only did she blame Kearny for destroying her husband's career, she convinced herself that the strain of the trial during her pregnancy had harmed her unborn, and now dead, son. Kearny shortly died himself, unforgiven by the angry, grieving mother.

SHE THEREUPON TRAVELED east to New York—and ran into a hurricane of popular emotion like nothing she or anyone else in America had ever experienced. The letter William Sherman had drafted at Monterey and sent off with the gold-laden Lieutenant Loeser had finally arrived at Washington, and President Polk had translated it into a special message to the American people. "The accounts of the abundance of gold in that territory are of such an extraordinary character as would scarcely command belief were they not corroborated by the authentic reports of officers in the public service, who have visited the mineral district, and derived the facts which they detail from personal observation," the president said. The entire California region was in a fit of excitement. "Labor commands a most exorbitant price, and all other pursuits but that of searching for the precious metals are abandoned. Nearly the whole of the male population of the country have gone to the gold district. Ships arriving on the coast are deserted by their crews, and their voyages suspended for want of sailors. . . . This abundance of gold, and the all-engrossing pursuit of it, have already caused in California an unprecedented rise in the price of the necessaries of life." Americans from every region of the country—eastern merchants and manufacturers, southern planters, western farmers—could expect to benefit from the gold discovery and the demand it created for those necessaries of life. Polk predicted that California and the other territories acquired from Mexico would "add more to the strength and wealth of the nation than any which have preceded them since the adoption of the Constitution."

Rumors of the California gold had been circulating for weeks, but skeptics could easily dismiss such rumors as self-interested efforts to drum up business. Polk's statement, backed by the can of gold, transformed the rumors into hard news. And it touched off a torrent of commentary and conjecture. "We are on the brink of the Age of Gold," asserted Horace Greeley of the *New York Tribune*. The *New York Herald* declared, "The Eldorado of the old Spaniards is discovered at last. We now have the highest official authority for believing in the discovery of vast gold mines in California, and that the discovery is the greatest and most startling, not to say miraculous, that the history of the last five centuries can produce."

New York's merchants eagerly calculated what part of the profits they might hope to claim. One merchant, Franklin Buck, watched his commercial colleagues lay in goods and passengers for the Far West. "Look out on the docks," he wrote his sister, appealing to her mind's eye, "and you will see from twenty to thirty ships loading with all kinds of merchandise and filling up with passengers." Buck, a Massachusetts man by birth and an heir to the sober Puritan tradition of ancestor Samuel Sewall (of the Salem witch trials), wasn't one to be swept away by every avaricious enthusiasm that came along. But this was more than he could resist.

> When I see business firms—rich men—going into it, men who know how to make money too, and young men of my acquaintance leaving good situations and fitting themselves out with arms and ammunition, tents, provisions and mining implements, there is something about it—the excitement, the crossing the Isthmus, seeing new countries and the prospect of making a fortune in a few years—that takes hold of my imagination, that tells me "Now is your chance. Strike while the iron is hot!"

Not all were so sanguine. The *Boston Courier*—reflecting that dour Puritanism—wondered whether reality was so golden as portrayed. The Spanish, after all, had owned California for two centuries without discovering gold, despite their adeptness at locating it elsewhere. Imagination strained to think that Americans, with no history in precious metals, should find gold within weeks of acquiring the territory. But Boston's doubts ran deeper than this. Even assuming that the reports were true in their entirety, they didn't augur well for California, or for America. "The last thing that we should desire for the prosperity and permanent welfare of a country would be the discovery of a gold mine in it. Hardly any thing can be more certain to repress industry, productive labor, thrifty habits, and social improvement in general." Were the mining regions of South America prosperous? Hardly—they were characterized by "ragged people, ruinous dwellings, neglected agriculture, sloth, ignorance, squalor, dirt, and dissipation." Americans would do well to heed the lesson of Spain's experience. "The romance of *El Dorado* cost the Spaniards more blood, treasure, fatigue, and suffering than all their real conquests and acquisitions in the Western world. It is to be hoped that our own times will not witness a copy of that delusion."

JESSIE FRÉMONT HAD expected a leisurely start to a genteel journey; what she encountered were mobs of argonauts (as they styled themselves, after Jason and his fleece-seeking shipmates) clamoring for space on the vessels heading down the Atlantic coast. For gold-seekers with money, the isthmus was the route of choice. The price of ocean passage, on the New York to Panama and Panama to San Francisco legs together, ran from $200 to $500 depending on the class of one's shipboard accommodations. And this was just the start. Under the crush of the gold-hunters, traversing the isthmus became a major operation and a major expense.

Fortunately for Jessie Frémont, money was no problem. Her father was happy to pay her way west. He was rather less happy for her to go unaccompanied by anyone older than Lily. Other Benton relatives were shocked that he even considered allowing her to travel so far, accompanied or otherwise. But he knew Jessie better than they, and knew it was futile to forbid what she had set her mind on—in this case, starting a new life with her husband in California. So her sister's husband, Richard Taylor Jacob, was pressed into service to escort her to San Francisco.

Jessie's maid was less amenable to persuasion. The young black woman had fallen in love with a young man who was distraught at the idea that his darling should leave him, and on such a perilous and lengthy journey, no less. As resourceful as he was desperate, he concocted a story that she was being spirited away against her will. In abolitionist circles in New York, claims of the kidnapping of free blacks for sale into slavery could be counted on to draw large and threatening crowds; just such a crowd gathered to protest this latest alleged atrocity. The young woman in fact was free, she wasn't being forced against her will, and she wasn't being sold into slavery. But she was so impressed with her sweetheart's determination that she told Jessie she couldn't accompany her to California. Jessie, too, had to admire the young man's audacity, although she was indignant at being accused of an act that was illegal and, worse, low. The Bentons had always opposed slavery.

If it was almost unthinkable for Jessie to travel to California without a male escort, it was wholly inconceivable for her to depart without a maid. An eleventh-hour search turned up a New England woman of indeterminate years, although apparently at least a score more than Jessie's twenty-five. Jessie distrusted the woman's looks. "She was a hard, unpleasing person to my mind," she recalled. But the steamer sailed the next day, and there was no one else.

Until the *Crescent City*, of the Pacific Mail steamship line, left the dock on the morning of March 15, Jessie kept up a brave face. But as the ship slipped down the Hudson estuary and out past Sandy Hook, the magnitude of the ocean and of the task she had set for herself briefly overwhelmed her. The ship carried nearly 350 passengers; all but Jessie, Lily, Jessie's new maid, and one Irish woman traveling with her husband were male. Jessie had never been to sea; in fact, she had never been much beyond the bosom of her family. "I had never been obliged to think for or take care of myself," she recalled, "and now I was to be launched literally on an unknown sea, travel toward an unknown country, everything absolutely new and strange about me."

That first night Jessie put Lily to bed early, soothing the same fears in her daughter she felt in herself. Then she too crawled under the covers, hoping that what she had told Lily—that things would look better the next day—would prove true. Sleep came slowly, then came and went repeatedly through the night. During one moment of semiconsciousness she heard footsteps in her cabin. Through half-closed eyes she saw a shadow, which became a human figure. The darkness eventually revealed the new maid—but not the new maid, for this woman was much younger, with lighter hair. Jessie, fearing an attack on her own person or Lily's, kept quiet while the woman rummaged through Jessie's trunk, pocketing everything that suited her larcenous tastes. After what seemed an age but certainly was no more than minutes, the woman left.

Jessie flew to the door and bolted it, and guarded it till morning against repeated knocks and calls from the same woman. When morning finally came, she reported the theft to the captain, who arrested the thief and put her under guard for the duration of the voyage. This left Jessie without a maid—for indeed the thief and the servant were one, the latter being the former in disguise—but relieved for the lack. (The woman in question would distinguish herself in San Francisco by being implicated in the great fire that destroyed the city in 1851.)

The eight remaining days to Chagres, the port on the Caribbean side of Panama, were marginally better. A storm laid Richard Jacob low, rendering him more a queasy burden than a source of strength. Jessie's double cabin, the best on board, soon seemed almost homey. Indeed, so comfortable did it become that she was tempted not to leave it. "When we reached Chagres," she said, "if it had not been for pure shame and unwillingness that my father should think badly of me, I would have returned to New York on the steamer."

THE SHIP'S CAPTAIN implored her to do just that, with reason. In more placid times the isthmus was merely unhealthy and unruly. Spain had tried to impose order during the three centuries of Spanish rule, and in the salad days of the empire succeeded well enough to get couriers and shipments of gold over the sixty or so miles of mountains and jungle that separated Chagres from Panama City. But when Castile nodded, outlaws, freebooters, adventurers, and other undesirables flocked to this crossroads of two continents and two oceans, and made merry havoc. Order deteriorated further when mainland Hispanic America threw off Spanish rule in the first quarter of the nineteenth century; the successor to sovereignty on the isthmus, the republic of New Granada, lacked the resources and imperial incentive to police the Panama strip.

The discovery of gold in California compounded the chaos. Thousands, then tens of thousands, of argonauts descended upon Chagres, overwhelming the town's ecological, economical, and political carrying capacity. Housing had never been plentiful; now it was nonexistent for most of the travelers. They slept in the streets, by the harbor, on doorsteps, and under awnings. The rough living heightened the danger the travelers incurred of contracting insect-borne diseases—chiefly yellow fever ("Chagres fever") and malaria. The town's sanitation system had sufficed, more or less, for a population of a few hundred; it failed appallingly under the load of several thousands. Cholera and typhoid were rampant.

Consequently, Captain Schenck of the *Crescent City* had ample cause for fearing that Jessie Frémont and Lily might never leave the isthmus alive. It would be far more prudent, he said, for the pair to return with him to New York. If Jessie's father and husband had known what this part of the passage would involve, under the crush of the argonauts, they never would have let her come.

Richard Jacob seconded the captain's argument, for his charges' sake and his own. He was traveling to California only because they were; his wife was back east and expecting a child. If Jessie would agree to turn around, his own journey would be shortened by more than half. And, by all evidence, his life might well be lengthened.

But Jessie, despite the trials of the journey so far, insisted on continuing. She had told John she would join him in California. Even now he must be battling his way across the winter mountains. She must meet him when he reached the promised land. Screwing up her courage, she handed Lily over the side of the ship to the crew manning the boat that would take them to shore, and followed her down. The reluctant Richard Jacob climbed in beside them.

"FOR THREE OR FOUR days before reaching Chagres," wrote J. D. Borthwick, "all hands were busy packing up, and firing off and reloading pistols; for a revolver and a bowie-knife were considered the first items in a California outfit. We soon assumed a warlike appearance, and though some of the party had probably never handled a pistol in their lives before, they tried to wear their weapons in a negligé style, as if they had never been used to go without them."

Borthwick, a Briton, was one of the thousands of gold-seekers who crossed the isthmus by the same route as Jessie Frémont. Like her and most others, he had embarked from New York (smaller numbers came from New Orleans and other ports); like her he encountered at Chagres the first real taste of what the trip to California entailed. To this point it had consisted of a sea voyage, and a generally pleasant one at that (an outcome not lost on later organizers of Caribbean cruises). But all the travelers had heard of Chagres and the isthmus, and all prepared for their first test. "Wondrous accounts constantly appeared in the New York papers of the dangers and difficulties of these few miles of land-and-river travel," Borthwick wrote, "and most of the passengers, before leaving New York, had been humbugged into buying all manner of absurd and useless articles, many of them made of india-rubber, which they had been assured, and consequently believed, were absolutely necessary." But how to carry them all, or even how to use them all, was a puzzle. "Some were equipped with pots, pans, kettles, drinking-cups, knives and forks, pocket-filters (for they had been told that the water on the Isthmus was very dirty), india-rubber contrivances, which an ingenious man, with a powerful imagination and strong lungs, could blow up and convert into a bed, a boat, or a tent—bottles of 'cholera preventive,' boxes of pills for curing every disease to which human nature is liable; and some men, in addition to all this, determined to be prepared to combat danger in every shape, bade defiance to the waters of the Chagres river by buckling on india-rubber life-preservers."

The setting of Chagres was stunning. "The eastern shore is high and steep, cloven with ravines which roll their floods of tropical vegetation down to the sea," wrote Bayard Taylor, a reporter for Horace Greeley's *New York Tribune* who was traveling to California to cover the biggest story of the decade. "The old castle of San Lorenzo crowns the point, occupying a position somewhat similar to the Moro Castle at Havana [another stop on Taylor's voyage], and equally impregnable. Its brown battlements and embrasures have many a dark and stirring recollection. Morgan and his buccaneers scaled its walls, took and leveled it, after a fight in which all but thirty-three out of three hundred and fourteen defenders were slain, some of them leaping madly from the precipice into the sea. Strong as it is by nature, and would be in the hands of an enterprising people, it now looks harmless enough with a few old cannon lying lazily on its ramparts."

The town itself was another story. "We found Chagres to be one of the filthiest places we ever saw," said Stephen Davis, a seventeen-year-old New Englander fleeing both the textile mills of his native region, in which he had already done time, and a new stepfather, from whom he anticipated trouble. School had promised an escape of sorts, but after the news of gold in the West, Stephen found it impossible to concentrate on his books and so abandoned the effort. During the voyage from New York he fended off an attempted robbery by one of the ship's stewards, who tried to divest him of his money belt while he was sleeping; upon reaching Chagres, he discovered that the thieves there operated more openly—indeed, legally. "Early in the morning went ashore in a skiff, for which we paid $2 each. . . . We engaged passage in a large flat-bottomed boat, with 15 others, for $10 each, to Gorgona."

Yet Davis counted himself lucky to be traveling by skiff and flat-bottom. More common as a means of reaching shore from the arriving ships was the native canoe, manned by "negroes in a state of perfect nudity (except for their hats)," as a Virginia doctor put it in a letter home. "We left the ship in a heavy sea, and some twelve of us got into a large canoe, made as all canoes here are, by hollowing out an enormous trunk of a tree some thirty feet long, five wide, and three deep. We sat down in the bottom of the boat, and came near being swamped several times by the large waves, some of which broke right upon our heads and drenched us through and through."

Most emigrants passed through Chagres as swiftly as possible. Frank Marryat, an English gold-seeker and traveler who at twenty-three had already been around the world, remarked drolly, "The town of Chagres deserves notice, inasmuch as it is the birthplace of a malignant fever, that became excessively popular among the Californian emigrants, many of whom have acknowledged the superiority of this malady by giving up the ghost a very few hours after landing." So notorious was the Chagres fever, in fact, that the life insurance policies purchased by many emigrants carried a Chagres-exclusion clause: if they slept ashore at Chagres, they voided their policies. Marryat's travels had revealed a hardy constitution, but even he made a point of leaving Chagres on the afternoon of the day he arrived. "All was noise and excitement—cries for lost baggage, adieus, cheers, a parting strain on a cornet-à-piston, a round dozen at least of different tongues, each in its owner's peculiar fashion murdering Spanish, a few discharges from rifles and revolvers, rendered the scene ludicrous, and had the good effect of sending us on the first step of a toilsome journey in a good humour."

FROM CHAGRES THE argonauts ascended the Chagres River to Gorgona, a distance of about fifty winding miles. Most of them breathed easier in the purer air outside the town; they also gazed in wonder at a lushness few had observed before. Frank Marryat wrote:

> There is an absence of variety in the scenery of the Chagres river, as throughout its whole length the banks are lined to the water's edge with vegetation. But the rich bright green at all times charms the beholder, and the eye does not become wearied with the thick masses of luxuriant foliage, for they are ever blended in grace and harmony, now towering in the air in bold relief against the sky, now drooping in graceful festoons from the bank, kissing their own reflections in the stream beneath.
>
> Every growing thing clings to and embraces its neighbour most lovingly; here is a bunch of tangled parasites that bind a palm tree by a thousand bands to a majestic teak, and having shown their power, as it were, the parasites ascend the topmost branch of the teak, and devote the rest of their existence to embellishing with rich festoons of their bright red flowers, the pair they have thus united.
>
> The teak, which here is a very bald tree, is much improved by the addition of these parasites, which give him quite a juvenile appearance, and form, in fact, a kind of wig, to hide the infirmities of age. Here is a dead and well-bleached sycamore tree, half thrown across the river, but still holding to the bank by its sinewy roots; and its extremity is an ant's nest, about the size of a beehive,

> and along the trunk and branches green leaves are seen to move about at a prodigious rate, under which ants are discovered on inspection.
>
> Immediately under the ants' nest are some glorious water-lilies, and close to these, by way of contrast, floats an alligator who has been dead some time, and hasn't kept well, and on the top of him sit two black cormorants, which having, evidently, over-eaten themselves, are shot on the spot and die lazily.

Jessie Frémont was better able to appreciate the scenery along the Chagres than many travelers. As the daughter of one of America's most powerful statesmen—a legislator well placed to facilitate, or hinder, the business of the Pacific Mail steamship line—she enjoyed a corporate solicitude extended to few others. After she rebuffed Captain Schenck's efforts to terminate her trip, she accepted his invitation to ride one of the ship's boats up the Chagres River. Consequently she only saw, rather than experienced, the dowsings the other travelers received in the dugouts, and observed only from a distance—but apparently no less carefully for that—what she described as the native vessels' crews of "naked, screaming, barbarous negroes and Indians."

Eight miles upriver from the mouth, Jessie and Lily were transferred to a smaller boat operated by the steamship company for its own officers and executives. In slack water the crew—consisting of blacks and Indians, but more mild-mannered than those in the canoes—rowed the boat upstream. Intermittently, and more the higher they went, the paddles had to be traded for poles. With great effort the crewmen pushed the craft against the current, often entering the water to propel the boat past a sunken tree, sandbar, or other obstruction.

By the time they approached Gorgona, on the third day of the ascent, the crew spent more time in the water than aboard. Richard Jacob determined to help, as Jessie related.

> We were near to the close of the last day's journey, within an hour of Gorgona, when my brother-in-law, being young and strong and

> a Kentuckian, in his impatience at the delay on one of those sand spits, jumped into the water and dragged the boat, in spite of the men, who told him that it would kill him.
>
> We did get off sooner than usual through his help, and he was very triumphant about it, when suddenly his eyes rolled back in his head and he fell prostrate from sunstroke just as we reached Gorgona; and throughout that whole night the physician with the engineering corps was doubtful if he could live.

In fact he did live, but the doctor declared that he must return to New York and civilization if he hoped to recover completely. Jessie insisted that he follow orders, which he did, not least because he realized he henceforth would be even less help, and more hindrance, than he had been so far. Predictably he implored Jessie to join him in the return; so did everyone else she encountered, who said it was impossible for her to continue unescorted.

"Quite secretly to myself I said so too when I began to see what the emigrants suffered," she conceded later. At Gorgona the traffic across the isthmus began to back up badly. Hundreds of people were camped on the hillsides above the village, huddling in tents, awaiting transport the rest of the way to the coast. Though the great majority were men, some were women and children; the suffering of the ladies and babes evoked in Jessie both sympathy for them and fear for herself and Lily.

But as often as the fear arose, Jessie's stubbornness stamped it down, and she pressed forward. The alcalde of Gorgona personally sought out the American senator's daughter and invited her to a celebratory feast. Jessie shuddered, and nearly became ill, at the sight of the pièce de résistance: "a baked monkey, which looked like a little child that had been burned to death." The alternate entrée—iguana—was only slightly more appetizing.

At Gorgona the emigrants left the river and set forth on foot—mules' feet, horses', or their own. Whether the track they followed was a road, a trail, or something less substantial was a matter of interpretation. "The distance from Gorgona to Panama was about twenty-one miles," Jessie explained. "It was *distance*, not a *road*; there was only a mule track—rather a trough than track in most places, and mule staircases with occasional steps of at least four feet, and only wide enough for a single animal—the same trail that had been followed since the early days of Spanish conquest; and this trail followed the face of the country as it presented itself—straight up the sides of the steepest heights to the summit, then straight down them again to the base."

The regular rains hardly helped matters, drenching the travelers and turning the soil into a greasy semiliquid. "Scrambling up ravines of slippery clay," wrote Bayard Taylor, "we went for miles through swamps and thickets, urging forward our jaded beasts by shouting and beating. Going down a precipitous bank, washed soft by the rains, my horse slipped and made a descent of ten feet, landing on one bank and I on another. He rose quietly, disengaged his head from the mud and stood, flank-deep, waiting till I stepped across his back and went forward, my legs lifted to his neck."

Mules carried much of the emigrants' baggage; porters carried the rest. "It was astonishing to see what loads these men could carry over such a road," J. D. Borthwick noted. It was especially astonishing in light of what Borthwick and most of his fellow travelers had come to expect of the natives. "It really seemed inconsistent with their indolent character, that they should perform, so actively, such prodigious feats of labor. Two hundred and fifty pounds weight was an average load for a man to walk off with, doing the twenty-five miles to Panama in a day and a half, and some men carried as much as three hundred pounds."

The human porters usually made it to Panama alive; and when they didn't, their bodies received comparatively respectful treatment. Not so for the mules. "We found the 'road' in a horrible condition," wrote Stephen Davis, "the mud being 4 or 5 feet deep in some places, and at frequent intervals were dead mules in various states of decomposition, which were now being torn and devoured by vultures."

The travelers' reward for a hard day slogging through the mud was a night at the Washington Hotel, an establishment much advertised along the route from Chagres. It boasted forty beds, although the assertion proved even more inflated than many in that immodest time and place. The beds "consisted of frames of wood five feet long," explained Frank

Marryat, "over which were simply stretched pieces of much-soiled canvas—they were in three tiers, and altogether occupied about the same space as would two fourposters." Moreover, in Marryat's case, they were already filled, leaving him to spend a miserable night outdoors, soaked, dirty, perched on a dead tree to avoid the wet ground, but tormented there by ants until he discovered a refuge among the packsaddles of a team of mules turned loose by their drivers till morning.

During the first several months of the Gold Rush, nearly all the traffic across the isthmus went from north to south—that is, from the Caribbean to the Pacific. But as early as the end of 1849, outbound gold-seekers met men returning from the mines. The encounter could be sobering. "Some were returning rich in gold dust and scales," wrote Frank Marryat, who ran into a group of returnees at the Washington Hotel, "but the greater part were far poorer than when they first started to realise their golden dreams. And these latter were as drunken and as reckless a set of villains as one could see anywhere. Stamped with vice and intemperance, without baggage or money, they were fit for robbery and murder to any extent; many of them I doubt not were used to it." The picture they painted of California was grim. "They foretold with a savage joy the miseries and disappointment that awaited all who landed there." Yet the outgoers tried to put the best face on things. "There are various reasons for some returning without gold," wrote one who refused to be discouraged. "Some are sick and spend their money to get well, and some lose all their money by gambling." The good news outweighed the bad: "All agree that there is gold enough for many years to come."

Once again, Jessie Frémont fared better than most travelers. She slept in a real bed, with a roof and screens to keep out the rain and ants—and snakes and rats and mosquitoes and leeches. Yet the atmosphere of the place weighed on her as on the others. "The nights were odious with their dank mists and noises," she wrote. Determined to bear up, at least in public, she kept her fears to herself—which caused the guardian assigned to her by the steamship line to assume she was stronger than she was. "As there were no complaints or tears or visible breakdown, he gave me credit for high courage, while the fact was that the whole thing was so like a nightmare that one took it as a bad dream—in helpless silence." But the nightmare diminished with the dawn. "There was compensation in the sunrise, when from a mountain top you look down into an undulating sea of magnificent unknown blooms, sending up clouds of perfume into the freshness of the morning; and thus from the last of the peaks we saw, as Balboa had seen before us, the Pacific at our feet."

Crossing the continental divide, Jessie felt she was crossing a chronological and emotional divide as well. Balboa in Darien recalled Prescott's history of the Spanish conquest, which she had read at home with her father and family. That happy time now seemed so long ago as to beggar the memory. "It lay before the date which should hereafter mark all things—before and after leaving home."

DESCENDING THE MOUNTAINS, the isthmian travelers emerged onto an open plain that ended at the ocean and the old city of Panama. The city showed its past—and its present. "Never were modern improvements so effectually applied to a dilapidated relic of former grandeur as here," remarked Frank Marryat wryly.

> The main street is composed almost entirely of hotels, eating-houses, and "hells" [saloons]. The old ruined houses have been patched up with whitewash and paint, and nothing remains unaltered but the cathedral. This building is in what I believe is called the "early Spanish style," which in the Colonies is more remarkable for the tenacity with which mud bricks hold together, than for any architectural advantages. The principal features in connection with these ancient churches are the brass bells they contain, many of which are of handsome design; and these bells are forced on the notice of the visitor to Panama, inasmuch as being now all cracked, they emit a sound like that of a concert of tin-pots and saucepans.
>
> At the corner of every street is a little turreted tower, from the top of which a small boy commences at sunrise to batter one of

> these discordant instruments, whilst from the belfries of the cathedral there issues a peal, to which, comparatively speaking, the din of a boiler manufactory is a treat. If those bells fail to bring the people to church, at all events they allow them no peace out of it.

The Panamanians were a diverse lot. "The natives are white, black, and every intermediate shade of color, being a mixture of Spanish, Negro, and Indian blood," observed J. D. Borthwick. (A less worldly emigrant put the matter less neutrally, saying the city "is inhabited by all of the hell hounds of god's creation, for they are some blacks, spanish jews with French.") Like most of the overwhelmingly male argonauts, Borthwick paid particular attention to the fairer sex. "Many of the women are very handsome, and on Sundays and holidays they dress very showily, mostly in white dresses, with bright-colored ribbons, red or yellow slippers without stockings, flowers in their hair, and round their necks, gold chains, frequently composed of coins of various sizes linked together."

Borthwick went on to describe a custom among the Panamanian women that struck him—with most other travelers through the isthmus—as very curious, if not downright dangerous.

> They have a fashion of making their hair useful as well as ornamental, and it is not unusual to see the ends of three or four half-smoked cigars sticking out from the folds of their hair at the back of the head; for though they smoke a great deal, they never seem to finish a cigar at one smoking. It is amusing to watch the old women going to church. They come up smoking vigorously, with a cigar in full blast, but, when they get near the door, they reverse it, putting the lighted end into their mouth, and in this way they take half-a-dozen stiff pulls at it, which seems to have the effect of putting it out. They then stow away the stump in some of the recesses of their "back hair," to be smoked out on a future occasion.

Borthwick estimated the native population of the city at about eight thousand; beyond this was the floating mass of perhaps three thousand transients. The latter included, along with the honest travelers, a considerable collection of sharps, pickpockets, and other birds of prey seeking a living from the birds of passage. Gambling was epidemic; even Jessie Frémont, simply through observation, became something of an expert at judging fighting cocks. The appetites of all were whetted by the gold that passed through Panama on its way back to the Atlantic world. "This morning 22 mule loads of gold dust started for Cruces, with over $1,000,000," wrote Stephen Davis in his diary, still wondering if he had seen what he thought he had seen.

THE LARGE NUMBER of transients in Panama reflected not simply the appeal of California gold but the peculiar manner in which the gold deranged traffic all along the Pacific coast of the Americas. During the spring and summer of 1849, California resembled what physicists of a later generation would call a black hole; in this case ships (rather than light) went into the harbor of San Francisco but didn't come out. Crews abandoned their vessels even before the anchors touched the bottom of the bay; despite the direst threats and most alluring promises, ships' captains found their vessels unmanned and themselves marooned on the golden shore. The effect was felt as far away as Nantucket, where an alarmed shipowner wrote to the captain of his whaling craft, "Keep clear of there by all means, or you will not have a crew to bring you out."

As a result, during that spring and summer, argonauts piled into Panama by the hundreds, then thousands, expecting to see the Pacific steamers promised them at New York—steamers that simply didn't come. Jessie Frémont, despite all the money at her disposal and all her family connections, found herself stranded with the rest of the mob. For weeks she waited, dreading that Lily would catch the fever and die—or worse, that she herself would die, leaving Lily alone in this godforsaken place. The point of the journey was to make a home in California with Lily and John; would they ever be reunited?

Her worries grew with the unexpected delivery of a letter from John. Since their parting at Westport on the banks of the Missouri, Jessie naturally had feared for his safety. She fancied herself modestly psychic; at one point she was seized by a feeling that he was in grave danger. "I became possessed with the conviction that he was starving," she wrote. "Nor could any effort reason this away." Now she learned the truth, which did little to assuage her fears.

John wrote of a disaster that had befallen his latest expedition. The expedition's stated purpose was to discover a route across the Rocky Mountains that would be passable for railroad trains in winter as well as summer. Frémont had been over the Sierras in winter, and was convinced that where he could go, trains could follow. But neither he nor anyone else he knew of had crossed the Rockies, on a latitude convenient to California, in the dead of winter. Such was precisely what he set out to do.

Frémont's unstated purpose was probably no less important. Publicly humiliated, deprived of his livelihood, he was determined to demonstrate that his career was not over, but just begun, that his heroism defied the slings and arrows of his outrageous misfortune. The very arguments against attacking the Rockies in midwinter became, by Frémont's inner calculus, reasons for making the assault. The greater the danger, the greater the glory.

After leaving the Missouri, Frémont and his men ascended the Arkansas River to Bent's Fort and Pueblo. It was early December, and the snows of winter already cloaked the peaks and clogged the passes. Trappers, traders, and other veterans of the mountains shook their heads on hearing Frémont's plan. To try the mountains in winter meant certain death, they said. But Frémont had ignored the pessimists who told him the Sierras were impassable in winter, and his success had taught him to trust his own judgment.

He needed a guide, a man who knew the mountains. Kit Carson would have been his first choice had Carson been available, but Carson had other obligations. Instead Frémont chose Bill Williams. "Old Bill" was legendary, first for his age, which was uncertain but obviously advanced for one of his hazardous profession; second for his knowledge of the southern Rockies, which surpassed that of any other white man and most Indians; third for his eccentricities, which included an awkward style of walking that made him appear constantly drunk (he *was* drunk often, but not constantly, and not in the mountains), a ludicrous manner of riding a horse, which made Ichabod Crane appear a professional jockey, and a wardrobe off-putting even by the casual standards of cleanliness common in the mountains; fourth, and finally, for his instinct for survival, which had gotten him through more winters and other hard times than he could count. (While some doubted Williams could count very well, he was sufficiently educated to have been a Methodist preacher in earlier life.) Frémont relied on Williams's survival instinct, although others preferred not to. Kit Carson later commented, "In starving times, no man who knew him ever walked in front of Bill Williams."

From Pueblo the party entered the mountains. The initial ascent was difficult but exhilarating, and not a little frightening. One of the men, describing the view backward and forward from one of the first passes, wrote, "The sight was beautiful, the snow-covered plain far beneath us, stretching as far as the eye could reach, while on the opposite side frowned the almost perpendicular wall of high mountains."

Into those mountains they plunged, and almost immediately discovered why the neighborhood regulars were so skeptical. The snows were deep and grew deeper daily; the drifts mocked the men's efforts to move forward and defied the mules to find forage. At one point the party spied what seemed to be grass pushing up through the snow where the wind apparently had blown away the drifts; on closer inspection the tufts proved to be the tips of tall trees buried to nearly their full height. The cold intensified with the increasing elevation and the advancing season. The wind shrieked through the passes and sliced through the clothing of the men. All the elements assaulted the expedition, which began to look like a ruined military column. "The trail showed as if a defeated party had passed by: packsaddles and packs, scattered articles of clothing, and dead mules strewed along," Frémont wrote Jessie.

Conditions only deteriorated. The storm became a constant blizzard. Williams lost the way, leading the group into a maze of mountains from which there appeared no exit. Frémont unwisely determined to save the baggage rather than leave it and evacuate the men as rapidly as possible to a lower elevation. He dispatched a party of four, including Williams, to the settlements of northern New Mexico, there to acquire fresh provisions and mules to replace those now dead in the snowdrifts. He himself remained in the mountains with the rest of his men.

Christmas came while Frémont and the others awaited relief. "Like many a Christmas for years back," he wrote Jessie, "mine was spent on the summit of a wintry mountain, my heart filled with gloomy and anxious thoughts, with none of the merry faces and pleasant luxuries that belong to that time. You may be sure we contrasted much this with the last at Washington, and speculated much on your doings and made many warm wishes for your happiness." Frémont intended to commence a career in law once he and Jessie and Lily were established in California; to this end he had brought some books on the expedition. "You remember the volumes of Blackstone which I took from your father's library when we were overlooking it at our friend Brant's? They made my Christmas amusements. I read them to pass the heavy time and forget what was around me. Certainly you may suppose that my first law lessons will be well remembered."

Days elapsed, then weeks, with no return of the relief party. Rations ran low, and the men's spirits sank even lower. One man, perhaps irrational from cold and hunger, perhaps simply weighing his options, deliberately chose to let himself freeze. "In a sunshiny day, and having with him the means to make a fire, he threw his blankets down in the trail and lay there till he froze to death."

Frémont decided he could wait no longer. The relief party might have lost the trail or been ambushed by Indians. Selecting a small group, and leaving the others with the baggage, he set out in the same direction as the first party. For several days the group struggled along before discovering a thin column of smoke wafting above a stand of trees. This must be the rescue party, they thought, and they hastened their painful steps toward the smoke. "We found them—three of them, Creutzfeldt, Brackenridge, and Williams—the most miserable objects I have ever seen. I did not recognize Creutzfeldt's features when Brackenridge brought him up to me and mentioned his name. They had been starving. King had starved to death a few days before. His remains were some six or eight miles above, near the river." (Unknown to Frémont at the time he wrote Jessie, the three survivors had eaten part of King's body.)

After obtaining horses from friendly Indians, the Frémont group and the three survivors hurried on to the New Mexican settlements. Though Frémont didn't detail it to Jessie, by the time he reached Taos he was nearly dead: utterly exhausted, frostbitten (one leg was threatened by gangrene), almost snow-blind. Unable to travel farther, he dispatched his most trusted lieutenant, Alexander Godey, to lead a party back into the mountains to rescue the men who remained there.

What the rescuers discovered was a human catastrophe. The two dozen men had waited for a week, then decided they must find their own way out. One by one they fell by the trail. "Manuel—you will remember Manuel, the Cosumne Indian—" Frémont wrote Jessie, "gave way to a feeling of despair after they had travelled about two miles, begged Haler to shoot him, and then turned and made his way back to the camp, intending to die there, as he doubtless soon did." Ten miles from camp another man surrendered to fate, threw down his gun and blanket, and tumbled into a drift to die. Overnight a man went crazy from hunger, wandered off from the main group, and was never seen again. Another man died quietly the next day; a companion, snow-blind and himself at death's door, stayed behind with him and soon succumbed also.

Frémont spared Jessie few of the grim specifics.

> Things were desperate, and brought Haler to the determination of breaking up the party in order to prevent them from living upon each other. He told them "that he had done all he could for them, that they had no other hope remaining than the expected relief, and that their best plan was to scatter and make the best of their way in small parties down the river. That, for his part, if he was to be eaten, he would, at all events, be found travelling when he did die." . . . At night Kern's mess encamped a few hundred yards from Haler's, with the intention, according to Taplin, to remain where

> they were until relief should come, and, in the meantime, to live upon those who had died, and upon the weaker ones as they should die.

How much cannibalism actually occurred, no one cared to discover. When Godey arrived with relief, he was content to load the living onto the mules he brought and leave the dead to the snows and whatever nonhuman scavengers might find them.

In all, Frémont lost ten men of his party of thirty-three. Yet he expressed no remorse, no questioning of his judgment in the mountains, no doubt as to whether the goal had warranted the sacrifice. Perhaps he felt that his own close call released him from self-criticism, in that he had suffered alongside his men. Perhaps he felt that those who died simply weren't as strong as he.

In any event, he turned his face to the west and the future. He told Jessie he would soon continue to the coast, where they would be together again. "When I think of you . . ." he concluded his letter, "I feel a warm glow at my heart, which renovates it like a good medicine, and I forget painful feelings in a strong hope for the future. . . . I make frequently pleasant pictures of the happy home we are to have, and often and among the pleasantest of all I see our library, with its bright fire in the rainy, stormy days, and the large windows looking out upon the sea in the bright weather."

THE SHOCK OF READING of her husband's ordeal was more than Jessie could stand. The emotional strain of caring by herself for Lily, the physical toll of the journey from New York and across the isthmus, and now the psychological trauma of reliving the near-death of her husband culminated in a collapse she attributed to "brain fever."

Debating doctors fought over her treatment. The favorite of the family she was staying with prescribed the Spanish practice of bleeding, the avoidance of drafts and all other fresh air, and the application of hot water inside and out. An American doctor en route to California prescribed an abundance of fresh air, the application of ice to the skin, and iced drinks. "These two, with their contradictory ideas and their inability to understand each other fully, only added to the confusion of my mind, and became part of my delirium," she wrote. The one thing they agreed on was croton oil, obtained with difficulty from a visiting British man-of-war to treat congestion in her lungs.

Her illness elicited a repetition of the pleas of those around her that she return to New York. In her weakness she entertained the idea once more. But then, in the dark hours before dawn on May 6, a cannon's report announced the arrival of the steamer *Oregon*, long awaited from San Francisco. By coincidence, a second Pacific Mail steamer, the *Panama*, arrived within the same hour after a voyage around Cape Horn. Finally the thousands of stranded travelers felt deliverance at hand. En masse they stormed the harbor where the vessels anchored, each argonaut demanding to be taken on board and transported to the goldfields. A full-scale riot threatened as it became clear that even the two ships together couldn't transport anywhere near the number clamoring to leave. Bribes were offered, blows exchanged. The situation was resolved by the only method able to command a consensus: a lottery. The winners danced gleefully at their deliverance; the losers waited sullenly for the next vessel.

Once again Jessie's connections came to her aid. The steamship company withheld a few berths from the lottery; one of these went to the senator's daughter. Ushered to the head of the line of embarkation, she and Lily were hoisted onto the *Panama* by the makeshift of an oversized bucket attached to a boom. The ship had been built for eighty; four hundred crowded aboard. Although Jessie and Lily were assigned a cabin, its stuffiness aggravated her cough and drove her above decks, where she rigged a tent out of a large flag. By now all knew who she was, and what she had gone through. "Everybody contributed something to make me comfortable; one a folding iron camp bedstead—some, guava jelly—some, tea—while one of my fellow passengers gave me from his own private stores delicate nourishing things which brought back my strength." Even the tent on deck was a comparative luxury; most on board could claim no more than a rectangle for sleeping, sketched on the deck in chalk.

The fresh ocean air healed her lungs (confirming the prescription of the American doctor), so that by the time the *Panama* reached San Diego, she was tolerably well. Yet the nearer she approached to California, the more she feared bad news that would say her husband hadn't made it safely to the coast. As the ship dropped anchor in the bay of San Diego and everyone else crowded to the rail, she went below, anticipating the worst and not wishing to hear it.

Her situation and Lily's had engaged the emotions of the entire ship; many of the passengers were nearly as anxious as she to learn the outcome of Colonel Frémont's journey. From behind her closed door she heard a rising commotion in the passageway outside; gradually the commotion became comprehensible. The colonel had arrived! He was safe in California! He had been seen at Los Angeles and would meet her at Monterey!

Jessie's relief overwhelmed her. After all he had endured, after all she had endured, they were finally to be reunited. A few days more, another week perhaps, and the new chapter of their life—the chapter that brought and kept them together at last—would begin.

4

To the Bottom of the World and Back

On January 12, 1848, while James Marshall and John Sutter watched the American River rise and wondered whether the waterworks at Coloma would hold against the flood, half a world away the people of Palermo revolted against Ferdinand II, the longtime king of Naples and Sicily. Six weeks later, after the discovery of gold but many months before the news reached Europe, Paris exploded in revolution. Louis Philippe was forced to abdicate, and the Second Republic was proclaimed. The unemployed who formed the backbone of the Paris mob demanded work; when the new government proved unable to provide it, the mob attacked the new government. June saw some of the bloodiest street-fighting in European history; casualties were too many to count but were estimated at ten thousand. Meanwhile revolution spread across Europe, engulfing Austria, Prussia, most of the lesser German states, and large swaths of the rest of Italy. Amid the upheaval, two German émigrés living in London, Karl Marx and Friedrich Engels, gave voice to the radical disaffection in their landmark polemic, the *Communist Manifesto*.

After reeling, the status quo struck back. In France, the June Days were followed by the Red Fear. Chastened moderates joined convinced conservatives to muzzle the press, ban secret societies, and outlaw most public meetings. The nephew of Bonaparte, Louis Napoleon, was elevated to the presidency on promises that he would save society and restore order—a project he commenced immediately, and which didn't conclude before he had made himself emperor, with powers (although not talents) to match his uncle's.

Jean-Nicolas Perlot was in Paris during the exciting, terrifying, and ultimately disillusioning events of 1848. Born in 1823 in the French-speaking part of Belgium, Perlot left home at twenty-two to seek his fortune in Paris, where an uncle found him a job as a *calicot*, or linen-draper's assistant. The great city was a lonely place for a newcomer and at times overwhelming. But for two years the job fed him and left him leisure to explore. He prowled cafes and booksellers; at night he attended a trade school that taught mathematics, surveying, and engineering.

Neither more nor less political than most young men who had to work for a living, Perlot kept his distance from the rioting and urban warfare of 1848. More important to him than the effects of the revolution on Paris politics were its effects on the French economy. Hard times had helped trigger the uprising, which in turn made the times harder. Workers went hungry and cut down trees on the Bois de Boulogne for fuel. Perlot's employer ran out of orders, and Perlot was soon out of work.

At just this moment arrived the news from America of gold in California. With business at a standstill and politics in turmoil, the El Dorado in the west was nearly irresistible. Of late a certain vogue had developed in Paris for the American frontier, largely as a result of the publication of French translations of the accounts of the expeditions of John Frémont, whom the French were happy to claim as one of their own. Now everything involving California was rushed into print and snatched from the bookstalls: correspondence from the few Frenchmen in California, memoirs by French sailors to the California coast, articles lifted from American publications.

As at Valparaiso and Sydney and Canton and New York, the gold reports sent an electric current through Paris and the surrounding country. Merchants hoped to profit from the sale of their wares at San Francisco; shipowners counted on an increase in traffic aboard their vessels; peasants and workers reckoned how to get to the goldfields to reap the harvest waiting there. Broadsides blossomed on walls across Paris, advertising passage on ships preparing to set sail; companies of gold-seekers calling themselves L'Aurifère, La Toison d'Or, La Ruche d'Or, L'Eldorado, and scores of other such names appealed to prospective argonauts to join up. Shopkeepers offered to outfit those preparing to go—for a suitable price, of course. Even as the dreams set soaring by the February phase of the 1848 revolution crashed to bloody earth, the news from California provided an alternate hook for hope. A bimonthly journal called *Le Californie* predicted a golden end to France's troubles:

> There is no French province which does not have products accumulated to the point of being irksome and which could be sold today with immense profit not only in California but in Valparaiso, Lima, and all Western America. Our agriculture, our commerce, our industry, and our capital of all kinds can draw greatest advantages from the movement initiated by the discovery of great treasure in California. Let us then not lose this chance to increase our riches and to efface from our memory the suffering of the past year. We cannot urge the French too strongly to profit in these marvelous discoveries so that they shall not pass into the hands of other peoples.

Jean-Nicolas Perlot put the matter more succinctly: "The gold fever succeeded the revolutionary or reactionary fever, or, at least, gave it rough competition."

Perlot watched in wonder as the advertisements went up. "The least lucky would have 100,000 francs, rather more than less," he paraphrased the promises. Twenty-five years old, unattached, caught in a threadbare craft growing thinner by the day, he let himself be persuaded. "The chance to tempt fortune thus presented itself; I seized it and decided to leave for California."

LEAVING WAS LESS simple than deciding to do so. The voyage to America cost a thousand francs, which Perlot didn't have. Yet if he was poorer than most of the French argonauts, he was more resourceful than many, and after much calculating and some negotiation he signed an agreement with the manager of one of the California companies, La Fortune, whereby Perlot would receive passage in exchange for serving as company steward on the way. Once in America he would have a standard share in the company's earnings, which would consist of the pooled revenues (that is, the value of the gold dust and nuggets discovered) less combined expenses. The overall term of the agreement was five years; at the end of that period the company would return him to Paris, if he so chose. Perlot was delighted at this arrangement. "I was saved, I was leaving!"

The company gathered at Paris and traveled down the Seine to Le Havre. Their ship, the *Courrier de Cherbourg*, was supposed to be ready for immediate departure, but was not. For a month the men put up at a boarding house, chafing at the delay and costing the company—that is, themselves—a distressing amount of money. Steward Perlot supervised the packing of provisions and kept a sharp eye out for cheating by the provisioners.

Finally the preparations were finished and the vessel made ready to sail. The scene on deck at the last hour featured hugs, kisses, tears, and bon voyages from the wives, mothers, fathers, brothers, and sisters of the brave adventurers.

Perlot, however, stood apart. "I had in this crowd neither relative nor friend, nor even an acquaintance, and none of these words of affection was addressed to me. I was leaving—would I ever return? Nobody asked himself this question, which interested nobody. As at my arrival in Paris, I had the bitter feeling of my isolation. Ought I, after all, to rejoice or regret not seeing anyone weep for my departure? I did not know. And nevertheless, witnessing these scenes of farewell, I began to be sorry that I too did not have someone to embrace, to shake by the hand." The one other Belgian aboard was the sole person similarly stranded. Perlot approached him. "After some seconds of silence, I told him what I was feeling. Without saying a word, he looked at me fixedly, then, covering his face with his handkerchief, he fled. I remained alone, mournful, my eyes turned toward Le Havre, which was slowly receding."

Perlot's companions aboard the *Courrier* were a diverse crowd. Two were the sons of the director of La Fortune. Two more were the company's doctor and engineer. Then there was "Clavel de Vérance, ex-Zouave, an imaginary nobleman, whom we nicknamed Portos, to humor him, for he was proud of his bodily strength, although it appeared as debatable as his coat of arms." A cafe-waiter had recently returned from Madrid to discover that waiters went begging in Paris. A Norman son of a schoolmaster had been a clerk in England but had grown restless there and retreated to his native village, which had nothing more to offer than when he left. A lumber-seller with a weakness for drink, a tanner fleeing his wife, a student fleeing the friars who ran his school, an army veteran named Magraff, who "called himself a nephew of the Duke of Baden, and perhaps he really was," and a man subsequently dubbed Tenerife, for his mountainous nose, filled other berths.

The ship also carried argonauts unattached to La Fortune. Badinier was a lumber dealer from Orléans who had been ruined by the recent revolution. Surprisingly, considering this personal history, he held no animus against the popular cause. "Quite the contrary. He was nicknamed 'Mirabeau' [after the great orator of the first French revolution] and 'the Father of the people,' because on any occasion, and even without any occasion, he talked to us about his love for the people and delivered harangues which were doubtless very beautiful, but which were Greek to us and perhaps to him too, so elevated was the point of view—and so incoherent the form." The Abbé Laubert "was going to evangelize the savages of California, and in the meantime he evangelized us. In his character as missionary, he wore a long red beard. He was an educated and liberal priest, perhaps a little heretical. Was that why he was going far from the oldest daughter of the Church [that is, France]? It might be. The explanation which he gave us of the birth of Jesus Christ, son of a ghost, although he swore he did not believe in incubi, completely passed my understanding."

NOT UNUSUALLY FOR a group of landlubbers, nearly all suffered the mal de mer their first days out. This eased Perlot's job as steward, since the collective failure of appetite freed him from having to distribute food rations. For almost a week a surly wind from the west confined them to the Channel; not till the seventh day did the lengthening swells indicate their entrance to the Atlantic. The slower tempo of the ship's rolling, combined with the acquisition of sea legs by the passengers, eased the seasickness. Appetites improved, and Perlot found his services in greater demand.

During a brief stretch of clear weather in the Bay of Biscay, the novices concluded that sailing was a fine means of travel. This conclusion abruptly proved premature, as Perlot related.

> It changed all at once from white to black. Then it was that we could judge what the Ocean is. This time we had a real tempest, for we had had, in the Channel, only a shadow of one. A fair number of us who, at that time, had only frowned, were weeping now when they looked toward the absent shore, convinced that their last day was come. Certainly, when seeing in the port of Le Havre great ships which gauged two or three thousand tons, I never would have imagined that the sea had enough power to make these colossi pirouette like nutshells.
>
> The motions of two ships in distress which we had in sight made us aware of the movements which ours was performing. One of them seemed hardly out of gunshot; we could perceive it only when it found itself, like us, on the top of a wave; sometimes launched toward the sky, we saw it almost upright on its prow or on its poop; sometimes it appeared to us completely upset and let us see only its keel.
>
> It was just the same with ours. Sometimes it stayed so thoroughly upright on its bow or stem that the deck fled from under my feet and I remained suspended from the rope which I had twisted around my arm; at other times, the roll put the deck on a vertical line and half the yards in the water. Then all at once, it dove between two waves and the surge passed over the deck, and I was astonished at not being engulfed.

The storm lasted three days, followed by fair weather that carried the craft to Madeira. The voyagers, like most making their first ocean crossing, were delighted to touch terra firma again. And Madeira was a delightful place to touch. "Madeira is a charming little island, a true earthly paradise," Perlot remarked. Yet cheap supplies, rather than the picturesqueness of the place, were the reason ships like the *Courrier de Cherbourg* put in at Madeira. Although La Fortune didn't buy much in new stores, others on the vessel did.

It was just as well Perlot and company didn't provision at Madeira. The ship's mate took aboard a quantity of tuna, which turned out to be bad. Nearly a quarter of the passengers and crew became acutely ill. None died, but most lost their taste for fish.

Amid the epidemic, Perlot devised a scheme for efficiently feeding his company. During the first weeks of the voyage his impatient partners insisted on receiving rations at whatever hour suited them; now he succeeded in imposing a more regular schedule. The men were divided into eight squads; each had its own kettle and mess kit, which served its seven or eight members. Each squad selected a cook, who at the appointed hour received the rations for the group and apportioned them out to the members.

In good weather the mess squads ate on deck, and accidents were few. But in stormy weather the men discovered another difference between life on land and at sea. They were forced to take refuge below, in a large room that served as a dormitory at night and a commons during the day. Here each squad clustered around its kettle, balancing and bracing themselves as well as they could against the rolling of the ship. They rarely held their positions for long. "How many times that damned wind came to disturb the order and the religious silence which ruled in that solemn moment!" wrote Perlot. "How many times we had the bitter experience of that truth, that there is many a slip 'twixt the spoon and the lip!" The rolling didn't merely disrupt the eating; it also frayed nerves and sometimes triggered violence. One man would splash soup on his neighbor and be cursed for his carelessness. Another would knock his neighbor down and receive a cuff in return. A third would topple the mess pot of an adjacent squad and provoke a general melee.

THREE DAYS OUT OF Maderia the *Courrier* sighted Tenerife, the summit of the Canaries, and then skirted southwest toward the Cape Verde Islands. Crew members told Perlot that the African coast was just over the eastern horizon; perhaps in the backlight of dawn he would see Cap Vert. But strain though he did, he failed.

Another week brought the social highlight of the voyage—in fact, the social highlight of nearly every voyage that passed from the Northern Hemisphere to the Southern, and one encountered by thousands of argonauts. As the ship approached the equator, those who had already been initiated into the service of King Neptune prepared to repeat the procedure on those who had not, in this case including the entire membership of La Fortune. The ritual, like all rituals, assumed a certain timeless quality, not least in Perlot's retelling.

> The day before the crossing, toward evening, the mate, armed with his telescope, attentively scrutinizes the horizon, then after several false alarms, cries to the man at the helm: "Hold the wind, the line is in sight." He says these words in a way that attracts attention, then takes a few more sights through the glass as if to be sure he is not mistaken. The news spreads, and everyone rushes to the deck, trying to perceive the line; they look, they squint their eyes, they rub them, they look again; in vain! They see nothing. Then the mate advances, glass in his hand, and obligingly offers to show you the famous line. You approach, you look; ah! this time you see very clearly a line which extends all the length of the horizon.
>
> The complaisant officer is careful, it's understood, to direct the instrument only toward the Equator; otherwise one would notice that, whatever part of the horizon is observed, one sees the line, and one would soon guess that this line is nothing but a hair

placed between the two large glasses of his telescope. No one thinks, however, of making this experiment; everyone has proved *de visu* that he is coming to the line.

The next day at dawn all awake to the rattle of hail on the deck. This is odd, as hail rarely falls in the tropics. Reveille sounds; there is no time to dress. "The men wear only shirt and trousers, and the ladies—I don't know exactly, but not much."

The captain appears, growling to discover the meaning of this importunate end to his slumbers.

A voice rumbles down from the heavens: "Who are you, audacious mortals, who do not fear to adventure upon my waters? Know that I am the Equator, and that I permit no one to cross me."

The brave captain answers, "We have been told, in our distant lands, that previously voyagers had encountered his Lordship the Equator and had been able, under certain conditions, to cross beyond without being destroyed by the fires with which he defends his realms."

"That's true," replies Equator from on high. "But those travelers had submitted to my conditions. Submit in your turn, and you will pass."

"What are your conditions?"

"I wish each person who passes here to change his name and be baptized in my waters. I wish him after the baptism to bear no name other than *shellback*."

The captain accepts the condition. He orders that all be baptized, and henceforth answer only to *shellback*.

As preparations are made for the ceremony, a few sharp-eyed passengers note a sailor descending from the top of the mainmast—interestingly, from near where the voice of Equator had seemed to emanate. He carries an empty sack—which looks as though it might once have held the dried beans that litter the deck.

The baptisms begin. Each neophyte is made to sit on a plank suspended by ropes over a tub of water. The godfather and godmother—veterans of the crossing—speak the sacramental words. At "Amen," a pail of water is emptied upon the neophyte's head, and the ropes are released, dumping him into the tub. The shellback clambers out, and the ceremony is repeated.

All are amused, and all goes smoothly till one neophyte, an independent passenger, decides that the assistants to the godparents have handled his wife more familiarly than necessary. Cross words are exchanged, then blows.

The captain intervenes, halting the ceremony. Those awaiting their turns are left to risk Equator's wrath unbaptized.

This breaks the spell of the ritual—and requires Perlot to return to the past tense, which he employs to relate the denouement.

> Before the end of the day, peace was made, and at four o'clock in the afternoon the baptismal banquet took place. A great table was set on the poop; we all seated ourselves there, officers, sailors, and passengers, and the dinner was splendid: food, beer, all kinds of wine were served to us with profusion, and the guests did honor to all; each one helped himself to his heart's content, knowing that he would not again find himself at such a feast during the rest of the crossing.

By banquet's end the sour feelings had sweetened. Everything indicated a happy conclusion to the day. But such was not to be. "The demon of discord, who had succeeded that morning in disturbing the baptismal ceremony, had promised himself to disturb the feast too." His agent in the disruption was the putative nephew of the duke of Baden, Magraff, who "had eaten well and drunk superlatively." Magraff asked for silence. The guests complied, expecting a toast. Not at all: he began complaining about the management of the company's business. This annoyed several of his fellows, who had drunk nearly as well as Magraff; fisticuffs commenced. The pugilists, however, were distracted by the republican Badinier, who seized the floor to declaim in favor of liberty, equality, fraternity, and California. His remarks excited approbation from the many and thoughts of mischief in a few. These latter snatched a spar from the deck and compelled Badinier to sit astride it, though he protested that he didn't merit the honor. They paraded him about the ship before depositing him in the privy.

"This folly ended the festival," Perlot wrote. "In sum total, it was a joyful day." He added, "The next day we were able to economize on breakfast and to a great extent on dinner. Nobody was hungry, but everyone was a little thirsty. Each one complained of pain at the roots of the hair."

IF HEAVY USE COULD have worn ruts in the ocean, the track the *Courrier de Cherbourg* followed thus far in its voyage would have been deep and smooth. The French vessel was one among hundreds that made the voyage to California in the few years after James Marshall's discovery. Scores of the ships shared the European origins of the *Courrier*; a larger number hailed from ports of the eastern United States. Yet whichever side of the Atlantic the argonauts' vessels started out on, their journeys converged near the equator off Brazil. And at that point they entered waters that, while not exactly unknown, were hardly as familiar to seamen as many other parts of the world's oceans.

From the fifteenth century until the end of the eighteenth, the heaviest traffic in the South Atlantic had been bound east for the Indies, around Africa's Cape of Good Hope. By comparison, the traffic around South America, for the Pacific, was far lighter. Magellan discovered the southwest passage to the Pacific in the early sixteenth century, but for another 250 years the length of the voyage and the relative absence of attractive destinations in the Pacific discouraged commerce via the Strait of Magellan and Cape Horn. As late as the 1770s, British explorer James Cook could cruise for many months in Pacific waters no European had ever visited.

The American Revolution didn't exactly revolutionize navigation of the South Atlantic and the Pacific, but it did change it. As long as the American colonies had been under British rule, American commerce with the Far East was hostage to the monopoly held by the British East India Company, whose vessels traveled via the Cape of Good Hope. American independence broke the monopoly and allowed American merchants and captains to chart their own course to China. An active trade soon developed around Cape Horn, with merchantmen from New York and Boston doubling South America on their way to Oregon (where they purchased furs), to the Sandwich Islands (Hawaii, where they wintered and acquired sandalwood), and on to Canton (where they traded the furs and sandalwood for tea).

In time the trade grew fiercely competitive. During any given sailing season, the first ship back to New York with its cargo of tea won premium profits, which might be so high as to buy a new ship outright. The pressure for speed drove shipbuilders to experiment with new designs; ships grew taller, leaner, longer. The culmination of the trend was the clipper ship, of which the state of the art in the late 1840s was the *Sea Witch*, with a recorded top speed of sixteen knots.

The demand for speed had a second effect, institutional rather than technological. For centuries sailing had been more art than science, as skippers consulted soothsayers, entrails, rheumatic elbows, and intuition to find fair winds and favorable currents. Such general features of atmospheric motion as the trade winds and the equatorial doldrums, and such gross oceanic motions as the Gulf Stream, were common knowledge; but the specific and detailed information that could give one ship a few days' edge over its rivals was either undiscovered or jealously—because profitably—held by its discoverer.

In the 1840s, however, the U.S. Navy began sponsoring systematic investigations of wind and current patterns. Spearheading the research was a young officer confined to land by injuries incurred in a stagecoach wreck; during his (ultimately incomplete) recuperation, Matthew Maury directed a team that sifted through tens of thousands of pages of ships' logs, collating by position the recordings of wind and current and producing a remarkably ambitious set of charts of the movements of air and water over and in the world's oceans. First published in 1847, Maury's *Wind and Current Charts* (with a companion volume: *Sailing Directions*) yielded immediate benefits to users.

Conventional wisdom *ante* Maury held that vessels from the East Coast of the United States bound for Cape Horn should swing far out into the Atlantic above the bulge of Brazil, that to get caught under Cape São

Roque risked endless days battling the trades that blew up from the cape to the northwest. What Maury discovered was that very close to the coast the wind and current changed. Breezes blew from the continent out to sea, and the current ran down to the cape—both contrary to conventional wisdom. One of the first captains who tested Maury's findings cut a third off the usual transit time from the Virginia capes to Rio de Janeiro. When this captain returned to Baltimore a whole month ahead of schedule, Maury became famous and his charts sold out.

As it happened, the ascending trajectory of intelligence regarding wind and wave intersected the similarly rising curve of shipbuilding technology at precisely the moment when both became immensely more valuable than before: that is, at the moment the discovery of gold in California burst upon the Atlantic world. Until 1848 the race in which the clippers and their nautical kin competed was essentially unidirectional: from China home to the Atlantic. They carried nothing out to the Pacific that depreciated with time; consequently their speed was wasted during half their round trip. The news from California changed the situation overnight. As everyone from Valparaiso and Sydney to New York and Paris appreciated, those who reached California first would claim the best gold mines and the largest markets for all the supplies the miners required. Speed immediately doubled in value, as did whatever delivered speed.

The gold discovery conferred a windfall on the owners of existing clippers and touched off a mad boom in the construction of new ones—"a perfect mania," said the *New York Herald*, which reported regularly on the merchant marine. Keels were thrown down by the dozen; more than 150 clippers were built in the half decade after 1848. Ship architects stretched the clipper principle ever farther: the craft grew longer, taller, slimmer, faster.

The gold discovery also conferred celebrity on the men who commanded the great ships. The clipper captains were icons of their day. Newspapers reported their comings and goings; small boys trailed them in the streets; gentlemen tipped hats to them in the finest hotels and restaurants.

Among the celebrated clan, none drew more attention than Robert Waterman. "A strutting dude of sail," was how a contemporary described the captain of the *Sea Witch*, the man who shattered all records to China and back. In his early forties, Waterman was of average height, perhaps five feet eight inches, and barrel-chested yet otherwise trim. Most captains wore beards; Waterman's face was bare, the better to show off his splendid jawline. The odd black ringlet trespassed upon his high forehead; his Roman nose seemed the prow of his visage. Tailored in wool or Chinese silk, top-hatted in beaver, Waterman turned the heads of men and women as he rolled—whether by carriage or, with that seagoing gait, by foot—up Fifth Avenue.

More than his appearance excited whispers. He had a reputation for fearsome discipline. "Bully Waterman" was the name he bore among the veterans of his cruises, and among those to whom they passed their tales. Even his defenders conceded that he was a "driver"; his critics called him a killer. Passersby wondered if the tales were true. He seemed so self-controlled, so refined. Was there a furnace behind that fashionable cravat, a volcano beneath the pearl buttons of his waistcoat?

Cordelia Waterman heard the whispers, though she affected not to. Anyway, she hoped the question of his captainly character was in the past. After his record runs in the *Sea Witch*—the best of which carried him from New York to Valparaiso in sixty-nine days, from Callao to China in 50 days, and from China to New York, via the Sunda Strait and the Cape of Good Hope, in an astonishing 75 days—Cordelia convinced her husband to retire. He was very young, by most standards of retirement, but between his regular pay as captain, the bonuses the *Sea Witch*'s owners paid for his records, the profits he earned from the cargo he carried on his own account, and some shrewd investments in real estate, he and Cordelia had more than enough to live quite comfortably. Early retirement had been implicit in the marriage agreement; four years after the wedding, Cordelia hoped—and expected—that her husband's sailing days were done.

But the brothers Griswold had different ideas. South Street merchants with a whole fleet flying their flag, Nathaniel and George Griswold were inspired by the gold discovery to commission the building of the arch-clipper of the clipper age: the *Challenge*. The builder they chose was William Webb, whose East River yard was the epicenter of clipper construction. Amid the California boom, Webb already had more work than he could handle, but two things about the Griswolds' proposal enticed him: their ship must be the fastest afloat, and money was no constraint. He whittled on a model, reckoned costs and profits, and agreed.

The maritime world immediately began to buzz about the *Challenge*. At a time when $60,000 was a handsome price for a ship, the Griswolds were spending $150,000. Their goal was to capture the record for the California run. Then, it was rumored (and not denied by the subjects of the rumor), the Griswolds would send their ship to England, where she would challenge (hence her name) any British vessel to a match race, the winner to receive the loser as prize.

The *Challenge* was a ship like no other. She was the longest in the world, at more than 250 feet. Her masts towered to 230 feet; her main yard was nearly 90 feet long. Her keel was of white oak, bolted with copper; her decks were of white pine, clear and straight-grained. Copper covered the keel; iron plates, painted yellow, sheathed her lower flanks. From the top of the plates to the rail was painted pitch black. Her form caused reporters nearly to swoon. "Her bow rises nobly," said one, "and although its lines are concave below, yet as they ascend they become gently modified, still preserving their regular form; and, on the rail, blend in perfect harmony with her general outline. . . . The bow is plain to nudity, compared with other ships, but beautiful beyond the power of words to describe."

To captain their prize vessel, the brothers lured Robert Waterman out of retirement. One last voyage, they explained to him—and to Cordelia—was all they asked. For his trouble—and hers—Captain Waterman would receive his regular fee, a share of the profits from the sale in California of the ship's cargo, and, if the *Challenge* broke the Cape Horn record by reaching San Francisco in ninety days or less, a bonus of $10,000.

THE GOLD FLEET FOR California comprised two distinct categories of vessels. In one category were those ships like the *Courrier de Cherbourg*, hired to haul argonauts like Jean-Nicolas Perlot and his fellows in La Fortune to the mines. The *Courrier*'s owners and its captain were happy to get the argonauts to California as quickly as was reasonable, but having little direct interest in the mining, they had no desire to risk life or vessel to trim a few days or even weeks from the voyage. In the second category were the clippers, for whom speed was all. The clipper captains were prepared to risk everything—ship, cargo, and crew—to make the fastest time possible around Cape Horn. And if the possible weren't fast enough, men like Robert Waterman were willing to attempt the impossible.

Waterman's crew would join him in the attempt, even if unwillingly. The crew was typically the weakest element of any clipper, for although the law of supply and demand worked well enough on the quarterdeck, with captains like Waterman selling their services to the highest bidder, it failed in the forecastle. Despite an acute shortage of ordinary seamen, shipowners refused to raise their pay above about ten dollars per month for the Cape Horn run. To some extent this was a matter of circular reasoning: observing the crews they obtained at this wage, they couldn't imagine paying such incompetents more. To some extent it was an acknowledgment of the strange effects California gold was having on the supply of sailors: with crews abandoning ship for the mines upon anchoring at San Francisco, owners often felt their crews ought to be paying *them*—for passage to California.

Nor was the problem simply low wages. Food was a chronic complaint: blandly monotonous at best, often wormy and rotten. Fresh water ran short. Rats ruled below deck. "They ate holes over-night through the hardwood cabin partitions, stole socks out of our shoes while we slept, also balls of twine and beeswax used in sail-making, and dragged them into their nests between the partitions where they seemed to produce a fresh family over-night," wrote one seaman. Worst of all was the arbitrary discipline doled out by the captains and mates. Service aboard a clipper (as aboard other ships) was a form of indentured servitude; but where servants on land could appeal to neighbors and the sheriff in cases of mistreatment, crewmen at sea had no recourse. Their rights were only such as their captain deigned to recognize; he was judge, jury, and executioner for infractions of his code of conduct.

Between the low pay and the grim conditions, it was no wonder owners had trouble filling out their crews, and hardly less wonder they relied on "crimps": human scavengers of the waterfront who cajoled, coerced, or drugged and dragged unsuspecting and unwilling victims aboard just in time for sailing. When the victims awoke, they were at sea, beyond the reach of any law but the captain's. Adding financial insult to physical injury, the crimps charged the owners per sailor delivered; the owners transferred the cost to the sailors, who had to work it off before receiving any pay of their own.

The crimps made good money filling the forecastle of the *Challenge*. When the ship cast off from its East River berth, its crew comprised fifty-six men, of whom half had never been to sea before; and of these, a substantial number had never wanted to go to sea. If not for the crimps they would have been home with their mothers or sleeping off their drunks in an East Side alley, a Bowery brothel, or the city jail.

Robert Waterman was accustomed to making sailors out of landsmen, but even he was shocked at the composition of this crew. A captain—especially a famous captain like Waterman—could wait until his ship had cast off before boarding; Waterman joined the *Challenge* below the Battery. He examined the crew and summarily fired the first mate, the man responsible for finding suitable hands. He might have put back into port had not a boat from an arriving ship brought aboard James Douglass, a first mate Waterman knew. Douglass said he was looking for work. This surprised Waterman; most seamen valued their shore time, and Douglass's vessel hadn't even tied up yet. But Douglass explained that the crossing from Liverpool had been rough, and he had been obliged to treat his men vigorously. On shipboard he was safe, but he feared reprisal on shore. Could Captain Waterman use a first mate?

Waterman certainly could, especially one with a reputation as a driver like himself. "Black Douglass" was what sailors called him; the name suited the man, and the man suited Waterman.

During the first weeks of the voyage, the men got a taste of the Douglass discipline. A clipper could be a daunting introduction to the nautical arts. To push reluctant landlubbers to the top of masts that soared and swayed two hundred feet above the deck, and to the ends of yards that swooped and dipped far out across the sea, often required the kind of encouragement Black Douglass delighted in. Fortunately for the sailors, the weather was settled and breezes light. First trips up the rigging could hardly have come under less threatening circumstances.

Yet this crew was more reluctant than most. Several pleaded seasickness despite the favorable conditions; after a couple of days Douglass suspected malingering. He applied his own cures: a heaver (a stout stick of wood used to twist and thereby tighten ropes), a belaying pin (a short post inserted in the rail, to which ropes were fastened), a thick end of rope, or simply his fists. The more pliable found relief aloft; others nursed their injuries and plotted revenge.

The mood darkened as the *Challenge* entered the tropics east of the Bahamas and encountered the doldrums; day after day the vessel drifted, sails slack, the swells hardly more than the ripples of a pond. The sun baked the deck, steamed the men in their berths, and simmered the water in the drinking tank. One man died of a mysterious illness; his funeral cast an ominous pall over the vessel.

Crossing the equator off the multiple mouths of the Amazon, Robert Waterman cursed his luck. A record run required at least the acquiescence of the weather; this weather was damnably recalcitrant. And the crew compounded the weather problem. A clipper could make the most of the lightest breezes, but only if its crew looked lively when summoned and if they efficiently followed the captain's commands. This crew was neither lively nor efficient. "I think it was the worst crew I've ever seen," Waterman recalled later. Staring south, he cursed again.

THE EQUATORIAL DOLDRUMS that delayed the *Challenge* also captured the *Courrier de Cherbourg*, albeit farther south. And though Perlot and his companions in La Fortune had no such precise deadline as Robert Waterman's ninety days, they were plenty eager to reach California. Every day lost to the absence of wind was a day deducted from golddigging, a day on which those who beat them to California would claim a larger portion of the wealth. For twenty-two days the calm held the ship fast—"twenty-two days which seemed to us as long as twenty-two years, and twenty-two years of purgatory." The savants among the crew said it was precisely these calms that led the ancients to conclude that the tropics were impassable; Perlot started to think the ancients were right.

Finally a skein of clouds crossed the horizon. It drew closer, and as it did, the faintest whisper of wind ruffled the sails. The sea surface wrinkled; slowly the ship began to move—at first south, then southwest. Perlot and the others savored their release from prison. "A steady and pleasant wind rocked us softly and led us to our heart's desire."

But the soft rocking gave way, before long, to motion more violent. As the ship crossed the Tropic of Capricorn, the weather turned foul. The north wind jumped to the south, bringing rain, which in turn was followed by a west wind and thick clouds. For eight days the weather was a torment—"never two hours of the same wind, and never a good wind." Eventually, however, by tacking west, then south, then west again, the captain was able to escape this turbulent region.

A northeast wind blew them to the latitude of the Rio de la Plata, which they sensed—by the color of the water, the sudden presence of seaweed, and the land-based birds—rather than saw. Several days later they did sight land: Patagonia. From the distance of six to eight leagues the coast seemed scarcely to rise out of the water, and the whole countryside had the appearance of a vast forest. Far in the interior, two volcanoes erupted. "The smoke of one of these volcanoes made a half-luminous trail in the evening, almost four leagues long; the other belched flames only at intervals."

The passengers enjoyed the fireworks for three days before a sudden west wind drove them out to sea. The wind grew to tempest strength, compelling the captain to heave to and causing the ship to drift steadily, helplessly east.

When the storm abated they once again headed southwest. Three more days brought them within sight of the Falkland Islands, although at first even the captain wasn't sure of the identity of those barren and windswept outposts of Britannia. Having seen neither sun nor stars for ten days, and with no accurate way to judge their drift during the storm, he didn't know where they were.

The wind continuing from the west, the *Courrier* beat painfully toward Tierra del Fuego, which seemed to Perlot "rather the land of snow than that of fire, with its cliffs as high as mountains." The coast now trended southeast, and the ship followed its curve to the strait of Le Maire, which separates the main island of Tierra del Fuego from a neighbor island called Staten. Before a cold but steady west-northwest wind, they cleared the strait and proceeded swiftly toward Cape Horn—which, Perlot and the other novices learned, was a rocky island rather than a true cape.

> Joy reigned on board; we were going to have the unexpected luck of doubling, unimpeded, the terrible Cape! And while still casting a last look on Staten Island, which was fleeing far behind us, each one got ready for a passing salute to the island, or rather the rock which bears this name, the terror of navigators, whom it reminds of so many wrecks: Cape of Storms! That evening we went to bed gay and happy, promising ourselves to get up early in order to enjoy the view of the redoubtable cape.

But the Cape of Storms had its honor to defend, and it refused to let the argonauts pass without a contest. Hardly had Perlot and the others retired for the night than they heard the mate shout for the sailors to scramble aloft; almost at the same time they felt the ship shudder before a frightful blast from the west. The blast brought waves such as they had never seen. "The billows rolled over the waist of the ship; almost every wave passed over the vessel."

The pounding continued all night; Perlot awoke to see the topsail, the only one that had been left set, in tatters—"as if someone had tried, with a machine made expressly, to make it into a canvas sieve." The captain abandoned all hope of holding the Cape. Putting the wind astern, he steered away from that perilous place. "I would leave you to guess if we made good time, pursued by a wind of unheard violence."

Yet retreat offered no respite.

> The ship literally leaped from one wave to another, so rapid was the headway and so short was the interval from the crest to the trough of the wave. Besides, what waves! Truly, only Cape Horn can raise waves to equal them. Each one, in descending, seemed certain to precipitate us into a gulf ready to swallow us—and nevertheless we always found ourselves, more or less soaked, it's true, on the top of the following wave. Each surge passed over the ship and left us a foot or two of water on deck.

For two days they flew before the storm. By the time the wind dropped enough to let them feel at least comparatively safe, they had lost 160 leagues to the guardians of the Cape. The captain repaired his rigging and attempted to regain some of the lost distance. Three days of tacking yielded modest progress. But the closer they approached to the Cape, the harder the wind roared. The captain hove to again. For twelve days they drifted backward, bow into the wind.

Once more they began tacking. The weather was clear, but very cold, and the wind persisted from the west. They gradually regained their westering, but only by circling far to the south.

Eventually the wind dropped; as it did, clouds set in. An icy fog enveloped the ship. "All the ropes were covered with a layer of grime an inch thick; it was impossible for us to put about that day and the next; it was not till the third day, toward noon, that, breaking the ice which encased the ropes, we succeeded in putting about and going back toward the northwest."

At this point they were at latitude 61 south, almost within sight of Antarctica. Though they didn't spy the mysterious southern continent, they did see and feel the effects of summer—*summer!* this tempestuous season was—at high latitudes.

It was the 18th of December. That day we had twenty-one hours of sunlight followed immediately by three hours of aurora clear enough to permit us to read and play on deck as in full daylight. The sun turned almost horizontally round us, but, although nothing stopped its rays, for no cloud altered the azure of the sky, we froze on deck, where we liked to stay in order not to miss the opportunity, if it was presented, of seeing a floating iceberg.

To the passengers' disappointment but the crew's relief, no icebergs were encountered. The disappointment was mingled with disorientation. "Our existence on board had become the strangest in the world," Perlot said. "The night was suppressed, or virtually so. Daily habits were found to be completely upset. Thus, the cook would have to stay permanently at his stove, if he had wanted to satisfy everybody. This one, who had just got up, claimed his breakfast, while that one, up for a long time, demanded supper in order to go to bed. One claimed that the sun had just risen; the other affirmed that it was going to set. Both were wrong, for it was noon."

Progress continued northwest. For nine days they held the same tack. Each day the sun rose a little higher above the horizon; each night the darkness lasted longer and the aurora diminished in brilliance. The cold gradually eased. On the tenth day they sighted one of the many islands off the west coast of Chile, which brought the immensely welcome realization that they had passed Cape Horn. "So we had been floating for several days in the waters of the Pacific Ocean, which seemed to want to justify its name, for we were sailing as peacefully as possible, though nonetheless with speed."

THE FRENCH CAPTAIN of the *Courrier de Cherbourg* probably didn't carry copies of Matthew Maury's *Wind and Current Charts* and *Sailing Directions*. If he had, he would have learned what he ended up discovering on his own: that the longest way around Cape Horn was sometimes the shortest. In his days at sea, before his injury, Maury conjectured that the prevailing winds between the Cape and Antarctica flowed in a circular, clockwise direction. His subsequent research confirmed this. In other words, whereas a ship coming from the Atlantic might meet ferocious headwinds near the Cape itself, by swinging south it could pick up winds blowing in the opposite direction.

Robert Waterman appreciated Maury's insight, but the captain of the *Challenge* had too much riding on a record passage to San Francisco to waste time swinging south. And he was behind schedule already. The weather was partly to blame, but so also the crew—or perhaps it was the officers. First mate Douglass cudgeled crewmen for minor infractions and on general principle; some submitted silently, but others struck back. One seaman named Fred Birkenshaw, after receiving one of Douglass's blows, took the opportunity of a diversion of the mate's attention and grabbed him from behind. Several other crew members rushed Douglass, snatching away his heaver and pummeling him with their fists. One man produced a knife; aiming for Douglass's throat or breast, he slashed but badly missed, merely stabbing Douglass in the leg.

Douglass screamed bloody murder, alerting Waterman for the first time to the mutiny. The captain may have realized that his life was in jeopardy too, or he may simply have responded from righteous wrath. In either case, he hurled himself from the quarterdeck into the midst of the melee. With his sextant he smashed one mutineer, a man named George Smith, who had Douglass's neck in a death grip. With fists, feet, and rope, Waterman attacked several others. He helped free Douglass, who, with his blood spurting across the planks, went into a frenzy of retribution. Seizing a heaver again, the mate laid about like a demon. The mutineers, losing their nerve, fled for their lives.

The mutiny lasted no more than a few minutes; Waterman took longer weighing his response. Some of the central participants were readily identifiable. George Smith bore the imprint on his scalp and skull of Waterman's sextant; the captain ordered him placed in irons. Fred Birkenshaw was identified as the leader of the insurrection, but was missing. A crew member said he had seen him dive over the side, apparently preferring death by drowning to a noose at the end of a yard.

Waterman interrogated Smith, who at first contended the violence was extemporaneous. But threats that his punishment would increase from continued lying brought forth an explanation that several of the crew had indeed been plotting for some time to murder Douglass and Waterman and take the ship to Rio de Janeiro, where they would melt into the swirling population of that busy port. Smith hastened to add that he had not been party to the plotting; he had simply overheard it.

Waterman thereupon seized several of the alleged conspirators. Under questioning they too admitted overhearing the mutiny plans; like Smith, all but one said they took no part.

Waterman disbelieved the denials of participation. He pronounced eight men guilty and ordered them flogged. Douglass carried out the sentences, with obvious relish. By the time the convicted were cut loose, they were nearly unconscious (they revived slightly when stinging salt water was thrown on their wounds), and the deck was covered with their blood and gore.

Needless to say, all this hardly endeared Waterman to his crew. Nor did he expect it to. The operative question was whether it terrified them sufficiently to do his bidding against their own will. The answer, as it emerged, was yes and no.

Between the Tropic of Capricorn and the Cape, the *Challenge* encountered generally favorable winds. The vessel skated across the waves as its designer intended, lifting Waterman's hopes of recouping the lost time and capturing the record. For several days the good luck held, and the ship cruised smartly through the Strait of Le Maire and clear to the Cape.

But then, as if it had been lying in ambush behind the Cape, a huge storm slammed the vessel. Giant rollers—"Cape Horn snorters"—bearing the momentum of five thousand miles of open water and towering to sixty feet, raised the great clipper high, then dashed it down. The keel and braces groaned under the repeated pounding; the masts bent and shuddered and swayed before the gale like the trees they once were. Foam from the wave tops mixed with sleet and snow to turn the air a spuming white. The water roared, the wind shrieked, and the guardians of the Cape, become demons from hell, howled derision at these mortals trespassing where mortals didn't belong.

Waterman had trespassed before and knew how to defeat the demons. But he couldn't do it alone. He needed men to climb the rigging, to furl or reef the sails that survived the blast, to cut away those the storm shredded. With sail the ship would survive; without sail it would perish—capsized or crashed on the rocks. At this latitude all could expect to go down with the vessel, frozen blue within minutes of hitting the water.

But to many of the men, death seemed more likely aloft. The lurching of the ship was bad enough on deck; two hundred feet of mast magnified the motion to appalling proportions. The wind, also, was more violent aloft, able to snatch a man from the footropes and cast him to the waves. Nor was the wind or the pitching the worst of the danger. The snow and spume encrusted the ropes in ice, cheating the sailors of purchase for hands and feet. The sailors too were quickly encrusted, their faces frostbitten, their fingers immobilized, the blood that oozed from cracks in the skin freezing before it coagulated. A man didn't have to be a coward to quail at the prospect of ascending in conditions like these.

Even the kindest captain, under duress of the common danger, might have felt obliged to counter these fears with other fears—of the first mate's wrath, for instance. Waterman was hardly the kindest captain, and he turned Douglass loose on the reluctant. The mate employed his heaver to drive the men from the forecastle to the deck, where they quickly discovered they risked being swept overboard by the waves that crashed across the bow. Between the blows of the mate and those of the ocean, most decided they were safer aloft. Up they went, as slowly and carefully as they dared. Douglass hastened their ascent by vowing to follow them up and beat them there.

Before long the reckoning of danger shifted. Furling the sails in such a tempest required coordination of the efforts of several men, coordination that would have tested the most experienced crew. The crew of the *Challenge* failed the test, horribly and repeatedly. The first man to fall was catapulted from his footrope by the billowing of an unsecured sail. He plunged into the churning waters with a scream that momentarily paralyzed all above and below. No rescue was attempted. If the fall hadn't killed him, the waves quickly carried him out of reach of a line; to lower a boat would simply condemn several more men to the silent below.

Even as it was, others soon joined the dead man. The same loose sail that felled him subsequently snapped two others from their perch. One hurtled overboard, joining his friend in the deep; the other plunged to his death on the deck, his crumpled body serving mute witness to the roaring danger that surrounded them all.

Shorter-handed than ever, the *Challenge* slashed, bucked, and wallowed through seas that grew larger by the minute. The winds reached hurricane strength—eighty, ninety, one hundred knots. But this was no hurricane, no storm that blew itself out in forty-eight or seventy-two hours. Day after day, for a week, for two weeks, for almost three weeks it continued. Clouds hid the sun and stars, making navigation impossible. Waterman had no idea where they were, whether his tacks to north and south held the ship's position east and west. Was the Cape behind or ahead? Was this Pacific water that crashed across the decks, or Atlantic? All thought of a record passage to California had been blasted away; survival was the sum of hope now.

And survival required more brutal measures than ever—by the logic that ruled the *Challenge*, at any rate. The deaths of the three men terrified all but the most hardened of the rest. Several more reported to sick bay, some with legitimate complaints—pneumonia, frostbite, broken limbs incurred from falls or being battered against rails or bulkheads by waves—some simply from horror. Others wedged themselves in their berths and refused to come out. Still others reported to deck but refused to go aloft.

Among the latter was George Lessing, who had won the name "Dancing Master" for his agility at evading ropes and heavers swung by Douglass. Amid the Cape Horn tempest Douglass ordered Lessing aloft. Lessing refused, saying he was sick. The mate thereupon forcibly delivered Lessing to Waterman, explaining that the seaman had refused a direct order. Waterman, cursing and swearing that he'd teach this wretch obedience, seized Lessing and threw him headlong into the scuppers, which were filled with icy slush and water. Douglass took over from there, grasping the seaman by the hair and holding his head below the surface. Just before the victim would have drowned, the mate pulled him up, dragged him to the rail, and tied him fast. For an hour Lessing—who wore only a flannel shirt and thin jacket, a pair of cotton trousers, and no shoes—was exposed to the cutting wind and the freezing water. Finally—whether on Waterman's order or Douglass's own volition was unclear—Lessing was cut down and allowed to report to sick bay. Probably he really had been sick; certainly the near-drowning and the exposure aggravated his illness. Within days he died.

By then the terror had claimed another victim. "Pawpaw" was an Italian immigrant who fell afoul of the crimps and wound up aboard the *Challenge* without shoes, experience at sea, or understanding of English. The lack of shoes left his feet especially subject to frostbite, which in turn made it nearly impossible for him to climb the rigging. The lack of experience intensified the horror he felt at the storm, at the brutality of the officers, and at the general circumstances in which he found himself. The lack of English made him slow to understand what was being demanded of him. This last deficiency infuriated Waterman during one maneuver on deck, when all hands had to work in unison. Pawpaw continued to pull after the captain ordered a halt. Waterman grabbed a belaying pin and pounded Pawpaw on the back and shoulders for his failure.

Pawpaw retreated to his berth and refused to return to deck at the next order. Douglass entered the forecastle, bodily dragged Pawpaw out, and, pointing aloft, made clear that he was expected to start climbing. Pawpaw replied in Italian, pleading that his frozen feet forbade any such effort. Douglass began beating him savagely with his fists; when Pawpaw tried to take refuge in the forecastle, Douglass followed, and beat him further. Pawpaw was still breathing when one of the ship's boys lifted him into his bunk. But he soon lost consciousness, and within an hour died.

Nor was even this the end of the terror. The second mate, Alexander Coghill, imbibed some of the ferocity of his superiors; when he discovered one of the crew trying to evade his watch, Coghill kicked him so hard the man was incapacitated for days. Waterman took a heaver to a Finnish crewman who complained that scurvy made it impossible for him to answer orders. Meanwhile two more men died in sick bay, of dysentery.

Then a crewman reported that Fred Birkenshaw, the mutineer who was said to have gone over the side, in fact was hiding out between decks. Evidently this crewman had decided that Birkenshaw ought to share the danger the others were enduring. Douglass didn't seem surprised, apparently having doubted the drowning story from the start. Now he delivered Birkenshaw to the quarterdeck, where Waterman ordered him placed in irons.

Birkenshaw initially indicated willingness to confess to his role in the mutiny, but during Waterman's interrogation he changed his mind. He said he had nothing to do with it. Waterman refused to accept this. He swung a heaver at Birkenshaw, who raised his arm to defend himself. "I felt the bones of my arm crack when he hit me," Birkenshaw recalled afterward. The captain then fashioned a hangman's noose from a rope and hitched it to a block and tackle. The noose went around Birkenshaw's neck; the block and tackle was raised till Birkenshaw's toes just touched the deck. As the seaman slowly strangled, Waterman asked him again about his role in the mutiny. Birkenshaw decided to confess. The captain let him down.

Yet Birkenshaw still tried to wriggle free. He implicated Coghill, the second mate, in the conspiracy, besides the several others Waterman had previously identified.

Waterman might have believed Birkenshaw—but realized he couldn't afford to. As shorthanded as the ship was, the captain needed the second mate, even if his loyalty was suspect. He sent Birkenshaw to sick bay (where, Birkenshaw later claimed, his broken arm was deliberately neglected), and kept Coghill at his post, albeit under close observation.

By this time, finally, the storm had abated. After eighteen days the Cape's guardians were exhausted. The sky cleared, and Waterman discovered that the *Challenge* was in fact in the Pacific, several degrees west of the Cape.

AFTER THE CAPE, the passage up the Pacific to California was anticlimactic for most ships. The *Courrier de Cherbourg* had a close call with some fog-shrouded rocks on the Chilean shore, and with an earthquake that shook the waters near Valparaiso; but otherwise Jean-Nicolas Perlot and La Fortune had leisure to count their blessings, recent and prospective. Six months and three days after leaving Le Havre, they arrived at Monterey.

Anything would have been anticlimactic for the *Challenge*. The weather improved, and with it Waterman's treatment of his men. The ship again made swift sailing, but not nearly swift enough for the captain to win his ten-thousand-dollar prize. The *Challenge* anchored at San Francisco on the 108th day from New York. For such consolation as the coincidence offered, the eighteen days by which Waterman missed his mark was precisely the duration of the storm off Cape Horn.

5

To See the Elephant

The amphibious assault on California—across the Pacific, via the isthmus, and around the Horn—was a chapter of world history. A great many of the invaders, including an initial majority, were from countries other than the United States; and even the Americans who entered California at Monterey or through the Golden Gate had spent most of their journey in international waters, mingling their aspirations and experiences on equal terms with those of their fellow inhabitants of the blue planet.

By contrast, the invasion of California by land was a fundamentally American affair. Some Mexicans came north over the border, but by far the majority of those who reached the goldfields afoot were from the United States. These were the quintessential Forty-Niners, migrants in the mode of westering that had marked American history from the early seventeenth century. Their numbers outstripped those of the seaborne assailants, and their place in American memory would loom even larger than their numbers warranted.

A prime reason for the outsized memory was the nature of the overland journey. Although much shorter in distance than the isthmus route, and far shorter still than the Cape route, the overland route was by certain measures the longest, for it required travelers to cross not just distance but ignorance. Since the early nineteenth century, explorers (including John

Frémont) and traders had traveled from the Mississippi Valley to the West Coast; more recently emigrants to Oregon had pushed out across the plains and mountains. But vast reaches of the continent west of the 100th meridian remained terra incognita to all but the aboriginal inhabitants—who knew enough to stay out of the most desolate zones. This was more than many of the argonauts knew. Although most of the Forty-Niners kept to well-trod trails, some of the more impetuous, reckless, or greedy struck out on their own, with results that made even the survivors shudder.

Those who chose the overland route did so for various reasons. Some shunned ships from fear of drowning, in much the way some travelers in a later era would shun airplanes from fear of crashing. For a larger number, the primary consideration was cost. The widely circulated *Emigrants' Guide to California*, printed in early 1849, explained that the least expensive sea voyages to California cost three hundred dollars per person, while the overland route would set the gold-seeker back but fifty or sixty. This overland estimate was a net figure; the cash outlay at the start of the journey was greater, perhaps three times as much, but the overlanders would arrive with wagons and teams of mules or oxen that would command top prices in California, where a substantial portion of the initial outlay might be recouped.

The cash required at the start prevented the really poor from making the trek, but within a broad band of middle means, the overlanders were a diverse group. They hailed from the North and from the South, from the East and from the West (as the West was then understood, extending from the Appalachians to the Mississippi Valley). They were farmers and townsfolk, merchants and ministers, lawyers and doctors and teachers, slaveholders and slaves, freedmen and abolitionists, white and black and brown and occasionally red.

All sought wealth; nearly all sought adventure too. The news from California was the most exciting most of them had ever heard; the rush to California promised to be the event of their lifetime. Like little boys hurrying to greet the circus, to catch a glimpse of the mighty elephant, the emigrants of 1849 couldn't bear to miss out—and in fact the phrase "to see the elephant" became a cliché on the trail. To neglect this opportunity would be to guarantee future regret; to seize it would be to partake of something truly historic and wonderful.

HUGH HEISKELL HEARD the news in Knoxville, Tennessee. Hugh's father, Frederick Heiskell, was a mainstay of the East Tennessee community: former owner and editor of the *Knoxville Register*; present proprietor of Fruit Hill, a twelve-hundred-acre farm ten miles from town; senator in the Tennessee legislature. Hugh was one of ten children (and one of thirty-five first cousins living within a day's drive of Knoxville). He showed promise as a gentleman farmer, and when Frederick went off to Nashville on government business during Hugh's twenty-second year, Hugh took charge of Fruit Hill with his mother, Eliza. Interestingly, during the precise months in the autumn of 1847 when James Marshall was digging a millrace at Coloma, Hugh Heiskell was doing the same at Fruit Hill. When the autumn rains came, Heiskell's luck was worse than Marshall's, for a flood burst the mill dam at the Tennessee farm, forcing Heiskell to excavate a new channel. "Hugh is making a perfect slave of himself," his mother reported to Hugh's father.

That was the problem, as Hugh saw it. In a state and a region that knew what slaves were, he had no desire to slave away at farming. "Farmers don't often dream; their sleep is too sound," he explained to his sister Margaret. He added, "Following a plough, staggering and stumbling over clods all day, is anything but poetry."

Hugh would have settled for prose: the prose of the lawyer. He studied law, evidently in the office of one of Frederick's friends. By early 1849 he had completed his studies and was ready to hang out his shingle.

But then came the news from California. In Tennessee as elsewhere, certain civic guardians tried to dampen the enthusiasm for the goldfields and thereby forestall the depopulation of their own communities. A newspaper in Franklin, Tennessee, reprinted a letter from a traveler to California: "I have seen those who started from the borders of Missouri hale and stalwart men, hobble down into the plains of California crippled for life. I have seen brothers, who in the madness of hunger have fought for the last bit of their father's dead body." The *Western Star* of Pulaski, Tennessee, lampooned the gold-seekers in verse, concluding:

> Yes, wise men will make your graves,
> And all your gold fall heir to,
> And say—"Poor fools, they're broke and gone,
> We know not, care not, where to."

But others celebrated the golden promise. One paper ran a letter from a Tennesseean just arrived in California: "Men are here nearly crazed with the riches forced suddenly into their pockets. . . . The accounts you have seen of the gold region are *not overcolored. . . . The gold is positively inexhaustible*." Various editors characterized the argonauts' rush to California as part of the march of civilization and religion. In the words of the Memphis *Daily Eagle*: "They go as agents of social comfort, moral progress, expanding civilization and diffused thought, and (noblest of achievements) run high up into the heavens of strange lands, the cross-crowned spire, symbol of a true faith and prophecy of a sure eternity. Those who go to California may not know it, but they are society's, or rather God's, agents to these wonderful ends."

Naturally—again as elsewhere—much of the enthusiasm reflected an expectation that the rush to California would be good for business. A Memphis merchant advertised:

> ***For California***
>
> Persons going to California would do well to call and examine our stock of the following articles, which we have received direct from England and the manufactories of the East, viz:
>
> Stub Twist and Damascus double and single bbl. Shot guns; Stub Twist Rifles and Shot Guns, combined; American Rifles, assorted sizes; Powder and Pistol Flasks and Shot Pouches; Every article of gun-trimmings; Shot and Lead; Long and short handled Fry Pans; Pick Axes, hand and chopping Axes and Hatchets; Curry Combs, Drawing Knives; Trace Chains and Harness;

Stretcher, Stay, Tongue, and Fifth Chains; Shovels, Spades and Hoes; Pocket Knives, every variety.

The co-owner of the Nashville *Daily American* advertised something of a different sort—his share of the paper.

A valuable investment can be had in the *American* office, in the way of a lease, for three years, of all my interest in the establishment, consisting of one-half. It will be a good investment for any-one who has not got the "California fever" so bad as I have.

Hugh Heiskell caught the fever. Despite the promise of his law practice, he opted for adventure and quick riches. Scores of emigrant groups were being organized in the area; Heiskell selected one headed by James Bicknell of Madisonville. Bicknell had been a farmer, a politician, a postmaster, a shopkeeper, and a soldier in the Fifth Tennessee Volunteers in the Mexican War. He was also the husband of Hugh Heiskell's cousin Elizabeth Heiskell. Elizabeth's brother Tyler Heiskell, a recent college graduate, was another member of the Bicknell company, as was Oliver White, a beginning doctor who decided that Madisonville, with four physicians already for its four hundred inhabitants, wasn't the place to commence a practice. Oliver White's brother Richard and four others rounded out the crew.

Early in the planning, James Bicknell contacted Donald Campbell, a former Tennesseean who had drifted down the Tennessee River into Alabama. Campbell had tried farming but found it unrewarding; consequently he welcomed the chance to dig for gold. Campbell organized a company consisting of himself, his three brothers, a slave youth named Alex, two young free blacks, and a handful of others. The Tennesseeans proposed to steam down the Tennessee to the Mississippi River; they would pick up Campbell's Alabama company on the way.

Hugh Heiskell and the others left Knoxville on April 16, 1849, aboard the shallow-draft steamer *Cassandra*. The boat carried them without incident to Decatur, Alabama, where the rapids of Muscle Shoals compelled the upper-river boats to turn around. Continuing passengers traveled overland via horse-drawn railcars to Tuscumbia. There the Bicknell company met their Alabama partners and embarked on a lower-river packet for Paducah, Kentucky. At Paducah they caught one of the steamboats on the Cincinnati–St. Louis run, vessels that for speed and style outstripped anything on the Tennessee. At St. Louis they switched to a Missouri River boat that carried them west up the Big Muddy to St. Joseph, Missouri, one of the principal jumping-off points for Oregon and California.

WILLIAM SWAIN WAS a less likely argonaut than Hugh Heiskell, in that while Heiskell had neither wife nor child, Swain had both. Swain had just begun a career as a schoolteacher in upstate New York, north of Buffalo, when he met Sabrina Barrett at a spelling bee. Within a year they were married. A year after that—while the news from California was working its way east—Sabrina bore William a daughter, Eliza.

Perhaps family life wasn't everything Swain had hoped. Perhaps, having lived his entire twenty-six years almost within the spray of Niagara Falls, he felt his horizons contracting prematurely. Swain had read the romances of Walter Scott and the truer but no less romantic tales of John (and Jessie) Frémont. At one point he considered a military career. But then his father died, and with his mother, Patience, and bachelor brother, George, he inherited the family farm. His share in the farm was his sole capital, which under the circumstances of multiple shareholding was essentially illiquid. Nor, on a teacher's salary, and supporting a wife and child, could he hope to save more than pocket money. Between the farm and his two families, his life appeared bleakly predictable.

Then came word of the gold strike. As everywhere else, staid voices tried to keep the young men home. "We are quite sure that it is the duty of newspapers to use all the means in their power to repress rather than stimulate the prevailing excitement," intoned the Buffalo *Morning Express*. But, again as everywhere else, the naysaying often fell on ears attuned to a sweeter siren, in this case rendered by a California correspondent to the same paper, who wrote, "Many men who began last June to dig for gold with capital of $50 can now show $5,000 to $15,000."

Such statements supplied the moral cover Swain needed to bolt the farm, abandon Sabrina and Eliza, and embark on the great adventure of his heretofore adventureless life. Sabrina pleaded with him to stay; Eliza seconded her mother, at least by Sabrina's interpretation of the baby's cries. Sabrina's plea doubtless reflected her love for her husband; it may also have reflected the fact that with William gone, she would be stuck in the house of her in-laws. But William wouldn't be deterred. Here was the chance of a lifetime—of *their* lifetime, he explained. He wouldn't be gone long: a year, two at the most, only long enough to make a few thousand dollars, which would allow them to buy a place of their own, away from Patience and George.

Swain had no trouble finding companions for the journey west. Frederick Bailey's story was similar to Swain's; at thirty he had a wife, son, and few prospects. John Root was nineteen and unattached. Michael Hutchinson, forty-three, was a childless widower.

The foursome embarked in mid-April 1849 from Buffalo. By steamboat they traversed Lake Erie to Detroit, planning to proceed by train across Michigan. "But after learning that the fare to Niles [Michigan], 180 miles to the west, was $6," Swain explained to brother George, "that we would have to travel from there by stage forty miles to New Buffalo and thence from there by steamboat to Chicago for $6 more; that it would take three days on that route; and that the cars and boats did not run on Sunday, we concluded to take the lake route on account of its cheapness." The lake steamer *Michigan* would carry them up Lake Huron, through the Straits of Mackinac, and down Lake Michigan to Chicago, in four days for $6. "We concluded that $6 or $8 saved in one day was better than gold-digging, and we took our passage on the steamer."

As with many for whom the journey to California was the first long trip of any kind, Swain's adventure began as soon as he left home. The Great Lakes astonished him. "The waters of Lake Huron and the Straits are the clearest and most transparent waters I have ever seen. In the bay a sixpence can be distinctly seen at a depth of twenty feet. And the fish, which are here in great abundance, are as good as the waters are clear. This I know experimentally, for the steward brought a full barrel of fresh whitefish and trout—large, fat, and sweet!" April wasn't still winter in the north, but neither was it spring. Swain's ship encountered floating ice and a driving snowstorm that forced the captain to seek shelter behind Beaver Island. "We cast anchor within a stone's throw of the shore, secure from everything but the falling snow. Here we lay the rest of the day and all night, living on whitefish and trout and good potatoes and plenty of other necessities."

Chicago was a bustling town, full of itself and its future. Swain looked up a family friend who had moved there. "When I told him I was going to California for gold, he laughed and asked me if I had enough money to get back with. He advised me—and urged me—to put the money I had into land in Chicago and go home again."

From Chicago the Illinois Canal led south to the Illinois River, and the Illinois to the Mississippi. The mule-drawn canal boat was crowded; the long, narrow cabin served as parlor, dining room, and bedroom for the passengers, who slept in berths along the walls and on the floor. At Peru, Illinois, Swain and the others switched to the steamboat *Avalanche* for St. Louis, which they reached on April 24. "The public buildings here are the most splendid specimens of architecture I have ever witnessed, and many of the private buildings are splendid habitations. But the business part of the city is dirty, with black, narrow streets filled with carts drawn by mules. It is a bare heap of stone and brick, covered with coal smoke, with which the air of the city is black all the time."

St. Louis was an education in another sense. "This is, as you know, a slaveholding state," Swain told George. Swain had heard and read about the peculiar institution; he was curious to observe it in the flesh. He saw notices of a slave auction to take place that day at the courthouse, and hoped to attend. But the demands of travel left his curiosity unsatisfied. "We had not time to witness the spectacle."

At St. Louis the Swain party—less John Root, who had forgotten his rifle at Detroit and now waited for it to overtake him—boarded the *Amelia* for the run up the Missouri to Independence. Another emigrant, J. Goldsborough Bruff of Washington, who made the same trip just nine days ahead of Swain, left a vivid picture of this stretch:

> We were on board amid such a dense medley of Hoosiers, Wolverines, Buckeyes, Yankees and Yorkers, including black legs and swindlers of every grade of proficiency and celebrity, as is seldom to be found, even on our western rivers. The decks, above and below, exhibited an equally stupendous assortment of wagons, horses, mules, tents, bales, boxes, sacks, barrels and camp kettles; while every cabin and state room was an arsenal of rifles, fowling-pieces, bowie-knives, hatchets, pouches, powder-horns and belts.

A heavy headwind, added to the snowmelt current, forced the *Amelia* ashore. Swain and the others helped the crew gather wood to stoke the boilers. Swain appreciated the exercise but fretted at the lost time. "The slow progress of our boat is discouraging to all on board," he wrote. Impatience cast a pall over both scenery and company. "The sandy deposits of river banks, the unbroken cottonwood forests on the river flats, the dirty water, and the confinement on board with so many persons have become completely disgusting." Just below Independence the *Amelia* ran onto one of the innumerable shifting bars that vexed navigation on the Missouri. "How long we shall lay here I cannot say, but certainly the prospect is anything but encouraging." After six hours, though, the captain managed to free the boat, and at eight o'clock in the evening of May 2, Swain's small company reached Independence.

MOST OF THOSE WHO headed for California read about the gold strike in their local newspapers. Lewis Manly had no such opportunity, for on his part of the Wisconsin frontier there were no newspapers. But when talk at the taverns and trading posts turned to the word from the West, he quickly decided he was as well suited to gold-digging as the next man, and he determined to make the journey to California.

In fact Manly was far better suited than most gold-seekers to both the rigors of the journey and the trials of the goldfields. By inheritance he was a rolling stone, a chip off some wandering blocks. His father's father had migrated from England to Connecticut, where Manly's father was born; the family then relocated to Vermont, where Lewis's father met his mother, an orphan of Welsh parents and a veteran of multiple moves herself. The couple remained in Vermont, hard by the Canadian border, long enough to have four boys, of which Lewis (christened William Lewis) was the first. But then the wanderlust resurfaced. Good things were heard about Michigan; with his uncle, Lewis was sent ahead with a horse and a wagon, which the nine-year-old drove across New York, Pennsylvania, Ohio, and half of Michigan during the winter of 1829–30.

Upon being reunited with his parents and brothers, Lewis received a rifle and instructions to go hunting and not return without a deer. As it happened, he downed dinner on his first shot, thereby earning a reputation locally as a budding Nimrod, and regular responsibility for stocking the family larder.

Michigan was a decided improvement over Vermont. The fields grew crops of wheat and flax rather than rye and rocks; the winters were shorter and less severe. But the land between the lakes harbored that annoying "fever 'n agur"—in the local dialect—and Manly caught it. Quinine and calomel failed to relieve his symptoms, and he decided to seek a healthier neighborhood.

He built a boat from boards he found, and paddled west along Michigan's rivers, halting occasionally to work for cash. He split logs for fences and cut timber for railroad ties (for the Michigan Central Railroad, the line William Swain would deem too expensive). He crossed Lake Michigan on a lumber schooner, getting thoroughly seasick—but, by his own assessment, defeating his malaria in the bargain. (A later generation of physicians might have said the malaria was falling into remission on its own, even as the motion sickness made its symptoms seem mild by comparison.) In Wisconsin he found work as a lead miner among immigrants from England's Cornwall district, who contributed their geological expertise to Manly's growing stock of practical skills. But lead mining, besides being hard and dirty, paid poorly; during the winter Manly supplemented his income by hunting and trapping. In the process he learned still more about surviving in the wilderness and among its denizens, including various Indian tribes.

In long summers scratching the dirt for lead, and in longer winters chasing pelts across the snow, he dreamed of a better life, or at least an easier one. Acquaintances had moved to Oregon and found the climate there mild, the fish and game abundant, and the land cheap. Manly started saving to purchase the necessary kit to join the trek to the Willamette Valley.

But before he acquired the requisite capital, the news from California altered his plans. For a lead miner, gold mining was a signal promotion; as Manly laconically recalled, "I felt a change in my Oregon desires and had dreams at night of digging up the yellow dust." A friend named Bennett felt a similar compulsion. "Nothing would cure us then but a trip," Manly wrote, "and this was quickly decided upon."

Because Bennett would be driving a wagon and team (to carry his family), he had to wait for the spring grass to grow. The two agreed that Manly should leave first and make preparations. They would rendezvous on the road. But between high water, which disrupted travel, and an undated letter, which left Manly unsure whether Bennett was ahead or behind him, the two missed their connection. Manly pondered whether to go on or back. Because Bennett had Manly's rifle and some provisions they had jointly purchased (leaving Manly with almost no money), for him to proceed without Bennett would be very difficult. Manly had nearly decided to go back when a passing party, led by Charles Dallas of Iowa, offered him work driving a team of oxen to California. Manly accepted.

Like Manly and the Bennetts (and many other emigrants from the upper Mississippi Valley), the Dallas party hoped to jump off for the West at Council Bluffs, Iowa. But Council Bluffs was new to the business of provisioning overlanders, and the first few hundred emigrants drained the town's merchants of their small store of travel supplies. Manly and the Dallas company were compelled to proceed south to St. Joseph.

It was one of the ironies of the Gold Rush that in going west, many thousands of northern emigrants—including William Swain and Lewis Manly—were forced to go south: to slave-state Missouri. Under other circumstances, probably no more than a relative handful of these northerners would have visited the South and personally encountered the slave system. Missouri opened their eyes and forced them to reflect on the difference between slave labor and free. One emigrant, Eleazar Ingalls of Illinois, asked himself why Missouri, which was blessed with bountiful resources, was so sparsely settled compared to its neighbors. "Is it not owing to, and one of the fruits of, the blighting curse of slavery?—the driving of free men of the northern states to emigrate to more uncongenial soil and climate, rather than settle in a slave state." Lewis Manly, after witnessing the auction of a young slave in St. Joseph, wrote that the auctioneer "rattled away as if he were selling a steer." The bidding started at $500 and ended at $800, with the unfortunate chattel being dragged off in chains. "With my New England notions," Manly remarked, "it made quite an impression on me."

SARAH ROYCE'S NOTIONS didn't come from New England, although some of them would wind up there when her son Josiah became a famous Harvard professor and one of the most distinguished philosophers of his day. If Sarah Royce's notions originated anywhere other than her own determined mind, they probably were born in old England, in the hometown she shared—at two centuries' remove—with William Shakespeare. From Stratford-on-Avon, Sarah emigrated with her parents to Rochester, New York, not far from where William Swain grew up. She married Josiah Royce, who, like Lewis Manly's father—and generations of other Americans—believed that the future lay in the West. In the case of the Royces, this meant Iowa, just beyond the Mississippi River. Sarah prepared to make a home there, but Josiah, like many others on the frontier, kept his eye out for better prospects still farther west. Upon news of the gold discovery, he thought he spied them in California, and announced that the family, which now included daughter Mary, should move again.

Sarah lacked her husband's enthusiasm for the uprooting, but she accepted the decision with quiet confidence and resolve. Recollecting the spring day in 1849 when they set out across Iowa, she wrote, "The morning of that 30th of April was not very bright; but neither was it very gloomy. Rain might come within an hour, but then the sun might come out—I would not consent to delay our departure for fear of the weather. Had I not made up my mind to encounter many storms? If we were going, let us go, and meet what we were to meet, bravely."

In fact the first day proved pleasant enough, with a warm sun beating back the clouds. The first night was another matter, at least in Sarah's mind. She had grown up in towns, and as evening fell she found herself scanning the horizon for a house or other habitation.

> Why did I look for one? I knew we were to camp; but surely there would be a few trees or a sheltering hillside against which to place our wagon. No, only the level prairie stretched on each side of the way. Nothing indicated a place for us—a cozy nook, in which for the night we might be guarded, at least by banks and boughs.
>
> I had for months anticipated this hour, yet, not till it came, did I realize the blank dreariness of seeing night come on without house or home to shelter us and our baby-girl. And this was to be the same for many weeks, perhaps months. It was a chilling prospect, and there was a terrible shrinking from it in my heart; but I kept it all to myself and soon we were busy making things as comfortable as we could for the night.
>
> Our wagon was large, we were provided with straw and plenty of bed clothes, and soon a very tolerable resting place was ready for us. Our little Mary had been happy as a lark all day, and now sank to sleep in her straw and blanket bed, as serenely as though she were in a palace, on a downy pillow.
>
> At first the oppressive sense of homelessness, and an instinct of watchfulness, kept me awake. Perhaps it was not to be wondered at in one whose life had so far been spent in city or town, surrounded by the accompaniments of civilization and who was now, for the first time in her life, "camping out."
>
> However, quiet sleep came at last, and in the morning there

was a mildly exultant feeling which comes from having kept silent through a cowardly fit, and finding the fit gone off.

More than the fit had gone off in the night. The six oxen that pulled the wagon wandered away, as did the family's two milk cows. Not till noon were all retrieved. Sarah absorbed the lesson: "The hard facts of the pilgrimage would require patience, energy, and courage fully equal to what I had anticipated when I had tried to stretch my imagination to the utmost."

The end of April was late to be leaving eastern Iowa, and delays on the road caused them to fall further behind schedule. Spring rains raised the creeks and required detours; mud mired the wheels and compelled repeated unloading and reloading of the wagon; thunderstorms battered the travelers—but occasionally, in the aftermath, raised their spirits. Sarah wrote in her diary on May 21: "Were overtaken during the afternoon by two tremendous storms of thunder, lightning and wind. Encamped just as the last one burst upon us, on the lee side of a beautiful grove; and at the close of the storm, as the clouds broke, the most brilliant and perfect rainbow I ever saw completely arched the lovely scene."

THE MISSOURI RIVER was where the journey west began in earnest. It was also where the emigrants learned the economics of overland travel. *The Emigrants' Guide to California* led travelers to expect to purchase supplies at Independence, St. Joseph, and the other river towns "on nearly as low terms as at St. Louis." This proved hopelessly optimistic, as Hugh Heiskell, among thousands of others, discovered to his dismay. "It ought to be generally known that at St. Joseph emigrants for California are most shamefully imposed upon," Heiskell recorded. "They are required to pay exorbitant prices for all they need." He illustrated: six to seven dollars per hundredweight of flour (the *Emigrants' Guide* quoted two dollars), five to six cents per pound of bacon, fifty to eighty-five dollars per yoke of oxen. Mules old enough to travel well were unavailable at any price, while immature animals of two to three years went for seventy-five to one hundred dollars each. "But such are considered to be too young to endure the journey." Yet there was little the emigrants could do. "This being the last point at which any thing can be procured for the trip, they are obliged to give whatever is asked."

Different people responded to the high prices in different ways. Heiskell's group grumbled and paid. Charles Dallas paid for provisions for the group Lewis Manly had joined, but then refused to pay the $50 demanded to ferry his company across the Missouri. He ordered a return north, where after a day's drive they encountered a ferryman willing to take them across for $30.

William Swain's New York threesome (John Root hadn't caught up yet) solved the supply problem by joining a more foresighted company. For $100 each, plus a wagon and team of oxen for the three, the New Yorkers became partners in a Michigan outfit calling itself the Wolverine Rangers. The Rangers had sent a purchasing agent ahead to buy provisions before the heaviest of the rush arrived; by joining the Rangers, Swain and his fellows benefited from the Michiganders' advance planning.

THE HIGH PRICES at the river towns were a worrisome problem for the emigrants, but hardly the most frightening. That distinction fell to the infectious diseases that followed the travelers upriver. Summer was always hazardous to health along populated rivers, where the wastewater of one community became the drinking water of communities downstream. But the summer of 1849 was peculiarly lethal, and with the springtime arrival of tens of thousands more people than the water and waste facilities of the river towns were accustomed to handling, it started early.

Cholera was the worst of the waterborne diseases. It struck with terrifying swiftness. A man or woman could appear hearty at breakfast, complain of queasy bowels at noontime dinner, and be dead by supper. The cause of the disease—the bacillus *Vibrio cholerae*—was unknown, and for this reason the reach of the illness seemed a matter of fate, bad luck, or divine disfavor. St. Louis, as the largest city in the path of the emigration, was the hardest hit. During June alone nearly two thousand people died of the disease there.

The towns above St. Louis did what they could to ward off the epidemic. Steamboats suspected of carrying infected passengers were turned away or compelled to unload across the river. In extreme cases, vessels were simply abandoned; after fifty-three persons died aboard the *Monroe*, the surviving passengers and crew fled for their lives.

But no quarantine could hold back the epidemic. For one thing, cholera's incubation period of up to five days meant that many apparently healthy people were already infected. For another, the river towns lived on the river traffic; any extended quarantine would have killed them. The Gold Rush was the chance of a lifetime for most Missouri Valley merchants; they were loath to spurn such a windfall of customers. The towns would take their profits and take their chances with the disease.

The emigrants were in a similar bind. They all knew about the epidemic, but they also knew that the chance for gold wouldn't come again. The compulsion for California caused some emigrants to accept questionable intelligence. Before boarding at Peru, Illinois, William Swain asked the captain of the *Avalanche* about health conditions downstream. "He says that there is nothing heard about cholera at St. Louis, no cases among the inhabitants there," Swain noted. The captain was lying; the epidemic at St. Louis was already raging, as anyone who made a living on the river knew. Other emigrants held their breath, almost literally, as they crossed the Missouri, hoping to leave the danger at the river's edge. "The cholera is prevailing to a considerable extent along the river," Hugh Heiskell wrote from the western side. "But so far we have escaped, and as we are now in a healthy region, we cherish the hope that Providence will still protect and preserve us, and that this fearful scourge will not overtake us."

It was an idle hope, for many others if not for Heiskell. The Missouri turned out to be no barrier to the epidemic, as Sarah Royce discovered a couple of days across the river. The Royces went over at Council Bluffs, where, because the emigrants were fewer than farther downstream, the cholera epidemic was less severe. And having survived the crossing uninfected, Sarah had reason to hope their party might be spared.

And so it was until they were well out onto the prairie. By then other distractions had driven thoughts of the disease from the travelers' minds.

Consequently, when the cholera appeared, its arrival was all the more dismaying. Sarah described the first casualty:

> The oldest of the men who had joined company with my husband complained of intense pain and sickness, and was soon obliged to lie down in the wagon, which, being large, gave room for quite a comfortable bed behind the seat where Mary and I sat. Soon terrible spasms convulsed him; the Captain was called, examined the case, and ordered a halt. Medicine was administered which afforded some relief.
>
> About this time a horseman or two appeared, with the intelligence that some companies in advance of us were camped at the ford of the Elkhorn River, not more than two miles distant, and that there was a physician among them. We therefore made the sick man as comfortable as we could, and went on. Arrived at the encampment, the Doctor pronounced the disease Asiatic Cholera. Everything was done that could be under the circumstances, but nothing availed, and in two or three hours the poor old man expired.

All mourned the deceased; Sarah faced the additional task of disinfecting her wagon and bedclothes. This was a distasteful and nerve-wracking job, as the hallmark of cholera, and the principal source of transmission, was profuse diarrhea and vomiting. Sarah washed everything as well as she could, and hung the blankets and linen out to dry. But she couldn't know whether she had washed them well enough or, even if she had, whether that would protect her and her family. Her diary recorded her fears (which echoed those of Jessie Frémont in Panama):

> Now indeed a heavy gloom hung round us. The destroyer seemed let loose upon our camp. Who would go next? What if my husband should be taken and leave us alone in the wilderness? What if I should be taken and leave my little Mary motherless? Or—still more distracting thought—what if we both should be laid low,

and she be left a destitute orphan, among strangers, in a land of savages?

THOUGH FEW OF THE emigrants realized it at the time, cholera was the greatest danger most of them would encounter on the journey west. And though that danger didn't disappear as the migration proceeded onto the prairies and plains west of the Missouri, it did gradually diminish.

It was replaced by another danger that loomed far larger in the minds of most emigrants than in actuality. Every overlander had heard stories of the Plains Indians, particularly the Pawnee ("a treacherous, hostile race," according to Eleazar Ingalls) and the Sioux; most anticipated their encounters with the aboriginal peoples with trepidation.

Sarah Royce met her first Indians a short distance beyond the Missouri. Looking to the west, she and the others descried a large number of moving objects on both sides of the road where it entered a range of low hills. At first Sarah thought that another wagon train, making early camp, had turned out its cattle. On closer approach, the moving objects proved to be Indians, several hundred of them, lining the road. As the Royce party approached, a small group of the Indians came forward to meet the emigrants. The captain of the Royce train in turn summoned several men among the emigrants to go forward and parley with the natives.

The latter presented a simple demand: before the travelers could pass, they must pay a toll. Whether or not this particular group of Indians put it in such terms, it wasn't lost on the Indians generally that the emigrants paid tolls to the owners of ferries and bridges; the principle here was the same. Hadn't the government of the United States itself designated this region as Indian Territory?

To the members of the Royce party, the principle was *not* the same. "The men of our company," Sarah wrote, "after consultation, resolved that the demand was unreasonable! that the country we were traveling over belonged to the United States, and that these red men had no right to stop us." The Indians were informed that they wouldn't get a penny from this train. The gold-seekers were bound for California, and if allowed to pass would do the Indians no harm. But if the Indians provoked a fight, they would get a fight, a fierce one.

A tense several minutes ensued. The Indian representatives returned to their main force; the emigrant delegation returned to the wagon train. The captain of the train directed that every man in the company display and prepare to use every weapon he owned. "Revolvers, knives, hatchets, glittered in their belts; rifles and guns bristled on their shoulders," Sarah explained. Then the captain gave the order to march.

> The drivers raised aloft their long whips, the rousing words "Go 'long, Buck!"—"Bright!"—"Dan!" were given all along the line, and we were at once moving between long but not very compact rows of half-naked redskins, many of them well armed, others carrying but indifferent weapons; while all wore in their faces the expression of sullen disappointment, mingled with a half-defiant scowl that suggested the thought of future night attacks, when darkness and thickets should give them greater advantage. For the present, however, they had evidently made up their minds to let us pass, and we soon lost sight of them.

The experience of most emigrants was similar. For many years the Indians of the region west of the Missouri had known the white men as traders, who engaged the Indians essentially as entrepreneurs dealing with entrepreneurs. Although there were occasional misunderstandings and acts of unorchestrated violence, both sides benefited from the trade, and neither had reason to disrupt it. The migration to Oregon that began in the early 1840s altered the situation somewhat. The emigrants weren't traders, and they did the Indians no good. But neither, at first, did they do the Indians much harm. They were merely passing through—nomads, for the moment, more or less like the Indians themselves.

The Gold Rush altered the situation further. To be sure, these latest emigrants also were just passing through, but there were vastly more of them than before. Their oxen, cattle, mules, and horses ate all the grass in sight and fouled the streams; their hunters shot buffalo, driving the herds away from the trail.

Yet the very numbers that made the emigrants worrisome to the Indians simultaneously protected the emigrants. As Sarah Royce discovered, as long as the emigrants stuck together, they had little to fear. The particular band the Royce party encountered could have overpowered this one group of emigrants, but there were many other emigrants who would have demanded retribution, and there were soldiers who would have responded to the demands.

Besides, though the emigrants were an annoyance and a potential threat, they were also an opportunity. Indians were happy to trade with the emigrants, supplying ponies, meat, and other provisions required for the cross-country trek, typically at prices well below what the merchants of the Missouri River towns charged. "We are getting among the Indians," William Swain wrote from the Kansas River. "They come into camp with all their native rigging on, all mounted on ponies splendidly rigged out, for which they ask from $30 to $50." Writing from farther west, Hugh Heiskell reported, "Camp full of Indians; great excitement. Most of the company trading, blankets for buffalo robes, powder & lead or tobacco for deer skins, lariats, &c."

From the emigrants' perspective, the presence and activities of the Indians were another aspect of the grand adventure of the Gold Rush. In this regard, such threat as the Indians posed, and the initial frisson they engendered, were part of their appeal. So were their wild customs. Indian funeral rites occasioned especial notice. Lewis Manly described a scene near Scott's Bluff on the North Platte:

> We found a large camp of the Sioux Indians on the bank of a ravine, on both sides of which were some large cottonwood trees. Away up in the large limbs, platforms had been made of poles, on which were laid the bodies of their dead, wrapped in blankets and fastened down to the platform by a network of smaller poles tightly lashed so that they could not be dragged away or disturbed by wild

> animals. This seemed a strange sort of cemetery, but when we saw the desecrated earth-made graves we felt that perhaps this was the best way, even if it was a savage custom.

William Swain, observing a similar scene, reached a generally parallel conclusion: "It was a revolting sight to me, but they probably consider this method as sacred as we do that of burying in the consecrated grounds at home."

NEXT TO THE INDIANS in the emigrants' catalog of exotica were the buffalo. Whether they had read Frémont's reports or the more recent *Oregon Trail* by Francis Parkman (which since the gold discovery had been reissued with a new title, *The California and Oregon Trail*), the emigrants all knew about the vast herds of buffalo that roamed the trans-Missouri plains. Nearly every man who fancied himself a hunter felt obliged to take part in a buffalo hunt.

William Swain's turn arrived on June 16, not far from Fort Kearny.

> This afternoon when I was in the rear I observed a commotion in front. The horsemen galloping along the train, the footmen, the drivers, all seemed anxiously inquiring for something. Soon the train formed a telegraphic line, on which the word "buffalo" was transmitted. All hands seized their guns and every man at liberty started for the head of the train. The drivers all mounted the wagon tongues and drove with one hand, having hold of the wagon cover with the other, while eyes and mouths were wide open in search of the subject of the commotion.
>
> I was driving, and from the tongue on which I stood I soon fixed my eye on the object of all the feeling and interest of the company: a troop of some twenty buffalo who had come across the river and were making for the bluffs across the head of our trail. They had far the start on our boys and were doing their best. Footmen ran and horsemen put the ponies under whip and spur.

> The plain was three miles wide, and the chase was very even for the first half way; but the buffalos' wind proved the best and all but three of the horsemen gave up the chase, one of whom came up on the buffalos. He was far in advance of the train when he saw them and had no arms but his revolver, and from that he shot four balls, two of which took effect but only made the buffalo run the faster.
>
> Thus ended our first buffalo chase. I confess I was much displeased, as I had made up my mind for some steak this evening.

The hunts were often more successful, though rarely less strenuous. Lewis Manly described several hunters on horseback pursuing a solitary bull. The horsemen caught the buffalo and plugged the beast with multiple balls.

> He still kept his feet, and they went nearer. Mr. Rogers, being on a horse with a blind bridle, got near enough to fire his Colt's revolver at him, when he turned, and the horse, being unable to see the animal quickly enough to get out of his way, suffered the force of a sudden attack of the old fellow's horns; he came out with a gash in his thigh six inches long, while Rogers went on a flying expedition over his head, and did some lively scrambling when he reached the ground.
>
> The other hunters worried the animal along for about half a mile, and finally, after about forty shots, he lay down but held his head up defiantly, receiving shot after shot with an angry shake, till a side shot laid him out.
>
> This game gave us plenty of meat which, though tough, was a pleasant change from bacon.

Significantly, Manly—a professional hunter rather than an enthusiast—declined to take part in the chase. But his professional curiosity was piqued by the bull's ability to absorb so much fire before succumbing. The answer soon appeared. "On examination it was found that many of the balls had been stopped by the matted hair about the old fellow's head, and none of them had reached the skull."

The Gold Rush marked the beginning of the end of the great buffalo herds. Tens of thousands of hunters turned loose on the plains, each determined to bag a buffalo—or two or ten—led to killing far in excess of any conceivable need. One emigrant witnessed a half-day's devastation and commented, "I presume that not less than fifty buffalo were slaughtered that morning, whereas not three in all were used. Such a wanton destruction of buffalo, the main dependence of the Indians for food, is certainly reprehensible, but still the desire of engaging at least once in the buffalo chase by the emigrant can scarcely be repressed."

ONE REASON FOR THE slaughter was that the emigrants were often simply bored. For nine hundred miles west of the Missouri, every day was essentially like the last. Rise before dawn, cook and eat breakfast, gather the animals, hitch up the wagons, head out, halt around midday, cook and eat dinner, march again to whatever camp the captain or scouts had discovered, undo what was done at dawn with the animals and wagons, cook and eat supper, set guards on the stock, go to sleep under the stars or the canvas.

The marching itself was slow, at the pace of the slowest oxen, no more than two miles per hour. All but the lead wagons choked on the dust; for this reason the lead rotated among the wagons of each train. Women and children, who typically had expected to ride in the wagons, often abandoned their seats to escape the dust and walked well to the side of the trail.

Once out on the plains, the scenery scarcely changed from day to day, week to week. The trail climbed gradually; the rolling plains leveled out. Occasional landmarks—Courthouse Rock, Chimney Rock, Scott's Bluff—afforded the only visible signs of progress. When mountains finally appeared on the western horizon, they grew so slowly that they seemed on the far side of the world.

Under the circumstances, the emigrants welcomed anything that broke the monotony. Practicing Christians were a majority on the trail, and many trains initially observed the Sabbath by resting. "We are determined to *not* travel on Sunday," Hugh Heiskell wrote, "unless some times we are compelled to do so in order to get wood & water. We rest, altho many things are done which would not look right at Fruit Hill—for instance, wood is cut, although if near we cut it Saturday evening; cooking, and sometimes sunning whatever may be damp in the wagon. Some in the company have washed. Our mess of nine will not." Whether this trailside sabbatarianism demonstrated the authenticity of the Mosaic law or simply its practicality, the halts refreshed the travelers and their livestock, and readied them for the new week. (Yet some of the observant among the emigrants grew anxiously indignant at the impiety of the nonobservant. Thomas Van Dorn of Illinois fretted and scolded in his diary on Sunday, May 13: "Over 100 teams have passed us today. It is a novel thing to see men in their career for gain rush forward like a herd of wild buffalo as though led on by some instinctive influence, with apparently no further aim in view." Yet Van Dorn and others—including Hugh Heiskell—eventually modified their theology under the duress of distance and desire to reach the mines. "Many are more pious than we are," Van Dorn noted on Sunday, August 19, his remorse yielding to a sense of triumph, "for the crowd we were with yesterday have all been left behind.")

Other breaks in the routine were based in patriotism rather than religion—although religion wasn't entirely absent. July 4 fell on a Wednesday in 1849, and nearly all the trains observed the anniversary of American independence. "At twelve o'clock we formed a procession and walked to the stand [a makeshift of a table spread with a blanket] to the tune of 'The Star Spangled Banner,' " William Swain recorded. "The President of the day called the meeting to order. We listened to a prayer by Rev. Mr. Hobart, then remarks and the reading of the Declaration of Independence by Mr. Pratt, and then the address by Mr. Sexton. We then listened to 'Hail Columbia.' This celebration was very pleasing, especially the address, which was well delivered and good enough for any assembly at home." A brief parade around the camp was followed by a banquet. "Dinner consisted of ham, beans boiled and baked, biscuits, john cake, apple pie, sweet cake, rice pudding, pickles, vinegar, pepper sauce and mustard, coffee, sugar, and milk. All enjoyed it well."

Further festivities followed. "After dinner the toasting commenced. The boys had raked and scraped together all the brandy they could, and they toasted, hurrayed, and drank till reason was out and brandy was in. I stayed till the five regular toasts were drunk; and then, being disgusted with their conduct, I went to our tent, took my pen, and occupied the remainder of the day in writing to my wife, in which I enjoyed myself better than those who were drinking, carousing, and hallooing all around the camp." The carousers doubtless would have differed, had they stopped to consider the matter, which they didn't. "At night the boys danced by moonlight on the grass, or rather on the sand."

ALL COULD AGREE that American independence ought to be celebrated, even if some disputed the role of drink in the celebration. Other issues elicited no such consensus. Slavery divided wagon trains just as it divided America as a whole. Hugh Heiskell's company of Tennesseeans and Alabamians had added various persons from the South and beyond, including an English couple named Thomas. The Thomases' distaste for slavery had been evident from the start, although it hadn't prevented them from joining a group that included slave-owners and slaves. At one point, however, they could abide the issue no longer. "A flare up in camp today," Heiskell wrote.

> Mr. Thompson was whipping Wash [his slave]. Thomas, running in, said he should not whip him. Thompson said if he interfered he would whip him too, & seizing a hatchet seemed ready to execute this threat. At this stage Mrs. Thomas, rushing in, addressed Thompson, "If you kill my husband you shall not live." Thomas, going back to his wagon, now came out with a pistol. Others now interfered with, telling Thomas he had no right to say anything to Thompson for whipping his Negro. "No!" says Mrs. Thomas [to

her husband], "You are in the States, you are not in England."
"Well, but what's the difference? Didn't the Americans all come from England?" And so ended the battle.

Other differences in mores simmered below the surface. When Lewis Manly's party had almost reached Fort Kearny, the members were surprised to see an unsaddled horse gallop into camp from the west and fall in with the party's horses as they grazed among the willows in the river bottom. Next morning two soldiers from the fort arrived, inquiring after the stray. Charles Dallas, speaking for the company, said he hadn't seen the beast, and the soldiers accepted his word. When the train approached the fort, Dallas tied the horse to his own, on the side away from the fort and any inquisitive eyes there. Then he dismounted and walked ahead, distracting the officers while the rest of the party drove on past. "I did not like this much," Manly recalled, "for if we were discovered we might be roughly handled, and perhaps the property of the innocent even confiscated. Really my New England ideas of honesty were somewhat shocked."

MANY ROADS LED FROM the emigrants' starting places—in Tennessee for Hugh Heiskell, upstate New York for William Swain, Wisconsin for Lewis Manly, Iowa for Sarah Royce—but only one road led from the plains into the mountains. The Platte River wasn't much to look at ("a mile wide and six inches deep," according to one saw; "too thin to plow and too thick to drink," by another), but it ran all summer in a region where many streams failed; its valley ascended in the right direction, namely west; and its ascent into the mountains was gradual enough for the most heavily laden wagons and teams. Whether the emigrants crossed the Missouri at Independence or St. Joseph or Council Bluffs, all reached the Platte at or before Fort Kearny (in the middle of what would become Nebraska). From Fort Kearny they followed the main stem of the river to its forks, then up the northern branch past Courthouse Rock, past Chimney Rock, past Scott's Bluff, to Fort Laramie.

The North Platte remained roughly the route to its juncture with the

Sweetwater, the ascent of which took the travelers to within a day's drive of South Pass. For most emigrants, this was the best part of the journey. The scenery above Fort Laramie was breathtaking, with the Laramie Range to the south and the Wind River Range to the north. A mile above sea level, the air possessed a clarity unmatched at lower elevations. Days were warm; nights were cool; the grass was plentiful; the water was sweet (hence the name of the river); the emigrants and their livestock had gained strength from the exercise of the road and not yet begun to lose it to fatigue.

For most of the emigrants, South Pass was a disappointment. North America was a grand continent, and grandeur was anticipated in its continental divide. But anyone who had crossed the Appalachians had surmounted passes more impressive. In a region of high, open valleys, South Pass was simply the highest point in one such valley above the Sweetwater, distinguishable only (and barely) by the fact that the lay of land shifted almost imperceptibly from east to west. "Our Guide Book gave very elaborate directions by which we might be able to identify the highest point in the road, where we passed from the Atlantic to the Pacific Slope," Sarah Royce wrote. "Otherwise we could not have noticed it, so gradual had been the ascent, and so slightly varied was the surface for a mile or two on all sides."

After South Pass the trail diverged again, requiring the emigrants to make some basic decisions. Before 1849 most travelers in this region had been bound for Oregon; from South Pass they steered north toward Fort Hall on the Snake River, then down the Snake to the Columbia River and the Willamette Valley. A few emigrants of 1849 followed the Oregon Trail to Fort Hall and the Snake before turning south and picking up the road west to California. The route from South Pass to the Snake wasn't easy, but it was familiar, with its camping sites and river crossings well marked on reliable maps. For those who liked to know where they were going, this northern branch of the trail had considerable merit.

Less familiar than the Oregon Trail, but still well known, was the Mormon Trail from South Pass to Salt Lake City. This was shorter than the Snake River route, trending more directly west. But because it had been blazed by those who intended to go no farther than the foot of the Wasatch Mountains, it had the signal disadvantage of depositing California-bound travelers on the eastern edge of the most forbidding desert in North America, the Great Salt Lake Desert. For nearly a hundred miles, the white salt shimmered in the brilliant sunlight—a stunning scene, but incredibly daunting and nearly impassable to any but the best prepared. The Mormon Trail had another drawback: the Mormons. The majority of orthodox Christians in the army of overlanders disliked and distrusted the heretical sect of Saints—for their heresy (including the strange and dangerous practice of polygamy), and for the desire for revenge the Mormons were presumed to harbor after their harsh treatment in Illinois and Missouri.

A third route was the one chosen by most Forty-Niners. After following the Oregon Trail for some distance, along what was called Sublette's Cutoff, this route split the difference between the Oregon Trail and the Mormon Trail. Veering south of the Oregon Trail and the Snake River, it remained well north of the Great Salt Lake, finally delivering travelers to the headwaters of the Humboldt River west of the Salt Desert.

Hugh Heiskell and William Swain followed this third route, which, not surprisingly, was called the California Trail. It encompassed the hardest going so far, largely because the river courses in the region ran north and south rather than east and west; as a result the wagons were constantly climbing out of one valley or descending into the next. A headlong pitch down to the Green River required the emigrants to lock their brakes and chain logs to the axles as land anchors against the descent. Moreover, because the rivers ran transverse to the route, for the first time the travelers were compelled to make waterless marches between streams. They were really in the mountains now, and the weather let them feel it. Days remained warm, but nights were sharply cold. The emigrants often awoke to frost on the ground and ice in the water buckets.

Yet the scenery was glorious. "The sun in magnificence rose above the mountain among the golden coloured clouds of dazzling brightness," recorded Hugh Heiskell one typical morning. Hot springs bearing such names as Soda Springs, Beer Springs, and Steamboat Springs bubbled, gurgled, and geysered from the earth. "Going down, we found a basin underground in the rock in which the water was agitated as a violent boiling caldron," Heiskell wrote. Describing the same spot, William Swain said the spring "presented the appearance of a pot of boiling water and made a noise like lard boiling violently."

Hardly less fascinating than the geography were certain of the human inhabitants. Pegleg Smith was a mountain man about fifty years old who operated a trading post on the Bear River with his wife, an Indian girl of perhaps sixteen ("who he appears to love," remarked Heiskell). Smith's nickname derived from a feat that amazed the emigrants when they heard of it. Some twenty years earlier Smith had been trapping when a bullet from an Indian rifle shattered his leg below the knee. He realized that only amputation stood between him and death by gangrene. Hardly hesitating, he took out his sheath knife and performed the amputation himself. Eventually he carved a wooden leg, on which he now clattered about his trading post. A socket carved in his stirrup allowed him to ride.

Hugh Heiskell found Smith "a hospitable, honest mountaineer." Even so, he had "peculiar ideas about some things, of course, owing to his habits from so long a residence among savages." One of these habits was a readiness to resort to violence. "Yesterday evening White & Nelse came home & told us that Pegleg had cowhided a fellow for trying to steal one of his horses." It seemed that one of the men from the train had grown drunk and quarrelsome, and when Smith ordered him away, he left in company with some of Smith's horses. Smith alleged theft; the accused claimed a misunderstanding. Observers were divided: "Oll and Nelse, who were there all the time, believe him guilty. The rest of us think not." But on the Bear River, Pegleg Smith's word was law. "At any rate they brought him back and gave him a cowhiding."

SARAH ROYCE SAW neither Pegleg Smith nor the hot springs that impressed Heiskell and Swain. The Royces had joined a company that was bound for Salt Lake City, and they decided to stay with it that far. Crossing the Wasatch Mountains west of Fort Bridger, they noted with concern the snow swirling about the ridgetops. It was mid-August, and the Sierras, which were higher than the Wasatch, were still months away. Yet the vista from Emigrant Pass (so named by the Mormons two years earlier) almost erased the foreboding.

> It was near sunset on the 18th of August when we got our first view of the Great Salt Lake, with its back-ground of mountains; and in its foreground the well laid-out city, of snug dwellings and thrifty gardens. The suddenness with which we came upon the view was startling. From narrow mountain gorges and rough crooked turns, our road abruptly led us through an opening, almost like an immense doorway, unarched at the top. Here we were on a small plateau some hundreds of feet above the valley, with nothing to obstruct one's view for many miles. It is impossible to describe how, in the transparent atmosphere, everything was brought out with a distinctness that almost ignored distance.

Despite the lateness of the season, the Royces spent ten days resting in Salt Lake City, allowing their oxen to regain strength and weight. Meanwhile Sarah and Josiah pondered what to do next. One veteran of the region claimed to know a route that led far south of the main emigrant road and would spare the travelers the Sierra snows. Yet he wouldn't be leaving for several weeks, and this seemed to Sarah and Josiah too long to wait. The Mormon elders and their many wives, observing the presence of Sarah and little Mary, urged the Royces in the strongest terms to stay the winter. The heat of summer had scorched what little grass the Great Basin offered; the hordes ahead of them had devoured most of what survived the sun. The Royces would probably die before they reached the Sierras. But even assuming the desert spared them, they were so late that the snows of the mountains would almost certainly trap them. The grim fate of the Donner party should be an object lesson to them. Besides, everyone else had either hurried ahead or decided to winter in the city; if the Royces continued, they would be traveling alone.

The advice failed. "We heard it, we coolly talked it over, and yet, so perverse were we, that on the 30th day of August, a solitary wagon, drawn by three yoke of oxen, and in charge of only two men [Josiah and an elderly fellow the family picked up], left Salt Lake City, bearing, as its passengers, one woman and one little child, and for freight only so much provisions as might last us till we could scale the mighty Sierras and reach their western feet."

ALTHOUGH LEWIS MANLY was even less eager than the Royces to winter with the Mormons, Charles Dallas had no such compunctions, and before his train reached South Pass, he informed Manly and the other drivers that he was going to halt for the season in Salt Lake City. They could stay or not, but he couldn't afford to pay them during the idle winter months.

"This was bad news for me," Manly recalled, "for I knew the history of the Mormons at Nauvoo and in Missouri, and the prospect of being thrown among them with no money to buy bread was a very sorry one." The other drivers shared Manly's fears, and the group called a council, to which they invited Dallas. Evidently they hoped to make him reconsider his decision, perhaps by threatening a strike, which would have left him in the middle of the wilderness with no drivers. He resented this attempt at pressure. "He became quite angry at us, and talked some and swore a great deal more, and the burden of his speech was: 'This train belongs to me and I propose to do with it just as I have a mind to, and I don't care a damn what you fellows do or say.' " He then stalked off, leaving the drivers to their grumbling.

For several days Manly and the others weighed their options. Going back east was ignominious and perhaps impossible, given their lack of supplies and money. Going forward to Salt Lake City was hardly more appealing, given what they assumed to be the Mormons' animus against unbelievers. "We began to think that the only way to get along at all in Salt Lake would be to turn Mormons, and none of us had any belief or desire that way." As gentiles, they might not even survive the winter among the Mormons. "If we were not very favored travelers"—and they would not be, given their unemployment and penury—"our lot might be cast among the sinners for all time."

Crossing South Pass into the country where the rivers ran toward the Pacific, Manly started formulating a solution to his and the other drivers' predicament. By the time they reached the Green River, the first sizable stream flowing west, he was quietly talking it over with them. "We put a great many 'ifs' together and they amounted about to this: If this stream were large enough; if we had a boat; if we knew the way; if there were no falls or bad places; if we had plenty of provisions; if we were bold enough to set out on such a trip, etc., we might come out at some point or other on the Pacific Ocean."

As though in answer to Manly's second question, a boat suddenly appeared. At one time someone had operated a ferry at this crossing of the Green River; all that remained was an abandoned boat—just large enough to hold a single wagon—filled with sand and lying on the bank. Manly and the others dug the boat out and employed it to float the Dallas train and a contingent of U.S. soldiers, their recent companions on the trail, across the Green. In the process Manly asked the unit's surgeon and the commanding officer about the river. Was it passable? Where did it go? Both men said its waters eventually reached the Pacific, and though it contained some cataracts, there were no waterfalls.

This made up Manly's mind. He would try the river. Somewhat to his surprise, Dallas presented no objection—probably because they were close enough to Salt Lake City that he could get along without his full crew of drivers. Dallas offered to buy Manly's horse for $60, and he agreed to sell Manly some flour and bacon, two ropes, and two axes.

Six others joined Manly in trading their whips for oars. Together they watched Dallas and the army party disappear to the west. "Each company wished the other good luck, we took a few long breaths, and then set to work in earnest to carry out our plans."

The first days down the Green River caused Manly and the others to congratulate themselves on their boldness and perspicacity. The river was smooth and swift, and though its direction was south rather than west, their speed—estimated by Manly, who had been elected captain by the other six, at thirty miles a day—far outpaced the plodding to which they had grown accustomed on the trail. Besides, river travel was exhilarating.

Whenever the sun grew hot overhead, a man had only to splash himself with the cold water to feel as though all was well in this beautiful world. By every indication, they had got the better of the bargain with Charles Dallas. "It looked as if we were taking the most sensible way to the Pacific," Manly wrote, "and we wondered that everybody was so blind as not to see it as we did."

Subsequent challenges simply added to the zest. They spied an encampment of Indians where a tributary joined the Green. The Indians beckoned the boaters to come to shore, as if warning against some danger below; but Manly guessed—and the others agreed—that this might be a ruse, and so they feigned ignorance and floated by. In the swiftest stretches two men pulled oars and the other five manned stout poles, cut from saplings on the shore, to push off from rocks. Manly, standing in the bow, gave a mighty heave against one especially large boulder, only to have his staff lodge in a crevice beside the big rock, and the rebound of the staff catapult him out of the craft and halfway across the stream. He landed with a great splash and disappeared beneath the surface. Briefly the men wondered if they had lost their leader, but Manly, a strong swimmer, came up laughing, and the men waved their hats and cheered for their intrepid captain.

Although the provisions purchased from Dallas were modest in quantity and boringly bland, nature opened her larder to the travelers. Antelope and other animals came to the river to drink, and Manly, drawing on his experience as a professional hunter, bagged more than the men could eat. One massive elk weighed in—by the estimate of a crew member named Rogers, a butcher by trade—at more than five hundred pounds. The antlers spanned six feet, and when the skull was suspended upside down by the antlers, Manly could walk beneath the arch they formed. The men spent an entire night cutting the meat into strips and drying it over a fire, to reduce its bulk for transport.

For several days the river traced a route through wide canyons, where the mountains sloped gently back from the banks; but then the mountains drew nearer and the canyons began to close in upon the boaters. At one point Manly, tired from his hunting and his general responsibilities, was napping in the bow when the men awoke him abruptly. Dead ahead rose a wall of rock many hundreds of feet high. Where the river went at its foot, none could see. Manly recalled a map the army party had used, which marked something called "Brown's Hole." Unfamiliar with the terminology of the mountain men who had christened the landmarks in this vicinity (a "hole" was simply a sheltered canyon), Manly grew alarmed that the river was about to disappear down a hole in the ground. "I told the boys I guessed we were elected to go on foot to California after all, for I did not propose to follow the river down any sort of a hole into any mountain." At the last possible moment, when the boat was about to be dashed into the base of the towering rock cliff, the stream turned sharply to the right, into a hitherto invisible gash of a canyon. The sky, so broad just moments before, now shrank to a sliver of light far overhead. The sun disappeared; the river ran in perpetual shadow between walls forbidding and dark.

Nor was the scenery all that changed. In many places rocks the size of houses had crashed—eons ago, or perhaps just yesterday—from the cliffs to the canyon floor, where they blocked the river and forced the waters to either side. Time and again Manly and the others had to get out of the boat and, with great effort and no little hazard, lower it by rope through the rapids. Where before they had glided down a smooth pathway, now they stumbled down a turbulent, treacherous flight of giant stairs. Their pace had been measured in miles per hour; now it was hours per mile.

The work was wearing; the men grew hungry. And the game all but disappeared. Only a few mountain sheep, scampering impossibly on the precipices above, far beyond the reach of Manly's rifle, gave sign that any animals lived within the canyon walls.

The travelers became disoriented. Unable to find the sun, unable to keep track of the twists and turns of the river, they had no idea which direction they were traveling, or how far. They didn't know if they were still within the bounds of the United States. (They were, but only because the Senate had ratified the Treaty of Guadalupe Hidalgo, bringing the entire Southwest under American rule). Manly, in an effusion of patriotism—and to leave a record lest they never escape the canyon—climbed to above the high-water mark and, in letters of gunpowder mixed with grease, wrote in large capitals: CAPT. W. L. MANLY, U.S.A.

Given the desolate nature of the place, it was easy to imagine they were the first white men to descend this stretch of the river. They were wrong, but not by much, as they learned shortly. Someone sighted scratchings on the canyon wall; upon closer inspection these proved to be letters, which spelled ASHLEY, 1824. Manly and the others had no way of knowing who this Ashley was, but it seemed unlikely that subsequent expeditions would have passed Ashley's signature without signing in themselves. (William Ashley, one of the great explorers of the Rocky Mountain region, had led a small party down this stretch of the Green River twenty-five years before Manly's group.)

By now Manly and the others understood why the canyon had seen so few visitors; but less than a mile farther on the lesson was driven home more forcibly. A massive block barred the stream; to maneuver the boat around it, Manly ordered the men out and the craft unloaded. The boat was lowered as far as the rope would reach, then it was let go. Manly and a couple of the others waited downstream to catch it as it approached. But midway the current tipped it over and pinned it—one gunwale down, the other tilted skyward—against the great rock. So strong was the current that, despite several hours' application of muscle and mind, the boat remained precisely where it initially stuck. "We could no more move it than we could move the rock itself."

All were stunned by this turn of events. Without a boat, in the middle of this canyon in the midst of nowhere, what would they do? It might be years, perhaps decades, before anyone even found their bodies.

But Manly hadn't been a woodsman for nothing. Some distance downstream from the imprisoned boat he spotted two pine trees clinging to the side of the canyon. Each was roughly two feet in diameter, and relatively straight in the main part of the trunk. Manly had made canoes before, and decided he could do it again. He and the others felled the trees, trimmed them to length, and set to hollowing them out. This last was the hard part; the men chiseled and chopped in shifts, by the thin light of the sky during the day, by the light of a fire at night. When they finally finished, after most of a week, they had two canoes, each fifteen feet long and two feet wide. For stability they lashed the two craft together.

The twin-hulled vessel floated, but low in the water, and after only half a mile on the stream Manly decided another canoe was needed. Luckily a third pine tree, taller than the first two, soon came into sight. Several more days and nights of chiseling ensued; these culminated in the launch of a second vessel, a single-hulled canoe nearly thirty feet long. As the only experienced canoeist in the party, Manly took charge of this craft, and in his flagship he led the small flotilla off hopefully.

The two canoes—swifter and more agile than the ferry scow—made good progress down the canyon, which became less obstructed the farther they went. Gradually the walls fell away from the river, the sky opened up again, and the current slowed. Once more game grew abundant; the party feasted on elk, deer, goose, and duck. The behavior of the waterfowl surprised Manly; upon being fired at, they refused to fly away but instead swam toward the hunter. He concluded that they had never encountered firearms, perhaps not even humans.

At one point the group saw signs that a herd of horses had been driven across the river. Manly and the others assumed—or hoped, really—that those driving the horses had been white men, perhaps traders or even emigrants for California. On no firmer basis than this, they let themselves think the worst was behind them.

But then the river entered another canyon, almost as wild and deep as the one they had managed to escape. Once more they encountered huge boulders in the water, which forced repeated portages. After several difficult miles they found an abandoned skiff, along with some cooking utensils and a notice stuck to an alder tree saying that the several undersigned, having concluded that the river was impassable, had decided to head overland for Salt Lake City. This intelligence naturally discouraged Manly's party. But judging their canoes more manuverable than the skiff, and looking to Manly's experience on the water, they decided to push on.

Things got worse. The river made a sharp turn, more than a right angle, and plunged over a low waterfall. Manly, having no time to reach shore, was forced to take his boat over. He made it safely, though drenched. So did the other canoe, to the surprise of all involved. The river then straightened out but shot steeply downhill. Manly skirted the main channel, creeping downstream next to the shore. But the others, ignoring his hand signals and shouts, tried to run the main channel. Midway they hit a standing wave—larger and more powerful than anything Manly had ever seen—which capsized the canoe, ejecting the occupants.

Two of them—like a surprising number of emigrants—didn't know how to swim. One of the two, who had fashioned a crude flotation device, splashed madly amid the powerful current but eventually found his footing and staggered to shore. The second man clung to the canoe for very life. As it dipped and rolled in the water, he alternately disappeared and resurfaced, his shock of black hair reminding Manly of a crow perched on the end of a log. Manly and one of the other men chased him downstream in the big canoe, with Manly standing in the stern for a better view. Finally they caught the runaway craft and hauled it to shore. The man still clinging to it was nearly dead of exhaustion, inhaled water, and hypothermia. They dragged him to land, expelled as much of the water from his lungs as they could, built a fire to warm him, and massaged his limbs to revive the circulation.

Gathering the others, Manly assessed the situation. By dumb luck the men's bedding and extra clothes had remained within the capsized canoe; it was wet but otherwise unharmed. Yet several guns had been lost. Though Manly directed a search of the river bottom, these were not recovered. The party's total armament—for hunting and protection against Indians—was reduced to two weapons: Manly's rifle and another man's shotgun. After the capsizing and the close brush with death, this sobered the group still further.

The next day, nearly dried out, they set off once more. The river grew smoother, giving each man time to dwell on his predicament and doubtless to wonder what had possessed him to leave home in the first place. Their glum reveries were broken by the sound of a gunshot from downstream. The shot was repeated, then again. Manly and the others had never heard of any white settlements in this part of the country, and from the looks of the terrain, the land wouldn't have supported any. Nor did they think any emigrants traveled this far south of the main roads west. That left Indians as the likely source of the gunfire. "If it were a hostile band," Manly reasoned, "we could not do much with a rifle and shotgun toward defending ourselves or taking the aggressive." On the other hand, they could hardly turn around and go back up the river. "We concluded we had not come into this wild country to be afraid of a few gunshots, and determined to put on a bold front and take our chances on getting scalped or roasted."

Around another bend they came into sight of three Indian lodges a little way back from the river. An Indian appeared with a rifle in his hands; he motioned for Manly and the others to come to shore. They did so, cautiously. When the man made no threatening gestures, Manly moved to within speaking distance.

They exchanged words. The only one the Indian spoke that was at all intelligible to Manly sounded like "Mormonee." Manly gathered that this band was friendly with the Mormons. As other Indians then appeared carrying various manufactured goods, including firearms, Manly concluded that they traded with the Mormons. He quietly suggested to his own men that a conversion-of-convenience to the Mormon faith might be prudent. No one's conscience protested, and so all seven put their right hands to their breasts and declared "Mormonee" with cheerful countenance. Their hosts seemed pleased.

By now the leader of the Indians appeared. Manly struck up a conversation with the chief, who indicated he was known to the whites as Walker. The conversation took place principally in signs, but enough was conveyed to convince Manly of Walker's good faith and general knowledge. Manly asked Walker how far it was to "Mormonee," meaning Salt Lake City. Walker responded with a galloping motion of the hands, and by laying his head sideways and closing his eyes three times. From this Manly inferred that the Mormon city was three sleeps, or four days, on horseback.

Manly asked a harder question: How far was it down the river to the big water of the West? As best he could, Manly explained that he and his party had come down the river through the canyons and hoped the worst was behind them.

Walker evinced astonishment at this. He shook his head vigorously, looking alternately down the river (which still trended south) and out to the west, and shaking his head the more. He led Manly to a sandbar by the river, and with a crooked stick began drawing a map. First he sketched a long, crooked line, about ten feet in length. He pointed from the line to the river and back, letting Manly know that the line represented the river. Pointing upstream, he drew several of the tributaries Manly and the others had encountered. Making a hoop of a twig and rolling it along the ground, he indicated the emigrant trail by which Manly and the others had reached the Green River; he also indicated other trails, which Manly had seen on maps. All these were just where they were supposed to be, convincing Manly that the chief knew whereof he spoke.

Walker began stacking stones on either side of the river, making miniature canyons. He raised his hands to the sky and said, "E-e-e-e!," to indicate the great height of the canyon walls. He left an open space, then built another canyon, and with similar gestures and sounds, indicated the second deep canyon Manly and the others had been through. The more Walker spoke, the more he impressed Manly with his apparently comprehensive knowledge of the region's geography.

Manly urged him to describe the river below their present location. Walker obliged.

> He began piling up stones on each side of the river, and then got longer ones and piled them higher and higher yet. Then he stood with one foot on each side of his river and put his hands on the stones and then raised them as high as he could, making a continued e-e-e-e-e-e as long as his breath would last, pointed to the canoe and made signs with his hands how it would roll and pitch in the rapids and finally capsize and throw us all out. He then made signs of death to show us that it was a fatal place.

Nor was this the sum of the dangers.

> Then Walker shook his head more than once and looked very sober, and said "Indiano," and reaching for his bow and arrows, he drew the bow back to its utmost length and put the arrow close to my breast, showing how I would get shot. Then he would draw his

> hand across his throat and shut his eyes as if in death to make us understand that this was a hostile country before us, as well as rough and dangerous.

Manly required no further convincing that the river trip was over. Only later would he learn that Walker was describing the Grand Canyon of the Colorado River (into which the Green emptied). But he was willing to take the chief's word—and gestures—that he and his companions would never reach California that way.

Two of the men, named Field and McMahon, were skeptical. They doubted whether Walker knew all he claimed to, or whether he was telling the truth. McMahon had seen a map of the country to the southwest, and he said it didn't look any worse than what they had already survived.

Manly told the two they were free to do as they pleased. But he pointed out that Walker had spent his whole life in this region and knew it as well as an easterner knew his father's farm. Neither was there any doubt regarding the translation. The sign language Walker used was quite similar to that of the Indians of Michigan and Wisconsin, with which Manly was thoroughly familiar. Manly said he trusted Walker, and said he preferred his chances with the Mormons to those in the canyon of death and among the murderous Indians.

McMahon and Field wouldn't be persuaded. But the others stuck with Manly. He had thirty dollars in his pocket; from this he offered to buy horses from Walker. The chief refused the money, which would do him no good this far from the white man's civilization; instead he offered two ponies in exchange for some clothing. One of the men let Walker have a coat, which he was pleased to put on despite the heat. The others supplied odds and ends of apparel.

Manly's group divided the remaining flour and dried meat with McMahon and Field. Then, wishing those two the best of luck, Manly and the others set out across the desert in the direction of Salt Lake City.

6

Where Rivers Die

In abandoning the Green River, Manly and his companions implicitly admitted what nearly every overlander concluded early or late: that in traveling to California, there was no avoiding the Great Basin. A giant bowl bounded on the east and south by the drainage systems of the Green and Colorado rivers, on the north by the Snake and Columbia, and on the west by the Sierra Nevada, the Great Basin was something few of the emigrants had even imagined before heading for California: a vast region where rivers don't run to the sea. Between the Strait of Georgia in what would become British Columbia and the Gulf of California in Mexico, the Columbia is the only river to pierce the mountain wall of the Sierra-Cascade chain—which was a principal reason the early western emigration was to Oregon. The rivers of the Great Basin, such as they are, die in the desert: in the Great Salt Lake or other briny bodies, or simply in the sand.

The lack of drainage to the sea is the result of the interaction of geology and climate. The Columbia was able to breach the Cascades because those mountains rose relatively slowly, and the rain and snow that fed that river gave it sufficient erosive power to defeat the tectonic forces that were building the mountains. The river's victory is carved in the walls of the present-day Columbia Gorge. The Sierras, however, are higher than the Cascades, and rose faster; and their rain shadow is longer. The ancient rivers to their east lost the battle between erosion and uplift; defeated, they turn back on themselves and expire in the desert sun.

Yet even in death there is life. The largest river of the Great Basin, the Humboldt, was the one stream absolutely essential to the Forty-Niners. To easterners it hardly rated as more than a creek, and a poor one at that. It meandered infuriatingly; at a stage of the journey when time meant everything to the emigrants, and every extra mile wasted their time, the Humboldt wandered across the desert floor as if it had all the time in creation.

But if the Humboldt was hard to love, it was harder to leave. The three-hundred-mile stretch of desert it spanned would have been impossible to cross without it. Some religiously minded emigrants thought Providence had placed the river along their path; those whose faith was less firm concluded, by the river's bitter end, that heaven was playing them a bad joke. Until they reached the Humboldt, the emigrants could choose among different trails and cutoffs; after they left the Humboldt, they again had choices. But for crossing the northern part of what would become Nevada, there was only the Humboldt.

Hugh Heiskell's party reached the headwaters of the Humboldt in early September. At first encounter, and after weeks of struggling across the alternating ridges and valleys north of the Great Salt Lake, the Humboldt was a welcome sight. "The road this evening has been one of the finest we ever traveled on, level as a floor and not traveled enough to make the dust very deep," Heiskell recorded. The next day was more pleasant still. "Decamping at half past 7 we continued down the bottom, the road better than the finest MacAddamized road in the world." As to the scenery: "This is a beautiful valley—a line of willow running through the middle, the branch [that is, the river] in this season of the year in places winding among them, at others sinking in the sand." The latter phenomenon—the sinking into the sand—would become distressing, but for now it was merely a curiosity. The livestock enjoyed themselves as much as the emigrants did. "The cattle are feeding on excellent pasture, grass in seed but not parched."

Yet all depended on the river, a vital thread stretched thin. "The river here about 20 feet wide, an average depth of 2 feet," Heiskell noted. Soon the thread showed signs of fraying. "Marching eight miles, we camped on the river, here affording less water—an ugly stream, pools along it nearly stagnant." Parts of the broad valley were still a healthy green from the willows, but larger parts were sickly pale, and pungent. "The whole plain is covered with alkali, the grass of a yellow color being impregnated with it, and pools of water standing are the color of lye. A strong odor of lye you smell as you ride across." William Swain, traversing the same stretch, was even less complimentary: "The river here is nothing more than a mud ditch winding through the alluvial deposit of the valley in the most crooked course that could be marked out for it."

The wretched river supported—after its wretched fashion—what seemed a wretched people. Regardless of the emigrants' perception of the character and customs of the Sioux and Pawnee of the Great Plains, they couldn't help being impressed by those Indians' stature, demeanor, and general presence. For the Digger Indians of the Great Basin, however, the emigrants had little but disdain. "Dent & Crocker were riding along the river hunting & came across three Indians (Diggers) in the willows," Hugh Heiskell wrote, "one of which they brought to the road, a poor miserable specimen of humanity, miserably dirty, with a shirt of fox skins—hair turned inside—which came nearly down to the knees. Naked from there down and barefooted." Goldsborough Bruff, the emigrant from Washington, added a pseudoscientific gloss to his loathing. On the large map he carried, he indicated the Great Basin and wrote: "Range of the Pah Utahs [Paiutes], the original & most numerous class commonly called the Mountain Diggers, perfectly untameable & the lowest species of the genus Homo, next to them is the baboon."

The Diggers' diet of grubs, insects, and snakes put off the emigrants as much as the natives' appearance did; equally damning in emigrant eyes was what the whites took for the Indians' treachery and theft. The Diggers rarely confronted the travelers directly, instead circling about the wagon trains, stealing cattle by night or shooting an arrow into an ox, knowing that the emigrants, in their hurry, would have to leave the animal behind. Nor was the cost confined to the livestock killed. To minimize depredations, the trains set guards at the sides of the trail and posted pickets at night. The extra effort wore into minds and bodies already taxed by fatigue, poor nutrition, and the overall strain of three months on the road.

The danger from the Indians disappeared only when the Humboldt led the travelers into country so barren even the locals avoided it. "We no longer see any traces of Indians," Hugh Heiskell wrote on September 28. "The country is too poor for even the miserable Digger Indians to live. The valley has opened out to an expansive level, covered with sage and not a spear of grass. The immediate bottom, narrow and ten or twenty feet lower than the common level, is now parched. . . . There is a ridge or range of mountains bounding the plain and parallel with the river, which produce the shrubby sage alone. We have noticed there is not a spring or stream emptying into the river since Martin's Fork [passed thirteen days earlier]. Our water here has an alkaline taste, which increases daily."

The travelers had entered the worst stretch of the entire journey. The last 150 miles of the Humboldt River took them through some of the driest, bleakest, most difficult country in North America. Water was short and bad, grass for the stock nonexistent. Days were brutally hot, nights numbingly cold. Nearly every river the emigrants had ever encountered grew stronger with each downhill mile; in this strange land, precisely the opposite occurred. The Humboldt (by now often damned as the "Humbug" River) grew weaker, as did those people foolish enough to follow it down. From their guidebooks they knew the river was about to expire in the Humboldt Sink—a concept they had had trouble envisioning when they first read or heard the term, but which now they envisioned all too easily. And, all too easily, they envisioned themselves expiring with it.

SO DAUNTING WAS the Humboldt Sink, and the desert surrounding it, that the emigrants were driven to desperate measures to avoid it. In its death throes the Humboldt turned south; at the last bend, ninety miles above the sink, some travelers struck away from the river, to the west, on the reasoning that nothing could be worse than the sink.

The Lassen Cutoff, as the western route was called, was truly a leap of faith. The horrors of the Humboldt were known—from the emigrants' own experience by now, and from the tales of earlier emigrants and explorers. Next to nothing was known for sure of the Lassen route.

To William Swain, the principal attraction of the Lassen route, besides the fact that it wasn't the Humboldt, was that it headed west, in the direction of the goldfields. Unfortunately this attraction faded after a couple of days, when the trail descended from the Antelope Hills to the edge of the Black Rock Desert, an enormous dry lake bed, or playa. To cross the playa compelled the travelers to veer toward the north.

The weather during the third week of September was beastly. Daytime temperatures soared well above 100 degrees; nights plunged below freezing. Between the two, the cold seemed better for the crossing, which required a forced march without water.

The jumping-off point for crossing the Black Rock was a place called Rabbit Hole Springs. Doubtless the name inspired thoughts of respite for the dry and weary. The reality was shockingly different. Goldsborough Bruff, just ahead of Swain on the Lassen trail, described what the thirsty travelers found:

> Along the edge of this plateau are a number of springs as they are called, but are actually wells, dug from 3 to 6 feet deep, and from 4 to 5 feet diameter, containing cool, clear water, but a little saline—about half filling the wells. Two of these springs were about 4 feet apart; in one was a dead ox, swelled up so as to fill the hole closely, his hind legs and tail only above ground. Not far from this was another spring similarly filled. There was scarcely space for the wagons to reach the holes, for the ox-carcasses. West of the plateau springs, the road followed an indentation formed by winter floods, down into the plain; and close on the right of it was a deep rugged gulch, containing 2 spring holes, choked up with oxen; while the ravine for 100 yards was thickly strewn with their carcasses. Here, and around the other springs, I counted 82 dead oxen, 2 dead horses, and 1 mule—in an area of 1/10 of a mile.

On this grim note, the emigrants set out upon the playa. Swain's party left at half past eight in the evening. "The moon was some two hours high," Swain wrote, "the night cold with a fresh wind blowing from the northeast." That wind would be painful by dawn, but for now it injected new life into animals and men. "Our cattle walked quickly along, and our train moved more gaily than for weeks past."

The gaiety dissipated as the rising moon revealed the desert's toll. "A destruction of property beyond my conception lined the road," Swain recorded. "Wagons and carts were scattered on all sides, and the stench of dead and decaying cattle actually rendered the air sickening." Several cattle from Swain's party staggered, stumbled, and were left to die.

The trail across the playa was uncertain, and the captain went ahead to scout. In the dark he got lost—or the rest of the party did. Whichever was the case, the main body trudged forward with little idea where they were going. By observing the North Star, Swain noted that they were turning ever farther north. He kept looking for tracks leading off to the left, back toward the west, but never saw them.

Through the small, desperate hours they pressed on—thirsty, frozen, losing livestock with each mile, wondering if they were losing ground as well. Not till the first faint light of dawn did their spirits rise. Five miles ahead, looming in the grayness, appeared the Black Rock for which the desert was named. At its foot was a spring, which meant their survival.

Only in such a hellish place would such a spring have been welcome. The water came out of the ground boiling hot and laced with minerals. Before cattle or men could drink it—nearly expiring from thirst though they were—they had to let it cool. But there was plenty, and all drank their fill.

Along the creek that drained the spring grew some grass, which infused faint life into the surviving cattle. The animals needed to rest, but with October approaching and the Sierras still far distant, every hour told. To Swain's continued dismay, the trail remained northerly. But there was no choice. To get past the Black Rock Range they had to traverse the aptly named, and north-trending, High Rock Canyon. "The bottom was level, probably three hundred feet wide, and covered with thick, fine grass," Swain wrote.

> The sides which rose perpendicular to the height of five hundred feet, stood in massive towers between which openings ran up to

> the back hills. The moon was shining vertically as we passed through, and the spirits of our people were enlivened by the sublimity of the scene. Singing, whooping, and halloing to one another were resorted to, to test the reverberating power of the cliffs which walled us in. The mocking rocks were apparently ready to join the glee of the boys, for they answered back their words and sent them ringing from cliff to cliff.

The oxen, by the evidence of their weariness, didn't share the glee of the boys, and despite good grass in the canyon bottom, the animals continued to weaken. To lighten their burden, Swain and his fellows jettisoned items that had seemed essential back on the Missouri, and might yet seem essential in California, but that threatened to anchor the wagons amid the sage and greasewood. Out went a blacksmith's anvil, the heaviest item aboard. The anvil's ouster eased the ejection of related tools and supplies (what good would they be without an anvil?): a pair of bellows, a large vise, hammers and tongs, a five-foot bar of cast steel. Also overthrown were saddles, ropes, chains, casks, and barrels.

With each day the nights grew only colder. "The ground was frozen this evening, and ice formed over the little brook by our camp," Swain wrote on October 7. The next day he noted, "This morn we put on our underclothes and rigged for winter, as the air is cold and the frost severe."

Yet that very afternoon the company caught a glimpse of salvation. "Today is the first time we have seen any timbered hills, except for some fir and juniper groves, since leaving South Pass. . . . This evening a mountain range covered with evergreen trees is to be seen eight miles to the north. The sight is indicative of a better country than that passed, and tells a pleasing tale of a clime far away. Today I had my first view of the summit range of the Sierra, from which we are sixty-five miles distant."

SARAH ROYCE AND her family refused the Lassen Cutoff in favor of the Humboldt Sink. They did so because they thought they knew more about that treacherous region than they really did.

There was reason for their false confidence. In Salt Lake City, Sarah and Josiah had acquired a handwritten guidebook authored by a Mormon who had recently made the trip to California. The book detailed the best route across the Great Salt Desert and down the Humboldt River, identifying waterholes, pastures, and campsites. The proof of its value was the safety and comparative ease with which the Royces crossed the fearsome Salt Desert. The guidebook was less specific regarding the Humboldt Sink and the waterless stretch between the Sink and the Carson River, the first stream beyond. But the Mormons who gave the book to the Royces—largely out of pity for Sarah and her little girl—assured them that before they got there, they would encounter a Mormon party returning from California, who would fill them in on that difficult stretch.

The Mormon party arrived on schedule. Its leader drew the Royces a map in the sand. Starting from the Humboldt Sink, he showed them how they should turn off the main road onto a wagon trace to the left, at two or three miles from the sink, and how this would take them, after another two or three miles, to a grassy meadow unknown to most emigrants and therefore still providing feed. Moreover, this meadow contained several shallow wells lately dug by the Mormons, and also unknown to the emigrants. Having just come from there, the mapmaker said the water was sweet and plentiful. To maximize the flow, the Royces might deepen one or two of the holes; overnight these would fill with fresh water.

The Mormon mapmaker was an experienced hand in the desert and mountains. He advised the Royces to camp at the meadows for two or three days, to let the cattle rest and graze freely. Meanwhile the party should cut grass and load it into the wagon, along with water to the top of every container they possessed. If the days were relatively cool, they should set out across the desert at noon; if hot, they should wait until evening. But in either case the larger part of the journey must occur at night. They should stop every few hours to feed, water, and rest the cattle. In this way they would be able to reach the Carson River within twenty-four hours of leaving the sink.

"After hearing his instructions, and having the road made thus plain to us, we went on with renewed cheerfulness and energy," Sarah recorded.

The energy carried them down the lower Humboldt to its final disappearance in the sand. This late in the season, the river expired just before reaching what in the springtime was Humboldt Lake, a shallow body of water spanning some ten miles.

But here an almost lethal confusion crept into their thinking. Conventional wisdom on the trail—as they had interpreted it—described the sink itself as being at the foot of the dry lake, where, they were told, several holes had been dug. This placed it about ten miles beyond the point where the river, in early October, literally sank into the ground.

Accordingly, when they reached the literal current sink, they gauged they had thirteen miles to go till the point where the Mormon trace trailed off to the left, leading to the Mormon meadow. They decided to stop for the night and leave very early the next morning, to reach the meadow before the heat of the day.

At two o'clock they awoke, brewed coffee over a sagebrush fire, finished the last of the previous day's rabbit pot-pie—the result of a rare success with a gun—and set off. The moonlight cast an ethereal glow across the barren landscape. Between the uncertain light and her overall weariness, Sarah began to see things that weren't there.

> Once it was an extended sheet of water lying calmly bright in the moonlight, with here and there a tree on its shores; and our road seemed to tend directly toward it; then it was a small lake seen through openings in a row of trees, while the shadowy outlines of a forest appeared beyond it; all lying to our left. What a pity it seemed, to be passing by it, when our poor animals had been so stinted of late. Again, we were traveling parallel with a placid river on our right; beyond which were trees; and from us to the water's edge the ground sloped so gently it appeared absurd not to turn aside to its brink and refresh ourselves and our oxen.

Dawn dispelled the mirages, and caused Sarah and Josiah to seek anxiously for the holes that would mark the Humboldt Sink. It was nearly noon before they reached them. The holes contained some brackish water, which they couldn't bring themselves to drink straight. They kindled another sage fire (one of the few saving graces of the desert was the ready tinder it provided), boiled the water for coffee, and gulped it down disguised. Then they hurried on, expecting to find the Mormon trace on the left at a distance of two or three miles; in less than six miles they would be at the meadow.

They traveled for an hour, with no sign of the trace. Then another hour, and still no sign. Another hour, and another, and another. Night was falling, with no Mormon trace and no Mormon meadow. In every direction they looked, they saw only desert—dry, barren, deadly.

With a sickening feeling, Sarah and the others realized their mistake. The sink the Mormons spoke of was the one where the river actually disappeared—ten miles before the holes that marked what the Royces thought was the sink. In the dark of the previous night, they had passed the Mormon trace without seeing it. Now they were far out upon the desert leading to the Carson River, but without a single mouthful of grass for the oxen, and with only a few quarts of water in a small cask.

What to do? Every instinct said go forward. They must be nearly halfway across the desert. If they could hold on for several more hours, twelve at most, they must reach the Carson River, and the desert would be behind them. As always, the calendar drove them forward; every day on the desert exposed them to greater risk in the mountains that still separated them from California.

But the animals were worn to the edge of existence. They had neither eaten nor drunk for many hours. While their masters debated what to do, they were collapsing in harness. Without food and water, they would never make it across the desert. And without them, their masters would soon perish.

All the rest of the night, Sarah and Josiah weighed their options. The next day Josiah and one of two young men who had joined them for the crossing ascended a hill a mile away, in hopes of finding something on the horizon to give them guidance. The horizon yielded nothing. Meanwhile Sarah, to keep the cattle from expiring, ripped open some mattresses in the wagon and fed the animals the bedstraw, handful by precious handful.

The answer to their dilemma had become inescapable. They must turn back and find the Mormon meadow. Yet though inescapable, this answer was almost unbearable. "Turn back!" Sarah wrote.

> What a chill the words sent through one. *Turn back*, on a journey like that; in which every mile had been gained by most earnest labor, growing more and more intense, until, of late, it had seemed that the certainty of *advance* with every step was all that made the next step possible. And now for miles we were to *go back*. In all that long journey no steps ever seemed so heavy, so hard to take, as those with which I turned my back to the sun that afternoon of October 4, 1849.

Yet turning back was no guarantee of safety. The cattle grew weaker with each mile, prompting Sarah to get out of the wagon and walk, to lighten the load. She refused to drink, sparing the water for Mary and the others. She slipped into a trance, unsure which part of what she saw was real and which part hallucination. Biblical images filled her head.

> I seemed to see Hagar, in the wilderness walking wearily away from her fainting child among the dried up bushes, and seating herself in the hot sand. I seemed to become Hagar myself, and when my little one, from the wagon behind me, called out, "Mamma, I want a drink," I stopped, gave her some, noted that there were but a few swallows left, then mechanically pressed onward again, alone, repeating, over and over, the words, "Let me not see the death of the child."

As the sun bore down upon them, Sarah prayed for some sign, some reason to hope that her baby wouldn't die in this desolate land. They passed through an area where the sagebushes were closer together than usual; in recent days, Indians or emigrants had camped there. Leftover embers apparently had set the sage smoldering, and as Sarah walked by, a few wisps of old smoke curled heavenward. Suddenly, just in front of her, a bush burst into flame. Hot and bright, the fire raced through the branches of the bush before burning itself out. Only ashes and a smoldering trunk remained. "It was a small incident, easily accounted for, but to my then overwrought fancy it made more vivid the illusion of being a wanderer in a far-off, old time desert, and myself witnessing a wonderful phenomenon. For a few moments I stood with bowed head worshiping the God of Horeb, and I was strengthened thereby."

The sun began to sink behind them; the horned heads of the oxen drooped lower and lower till their noses scraped the sand with each weary step. And then, from a hundred yards in front, came the cheers of the two young men. "Grass and water!" they shouted. They had found the Mormon meadow. For now at least, the God of Hagar and Horeb—and Joseph Smith—had preserved this small wandering tribe.

For the rest of that day and all the next the travelers let the animals drink, eat, and recover. The men cut grass while Sarah repacked the wagon to make more room for the men's cuttings. On the following day the party set off west. "The feeling that we were once more going forward, instead of backward, gave an animation to every step which we could never have felt but by contrast." The change of direction was lost on the animals, which needed more rest and recuperation than they had received at the meadow. Sarah allowed herself to nap in the wagon; she woke to hear her husband speaking to one of the oxen: "So you've given out, have you, Tom?" Sarah looked out to discover Tom prostrate on the ground. Josiah unhitched him, and likewise his partner in harness, almost equally far gone. With a gesture of thanks for having drawn them so far and so faithfully, their masters left them to die. Four animals now pulled what had strained six. Sarah guiltily resolved to walk the rest of the way. "Nothing could induce me to get into the wagon again."

As darkness fell they entered the worst of the desert. No moon illumined the path, but the shimmering starlight revealed more than the travelers cared to see. The carcasses of cattle lined the road, increasing in number with the miles. Presently a pair of abandoned wagons came into view. The owners, evidently despairing of reaching the Carson with their vehicles, had loaded the absolute essentials onto the few animals that could yet walk, and pushed ahead.

Farther on, the ruin of human dreams touched Sarah in a special way. Grand Conestoga wagons, employed by traders to haul merchandise, towered against the canopy of the stars, looking as tall as houses. They carried—or *had* carried—all manner of merchandise, of which the remnants were now strewn about the desert floor. Pasteboard boxes, wrapping paper, trunks and chests, pamphlets and books reminded Sarah of home even as they reminded her how far from home she was.

The cumulative effect of one wreck after another was profoundly discouraging. "We seemed to be but the last, little, feeble, struggling band at the rear of a routed army," Sarah recalled.

The remaining oxen could be moved only by baiting: by holding grass before their noses and making them walk to receive it. The water ran out shortly before daylight, foretelling an imminent end to the animals, and to the humans not long thereafter. The cattle were too tired to complain; neither did the humans speak. Instead Sarah and the others constantly scanned the horizon, seeking any change in the flat, forbidding aspect, any sign that this terrible waste didn't stretch to the ends of the earth.

Finally Sarah saw something. "Was it a cloud? It was very low at first, and I feared it might evaporate as the sun warmed it." She asked Josiah what he made of it. "I think it must be the timber on Carson River," he said.

At that moment one of the lead cattle offered his opinion: a weak, but no longer desperate, lowing sound. Sarah, misunderstanding, expected him to collapse and die. But then the other lead ox emitted a similar sound, and all four animals lifted their heads to sniff the air—and the scent of water it carried.

It was then that Sarah knew they had survived the desert. Reaching the river required hours more; and of course the ramparts of the Sierras remained. But young Mary wouldn't lose her parents, nor her parents Mary, on the sands of the Carson Desert.

NONE PAID MORE for ignorance than the party of Lewis Manly. Traveling north toward Salt Lake City, glumly expecting to have to winter among the Mormons, Manly and the others were delighted—and Manly amazed—to meet a wagon train that included his original partner, Bennett, whom he had missed east of the Missouri. Bennett recounted that he had linked up with a company upon which fell all the troubles of the trail. Cholera had carried off some of the travelers; the survivors quarreled among themselves; the solemn compact to stick together was voided by those who thought they stood a better chance alone. Division reached the point of sheer spite: when one half-owner of a wagon insisted on cutting the vehicle in two (thinking to convert his half into a cart), the other owner agreed, but sawed the wagon in half lengthwise, rendering it unusable to both. The catalog of troubles delayed the train so long that the central route to the diggings would be impassable by the time the Sierras were reached. Bennett and some others determined to angle south, along the road to Los Angeles, which might be traversed all winter.

Manly decided to join them, not least since Bennett still had much of what the two had purchased together. Most of Manly's partners from the Green River, having no such stake with Bennett and rather less confidence than Manly that Bennett and the others knew where they were going, declined an invitation to come along.

Fresh problems surfaced almost at once. Some members of the group circulated a map purporting to show a shortcut to the goldfields, one that avoided the Sierra passes but entered California much closer to the mines than the Los Angeles route did. The more impatient members of the group, including Manly and Bennett, voted to secede from the main train and attempt the shortcut.

Within days they began to regret their decision. Pastures and water holes marked on the map weren't where they were supposed to be; ridges and canyons absent from the map blocked the trail. Before long the seceders realized they were on their own—not exactly lost, for they knew more or less where they were and where they wanted to go, but without any information as to how to get there, or what lay between them and their goal.

They groped forward. After three days ascending a ridge, they found themselves on the brink of a steep canyon running as far to north and south as they could see. There appeared to be no way to get the wagons down into the canyon or, once in, to get them out. For days they were stymied; several members lost courage and retreated toward the trail they had left. At last a scouting party reported that it had found a way through the canyon. The route wouldn't be easy, but neither was it impossible.

Manly and the others set off. The route led north, which troubled Manly, as California was still so far to the west. Until the canyon was behind them, nothing could be done; but when the trail continued north beyond the canyon, he felt obliged to speak up. He told Bennett and the others they must turn west if they ever hoped to reach California. By all indications, the trail they were on simply led back to Salt Lake City. A council was called, the case was heard, and Manly's motion carried. Leaving the northbound track, the party turned left toward the trackless west.

Although they didn't know it, Manly and the others were entering the heart of what geologists would call the Basin and Range Province. The tectonic stresses on this portion of the North American plate have caused parallel ranges of mountains to rise and the intervening basins to fall. These ranges and basins run north and south, so that a traveler going from east to west crosses range and basin and range and basin and range and basin from Utah all the way to California. The Humboldt River provided the only east-west corridor across the basin and ranges, having had, over the ages, sufficient power to cut through the rising ranges (though not enough to slice the more rapidly rising Sierras). This was what made the Humboldt route so vital to most emigrants, despite its numerous disadvantages. Farther south, where Manly now was, no such avenue existed north of the Grand Canyon, which—as Chief Walker explained to Manly—was essentially impassable.

Manly spent the last several weeks of 1849 traversing and exploring the basins and ranges. Bennett didn't need him as a driver, so he became a scout. He roved far ahead of the wagons, and far to either side of their path. While the drivers sought the lowest points of the ranges for crossings, Manly sought the highest points for lookouts.

The vistas were breathtaking—and heartbreaking. "I reached the summit about nine o'clock," he said of one scouting trip, "and had the grandest view I ever saw. I could see north and south almost forever." A high, snowy mountain commanded the western horizon; to left and right of that summit the edge of sight sloped downward. "A few miles to the north and east of where I stood, and somewhat higher, was the roughest piece of ground I ever saw. It stood in sharp peaks and was of many colors, some of them so red that the mountain looked red hot. . . . It was the most wonderful picture of grand desolation one could ever see."

That desolation, and its incredible vastness, were what made the vista heartbreaking. No one in Manly's train had any idea how far away California was; with each ridge surmounted, they succumbed to thinking the Sacramento Valley was just over the next. From Manly's high perch he now perceived the true nature of their predicament: the fact that the ranges and basins rolled on and on to the west like frozen waves on the sea of time. "The more I looked, the more I satisfied myself that we were yet a long way from California, and the serious question of our ever living to get there presented itself to me as I tramped along down the grade to camp. I put down at least another month of heavy, weary travel before we could hope to make the land of gold, and our stock of strength and provisions were both pretty small for so great a tax upon them."

Like every other argonaut sooner or later, Manly pondered what he had left behind in the East. "I thought of the bounteous stock of bread and beans on my father's table, to say nothing about all the other good things, and here was I, the oldest son, away out in the center of the Great American Desert, with an empty stomach and a dry and parched throat, and clothes fast wearing out." Nor, in all likelihood, had he met the worst of it. "I might be forced to see the men and women and children of our party choke and die, powerless to help them. It was a darker and gloomier day than I had ever known it could be, and alone I wept aloud, for I believed I could see the future, and the results were bitter to contemplate."

Manly shared with the others his assessment of the distance left to travel, until Bennett told him to desist. "Lewis, if you please," Bennett said, "I don't want you hereafter to express your views so openly and emphatically as you did last night about our prospects. When I went to bed I found Sarah [Bennett's wife] crying, and when pressed for the cause, she said she had heard your remarks on the situation, and that if Lewis said so it must be correct, for he knows more about it than all of you. She felt that she and the children must starve."

For weeks the party struggled across the desert. Days would pass without water; when finally found, it was often of the vilest sort. Manly was faint with thirst one evening when, walking long after sunset, he literally stumbled on his salvation. "I poked around in the dark for a while and soon found a little pool of it, and having been without a drop of it for two days, I lay down and took a hasty drink. It did not seem to be very clear or clean, but it was certainly wet, which was the main thing just then." Later he rejoined the rest of the party at the edge of a lake bed that was covered by the thinnest film of water—no more than a quarter-inch. By digging holes they managed to collect just enough to drink.

Food was even more problematic. Game had long since disappeared; though he continued to carry his gun, Manly realized one day that the same load had filled his rifle's chamber for a month. "Very seldom could a rabbit be seen, and not a bird of any kind, not even a hawk, buzzard, or crow made their appearance."

Infrequently they found food cached by Indians. Manly warned against eating it, remarking that the natives were as hungry as they were, and certain to resent such theft. Remembering Walker's warning about the unfriendly character of the Indians, Manly had no desire to antagonize them unless absolutely necessary.

Yet the hungry members of the party did more than steal the Indians' food. At one point some men from the train happened upon a lone native, whom they captured. For days they held the man hostage, forcing him to act as their guide. But eventually he escaped, leaping down a cliff and between some rocks where only a mountain sheep could have followed.

In their extremity, Manly's party were reduced to killing their oxen. One instance was precipitated by Indians who ambushed the train—which, between breakdowns and decisions to turn back, had dwindled to seven wagons. The Indians shot three of the oxen with arrows. Two of the animals survived after the arrows were removed; the third was wounded mortally. Lest the ambushers benefit—and the owners lose—Manly and the others killed and butchered the animal themselves. Some feared eating the meat, thinking the arrow had been poisoned. But Manly pointed out that the Indians hoped to eat the meat and wouldn't have tainted their own supper.

Shortly Manly's group was slaughtering their oxen without the encouragement of the Indians. The reward hardly repaid the effort. "Our animals were so poor that one would not last long as food. No fat could be found on the entire carcass, and the marrow of the great bones was a thick liquid, streaked with blood resembling corruption."

The hunger became all-embracing. Not long after leaving the Los Angeles trail, Manly's party had been passed by a group of young men from Kansas calling themselves the Jayhawkers. This impetuous bunch had driven swiftly by, and then—after having got lost—driven by again, less swiftly. One day Manly came across the carcass of an ox they had killed. The best cuts of beef—a very relative term under the circumstances—had been carved and packed off. But some leavings remained on the bone. How long the carcass had been lying in the sun, he couldn't say. Nor did he ask. "I was so hungry that I took my sheath knife and cut a big steak which I devoured as I walked along, without cooking or salt. Some may say they would starve before eating such meat, but if they have ever experienced hunger till it begins to draw down the life itself, they will find the impulse of self-preservation something not to be controlled by mere reason. It is an instinct that takes possession of one in spite of himself." Later Manly found some scraps of bacon rind left on the ground. "As I chewed these and tasted the rich grease they contained, I thought they were the sweetest morsels I had ever tasted."

Manly's party by now was thoroughly lost. They wandered semideliriously through a maze of mountains and valleys. They wanted to go west, but the valleys kept pushing them north and south. Each mountain range crossed revealed another ahead. How many more ranges separated them from California, God alone knew.

More discouragingly, the mountains kept getting taller and more rugged, and the valleys lower and more hostile. In one valley, during the last week of 1849, Manly made an appalling discovery. "As I reached the lower part of the valley, I walked over what seemed to be boulders of various sizes, and as I stepped from one to another the tops were covered with dirt and they grew larger as I went along. I could see behind them and they looked clear like ice, but on closer inspection proved to be immense blocks of rock salt, while the water which stood at their bases was the strongest brine." Encountering yet again the Jayhawkers, he compared impressions with them. "One fellow said he knew this was the Creator's dumping place, where he had left the worthless dregs after making a world, and the devil had scraped these together a little. Another said this must be the very place where Lot's wife was turned into a pillar of salt, and the pillar had been broken up and spread around the country. He said if a man were to die he would never decay on account of the salt."

The sole redeeming feature of the place was the moderate temperature. Snow covered the mountains that towered above the valley (Telescope Peak, the prominence Manly had seen from more than a hundred miles away, rises to 11,000 feet), but on the valley floor the sun shone warm, despite the imminence of the new year. Ironically, if their luck hadn't been so bad thus far, Manly's party would have arrived earlier and risked being broiled. But now the temperature was quite comfortable.

Manly and the others had no way of knowing that they had reached the lowest point on the North American continent, nearly 300 feet below sea level. The same pressures that thrust the ranges (including the Amargosa Range just behind and the Panamint Range just ahead) toward the heavens drove the basins toward hell. Like a sheet of paper or aluminum foil, the earth's crust crumpled as the North American plate crashed into the Pacific plate; in the collision, parts of the plate went up, other parts went down.

And in fact the part underlying Death Valley (where Manly stood, although the valley had yet to earn its name) had plunged much farther than topography revealed. The rock salt on the valley floor, deposited over millions of years by evaporation of water flowing off the mountains, was more than a thousand feet thick. Had Manly stood on bedrock, he would have been that much lower, and the mountains would have appeared that much higher. Though Manly couldn't even guess the depth of the salt bed, he could see its extent. "It looked to me as if the whole valley, which might be a hundred miles long, might have been a solid bed of rock salt."

With each day and mile, the hunger deepened and put all on edge.

Manly half expected some of his companions to lose their minds. "A man in a starving condition is a savage. He may be as bloodthirsty and selfish as a wild beast, as docile and gentle as a lamb, or as wild and crazy as a terrified animal, devoid of affection, reason, or thought of justice. We were none of us as bad as this, and yet there was a strange look in the eyes of us sometimes, as I saw by looking round, and as others no doubt realized, for I saw them making mysterious glances even in my direction."

Despair drove some of the stronger to abandon the others. Four hired drivers announced that they were going off on their own. None could gainsay their choice, as they were unattached by blood or long acquaintance with those left behind. They were apportioned their small share of the common supplies, which they packed on their backs, and they disappeared south down the valley floor, toward a place where the mountains seemed somewhat lower than elsewhere.

Manly and the others tried a more westerly route. With painful steps they struggled from the floor of the valley up one of the long slopes of alluvium that marked the places where the side canyons debouch into the valley. If they had understood that these features are the work of flash floods, themselves the result of furious rainstorms at the heads of the steep, narrow canyons, the irony of their inescapable thirst would have rendered their steps still more painful. Manly scouted the way, working uphill across the alluvial fan to the side canyon at its head, and up the canyon's broken floor. Higher and higher he climbed; narrower and narrower the canyon became. Then, to his surprise and encouragement, the canyon began to broaden out, promising easier passage for the wagons. He rounded a corner—and his encouragement evaporated. The canyon abruptly terminated in a large bowl with nearly vertical sides, from which there was no wheeled escape. A man might climb out of the bowl, but the wagons never could.

With this grim intelligence he returned to the where the wagons still struggled up the canyon. "They could hardly endure their disappointment." Starving, they now had to give up every step won with such sacrifice coming up the slope. One of the oxen refused to retreat, instead surrendering on the spot. It was killed and butchered.

That night a council was held. Clearly the end was near. They could live as long as the oxen did, and then till the meat of the oxen ran out. But they couldn't move, because the oxen couldn't move. They certainly couldn't make it over the mountains—and over whatever lay beyond the mountains.

After much morose and circular discussion, Bennett suggested a plan. Suppose two of the youngest, strongest members of the party struck out on foot. They could be supplied with all the food the others could spare; considering the dire straits, this would hardly weigh them down. They would cross the mountains and seek help, which they would lead back to where the rest of the party waited.

Bennett's proposal was better than anything else on offer, but the others hesitated to embrace it. Although none seems to have said so aloud, doubtless some were wondering what guarantee they had that the help-seekers would return—assuming they survived the trek to the nearest settlement, wherever that might be.

Bennett broke the hesitation by recommending Manly. He knew Manly and trusted him. If anyone could get out, Manly could. And if Manly got out, he could be relied on to return. Manly agreed to go. John Rogers, the last of the Green River crew, volunteered to join him.

Another ox was killed and butchered. So wasted was the animal that the meat it furnished, when dried, barely exceeded what Manly and Rogers could carry in their improvised knapsacks. A collection was taken of all the money the party had, and given to Manly and Rogers. The parting was tearful, both sides fearing they would never more see the others alive. Sarah Bennett was the last to squeeze Manly's and Rogers's hands, asking God to bless these two young men and let them bring food back to her starving children.

With Rogers, Manly again traced the route up the western canyon. The two surmounted the walls of the bowl that had turned him back before; by dark they were near the top of the canyon. At that elevation the night air was sharp; they slept huddled together for warmth. The next morning they reached the summit. To the east they could see the entire country they had traveled since early November; to the west, above a hazy valley even wider than any crossed thus far, stood yet another range of mountains, higher than any previous range, and dim in the distance. "It seemed to me the dim snowy mountains must be as far as 200 miles away."

Perhaps compensating for previous disappointment, Manly this time overestimated. Mount Whitney and the Sierra summits were only about a hundred miles away. Even so, he and Rogers could tell they would never cross those mountains and return in time to save the men, women, and children left behind.

Toward the south the mountains were lower and less formidable; in that direction the two proceeded. After a day they passed the corpse of one of the Jayhawkers. So hard was the soil, and so hurried the dead man's companions, that no attempt had been made to bury him. Thus far no scavenging animals had visited the body; from the looks of the country, not even scavengers came this way.

More than once Manly and Rogers detoured toward water only to find it too salty or alkaline to drink. They pressed on, the temperature rising as their elevation diminished. They grew so thirsty they had to chew pebbles to induce saliva; where they found a spear of grass, they sucked it for all the moisture it contained.

They tried to eat but choked on the jerked beef. Though they chewed and chewed, the lack of saliva left the meat as tough as leather, and they had to disgorge it. After weeks on the verge of starvation, this final irony was the most bitter of all. "It seemed as if we were going to die with plenty of food in our hands, because we could not eat it." They were exhausted, but sleep wouldn't come, held at bay by their hunger and thirst.

They decided to split up, the better to search for water. If one discovered anything, he would fire his rifle to alert the other. Eventually Manly heard the report of Rogers's gun; his partner had found a thin sheet of ice, no thicker than a pane of window glass, that had frozen overnight. They sucked the ice, then melted more to drink. Before it was gone they managed to force down a few bites of meat.

Farther on they met additional Jayhawkers—alive, although these told of another member of their party who had expired. The survivors were utterly discouraged and were wandering south to avoid the mountains, for fear of snow in the passes. Several supplied Manly and Rogers with addresses of their next of kin, to be notified of their loved ones' death.

By now Manly and Rogers were out of the mountains and onto the Mojave Desert, which, although deadly in the hotter months, saw irregular traffic during what passed for winter. The first sign of human activity was a rude corral woven from willow branches near a spring. Next the two men saw the remains of domesticated animals, including several horse heads. Though they lacked an explanation for the presence of the heads and the absence of the rest of the carcasses, they interpreted these as good signs.

Yet they were hardly beyond danger. Their supply of meat ran out, and they were reduced to eating a crow Rogers shot. "That abominable crow!" Manly wrote. "His flesh was about as black as his feathers, and full of tough and bony sinews. . . . Ever since that day, when I have heard people talk of 'eating crow' as a bitter pill, I think I know all about it from experience."

Inevitably, the endless miles and insufficient rest and nourishment levied their toll. One morning Manly felt a sharp pain in his left knee. The more he walked the worse it got. He told Rogers to go on ahead, arguing that those left behind might already be dying.

But Rogers refused, saying they would get out together or not at all. After resting, they hobbled on. They struggled up the north side of the San Gabriel Mountains, where they saw a small pack of prairie wolves snarling over some unrecognizable prize. "We regarded this as another encouraging sign, for these animals only live where some sort of game can be found, and they knew better than we that it was not for their health to go into the barren desert."

Shortly they topped the summit of a pass—and felt an immense wave of relief.

> There before us was a beautiful meadow of a thousand acres, green as a thick carpet of grass could make it, and shaded with oaks, wide branching and symmetrical, equal to those of an old English park, while all over the low mountains that bordered it on the south and over the broad acres of luxuriant grass was a herd of cattle number-

Sutter's Fort, before the Gold Rush

The mill at Coloma. The man in the foreground may (or may not) be James Marshall.

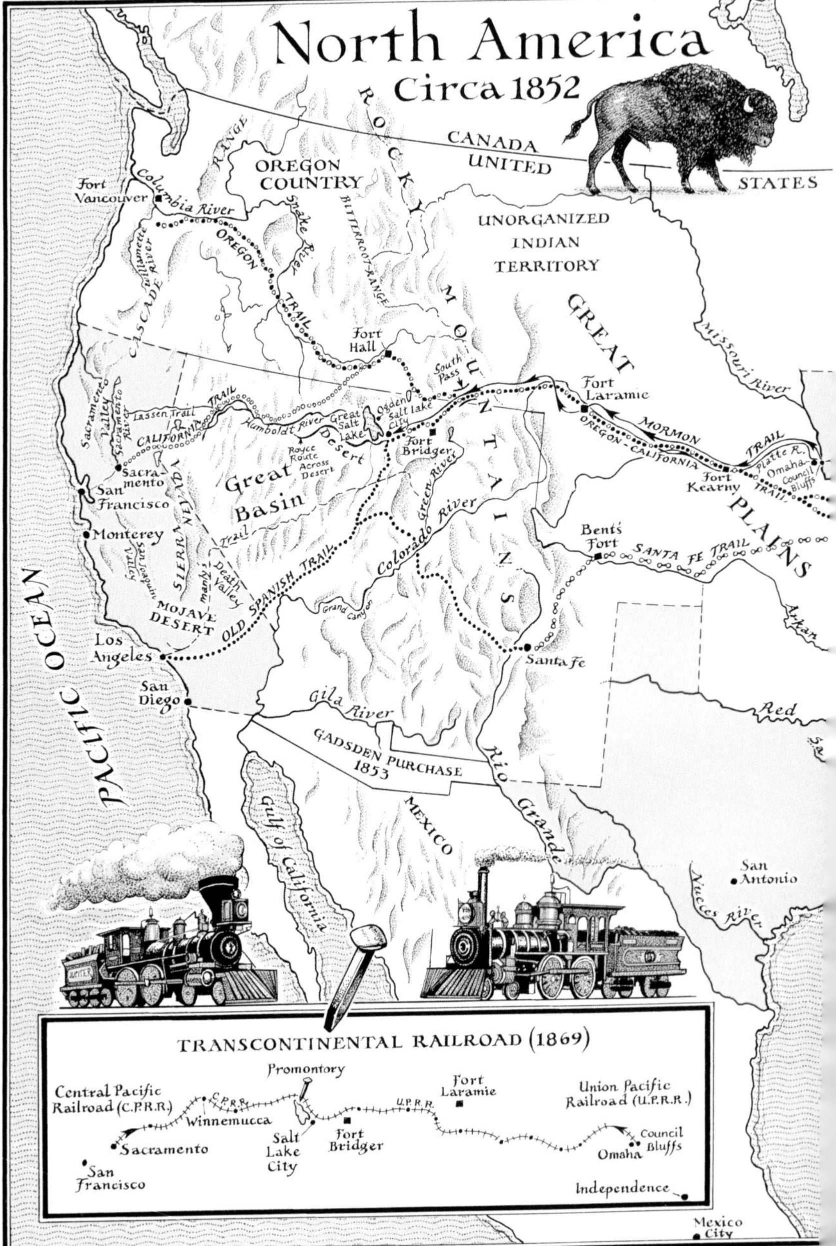
North America
Circa 1852
CANADA
UNITED STATES
OREGON COUNTRY
UNORGANIZED INDIAN TERRITORY
ROCKY MOUNTAINS
RANGE
BITTERROOT RANGE
CASCADE
Fort Vancouver
Columbia River
Willamette River
Snake River
OREGON TRAIL
Fort Hall
South Pass
GREAT PLAINS
Missouri River
Fort Laramie
MORMON TRAIL
OREGON - CALIFORNIA TRAIL
Platte R.
Omaha
Council Bluffs
Fort Kearny
Sacramento Valley
Sacramento River
Lassen Trail
CALIFORNIA TRAIL
Humboldt River
Great Salt Lake
Great Salt Lake Desert
Ogden
Salt Lake City
Fort Bridger
Green River
Royce Route Across Desert
Great Basin
Sacramento
San Francisco
Monterey
SIERRA NEVADA
San Joaquin Valley
San Joaquin River
Manly's Trail
Death Valley
Colorado River
Bents Fort
SANTA FE TRAIL
OLD SPANISH TRAIL
Grand Canyon
MOJAVE DESERT
Los Angeles
Santa Fe
San Diego
PACIFIC OCEAN
Gila River
GADSDEN PURCHASE 1853
Red
Rio Grande
MEXICO
Gulf of California
San Antonio
Nueces River
Mexico City
TRANSCONTINENTAL RAILROAD (1869)
Central Pacific Railroad (C.P.R.R.)
C.P.R.R.
Promontory
U.P.R.R.
Fort Laramie
Union Pacific Railroad (U.P.R.R.)
Winnemucca
Sacramento
San Francisco
Salt Lake City
Fort Bridger
Council Bluffs
Omaha
Independence

British North America
Lake Superior
Lake Michigan
Lake Huron
Lake Ontario
Lake Erie
Niagara Falls
Rochester
Buffalo
Boston
New York
Chicago
MORMON TRAIL
Nauvoo
St. Joseph
Fort Leavenworth
Independence
Mississippi River
St. Louis
Ohio River
Knoxville
River
River
bine River
ATLANTIC OCEAN
Gulf of Mexico
Scale of Miles
0 100 200 300 400
OVERLAND ROUTES
KEY
Mormon Trail
Royce Trail (Salt Lake Desert)
Oregon-California Trail
Oregon Trail
Lassen Trail
California Trail
Old Spanish Trail
Santa Fe Trail
Manly's Route (Death Valley)
Illustrated Map by Laura Hartman Maestro © 2002

Ready for anything

Entering the mountains

The *Challenge*, after surviving Cape Horn

Jean-Nicolas Perlot

A long tom—and a rare woman—in the placers

Chinese miners, and partners, sluicing

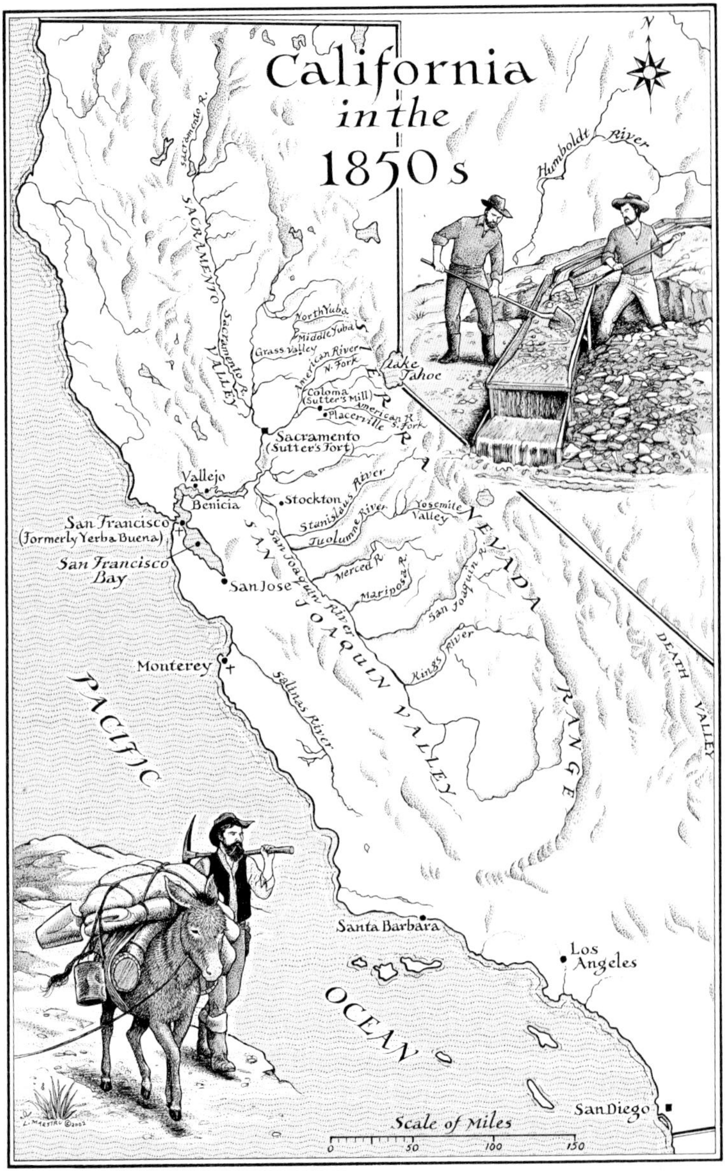
California in the 1850s
N
Humboldt River
Sacramento R.
SACRAMENTO VALLEY
Sacramento R.
North Yuba
Middle Yuba
Grass Valley
American River
N. Fork
Lake Tahoe
Coloma (Sutter's Mill)
American R.
S. Fork
Placerville
Sacramento (Sutter's Fort)
SIERRA NEVADA RANGE
Vallejo
Benicia
Stockton
Stanislaus River
Tuolumne River
Yosemite Valley
San Francisco (Formerly Yerba Buena)
San Francisco Bay
San Jose
SAN JOAQUIN VALLEY
San Joaquin River
Merced R.
Mariposa R.
San Joaquin R.
Kings River
DEATH VALLEY
Monterey
Salinas River
PACIFIC OCEAN
Santa Barbara
Los Angeles
San Diego
Scale of Miles
0
50
100
150

ing many hundreds, if not thousands. They were of all colors, shades, and sizes. Some were calmly lying down in happy rumination, others rapidly cropping the sweet grass, while the gay calves worked off their superfluous life and spirit in vigorous exercise, or drew rich nourishment in the abundant mother's milk.

All seemed happy and content, and such a scene of abundance and rich plenty and comfort bursting thus upon our eyes, which for months had seen only the desolation and sadness of the desert, was like getting a glimpse of Paradise, and tears of joy ran down our faces. If ever a poor mortal escapes from this world, where so many trials come, and joys of a happy Heaven are opened up to him, the change cannot be much more than that which was suddenly opened to us on that bright day.

MANLY AND ROGERS knew they were saved. Where cattle lived, people lived. Whether the men, women, and children still left back across the desert and the mountains, camped on the floor of that terrible salt valley, could be saved was another matter, and one that quickly broke Manly's and Rogers's reverie. They hastened forward as fast as the still-hobbling Manly could walk. They encountered a Mexican couple, who gave them cornmeal, and an American, who gave them directions to Los Angeles, some thirty miles to the west, where he said they might get help. The cornmeal caused them acute intestinal distress after so long on an all-meat (and vanishingly stringent) diet; the directions led them to another American, a man named French, who informed them that Los Angeles was deserted. Everyone had gone to the goldfields. They would find no help there. But French guided them to the mission of San Fernando, where for sixty dollars they purchased food, three horses, and a mule.

The journey back to the salt valley went much faster than the trip out, because of the horses and because Manly and Rogers knew where they were going. They tried one shortcut, which almost failed when a dry streambed they were ascending was blocked by huge boulders. Night was falling; they had traveled all day without water. The horses were ready to drop from thirst and exhaustion. There was no turning back, for the horses would expire before they could reach the most recent water hole. And in any event, to detour would surely condemn the people in the salt valley to death, if they weren't dead already.

The mule was nimbler than the horses. At one giant stair-step that the horses refused to try, she skipped right up. Manly and Rogers decided to abandon the horses to their misery and move on. "One who has never heard the last despairing, pleading neigh of a horse left to die can form no idea of its almost human appeal," Manly remembered.

Not much farther on, even the mule appeared stumped. A sheer rock face ten feet high—a dry waterfall—spanned the canyon. For a man to climb it would be difficult; for a mule, impossible. Yet the mule exuded uncanny confidence, which almost alone prevented her human partners from despairing. In the darkening shadows they piled rocks along one of the canyon walls, building a bridge to a narrow ledge by which the mule might—just might—cross to the top of the falls. "It was a trying moment. It seemed to be weighted down with all the trials and hardships of many months. It seemed to be the time when helpless women and innocent children hung on the trembling balance between life and death." The mule crept forward, finding footing where no horse and few men could. At the last step she hesitated, as if finally asking herself whether this was a good idea, then jumped across to the top of the falls and safety.

After an anxious, cold night in the mountains, Manly and Rogers came out on the floor of the salt valley. They saw no sign of those they had returned to save. After several miles they found the body of one of the men, sprawled in the sand, a makeshift canteen at his side. Their worst fears crowded upon them. Was no one left alive?

Farther on, Manly and Rogers sighted the wagons, apparently empty and as still as death. Thinking that Indians might have attacked the party, and remained nearby, the two let the mule approach first. Her senses were sharper than theirs, and she would smell trouble before they did. But the mule neither brayed nor shied. Counting his bullets, Manly fired a shot into the air to see what reaction the report might bring; he kept enough in reserve to kill at least a few Indians if any appeared.

The gunshot elicited no echoes from the distant mountains, nor any immediate response from the wagons. Yet after several long moments, a man emerged from beneath one of the vehicles. Dazed by the light, he looked all around before finally locating the source of the noise. "The boys have come! The boys have come!" he shouted.

This raised other figures and other voices. Bennett and Sarah appeared, rushing forward to embrace Manly and Rogers. But the number of the party was considerably diminished. Manly told about meeting the dead man that morning; where were the rest?

Bennett explained that no sooner had Manly and Rogers departed than some of the others predicted that the two would never return, and would be damned fools if they did. These skeptics decided they would rather die trying to escape than awaiting a rescue party that would never come. They packed their goods on their oxen and headed off, a few at a time. The dead man whom Manly and Rogers had discovered that morning had left with the last group. Whether the others shared his fate, undiscovered, Bennett didn't know.

Preparing the survivors for the trek to Los Angeles required a couple of days. The wagons would remain behind; food and children would be packed out on the mule and on those oxen not slaughtered for food. None of the survivors underestimated the trials that still separated them from safety, but, traveling with men who knew the route, they could be confident of ultimate success. At the crest of the range that had so long stood in their way, they gazed back upon the fearful valley. "We took off our hats," Manly recalled, "and then overlooking the scene of so much trial, suffering, and death, spoke the thought uppermost in our minds, saying: 'Good-bye, Death Valley!' "

THE RESCUE OF THE survivors of Death Valley—the name stuck—was a private matter. Other rescues were publicly organized. In 1849 the memory of the Donner party was fresh among the Americans in California; many sensed that there, but for the grace of God and the luck of the trail, went they. The massive influx of gold-seekers, which continued far into autumn, raised the specter of a Donner-like disaster multiplied by a thousand. To prevent such a fiasco, the governor of California, Persifor Smith, sent rescue parties back east along the trails.

Most emigrants didn't require rescuing but nonetheless appreciated the effort. "We bid a long and hearty goodbye to this team-killing, back-breaking, leg-soring mountain," William Swain wrote on October 12, just west of the Sierra summit, "and arrived in camp at sundown, where we indemnified ourselves in part with a pot of smoking beef soup, the material for which was received from a relief train sent out on the route by Governor P. Smith with a drove of beef cattle to be distributed among the emigrants as their necessities required."

More important than the soup meat, in Swain's case, was the intelligence the relief party brought. The soup tasted better than the news. Swain and the Wolverine Rangers learned that they were much farther from the diggings than they thought. Swain's concerns about the northerly trend of the Lassen trail had proved well-founded; by the relief party's calculation they were 380 miles from Sutter's Fort. To make matters worse, that distance included rugged ridges, broken plateaus, and not much of a road.

So discouraging was this news, at what had seemed the moment of triumph, that the feeling of common purpose that had held the Rangers together across the plains, the Rockies, and the Great Basin suddenly dissolved. Those who knew they could travel faster determined to do so; calling a meeting of the association, they moved to disband. The motion carried. In groups of four, the members split up the common property, with each foursome getting a wagon, a team, and an equal share of what provisions remained. "Mr. Hutchinson, Mr. Bailey, Mr. McClellan and self drew a team and wagon together and shall travel the remainder of the way on our own hook," Swain recorded.

Through the country of the Pit Indians (so called for the pits they dug to trap game and unwary enemies), Swain and the others trudged, keeping watch night and day to prevent the theft of animals or food. The last week of October and first week of November brought snow on the ridges and rain in the valleys; they slogged through mud up to the axles. As the government beef ran low, they missed meals once again. But finally, at sundown on November 8, Swain and his partners reached the Sacramento River at Lassen's Ranch.

HUGH HEISKELL AND Sarah Royce met the relief parties on the eastern slope of the Sierras, where the central emigrant trail climbed out of the Great Basin. Heiskell and his Tennessee and Alabama companions had fared better than many overlanders, crossing the Carson Desert without undue hardship, and they subsequently made the ascent of the Carson River into the Sierras in good shape and time. The last stretch over the top slowed them, with the steep trail requiring a doubling of teams to pull the wagons up. Not far from the crest a relief party with extra oxen arrived. "They brought us 6 yoke of cattle to assist us," Heiskell wrote. "We could have [a word is missing here: managed?] without danger, but we will not insult Uncle Sam by refusing his aid."

Sarah Royce and her family couldn't have survived without the government aid. Heiskell and the others told the relief parties about groups farther east who were having serious difficulty. At the rate these stragglers were going, they would never make it over the mountains before snow blocked the pass.

Sarah realized the danger, yet there was nothing to do but plod on. She and the others were inching up the Carson River when they discerned approaching dust on the trail ahead. As all the white people in that country were going the other way, she and Josiah feared Indians. But there was nothing to do about this either, except put on a brave face and hope for the best. Presently the cause of the dust appeared: two riders in loose garments that blew in the breeze, lending the riders the appearance—to Sarah, with her biblical inclinations—of angels. "Their rapidity of motion and the steepness of the descent gave a strong impression of coming down from above, and the thought flashed into my mind, 'They look heaven-sent.' "

On reaching the Royce party, one of the riders addressed Josiah: "Well, sir, you are the man we are after!"

"How can that be?" answered Josiah.

"Yes, sir, you and your wife, and that little girl, are what brought us as far as this." The man explained that his orders were to go no farther than the summit. But a woman there said she knew of another party, containing a woman and a small girl, back down the trail and in trouble. The woman who provided the information wouldn't rest until the man agreed to rescue that woman and girl. "You see, I've got a wife and little girl of my own," he explained, "so I felt just how it was."

The man went on to say that the Royces would never get their wagon over the summit. Their oxen couldn't handle the climb, and it was already snowing in the heights. Indeed, a snowstorm had lately closed the pass temporarily; when the next storm would arrive, perhaps closing the pass for the winter, could only be guessed. They must abandon the wagon and pack what they could on the oxen and on two mules the rescuers had brought. Only by this means could they hope to cross the mountains.

Sarah reflected on how, when leaving her Iowa home, she had shuddered to think that all her worldly possessions were reduced to what would fit in a wagon. Now not even the wagon survived. Yet life was more precious than possessions; if they reached California alive and together, that would be enough.

Packing the oxen and managing the mules was no small task, but several days later saw them near the Sierra crest. So much faster was pack-travel than driving wagons that they caught Hugh Heiskell's train just before the top. "Rice [that is, Royce] came in with his oxen packed and his wife riding a mule—furnished them by Uncle Sam—& carrying a child," Heiskell wrote on October 18.

The next day the combined party reached the summit. Speaking for every emigrant who achieved that goal, Sarah recalled the glorious moment. "I looked down, far over constantly descending hills, to where a soft haze sent up a warm, rosy glow that seemed to me a smile of welcome; while beyond, occasional faint outlines of other mountains appeared; and I knew I was looking across the Sacramento Valley."

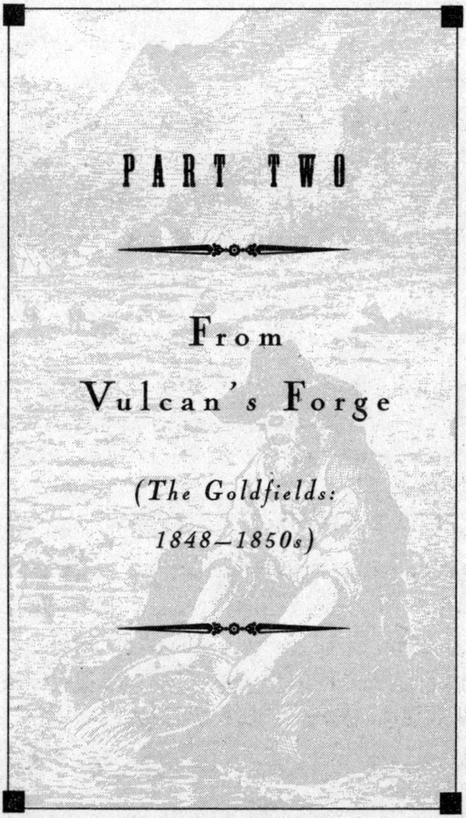

PART TWO

From Vulcan's Forge

(The Goldfields: 1848–1850s)

Never, since the Roman legionry shadowed the earth with their eagles, in search of spoil—not even when Spain ravished the wealth of a world, or England devastated the Indies for its treasures—never has such a gorgeous treasury been opened to the astonished world.

—James Hutchings, gold-hunter and publisher

And so they came, in wave after wave after wave. The Pacific wave splashed tens of thousands of argonauts ashore; the larger rollers from the isthmus and around Cape Horn carried scores of thousands more; the great breakers that crashed across the plains and desert and mountains flooded California with a hundred-and-a-half-thousand immigrants. By 1853 the tally of gold-hunters had passed a quarter million. At that point the Americans, including Sarah Royce and Lewis Manly and the others, composed perhaps two-thirds of the total. The Latin Americans, including Chileans like Vicente Pérez Rosales, made a tenth of the total. The contingent from France, including Jean-Nicolas Perlot, and from other parts of Europe made another tenth. Yee Ah Tye and his Chinese compatriots were somewhat less than a tenth, while Tom Archer and the Australians were about a third of the Chinese. (Much guesswork goes into these numbers, as the new Californians were too busy digging gold to queue up for counting, but the figures give an idea of the size and composition of the immigration.)

Although the difficulty of their journeys had varied drastically—Tom Archer's Pacific voyage was a pleasure cruise compared to the Great Basin ordeals of Sarah Royce and Lewis Manly—nearly all the immigrants felt tremendous relief on reaching California. When they stepped ashore at Monterey or San Francisco, or gazed down upon the Sacramento Valley from the summit of the Sierras, most sensed a huge burden lifting from their souls. Their bones wouldn't bleach on the desert; their flesh wouldn't feed the fishes; their children wouldn't be orphaned for their parents' reckless decision to leave home. They had survived; they had triumphed.

But they soon discovered that their struggle had just begun. For those who came by sea, the journey from harbor to mines could be as difficult and dangerous as the journey from home to California. And when the argonauts reached the diggings, the place where, in their dreams, they had imagined plucking gold nuggets from the ground, they encountered another set of challenges. They had to master the art of mining, which turned out to involve much more than simply pocketing nuggets. Where the inherited techniques of the art fell short of the argonauts' need, they had to invent new ones, often complicated and costly.

And they had to do all this amid a human welter none had ever experienced. The gold-hunters scrambled over each other at San Francisco; they elbowed and jostled one another in the mining camps. They competed fiercely in the river bottoms and gravel bars for the best claims. Time was money, and none had a moment to lose.

A few found what they came for, filling their pockets easily and heading home convinced that California was God's apology for ousting Adam and Eve from the Garden. But the many more toiled in a decidedly post-Edenic state, with uncertain and often diminishing success.

Had the immigrants known what a task the gold-hunting would be, their spirits might have failed. Yet had they been the kind to weigh trials in advance and be daunted, they wouldn't have come in the first place. And so, with the same determination—and in many cases blithe ignorance—that had launched them out upon the stormy oceans and over the endless plains and desert, they embarked on the next phase of their great adventure: the apportioning of El Dorado.

7

With a Washbowl on My Knee

Some two hundred million years before Sarah Royce and Hugh Heiskell and the other overlanders crossed the Sierra summit, giant bubbles began forming far beneath the surface of the earth. These weren't bubbles of air, but of molten rock, and although their weight totaled perhaps a quadrillion tons (give or take a few hundred trillion), they were lighter than the surrounding material and accordingly buoyant. The bubbles had their genesis in the constant recycling of the earth's crust, from its fiery emergence out of the mantle beneath what would become the Atlantic Ocean, through its conveyorlike transport across the earth's surface, to its plunging return to the abyss. As it plunged, the crust grew hot again and started to melt; the melting produced the bubbles that floated slowly—very, very slowly—upward.

In some places the bubbles reached the surface. Where they did, the molten rock spilled forth as lava, covering the landscape in sheets of liquid flame. But the greatest part of the molten rock never got that far. Cooling as it ascended, it froze in place, creating what geologists would call the Sierra Nevada batholith, a giant body of granite underlying twenty-five thousand square miles of the future states of California and Nevada.

The melting, bubbling, and cooling was a messy process. Different minerals in the rock liquefied at different temperatures; these minerals were then mobilized by water squeezed from the rock under the enormous pressure. As the rock cooled, the minerals precipitated out in streaks or veins. Eons hence, humans would learn to separate and concentrate chemical elements by similar distillation methods; in doing so they would be puny mimics of the planet beneath their feet. The results of the subterranean refining process were striking. Gold, for example, occurs in the crust of the earth at an average concentration of five parts per billion. But the melting and cooling that produced the Sierra batholith yielded veins of gold-bearing quartz in which the gold occurred in concentrations as high as one hundred million parts per billion.

Yet most of this gold was trapped far below the surface of the earth, where it remained for tens of millions of years. About four million years before the arrival of the Royces and the rest, however, the crust that contained the batholith and the golden quartz began to crumple and heave, as its forward edge crashed down into the mantle. Along a front stretching four hundred miles from north to south, the batholith was raised thousands of feet into the air; so too were the veins of gold.

Then the forces of erosion went to work. During chilly spells—spells long by human standards but fleeting in geological terms—glaciers ground away at the granite, producing such sculptures as Yosemite Valley. In warmer eras, water did the heavy work, aided by seasonal ice that crept into crevices and chiseled off pieces of the batholith, tumbling them down into the riverbeds where the rushing water pummeled them. (Similar action farther east deposited the boulders that slowed Lewis Manly's journey through the Green River gorge.)

The gold, having been chemically distilled beneath the surface, now was mechanically sifted from the quartz that encased it. The glaciers, the winter ice, and especially the rushing water attacked the veins, grinding them to gravel, sand, and dust. In the steeper regions, the water carried all the rubble indiscriminately: large pieces and small, heavy pieces and light. But wherever the water slowed, the densest material drifted to the bottom, catching behind boulders, accumulating in eddies, piling up along the inside of river bends. The gold, seven times heavier than the quartz, sank while the quartz was carried away.

Where the gold sank it waited—waited, in nearly all cases, to be buried anew by additional debris borne down from the higher elevations. Time and again the riverbeds shifted; the caches of gold were entombed under tons of gravel and sand and mud. Forests grew atop the tombs, quiet and serene by the measure of biological time, amid a landscape that remained violently unsettled in geological time.

Eventually those forests attracted an inquisitive species, a biped drawn to the forests for their timber, but possessing a peculiar penchant for shiny yellow metal. When this species began scratching about in one of the streams as yet unburied, biological time and geological time abruptly intersected, and entered historical time.

"THE GOLD IS IN fine bright scales and is very pure," William Sherman wrote a friend, regarding the diggings on the American River.

> It is separated from the earth and gravel by washing in the pans by hand, but the better plan is in a kind of inclined trough with cleats nailed across the bottom. A grate is placed over the highest part of this trough, upon which the gravel is thrown, afterward the water. The gold passes into the trough, the gravel and stones are removed, and by a constant dashing of water and rocking the machine, the earthy matter is washed off, leaving the gold mixed with black sand in the bottom of the machine. These are separated by drying them in the sun and blowing off the sand, leaving the gold pure. You would be astonished at the ease with which the precious metal is obtained; any man by common industry can make $25 a day.

The ease of the gold-gathering was certainly astonishing, but the principle behind it wasn't surprising, or at least it wouldn't have been surprising had Sherman and those in the streambeds understood the geology of gold. The heat of the earth—the heat that drove the crustal plates to their collision at the western edge of North America, the heat that then melted the rock and boiled out the precious metal—had done the hard work over two hundred million years; all that remained for humans was to harvest what the earth had already collected. In time a practical knowledge of gold's geology would develop along the Sierra front, and prospectors would acquire a keen sense for which formations were likely to yield pay dirt. But in the beginning they operated blindly, groping about the placers (pronounced *plassers*, derived from the Spanish *placer*—"to please"—and referring to the deposits of gold in streambeds) for each new nugget, each fresh niche of gold dust.

The gold-hunters at first employed the most rudimentary and unspecialized equipment. A sheath knife loosened nuggets; a shovel shifted gravel. Shortly the miners (for so they were called, even though few initially went near anything easterners associated with "mines") ascended to the next rung of technology: ordinary tools turned to novel ends. A pan or a washbowl was filled with a slurry of sand and water. The vessel was rocked back and forth by hand, causing the water to spill over the sides, carrying with it the comparatively light quartz sand and leaving behind the much heavier gold. Where necessary, a final sifting was accomplished by letting the leavings dry and blowing away the last of the sand.

Local Indians soon joined the hunt, once they discovered what the whites would pay for gold. The Indians often used sticks instead of shovels, and baskets in place of washbowls. And they made a family affair of the undertaking. "The system they employed for washing the earth was the same as that still used by our panners of gold, but more methodical," wrote Vicente Pérez Rosales.

> With sticks hardened in the fire, or an occasional worn-out tool of civilization, the men dug until they came to the *circa*, one of the strata most largely composed of sand and of the heavy bodies deposited in the valleys by the water that drains into them. This sand the children loaded into tightly woven grass baskets and carried to the banks of the stream where a row of women with fine trays of the same material washed it, wrapping the gold in small packages to the value of about two Spanish gold pieces, for use in trading.

From stick and sheath knife, washbowl and basket, the next step up the ladder of mining technology was the cradle. Pérez Rosales and his Chilean companions had made their way to Weber Creek, a tributary of the American River above Sutter's Fort. They observed the Indians' method of gathering gold and briefly tried copying it (using pan and scoop rather than basket and stick). The results were disappointing. "For the first three days the harvest was meager," Pérez Rosales wrote. Then they discovered some of their neighbors using the "California cradle."

> The cradle is a very simple and ingenious apparatus that has all the advantages of a scoop on a colossal scale, but is no larger than an actual cradle a yard and a half long by half a yard wide, placed so that the head rests on a base a fourth higher than the one at the foot. These bases are nothing more than wooden arcs that facilitate the rocking of the cradle. The upper end of the latter holds a rough sieve built of pieces of wood bored full of holes; the foot has no bottom. Along the floor of this singular device at intervals of four inches are nailed strips of wood a quarter of an inch square. These prevent the escape of the heavy particles mixed with the mud that runs down the inclined floor.
>
> The method of using this primitive but highly important machine is so simple and easy that the dullest observer can take his diploma in the science in no time at all. One man feeds the gold-bearing earth into the sieve, another pours buckets of water over it, a third rocks the cradle, and finally still another takes out by hand the stones that are too large to pass through the strainer, examines them, and throws away such as do not contain gold. The water rinses the earth through the seive, the mixture drops down and flows over the sloping bottom, and the gold and other more or less heavy bodies lodge in the cleats provided by the crosswise strips of wood. Every ten minutes the work is interrupted and the gold dust and nuggets mixed with iron that have been caught in these small angles are collected. This material is then placed in a hand trough for separation later, and the operation continues all day long.

Pérez Rosales and the Chileans found the cradle—the device Sherman described to his friend—to be a vast improvement over the pan. "In this device we lovingly rocked the infant gold and beheld it wax portentously. . . . Our daily harvest varied between ten and twenty-two ounces of gold."

Although much better than the pan, the cradle suffered from the inefficiency implied by the frequent interruptions of the washing to clean the gold from the cleats. A variant of the cradle solved this problem, as Jean-Nicolas Perlot and his French partners discovered on their arrival at the gold regions.

> This new invention was called the long-tom. It consisted of three planks nine to twelve feet long, nailed together, one of which served as bottom for this sort of boat; one of the ends was cut in an elongated bevel, and a sheet-iron plaque pierced with fairly big holes was nailed on this bevel. This boat was set at a slope, so that the iron sheet was horizontal. On it they threw the dirt to be washed, which they stirred with a shovel whose end was cut square. Water was thrown on the upper part of the boat with a bucket, or else it was brought there, either by a canal, or by a hose of strong canvas. This long-tom was supported from below by a sort of square wooden box with a flange all around and inclined in the same direction as the boat.
>
> Into this receptacle fell the water and all that which could pass through the holes of the plate; the remainder was thrown aside with the shovel. It was enough to wash in the pan, twice a day, the little gravel which was at the bottom, in order to gather all the gold which had been moved during the day.

HAD THE PRIMARY GOAL of mining operations been to maximize the yield of gold per cubic yard of ore (which is, of course, what the composite of sand, gravel, and gold was, though the argonauts didn't initially use the term), the miners should have stuck with the washbowl—or the grass basket. The Indians, with their methodical approach, sifted the gold-bearing materials far more thoroughly than the whites did with their cradles and long-toms.

But the yield-per-yard mattered less than the yield-per-day. "Time is money," Perlot heard again and again, and all evidence indicated that this was true. At bottom the obsession with time derived from the peculiar property arrangements in the goldfields. No one owned the gold until someone discovered it. Upon ratification of the Treaty of Guadalupe Hidalgo, nearly all the land in the gold regions became American public land, held in common by the people of the United States. The minerals on or under that land might be claimed by anyone. But a claim was valid only as long as it was being exercised—that is, as long as the claim was being physically worked. Neither an individual nor a company could set aside property to be worked later; if not worked now, someone else might legally come in and begin taking out the gold. Yet because new fields were being discovered all the time, no one was interested in wringing the last ounce of gold out of any existing claim; better to take what came easily, then move to another site and skim the cream there.

John Frémont discovered the evanescent nature of mineral rights in California upon his return there in 1849. He also discovered—and indeed epitomized—what became a principal theme of life in the new land: that luck was as important as industry in tapping the wealth of the new land.

Frémont almost literally stumbled into the Gold Rush. Before his frostbitten leg was fully recovered from the disaster in the Rockies, he headed haltingly west to meet Jessie. En route he encountered a large group of Mexicans from the border province of Sonora, going the same way. He had no idea why they were traveling to California, and had to ask. To dig the gold, they replied. Wasn't that why everyone was going to California?

This was the first Frémont heard of the gold discovery, and he plied the Sonorans for details. How much gold was there in California? Where was it found? The Sonorans couldn't say. They knew only that gold had been discovered at Sutter's mill and that people were getting rich.

Impulsiveness was an essential part of Frémont's character. Sometimes it surfaced as boldness, sometimes as rashness; in this case it inspired a stroke of genius. Frémont had never seen the Sierra tract that had been purchased for him; indeed, until now he was convinced he'd been swindled. And he knew nothing of these Sonorans, whose golden tales he had no immediate way of verifying. But he had seen enough of the Sierras to guess that if there was gold at Sutter's mill, there was gold in the streams of the Mariposa. And these Sonorans, sons (and daughters, for some of the miners brought their wives) of a district where mining was centuries old, appeared to know what they were talking about. On the spot he engaged twenty-eight of the Mexicans to work for him. He would outfit and feed them; they would hunt gold on his property. He and they would split the profits.

While Frémont continued to the coast to meet Jessie, the Sonorans proceeded to the Mariposa to start mining. The placers there soon began yielding gold in promising, then eye-popping, then brain-boggling, quantities. Even the half-share sent to Frémont was a prince's ransom. Jessie described "the astonishment and pleasure of receiving buckskin bags filled with gold dust and lumps of gold." The first installment was a hundred pounds of gold, worth $18,000. Additional installments followed regularly.

Frémont often acted as though a personal version of Manifest Destiny applied to him, as though Providence, already looking out for Americans, kept special watch over him. This attitude had carried him across the snowy Sierras to his first meeting with John Sutter; it had allowed him (with Jessie as co-conspirator) to defy the War Department; it had encouraged him to flaunt his disdain for the Mexican government of California. It had got him into trouble when he challenged General Kearny, and had almost killed him (and did kill several of his followers) when he tried to cross the winter Rockies. Some of those who knew him, starting with William Sherman, interpreted this trait in Frémont as unwarranted conceit. But now not even Sherman could gainsay that Providence or destiny or something was smiling on Frémont. From disgrace and near-death he was fast becoming as rich as Croesus. Who wouldn't feel blessed?

JESSIE SHARED the feeling. Several days after touching at San Diego, her ship from Panama anchored at San Francisco. Getting ashore was a challenge, as the boat crews that transported the passengers to the beach promptly abandoned their craft and headed for the mines. But, as before, her name preceded her, and one of the town's enterprising businessmen rowed out to fetch her and Lily.

San Francisco was a wild place that summer of 1849, a village fast becoming a city, a vortex of human activity that never ceased nor even much slowed. In the year since Sam Brannan had paraded about the plaza shouting of gold on the American River, San Francisco had undergone a revolutionary transformation. The first effect of the gold discovery was to empty the town, as everyone left for the goldfields. This effect lasted several months, or as long as was required for the news of the discovery to reach the outside world and for the outside world to reach back. By early 1849, as the Pacific fleet of argonauts from Latin America and Australia started to arrive, the town began to fill up again, but with a population unlike that of any other American city. Not only was this new group more cosmopolitan—or foreign, to put the matter plainly—it consisted almost entirely of people who didn't want to be there. The argonauts saw San Francisco as a way station to the mines; the sooner they could leave the town and get digging, the better.

The transformation continued with the arrival of the ships from the isthmus and around Cape Horn. The large number of Americans in this part of the argosy diluted the foreign influence but, accompanied as the Americans were by Europeans, not all that much. Meanwhile the transient atmosphere increased with the increase in the number of transients. If anything, the desire to keep moving grew more frantic, as each shipload of argonauts arrived and learned how many others had preceded them.

The incessant rush lent a peculiar disorder to the place. Nothing appeared permanent; most of the buildings were actually tents: canvas tossed over a few boards and tied down against the winds that arose off the Pacific each afternoon and blew sand and dust everywhere (and set such tender-lunged newcomers as Jessie Frémont coughing). The few trees that had graced the virgin peninsula had nearly all vanished, cut for lumber or firewood. Merchants lacked warehouses for the goods they sold the argonauts, and so they simply piled their wares in the street. Some of the argonauts slept in tent-hotels; others camped in the open. Viewed from the dunes that stood behind the city, San Francisco that summer looked like nothing so much as the bivouac of an army on the move—which essentially was what it was.

This was hardly what Jessie had envisioned when she dreamed of her new home in California, the refuge she would create for herself and John and Lily. If anything, it reminded her of Chagres and Panama City, albeit without the tropical diseases. Consequently, she stayed in San Francisco only long enough for John to arrive from Los Angeles. On her tenth day there he appeared, and they shared a warm and weepy reunion, with each filling the other in on the details of their eventful six months apart. Shortly thereafter they moved to Monterey, where they took up residence in the house of John's erstwhile bête noire, José Castro, who had retreated to Mexico.

Monterey was more in keeping with Jessie's domestic vision. The town was very quiet, suspended, so to speak, in the first phase of the gold-induced transformation—the phase in which everybody left. The difference was that no one replaced Monterey's departed, as the old capital was utterly eclipsed by San Francisco, which was much more convenient to the goldfields. At the time of Jessie and John's arrival, in the summer of 1849, about the only men in Monterey were those required by law or unbreakable contract to be there. These included some American soldiers, among them, as Jessie put it, "a long thin young captain" with red hair named Sherman.

There were a larger number of women, nearly all of them native Californians. At first they kept their distance from Jessie. She understood why: "My name represented only invasion and defeat." But before long the common bond of motherhood brought them together. They traded milk and flour and fabric and advice. The one thing Jessie never learned to appreciate was the Californians' addiction to cigars, which she declined as often as the other mothers offered a puff.

Daily life in Gold Rush California posed peculiar problems. Even after the Frémonts' gold began pouring down from the Mariposa, many things Jessie took for granted back east were simply unavailable (starting with banks to hold their money: she stored the gold under the mattress, and then in trunks). She sought to hire a chambermaid, and by dint of much effort found a woman willing to work for $240 a month and perquisites. This wage was more than ten times the going rate in the East, but Jessie agreed to pay it. She also agreed to the woman's demand for housing for herself and her children. But when the woman began borrowing Jessie's dresses for copying by her—the maid's—seamstress, Jessie demurred. The woman indignantly resigned, leaving Jessie to tend to her own and Lily's needs herself.

The one servant Jessie was able to retain arrived under a cloud. This woman appeared at the door with babe in arms, and inquired hesitantly whether Jessie needed a cook. Jessie said she did. "Would you take one from Sydney?" the woman asked. Jessie didn't understand the question at first. The woman explained that her ship from Australia had arrived the day before, and she already had been turned down for work on account of the suspicions surrounding that colony of felons. Jessie nonetheless said she would hire the woman. When the woman asked why, Jessie responded, "Because your baby is so clean, so well-kept, and looks so well. He answers for it that you are clean, patient and kind." The woman promised that Jessie would never regret hiring her. "And I never did," Jessie recollected.

Despite the inconveniences, Jessie's new life suited her quite satisfactorily. During the dry season—from late spring to fall—she, John, and Lily traveled out from Monterey in a special six-seated carriage built in New Jersey and shipped around the Horn. The vehicle comfortably slept the three of them, and they would ramble north to San Francisco and then south to San Jose, stopping at ranches or simply under the stars. When draft animals to pull the carriage proved—like so much else in that time and place—hard to procure, the Benton name worked its customary magic. John had been reduced to hitching pack mules to the carriage, and predictably they balked in the harness. He tried to buy a harness-trained team from some passing Texans, only to have the Texans say they liked the team themselves and had no desire to sell. Jessie, however, overhearing one of the men address another, thought she recognized the name. She told John to ask the man if his mother was from North Carolina, and if her name was

Caroline. The surprised man said yes to both questions, prompting Jessie to explain that the man's grandfather was an old friend of her father's. On learning this, the man insisted that the Frémonts have the mules.

Jessie had never known such carefree pleasure.

> We were in the most delightful season of the year; no rains, no heavy dews; the wild oats were ripe, and gave the soft look of ripe wheat fields to the hillsides; the wild cattle were feeding about or resting under the evergreen oaks, which looked so like orchard trees that one was disappointed not to find the apples on the ground beneath them; the sky was a deep blue, without a cloud. We were young and full of health, and in all the exhilaration of sudden wealth which could enable us to realize our greatest wishes.

But the wealth on which this idyll rested was fragile. Small armies of argonauts were invading the Mariposa, stripping the richest placers of their gold. Frémont would have required an army of his own to defend the deposits. The best he could come up with was his contingent of Sonorans, who protected his interests (and theirs) by mining faster and better than the squatters. Unfortunately for him, before a year had elapsed the Sonorans decided to return to Mexico, putting Frémont's income in jeopardy. The Sonorans reckoned that they had had enough of mining, in both the positive sense of having made the money they came for and the negative sense of suffering mistreatment at the hands of Anglo miners who resented the competition. An American traveling west across northern Mexico, encountering a group of Mexican miners returning east and south, summarized their situation: "They all appear to have plenty of money with them and speak very hard of the Americans that are in the diggings. We think the Americans have drove them out." These particular Mexicans may or may not have included Frémont's former partners, but they almost certainly shared those miners' experiences.

The animus against foreigners in the mines would become a theme; for now it represented a disruption of the Frémont cash flow. Yet John, who handled the business of the mines—to the eventual dismay of the more astute Jessie—adopted the attitude that what came easily went easily. So casual was his approach that on the day of settling up with the Sonorans he declined to travel to the Mariposa himself. He simply sent a messenger with the key to the storehouse and told the Mexicans to gather up as much gold as they were owed. "This they did with scrupulous honor, not taking an ounce more than their stipulated portion," Jessie had to admit.

JEAN-NICOLAS PERLOT was among those who mined the Mariposa without Frémont's permission. (French-speakers felt some of the antiforeign animus, but not nearly as much as Latin Americans and Asians.) It was at least a little ironic that Perlot did so, for it was Frémont's fame in France that attracted many of the French companies to the Mariposa. Most, however, laid plans to head for that district without appreciating its remoteness or the difficulties of getting there. For Perlot these difficulties were compounded by the dissolution of La Fortune. Through corruption or simple mismanagement—human failings that afflicted many of the mining associations—Perlot's company had fallen into debt and then bankruptcy. Supplies that were supposed to reach Perlot and the others in California never arrived, and the company's cash was soon exhausted. "The blow was terrible," Perlot wrote. "There we were, thrown on the shore like castaways, without money, without resources, in an unknown land whose language we did not understand. Each one asked what would become of him and found no reply." The company disbanded, with several members forsaking their dreams of gold for work on farms near the coast. Perlot, however, persevered. "I wanted, at the very least, to get to the placers and to try them, cost what it might."

The cost proved more than he guessed. The Mariposa was part of what were called the "southern mines," separated—somewhat arbitrarily—from the "northern mines" above Sutter's Fort by the Mokelumne River. (After gold was discovered even farther north, the mines around Coloma were sometimes called the "central" mines.) While the route to Sutter's was well marked, the road to the Mariposa was substantially less so. Those with cash could pay for transport by boat up the San Joaquin River to Stockton, the gateway to the southern mines. Those without, like Perlot, walked. Locals warned him that the journey would be very arduous. "It was a matter of covering two hundred and six miles (sixty-eight leagues) across an uninhabited and pathless land, of avoiding Indians, bears, panthers, wildcats, coyotes, and snakes of all kinds, including rattlesnakes." The French consul at Monterey cautioned Perlot against attempting the trip. "But I made him understand that my mind was made up."

The journey was as trying, in its briefer way, as anything the overlanders from the eastern United States endured. After traversing the Coast Range, Perlot and the few former members of La Fortune who accompanied him had to cross the forbiddingly immense and barren Central Valley. "Not a cloud impaired the clarity of the air, and the view stretched unbroken as far as the limit where the earth and sky seemed to unite and mingle. It was the first time I found myself on a plain where the earth's curvature alone ended the view. . . . This limitless plain was covered only by a thin grass which the ardor of the sun had already almost dried out. Here and there, sand covered great surfaces where the print of no step was visible, perhaps because the wind, in lifting this sand, ceaselessly leveled the ground." Perlot spied a river, a silvery stream that beckoned them forward. But with every step the river retreated, finally revealing itself to be a mirage.

After crossing the valley, Perlot's small band lost their way in the foothills of the Sierra. They encountered an odd pile of dirt, like an overgrown molehill, then another, then a dozen, then a score. "These hillocks became so numerous to the right and left that the trail almost resembled the path in a cemetery; only the tombs and the crosses were lacking." Each man asked himself the meaning of these strange excavations, when all at once the answer became gruesomely clear. "We saw a piece of clothing hanging out from one of these graves; we approached and saw that some animal, in digging, had exposed the leg of a corpse buried fully clothed. Instinctively, we pushed the earth back with our feet, having no other instrument, and covered this half-devoured leg." Perlot later learned that the dead, who numbered three or four hundred, had starved the previous winter after heavy rains had prevented provisions from reaching the Mariposa mines and the miners had waited too long before coming out. That they were buried, if only after a fashion, owed at least partly to a plea Perlot discovered nailed to the trunk of an oak. "It was written in longhand, in English, in French, and in Spanish. It begged the passersby, whether they were arriving at the placers or returning to the coast, to be so good as to bury the dead they might encounter on their way. 'God has willed,' it said, 'that civilization should begin, in this place, with this duty which a man owes to his kind, to his brother, in order that he may never forget it. Every man believing in a God knows that to bury the dead is a duty. I entreat you to fulfill it, you who are civilized.' "

After further struggle, Perlot and his friends reached the Mariposa. They were exhausted, hungry, and destitute. They wished to gather gold but lacked the money to purchase pans and shovels. Having left France with the dream of becoming independently wealthy, they found themselves reduced to wage labor. "We were mercenaries," Perlot lamented. "We no longer belonged to ourselves."

Instead they belonged to a trio named McDonald, Thomson, and Dick, who—without asking leave of Frémont—were setting up a long-tom. The group's first task was excavating a ditch to the device. The labor was backbreaking. "Two workers threw out the dirt, one to the right, the other to the left; the two others, placed in the middle, threw it from the other side of the trench which was only four feet wide; when a stone or a rock was too big, it was rolled to one side or else was allowed to fall into the trench." After two days the excavation was finished and the washing began. Shovelful by shovelful, Perlot and his companions threw the dirt they had excavated into the long-tom, where the diverted water coursed over it. Their bosses collected the gold that caught in the bottom, and on Saturday evening, at the end of a backbreaking week, Perlot and the others received their pay: for each man, a little more than half an ounce of gold for each day worked.

LABORING FOR WAGES wasn't what Perlot had intended, but it kept body and soul together. Not every argonaut was so lucky. Hugh

Heiskell, after conquering the Great Plains, the Rocky Mountains, the Humboldt River, the Carson Desert, and the Sierra Nevada, died at the very entrance to the goldfields. Doubtless the fatigue and unbalanced diet of the overland journey had lowered his resistance to disease; certainly the unsanitary conditions at Weaverville, the first gold camp many of the emigrants encountered, and the place where Heiskell and his Tennessee company decided to winter, were the source of the infection that claimed him. Cholera was the likely culprit, although the single account of Heiskell's death—a letter written by his cousin Tyler, who had gone for supplies to Sacramento, the town that was gathering beside Sutter's Fort—prevents a positive identification of the cause of death. "I did not see him during his illness, nor did I know but what he was well till I got back from Sacramento," Tyler explained to Hugh's parents. "The distance is 60 miles, and the means of communication in no regular way, and any message or note seldom reaches its destination. He had the medical attention of Dr. White, whom I consider inferior to no other, but availed not to saving his life. The attention of a good nurse was wanting to some extent, though his friends who were with him did all they could—most of them being sick."

Tyler assured Hugh's parents that their son had met his end bravely. "He was conscious that his time had come for him 'to depart hence and be no more on earth forever,' and remarked but a short time before he expired, 'Doc, I will die.' " (Obviously Tyler had this from White.) "Though it is the severest affliction in human life, 'tis a consolation to Christian parents to know and be assured that an affectionate son, though dead and far from his home and friends, was prepared to meet the dreaded hour."

FATE IS OFTEN ARBITRARY, but Heiskell's death epitomized the unusual arbitrariness of life in Gold Rush California. A man could surmount every challenge of the two-thousand-mile trail and still be felled at the mouth of the mines. All he had to show for his courage and perseverance was a stone over his grave; all his loved ones had, if they were lucky, was a letter recounting his final moments.

Heiskell's death also revealed the abysmal living conditions in the mining camps. Like Heiskell, most of the overlanders went more or less straight to the mines from the trail, and so the mining camps—as the towns that sprang up around the placers were called—represented their first encounter with community life in California. But this was community life of a kind none had experienced in the East. The populations of the camps were less transient than that of San Francisco—these, after all, were destinations, not a way station—but they were unsettled just the same. The frenzy to be digging was even more compelling than in San Francisco, for before the argonauts' very eyes the best placers were being snatched up. To waste a moment for such mundane chores as washing clothes, building latrines, or even cooking decent meals was to jeopardize all they had struggled so hard to accomplish. Tomorrow we bathe; today we dig.

The result was predictable: regular outbreaks of disease, made worse by the weariness and reduced resistance of those who had been so long under strain. Cholera was familiar, but no less deadly for its familiarity. Scurvy and other diet-deficiency diseases became common. And when the miners got sick, they could hardly count on medical attention. Hugh Heiskell was fortunate to have a physician look after him, even if Dr. White's ministrations failed to prevent his death. Doctors willing to be doctors were as hard to find in the mining camps as chambermaids at the coast; like nearly everyone else who had come west, they wanted to look for gold. When they did deign to see patients, their services were very expensive. "Physicians are all making fortunes in this country," one miner moaned. "They will hardly look at a man's tongue for less than an ounce of gold! I have known doctors, although they are scarcly worthy of the title (for most of them here are quacks), charge a patient as much as $100 for one visit and prescription."

The high price of services was mirrored by the high price of goods. One of the most salient aspects of mining camp life, and the one that provoked the most consistent complaints from the miners, was the exorbitant cost of food and other essentials of life. Tom Archer, reflecting on his experiences in a camp near the Mariposa, explained, "The price of provisions had become so high that our paltry earnings were not nearly sufficient to pay for the food we required to keep us alive. Flour was $1 a lb., pork the same, Chilian jerky (dried beef) half a dollar to 75 cents, tea $5, coffee $3, frijoles (dried beans) about half a dollar, and everything else in the same proportion." Archer and a partner worked for three months, spent every dollar they made in the diggings on bare necessities, and still found themselves $500 in debt. (Camp merchants didn't usually operate on credit, but the one Archer patronized knew his brother and felt obliged to give Tom a hand.)

The high prices in the camps reflected the high cost of transporting goods there; they also reflected the ability of merchants to exploit the shortages created by the huge influx of customers. Vicente Pérez Rosales, traveling via New Helvetia en route to the mines, noted the success of the man who got the rush going. Near the fort, Pérez explained, was "a large store with a huge sign that read 'Brannan and Company.' " The proprietor was "the possessor of one of the securest fortunes in California at that period," for he had what everyone needed, and charged what the traffic would bear. "The store, situated right on the road to the placers, was admirably supplied with all that could be desired for the tasks incidental to mining. I say nothing about prices, since they gave the retailer only the infinitesimal profit of five hundred or a thousand per cent or so." (Brannan's success naturally elicited envy in those required to pay the prices he demanded. Pérez couldn't resist relating the conventional wisdom about Brannan's flagging Mormonism: "It seems that he had no sooner won his wealth than he discarded his religion without replacing it by another, although gossip had it that in order to hush his conscience he frequently said prayers to Saint Polygamy.")

The high prices aggravated the health problems of the miners, who might have eaten something besides beans and bacon, salt pork and jerky, biscuits and hardtack had the prices been lower. The miners' health was further eroded by the lack of adequate shelter. At least until the first winter, miners typically camped in canvas tents or brush lean-tos. (Pérez Rosales and his Chilean partners slung serapes over branches.) Although such accommodations sufficed, more or less, during the dry season, the autumn rains invariably caught many miners out. Before they could arrange something more substantial, they got cold and wet and often sick. Their indoor options were sharply circumscribed by what they could afford, which often was nothing better than a spot on the floor of one of the hotels that sprang up in each camp.

Yet camp life wasn't without its pleasures. Foremost, of course, was the thrill of a rich strike. Every miner heard of fellows finding placers that paid fabulously—the pair on Weber Creek who collected $17,000 in dust and nuggets in seven days; the six miners (working with fifty Indians) who gathered 273 *pounds* of gold on the Feather River; the Irishman who took $26,000 out of Sullivan Bar. It was in the nature of such stories that they almost always happened last month or over the next ridge, but they remained sufficiently credible as to keep the miners at their labors, and to keep them hoping that such good fortune might befall them.

Gambling of other sorts took place in the camps on a more institutionalized basis. Saloons appeared as quickly as the miners, and despite the high cost of living, miners could always find a dollar or two, or ten or a hundred, for booze and cards. Monte and faro were the indoor games of choice, but miners would wager on just about anything: horse races, cockfights, dogfights, bear fights, bear-and-bull fights. Humans fought frequently in the camps, especially after an evening in the saloons; occasionally they wrestled and boxed for the entertainment of paying—and betting—customers. In time, most of the diversions and vices of the outside world found their way to the camps: vaudeville, stage plays, concerts, opera, prostitution. Pretty nearly whatever a man wanted, and could pay for, he could get.

WHAT WOMEN WANTED, and could get, was another matter. Especially in the early days of the Gold Rush, there weren't enough women in the mining camps to have much effect on life there. Those who did find themselves in the camps, like Sarah Royce, had to struggle to create a space in an overwhelmingly male world.

Sarah settled at Weaverville about the same time Hugh Heiskell did. Josiah briefly attempted mining, but amid the crowd in the diggings he had little luck. He decided instead to try his hand as a merchant, having had some experience in the retail trade back east. Taking the last of his and

Sarah's money from the overland journey, he headed down to Sam Brannan's store to purchase supplies.

In his absence Sarah began to establish a home. Her standards—at least at first—were higher than those of her neighbors. Instead of a tent or lean-to, she wanted a house, with walls and doors. Instead of dinner cooked over a fire and eaten on stumps, she wanted a kitchen with table and chairs. Sketching out her design, she sought to engage some men to build it. But no one would work for her. "All were so absorbed in washing out gold, or hunting for some to wash, that they could not think of doing anything else," she wrote. She had to settle for a large tent, divided into two rooms: the rear one for living, the front one for the store Josiah opened with a few partners on his return from Sacramento.

Sarah spent her days in the store, with Mary underfoot or venturing cautiously outside. The experience put Sarah into contact with the full diversity of mining camp life. Several of her neighbor-customers were men of intelligence and education. One was a doctor, another a lawyer, another a scientist. There were merchants, mechanics, farmers, teachers. Each had come to test his luck at mining, driven by a dream of a better life than he could find at home. Often they were touched by the sight of Sarah and Mary, and stole moments on their way to and from the diggings just to watch. "Excuse me, madam," said one, passing the Royce tent one day. "May I speak to the little girl? We see so few ladies and children in California, and she is about the size of a little sister I left at home."

With such folk as these, Sarah might have come into contact back east. "But, mingled with these better sort of men who formed the majority, were others of a different class," she explained.

> Roughly-reared frontier men, almost as ignorant of civilized life as savages. Reckless bravados, carrying their characters in their faces and demeanor, even when under the restraints imposed by policy. All these and more were represented in the crowd who used to come for their meat and other provisions in the early morning hours. There were even some Indians, who were washing out gold in the neighboring ravines, and who used to come with the others

> to buy provisions. It was a motley assembly, and they kept two or three of us very busy; for payments were made almost exclusively in gold-dust, and it took longer to weigh that than it would have done to receive coin and give change. But coin was very rare in the mines at that time, so we had our little gold scales and weights, and I soon became quite expert in handling them.

Sarah avoided the rougher aspects of camp life whenever possible. She eschewed liquor and gambling. But she couldn't keep entirely clear of the rowdiness. Like many camps, Weaverville was situated on two sides of a canyon. On the slope opposite the Royce residence was a saloon. At night the revelers regularly interrupted her and Josiah's slumber, but one evening in particular stuck in her memory. "That was past midnight, one rainy, dark night, when we were startled from sleep by a loud shout, followed by various outcries, several running footsteps, and three or four pistol shots." She and Josiah peered through the dimness to discern the cause of the shooting, but buildings and trees blocked the view. "The next morning we were told by one who had inquired, that a gambler who had lost several times, and saw himself about to lose again, had snatched all the money from the table by a sudden movement, and fled out into the darkness before any one had been aware of his intentions. Then, two or three had followed with shots; but he had escaped them."

In some cases the boisterousness reflected nothing more than the need of men, mostly young, who spent long days at hard labor, to blow off steam. In other cases, however, it appeared—to Sarah, at any rate—to indicate an undercurrent of discontent and sadness that ran through the camp.

> Discontent: for most of them had come to California with the hope of becoming easily and rapidly rich, and so, when they had to toil for days before finding gold, and, when they had found it, had to work hard in order to wash out their "ounce a day," and then discovered that the necessaries of life were so scarce it took much of their proceeds to pay their way, they murmured, and some of them cursed the country, calling it a "God forsaken land," while

> a larger number bitterly condemned their own folly in having left comfortable homes and moderate business chances, for so many hardships and uncertainties.

> The sadness had a different tone.

> The sounds of sadness were deeper and more distressing than those of mere discontent, for they were caused by sickness and death. Many ended their journey across the plains utterly prostrated by over-exertion, and too often poisoned by unwholesome food and want of cleanliness.

Some of Sarah's neighbors, a crew from Missouri, had traversed the continent without once removing their clothes, not even their boots, and subsisting the whole time on salt meat and hardtack. "Of course disease claimed them as natural prey." One died soon after arrival; the rest fell critically ill.

So did others more fastidious (including Hugh Heiskell, although Sarah seems not to have known him by name). Josiah contracted cholera upon his return from Sacramento. Sarah herself came down with the disease several days later. But through good luck, and perhaps because their strength had revived somewhat since reaching Weaverville, both survived.

TOM ARCHER FOUND life in California to be almost as arbitrary as Hugh Heiskell did, although in Archer's case it was his friend Ned Hawkins who paid the ultimate price. Archer and Hawkins might have been excused for thinking all of Australia had come to California. Their ship had hardly anchored in the cove of San Francisco when a boat from a vessel out of Hobart dropped by to wish g'day. After conversing with Archer for some time, one of the Hobarters asked him his name. Upon being told, this fellow declared that he had been thinking that Archer looked familiar: Archer's very brother was the captain of the Hobart ship. "I soon found myself on board the *Harriet Nathan* of Hobart Town," Archer afterward told his children, "shaking hands with her captain, your Uncle John, whose surprise at seeing me was, as may be imagined, very great." Ned Hawkins ran into a brother-in-law, a man named Bertelsen who, though a nautical novice, had recently been promoted to first mate of another Australian craft when the entire regular crew abandoned ship for the mines.

Maybe it was all the familiar faces and accents, or perhaps it was that the land they came from was as rough and raw, in its own way, as California, but most of the Australians had few complaints about the lack of civic life and amenities in San Francisco. As Tom Archer wandered the city, he concluded that San Francisco's shortcomings simply gave scope to what he called "the true and very enviable Yankee philosophy" that characterized the American approach to adversity. Archer was walking about one day, after some heavy rain.

> I saw a mule wagon sunk beyond its axle in one of the streets, and remarked to an American standing by that the streets seemed rather soft. "Reckon you're right," was the answer, "but they ain't so bad here as at the other side of town, where I was walking along and saw a hat lying in the middle of the street, went and picked it up, and there was a man's head below it. 'Waal,' says I to him, 'How in tarnation did you get there?' 'Oh, that ain't nothin',' says he. 'I've got a mule under me.' " This was told with the utmost gravity, and the man moved on without further explanation as to the fate of the hat, the mule, or the rider.

Archer and Hawkins had reached California financially sound, and, having learned that the most convenient route to Sacramento and the northern mines was the Sacramento River, they purchased a ship's longboat (these sold cheap, with so many ships abandoned). They piled their provisions aboard and headed northeast across San Francisco Bay, accompanied by a man named Mackenzie, another named Hicks, the two Chinese and the two aborigine boys Hawkins had brought over from Australia, and the two aborigines who came with Archer.

Between the provisions and the ten persons, the boat rode low in the water. But the breeze was fair, filling the boat's small sail, and they made the crossing of the northern arm of San Francisco Bay to the Strait of Benicia in fine shape. They landed at the town of Benicia, whose promoters proclaimed that it would supplant San Francisco as the hub of the region. So far it hadn't, and the Australians spent no more time there than they required to purchase a few additional supplies. They sailed and rowed east across Suisun Bay toward the mouth of the Sacramento. But night fell and the tide ebbed while they were still several miles from the river, and they decided to drop anchor till dawn. All bundled themselves against the cold wind, shut their ears to the honking of the waterfowl that made the Sacramento delta their home, and tried to sleep.

They were shocked awake when they felt the boat listing sharply and the bay water rushing in. The anchor had got stuck in the mud of the bay floor as the tide changed, and the flood tipped them over. All were tumbled into the watery blackness—freezing, disoriented, and uncertain where the nearest land lay, or how far. Mackenzie managed to clamber atop the capsized boat, as did one of Hawkins's aborigine boys and both of Archer's. Hicks was nowhere to be seen, which wasn't surprising in that he was a known nonswimmer. But Hawkins, a strong swimmer, was missing, too. Archer could also swim, and made it onto the boat's bottom. (The two Chinese apparently had debarked at Benicia.)

Look and call as they might, the survivors found no trace of Hawkins, Hicks, or the missing boy. Archer hardly knew Hicks or the aborigine boy, but the loss of Hawkins, his companion from the outback, hit him with tragic force. And it was all the more tragic for the mystery it entailed. "I have never been able to understand his having disappeared without attempting to reach us, or making any reply to our calls. But so it was, and thus ended the life of one of the most manly, most generous, and most kindhearted friends I ever had."

Soaking wet, splashed by wave and cut by winter wind, the survivors faced imminent death by exposure. Fortunately, the night was nearly spent; at first light Archer and Mackenzie determined that they must swim for land. "Telling the black-boys, who could all swim, to follow us, we struck out for the shore, agreeing to keep low down in the water, and swim very slowly, so as to save our strength as long as possible. The friction of the water, and the shelter it gave us from the icy, bitter wind, and the exercise of swimming, restored our circulation to some extent, and we had progressed three or four hundred yards when it occurred to me that, though not very tired, I might as well put my feet down and try for the bottom. I did so, and to my amazement and joy, found that I could touch it with my toes and still keep my chin above water." Mackenzie, shorter than Archer, had to swim farther, but soon he too could stand up. The pair then looked back for the boys, only to discover that they had disappeared. Archer and Mackenzie shouted and scanned the surface of the water, but saw nothing. (As Archer learned later, the boys, despairing of reaching shore, had swum back to the boat to await rescue. Two of them hung on there till a passing craft found them. The third, frozen and exhausted, was washed overboard by the waves and drowned.)

All that Archer owned was lost in the boat, even the clothes on his back, jettisoned before the swim to shore. Making his way to Benicia, he begged two suits of clothing from a merciful merchant, one for himself and one for Mackenzie. The two decided Sacramento wasn't the place for them—a decision fate seemed already to have made—and they determined on Stockton instead. A man with a whaleboat was going that direction; in exchange for their labor rowing he let them come along.

Stockton had pretensions but little substance. The streets were quagmires, the buildings flimsy and miserable. Yet it offered work to willing hands, and Archer and Mackenzie took up the building trade. For a half ounce of gold per day they hammered and sawed, and saved. They also observed. One day they encountered a group of about fifty Chinese marching, or rather jogging, into the town from the west. Each one carried a pole over his shoulder; from the poles hung what appeared to be their entire possessions. Inquiring, Archer learned that they had been expelled from the diggings by whites who "jumped" their claims. "This, I thought at the time, was somewhat odd in a 'free country,' but I got more used to such things by and by."

Archer and Mackenzie eventually gathered the wherewithal to purchase a minimal kit of mining tools. They ascended the Stanislaus River to a region crowded with miners. For two weeks they panned here and there, with no success. All the good stretches of streambed had been taken; what was left hardly repaid the effort. Their resources were dwindling, and their future once more looked grim. But then the clouds parted.

> One morning a report spread abroad that payable gold had been found in a small gulch which came down from a hill close behind our tent, and after breaking through a low rocky plateau, disappeared in a sandy flat which skirted the Stanislaus River. A rush at once set in, scores of people appeared from all quarters, and in a few hours the whole upper part of the gulch was claimed and marked off, before we "new chums" were aware of what was going on.
>
> It occurred to me, however, that although the gulch was now dry, it must be a perfect torrent during the heavy rains and the melting of the mountain snows, and I could not see why the gold should not have been washed down through the rocky gorge, and deposited in the sandy flat below. We therefore marked out a claim just below the gorge, and dozens of others followed our example.
>
> We then set to work and dug down about three feet, to the bed rock, without discovering a speck of gold. Nothing daunted, however, we continued for days working on, encouraged by the success of some few of our fellow diggers around us, when—joy of joys!—after our claim was more than half worked out, we came upon a lead [pronounced *leed*, a vein] of the most beautiful, "nuggety" gold, extending in patches from the roots of the grass down to the bed rock, and varying in size from dust and pinhead specks up to quarter-ounce nuggets.

ARCHER'S INSIGHT WAS characteristic of the empirical science practiced in the goldfields. The first miners correctly inferred that the gold found its way to the stream bottoms by the erosive action of water, and the first digging was done along current watercourses. Subsequent arrivals, including those forced to look elsewhere after all the good beaches and bars were taken, reckoned that where rivers had formerly flowed, gold might remain. These dry streambeds, of ancient or recent vintage, attracted the second set of miners, men like Tom Archer. The digging they required was typically difficult and extensive, as the overburden of nonpaying dirt had to be removed before the pay dirt was struck.

Sometimes the pay dirt was very rich, as in Archer's case. Sometimes it was less so. Jean-Nicolas Perlot eventually managed to amass enough capital to prospect for himself. But getting started required deciding where to dig. "I saw many places, but I was always faced by the same difficulty: How to distinguish the good from the bad? And in a good claim, how to know where the rich vein is? How, under six or ten feet of earth, to foresee where to find the most auriferous dirt, the *balux*?" With other miners, Perlot carefully observed those who seemed to be doing well. In the case of the Mariposa, the best miners were the Sonorans, of whom three worked nearby. "They were miners in their own country; they should know the secrets of the craft; they had not established themselves by chance on the claim they were occupying. They had examined the rock at each turn of the river, had sounded it, had consulted among themselves; then by way of conclusion had started to dig a pit on the flat, at the foot of the hillside, and fairly far from the riverbed. They had come to a good conclusion, it seemed, for they were finding gold." How did they know what they knew? Perlot tried to ask them. But his Spanish was no better than their French. "Whether they did not understand me or did not want to understand me, I could draw nothing from them." He returned to his observations.

After a time he and a partner named Bérenger—the last of La Fortune—attempted to employ what Perlot had learned. Perlot proposed digging a test hole "at the bottom of a big flat where I thought I had observed that the river, in times past, must have deposited the same alluvium as where the three Mexicans were working; there was, in fact, the same lay of the land." Bérenger agreed that this was a sound plan. They began digging the test hole. To their chagrin, fellow miners and passersby, including some former partners, laughed at their efforts and derided their choice of claim. "However, we continued to dig without paying attention to these remarks and, at the depth of six feet, we observed that the gravel contained gold." Two feet farther down they hit bedrock.

They tested the gravel. The first pan yielded a quarter ounce. "What a windfall!" Their fortune seemed to be made. "We washed what we had extracted from the gold bed, counting on a marvelous result."

Alas, reality was otherwise. Additional assays showed the ore to be only modestly endowed with the tantalizing yellow metal. "Farewell to our dream of a speedy fortune!" For three days Perlot and Bérenger dug a ditch connecting their test hole to the river; for four days they washed the gold-bearing gravel their ditch uncovered. They continued in this way: three days of ditching, four days of washing. Six weeks exhausted the claim—not to mention the claimants—and yielded the equivalent of somewhat less than a half ounce of gold per man per day. As they had earned more than this as wage-workers, they had reason to be disappointed. To make matters worse, by the time they finished, the area on all sides of them had been taken up. They were forced to move on, and start over again.

DITCHING WAS THE ANSWER when pay dirt was covered by the detritus of old streams, but when present streams covered the golden sands, the solution was damming. William Swain, after entering the Sacramento Valley from the north, and late, not unnaturally decided to try his hand in the northern mining region. In mid-November a man couldn't expect to do any serious mining before spring, so Swain and a small remnant of the Wolverine Rangers filled their days planning for when the rainfall diminished. Local experts, unobtrusively cultivated, guided them to a promising location. "We judged the South Fork of the Feather River to be the most likely to yield a pile another summer," Swain wrote home, "for the following reasons: the main part of the Feather River and all the southern rivers have been overrun and consequently the best and richest placers found and worked. The South Fork of the Feather River was reported to be rich, and the gold on it coarse and not much worked. There is good timber for building (not the case on many of the streams of California), which with us is an important consideration as we believed our health next summer depended upon having dry, warm, and comfortable habitation during the rainy season."

This last point had been underscored for Swain by the recent death from disease of two of the Rangers, and he took no little pride in the dwelling he and his companions constructed, and the life they led therein.

> Our house is a log cabin, sixteen by twenty feet. It is covered with boughs of cedar and is made of nut pine logs from one to two feet in diameter, so that it is quite a blockhouse. It has a good door made of cedar boards hewn out of cedar logs, but no window. [Glass was a luxury beyond reach at this stage of Swain's finances and California's development.] It faces the south and is on the north side of the river. In the east end is a family fireplace, in which large logs are burning night and day. At the west end is a bedstead framed into the logs of the cabin and running from side to side. The cords of the bedstead are strips of rawhide, crossing at every three inches, thus forming a bottom tight enough to hold large armfuls of dry breaks gathered from the sides of the mountains, which make a substitute for feather beds. On these are blankets and buffalo skins. Altogether it makes a comfortable bed. Moore has a bunk in one of the other corners.
>
> Over the fireplace are our rifles, which are ever ready, cocked and primed, and frequently yield us good venison. In the other corner may be seen our cupboard with its contents, which consist of a few wooden and tin dishes, bottles, knives and forks and spoons, tin frying pan, boiler, and coffee pot.
>
> Around the sides of the cabin at various points are the few articles of clothing belonging to the different members of the company. Under the bed are five cakes of tallow, under the bunk are three or four large bags of flour. Along the point of the roof is a line of dried beef and sixty or seventy pounds of suet. And out at the corner of the house in a trough made of pine may be found salt beef in the pickle, in abundance.
>
> At ten in the evening you might see in this cabin, while

> everything is still, a fire blazing up from the mass of fuel in the large fireplace, myself and Hutchinson on one end of the bedstead, Lt. Cannon on the other, Mr. Bailey stretched before the fire in his blankets on the ground floor, and Moore in his bunk. On the roof the incessant rain keeps up its perpetual patter, while the foaming stream howls out a requiem of the rushing torrent as it dashes on its way to the valley.

It was this rushing stream that Swain and the others planned to tackle when the rains let up. The logic of placer mining dictated digging at the lowest point of any streambed, where gravity concentrated the gold. Unfortunately, in the case of a currently active stream, this lowest point was almost always underwater. Yet if a person could build a dam and divert the flow, the streambed would be laid open to mining.

In practice, nearly all dams were beyond the capacity of single individuals. California mining quickly evolved from an occupation that could be undertaken by individuals (the washpan stage) to one that required two or three persons (the ditching and long-tom stage) to one that required teams of several individuals (the damming stage). Nor was cooperation the only new requirement. Capital was also needed. A miner with a washpan—and decent luck—might start making money his first day in the diggings, but building a dam required the ability to work for weeks or months before the gold started coming in. The high prices of provisions in the mining camps made this an expensive affair.

The high prices drove Swain and his partners out of their cabin and into the icy river even before the winter rains ceased. For weeks in January and early February 1850 they piled rocks for their dam and excavated a diversionary race for the overflow. Eventually they accomplished their preliminary goal. "Our dam is finished," he wrote on February 17, "and the river, which is high and will probably be so for some months, is running through our race leaving its old channel bare." At this point—after all this effort and expense—Swain found himself where Jean-Nicolas Perlot had been before digging his first test hole. "We have to remove some three feet of gravel and stone before we find the foundation rock where the gold always lies," Swain observed. Actually, Swain was worse off than Perlot, for the dams were never watertight. "On account of the water which leaches from the race to the channel, we have not been able to test it." But they hoped to do so shortly.

The weather refused to cooperate. The rains lasted longer that winter than usual, preventing Swain and the others from discovering whether they were rich or ruined. "Four weeks ago we thought the rain over, but March has been the worst month of the season," he wrote on March 17. "The waters are up, and our prospects for mining soon are dark, at least for two months to come." The larder drew lower, and their wallets emptier, with each passing day.

They decided they couldn't wait two months. Splashing through the high, bone-numbing water, they retrieved sufficient samples for an assay. The results were disappointing. On April 15, Swain recorded, "We finished our job on the Feather River and tested it, although under great disadvantages. I am satisfied it will *not pay* to work it out." They had moved a river and many tons of rock, only to discover that the yield was too poor to bother with.

Perhaps it was his youth, perhaps a congenital optimism, but Swain refused to lose heart. "The job cost us a great deal and much hard work. Many a one has acquired a large fortune with half the exertion we have made, but we are not discouraged; on the contrary, we are confident of success." Still, he couldn't help admitting that it was "rather provoking to be disappointed in high hopes."

8

A Millennium in a Day

River mining—as the method that involved ditching, damming, and other manipulation of stream flows was called—became more elaborate with each passing season. The dams grew longer and higher and more specialized. Sometimes they diverted the river entirely, baring the bed from bank to bank; sometimes they shunted the flow to one side, baring half the bed at a time. Pumps were installed, powered by the diverted current to remove the water that invariably seeped through the rock-and-earthen dams.

In many places, flumes complemented or replaced the diversionary ditches. Constructed of boards nailed together in U-shaped cross section, a flume received the water turned aside by a dam, carried it downstream parallel to the riverbed, and returned it to the channel below the claim of the company that built it—often dumping it right where the next set of claimants was building its own dam. Great effort and much duplication of expense went into the construction of the multiple systems. Magazine publisher James Hutchings calculated the cost of the ten dams along one stretch of the Feather River at $80,000, and noted that this amount bought insubstantial waterworks that lasted only a single season before being swept away in the following spring's high water. "Should that sum be used," Hutchings suggested, "to construct one permanent dam that should last not only for one, but for many seasons—besides the advantages it would offer to other claim owners by not backing the water upon them, as now—it would be a piece of economy that must commend itself to the thoughtful consideration of all persons interested in river mining."

As the miners grew adept at building flumes, they realized that in addition to carrying water away from places where it wasn't wanted, the wooden aqueducts might be employed to deliver water to places where it *was* wanted. This idea was no more than an extension of the principle behind the ditch Jean-Nicolas Perlot dug to wash his claim on the Mariposa, but it was an extension that opened up whole new areas to mining. In due course flumes five, ten, twenty miles long snaked beside canyon walls and crisscrossed gorges on trestles, carrying water intended to mitigate the miners' ultimately unquenchable thirst for gold. A Yuba County flume fairly flew across one canyon, reaching a height of two hundred feet above the ground and resting on the tops of tall trees along the way.

As the flumes freed the miners from proximity to rivers—and as the placer deposits on those rivers dwindled—the gold-hunters discovered that entire ridges and hillsides consisted of gravels laid down by ancient streams, long since diverted by natural forces. Digging revealed that those gravels contained gold-bearing placers, and that—just as with the contemporary placers—the ancient placers were richest where the gravels touched bedrock. But where bedrock for the contemporary placers might be six inches or six feet below ground level, the ancient bedrock might be sixty feet or six hundred feet below ground.

Reaching the ancient placers required removing the gravel that entombed them. Some miners resorted to the straightforward expedient of shovels. They dug "coyote holes" down to pay dirt, which they hoisted to the surface and washed by regular methods. But any large-scale exploitation of the ancient placers required a new method—a method capable of moving mountains as none but geological forces had moved them till now.

Hydraulic mining—as the new method was called—entailed magnifying and focusing the erosive power of water. The germ of the idea came to a Frenchman named Chabot, who employed a piece of hose some forty feet long to direct a stream of water from behind his dam to the bottom of his diggings. The water from the hose washed away worthless overburden and allowed access to the richer material below.

Chabot's idea inspired Edward Matteson (sometimes spelled Matterson) to improve it the following season. Perhaps Matteson remembered fire hoses he had seen back home in Connecticut, for his innovation was to add a nozzle, much like the nozzle of a fire hose. This concentrated the energy of the water and allowed Matteson to aim the concentrated stream where he wished. To his delight he discovered that the blast of water tore into the earth, removing in minutes what would have taken days or weeks to dispose of with pick and shovel. Matteson's neighbors appreciated the superiority of his technique and adopted it themselves.

Further improvements followed. Where a fall of several feet produced an impressive force, a fall of hundreds of feet produced an astonishing force. And the force was the more astonishing when the hoses exploded in the hands of their operators. Reinforcement—coils of rope, hoops of iron—remedied the situation. Iron pipe, although expensive and initially prone to splitting, permitted even greater pressures, and still more amazing results. Nozzles were replaced by "monitors": swivel-mounted cannons that allowed the "hydraulickers" to bombard hillsides with barrages of water, creating flash floods that carried away eons of earth, sand, and gravel.

Supplying the artillery with ammunition was no small chore. The pressure at the nozzle was directly proportional to the "head" of water: the vertical distance from the nozzle to the reservoir that supplied it. A dam had to be built upstream and pipes laid to the claim. In steep country a single partnership might control enough land to keep the waterworks in-house, but more commonly the hydraulickers purchased water rights from others. The rights were often sold by the day; as a result, once the spigots were opened, the hoses generally roared from morning's first light to evening's last, and frequently by moonlight.

Reducing a hillside to rubble was straightforward, if violent; but capturing the gold the rubble contained required greater subtlety. Because the techniques employed in the placers would have been overwhelmed by the sheer volume of material brought down by the water cannons, new techniques of capture were needed. "Sluices" were scaled-up versions of the long-tom, and in fact had been introduced in the placers before being adopted and expanded further by the hydraulickers. A sluice box looked much like a flume, except that its bottom was perforated, split, riffled, cleated, or otherwise roughened to catch the heavy gold while letting the light sand and gravel wash by. In a hydraulic operation, sluice boxes might be arrayed in a continuous line several hundred feet long. In some operations, "ground sluicing" was employed. Here the sluice was simply a ground channel into which boulders had been strategically placed. As the slurry flowed through the channel, the gold lodged behind the boulders. From time to time—as with the long-toms and the sluice boxes—the flow of water was shut off and the gold collected.

Hydraulic operations were breathtaking in their capacity—and rapacity. A correspondent for a Sacramento paper visited a site before the novelty wore off.

> A claim at Iowa hill had been worked into the hill by the application of hydraulic power, until it was *one hundred and twenty feet from the top of the hill to the bedrock in the claim.* With a perpendicular column of water 120 feet high, in a strong hose, of which they work two, ten men who own the claim are enabled to run off hundreds of tons of dirt daily. So great is the force employed that two men with the pipes, by directing streams of water against the base of the high bank, will cut it away to such an extent as to cause immense slides of earth, which often bring with them large trees and heavy boulders. . . . After these immense masses of earth are undermined and brought down by the streams forced from the pipes, those same streams are turned upon the tons of fallen earth, and it melts away before them, and is carried through the sluices with almost as much rapidity as if it were a bank of snow. No such labor-saving power has ever been introduced to assist the miner in his operations.

Hydraulic mining certainly saved labor. A government report compared the various methods of gathering gold: "The man with the rocker might wash one cubic yard of earth in a day; with the tom he might average two yards; with the sluice four yards; and with the hydraulic and sluice together fifty or even a hundred yards." An engineering estimate reckoned the savings slightly differently. Assuming wages in the goldfields averaged $4 per day (this was by now a fair estimate), the cost of processing a cubic yard of soil with a washpan was $20; with a rocker, $5; with a long tom, $1; with hydraulic methods, 20 cents.

But the savings in labor came at the cost of capital. The waterworks that supported hydraulic mining were very expensive, and the expense exerted its own form of tyranny. Interest rates in California were outrageous by American standards of the period, reaching 10 percent per month. Moreover, with water rights running up to $75 per day, time truly *was* money, and every day that could be saved might mean the difference between profit and loss. As a result, in some cases even the enormous wrecking power of the hydraulic cannons was deemed insufficient. Where the soil refused to melt like snow—where the ancient gravels had congealed into a natural form of concrete—the miners added blasting powder to their kit. The miners—sappers now—burrowed into the hillside that was to be reduced, and laid depth charges to soften the hard-pack. A government report described the system in operation in Yuba County:

> The quantity of powder for the blast depends upon the depth of the bank and the surface area to be loosened. If the bank is 50 feet deep a tunnel four and a half feet high and two and a half wide may be run in 75 feet; a cross-drift 60 feet long is cut across the end at right angles, and another similar cross-drift of equal length 55 feet from the mouth of the tunnel. 300 kegs may be used in such a blast, all distributed along in the cross-drifts and in the tunnel beyond the first cross-drift. 20 kegs near the intersection are opened by taking out the heads; the others are left closed, with the certainty that they will all be opened by the explosion of the 20. From the intersection to within 10 feet of the

> mouth wooden troughs two inches wide and deep inside are laid, and a liberal supply of powder is poured in, leading to an open keg. The 10 feet next to the mouth are laid carefully with a fuse, and for that distance the tunnel is filled in with dirt. When the blast is fired a dull, heavy sound is heard, the earth rises slowly about 10 feet; it then settles down, leaving a dust behind it, and on examination an area about 120 feet square will be found all shattered.

The water-gunners then moved in, completing reduction of the ridge.

THE SPONSOR OF this mining report was the United States Treasury Department. The Treasury's interest in California mining was to determine how much gold was coming out of California, and how much might continue to come out; for if time was money in the goldfields, gold was money in the rest of country. The Treasury—the keeper of the nation's currency, the minter of its gold—needed to know what to expect. County by county, mine by mine, the report listed the money sunk into the mines and the gold extracted. It described the techniques of placer mining, river mining, and hydraulic mining; the size of sluices and the length of flumes; the number of men and quantity of powder at work tearing down the terrain, washing the dirt, and retrieving the gold. To eyewitness observations were added the opinions of practical and scientific authorities. The result was an impressive tome, an encyclopedia of California's current mineral wealth and a guide to its golden future.

In the section on the southern mines, the report included an account of the tract belonging to John Frémont.

> The Mariposa Estate, or Frémont Grant, as it is sometimes called, contains 44,380 acres, or about 70 square miles. It reaches 12 miles from east to west, and 12½ miles from north to south. Its greatest length, from northwest to southeast, is about 17 miles, and its average width nearly 5 miles.

From the first days of the Gold Rush, the report explained, the Mariposa had yielded large quantities of gold to placer and river miners. More recently the hydraulic miners had been at work.

But the striking characteristic of the Mariposa was the existence of veins of quartz mixed with gold, veins that came to the surface in several places about the tract. Such veins had drawn attention from the time the first prospectors stumbled upon them, for they appeared to be the source of all the placer deposits, the parent formation from which the ancient and modern gravel deposits derived their riches. The report described the richest part of the primary vein on Frémont's property:

> Near the mill the vein forks, one prong running westward in the line of the main lode, and the other running north of west. At a distance of 300 yards from the forks, the two prongs are not more than 60 yards apart. Each fork is about 3 feet thick. The rock is a white ribbon quartz; the walls are a black talcose slate. . . . East of the fork the gold is in fine particles, while west of the fork the gold is collected in rich pockets, which are separated from one another by large masses of very poor quartz. . . . One pocket paid $30,000, another $15,000, and numerous others sums varying from $100 to $1,000. The great richness of the vein is proved by the facts that the decomposed quartz at the surface was worked or washed for a distance of half a mile, the ravines immediately below the lode were famous for their richness, and drifts have been run a quarter of a mile underground. It is said before Frémont obtained possession, squatters took $200,000 from the mine.

On this last sentence hung a tale of which the report's authors knew but the outline. Frémont's troubles with pirate placermen like Jean-Nicolas Perlot were merely the beginning of a long fight for control of the Mariposa. Much of the fight involved the terms of the grant defining the tract. Frémont had acquired title from Governor Juan Alvarado, who had received from the Mexican government the right to select ten leagues from within a larger portion of the Sierra foothills. Alvarado had other matters more pressing, however (the war with the United States being one), and when Frémont bought the title, the selection remained unmade. In Alvarado's time, and at the time Frémont took title, all parties assumed that the value of the grant, like the value of most land in California, lay in the pasturage it contained. Accordingly, Frémont initially instructed his surveyors to select land along the Mariposa River, where cattle might obtain water in an arid landscape.

The discovery of gold complicated matters, and the transfer of sovereignty from Mexico to the United States complicated them more. In principle, the Treaty of Guadalupe Hidalgo committed the United States government to honor contracts concluded and titles obtained under Mexican rule; in practice, American administrators insisted on close scrutiny of all such transactions and documents. Frémont, not having registered with the Mexican government the precise boundaries of his grant, found his claim scrutinized with special care.

Then there was the question of whether ownership of land entailed ownership of the minerals on and under the land. In the Mexican conception, based as it was on grazing and ranching, land titles didn't normally convey mineral rights. Even if Frémont could defend his title under Mexican law, he might not win the gold. On the other hand, shortly after Marshall's gold strike and the transfer of authority from Mexico to the United States, the new American regime abolished Mexican practices as they applied to mineral rights. Whether this made Frémont's position better or worse wasn't immediately apparent. The one thing certain was that the Frémont claim was a legal mess.

Meanwhile the squatters helped themselves to Frémont's gold—or the gold he considered his. His Sonoran partners protected his interest while they remained, but their departure left him looking for new allies. In his hurry—Frémont was always in a hurry, but the thought of gold going off his property in other people's pockets made him move even faster than usual—he confounded things still more. He authorized an agent to sell leases in England to companies desiring to dig California gold. At the same time he gave power of attorney to his father-in-law, Senator Benton, who also sold leases. Unfortunately, the various leases overlapped, and the leaseholders sued one another and Frémont.

To add a final twist to the knot, Frémont, belatedly realizing that the value of the Mariposa property lay in gold rather than grass, changed his mind about where his boundaries should run. Redrawing the map, he included several of the most valuable deposits within the portion he claimed for himself.

Frémont's fight for the Mariposa would keep his lawyers busy for a decade, long after the best placers ran out. What gave the matter its staying power was the discovery of the veins of quartz and gold the government mining report described in such detail. Although the miners on the Mariposa didn't understand the geological history of these formations—how they were formed in the heat and pressure that accompanied the creation of the Sierra batholith—the miners recognized that the quartz veins were the source of the placer deposits downhill and downstream. And as they discovered the extent of the system of veins, which ran north along the Sierra front from the Mariposa to Coloma, they christened it the "Mother Lode."

The Mother Lode inspired awe in the gold-hunters. The mere thought of this huge body of ore lying beneath the foothills set the crustiest miner quivering. In some cases awe induces respect; in this case it elicited avarice, and the miners began to plot how to rip the gold from the womb of its mother.

QUARTZ MINING, as the techniques they devised were called, was more complicated than the other forms of mining. In placer mining, river mining, and hydraulic mining, nature had already separated the gold from the quartz; the miners needed only to effect the final sifting. In quartz mining, they had to do the separating themselves. The process involved several steps and required a working knowledge of physics and chemistry, not to mention geology and mechanical engineering.

Quartz mines varied from locale to locale, depending on the lay of the land and the veins beneath, and on the predilections of the miners. As part of his effort to educate the public about life in California, publisher James Hutchings sent a correspondent down a typical mine. The correspondent, noting that the principal vein at this mine entered the earth at an angle of more than forty degrees, explained that the workers had dug a vertical shaft from a point on the hillside well above the outcropping of the vein. The idea was to intersect the vein (alternatively called the lead or ledge) and attack it in two directions at once: back up toward the surface and down toward the nether regions. A horizontal tunnel was fitted with a miniature, miner-propelled railway for transporting the ore from the vein to the vertical shaft for hoisting to the surface.

With some trepidation—the hole was very dark, and appeared bottomless—the correspondent received permission to enter the miners' lair.

> We descended their shaft—but not before the workmen had offered and we had accepted the loan of an India-rubber suit of clothing—and on reaching the bottom of it we found a considerable stream of water running in the centre of the railway, constructed along the tunnel to the shaft. This water was removed by a pump in one corner of the shaft, working by steam power, both day and night.
>
> On we went, trying to keep a sure footing on the rail track, inasmuch as watertight boots even then became a very necessary accompaniment to the India-rubber clothing. Drip, drip, fell the water, not singly, but in clusters of drops and small streams. . . . The miners, who were removing the quartz from the ledge, looked more like half-drowned sea lions than men.
>
> We did not make ourselves inquisitive enough to ask the amount of wages they received, but we came to the conclusion that they must certainly earn whatever they obtained. Stooping, or rather half lying down upon the wet rock, among fragments of quartz and props of wood, and streams of water, with pick in hand, and by a dim but waterproof lantern, giving out a very dim and

> watery light, just about bright enough, or rather dim enough, and watery enough, as Milton expresses it, "to make darkness visible," a man was at work, picking down the rock—the gold-bearing rock—and which, although very rich, was very rotten, and consequently not only paid well, but was easily quarried, and easily crushed; and although this rock was paying not less than three hundred and fifty dollars a ton, we could not see the first speck of gold in it, after a diligent search for that purpose.

Although that $350 rock was very rich, there was some question as to how deep it went. The correspondent's guide invited him to see for himself.

> We had the satisfaction of descending the Osborne Hill lead, under the guidance of Mr. Crossett, and after bumping the head against the rocky roof above, and holding on by our feet to the wet and slippery floor of rock below, on which we were descending, at an angle of forty-two degrees; now clinging to the timbers at the side . . . now winding among props, and over cast-iron pump tubes, now making our way from one side of the inclined shaft to the other, to enable us to travel as easy as possible.
>
> On, on; down, down we go, until we hear the sound of muffled voices issuing from somewhere deep down amid the darkness, and uttering something very indistinct and hard to be understood; when again we cross over to and enter a side drift; where in the distance we see lights glimmering, in shadow and smoke, and hear the voices become more and more distinct, until my guide asks the question, "How does she look now, boys?"
>
> "All right—better, sir."

The *Hutchings'* correspondent inquires whether they have reached the bottom. By no means, the guide replies: they are only 160 feet below the surface. They descend farther, past 200 feet, to nearly 300. The correspondent inquires whether the quartz still pays off, this deep. "Yes," the guide says. "The deeper we get, the richer the quartz becomes."

The correspondent stops to ponder what drives men to such depths.

> Except from the lights in our hands all is dark, and as still almost as the tomb, with the exception of the distant creaking of a pump, and the steady dripping of some water at our elbow. Rock here, there, and everywhere. . . . Men have been picking and drilling and blasting through solid rock: by day and night, in winter and summer, led forward by the talismanic power of gold, or at least the hope to obtain it.

The guide says it's time to return to the surface. As they catch their breath after the long climb back up, they observe the loads of ore that have been pulled, bucket by windlass bucket, from the depths they've just visited. The ore is loaded into another set of railway carts and rolled to a nearby mill. There the chunks of ore are dumped on the ground, where men with sledges break them into pieces no larger than a human fist.

But this is not fine enough, for the quartz still clings jealously to the gold. Workers shovel the ore into the hopper of a several-armed stamping machine. Each arm consists of a massive, vertical wooden post, much taller than a man, mounted in a frame so that it can slide up and down freely. A cam connected to a rotating shaft, itself connected to a steam engine, raises each arm, then allows it to fall. The bottom of each arm is sheathed in cast iron; together with the wood, the iron gives the whole arm a weight of perhaps a thousand pounds. Beneath the iron of the arm is a cast-iron bedplate, upon which the ore tumbles from the hopper. As they rise and fall, the several arms together shake the earth and set the hillsides rumbling with their muffled thunder; the ore upon which their weight is brought to bear is ground to powder.

This powder is given a first washing to claim the gold knocked free so far. A sluice separates the gold from the quartz. The process is made more efficient by the application of quicksilver—mercury—to the sluice; gold has a greater affinity for quicksilver than for quartz, and readily forsakes the latter for the former. (This part of the process has been borrowed from the more sophisticated placer miners, who have learned to employ mercury in their own sluicing devices.)

To improve the efficiency still further, the powdered ore left over from the first step of crushing and separation is crushed a second time, by a second pulverizing device. This machine is the soul of simplicity and has been in use for centuries in Mexico. Called an *arrastra* (from *arrastrar*, "to drag"; also called "rastra" and other corruptions), it consists of a circular bed of stones over which is dragged—by mule-power—another stone. The powdered ore, mixed with water to form a paste, is ground exceedingly fine. (Other *arrastras* are powered by steam engines. A variant employing a wheel that rolls around the circular bed is called a "Chili mill"—after the country, Chile—of its origin.) For an average batch of ore weighing five hundred pounds, the grinding takes three to four hours.

The reporter describes the final part of this step of the operation.

> About three quarters of an hour before the whole is thoroughly ground, a sufficient quantity of quicksilver is added; but the amount is regulated by the richness of the quartz in the process of grinding. If, for instance, the five hundred pounds of tailings placed in the rastra is supposed to contain about three quarters of an ounce of gold, about one ounce of quicksilver is generally used—or about twenty-five per cent more of the latter than the former. Some judgment is required in this—too much quicksilver being a disadvantage, inasmuch as the amalgam [of the gold and quicksilver] should be kept hard to make it effectual in saving the gold.

Water is added to the mix to produce a slurry, which carries off the quartz, leaving the gold and quicksilver to sink to the bottom. More ore is added, and the process repeated. At intervals varying from a week to a month, the *arrastra* is entirely drained, and the gold and mercury retrieved. The amalgam of these two elements is heated in an enclosed furnace, or retort. The mercury vaporizes first, leaving the gold behind. A condensing column captures the mercury for reuse.

To the *Hutchings*' correspondent, quartz mining guarantees the future of California. The placers dwindle, but the veins that gave rise to the placers are inexhaustible. "As California is one vast network of quartz leads, a thousandth part of which have never even been prospected, and as the bottom of a single lead has not yet been found, it is not an uncertain venture to say that this department alone is capable of giving employment to several millions of people."

BUT WHAT KIND of employment? That was the question that confronted most miners sooner or later. As the scale of mining operations increased, the opportunities for individual miners diminished. The placer miner with a washbowl was the epitome of personal initiative; he succeeded or failed on his own ambition, energy, and luck. While only a few enjoyed the kind of luck many had taken for granted on leaving home, the rest sorted themselves according to their ambition and energy. Some maintained their independence, but as placer mining gave way to river mining, hydraulic mining, and quartz mining, most of those who stayed in the goldfields found themselves working for wages for someone else.

Many did not stay in the goldfields. Argonauts who had something to go home to often left within a season of their arrival. William Swain spent the spring and summer of 1850 on the Feather River, but by the end of the year he was headed back to New York to his wife and daughter. "I have with me about $500 in gold dust and about $10 in specie," he wrote to his brother. "I also have a very fine double-barrel fowling piece which I should take great pride in bringing home with me, if I should get home." This last was no sure thing, as Swain was traveling via Panama (reversing the route of Jessie Frémont) and had heard worrisome tales of the Chagres fever. To make matters worse, cholera had broken out on board Swain's ship, and he himself felt shaky at the time of writing. Yet though his California dream had failed to come true, he didn't regret the journey. "I have seen many hardships, dangers and privations, and made nothing by it, i.e., accumulated no property; but if I arrive home with my health, I shall ever be glad that I have taken this trip. Absence from my friends has given me a true valuation of them, and also it has taught me to appreciate the comforts and blessings of home."

Those argonauts who stayed in California often did so because they had less to return to. Jean-Nicolas Perlot succeeded no better on the Mariposa than Swain did on the Feather River, but without wife or child or job back in Europe, he saw little reason to risk recrossing the Atlantic. Not that Perlot was immune to homesickness—far from it. During his first winter in the mines, while rain halted work, he walked to the town of Mariposa after hearing that a company of Belgians who were leasing one of Frémont's quartz mines had arrived. Perlot hoped the newcomers might have word of his hometown, perhaps of his parents or siblings. "But they were ignorant of all but the existence of my native place, and consequently could give me no news."

Indeed, the Belgians at first refused to believe that Perlot could be a compatriot of theirs. "He a Belgian! Never in his life!" protested one, put off by Perlot's unkempt appearance. "What the devil! There is no savage like that in Belgium!"

"I see that you have a high idea of the Belgians, and I'm not one to contradict you," Perlot responded. "But wait a bit. You arrived two days ago, and you are staying at the hotel. You have a fine new greatcoat, nicely polished boots, neatly combed hair, and you are freshly shaven. But your company will hardly last, and doubtless you will become a miner. Wait until you have led like me the life of the placers for nine months, spending the day in a ditch, your pick in your hand, the night under a live oak, cooking your own stew, yourself providing for all your needs; then you will see what will become of your greatcoat, your hair, your beard, your face. You will realize that under these conditions a man, even a Belgian, can well have some resemblance to a savage."

To such was the placer miner reduced—and to forever chasing rumors of rich strikes over the next ridge. On this same visit to Mariposa, Perlot heard of some newly discovered deposits at a place called Bear Valley. He determined to have a try at them, and with a temporary partner named Thomas set out at once.

> We had no need to ask the way; the news, spreading rapidly, of the discovery of the new mines had produced among the population of the area an extraordinary effervescence. From all points of the horizon, men on foot and on horseback were heading for Bear Valley; it was necessary only to keep them in sight. The riders passed with all the speed of their mounts. Several, in the hurry of their departure, had improperly cinched their mule, and it sometimes happened that the saddle turned and so came to rest under the belly of the beast. We saw one, among others, to whom the accident happened, and who, resaddling his mule in haste, left at the end of the train without noticing that he had put the saddle on hindside beforemost.

Perlot and Thomas moved as quickly as they could drive the mule—saddled correctly—that carried their provisions. Though they had learned to discount rumors, they couldn't help being enticed by reports relayed back up the trail by their fellow hopefuls, to the effect that a single pit in Bear Valley was yielding thousands of dollars of gold.

Topping the last ridge, they looked down on a valley swarming with miners. "All around the pit of which they had told us, and in a radius of a thousand paces, the land was claimed in the name of one or another; a square of twenty-five feet on a side indicated each claim. We saw, on all sides, miners with pick or shovel in hand, occupied in digging."

Venturing to the celebrated pit itself, Perlot saw a hole six feet wide by fifteen feet long by ten feet deep. The Mexicans who had discovered it were indeed becoming rich. The hundreds of more recent arrivals were betting their time and labor that it wasn't an isolated deposit.

Yet with each shovelful that came up, the uniqueness of the Mexicans' strike grew increasingly obvious. "It was a pocket in the rock, and nothing more," Perlot concluded. "The nearest neighbors had no more chance of finding one like it on their claims than the ones farthest away." Thomas agreed that their hopes were forbiddingly slim.

Even so, they had to try. "We wanted to get it out of our minds." They staked a claim, and for two days dug hard and deep. On the third day they declared themselves convinced, and gave up the quest.

The denouement of the Bear Valley boom summarized the plight of the placermen.

> Except for the happy proprietors of the famous pit, who had worked it as far as thirty feet in depth and had found twenty-two thousand dollars there, the others had been no luckier than we. Fifteen days after the discovery, there were more than four hundred miners occupied everywhere in turning the soil. . . . At the end of a month there remained twelve of them: those who were working in the pit in question.

Perlot clung to his independence, but he found himself increasingly isolated in doing so. As the larger operations moved in, the last of his fellows from La Fortune gave up hope of making daily bread by his own efforts. "Bérenger left me and went to work by the day for one of these companies; he earned four dollars a day. I bought back from him his share of the provisions we had left; then I found myself alone."

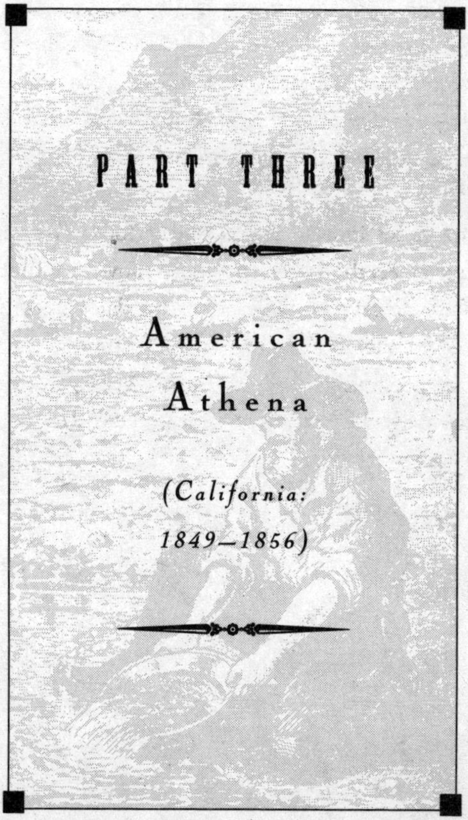

PART THREE

American Athena

(California: 1849–1856)

Plutus rattled his money bags, and straightaway the world ran to gather the falling pieces. The meanest yet most powerful of gods waved his golden wand, and lo! the desert became a great city. This is an age of marvels, and we have seen and mingled in them. Let the pioneer rub his eyes: it is no mirage, no Aladdin's palace that he sees, but real, substantial tenements, real men and women, an enduring, magnificent city.

—Frank Soulé, San Francisco journalist

Amid their digging for gold, the immigrants confronted another challenge, one most of them hadn't considered before heading for California, but which proved even greater than the problem of how to get the gold from the ground. They had to build a society, to fashion the civil and political institutions that would allow this heterogeneous horde to live cheek by jowl, hip to knee, without murdering one another more often than necessary. It was a formidable task, the likes of which had rarely been attempted, and probably never at such a pace on such a scale. The newcomers all shared a desire to get rich, but the Americans and Latin Americans and Europeans and Australians and Asians shared precious little else. How could they hope to construct a coherent society from such a congeries of peoples? How indeed, especially when the one thing they shared militated against social coherence? The vast majority came to California not to make lives but merely livings, not to sink roots in the new land and build homes but to strip the land and return to their real homes. And what were the newcomers to do with the people who preceded the invasion: the native Indians and Californians, who had their own ideas about how to organize society? What were the natives to do with the newcomers?

Compounding California's problems were the problems California created for the rest of the United States. Upon the signing of the Treaty of Guadalupe Hidalgo, nearly everyone in America assumed that the peopling of California would be a slow process, as the peopling of the territories acquired earlier by the United States had been. Fashioning governments for those earlier territories, and admitting them to the Union as states, had sometimes stretched the imagination of America's political leaders; but the feat had always been accomplished, not least on account of the ample time allowed for it. The Gold Rush guaranteed that time would *not* be allowed in California's case. Within the year of President Polk's announcement of the gold discovery, California contained more people than many existing states, and those people demanded admission to the Union. They got what they demanded, but not without setting off a fight in Congress and in the country at large that shook the republic to its foundations.

9

The Miracle of St. Francis

The struggle to build a new society in California was waged in every mining camp along the Sierra front and in every lowland community that sprang up to service the mines. But the contest was most spirited in San Francisco, the first city of California (and indeed the first city on the western coast of North America), for it was in San Francisco that the contradictions of life in Gold Rush California became most painfully evident. The principal contradiction was something that made San Francisco unique in American history to that point: it was at once urban and a frontier. San Francisco's troubles were the troubles of the frontier, where civilization had to be carved from the wilderness and humanity's rule imposed on nature's unruliness. But this was a frontier full of people: 50,000 by 1853. The saving grace of most frontiers was the room they allowed for error, for the uncertainties and false steps that mark every infant society. San Franciscans lacked that luxury; crowded on the peninsula, between the bay and the sand hills, they inflicted their errors on one another.

THE MISSION OF San Francisco, often called Dolores after the sorrows of the Virgin, was established in 1776 on a site two miles southwest of the cove of Yerba Buena. During the next half century the mission received occasional visits from merchant vessels and the odd warship, representing Spain, the United States, Britain, Russia, or France, once captains entering San Francisco Bay discovered the cove's virtues as a sheltered anchorage. In 1835 an American named W. A. Richardson erected the first structure at the cove, a tent-house fashioned from a ship's foresail and resting on four redwood posts. From this headquarters Richardson took up the hide and tallow trade. The following year another American, Jacob Leese, built a wooden structure at a location later occupied by the St. Francis Hotel. The Leese house was neither large nor elaborate, its small size and lack of sophistication indicated by the fact that the building materials were landed on the beach on July 2 and construction concluded in time for Leese to receive guests to commemorate American independence on the morning of July 4. They had quite a party. "Our fourth ended on the evening of the fifth," Leese recorded in his diary.

The village, called Yerba Buena, grew slowly. In 1838 the first baby was born there, to Jacob Leese and his wife, the sister of General Mariano Vallejo, one of the wealthiest and most powerful of the Mexican Californians. The following year a violent earthquake shook the region. This novelty to the newcomers did only slight damage to the few and generally flexible buildings at Yerba Buena, but it reminded the Californians of a very large earthquake that had struck the region in 1812, killing many people and leveling the mission of San Juan Capistrano. Local Indians recalled their tradition that San Francisco Bay had originally been a freshwater lake but had been joined to the sea when a huge earthquake breached the hills that still formed the spine of the San Francisco peninsula. (San Francisco journalist Frank Soulé, writing in the mid-1850s and noting that no comparable earthquake had struck since the 1839 tremor, held his breath: "God help the city if any great catastrophe of this nature should ever take place!" On the other hand, at least one gold-hunter hoped for more shaking. "Last Wednesday we had several quite smart shocks of an earthquake. Perhaps it shook out some large lumps of gold which I may stumble over.")

In 1844, Yerba Buena comprised perhaps a dozen houses and no more than fifty permanent residents. Two years later, at the time of the American conquest, there were about fifty buildings and perhaps two hundred residents. The village continued to grow under the American occupation, with the arrival of Sam Brannan's boatload of Mormons from New York nearly doubling the population. The first newspaper appeared, albeit with difficulty. "Our type is a spanish font picked up here in a cloister, and has no VV's [W's] in it, as there is none in the spanish alphabet," the editor explained. "I have sent to the sandvvich Islands for this letter; in the mean time vve must use tvvo VV's. Our paper at present is that used for vvrapping segars; in due time vve vvill have something better." In January 1847 the alcalde—now appointed by the Americans but retaining the powers of the Mexican office—rechristened the village as San Francisco, to take advantage of the general name recognition of the bay. Early the following year the label "Golden Gate" appeared in a report produced by John—and Jessie—Frémont, who at the time of writing had no idea of the full aptness of the name.

And then Sam Brannan brought news of gold on the American River, and everything changed. Overnight the town was abandoned, with all able bodies heading for the mines. For months—from the late spring through the autumn of 1848—it remained virtually empty. Then the first wave of immigration hit, borne by the gold-hunting fleets from South America, Australia, the Central American isthmus, and Cape Horn. The largest part of the wave washed right over San Francisco to the goldfields. Passengers and crews abandoned their ships in the harbor, leaving a forest of masts protruding from a plain of decks jammed gunwale to gunwale and bowsprit to taffrail; the new arrivals tarried in town only long enough to ask directions for the mines and supply their needs for the last 150 miles.

Yet that was enough to start the city growing rapidly. The transients had to eat and drink: restaurants and saloons sprang up to fill their bellies and quench their thirst. They had to sleep: hotels appeared beside the restaurants. They had to purchase their supplies: shops and warehouses were constructed. Streets were pushed into the dunes behind the old village; the built-up area spilled south toward the mission and north toward

Washerwoman's Lagoon. Piers were built into the bay to ease the unloading of passengers and cargo. In this process particularly, San Francisco confirmed its preeminence over potential rivals as entrepôt to the mines. While small oceangoing vessels—barks and schooners—could sail much farther up toward Sacramento and Stockton, the largest ships, including great clippers like the *Challenge*, were confined to the deep water of San Francisco Bay. Behind the piers, low-lying areas were filled in, often with sand and dirt scraped from the city's high spots by a steam shovel transported around the Horn and called "Steam Paddy," after the Irishmen its kind replaced. At first the inhabitants of the city avoided the hills they couldn't flatten—Telegraph, Nob, Russian, Rincon—but as the level lots ran out, the hills were overrun as well, and eventually acquired a certain cachet.

Proprietors and employees in the various service enterprises formed the core of the city's new population, small in number next to the transients but not inconsequential. To attract and keep the employees, to prevent their running off to the mines with everyone else, the proprietors had to pay wages unthinkable just months before. Unskilled workers, who had been happy with a dollar a day, now got ten. Skilled workers turned up their noses at twenty. But no one wept for the proprietors, whose prices were rising even faster than the wages they were paying.

WHAT DROVE THE growth was the gold—both the actual gold coming down from the mines and the prospective gold that drew the argonauts to San Francisco on their way to the mines. The city's economy ran on gold; the obsession of all was how to get it. This obsession cast a distinctive—and, in the opinion of those attuned to a more settled existence, unhealthy—glow over city life. Sarah Royce visited San Francisco and was shocked at the temptations awaiting the unwary.

> In the immense crowds flocking hither from all parts of the world there were many of the worst classes, bent upon getting gold at all hazards, and if possible without work. These were constantly lying

> in wait, as tempters of the weak. A still greater number came with gold-getting for their ruling motive yet intending to get it honestly, by labor or legitimate business. They did not intend, at first, to sacrifice their habits of morality, or their religious convictions. But many of them bore those habits and held those convictions too lightly; and as they came to feel the force of unwonted excitement and the pressure of unexpected temptation, they too often yielded, little by little, till they found themselves standing upon a very low plane, side by side with those whose society they once would have avoided. It was very common to hear people who had started on this downward moral grade, deprecating the very acts they were committing, or the practices they were countenancing; and concluding their weak lament by saying, "But here in California we *have* to do such things."

There was more to this rationale than the stern Sarah allowed. Especially at first, many of those in San Francisco had no alternative to the dens of iniquity. On cold, rainy evenings the saloons and taverns were among the few places in the city with tight roofs and warm fires; for more than a few harried souls, the saloons were in fact their lodgings, where they rolled out sleeping mats after last call at the bar. Even when housing conditions began to improve, men typically slept several to a room. To stay away from one's room until as late as possible was the only way of preserving mental and—considering the contagions of such close quarters—physical health. Saloons often afforded the sole refuge.

Necessary or not, the hyperactive public life of San Francisco deranged many private morals. A just-arrived argonaut reflected on this remarkable place, and informed his family back home: "The usual order of things seemed to be entirely reversed. All one's ideas of economy, of carefulness, of religion, of morality, were first astonished, then mollified down to a par with what one saw going on around him, and I can assure you it is astonishing how soon and easy one can get into expensive habits and get what is called liberal ideas about the rules of decent society." Another observer, Frank Soulé, who like fellow Mainer Sam Brannan had swapped one coast for the other, and was now a journalistic conscience of San Francisco, lamented the low state of affairs:

> No place in the world contains any thing like the number of mere drinking-houses [as opposed to restaurants] in proportion to the population, as San Francisco. This, perhaps, is the worst feature of the city. The quantity of ardent spirits daily consumed is almost frightful. It is peddled out in every gambling-room, on the wharves, at almost every corner, and, in some streets, in almost every house. Many of the taverns are of the lowest possible description—filthy dens of vice and crime, disease and wretchedness. Drunken men and women, with bloated bodies and soiled garments, crowd them at night, making the hours hideous with their bacchanalian revels. Americans and Europeans, Mexicans and South-Americans, Chinese and even negroes, mingle and dissipate together, furnishing a large amount of business for the police department and the recorder's court.

The saloons typically doubled as gambling houses, or "hells." Most Americans of the mid-nineteenth century considered gambling a vice, lesser or greater than drinking depending on one's temperament and upbringing. But given that the entire enterprise of the Gold Rush was a gamble, in which the stakes could include one's life, conventional taboos against gambling lost much of their force in California. Bayard Taylor—having won his own gamble against Chagres fever and the other hazards of the isthmus—conducted a personal survey of several gaming houses clustered around the San Francisco plaza.

> Denison's Exchange, the Parker House and Eldorado stand side by side; across the way are the Verandah and Aguila de Oro; higher up the plaza the St. Charles and Bella Union; while dozens of second-rate establishments are scattered through the less frequented streets. The greatest crowd is about the Eldorado; we find it difficult to effect an entrance. There are about eight tables in

the room, all of which are thronged; copper-hued Kanakas [Polynesians], Mexicans rolled in their sarapes and Peruvians thrust through their ponchos, stand shoulder to shoulder with the brown and bearded American miners. The stakes are generally small, though when the bettor gets into "a streak of luck," as it is called, they are allowed to double until all is lost or the bank breaks. Along the end of the room is a spacious bar, supplied with all kinds of bad liquors, and in a sort of gallery, suspended under the ceiling, a female violinist tasks her talent and strength of muscle to minister to the excitement of play. . . . At the Aguila de Oro there is a full band of Ethiopian serenaders [black minstrels], and at the other hells, violins, guitars or wheezy accordeons, as the case may be. The atmosphere of these places is rank with tobacco-smoke, and filled with a feverish, stifling heat, which communicates an unhealthy glow to the faces of the players. . . .

They are playing monte, the favorite game in California, since the chances are considered more equal and the opportunity of false play very slight. The dealer throws out his cards with a cool, nonchalant air; indeed, the gradual increase of the hollow square of dollars at his left hand is not calculated to disturb his equanimity. The two Mexicans in front, muffled in their dirty sarapes, put down their half-dollars and dollars and see them lost, without changing a muscle. Gambling is a born habit with them, and they would lose thousands with the same indifference.

Very different is the demeanor of the Americans who are playing; their good or ill luck is betrayed at once by involuntary exclamations and changes of countenance, unless the stake should be very large and absorbing, when their anxiety, though silent, may be read with no less certainty. They have no power to resist the fascination of the game. Now counting their winnings by thousands, now dependent on the kindness of a friend for a few dollars to commence anew, they pass hour after hour in these hot, unwholesome dens. There is no appearance of arms, but let one of the players, impatient with his losses and maddened by the poisonous fluids he has drank, threaten one of the profession, and there will be no scarcity of knives and revolvers.

More respectable than the saloons and gambling halls were the restaurants. From the start, San Francisco boasted a diversity of cuisines to match the diversity of its population: American, Chilean, Peruvian, Polynesian, Mexican, French, Chinese, Italian, German, English. Vegetables and fruit were initially scarce, but beef and seafood were plentiful ("California beef is the best in the world, both in flavor and fatness," wrote Thomas Van Dorn), as was game of all sorts. Prices were high; dinner at Delmonico's, or at the Sutter, Franklin, or Lafayette houses, cost from five to fifteen dollars, depending on the quality and quantity of wine. Lesser establishments got one to three dollars for a meal.

The better restaurants did an enormous business. In July 1851, M. L. Winn, who had made his start in San Francisco manufacturing candy and selling it on the street, opened a restaurant called the Fountain Head. Eighteen months later he added a second restaurant, the Branch. By the spring of 1854 the *Commercial Advertiser*—one of several papers published in San Francisco—would report that the two establishments served an average of 3,000 patrons daily, with 5,000 being unremarkable on a busy day. Winn's monthly beef bill ran to $8,000; for flour he paid $4,000. His ice bill for one month was $2,000; this allowed him to serve as many as 1,500 glasses of ice cream in a day.

THE DATE OF THE opening of the Fountain Head was not happenstance. Just two months earlier, a predecessor restaurant Winn owned burned to the ground, along with much of the rest of San Francisco.

Fire was the most harrowing civic problem of Gold Rush San Francisco. Especially at the start, when San Franciscans were too busy to build with stone and mortar, and instead threw up tents and wood-frame structures, the city suffered repeated conflagrations. The first occurred on Christmas Eve of 1849. It began at six o'clock in the morning, in Denison's Exchange, on the east side of the plaza, and spread in both directions, destroying a whole line of structures along Washington Street, between Montgomery and Kearny. A million dollars of property was consumed by the flames; more would have been lost if not for the decisiveness of the firefighters in razing buildings in the fire's path, creating a fuel-free zone that starved the blaze.

Partly because the city was so new, and partly because the buildings lost were so insubstantial, almost no one wasted time mourning the destruction. Within weeks the ruined structures were replaced by fresh ones, and, amid the city's continuing growth, they were joined by many others. Consequently, when a second fire broke out, on May 4, 1850, it wreaked havoc even greater than the first. "Before eleven of the forenoon, three immense blocks of buildings, with a few trifling exceptions, were totally destroyed," Frank Soulé explained. "A great many buildings were torn down or blown up by gunpowder to stay the progress of the flames; and, among others, nearly the whole erections in Dupont Street were voluntarily destroyed to prevent conflagration spreading on that side." Less civic-minded than the Dupont owners were those city-dwellers who refused to join the bucket brigades without being paid in advance. At least some of the reluctant busied themselves mining the ashes of buildings already lost. One recent arrival found his first gold amid the smoking ruins; sending his wife a lithograph of Portsmouth Square, with the destroyed hotels and other buildings marked in pencil, he enclosed a coarse grain of gold. "I put into this a little piece of gold that I picked up on the square. . . . The place I picked it up is marked by a cross thus X." Others caught on to the idea, and soon scavengers were sifting the rubble for the gold dust that had been secreted in the buildings now burned.

As before, reconstruction commenced almost before the flames died out. "New buildings were begun to be erected while the sites of the old were hot with smoking ashes," Soulé said. "While even one extremity of the old tenement was still blazing, people were planning the nature of the new erection, and clearing away the embers and rubbish from the other scarcely extinguished end." The energy of the rebuilders was greater than their ability to learn from experience. "In a wonderfully short time the whole burned space was covered with new buildings, and looked as if no fire had ever been there; although it was generally remarked that these were even more unsubstantial and inflammable than those which had just been destroyed."

The bulk of the new construction was completed in time for the city's third fire, which broke out only six weeks after the second. This one apparently started in the creosote-clogged chimney of an old house that had been converted into a bakery; the brisk summer winds fanned the flames and spread them to adjacent buildings. Property damage exceeded that of all the previous fires together and was estimated at five million dollars. This time San Franciscans took at least partial heed of their recent history; the buildings that went up over the ruins included a larger portion of masonry structures than before. And the inhabitants of the city began organizing into fire companies, with pump engines, hoses, and ladders purchased ahead of the next round of burning.

These preparations paid off three months later, in September 1850, when a fourth fire broke out. The fire companies quickly answered the alarm and, despite running low on water, managed to hold the losses to less than a million dollars. The citizens once more rebuilt, and congratulated themselves on having found the answer to this civic scourge.

JESSIE FRÉMONT MISSED the first four fires, but not the fifth. During the spring of 1851, awaiting the birth of her third child, she moved with John and Lily to San Francisco, to a prefabricated house shipped from China and fitted together on site like the pieces of a puzzle, without nails. The baby—a boy—arrived on April 19 and was named after his father.

Besides the name, John Jr. inherited his father's knack for surviving close calls. On the fifteenth day after his birth—and on the first anniversary of the great fire of May 4, 1850—the city once more burst into flames. This fire was the worst of all, and was made more terrible by the misplaced confidence that had crept over the city since the last fire. Heinrich Schliemann, a German merchant operating out of St. Petersburg (and the man who would become famous as the uncoverer of ancient Troy) was brand-new to the city. "I arrived here last night and put up at the Union Hotel on the Plaza," he recorded.

> I may have slept a quarter of an hour, when I was awakened by loud cries in the street: "Fire, fire," and by the awful sounds of the alarm-bell. I sprang up in all haste and, looking out the window, I saw that a frame building only 20 or 30 paces from the Union Hotel was on fire. I dressed in all haste and ran out of the house, but scarcely had I reached the end of Clay Street when I saw already the hotel on fire from which I had just run out. Pushed on by a complete gale, the fire spread with an appalling rapidity, sweeping away in a few minutes whole streets of frame buildings.
>
> Neither the iron houses nor the brick houses (which were hitherto considered as quite fireproof) could resist the fury of the element: the latter crumbled together with incredible rapidity, whilst the former got red-hot, then white-hot and fell together like cardhouses. Particularly in the iron houses people considered themselves perfectly safe, and they remained in them to the last extremity. As soon as the walls of the iron houses got red-hot, the goods inside began to smoke. The inhabitants wanted to get out, but usually it was already too late, for the locks and hinges of the doors having extended or partly melted by the heat, the doors were no more to be opened.

Jessie Frémont smelled the smoke about the time she heard the shouts and alarm bells. Her husband fetched blankets and a grass hammock on which his wife and namesake might be evacuated if necessary (Lily was expected to run). He then organized the servants and some neighbors into an emergency crew that hung water-soaked carpets and canvas over the sides of the house. A fortuitous shift of wind aided their efforts, and although the fire did more damage than any of the previous ones—dozens of people were killed, and the entire business district was destroyed—the Frémonts' home was spared.

Almost unbelievably, yet another fire broke out the following month. This time the Frémonts weren't so lucky. Jessie and Lily watched from the window as the fire companies battled the flames, which seemed to be moving away from the Frémont home. A sudden reversal of wind took all by surprise. A maid grabbed the baby and seized Lily by the arm, and raced away. A manservant scooped up Jessie and carried her off as the first sparks fluttered down onto the roof. Taking refuge with a neighbor, Jessie encountered a Frenchwoman who had likewise only just escaped the flames, and was nearly in shock. "Her wild fevered gaze was fixed on her burning home," Jessie recalled. "Suddenly, with a crazy laugh, she rose and offered me her seat—'C'est votre tour, Madame; your house goes next,' she said." And so it did.

John Frémont had returned to the Mariposa after the May 4 fire, relieved that his family had survived unharmed; on hearing of another fire he saddled his swiftest horse and raced back to San Francisco. When he saw the smoldering ruins of his house he naturally feared the worst. Only after some frantic searching did he find Jessie and the children, lodged with a friend among the sand dunes behind the city.

Jessie put on a brave face, but the destruction of her home was a jolting reminder of how unsettled life in this new country could be. The gold from the Mariposa continued to pour in, but all their money couldn't buy them the most basic form of security. "It is more disagreeable than you can realize without the experience, to be burnt out," she confided to a friend, several weeks after the fire. She was grateful that the servants and some neighbors had managed to save most of the family's irreplaceable personal items. "Still, the new house was a sudden unchosen place, and I felt shipwrecked."

AS SAN FRANCISCANS REBUILT yet again, they took two lessons from the fires. The first was that fire prevention was something absolutely essential to stable civic life. Reconstruction after the sixth fire went more slowly than before; new buildings featured solid brick walls up to three feet thick, iron shutters and doors with sufficient play to allow for expansion, and large rooftop tanks of water piped to allow dowsing of the premises at the first spark. As a result, although the corporate seal of the city still sported the mythic Phoenix, the bird got a rest during the next few years.

The second lesson was that not all those fires were accidents. The frequency of the blazes, and especially the fact that the May fire of 1851 occurred on the exact anniversary of the May fire of 1850, inclined many San Franciscans to smell arson in the smoke. Fire may have been the city's foremost problem, but crime came a close second.

Yet it was a problem the city was slow to confront, for reasons related to the gold fever but also to the demographic diversity of San Francisco. Crime initially concentrated in parts of the city frequented by foreigners, leaving the American majority to go about their business unmolested. Only when the transgressions touched closer to home did they take notice.

Vicente Pérez Rosales experienced the process personally. With his fellow Chileans, Pérez felt the hostility many Americans directed toward foreigners, who were accused of stealing wealth—that is, gold—that ought to be reserved to citizens of the United States. The hostility prompted recurrent efforts to keep foreigners out of the goldfields, ranging from a foreign-miners' tax to physical intimidation. The xenophobia was far from universal; merchants like Sam Brannan and mine owners looking for cheap help were happy for immigration from any source. But the antiforeign feeling persisted among those who suffered from the competition.

As it applied to the Chileans—and other Latin Americans, with whom the Chileans were casually lumped—the xenophobia gave rise to a belief that Chileans lay behind much of what went wrong in California. One day Pérez Rosales's compatriot Álvarez—the one who led the abortive mutiny on the *Stanguéli*—happened to be near a group of Americans who lost a shovel; the Americans accused Álvarez of theft, calling him, for good measure, a "son of a nigger." Álvarez spoke no English, and the Americans no Spanish, but when they wrapped a rope around his neck and threw the loose end over a tree limb, their meaning became clear.

Pérez Rosales reached the scene of the hanging at this critical juncture, and reckoned desperately how he might save his shipmate. Knowing that Americans respected Frenchmen more than Chileans, and guessing that these rowdies couldn't tell a Chilean accent from a French one, he cast himself as a countryman of the immortal Lafayette. He declared that Álvarez was the only protector the French in Chile ever had, that Álvarez had once saved him from death, and that surely the Americans would wish to honor the memory of the Revolutionary War hero by sparing Álvarez now.

The ploy worked, and Álvarez was set free. But the Chileans continued to encounter trouble. Their skill in the goldfields earned them the resentment of their neighbors, who by force and other means drove them off the best claims and in many cases out of the diggings entirely. A sizable contingent returned to San Francisco, some to try their hand at commerce there, most to seek passage home. (One enterprising Chilean merchant named Wenceslao Urbistondo set the pattern for what became a striking feature of San Francisco's urban topography. Urbistondo owned a ship that had been abandoned by its crew and was now hemmed in by a hundred others likewise marooned. Realizing that the ship had become, for all intents and purposes, a permanent part of the landscape, he made it even more so. He felled his masts to build a bridge to shore, effectively extending the street that had ended at the waterfront. Other shipowners followed his example, and eventually dirt and sand were hauled in to fill the spaces between the hulks. Soon Yerba Buena Cove began disappearing beneath the advancing city.)

By midsummer of 1849 about a thousand Chileans, joined by a smaller number of Peruvians and Mexicans, formed a colony at Clark's Point, just north of the cove. Their reputation as gold miners preceded them, and they were generally believed to be richer than the run of their neighbors. The larcenous among San Francisco's inhabitants eyed them hungrily.

Leading the larcenous was a band of rowdies called the "Hounds." The hard core of this gang were Mexican War veterans from New York who had been mustered out in California and hadn't returned home. Several of the Hounds had been schooled in the notorious Five Points and Bowery gangs of New York City, and they established headquarters in a large tent they dubbed "Tammany Hall." Claiming to be a mutual defense association (hence the name they subsequently adopted: "Regulators"), they in fact preyed upon their neighbors, especially the Chileans.

For a time their depredations went unheeded by San Francisco's honest folk. Thomas Cary, one of those honest folk, pondered this tolerance for crime.

> It will be asked why the more respectable part of the community did not exert themselves to put a stop to these proceedings. The answer is simple. The influential citizens, the merchants, lawyers and others, lived around what had been known as Yerba Buena Cove, while the Mexicans and Chileans lived at the back of the town among the sand-hills. They, therefore, knew little of what was going on out of sight and out of hearing. Everyone was too much interested in his own affairs to trouble himself about the misfortunes of others, and besides this, the Spanish-Americans were looked upon at that time very much as the Chinese are at the present moment [Cary was writing in the 1880s], as interlopers who should properly have been sent back to their own country, and these "Hounds," or "Regulators" as they now called themselves, professed to be the guardians of the community against the encroachments of all foreigners.

With no one else to look out for them, the Chileans looked out for themselves. "Compliant in their own country," Pérez Rosales explained of his compatriots, "Chileans cease to be so abroad, even in the face of a pistol aimed at their hearts, provided only they can lay hand on the knife at their belts." Pérez added that the Chileans "detested the Americans, whom they constantly averred to be cowards."

In late June 1849 two young men linked to the Hounds entered the shop of a Chilean merchant. Employing a favorite tactic, they began quarreling with the shopkeeper over a debt they said he owed them, and which he denied owing. As their attempted extortion grew louder and more threatening, the shopkeeper pulled a pistol. One of the pair tried to grab the gun; the other headed for the door. In the struggle for the pistol, the weapon went off and the fleeing man was shot. He died the next day.

The Hounds proclaimed their intention of bringing the murderous Chileans to account. Contriving a set of ill-matched military uniforms, they began parading and drilling. During the first two weeks of July, tensions between Americans and Chileans escalated sharply.

On July 15 a company of the Hounds crossed the bay to Contra Costa for additional drilling and marching. On their return, the company leader, a man named Sam Roberts—who, as it happened, had lived in Valparaiso and shipped aboard a Chilean man-of-war—discovered his Chilean girlfriend, a prostitute appropriately named Felice, entertaining another man. Roberts viciously assaulted the fellow, beating him with his riding whip and raking his face with his spur. Roberts then returned to Tammany Hall and summoned reinforcements for a general venting against the Chileans. For the rest of that day and into the night, the gangsters marauded through Clark's Point, breaking, burning, looting, shooting, slashing. Several people were wounded; at least one died.

This orchestrated anarchy finally aroused the American community of San Francisco. Leading the response was Sam Brannan, who had expanded his mercantile operations to San Francisco, and who now called for stern measures against the Hounds. "Boiling with indignation," as Pérez Rosales described Brannan, "he strode up to the roof of his house and shouted for the town to gather below. Briefly and energetically he asserted that it was high time to make an example of the perpetrators of these unheard-of outrages against the citizens of a friendly nation that daily exported to San Francisco not only the finest flour, but the best hands in the world at making bricks!" More than two hundred citizens answered Brannan's call. Armed with their own weapons and with sixty muskets supplied by one of Brannan's merchant allies, the posse went after the Hounds, arresting twenty, including Sam Roberts.

Another public meeting, at Portsmouth Square, nominated and elected two judges to try the cases. A prosecutor was appointed and a grand jury empaneled. Roberts was convicted of conspiracy, riot, robbery, and assault with intent to kill. Eight others were convicted on one or more of the same counts. Roberts and a second man were sentenced to ten years at hard labor; the rest received lesser sentences.

For various reasons, starting with the lack of a prison but including a feeling that popular justice had made its point by the arrests and convictions, Roberts and the other prisoners never served their sentences. Yet the Brannan-led crackdown broke the strength of the Hounds as an organized gang and was widely interpreted as a positive precedent.

A PRECEDENT IT WAS, but hardly a solution. The decline of the Hounds simply made room for other thugs, including a gang of Australians known as the Sydney Ducks, or Sydney Coves, who by 1850 had a reputation worse than the Hounds'. To some extent the Australians' evil name owed to their country's history as the outdoor prison for British felons, but to some extent it was honestly—which was to say, dishonestly—earned in California. Frank Soulé explained the Australians' preeminence in crime:

> The voyage from Sydney to San Francisco was neither a very tedious nor an expensive one; and great numbers of "ticket-of-leave" men and old convicts who had "served their time," early contrived to sail for California. There the field seemed so rich and safe for a resumption of their quondam pranks that they yielded to the temptation, and forthwith began to execute villainies that in magnitude and violent character far exceeded those for which they had been originally convicted. Callous in conscience, they feared nothing save the gallows.
>
> But that they had little reason to dread in merciful, gentle, careless California, where prosecutors and witnesses were few, or too busy to attend to the calls of justice; where jurors, not knowing the law, and eager to be at money-making again, were apt to take hasty charges from the bench as their sole rule of conduct; where judges, chosen by popular election, were either grossly ignorant of law, or too timid or careless, corrupt or incapable, to

> measure out the full punishment of crime; and where the laws themselves had not yet been methodically laid down, and the forms and procedure of legal tribunals digested into a plain, unerring system.

The center of the Australian criminal activity was the "Sydney Town" district between Broadway and Pacific Streets. Saloons and brothels were the principal establishments of the neighborhood; prostitutes and professional gamblers (by no means all of them from Australia) were the primary entrepreneurs. In this congenial atmosphere the Sydney Ducks plied their criminal trade. Armed robbery was a daily occurrence; resistance often resulted in murder. Decent men and women weren't safe in the district at any hour of day or night. When the police dared to enter, they did so only en masse and retreated quickly to their fortified station houses.

As in the case of the Hounds, the American community initially ignored the Ducks. But when the Australian gangsters began roaming beyond Sydney Town, committing burglaries in the neighboring districts, the prominent merchants and their friends were forced to take notice. And when evidence relating to the great fires pointed to Australian complicity—with the Ducks profiting by plunder and looting amid the general confusion of the fires—these city fathers felt compelled to take action.

They were urged on by the city mothers. As San Francisco continued to evolve—from the caravansary of 1849 to the commercial hub of 1851—its permanent population continued to grow. Merchants, artisans, and professionals made the city their home, and many brought their wives and children (typically via the isthmus, where the anarchic crossing conditions of 1849 had been replaced by relatively reliable transit service). As the ladies took up residence, they smoothed off some of the city's rough edges and contributed to an expansion of cultural opportunities. Thomas Cary described what had changed—and what hadn't:

> With the families came a sense of home-life, and the general recklessness which had been a marked feature in the early days was beginning to disappear. The gambling houses were still open to the

public, and did a thriving trade, but were not, as formerly, frequented by all classes of men, many of whom went there because there was nowhere else to go. There were theatrical entertainments and concerts, not terribly good, to be sure, but affording amusement to those who for a long time had seen no other tragedy than a street-fight with pistols, or heard better music than a brass-band in a gambling saloon.

The comforts of life, and of good living, had also improved very much, both in private houses and in restaurants. Farmers and gardeners had found they could make more money by digging for vegetables and raising fruit than they could get by prospecting for gold at the "diggings." The absurdly high prices which had formerly been charged were reduced to what at the time appeared to be quite reasonable, and strangers from Europe or the Atlantic States were surprised to find, together with the activity and bustle of a western city, all the luxury and gayety of a highly civilized metropolis.

This, however, was the bright side of the picture. The continued increase of crime in San Francisco made it evident to every thinking man that the time was not far distant when self-preservation would make it necessary for the people to assert their rights and take the law into their own hands.

The anniversary fire of May 1851 prompted these thinking men to reenage the engines of popular justice. In early June a self-appointed association styling itself the Committee of Vigilance adopted a charter pledging its members to "the maintenance of the peace and good order of society, and the preservation of the lives and property of the citizens of San Francisco." The members bound themselves to uphold the law and back the legal authorities. "But we are determined," they added significantly, "that no thief, burglar, incendiary or assassin shall escape punishment, either by the quibbles of the law, the insecurity of prisons, the carelessness or corruption of the police, or a laxity of those who pretend to administer justice."

The Committee of Vigilance soon had opportunity to demonstrate its seriousness. On the evening of June 10 a store near the waterfront reported a small safe missing. Shortly thereafter a Sydney Duck named John Jenkins was seen leaving the neighborhood of the theft with an unwieldy and obviously heavy object slung over his back. On being accosted, he stole a boat and rowed out into the bay. Several other boats gave chase and eventually caught Jenkins, but not before he dumped his burden into the bay. The water, however, was shallow, and the object was retrieved; it proved to be the missing safe.

Jenkins was taken to the meeting room of the Vigilance Committee. The bell of the Monumental Engine Company sounded the alarm: two quick clangs, followed by a minute's rest, then repeated. Some eighty members of the committee converged on the meeting place, and upon Jenkins. For two hours the committee weighed the evidence against the accused; at midnight it handed down the verdict and the sentence: guilty, and death by hanging. The condemned man was asked if he had a last wish. He requested, and received, a cigar and a glass of brandy. Shortly before one o'clock on the morning of June 11, Sam Brannan announced the verdict to the city at large. He inquired of the several hundred people gathered outside the informal courtroom whether they endorsed the judgment of the committee. "Great shouts of *Ay! Ay!* burst forth, mingled with a few cries of *No!*" recorded Frank Soulé.

Just before two o'clock, Brannan and other committee members brought the prisoner out for the execution. They marched him to the south end of the old adobe building at the northwest corner of the plaza. At this point the sheriff and some deputies made a feeble attempt to intervene. "They were civilly desired to stand back, and not delay what still was to be done," Soulé wrote. The sheriff complied. The crowd, by now grown to more than a thousand, applauded by look and gesture as the committee completed its business. A noose was placed about Jenkins's neck, and his arms were tied behind his back. The loose end of the rope was thrown over a beam projecting from the adobe building. Several men seized the rope and yanked it sharply, pulling Jenkins off his feet and hoisting him in the air. Within minutes he was dead. But those holding the rope didn't let go, instead keeping the corpse high where all could see it. When the original hangmen tired, others took their place; the body was kept swinging till nearly dawn.

Later that morning the sheriff, his confidence somewhat restored with the coming of day and the dispersal of the crowd, ordered an inquest. Brannan was summoned as first witness. He defended the actions of the Vigilance Committee, irregular though they might have been. "I believe the man had a fair and impartial trial," he declared. "He was tried before from sixty to eighty men. I believe the verdict of guilty was unanimous, and they came to the conclusion unanimously to hang him." Asked how the jury was empaneled, Brannan responded, "They empaneled themselves." How were the members of the committee selected? "A man is admitted to the committee on a motion by a friend who vouches for his character, and that he will devote a portion of his time to watching for burglars and other scoundrels." Was secrecy involved in the selection? "I don't know of any other secrecy than that of an honest man." Then perhaps Mr. Brannan wouldn't mind revealing the names of the committee members? "I object to give the names of any of the committee. I have understood that threats have been made against their property and lives. I have heard the threats made, have heard it said that my own house would be burned. Threats have come to me from the prisoners in the county prison that I should not live ninety days."

The next day the inquest board reported its finding that Jenkins had met his death "by violent means, by strangulation, caused by being suspended by the neck." The responsible parties were members of "an association of citizens styling themselves a Committee of Vigilance." The board went on to identify Brannan and nine others as leaders of this committee. However, the inquest board at this time declined to recommend legal action against Brannan or the others.

Lest the board change its mind, the Vigilance Committee passed a resolution condemning the "invidious verdict"—such as it was—of the inquest board. The resolution was signed by 184 members who claimed equal responsibility for Jenkins's execution with Brannan and those named by the board.

The authorities remained aloof, if not intimidated, while the Vigilance

Committee took up another case. James Stuart, like the other Ducks, had come to California from Australia; since his arrival he had been implicated in numerous robberies, murders, and lesser crimes. Seized by the committee, he was tried and condemned to hang. At first he affected unconcern, declaring the whole business "damned tiresome." But en route to the scaffold, in this case a derrick at the end of a dock, he nearly fainted from fear. His captors carried him the rest of the way and supported him as the hemp entwined his neck. "He did not struggle much," remarked Soulé. "After hanging a few seconds his hat fell off, and a slight breeze stirred and gently waved his hair. This was a sorry spectacle—a human being dying like a dog, while thousands of erring mortals, whose wickedness only had not yet been found out, looked on and applauded! But necessity, which dared not trust itself to feelings of compassion, commanded the deed and unprofitable sentiment sunk abashed. Reason loudly declared—*So perish every villain who would hurt his neighbor!* and all the people said *Amen!*"

10

Sutter's Last Stand

San Francisco's troubles hardly ended with the emergence of the Vigilance Committee; indeed, the assertion of the committee's extralegal authority simply stored up problems for the future. And California's leading city was hardly alone in its travails. A dozen towns of the Sacramento and San Joaquin Valleys, not to mention a hundred mining camps, faced many of the same problems of dislocation, overcrowding, fire, crime, and violence that made San Francisco such a raucous place during its first few years. Some of those communities confronted challenges San Francisco was spared. Low-lying Sacramento was regularly ravaged by flood and by a higher incidence of contagious disease than afflicted the better-drained, better-ventilated city on the bay. Several of the mining camps gave "Judge Lynch" a far freer hand than he enjoyed in San Francisco; Hangtown proudly took its name from this form of summary justice, rechristening itself as Placerville only after things calmed down.

Yet the local turbulence had a larger context, for even as San Francisco and the other communities struggled to gain their bearings, California sought to define itself as a state. California was unique in the speed with which it went from being foreign-owned and fairly empty to being American and brimmingly full. For half a century the norm for new states had been to serve apprenticeships as territories. But that norm was based on the premise that populating each new frontier was a slow business, and that the creation of state governments might be equally slow and deliberate. Nothing happened slowly in California after 1848; populating itself overnight, the land of gold skipped the territorial stage and went straight to statehood. Yet though straight, the process wasn't straightforward. Most of the new Californians couldn't be bothered with politics when gold glittered on the ground; they had come west not to squabble over a constitution but to get rich. Even so, those who did take time to squabble found plenty to squabble about.

PEOPLE WHO KNEW John Sutter before January 1848 had difficulty seeing him as a tragic figure. The resourceful Swiss appeared the epitome of survival, one more likely to visit tragedy, or at least suffering, on others—his wife and children abandoned in Bern, the Indians who toiled as peons around New Helvetia—than to experience it himself. But the few years after the gold discovery overturned all manner of ideas about success and failure in California, and if some observers had difficulty feeling sorry for Sutter, he had no trouble feeling sorry for himself.

Sutter's failure to persuade Richard Mason and William Sherman to ratify his claim to the land around Coloma was just the start of a series of setbacks. As the word of the gold on the American River spread, he found it impossible to keep his employees at the fort. The Mormons at Coloma fulfilled their commitment to finish the sawmill before leaving for the "Mormon Diggings" downstream, but the mill didn't cut much wood. High water on the South Fork—which had almost destroyed the mill before it was even completed—forced James Marshall to suspend sawing in the spring of 1848; by the time the water fell, no one in the area wanted to do anything but dig for gold.

Sutter succumbed to the temptation himself, after his feudal fashion. He led a troop of a hundred Indians and fifty Hawaiians into the foothills, where, according to his plan, they would do the digging and he would direct them and take the profits. The enterprise proved a fiasco. Other miners, adopting the individualistic attitude that characterized the early days in the diggings, resented Sutter's communal approach. They forcibly resisted his attempts to claim mining rights based on the number of his employees, and assaulted his men, driving many of them off. Alcohol claimed some of the others, who got too drunk to work.

Alcohol claimed Sutter, too. He had always had a taste for spirits. Sherman, in his account of the Independence Day dinner at New Helvetia, wrote, "Before the celebration was over, Sutter was very 'tight.' " When Sutter read Sherman's account, he complained, "I was no more intoxicated than he. Men cannot drink liquor without feeling the effects of it. I believe it was in bad taste for an officer of the Army to partake of my hospitality and then make flippant remarks about it, accusing the host of drunkenness." Sherman liked Sutter personally, and, learning of his host's annoyance, he amended "very 'tight' " to "enthusiastic" in the revised edition of his memoirs. Yet Sherman wasn't the only one who noticed. A verse circulated in California:

> I went to eat some oysters, along with Captain Sutter;
> And he reared up on the table, and sat down in the butter.

In the leisurely days before the gold discovery, Sutter's weakness for liquor wasn't a particular problem. But under the press of the Gold Rush, it placed him at a severe disadvantage.

Sutter's tippling revealed other character flaws—or, more precisely, traits of character that were ill-suited to the new circumstances. He had never been careful with money. He was a trusting soul, willing to wait when his debtors had cash-flow problems. In California before 1848, time was something everyone had plenty of, and personal relationships counted for more than the markings in a ledger book. But all that changed with the gold discovery. Time was money (as Pérez Rosales was repeatedly reminded), and, amid the flood of strangers, money was something that had to be watched very carefully. Sutter couldn't manage the feat. Heinrich Leinhard, an old-country associate who became Sutter's right-hand man at New Helvetia, remarked of the invaders, "Most miners were so greedy, treacherous and unreliable that no man's life was safe. Law and order were unknown, fights occurred daily and anyone who could not protect himself with his fists was unfortunate. Every man carried a gun." Sutter was simply out of his element. "He was so careless with his gold," Leinhard said, "that I was amazed that all of it was not stolen, when he had so many men of questionable character among his associates."

Within months, Sutter was forced to admit that mining wasn't for him. He paid his remaining Indians and Hawaiians and returned to the fort. When he got there he discovered that the greed of the diggings had spread downstream. The newcomers slaughtered his cows and sheep for food; they cut his grain for their horses and mules; they dismantled his fences for firewood. Two hundred barrels for packing salmon were gone; likewise the fort's cannons, church bells, and even the counterweights from the main gate. "There is a saying that men will steal everything but a milestone and a millstone," Sutter recalled disconsolately. "They stole my millstones. . . . The country swarmed with lawless men. I was alone; there was no law."

AMID THE THIEVES, however, one newcomer gave Sutter reason for hope. For fourteen years Sutter had had no contact with his family back in Switzerland. His creditors there attached what little property his wife possessed, and she and the children had to move in with her relatives. For a few years Annette Sutter awaited her husband's letter saying that he had found his niche in the New World and that she and the children should join him. But no letter came, and eventually she realized that no letter would. Then, in 1848, the news arrived of gold in California. Not every report included the name of the man who sponsored the portentous sawmill, but some did, and Annette rediscovered her long-lost husband. Although she was too old to make the trip to California, her son August, seven at the time of his father's departure and now twenty-one, was perfectly capable of the journey. With a kiss and what money she could spare, she sent him off to the land of gold to find his father and their salvation.

August reached San Francisco in September 1848. He doubtless was heartened to know that everyone had heard of his father; but he must have been shocked at *what* they had heard. Sutter's reputation for heavy drinking was accompanied by reports of the most undignified behavior at New Helvetia. According to one of Sutter's neighbors, New Helvetia was a place "where orgies and debauchery occurred as regularly as Saturday comes after Friday." By everything August learned, his father had never intended to return to Switzerland, nor to send for his wife or children. August could only wonder how he would be received by a father who had deserted and evidently forgotten him. Beyond the emotional issues were the financial ones: every second person August met seemed to have a claim against his father. August's hopes fell further on arrival at New Helvetia, where, with his father gone gold-digging, the interlopers were busy dismantling the Sutter estate.

When Sutter returned from the mountains, father and son had a teary reunion. Sutter offered excuses for not writing or sending for his family; August, wanting to believe his father, evidently accepted them. The two considered how they might solve the old man's money problems, and at the urging of some of Sutter's associates, who hoped (partly for their own sake) to keep his creditors at bay, Sutter signed over most of his property to his son. Neither the Sutters nor the advisers seriously expected to fool anyone; they chiefly sought to buy time—the time Sutter had always required to do business, and which was in such short supply at present.

Sutter's principal problem, besides his boozing and a temperament maladapted to the changed circumstances, was his lack of cash flow. His assets were substantial, in that he (or now August) owned a large amount of real estate at New Helvetia and in the vicinity. By everyone's reckoning, that real estate would be worth a great deal of money as Sacramento, the town that was already emerging there, developed. Sutter, assessing his situation in these terms, was encouraged enough to leave his affairs in August's hands and head back to the mountains. Although his mining venture had proved unprofitable, he had established a store at Coloma (in the double cabin built for Jennie Wimmer's family, since departed), and it was doing a brisk business. Besides, although he apparently didn't confide this to August, he had an Indian mistress in the mountains to whom he was eager to return.

So off he went to Coloma—only to be marooned there when winter snows rendered the road back down impassable. In his absence, Sacramento grew rapidly, but on land he (or August) did *not* own. "Had I not been snowed in at Coloma," he declared later, "Sacramento never, never would have been built." This was debatable, in light of Sutter's demonstrated ineptitude at property management. But regardless of the cause, what quickly became California's second city arose on the doorstep of Sutter's Fort, and Sutter could do little except gnash his teeth and drown his sorrows. He did try to promote an alternative townsite a few miles downstream. And though Sutterville had some significant advantages over Sacramento—the chief one being several additional feet of elevation—Sacramento was where the ferry crossed the river, it was closer to the mouth of the American River, and, ironically, it was more convenient to Sutter's Fort, with the associated stores, shops, and stables. Consequently, the real estate boom bypassed Sutter, who had only the grim satisfaction of standing on dry ground at the stillborn Sutterville when spring floodwaters inundated Sacramento, as they regularly did.

WHATEVER HIS PERSONAL foibles, the larger reason for Sutter's inability to capitalize on the gold strike was his failure of vision. He possessed a vision for California, but it was based on conditions *ante aurum*. The agricultural empire he created at New Helvetia probably would have thrived, and he grown old and rich, if not for the stampede to the mines. His empire, his vision, required cheap labor (the corollary of ample time), which vanished in the twinkling of the gold in the bed of the American River. Sutter lacked the driving audacity, the willingness to risk all in the service of a personal El Dorado, that marked the successful entrepreneurs of the dawning age of gold. New Helvetia was the vision of the past, El Dorado of the future.

In regard to vision, Sam Brannan had everything Sutter lacked. It was significant that Brannan's business was business—that is, trade—rather than land, for it prepared him for the commodification—that is, treating everything as for sale—that pervaded life in California after 1848. It was also significant that Brannan could be as cunning as anyone west of the Sierras. Brannan cajoled and threatened August Sutter into supporting Sacramento against his own father's competing Sutterville; then he turned around and threatened to abandon August, and stuck with the son only after extorting two hundred town lots from him.

Brannan and the elder Sutter shared a taste for brandy, but little else. In a murder trial at Sacramento, Brannan volunteered his services as judge. Sutter was a juror. The two passed a bottle back and forth, engaging alternately in judicial and juroral misconduct. Brannan was convinced that the defendant was guilty, and at one point leaped up to make an argument supporting the prosecution. The defendant—a man locals called "the Philosopher"—objected. "Hold on, Brannan!" he said. "You're the judge." "I know it," Brannan replied, "and I am prosecuting attorney, too!" At another point in the trial, Sutter, who had known and liked the deceased, was angered to hear the defense cast aspersions on his late friend. Rising unsteadily in the jury box, he lodged an objection. "Gentlemen," he said, "the man is dead and has atoned for his faults, and I will not sit here and hear his character traduced." Sutter thereupon grabbed the brandy bottle and headed for the door. Brannan—perhaps from prospective thirst as much as from regard for courtroom procedure—ordered him to sit down. Not surprisingly, the case ended in a mistrial. (Tried a second time, the Philosopher was acquitted.)

Outside the courtroom, Brannan and Sutter were bitter enemies. Actually, the bitterness was mostly Sutter's, who had to watch as Brannan became the grandee Sutter had lately been. Sutter was convinced that Brannan was the one who ruined Sutterville. "Brannan moved his store from the fort to the river, where Sacramento now is," Sutter recalled. "That was the reason he wanted the town there. The merchants of Sutterville were his rivals. . . . Jealousy built Sacramento." (Yet envy—Sutter's envy—got in a couple of licks. Sutter seems to have been the source of a story that initially revealed Brannan's Mormonism as the conversion-of-convenience it proved to be. When Brigham Young heard that Brannan had been tithing the miners at the Mormon Diggings, he sent an envoy to fetch the church's money. In the version circulated by Sutter, Brannan replied, "You go back and tell Brigham Young that I'll give up the Lord's money when he sends me a receipt signed by the Lord.")

Brannan's success transcended his dealings with Sutter. As the rush to the mines continued, Brannan's Sacramento store did a huge business, as much as $5,000 per day. With the proceeds he opened additional stores throughout the gold country and constructed hotels, warehouses, and other buildings in Sacramento and San Francisco. In San Francisco he organized the consortium that built the city's first large wharf. Costing $200,000, it quickly repaid its owners and greatly augmented Brannan's wealth. It was Brannan who initiated the first overland mail service to the East, and Brannan who brought the first steam locomotive to California (by ship around Cape Horn). Brannan was probably California's first millionaire, which fact alone made him, in the opinion of many of his fellow Californians, worthy of the highest regard.

And so he regarded himself. He insisted on the finest tailored clothing, now that he could afford it, and he had his barber trim his whiskers in the "imperial" fashion of the courts of central Europe: long side-whiskers and a neat tuft beneath the mouth. His heavy-lidded, almost lazy, dark eyes had sometimes seemed out of place on one as quick to get ahead as he; but now that he had outpaced the pack, their careless arrogance suited a man who had every reason for self-satisfaction.

YET SUTTER HAD a final hurrah. By the summer of 1849 the Swiss native had lost control of everything but a farm on the Feather River, to which he retreated from the swirl of swindle and confusion. He emerged only on the call of the acting governor of California, General Bennett Riley, for a convention to write a constitution for the state. Riley's action was irregular, in that California wasn't a state, or even a territory. The federal Congress, accustomed to the slow pace of settlement of the regions previously acquired from foreign countries, and consumed by matters it considered more important, had adjourned without organizing a territorial government for California. But already California contained more people than were required for statehood, and thousands more were arriving every week. The institutions left over from the Mexican era were clearly inadequate to the task of governing this rambunctious group, besides being distasteful to Americans reared on more democratic forms. So Riley, without authorization, summoned a constitutional convention, hoping the end would justify the means. "As Congress has failed to organize a new Territorial Government, it becomes our imperative duty to take some active measures to provide for the existing wants of the country," he explained. The goal of the project being "a more perfect political organization," the governor expressed his earnest desire "that all good citizens will unite in carrying it into execution."

Forty-eight delegates gathered at Monterey in early September 1849. As a group they summarized much of the diversity of the current population of California. Seven were native-born Californians; these included one Indian (Manuel Domínguez of Los Angeles). One delegate had been born in Spain, one in France, one in England, one in Scotland, one in Ireland, one (Sutter) in Switzerland. Thirty-five were born in the United States, with their time of residence in California ranging from four months to twenty years. The Americans from free states outnumbered those from slave states twenty-one to fourteen. By occupation, there were fourteen lawyers, twelve farmers (a few of the Americans preferred the label "agriculturist," while San Francisco–born José Antonio Carrillo, at fifty-three the oldest delegate, identified himself as a "*labrador*"), eight merchants, five military officers, two printers, one physician, one banker, one "negotiant" (this was Pedro Sansevaine, originally of Bordeaux), and one person (Benjamin Moore of Florida) who listed his occupation as "elegant leisure." (The degree of elegance of Moore's leisure was a matter of interpretation. He brandished a Bowie knife the size of a small sword and was typically at least semi-inebriated.) That none of the delegates identified themselves as miners, despite the fact that many of them had been in the mines, reflected the feeling almost universal in California that mining was a temporary occupation, a source of wealth rather than identity.

As in most such gatherings, assorted motives inspired the delegates. Tennessee-born William Gwin had been a congressman from Mississippi before traveling west; he wanted to become California's first senator and judged the constitutional convention the appropriate place to begin campaigning. ("Dr. Gwin laid before me his whole plan, which is this," recorded J. Ross Browne, the convention's note-taker, here acting unofficially. "He came out to California to form a constitution and identify himself with the political interests of the country. After forming a constitution he will undoubtedly be made Senator of the United States from California.") The native Californians present hoped to place a check on the enthusiasms of the Americans, preserving as much of the old system as possible, and in particular preserving their landholdings against the newcomers. (In their daydreams some of them may have hoped for more. José Carrillo, who had been an influential official under the Mexican regime, consorted regularly with former General Castro, now returned from exile. "I was gravely informed by a Californian who sat opposite me that he [Castro] meditated the reconquest of the country!" reported Bayard Taylor, attending the convention as an observer.)

The delegates gathered in Colton Hall, named for a former alcalde of Monterey who paid for the building with funds from the sale of town lots. It had two stories and was constructed of the same yellow sandstone that characterized the best buildings in Monterey. The sessions were held in a large meeting room that filled the second story. The delegates sat at four long tables, a dozen per table, and were cordoned off from spectators by a rail that ran the width of the room. Two American flags hung down behind a rostrum at the delegates' end of the room; these flanked an unusual portrait of George Washington, rendered by a local artist working chiefly—to judge by the visual evidence—from imagination. A door at the center of the room opened onto a balcony, which overlooked Monterey Bay. Delegates weary of sitting, or of listening, could step outside to enjoy the ocean air and the seaside sunsets.

Perhaps because all were sensitive to the irregularity of the proceedings, and perhaps by deliberate contrast to the anarchic state of affairs in California at large, the delegates adhered—at least at first—to strict protocol. They swore to defend the Constitution of the United States. They appointed clerks, translators, and sergeants-at-arms. They elected Robert

Semple as president of the convention and William Marcy as secretary. They appointed local clergymen to open the sessions with a prayer: Padre Antonio Ramírez for the Catholic Californians, and the Reverend S. H. Willey for the predominantly Protestant Americans.

As their initial order of substantive business, the delegates adopted a bill of rights, based on the federal Bill of Rights and the Declaration of Independence. (Perhaps to prevent Californians' suffering the common American misconception that life, liberty, and the pursuit of happiness are guaranteed under the federal Constitution, the California convention incorporated Jefferson's formula as the first section of the first article of their state constitution.) The California bill of rights also included a ban on slavery. "Neither slavery, nor involuntary servitude, unless for the punishment of crimes, shall ever be tolerated in this State," asserted the pertinent section.

The inclusion of this section was a bit of a surprise. The drafting committee had refrained from mentioning slavery, out of concern that the large southern-born contingent would object and perhaps tie up the convention at the outset. But when William Shannon, of Ireland via New York, offered the antislavery clause as an amendment to an initial draft of the constitution, the convention adopted it unanimously. For some of the southerners this may have been a tactical maneuver, a concession for which they hoped to be repaid later in the convention. For others it represented an acknowledgment that California was inhospitable to slavery. Where so many free men worked the mines, very few of them wished to incur the stigma slavery placed on manual labor. (Alternatively, as one veteran of the mines put it: "In a country where every white man makes a slave of himself, there is no use in keeping niggers.") Editorial opinion in California was strongly against slavery, and a recent mass meeting in Sacramento had resoundingly condemned the institution.

Yet the racial question, as distinct from slavery, wasn't so easily dismissed, and in fact became a central focus of the convention's debates. Even before the convention could vote on the Shannon amendment, M. M. McCarver, from Kentucky via Oregon, moved to amend the amendment, proposing to add, "Nor shall the introduction of free negroes, under indentures or otherwise, be allowed." McCarver's motion was ruled out of order until the convention voted on the Shannon amendment. The next day McCarver offered a reworded substitute; again he was put off, this time with the understanding that his views would be considered later. On September 19 he tried again, and succeeded in sparking a heated discussion. "No population that could be brought within the limits of our territory could be more repugnant to the feelings of the people, or injurious to the prosperity of the community, than free negroes," McCarver asserted. "They are idle in their habits, difficult to be governed by the laws, thriftless, and uneducated. It is a species of population that this country should be particularly guarded against."

Robert Semple—also from Kentucky, via Missouri—concurred. Saying he had canvassed opinion regarding such a measure, the convention president declared, "I found no man in my district who did not approve of it." Semple suggested that in the absence of a ban on blacks, the southern states would dump their unwanted Negroes on California. "I can assure you, sir, thousands will be introduced into this country before long, if you do not insert a positive prohibition against them in your Constitution—an immense and overwhelming population of negroes, who have never been freemen, who have never been accustomed to provide for themselves. What would be the state of things in a few years? The whole country would be filled with emancipated slaves—the worst species of population—prepared to do nothing but steal, or live upon our means as paupers." As president of the convention, Semple felt particular responsibility for ensuring ratification of the document it produced; he suggested that an anti-Negro clause would be very popular. "It will be a strong recommendation to the Constitution, and give it many votes in the community which may not otherwise be cast for it."

Shannon differed strenuously. In the first place, he said, Semple deluded himself to think eastern slaveholders would go to the trouble and expense of sending their slaves clear to California to emancipate them. Why not simply ship them across the Ohio River? More fundamentally, the proposed ban was ethically repugnant. "Free men of color have just as good a right, and ought to have, to emigrate here as white men." The ban would deprive the Negroes of their right to make a living in California, and it would deprive California of the value of their labor.

William Wozencraft, born in Ohio but lately of Louisiana, thought Shannon naïvely mistaken in contending that Negroes could bring anything of value to California. "Why, sir, of all the states that I have any knowledge of, whether free or slave states, it is admitted by all, whether philanthropists for blacks or for all mankind, that the free negro is one of the greatest evils that society can be afflicted with." As to the matter of rights, Shannon should consider the rights of white workingmen, and of the people of California generally. "We should protect them against a class of society that would degrade labor, and thereby arrest the progress of enterprise and greatly impair the prosperity of the state."

Kimball Dimmick of New York rallied to Shannon's defense. Whatever the experience of other states, Dimmick said, California was different. "We occupy a peculiar position. We are forming a constitution for the first state of the American Union on the shores of the Pacific. The eyes of the world are turned toward us. The constitution which emanates from our hands is to be subjected to the scrutiny of all the civilized nations of the earth." The recent revolutions in Europe, and the rumblings in several American states against slavery, revealed that the spirit of liberty was alive and advancing. "Let it not be said that we, the first great republican state on the borders of the Pacific, who have it within our power to spread the blessings of free institutions even to the remotest shore of the Eastern world—let it not be said that we have attempted to arrest the progress of human freedom. Let this constitution go forth from this convention, and from the new state, a model instrument of liberal and enlightened principles."

The debate continued for hours, with additional speakers joining in and the original speakers reiterating and reformulating their arguments. In the end, the convention, sitting as a committee of the whole, approved McCarver's anti-Negro proposition. But the vote was close, and when the convention, as the convention, ultimately passed judgment on the work of the committee of the whole, the provision was dropped.

The other topic of sustained debate was the boundary of California, in particular the eastern boundary. The western boundary was as undeniable as oceans generally are. The northern border—the 42nd parallel, separating California from Oregon—had been fixed by treaty with Spain in 1819. The southern border was the frontier with Mexico, as of the Treaty of Guadalupe Hidalgo. But the eastern border was undetermined. Conceivably it might lie as far east as the western border of Texas, which itself was subject to dispute. It certainly was no farther west than the summit of the Sierras. Congress hadn't spoken in the matter; consequently the California convention felt compelled to do so.

Several considerations informed the discussion. Slavery was one, which reentered the convention hall through the back door of the boundary debate. Some of the southerners fantasized about dividing California, sooner or later, along the 36° 30' line of the Missouri Compromise, with slavery being allowed south of the line. Such an outcome presumably would result more readily if California were larger rather than smaller; hence this group wanted a more easterly border. On the other hand, if the north-south division did *not* occur, then a generous eastern border would serve only to lock slavery out of a larger region. This was precisely the hope of the more ardent antislavery men at the convention: better to settle the slavery question here and now for the entire region taken from Mexico. Yet an overly ambitious boundary might stir up the pro-slavery forces in Congress, the body that would have to approve any California constitution. Finally, the presence of some thirty thousand Mormons around the Great Salt Lake complicated jurisdictional questions. The Mormons hadn't sent any delegates to the Monterey convention, nor been asked to send any. How could the Monterey convention presume to speak for them? For that matter, did it *want* to speak for them? Mormons were hardly the most popular people in North America, as their unfortunate and turbulent history demonstrated. Many in California wished nothing to do with them.

The delegates probed all aspects of the issue, declaiming on the merits of this line or that, even as they understood that their projections regarding the consequences of alternative boundaries were merely guesses. Sarcasm (Why not make the boundary the Mississippi River? asked one opponent of the more grandiose schemes. For that matter, why not include Cuba?) mingled with seriousness; pragmatism (Whatever we decide, Congress will have the final say) contested with principle. Ultimately the convention accepted what became the modern boundary of the state: the 120th meridian south from the 42nd parallel to the 39th, thence southeast to the Colorado River, thence to the Mexican border.

Minor issues consumed less time but hardly less emotion. Whether and how much the delegates ought to be paid for their efforts was one sore point. Some patriots volunteered to work for free, but others noted that time devoted to the public weal was time taken from private profit. The convention settled on a per diem allowance of $16 per day, and $16 per 20 miles traveled to and from Monterey. Several members proposed to ban state-run lotteries. An astonished Roman Price, a retired U.S. naval officer and a delegate from San Francisco, thought this the height of absurdity, considering Californians' passion for all other sorts of gambling. "The people of California are essentially a gambling people," he declared. Henry W. Halleck, representing Monterey, retorted, "We may be a gambling community, but let us not in this constitution create a gambling state." The lottery ban survived. A proposal to disfranchise duelists led to a sharp exchange that almost culminated in demands for satisfaction; evidently convinced of the need, the delegates adopted the measure. Various members expressed what another lampooned as a "holy horror of banking"; the antibank faction tried to prohibit the chartering of banks entirely, but other delegates succeeded in softening the ban to allow "associations" for the deposit of gold and silver—which associations, however, could not issue banknotes or anything else that might circulate as money. A proposal to permit women to keep control of their property upon marrying led to discussion of the relative merits of the common-law and civil-law traditions. "I am not wedded either to the common law or the civil law," observed Halleck, "nor, as yet, to a woman; but having some hopes that some time or other I may be wedded, and wishing to avoid the fate of my friend from San Francisco [a crotchety old misogynist], I shall advocate this section in the constitution, and I would call upon all the bachelors in this convention to vote for it." Enough did to win the measure's approval.

THE DELEGATES BROUGHT their work to a close on October 12, six weeks after the convention began. That night was devoted to a grand ball hosted by the people of Monterey (but paid for by contributions of $25 each from the delegates). Bayard Taylor described the celebration:

> The hall was cleared of the forum and tables and decorated with young pines from the forest. At each end were the American colors, tastefully disposed across the boughs. Three chandeliers, neither of bronze nor cut-glass, but neat and brilliant withal, poured their light on the festivities. At eight o'clock—the fashionable ball-hour in Monterey—the guests began to assemble, and in an hour afterward the hall was crowded with nearly all the Californian and American residents. There were sixty or seventy ladies present, and an equal number of gentlemen, in addition to the members of the convention. The dark-eyed daughters of Monterey, Los Angeles and Santa Barbara mingled in pleasing contrast with the fairer bloom of the trans-Nevadian belles. The variety of feature and complexion was fully equalled by the variety of dress. In the whirl of the waltz, a plain, dark, nun-like robe would be followed by one of pink satin and gauze; next, perhaps, a bodice of scarlet velvet with gold buttons, and then a rich figured brocade, such as one sees on the stately dames of Titian.
>
> The dresses of the gentlemen showed considerable variety, but were much less picturesque. A complete ball-dress was a happiness attained only by the fortunate few. White kids [kid gloves] could not be had in Monterey for love or money, and as much as $50 was paid by one gentleman for a pair of patent-leather boots. Scarcely a single dress that was seen belonged entirely to its wearer, and I thought, if the clothes had power to leap severally back to their re-

> spective owners, some persons would have been in a state of utter destitution. . . .
>
> Gen. Riley was there in full uniform, with the yellow sash he won at Contreras; Majors Canby, Hill and Smith, Captains Burton and Kane, and the others stationed in Monterey, accompanying him. In one group might be seen Captain Sutter's soldierly mustache and clear blue eye; in another, the erect figure and quiet, dignified bearing of Gen. Vallejo. Don Pablo de la Guerra, with his handsome, aristocratic features, was the floor manager, and gallantly discharged his office. Conspicuous among the native members were Don Miguel de Pedrorena and Jacinto Rodriguez, both polished gentlemen and deservedly popular. Dominguez, the Indian member, took no part in the dance, but evidently enjoyed the scene as much as anyone present.

The dancing lasted till midnight, when dinner was served. The guests feasted on turkey, roast pig, beef, tongue, and paté, washed down with assorted wines, liquors, and coffee. The dancing thereupon resumed, and continued till dawn.

After a few hours' sleep, the delegates regathered to sign the constitution. One by one they affixed their names to the document. At the appropriate moment, the guns at the fort of Monterey boomed a salute to the delegates and to the new constitution—thirty-one times, for the thirty-first state.

John Sutter may still have been merry from the night before, but the symbolism and significance of the moment overwhelmed him. "All the native enthusiasm of Capt. Sutter's Swiss blood was aroused," Taylor recorded. "He was the old soldier again. He sprang from his seat, and, waving his hand around his head, as if swinging a sword, exclaimed: 'Gentlemen, this is the happiest day of my life! It makes me glad to hear those cannon: they remind me of the time when I was a soldier. Yes, I am glad to hear them—this is a great day for California!' Then, recollecting himself, he sat down, the tears streaming from his eyes."

To Sutter was accorded the honor of leading the delegates to the quarters of Governor Riley. "General," Sutter declared, "I have been appointed by the delegates elected by the people of California to form a Constitution, to address you in their names and in behalf of the whole people of California, and express the thanks of the Convention for the aid and cooperation they have received from you in the discharge of the responsible duty of creating a State Government."

To which Riley replied, "Gentlemen, I congratulate you upon the successful conclusion of your arduous labors, and I wish you all happiness and prosperity."

11

Shaking the Temple

To carry the new constitution east to Washington, Californians chose John Frémont. The master of the Mariposa was California's leading citizen—which said as much about California as about him. Whether many of those who voted for the state legislature specified under the Monterey constitution recalled Frémont's arrest for mutiny in California and his subsequent court-martial is unclear; nearly all those voters were far from California at the time and next to none had ever dreamed of going there. If they did remember Frémont's clash with the army and the president, they apparently were more impressed with his role in exploring the West and conquering California. Those who didn't remember or never knew could simply admire the enormous wealth that was pouring from Frémont's part of the Mother Lode into the Pathfinder's pockets. By this measure alone, Frémont was the embodiment of success in Gold Rush California; and when the new legislature met, it was proud to select Colonel Frémont to be California's first senator.

Yet Frémont's election was as much Jessie's doing as his own. John Frémont was elected senator not only for his wealth and fame, but also for his opposition to slavery. And his opposition to slavery, while principled enough, had become an article of his political faith primarily at the insistence of his wife. This was somewhat surprising, given that Missouri, the home of the Bentons, was a slave state (as all those overlanders noticed). But the Benton household rejected slavery. Jessie's mother set the tone on the issue. As Jessie recalled, her mother "gave freedom to her slaves because of her conscientious feeling on the subject." Elizabeth Benton's conscience in turn dictated the actions of Thomas Benton. "While he did not share these ideas from the same religious and logical thoughts that made them obligatory on my mother, he yet made it thoroughly easy for her to carry out her feelings." Twice the Bentons turned down large inheritances because they came encumbered by slaves. Whatever John Frémont's original feelings on slavery, he discovered at the time of courting Jessie that there would be no slaves in her household.

Jessie's California acquaintances learned the same thing in Monterey. No wages could persuade any of the few American women in the area to do the Frémont wash, so Jessie tried to get some Indian women to take on the task. They agreed, but followed their own custom of beating the dirty clothes between flat stones in a stream, employing as soap a native plant called amole. "Everything looked very white and smelled fresh, but they had been merely washed and dried; there was no starching, no ironing, and a very distorted-looking lot of garments they were," Jessie recalled. The Indians had never heard of pressing clothes and, upon having the concept explained, wondered why on earth anyone would go to the trouble. They certainly wouldn't and, saying so, departed. Jessie had just about resigned herself to becoming the family's laundress when a neighbor from one of the southern states loaned her a black woman servant to do the job. Jessie's initial delight evaporated when the lender insisted that the Frémonts purchase the woman, a slave. "We gave her up," Jessie wrote. "It required no thinking or effort to make this decision; it was simply following out the habit of mind which came from my education and the example shown me at home."

The daughter of the distinguished senator, the wife of the famous explorer and soldier, was always in the public eye in California, and this decision increased the scrutiny. Jessie determined to demonstrate that even on this frontier, where good help really *was* hard to find, one could maintain a respectable household without bound labor. "Everyone knows the important part of a good dinner in diplomacy," she recounted. "The great Napoleon knew and acted on this." So did Jessie Frémont. The public eating houses in Monterey were expensive and of notoriously poor quality; Jessie made a point of hosting dinners for the delegates. She and two Indian men—who worked for wages—set a hearty and festive board, served on the best Frémont china ("I had to get used to Juan and Gregorio breaking a great deal of this"). "Our house and table were open, after the hospitable fashion of a new country, to all who had been, or would like to be, friends, and they saw for themselves that it was quite possible for the most cheerful hospitality to exist without the usual working forces." She recalled one fence-sitter making up his mind: "All these women here are crying out to have 'suv-vents'—but if you, a Virginia lady [Jessie didn't bother to correct him], can get along without, they shan't have them—we'll keep clear of slave labor."

In another sense as well, the Frémonts were considered a test case regarding slavery. The Mariposa mines seemed suited to slave labor if anything in California was. Advocates of slavery told John that his labor troubles—this at a moment when the Sonoran miners were about to go home, and no replacements had been found—would end if he could simply *purchase* replacements. But Jessie wouldn't hear of it, and neither would he.

As a result of their opposition to slavery, the Frémont household in Monterey became a meeting place for the antislavery men of the constitutional convention—which was another reason Jessie placed such store in setting a good table. And when the convention decided against slavery, John became a leading candidate for one of the state's two Senate seats.

How much encouragement he required from Jessie to make himself available for election is unknown. His ambition still burned, but till now it had sought, and found, outlets in activities suited to the soldier and explorer. Politics was something else—something that came far more naturally, by temperament and upbringing, to her than to him. Although she took pains to avoid appearing pushy, her ambition was evident to those who knew them both. Edward Bosqui, who for a period managed Frémont's Mariposa mines, explained, "Mrs. Frémont was a highly accomplished woman of fine intellect, with a towering ambition and courage equal to her husband's." Another acquaintance put the matter more bluntly, calling Jessie "the better man of the two, far more intelligent and more comprehensive." Almost certainly, John's decision to enter politics was Jessie's decision also.

John's election took place in December 1849. Following the adjournment of the Monterey convention, the constitution was referred to the voters of California for approval. Only about 13,000 trooped to the polling places, the rest apparently being too busy gathering the last gold before the winter rains shut down the mines. But by a margin of fifteen to one they ratified the new charter. They also selected the members of California's first legislature, which convened at San Jose on December 17. (The opening of the session had been scheduled for December 15, but those winter rains, now arrived, postponed a quorum.) An early order of business was the election of California's two senators. Frémont was elected on the first ballot, with 29 of 46 votes. William Gwin was chosen on the second ballot, with 24 votes.

Jessie received the good news at Monterey a short while later.

> One evening of tremendous rain, when we were, as usual, around the fire, Mrs. M'Evoy, with her table and lights, sewing at one side, myself by the other, explaining pictures from the *Illustrated Times* to my little girl, while the baby rolled about on the bear skin in front of the fire, suddenly Mr. Frémont came in upon us, dripping wet, as well he might be, for he had come through from San Jose—seventy miles on horseback through the heavy rain. He was so wet that we could hardly make him cross the pretty room; but "beautiful are the feet of him that beareth glad tidings," and the footmarks were all welcome, for they pointed home. He came to tell me that he had been elected Senator, and that it was necessary we should go to Washington on the steamer of the 1st of January.

WHEN JESSIE FRÉMONT arrived at Washington in March 1850, no one greeted her more warmly than Thomas Benton. And no one inspected her more closely. Jessie's father had followed the trials of her outbound isthmus crossing (hearing from the steamship people details Jessie omitted from her letters) with concern matched only by the knowledge that there was nothing he could do about it (beyond ensuring that the steamship folks looked after her as much as she would allow). He knew of the fabulous fortune John had fallen into at the Mariposa, and of course now he knew that John had been elected California's first senator. He wondered what Jessie's role in the election had been; he himself had never thought of John as the political type. And he wondered what California had done to his daughter. She couldn't have grown more willful; that would have been impossible. But as he watched her get off the train from New York, where their steamship back from Panama had landed, she seemed more capable, more calmly confident. Perhaps she shared with him the sentiment she later put to paper: "I had done so many things that I had never done before that a new sense of power had come to me." But she didn't really have to tell him, for he could see it himself.

She had every reason to feel confident. Beyond the knowledge of competencies she hadn't known she possessed, she occupied what to most observers must have seemed a charmed position in American life. She was one of the wealthiest women in the country, and growing wealthier by the week. Her father was one of the nation's most powerful men—in fact, the senior member of the Senate, by length of service. And her husband was now a senator also, at the start of what promised to be an illustrious political career. Travel to and from the West Coast was getting easier, as the recent journey back had demonstrated; Jessie could readily imagine herself splitting time between California, her new home and the seat of her and John's wealth, and Washington, her old home and the seat of national power.

There was one hitch in this scenario, however. John wasn't actually a senator yet, and he wouldn't be until Congress accepted the Monterey constitution and officially made California the thirty-first state.

And this was by no means a sure thing. The roots of the opposition to California's admission ran to 1846, when Democratic congressman David Wilmot of Pennsylvania introduced a measure to ban slavery in any territory acquired from Mexico in the war just begun. The Wilmot Proviso passed the House of Representatives yet failed in the Senate, a circumstance that both reflected and exacerbated the tension between North and South. For years the North's population had been growing faster than the South's; the greater numbers in the North gave that region a distinct advantage in the population-apportioned House. But a balance held in the Senate, where the fifteen northern states were matched by the fifteen southern states. The voting on the Wilmot Proviso reminded northerners of the imperfectly democratic character of Congress, in which southerners wielded more power per person than northerners, and it inspired many northerners to try to break the southern hold by admitting more free states. The Wilmot voting reminded southerners of the same thing, with the opposite effect. Southerners recalled that congressional democracy was deliberately imperfect—how else to guard states' rights?—and they feared a northern plot to overturn the system so carefully crafted by the Founders.

Until John Frémont and the other members-elect of California's congressional delegation arrived at the national capital in 1850, the debate over the Wilmot Proviso remained theoretical: an argument about what to do when the time came to organize the territory taken from Mexico. The arrival of the California delegation made plain that the time had come. Indeed, the time was past, for the Californians had organized themselves. Congress now had to accept their accomplishment or reject it.

But things weren't that simple, for the California question reopened the entire sectional dispute. Twice in living memory, thrice in American history, crises between North and South that threatened to disunite the states had been resolved by compromise: at the Constitutional Convention of 1787, when the three-fifths formula settled the argument over how to count slaves toward representation; in the Missouri Compromise of 1820, which divided the Louisiana Territory between future slave states and free at the line of 36° 30'; and with the Compromise of 1833, which saved face for both sides in the nullification controversy between South Carolina and the supporters of states' rights on one hand, and the Jackson administration and the partisans of federal power on the other. Perhaps a fourth compromise would resolve the California question, but any such compromise wouldn't come easily. Seventeen years had passed since the settlement of 1833, thirty years since the Missouri Compromise. In that time the rift between North and South had grown wider and deeper, and the conciliatory spirit in Congress that made those earlier settlements possible had been diminished by retirement and death.

As it had for most of the nineteenth century, the nation looked to three members of Congress for guidance, three statesmen who towered above the rest. Henry Clay literally did tower above his colleagues. Monumentally tall, with a high forehead, piercing eyes, and flowing hair, he was a sculptor's model of a statesman. As a Kentuckian, a man of the West, Clay had guided the North and South to amicable settlements in the compromises of 1820 and 1833, and he believed he could do the same now. He wrapped California in a compromise package of several legislative parts. First, California would be admitted as a state, with the Monterey (antislavery) constitution. Second, territorial governments would be organized for the rest of the Mexican cession (construed as New Mexico and Utah) without restriction on slavery. Third, the disputed boundary between Texas and New Mexico would be arbitrated. Fourth, the federal government would assume Texas's debts. Fifth, slavery would continue to be allowed in the District of Columbia (where, in the capital of democracy, it had come under attack as especially inappropriate). Sixth, the slave *trade* within the federal district would be abolished (the commerce in flesh being judged the most egregious aspect of slavery). Seventh, the fugitive slave law would be stiffened. Eighth, Congress would explicitly disavow any interference with the slave trade in or between slave states.

It was a lot to ask, as Clay conceded. "But it is impossible for us to be blind to the facts which are daily transpiring before us." Everywhere the spirit of section raged, goaded by the spirit of party. "It is passion, passion—party, party—and intemperance; that is all I dread in the adjustment of the great questions which unhappily at this time divide our distracted country. At this moment, we have in the legislative bodies of this Capitol, and in the States, twenty-odd furnaces in full blast in generating heat and passion and intemperance, and diffusing them throughout the whole extent of this broad land. Two months ago, all was calm in comparison with the present moment. All now is uproar, confusion, menace to the existence of the Union and to the happiness and safety of this people."

Because California had precipitated the current uproar, Clay concentrated on the candidate state. Senators from the South complained that their section was being shut out of the prize for which all Americans had fought against Mexico. Clay asked the distinguished gentlemen to consider who, precisely, was shutting them out. Was it Congress? Was it the North? "No, sir, the interdiction is imposed by California herself. And has it not been the doctrine of all parties that, when a State is about to be admitted into the Union, that State has a right to decide for itself whether it will or will not have within its limits slavery?" Did Congress claim the right to prevent New York from abolishing slavery within its own borders? For that matter, did Congress claim the right to force abolition on Virginia? It did neither. Likewise, then, Congress should not presume to dictate to California regarding slavery.

Clay spoke at considerable length—for two days, in fact—on the rest of his compromise package. He would have continued into a third day, but when a weary colleague moved to adjourn, Clay promised, "I begin to see land. I shall pretty soon arrive at the end." In getting there he acknowledged the deficiencies of any set of compromises, yet he contended that the alternative to compromise was something far worse. Extremists spoke of secession as though that could be accomplished without violence. They were woefully wrong. "War is the only alternative by which a dissolution could be accomplished. . . . In less than sixty days, war would be blazing forth in every part of this now happy and peaceable land." And it would be such a war as no one in America had ever seen. "We may search the pages of history, and none so furious, so bloody, so implacable, so exterminating, from the wars of Greece down, including those of the Commonwealth of England, and the revolutions of France—none, none of them raged with such violence, or was ever conducted with such bloodshed and enormities as will that war which shall follow that disastrous event—if that event ever happen—of dissolution."

Clay closed with a plea.

> I conjure gentlemen—whether from the South or the North, by all they hold dear in this world—by all their love of liberty—by all their veneration for their ancestors—by all their regard for posterity—by all their gratitude to Him who has bestowed upon them such unnumbered blessings—by all the duties which they owe to mankind, and all the duties they owe to themselves—by all these considerations I implore them to pause—solemnly to pause—at the edge of the precipice, before the fearful and disastrous leap is taken in the yawning abyss below, which will inevitably lead to certain and irretrievable destruction.
>
> And, finally, Mr. President, I implore, as the best blessing which Heaven can bestow upon me upon earth, that if the direful and sad event of the dissolution of the Union shall happen, I may not survive to behold the sad and heart-rending spectacle.

NO ONE EVER called John Calhoun handsome, yet his appearance was even more arresting than Clay's. Dubbed the "Cast-Iron Man" in honor of his unyielding character, the South Carolinian earned the label almost equally by his visage, which brought to mind the prophet Ezekiel, had the latter shaved his beard and put on a collar and cravat. (Milton's Satan was another image that came to the mind of at least one man who knew Calhoun.) By 1850, though, Calhoun was a shadow, or specter, of his former self; tuberculosis was drawing him ineluctably to the grave. He could only croak a whisper, and then not for long. The Senate readily granted permission when he asked if a colleague might read his reply to Clay.

Calhoun concurred with Clay that the Senate confronted a single central question—"the greatest and the gravest question that can ever come under your consideration: How can the Union be preserved?" But he differed with Clay on almost everything else. The present danger arose not from any extremism in the South, he said, but from the intolerance of the North. The antipathy of the North for the South had been evident for decades, and was manifest most recently in the conspiracy to admit California. For conspiracy it was, plotted between the executive branch, whose agent in California had authorized the irregular Monterey convention, and the antislavery elements in the federal legislature, who wished to force California on Congress.

The case of California, Calhoun said, was premised on the "monstrous assumption" that sovereignty over the territories resided with the people of those territories, rather than with Congress. This was utterly false. Had California—like Texas, for example—won independence from Mexico on its own, then it would have had the right to fashion its own government. But California was acquired from Mexico by American blood and American treasure. The American government, therefore, controlled the destiny of California. "The individuals in California who have undertaken to form a constitution and a State, and to exercise the power of legislating without the consent of Congress, have usurped the sovereignty of the State and the authority of Congress, and have acted in open defiance of them both. In other words, what they have done is revolutionary and rebellious in its character, anarchical in its tendency, and calculated to lead to the most dangerous consequences." The supporters of California's admission had laid before the Senate a document purporting to be a constitution, and they spoke of California as having rights, as though it were already a state. Nothing could be more wrong. "Can you believe that there is such a State in reality as the State of California? No; there is no such State. It has no legal or constitutional existence. It has no validity, and can have none without your sanction."

In opposing California, Calhoun said, the South simply asked for justice—no more than it deserved, but neither any less. The South was satisfied to remain in the Union, but only so long as its rights were honored. Gentlemen spoke of settling differences between the sections. "Can this be done? Yes, easily; but not by the weaker party, for it can of itself do nothing—not even protect itself—but by the stronger. The North has only to will it to accomplish it." The North must concede the South's equal rights in California and the other the acquired territories. It must fulfill its duty regarding fugitive slaves. It must cease agitation of the slave question.

Calhoun mocked the calls of northerners for "Union." "The cry of

'Union, Union, the glorious Union!' can no more prevent disunion than the cry of 'Health, health, glorious health!' on the part of the physician can save a patient lying dangerously ill." Besides, the cry of "Union" commonly came not from those dedicated to its preservation but from those bent on its destruction, through such crimes as the imposing of California on the rest of the country. Calhoun gave a grim warning, and ominously washed his hands of what might follow.

> California will become the test question. If you admit her, under all the difficulties that oppose her admission, you compel us to infer that you intend to exclude us from the whole of the acquired territories, with the intention of destroying irretrievably the equilibrium between the two sections. We would be blind not to perceive, in that case, that your real objects are power and aggrandizement, and infatuated not to act accordingly.
>
> I have now, Senators, done my duty in expressing my opinions fully, freely, and candidly, on this solemn occasion. In doing so, I have been governed by the motives which have governed me in all the stages of the agitation of the slavery question since its commencement. I have exerted myself, during the whole period, to arrest it, with the intention of saving the Union, if it could be done; and, if it could not, to save the section where it has pleased Providence to cast my lot, and which I sincerely believe has justice and the Constitution on its side. Having faithfully done my duty to the best of my ability, both to the Union and my section, throughout this agitation, I shall have the consolation, let what will come, that I am free from all responsibility.

DANIEL WEBSTER FOLLOWED Clay. From youth, the New Englander's swarthy appearance seemed an apt complement to his dark intensity. "He was a black, raven-haired fellow," recalled one who knew him then, "with an eye as black as death, and as heavy as a lion's—and no lion in Africa ever had a voice like him, and his look was like a lion's—that same heavy look, not sleepy, but as if he didn't care about any thing that was going on about any thing; but as if he would think like a hurricane if he once got worked up to it." Webster's reputation grew until he came to be considered the greatest orator in an age that prized the ability to speak. Generations of schoolchildren memorized the closing line of his address in the nullification debate: "Liberty and Union, now and forever, one and inseparable!" Thenceforth he was regularly referred to as "the God-like Daniel." A British observer was moved to declare, "That man is a fraud, for it is impossible for anyone to be as great as he looks."

Accordingly, an expectant hush fell over the Senate when Webster rose to answer Calhoun. "I wish to speak today," he said, "not as a Massachusetts man, nor as a northern man, but as an American." Southerners groaned at this appropriation of the national label, but such was Webster's manner that none openly disputed it. "We live in the midst of strong agitations, and are surrounded by very considerable dangers," he went on.

> The imprisoned winds are let loose. The East, the West, the North, and the stormy South, all combine to throw the whole ocean into commotion, to toss its billows to the skies, and to disclose its profoundest depths. I do not affect to regard myself, Mr. President, as holding, or as fit to hold, the helm in this combat of political elements; but I have a duty to perform, and I mean to perform it with fidelity—not without a sense of surrounding dangers, but not without hope. I have a part to act, not for my own security or safety, for I am looking out for no fragment upon which to float away from the wreck, if wreck there must be, but for the good of the whole, and the preservation of the whole; and there is that which will keep me to my duty during this struggle, whether the sun and the stars shall appear, or shall not appear, for many days. I speak today for the preservation of the Union. Hear me for my cause!

Webster inquired how the current crisis had come about, the present tempest arisen. He made no claim that high ideals drove the peopling of

California. "In January of 1848, the Mormons, it is said, or some of them, made a discovery of an extraordinarily rich mine of gold; or, rather, of a very great quantity of gold, hardly fit to be called a mine, for it was spread near the surface—on the lower part of the south or American branch of the Sacramento." Webster's geography was a little shaky, but not the thrust of his argument. "The digging commenced in the spring of that year, and from that time to this, the work of searching for gold has been prosecuted with a success not heretofore known in the history of this globe." From all over the world, and from all across the United States, gold-seekers flocked to the mines. Yet even as their numbers mounted, and with their numbers their need for the security of government, Congress had failed to act. So they took responsibility on themselves. They called a convention at Monterey and wrote a constitution that they subsequently submitted to the people of California, who approved it. All the Californians asked now was the belated blessing of the federal government on their efforts.

It was not their fault that in seeking admission they had reopened the question of slavery. Yet in a certain sense the question had *not* been reopened, for nature herself decreed where slavery might profitably be practiced, and where not. The law of nature—"of physical geography, the law of the formation of the earth"—spoke with an authority the institutions of man could only envy. "That law settles forever, with a strength beyond all terms of human enactment, that slavery cannot exist in California." Here Webster explained that he was speaking of slavery on a large scale: plantation slavery. Domestic servants might be taken west and kept indefinitely. But slavery as a general institution could never thrive there.

Webster concluded from this—to the surprise and discomfiture of some of his northern supporters—that the Wilmot Proviso was superfluous, and in fact counterproductive. Providence had made any such prohibition on Western slavery unnecessary, and the very act of prohibition needlessly antagonized the South. The South had a right to feel aggrieved.

But not so aggrieved as to speak of secession, the way Calhoun did. "I hear with pain, and anguish, and distress, the word secession, especially when it falls from the lips of those who are eminently patriotic, and known to the country, and known all over the world, for their political services." With Clay, Webster denied the possibility of peaceable secession.

> Peaceable secession! Sir, your eyes and mine are never destined to see that miracle. The dismemberment of this vast country without convulsion! The breaking up of the fountains of the great deep without ruffling the surface! Who is so foolish—I beg everybody's pardon—as to expect to see any such thing? . . . Peaceable secession! Peaceable secession! The concurrent agreement of all the members of this great Republic to separate! A voluntary separation, with alimony on one side and on the other. Why, what would be the result? Where is the line to be drawn? What States are to secede? What is to remain American? What am I to be—an American no longer? Where is the flag of the Republic to remain? Where is the eagle still to tower? Or is he to cower, and shrink, and fall to the ground? Why, sir, our ancestors—our fathers, and our grandfathers, those of them that are yet living among us with prolonged lives—would rebuke and reproach us; and our children, and our grandchildren, would cry out, Shame upon us! if we, of this generation, should dishonor these ensigns of the power of the Government, and the harmony of the Union, which is every day felt among us with so much joy and gratitude.

This wild talk must cease, and be supplanted by earnest effort, motivated by all the goodwill honest men could muster.

> Instead of speaking of the possibility or utility of secession, instead of dwelling in these caverns of darkness, instead of groping with those ideas so full of all that is horrid and horrible, let us come out into the light of day; let us enjoy the fresh air of liberty and union; let us cherish those hopes which belong to us; let us devote ourselves to those great objects that are fit for our consideration and our action; let us raise our conceptions to the magnitude and the importance of the duties that devolve upon us; let our compre-

hension be as broad as the country for which we act, our aspirations as high as its certain destiny.

JOHN AND JESSIE FRÉMONT observed the debate from the Senate gallery and participated from the sidelines. To all who would listen they explained that right and justice were with the Californians. "The Government of the United States has been three years indebted to the people of California for property taken and services rendered, and during this time they have been without representation, and without protection" asserted a letter published in the *National Intelligencer* over the signature of John but which almost certainly was edited, if not drafted, by Jessie.

Jessie had an additional stake in the debate, for her father was one of the leading antagonists. On the afternoon of June 10, Thomas Benton rose to address the Senate. Since March, Clay's package of proposals had been referred to an ad hoc committee (called the Committee of Thirteen) and crafted into a single bill, largely at the instance of Henry Foote of Mississippi, who wished to ensure that the concessions to the South not be separated from the rest of Clay's package. Clay initially opposed the one-bill approach; after Foote spoke in favor, Clay derided Foote's "omnibus speech, in which he introduced all sorts of things and every sort of passenger, and myself among the number." But such was Foote's influence that Clay felt obliged to go along (in the process adding a term—omnibus—to the American political lexicon).

Benton refused to join Clay on the omnibus ride. As the elder statesman of the Senate, Benton took very seriously the dignity of the upper house, and he felt insulted at being presented with an all-or-nothing choice. Besides, as a staunch opponent of slavery, he resisted the concessions to slaveholders the Clay formula entailed. Moreover, as one with a long history of supporting Western expansion, he resented that California should be held hostage to such extraneous matters as slavery in the District of Columbia. Finally, he didn't like Clay, and he absolutely despised Foote, whose tongue was as sharp as Benton's temper was short.

At one point the Benton-Foote feud turned almost deadly. On

April 17, Foote assailed Benton as a "calumniator." Benton responded by rising from his desk on the Senate floor and striding angrily toward the Mississippian. Foote, a small, slight man, feared the worst from the bruising Benton. He pulled a revolver, aimed it at Benton, and cocked it.

As colleagues hastily intervened, Benton threw them aside. "Let the assassin fire!" he shouted. "A pistol has been brought here to assassinate me!"

Foote responded that he was only defending himself, being no match physically for Benton.

Benton refused to be mollified. "No assassin has a right to draw a pistol on me!" he bellowed.

By now the gun had been taken from Foote, and the mortal danger passed. Several senators demanded Foote's expulsion; others were willing to settle for an investigation. The investigation proved nothing except that the debate over California was as ugly and explosive as anything the legislators had ever experienced.

In Benton's speech of June 10, he showered scorn upon the Foote-Clay omnibus. "This batch of bills is not to be a law freely made by Congress," he asserted, "but a compact to be swallowed, and swallowed whole, under the penalty of party execution and political damnation." The committee responsible for the omnibus bill had crafted a "monster." Benton intoned, "I proceed to the destruction of this monster."

Benton's heaviest blows were directed at the link between California's admission and the sundry complaints of the slaveholders. "The California bill is made the scape-goat of all the sins of slavery in the United States—that California which is innocent of all these sins." In case his listeners had forgotten what a scapegoat originally was, Benton reminded them: "an innocent and helpless animal, loaded with sins which were not his own, and made to die for offences which he had never committed." Benton continued, "So of California. She is innocent of all the evils of slavery in the United States, yet they are all to be packed upon her back, and herself sacrificed under the heavy load." California should have been admitted as soon as her constitution arrived, but the men now promoting the omnibus refused. "She has been delayed long, and is now endangered by this attempt to couple her with the territories [New Mexico and Utah], with which she has no connection, and to involve her in the Wilmot Proviso question, from which she is free." Nor was that all. "Now she is joined to Texas also, and must be damned if not strong enough to save Texas." And there was still more: the question of slavery in the District of Columbia, and of the fugitive slaves. "The conjunction of these bills illustrates all the evils of joining incoherent subjects together. It presents a revolting enormity, of which all the evils go to an innocent party, which has done all in its power to avoid them." California wanted nothing to do with the slavery quarrel, as she had demonstrated in her convention. "Existence and relief, is her cry!" the Senate must answer, affirmatively.

Benton's blows accomplished their purpose. Encouraged by their senior colleague, the opponents of the omnibus bill amended it, reamended it, rescinded the amendments, and cast such a spell of confusion about the whole business that when it finally came to a vote on July 31, it failed. "The omnibus is overturned!" Benton cried triumphantly.

Yet the overturning oddly facilitated the transport of the passengers separately. After half a year of debate, during which other legislation ground to a halt, Washington grew tired of the quarreling. The sudden death of President Taylor—felled by acute indigestion after an Independence Day feast—facilitated compromise by bringing Millard Fillmore to power. Where Taylor had been a southerner with northern principles, Fillmore was a northerner with southern principles. More to the immediate point, he was an unelected president and therefore more willing than Taylor to defer to the leaders of Congress, especially fellow Whigs Clay and Webster.

Clay was disappointed at the failure of the omnibus, but phlegmatic. "I was willing to take the measures unified; I am willing now to see them pass separate and distinct." Wisely (understanding that no small part of the animus against the omnibus was directed at him personally) and wearily (he was feeling the effects of the same consumption that afflicted Calhoun), Clay let an ally, Stephen Douglas of Illinois, conduct the salvage operation. Piece by separate piece, Douglas guided to passage what came to be called the Compromise of 1850. California was made a state. New Mexico and Utah were made territories, without prejudice regarding slavery. The boundary between Texas and New Mexico was made final. Texas received $10 million. The slave trade was banned from the District of Columbia. The fugitive slave law was strengthened.

The ailing Clay took comfort in this final compromise and received the plaudits of his colleagues. "Let it always be said of old Hal that he fought a glorious and patriotic battle," Douglas declared. "No man was governed by higher or purer motives."

For Webster, the essence of the outcome was the preservation of the Union. "Whatever party may prevail hereafter," he said, "the Union stands firm."

12

Children of the Mother Lode

Congress could grant California statehood, but it couldn't civilize the place. For all the—finally successful—efforts of John and Jessie Frémont and other advocates of statehood to portray their new home as settled and deserving of recognition as the equal of the existing states, California in the early 1850s remained very much a wild child. Just as San Francisco, that urban frontier, was sui generis among American cities, California was unique among American states—for a different, although related reason. In nearly every other state, farmers formed the majority of the citizenry; spread more or less evenly over the land, they cast a broad umbra of the social order that typically distinguished the states from the territories and the outright wilderness. In California, by contrast, the citizenry consisted mostly of miners and townsfolk; clumped in the state's few cities and the many mining camps, they left most of the rest of California (a land area larger than every other state except Texas) looking much like the territories and the wilderness—with the problems typical of regions in that prestatehood form of existence. Here the principal challenge was less to establish order among people newly arrived than to relate the new arrivals to the people who were already there.

. . .

THOUGH HINDSIGHT MAKES the destruction of California's Indians appear inevitable, it by no means seemed so in the immediate aftermath of James Marshall's discovery at Coloma. During the previous eighty years the numerous tribes of California had achieved a rough accommodation with the Spanish and the Mexicans; their numbers dropped from perhaps three hundred thousand to about half that, largely as a result of introduced diseases, but the direct pressure from the whites wasn't overwhelming. Indians who lived near the missions and pueblos worked for and with the intruders, and if coercion was often involved, so too was cooperation. When the whites became especially pushy, the Indians could withdraw to the interior. This wasn't an option exercised lightly, as it involved abandoning ancestral lands and encountering other tribes who didn't appreciate the newcomers, even if—often *especially* if, in light of historic grievances—they were Indians. But California was a large place, the inhabitants were relatively few, and with adjustments all could fit.

In the first year or so after the gold discovery, life among the Indians proceeded much as before. Indeed, the gold provided new opportunities for the Indians. William Sherman's observation on visiting the mining region in the summer of 1848, that half the estimated four thousand miners were Indians, suggested how quickly and well they were adapting to the changing circumstances. With their willow baskets they sifted the gold from the gravel and sand as efficiently as anyone. Some worked for themselves, others for such as Sutter. Very briefly, conniving whites were able to fool some Indians regarding the value of this yellow dust—one tale told by whites was that it was used it to plaster the walls of whites' homes—yet the Indians soon caught on to the market price of gold and got what everyone else was getting. Life in the mines was no egalitarian picnic for the Indians; whites often despised them, and cheated them whenever possible. But by and large the Indians were able to look out for themselves.

Things changed with the huge influx of 1849. More miners meant more competition for claims; in the competition the Indians were typically thrust aside. In this regard they suffered similarly to the Chileans, Mexicans, Chinese, and other foreigners. American miners, predictably for the age of Manifest Destiny, and especially after the war that won California for the United States, believed the mines belonged to them. They saw no reason to share the spoils with the indigenous peoples any more than with those against whom the war had been fought, or with foreigners who had taken no part in the war. American miners would defend one another against jumped claims and gross fraud—probably less from any sense of injured morality than from a recognition that what was done to their compatriots could be done to them. But they had scant such concern for those outside their circle of national and cultural affinity.

The Americans pushed, and the Indians either retreated or pushed back. Which course they chose—retreat or resistance—depended on the number of white miners involved, on the determination of particular Indians to defend their territory, and on the chance occurrences that shape history generally. As luck would have it, some of the fiercest tribes in all of California inhabited the southern mining district east of John Frémont's Mariposa estate. (This was a principal reason, of course, that the tract had been foisted upon Frémont in the first place.) The fierceness of the locals kept white miners at bay initially, allowing the Indians to take the leading role in working the placers. But the Indians had no use themselves for the gold they collected; they benefited only by trading it to white merchants who had the guns, bullets, knives, and other items the Indians desired.

These merchants were much like other Indian traders throughout the West. As middlemen the traders possessed some of the qualities of the cultures on either side of them. Among the whites they behaved as whites, among the Indians as Indians. It was a difficult balancing act, and often a dangerous one. Pegleg Smith—of the Bear River trading post visited by Hugh Heiskell and William Swain—lost a leg to his occupation. James Savage of California eventually lost his life.

Savage was a picturesque character. "He is a man of about 28 years of age, rather small but very muscular and extremely active," recorded Robert Eccleston, who had come west with a group calling itself the Frémont Association and had taken up a claim in the vicinity of the Mariposa. "His features are regular, and his hair light brown, which hangs in a negligé manner over his shoulders. He, however, generally wears it tied up. His skin is dark tanned by the exposure to the sun. He has, I believe, 33 wives among the mountain females of California, five or six only, however, of which are now living with him. They are from the ages of 10 to 22 and are generally sprightly young squaws. They are dressed neatly, their white chemise with low neck and short sleeves, to which is appended either a red or blue skirt. They are mostly low in stature and not unhandsome." At a time when women were scarce among the Americans, Savage's luck with the ladies, even if they were Indians, made him an object of envy.

Savage had served in Frémont's battalion during the Mexican War, and he went to work for Sutter soon afterward. He was at New Helvetia when gold was discovered at Coloma. A short while later he left Sutter's employ, heading south into the foothills along the Tuolumne River, where he employed a gang of Indians to mine for gold. He also entered the trading business, establishing several trading posts along the Merced, Fresno, and Mariposa Rivers. By all accounts he got on well with both whites and Indians. He helped negotiate a treaty with the Yokuts tribe, the predominant group on the Fresno River. The measure of his diplomatic skills was his business success; he soon acquired a modest fortune from his mining and trading operations. (Another measure of success was all those wives, who were often part of his business arrangements, offered by Savage's Indian interlocutors as deal-closers, and accepted by him as surety for the Indians' fulfillment of their ends of the bargains.)

Consequently it was significant when Savage in 1850 began detecting rumbles of Indian discontent. One of his wives heard from her people that the tribes above the Mariposa were plotting to drive all the whites from the area. A particular group, a fearsome band called the Yosemite—their name meant "grizzly bear" and summarized their reputation as raiders—seemed to be at the center of the trouble.

Savage affected to ignore the rumors. He conspicuously journeyed to San Francisco for supplies, inviting along one of the most vocal opponents of the whites, a chief called José Juárez. Savage wished to gain further intelligence about any incipient uprising; he also hoped to impress José Juárez with the power the whites could bring to bear against the Indians. The two reached the city in time for the celebration of California's admission to the Union, which they observed by getting drunk, and then getting into a fight with each other. Neither sustained serious injury, but the outing had the opposite effect to what Savage intended, and, rather than easing the bad feeling between the whites and the Indians, aggravated it.

On arrival back at the Mariposa, Savage learned that scattered violence had already begun against isolated settlements. He summoned leaders among the local Indians to share a peace pipe, and expressed his desire that they not do anything they would regret. He explained how numerous the whites had become in California, and how they would avenge any of their white brothers killed by the Indians. Turning to José Juárez, he asked the chief to confirm what he said about the great numbers and power of the white men at San Francisco.

To Savage's surprise, José Juárez derided the danger from the whites at the city. They were very many, he said, but they were too busy making money to worry about what happened so far away. They had big ships with many guns, but the ships couldn't sail into the mountains. He then launched into an impassioned advocacy of war against the whites. The blow must fall at once, he said, while Indians in the mountains still outnumbered the whites there. More whites were coming all the time. Soon it would be too late. The Indian audience seemed persuaded by José Juárez's remarks; another chief, called José Rey, declared that his people were ready to go to war at once. Beyond the satisfaction of reclaiming their homeland from the white interlopers, José Rey promised the plunder of the white man's gold, trade goods, and other property. The first to take up arms would win the most booty.

After this audacious declaration, Savage expected additional violence at once. But rather than attack, the Indians of the Mariposa, including women and children, disappeared into the mountains—which worried Savage even more, for it appeared to presage a major offensive. Gathering a small party of armed men, he headed into the mountains after the Indians, hoping to talk them out of war. An all-night march carried the pursuers to the Indians' hilltop camp, but the Indians refused to let Savage, even alone, come near. So he shouted at their leader, a chief named Baptiste, from an adjacent hill. Adam Johnston, a special government agent for Indian affairs, recounted the conversation:

> Savage said to them it would be better for them to return to their village—that with very little labor daily, they could procure sufficient gold to purchase them clothing and food. To this the chief replied it was a hard way to get a living, that they could more easily supply their wants by stealing from the whites. He also said to Savage he must not deceive the whites by telling them lies, he must not tell them that the Indians were friendly; they were not, but on the contrary were their deadly enemies, and that they intended killing and plundering them so long as a white face was seen in the country.

Disappointed, Savage returned to the Mariposa, where he discovered that an Indian attack on the Fresno River had already occurred. Adam Johnston investigated. "We reached the camp on the Fresno a short time after daylight," Johnston explained to Governor Burnett. "It presented a horrid scene of savage cruelty. The Indians had destroyed everything they could not use or carry with them. The store was stripped of blankets, clothing, flour, and everything of value; the safe was broken open and rifled of its contents; the cattle, horses, and mules had been run into the mountains; the murdered men had been stripped of their clothing, and lay before us filled with arrows; one of them had yet twenty perfect arrows sticking in him."

Johnston's report had the desired effect, producing an official call for two hundred men to mobilize in pursuit of the aboriginal insurgents. The mustering was complicated by two factors. First, the Indians had stolen or scattered most of the horses and mules in the region, compelling the militiamen to find substitutes. Second, even in the face of imminent war, many of the miners couldn't tear themselves from the diggings. Ben McCullough, on leave from the Texas Rangers, with whom he had become famous for his exploits against the Comanches, was asked to lead the Mariposa Battalion, as the militia group was called. McCullough declined the command, saying it would bring him neither honor nor pecuniary advantage. (Another Texas Ranger, Jack Hays, currently sheriff of San Francisco

County, was shamed into joining. "He says if we come to fighting, he will be in with us," Eccleston recorded.)

Eventually, however, the two hundred were enrolled, and the campaign began. Savage served as guide. "From his long acquaintance with the Indians, Mr. Savage has learned their ways so thoroughly that they cannot deceive him," noted T. G. Palmer, an obviously impressed member of the company. "He has been one of their greatest chiefs, and speaks their language as well as they can themselves. No dog can follow a trail like he can. No horse can endure half so much. He sleeps but little, can go days without food, and can run a hundred miles in a day and night over the mountains and then sit and laugh for hours over a camp-fire as fresh and lively as if he had just been taking a little walk for exercise. With him for a guide we felt little fear of not being able to find them."

Savage found his quarry, but only after a wearing chase into the heart of the mountains. With the Indians still a few miles off, he called a halt and ordered the men to dismount and tie their horses to bushes. He selected sixty for the attack, leaving the others to guard the horses and baggage. "About two o'clock we started in Indian file, as still as it was possible for sixty men to move in the dark," Palmer recorded. "For three long hours did we walk slowly and cautiously over the rocks and bushes, through the deepest ravines and up steep and ragged mountains, until within half a mile of the enemy. Here every one took off his boots, when we again pushed forward to about two hundred yards from the camp. Another halt was called to wait for daylight, while Savage went forward to reconnoiter."

Savage discovered that the Indians were more numerous than he thought. At least three tribes were represented, including some 150 of the formidable Chowchillas. Savage had hoped to surprise the village and take the Indians prisoner, with few casualties, but circumstances now forced a change of strategy. "Daylight by this time began to appear," Palmer wrote.

> We had been lying in our stocking-feet on the ground on the top of a mountain within a few paces of the snow for more than an hour, almost frozen by the intense cold, not daring to move or

> speak a word. It was not yet light enough to see the sight of our rifles, when an Indian's head was seen rising on the hill before us. For a moment his eyes wandered, then rested on us, and with a yell like a coyote he turned for the Rancharia [village]. Never did I hear before such an infernal howling, whooping and yelling, as saluted us then from the throats of about six hundred savages, as they rushed down the hill into the gim-o-sell bushes below.
>
> Our huzzahs could, however, hardly have sounded more pleasant to them, as when finding we were discovered, we charged on their town. Fifty rifles cracked almost instantaneously; a dozen Indians lay groaning before their huts, and many supposed we had undisturbed possession. Our firing had ceased and we were looking around for plunder, when a rifle fired from the bushes below struck a young Texan, Charley Huston, standing by my side. He fell with a single groan, and we all supposed him dead. My first impression was that I was shot, for I plainly heard the ball strike and almost felt it. This was a surprise that almost whipped us, for not knowing that the Indian had fire-arms, we were only expecting arrows. Before that shot was fired, I had always entertained the idea that I could run about as fast as common men (and I was one of the first in the charge), but by the time I had collected my wandering senses, I was nearly alone, the majority of the party some thirty paces ahead, and running as if they never intended to stop.

With difficulty, Savage halted the headlong retreat and regrouped the men. While the Indians fired from the trees and then disappeared, he organized a second charge on the village, which succeeded against little opposition. He thereupon ordered the place put to the torch. "We burned a hundred wigwams, several tons of dried horse and mule meat, a great number of bows and arrows, and took six mules," Palmer explained.

As the Mariposa war commenced, so it continued. Rarely were the white militiamen able to kill or capture Indian warriors, and even the Indian women and children melted into the mountains. But the Indian stores of food were less portable and therefore more vulnerable. Acorns were one staple of the Indian diet; so also the seeds of various pine trees, and wild oats and rye. Certain insects and their larvae were dried and stored, along with worms. "We had not the time, nor had we supplied ourselves sufficiently, to hunt them out," explained Lafayette Bunnell, a member of the Mariposa Battalion. "It was therefore decided that the best policy was to destroy their huts and stores, with a view of starving them out." This policy was pursued with a vengeance. "Burnt over 5000 bushels of acorns, and any quantity of old baskets," Robert Eccleston wrote in his diary. Another entry noted similarly: "We burnt over 1000 bushels of acorns and also a good many old Rancharias, some of which were not long deserted."

In the best of times, Indian life along the Sierra front was precarious. Winters were often lean, with cached provisions barely lasting till spring. The scorched-earth policy of the Mariposa Battalion threatened entire tribes with starvation; though the Indians might never lose a battle, they could easily lose the war.

The whites complemented their campaign of destruction with promises of support for those Indians who came down from the mountains and made treaties of peace with the new rulers of California. Some tribes, perhaps hungrier than the rest, accepted the terms of surrender and met with the peace commissioners appointed by the federal government. Others held out longer. The Chowchillas remained at large until the death of their chief José Rey, which evidently dispirited them. "Their courage must have died with José Rey," Lafayette Bunnell surmised.

The last of the holdouts were a band of the Yosemite tribe. With the aid of some Indians who acted as scouts, the Mariposa militiamen captured the old Yosemite chief Teneiya. Shortly after his capture Teneiya came upon the body of his favorite son, who had been killed under circumstances even some of the whites found distressing. The young man had been captured, but was allowed to attempt an escape, whereupon he was gunned down by a member of the battalion—"who had been led by an old Texan sinner to think that killing Indians or Mexicans was a duty," an angry Bunnell explained.

The sight of his dead son pushed Teneiya to the point of despair. "*Kill me*, sir captain!" he implored of the officer in charge (in Spanish, as Bunnell recalled the speech). "Yes, *kill me*, as you killed my son; as you would kill my people if they would come to you! You would kill all my race if you had the power. . . . You have made me sorrowful, my life dark. You killed the child of my heart; why not kill the father?" But then he offered a warning.

> Wait a little; when I am dead I will call to my people to come to you. I will call louder than you have had me call, that they shall hear me in their sleep, and come to avenge the death of their chief and his son. Yes, sir American, my spirit will make trouble for you and your people, as you have caused trouble to me and my people. With the wizards, I will follow the white men and make them fear me.
>
> You may kill me, sir captain, but you shall not live in peace. I will follow in your footsteps; I will not leave my home but be with the spirits among the rocks, the water-falls, in the rivers and in the winds. Wheresoever you go I will be with you. You will not see me, but you will fear the spirit of the old chief, and grow cold. The great spirits have spoken! I am done.

A curse from the Yosemite chief carried more weight in that part of the country than a similar threat from other Indian leaders would have. The Yosemites inhabited a valley on the upper Merced River that was so deep, and guarded by such towering cliffs and rockfalls, that it was thought to be enchanted. "We are afraid to go to this valley, for there are many witches there," the chief of another tribe told the Mariposa militiamen.

To guard against the evil spirits, the militiamen enlisted Teneiya. At first he went unwillingly, but as he grew convinced that continued resistance would lead only to the utter destruction of his people, he accepted the need to bring the rest of the tribe down from the granite-guarded valley.

By most reckoning, the Mariposa contingent to which Lafayette Bunnell belonged was the first group of white men to penetrate Yosemite Valley. Others had seen some of the prominent features from afar; indeed, Half Dome's distinctive profile could (and can, when the air is very clear) be discerned from the San Joaquin lowlands, eighty or ninety miles away. But none had ever entered the valley carved by the great glaciers; none had approached Half Dome or El Capitan or the cliffs from which the magnificent waterfalls leap. Bunnell was one of those who had observed the tops of the ramparts from afar, and had wondered what they looked like close at hand. Now he knew. "The immensity of rock I had seen in my vision on the Old Bear Valley trail from Ridley's Ferry was here presented to my astonished gaze. The mystery of that scene was here disclosed. My awe was increased by this nearer view." He added, "The grandeur of the scene was but softened by the haze that hung over the valley—light as gossamer—and by the clouds which partially dimmed the higher cliffs and mountains. This obscurity of vision but increased the awe with which I beheld it, and as I looked, a peculiar exalted sensation seemed to fill my whole being, and I found myself in tears with emotion."

At the same time, Bunnell understood an answer Teneiya had given when asked why, after the other tribes made their peace with the whites, so few of the Yosemites had done so. "This is all of my people that are willing to go with me to the plains," Teneiya said. Now having seen their awe-inspring home in the mountains, Bunnell appreciated their unwillingness.

Finally even the Yosemite holdouts surrendered. Starving, haggard from incessant flight, they reluctantly gave up their home and their way of living, in exchange for promises of food on a reservation. One of the young chiefs, who at first defied Teneiya, explained their change of heart. "Where can we now go that the Americans will not follow us? Where can we make our homes, that you will not find us?"

THE PLIGHT OF THE Yosemites was painfully poignant, not simply for losing their beautiful home but also for the fact that until the recent war they had largely been spared—by their isolation—the vices of the white man's liquor and the white man's injustice. Teneiya was asked what was lacking to make the Yosemites a happy people. One thing only, he replied: "The whites would not leave us alone."

The whites wouldn't leave the Indians alone, nor would they allow the

Indians the time to adapt to changing circumstances in California. Perhaps the sheer numbers of whites doomed the Indians, as comparable numbers did in other parts of what became the United States. Yet the Indians had managed to adapt to the Spanish and Mexicans, and at the beginning of the Gold Rush they showed signs of adapting to the Americans. In the end, however, the Americans' hurry made any permanent arrangement impossible. Governor Burnett bluntly described why the Indians had to go. "The white man, to whom time is money, and who labors hard all day to create the comforts of life, cannot sit up all night to watch his property. . . . After being robbed a few times, he becomes desperate, and resolves upon a war of extermination." Needless to say, Burnett here elided the whites' role in provoking the Indians to robbery and other forms of resistance, but he correctly identified the reason—"time is money"—for the lack of that patience in whites which alone might have made accommodation possible. And he forecast the ultimate result: "A war of extermination will continue to be waged between the races until the Indian race becomes extinct."

In fact no general war of extermination took place, and the Indians were not—quite—extinguished. Violence against Indians was a regular aspect of life in California, but, as in other parts of the United States, disease and displacement claimed a larger toll. By 1860 the number of California Indians had fallen to about thirty thousand, or one-fifth of what it had been at the time of the gold discovery. Sporadic resistance to white encroachment continued, but after the mid-1850s it was nothing many whites worried about.

The destruction of the Indians produced collateral damage among whites. Despite his part in waging the Mariposa war, James Savage proved too Indian-friendly for some of his fellow Anglos. In 1852 the Yokuts tribe complained of encroachment by white miners upon the reservation they had agreed to accept from the federal government. Savage thought the Indians had cause for complaint, and he took their side. But a man named Walter Harvey, who was both a competing trader and a Tulare County judge, raised a band of volunteers against the Yokuts. A lopsided skirmish ensued in which more than two dozen Indians were killed or wounded, against a single white man hurt. Savage reiterated his support for the Indians, criticizing Harvey in language a third party characterized as manifesting "high indignation." Harvey, who apparently considered himself a hero in the engagement, took offense at Savage's remarks and threatened to kill him.

Harvey found his opportunity a short while later. As Savage hastened to catch up with a group of whites heading for a grand council of the Yokuts, Harvey lay behind the group in wait for him. On the banks of the Kings River, the two men met. An angry argument followed. Bystanders got between the pair, but Harvey nonetheless pulled a pistol and shot Savage dead.

The news of Savage's death sent a shudder through the tribes of the region. Savage had been no saint, and his concern for the Indians' welfare reflected a large measure of his own self-interest. But at least they had that much in common. Harvey, by contrast, seemed bent on the Indians' rapid destruction, and his murder of Savage suggested strongly that his malignant designs were in the ascendant. Hundreds of Indians turned out for Savage's funeral, gathering to mourn the passing of an ally—and, one surmises, to lament the passing of their own way of life.

THE INDIANS WEREN'T the only ones to be thrust aside by the gold-seekers, although their demise was by far the most drastic demographic consequence of the Gold Rush. Native-born Californians of Mexican descent were also displaced; and if their displacement was rarely fatal, it was in its own way only slightly less definitive.

In the era before the Gold Rush, Mariano Vallejo was nearly everything a Californian could wish to be: wealthy, powerful, respected, blessed with family and friends. Moreover, when he saw where history was heading in his native land, he boldly tried to persuade his fellow Californians to embrace the new American regime. Yet all his wealth, power, and courage availed him little, and the gold-triggered tide rolled over him just as surely as it drowned the Indians.

Mariano Vallejo was the son of Ignacio Vallejo, a Spanish soldier who accompanied Junípero Serra at the founding of the San Francisco presidio in 1776. Ignacio had studied for the priesthood before assuming the military vocation, and the medical training he received in the seminary proved useful when the wife of a friend went into labor. Ignacio safely delivered the baby girl; asked what he would take for payment, he said he wished her hand in marriage when she came of age. Fourteen years later the soldier and the maiden were married at Santa Barbara; several years (and seven children) after that, in 1807, Mariano Guadalupe Vallejo was born at the presidio of Monterey.

Mariano came of age with Mexican California. He was fifteen when Mexico broke free of Spain; he was twenty-six when, in keeping with the family military tradition, he was named commandant of the San Francisco presidio. Shortly thereafter he received orders to establish a new presidio north of San Francisco Bay. The timing, and Vallejo's geographic sense, couldn't have been better, for no sooner had he selected the site of Sonoma than the mission there was secularized, giving him effective control over the mission's large herds and pastures. In addition, he personally received a ten-league grant, which became the basis of a private empire that ultimately comprised 175,000 acres. By one estimate, Vallejo's income from hides and tallow approached $100,000 per year.

He cut a striking figure, not least on account of the sidewhiskers that had been his trademark since early manhood. These were not the modest salients south of the temple that adorned the cheeks of many Spanish and Mexican gentlemen, but an aggressively curving pair of scimitars that started at the scalp line in front of each ear and threatened mayhem beneath his nose. As he added years and pounds, his cheeks grew fuller, but so did the whiskers, which evolved into twin peninsulas covered, as it were, by thick forests and separated by a narrow and diminishing strait.

Vallejo and his whiskers held court at a splendid hacienda on the plaza at Sonoma. With adobe walls four feet thick, it had broad second-story balconies that sheltered the inhabitants from summer sun and winter rain. From this headquarters Don Mariano rode out across the Valley of the Moon, as the vicinity of Sonoma was called, with a cavalry escort to patrol his empire. He ruled his fiefdom with a firm hand and a rough sense of humor, enforcing his writ by such sanctions as sending landlubbing recalcitrants to sea to suffer the mal de mer and other terrors of the deep.

Vallejo's reputation spread throughout California and even across the Pacific. John Sutter heard of Vallejo in Hawaii, and before Sutter left Honolulu in 1839 for Monterey he insisted on having the American consul write him a letter of introduction to Vallejo.

Despite the letter, something about Sutter put Vallejo on guard. Perhaps Vallejo found Sutter too facile and accommodating. Probably he sensed in Sutter an ambition that might threaten his own. Certainly he noted the fact that Sutter carefully cultivated the governor of California, Juan Alvarado, who had been trying for years to rein Vallejo in. Vallejo determined to keep an eye on the Swiss newcomer, by keeping him close. He offered to sell Sutter a fine ranch near Sonoma, at a very attractive price. Sutter, however, had been warned by Alvarado that Vallejo might try something like this, and he had his answer ready. He said he appreciated the kindness of Don Mariano in making the offer, but for reasons of trade and communication he preferred to locate on a navigable river. The Sacramento was just such a river—and was, as Vallejo didn't need to be told, safely distant from Sonoma and Vallejo's embrace.

Though Vallejo never trusted Sutter—"that Swiss adventurer," he called him—the two probably could have reached an accommodation. They shared an Old World heritage; they also shared the belief, inspired by that heritage, that land held the key to wealth and security. What Sutter wanted, a landed empire, was no more than Vallejo already had. And California had land enough for them both.

It did, at any rate, until the arrival of the Americans. Vallejo got his first inkling of what was in store at the same time Sutter did, and from the same source: John Frémont. Vallejo watched Frémont descend from the snowy Sierras in 1844 and prance about the province, scorning Mexican authority with each step of his horses and men. He observed Frémont's return the following year, when the American officer gave every indication of intending to conquer California, pending only the formality of a declaration of war. Frémont's slowness in withdrawing to Oregon after being ordered to leave California, and his general insolence toward all things Mexican, intimated danger to anyone with a stake in the status quo. Vallejo would have been more than human—or Californian—not to resent Frémont's very presence.

Yet Vallejo saw farther than most of his fellow Californians. Frémont, Vallejo judged, embodied the inevitable, whether Californians wished to admit it or not. At a time when most Californians swore resistance to yanqui expansionism, Vallejo took the astonishing step of advocating attachment to the United States. The United States, he said, represented the future of North America, and America's institutions represented the best guarantee of the future of California. "When we join our fortunes to hers, we shall not become subjects but fellow citizens, possessing all the rights of the people of the United States," Vallejo declared. "We shall have a stable government and just laws. California will grow strong and flourish, and her people will be prosperous, happy, and free. Look not, therefore, with jealousy upon the hardy pioneers who scale our mountains and cultivate our unoccupied plains; but rather welcome them as brothers, who come to share with us a common destiny."

The problem was that the Americans didn't act like brothers. At the outbreak of the Bear Flag revolt the rebels attacked Sonoma, the seat of Vallejo's empire. They caught Don Mariano by surprise, rolling him out of bed at gunpoint and taking him prisoner. The flag of Mexico was torn from its staff above Vallejo's hacienda; the Bear Flag was raised in its place.

The rebels then delivered Vallejo to Frémont, who transported him to Sutter's Fort, where Frémont ordered Sutter to imprison him. This turn of events didn't improve Vallejo's opinion of Sutter, but he placed the primary blame on Frémont. "In spite of the fact that he was wearing the honorable uniform of an officer in the American army," Vallejo recalled afterward, "he had no compunction about stooping to the extreme of associating himself with those robbers who on June 14th assaulted and robbed the peaceful residents of the Sonoma frontier."

To the ignominy of arrest was now added the discomfort of detention. Vallejo stifled in the small cell he shared with three others, including his brother Salvador. For six weeks Vallejo sweltered—and alternately shivered, from the malarial fever his imprisonment brought on. Such news as filtered into his cell made him fear the worst regarding the situation at Sonoma, for when rebels ruled, the property of the law-abiding was forfeit. Beyond the fear and the fever was Vallejo's mortification at having encouraged California's attachment to the land of these brigands and dishonorable officers.

Eventually Vallejo was released—significantly, on the order of Robert Stockton rather than Frémont, who had departed south in pursuit of glory. Vallejo emerged from his cell, blinking in the light and shaking from disease, to discover that the rebel-robbers had indeed continued their depredations during his imprisonment. "I left Sacramento half dead and arrived here almost without life," he wrote from Sonoma. "I have lost more than one thousand live horned cattle, six hundred tame horses and many other things of value which were taken from my house here and at Petaluma. My wheat crops are entirely lost." Tallying up additional damage, and reflecting on how the marauding made his American sympathies seem foolishly naïve, he reiterated, "All is lost."

In fact, Vallejo had much more to lose. The discovery of gold brought an army of invaders who showed no more respect for Vallejo's holdings than for Sutter's. "The good ones were few and the wicked many," Vallejo remarked. Even so, he might have held on to what was left of his empire, if only because Sonoma was farther from the mines than New Helvetia. But what he couldn't fend off was "the great crowd of shyster lawyers," as he put it, who came after the argonauts and immediately "set out to find means of depriving the Californians of their estates and property." Likening the lawyers to the notorious Sydney Ducks, Vallejo declared, "The bandits from Australia stole our cattle and horses, but these thieves in frock coats, wrapped about with the mantle of the law, took away our lands and buildings and, with no scruple whatsoever, enthroned themselves as powerful monarchs in our houses."

Vallejo sought, through participation in the new government of California, to limit the damage. As a delegate to the Monterey convention he impressed his fellow delegates with his seriousness and grasp of the issues, and his understanding of those aspects of American history that touched on property rights. "He is better acquainted with our institutions and laws than any other native Californian," Bayard Taylor reported. (Vallejo also brought to the convention a sly sense of humor. When the delegates considered putting a bear on the state seal, in memory of the Bear Flag revolt, Vallejo, with different memories of that period, offered an amendment proposing that if a bear must grace the seal, "it be represented as made fast by a *lazo* in the hands of a vaquero." Vallejo's amendment got 16 votes—mostly from other Californians—out of 37 cast.)

Vallejo threw himself into the politics of the new state. Elected a state senator, he worked to bring the capital to a site on the Carquinez Straits, a town he wished to call Eureka but which his friends insisted on calling Vallejo. He donated 150 acres and pledged $500,000 toward the construction of public buildings, including a capitol, a governor's mansion, a university, and an insane asylum. Construction began, and the lawmakers arrived. But they found the virgin town to be insufficiently entertaining, and when the fleshpots of Sacramento beckoned, they moved there, leaving Vallejo the town forlorn and Vallejo the man wiser and $100,000 poorer.

As a *patrón* of the old regime, Vallejo had been accustomed to lavishing generosity on family, friends, and protégés. He continued to do so even after the Gold Rush drove prices to ten times what they had been before. He spoiled his children, of whom he had a large but indeterminate number (counting, or rather estimating, his illegitimate offspring). When he bought a silver-studded saddle for himself, for $2,000, he bought a similar, smaller version for his son Napoleon, for $1,500. He loaned money on the unsecured promises of borrowers, considering collateral beneath him. When his own cash grew short, he borrowed against his land.

As long as the prices he received for his cattle and crops stayed high, he continued to prosper. But when prices subsequently fell—when the supply of food and other provisions started to catch up with the gold-driven demand—Vallejo found himself short. His mortgages came due, and the property behind them had to be sold. Piece by piece his empire was dismantled.

The greater disaster, however, occurred in the courts. Congress and the

American legal system, acting at the behest of those "shyster lawyers," redefined the Treaty of Guadalupe Hidalgo to place the burden of proving land ownership on the Californians. Vallejo spent tens of thousands of dollars defending his titles in various lower courts, with diminishing success. The coup de grâce came in 1862 when the U.S. Supreme Court ruled against him regarding the most important of his remaining properties, leaving him with large debts and a small fraction of his former assets.

Vallejo had braced himself for this outcome. "I think I will know how to be decently poor when the time comes," he said, "just as I have known how to be rich."

VALLEJO'S SAD EXPERIENCE was peculiar among the native Californians in the size of the fortune he had to lose, but it was not unique in kind. Within a decade of the gold discovery, the Californians were pushed to the margins of society in the land of their birth. The ten or twelve thousand Californians suffered no important decline in absolute numbers—certainly nothing like the destruction of the Indians—but, overwhelmed as they were by the influx of Americans, they lost political power, and with it, in many cases, property.

Explaining *why* the Californians became marginalized is more difficult than merely observing that they did. As Vallejo's experience demonstrated, their inability to assimilate wasn't due to a lack of trying—if anything, he was more American than many of the Americans. In Vallejo's case, as doubtless in others, some of the inability owed to a failure to master the commodification of life the Gold Rush wrought. In this regard, Vallejo was the same sort of casualty as John Sutter.

But the Californians labored under an additional difficulty: racism on the part of the American newcomers. This surprised some of the Californians, who considered themselves as European as Jean-Nicolas Perlot. Salvador Vallejo, who shared his brother Mariano's cell at Sutter's Fort, grew livid every day when the American who had custody of them came around and said, "Let me see if my greasers are safe." Salvador cursed the man—whom he called a "mulatto" and a "Pike county blackguard"—for defaming two gentlemen of the "purest blood of Europe." But surprising or not, discrimination on grounds of perceived racial difference was a fact of life in California, as it was in most of America at this time. California Anglos generally considered men and women of Hispanic background to be more or less inferior, and they made few distinctions among those they called "greasers" or—as Vicente Pérez Rosales's friend Álvarez discovered—"niggers."

Most of the victims of Anglo racism—including Pérez Rosales—responded the way victims of bigotry generally do: by trying to ignore it and getting on with their lives. A much smaller number adopted a violent recourse, taking up arms in their own defense. One responded so violently as to become a legend in the goldfields and a myth in much of the Spanish-American world.

Separating myth and legend from fact in history is never easy; in the case of Joaquín Murrieta it is complicated by the conflicting hearsay and other secondhand testimony that constitutes almost the entire record of his brief and violent life. Some historians have thrown up their hands and suggested he never existed at all; others contend that he was a pastiche of several individuals, a composite created by Anglos to bear the sins of Mexicans generally.

Yet the best evidence indicates that there really was a Joaquín Murrieta, and that he was born in Sonora around 1830. He came to California in 1848 or 1849, in the same migration of Sonorans that brought the first miners to Frémont's Mariposa estate. Whether he actually worked on Frémont's property is unclear, but unlike those Sonorans who headed back south in 1849, Joaquín stayed.

Why he turned to crime is equally unclear. A popular version of the Murrieta legend holds that Anglos raped his wife, murdered his brother, and horsewhipped Joaquín himself, thereby driving this heretofore peaceable soul to seek vengeance. (In the extreme version of the legend, Joaquín took pains to avenge himself only on those persons responsible for the assault on his wife and the murder of his brother.) How much of this is true is impossible to tell; but whatever personal insults he suffered, Murrieta doubtless felt the same sense of injury many of his countrymen did. Most

Mexicans believed—as did some of those Americans not beguiled by the mystique of Manifest Destiny—that California had been stolen from Mexico, and therefore that Mexican miners had every right to the gold they discovered in California. When American miners treated the Mexicans as interlopers, and when the California legislature in 1850 passed a foreign-miners' tax, many of the Mexicans understandably felt aggrieved.

Yet even if there was a real Joaquín Murrieta, it is by no means certain he was responsible for everything attributed to him. Robberies and other violent crimes were epidemic in the mining districts, where men carried fortunes, very large by the standards of most frontier regions, on their persons; where the multiethnic and multiracial composition of the populace inhibited any general sense of fellow feeling; where a large majority of the populace was young, male, single, and uninterested in settling there permanently; and where those young, single, unsettled males were too busy seeking their own fortunes to have time to create the regular institutions of social order. But a hungry winter in the southern mines (in the same region where Jean-Nicolas Perlot encountered the hundreds of graves of starved miners) helped provoke an outbreak of armed theft and associated violence in January 1853 that was unusual even by the anarchic standards of the gold country. Many Mexicans made a partial living rounding up and selling wild horses; whenever horses went missing it was easy for Anglos to blame the Mexicans. When other items went missing, it was easy to blame the Mexicans as well. Joaquín Murrieta provided a name and an identity on which to hang many crimes that winter.

The crime wave was thoroughly covered by the newspapers of Calaveras and Mariposa Counties and the surrounding region. "For some time back, a band of robbers have been committing depredations in the southern section of our county," a Calaveras weekly declared in January. The principal victims had been Chinese; the perpetrators appeared to be Mexicans. "During the week a party of three Mexicans entered a Chinese tent at Yackee [Yaqui] Camp, near San Andres, and ransacked everything, despite the opposition of the inmates, carrying off two bags of gold dust, one containing $110 and the other $50." The article went on, "Three armed Mexicans—supposed to be the same who committed the above outrage—

entered another Chinese tent in the same vicinity, assaulted its inhabitants, holding loaded pistols to their heads to keep them quiet, and robbed them of two bags of gold dust, $90 and $60. One of the Chinamen, named Akop [Ah Kop], refused to give up his money and attempted to defend himself, when one of the ruffians drew his knife and ran the unfortunate celestial through the body, causing almost instant death." A second paper summarized "the dreadful murders and outrages committed in the lonely gulches and solitary outposts" of the county, and put a name on the chief perpetrator. "The band is led by a robber, named Joaquín, a very desperate man, who was concerned in the murder of four Americans, some time ago, at Turnersville."

The violence continued during the following weeks. "We publish today the details of fourteen horrible murders, all committed within seven days, in Calaveras county," explained a shocked editor on February 16. "A condition of society exists in that important region far worse than that which prevailed in the early days of its settlement. No man dare travel a step unless armed to the teeth, or sleep without having fire-arms already in his grasp; life is not safe for a day and the utmost excitement prevails at every camp." A San Francisco paper, the *Whig*, supplied a biography of the reported brigand leader.

> Joaquín was born in the Villa de Catoce, in the department of Jalisco. He is aged about 35 years, and has ranked among the most crafty and daring guerrillas of Mexico. He is chief of a notorious band of robbers now infesting the vicinity of Mexico, and though living in California, has a regular chain of communication with his associates in his native country. He has been known to enter the capital cities disguised as a friar—has been arrested several times, but through the expertness and influence he wielded among the soldiery, he has been discharged. He is about six feet in height, and of immense muscular strength; is well versed in the use of arms, and in disposition cruel and sanguinary. He has a dark, sallow complexion, and during the Mexican war was known to wear a coat of armor. He has committed numberless murders, has

> burned many ranches, and has resided in San Francisco. He has frequently obtained information of Mexicans leaving California with money, who have been dogged and robbed by detached portions of his band. In some instances they have been robbed upon their arrival at Mexico—the news of their departures and the sums of money they had about them, having been forwarded by means of the associates living along the road.

That such details of Joaquín's background and activities were at this point almost entirely conjectural didn't diminish the alarm the undeniable violence aroused in the populace of the mining regions. And not only there: Joaquín was said to have been sighted along the Salinas River and as far south as San Diego. Almost needless to say—but only almost, as the opposite enjoyed credence at the time—no one person could have committed all the crimes attributed to Joaquín, or been everywhere he was said to have been. Yet it was human nature (besides making good copy for the papers) to personalize the crime wave, laying responsibility on a single mastermind, the more lurid and bloodthirsty the better. Imaginative drawings of Joaquín—swarthy, armed to the teeth, but handsome in a piratical sort of way—began circulating, along with elaborations of his great strength and his imperviousness to capture. "When shot at," the *Calaveras Chronicle* explained, "he receives the balls in the breast with a complacent smile. It has been a matter of surprise to his pursuers that the balls fired at him have no effect. We learn from a gentleman who shot from a short distance that he wears a coat of mail beneath his clothes. To what base use has the armor of the days of chivalry come!"

Predictably, a hue and cry arose for the capture of the bandit chieftain. A posse was formed at Mokelumne Hill, and set out on the trail. But they had no luck. "I have been engaged a week in hunting Mr. Joaquín and his party," the posse leader reported on their return, "and we had a right lively time of it after the greasers. We followed them all over the country, and, while we were on their trail, they killed and wounded 15 Chinamen and stole seven or eight thousand dollars. We got one or two chances at them, but they were so well mounted that they beat us running all to hell."

By now Joaquín's reputation had spread across the state, and his capture became a political priority. Legislators from Mariposa County convinced their colleagues in the state assembly that a general manhunt was required. An outfit of rangers, modeled on the Texas Rangers, was commissioned, and Harry Love, a veteran of the Texas border, was appointed first captain. Love hired several assistants—a mix of Indian fighters, frontier lawmen, and gunslingers—at $350 per month, and raised a company of men. To give the Rangers an added incentive, Governor Bigler placed a bounty of $1,000 on Joaquín's head.

Love and the California Rangers chased Joaquín across the Mother Lode country; when they heard that the bandits had escaped toward the west, Love and the Rangers followed them there. At San Jose they surprised and captured a man thought to be one of Joaquín's accomplices. As Love explained to Governor Bigler, "I have arrested a Mexican, Jesus, a brother in law of Joaquín's. He says he will take & show us to Joaquín if we will release him. I will try him a while to see what it will end in." The kind of encouragement to cooperation the prisoner received is unknown; considering the background of Love and the Rangers, he might reasonably have believed they would kill him.

In any event, on the intelligence thus acquired, Love and the Rangers trailed the bandits to a camp in the foothills of the Coast Range. They found a large herd of horses, including some that had been stolen, but initially no bandits. A Stockton paper, which had the story from one of Love's men, reported what happened next:

> Capt. Love was about sending the horses he had captured to the settlements, when he spied the smoke of a camp fire some three miles distant on the plains. The rangers proceeded immediately to the spot, and got within three or four hundred yards before they were perceived. Then there was a hurrying to and fro in the Mexican camp, some running for the horses which were picketed outside, others starting for their pistols which were near by. Capt. Love, however, galloped into the camp and stopped those who were after the horses, and interrogated them, each one of them

> giving him a different answer. By this time the main body of the rangers had arrived. As Capt. Burns entered the camp, he looked at the leader and cried exultingly, "This is Joaquin, boys; we have got him at last."
>
> At the mention of the word Joaquin, seeing that he was recognized, the Mexicans threw off their cloaks and serapes and commenced firing and retreating. Joaquin, himself, was unarmed, having evidently just been awakened from a sound sleep, and in his hurry to get his horse forgot his weapons. However, he made a bold dash for the animal, jumped upon him unsaddled, hastily threw his lariat over the animal's nose and leaped down off the bluff, 14 or 15 feet in height, into the dry bed of the creek. One of the rangers followed him immediately down the bank and another down the side of the creek to cut him off. They had fired at him several times but without effect, and seeing that there was a danger of his escaping, they aimed at the animal and succeeded in bringing him down. Joaquin then commenced running, and had gone some thirty yards when he received two shots, and as he was falling cried *No tire mas, yo soy muerte*—Don't shoot any more, for I'm dead. He immediately expired.

Love was fairly certain he had the right man—or right body, at this point. But in order to verify the identity of the deceased, for the dual purpose of reassuring the citizens of California and claiming the $1,000 bounty, he cut the head off Joaquín's body and preserved it in a large jar filled with whiskey. He carried the head about the neighborhood of the robberies and murders, obtaining testimony from victims and others that this was indeed the terrible bandit leader. "There is not the least doubt that the head now in my possession is that of the noted Joaquín Murrieta, the chief and leader of the murderers and robbers of the Calavaras, Mariposa and other parts of the state," he informed Governor Bigler.

Bigler and the legislature were convinced, at least sufficiently to pay out the reward. But others wondered. Crimes of violence continued in the southern mines, if on a somewhat diminished scale. Reports circulated that

Joaquín had escaped and gone back to Sonora. The uncertainty added to a sense of romance that began to spring up around the bandit leader, especially among those with complaints against the status quo. Within a year an author named Yellow Bird, an unsuccessful gold-seeking son of a Cherokee chief, published a book called *The Life and Adventures of Joaquín Murrieta, the Celebrated California Bandit*, which made Joaquín out to be the Robin Hood of El Dorado. (A book by that name—*The Robin Hood of El Dorado*—eventually entered the genre as well.)

As for the head in the jar, it did the rounds of the mining country, an object lesson in the wages of crime—or, alternatively, a relic of the martyred Mexican hero. It wound up on the shelf of a San Francisco museum, where it remained until 1906, when it was lost in the great earthquake and fire.

LIKE LATINOS, THE CHINESE of Gold Rush California suffered from the bigotry of the Anglo majority. But in the case of the Chinese, it was not always easy—and historically it may be beside the point—to distinguish racism from ethnocentrism, xenophobia, and plain incomprehension. Most Americans in the 1850s had scarcely a clue what to make of the Chinese. Prior to the Gold Rush, few Americans had ever encountered a Chinese outside the pages of Marco Polo; as a people, the Chinese seemed almost as exotic as Martians would have seemed to a later generation of Americans. The majority of Chinese, of course, were non-Christians, which made them immediately suspect in an era in America when even Catholics were eyed with suspicion. Many of the Chinese spoke little or no English, and although this by itself didn't distinguish them from thousands of Chileans and Mexicans and French and Belgians in California, the Chinese language and especially the Chinese script appeared downright bizarre next to the tongues and orthography of Mother Europe. Chinese dress and tonsure—the long pigtails, or queues, evoked endless comment—made the Chinese recognizable at a distance. Their eating habits—they ate *dog*!—and their use of opium put additional distance between them and others in California. (The irony of despising the Chinese for using opium, which

American merchants joined the British in selling to China, was lost on most Americans in California.) Finally, in an era when racial thinking was unabashed and nearly universal, most whites had no difficulty classing the Chinese as inherently inferior.

American stereotyping of the Chinese limited their opportunities as a group; yet at the same time, it enhanced the opportunities available to certain Chinese individuals. Yee Ah Tye was one of those so advantaged.

Not long after the immigration from China began, the Chinese in San Francisco organized into four associations, or houses. The associations corresponded to the regions from which the various Chinese emigrated, and new arrivals were easily sorted into the appropriate associations on the basis of their dialects. In some respects the associations acted much like the joint-stock companies of many of the other argonauts, with members pledging mutual protection and assistance. For the Chinese, a particular obligation of the associations was the return to China of the bones of any argonaut who died in America, that he might be honored by his descendants.

Partly because of his command of English, and partly because of an evident appreciation of power and its uses, Yee Ah Tye became the principal agent of the Sze Yup association not long after his arrival. The association agents represented the interests of the associations to the civic authorities; they also presided over disputes among association members. In this latter regard they sometimes acted extralegally but with the acquiescence of the authorities, forming a kind of vigilance committee for Chinese.

On occasion the leaders of the Chinese associations overstepped their bounds. A San Francisco grand jury registered its concern in a report on the Chinese situation:

> We find in existence in this community a society of Chinese called the Four Great Houses, established for the purpose of forcing trade to their different establishments and to prevent passengers among their countrymen from purchasing tickets from any but themselves, and punishing with fines and the bastinado all who may transgress their laws. Several on this account were most cruelly

> beaten. . . . They have regular meetings, which are presided over by the heads of the four great houses, viz., Sam Wo, Ah Tie [Yee Ah Tye] and the two Ah Chings. They have posted up printed handbills in their own language and signed by themselves, forewarning all from transgressing their laws and threatening their punishment.

Yee was the most notorious of the association leaders. The *San Francisco Herald* called him a "would-be Mandarin" and a "petty despot" who "inflicted severe corporeal punishment upon many of his more humble countrymen . . . cutting off their ears, flogging them and keeping them chained for hours together." The *Alta California* dubbed him a "Grand Inquisitor" who was "endeavoring to coerce his brethren into such measures as he may suggest and dictate." Various reports indicated that Yee had put a bounty on the head of a Chinese who defied him; this man then sought protection from the civil authorities. Within a week, however, the *Alta California* explained that the quarrel had been "satisfactorily settled outside of the judicial tribunal." In another case, Yee struck a deal directly with the court. Convicted of assault and battery, he was sentenced to five days in the city jail. But he appealed the sentence, posted bond of $1,000, and was allowed to remain at large.

That he commanded this kind of money indicated that things were going well for him—whether by fair means or foul. (The California press wasn't unbiased in reporting on Chinese affairs, but the direction of the bias in matters internal to the Chinese community was neither obvious nor consistent). Unfortunately for Yee and the Chinese community in general, their very success provoked the displeasure of many Americans. American miners repeatedly drove Chinese miners from the goldfields, as Tom Archer noted in Stockton. American workers constantly accused Chinese workers of stealing jobs and driving down wages. American politicians and editors regularly recommended barring the Chinese from California.

A specific proposal in 1852 to prevent Chinese immigration prompted a response from the association leaders. In an open letter to Governor John Bigler, a loud advocate of the measure, the leaders began by noting that in

China "all great men are learned men, and a man's rank is according to his education." (Thomas Cary, no fan of Bigler's, was moved to comment, "There is a delicate sarcasm in these remarks, for his Excellency John Bigler was as good a specimen of an illiterate pot-house politician as could be found in the ranks of Democracy anywhere between New York and San Francisco.") The governor and others stereotyped the Chinese as "coolies": contract laborers who worked for a pittance and thereby undermined the wages of honest Americans. The Chinese leaders answered the charge: "If you mean by 'coolies,' laborers, many of our countrymen in the mines are coolies, and many again are not. There are among them tradesmen, mechanics, gentry (being persons of respectability, and who enjoy a certain rank and privilege) and schoolmasters, who are reckoned with the gentry, and with us considered a respectable class of people. Some are coolies, if by that word you mean bound men or contract slaves." But even the bound men came of their own free will. "The poor China man does not come here as a slave. He comes because of his desire for independence, and he is assisted by the charity of his countrymen, which they bestow on him safely because he is industrious and honestly repays them."

The association leaders granted that Chinese ways weren't the same as American ways. "But in the important matters we are good men. We honor our parents; we take care of our children; we are industrious and peaceable; we trade much; we are trusted for small and large sums; we pay our debts, and are honest, and of course must tell the truth." Some Chinese intended to go back to China after making money in the goldfields; others would stay in California—if given the chance. "If the privileges of your laws are open to us, some of us will doubtless acquire your habits, your language, your ideas, your feelings, your morals, your forms, and become citizens of your country—many have already adopted your religion as their own—and we will be good citizens. There are very good China men now in the country, and better will, if allowed, come here after—men of learning, and of wealth, bringing their families with them." The Americans shouldn't pass laws against the Chinese. "Let us stay here—the Americans are doing good to us, and we will do good to them."

13

Reflections in an All-Seeing Eye

When Daniel Webster declared, after passage of the Compromise of 1850, that the Union stood firm, the great orator was engaging in exhortation rather than description. The California compromise, far from soothing sectional passions, inflamed them. Many northerners were incensed by the opening of Utah and New Mexico to slavery, and were even more outraged by the Fugitive Slave Act, which compelled free-state complicity in the return of escaped slaves. "The consummation of the iniquities of the most disgraceful session of Congress," Charles Francis Adams of Massachusetts called the compromise. Southerners were no less angry. Governor Whitemarsh Seabrook of South Carolina castigated the California compromise as "another triumph of the fell spirit of abolitionism." Robert Rhett eulogized his and Seabrook's fellow South Carolinian, John Calhoun—who died while the debate over the California compromise still raged—as the finest friend the Union ever had, which made it the more fitting that Calhoun died when he did, just after that final brilliant speech against the Clay package. "It was the last flash of the sun, to show the ship of State her only port of safety, as darkness and the howling tempest closed around her." Had Calhoun lived long enough to see the compromise pass, Rhett asserted, he would have been forced to admit defeat in his defense of the South, and thereby defeat of the Union.

Clay and Webster followed Calhoun to the grave in 1852. The former succumbed to consumption, the latter to liver disease. Yet in a political sense, and certainly in a symbolic one, Clay and Webster were felled by the demons of sectionalism the fight over California unleashed. Their Whig party splintered, and the whole idea of compromise—the idea on which Webster and especially Clay had built their political careers—acquired an evil name. From the wreckage of the Whigs arose a new party, the Republicans, pledged to no more truckling to slavery—a pledge that in turn provoked southern vows to secede if the Republicans ever came to power.

Stephen Douglas thought he could tame the demons of sectionalism, or at least make them work to his benefit. California was rending the nation; California therefore should help bind the nation together—by ribbons of steel. Douglas sponsored a Pacific railroad, a line linking the East to California. The idea, of course, had tremendous appeal in California, where travelers to the East dearly desired to trim the monthlong journey via the isthmus—the route of choice by now—to a week or less by train. Yet the other states would benefit almost as much as California, in Douglas's view at any rate. Both North and South would profit from easy access to California and its vast treasure, and in the joint benefit the two sections would rediscover the larger interests they held in common. A side effect of a transcontinental railroad would be the populating of the plains beyond the Missouri River; and when had the opening of new lands to settlement ever been bad for America? The fact that a railroad to California from Chicago, the obvious eastern terminus, would particularly benefit Illinois, including a certain Illinois senator with property in Chicago, was a happy accident. And if that statesman, who was now taking the lead in bestowing all these boons on his fellow Americans, were subsequently spoken of as a candidate for president, who was he to gainsay the wisdom of the American people?

Yet getting the railroad going was no small matter, even for one as shrewd as Douglas. Investors shrank from putting money into a political no-man's-land; a precondition of construction was the political organization of the territory between the Missouri River and the Rockies. Under the terms of the Missouri Compromise, this territory should have been off limits to slavery, as it lay above the line of 36° 30'. But the Compromise of 1850 had gone far toward erasing that line, by allowing that Utah might one day enter the Union as a slave state. (Strictly speaking, the Missouri Compromise dealt only with the region east of the Rockies, but many had come to expect that the underlying principle would apply beyond the mountains.) Moreover, southerners were calling for the wholesale abrogation of the Missouri Compromise, which with hindsight they interpreted as a bad bargain. Douglas, who chaired the Senate committee on territories, lacked the votes to organize Nebraska, as the trans-Missouri region was called, without some southern support. That support might be won, but at a price: repeal of the Missouri Compromise, and hence the opening of the new territory to slavery. David Atchison of Missouri spoke for many southerners when he said he'd see Nebraska "sink in hell" before he'd vote to organize it as a free territory.

The southerners had additional leverage against Douglas. Employing the reports of John (and Jessie) Frémont against the Pathfinder, they argued that a northern railroad route to California was impractical. Hadn't Frémont himself nearly perished in the snow? A California railroad, they said, should traverse the southern portion of the Mexican cession, where the mountains were lower and the winters less severe. (The deserts were harsher, but this was chiefly a problem for livestock of flesh and blood, not iron horses.) To bolster their position they persuaded the administration of Franklin Pierce to purchase a parcel of land from Mexico—the Gadsden Purchase—which held the key to the southern route.

They may have been bluffing, for the southern route entered California far from the goldfields and the important cities of the state. Yet if they were bluffing, the bluff worked. Douglas introduced a bill organizing Nebraska into two territories—Nebraska in the north and Kansas in the south—without regard to slavery. The measure also repealed the Missouri Compromise.

Douglas guessed that his bill would "raise a hell of a storm," but even he had no idea of the tempest he was loosing. Northern editors savaged the Douglas bill; from several northern states "anti-Nebraska" meetings sent petitions and resolutions to Congress. "This crime shall not be consummated," said one, characteristic of most. "Despite corruption, bribery, and treachery, Nebraska, the heart of our continent, shall forever continue free." A Whig senator from Maine, William Fessenden, called the Douglas bill "a terrible outrage," and added, "The more I look at it the more outraged I become. It needs but little to make me an out & out abolitionist."

But the Whigs were a dying breed, as the canny Douglas knew. And the Kansas-Nebraska bill finished them off. On the vote, in the spring of 1854, northern Whigs unanimously rejected the bill while southern Whigs voted strongly in favor. Douglas and the Democratic leadership meanwhile enforced something much closer to party discipline (a majority of northern Democrats joined nearly all southern Democrats in favor), and the bill became law.

This made matters only worse. By leaving the future of slavery in Kansas and Nebraska in the hands of settlers in those territories, Congress guaranteed a bitter contest between free-soilers and slavery men there. The battle centered in Kansas, whose eastern districts looked much like Missouri in terms of climate and terrain that might support slavery. (Douglas's decision to divide Kansas from Nebraska seemed to many an implicit offer of Kansas to the South, with Nebraska reserved to the North.) The contest quickly turned bloody. "Since there is no escaping your challenge," William Seward of New York told his southern colleagues in the Senate, "I accept it in behalf of the cause of freedom. We will engage in competition for the virgin soil of Kansas, and God give the victory to the side which is stronger in numbers as it is in right." The slavery men in turn accepted Seward's challenge, supporting hundreds of pro-slavery settlers who streamed into Kansas from Missouri. For some of the southerners, the campaign against the free-soilers elicited memories of an earlier crusade. "We will be compelled to shoot, burn & hang, but the thing will soon be over," Missouri senator Atchison told Jefferson Davis of Mississippi. "We intend to 'Mormonize' the abolitionists."

The free-soilers weren't without resources and sanguinary zeal of their own. Emigrant-aid societies sprang up in New England and elsewhere, organized for the purpose of transporting antislavery men to Kansas. Amos Lawrence, of the Lawrence, Massachusetts, textile family, sponsored one such emigrant-aid group, and for his money had Lawrence, Kansas, named for him. This appeared a doubtful distinction when a small army of Missourians sacked the town in the spring of 1856. In response a squadron of free-soilers led by John Brown abducted five pro-slavery men near Pottawatomie Creek and split their skulls with broadswords.

LELAND STANFORD WAS no friend of Stephen Douglas, but what Douglas started, Stanford, with the help of many others, would finish. Stanford was part of the second generation of emigrants to Gold Rush California: those who went west looking not for gold but for the collateral opportunities the precious metal created. A New Yorker transplanted to Wisconsin, Stanford resisted the lure of gold in 1849; he was engaged to be married and, having just established a law practice, he—and presumably his fiancée, Jane Lathrop—preferred its steady income to his chances in the goldfields. But an 1852 fire burned up his law books and burned down the businesses of his best clients, and caused him to recalculate life's risks. Several of his brothers had gone to California, and they wrote him regularly. "Mining is not so good now as formerly," Thomas Stanford explained. "Gold is not found in so large quantities as in times gone by. Miners have to work hard to get from three to five dollars per day." But Dewitt Stanford offered an alternative, saying that a general store established at Mormon Island by Josiah Stanford, the eldest brother, and operated by Josiah, Dewitt, Charles Stanford, and a fourth partner named Peck, was doing a thriving business. "Our trade amounts from $1500–$2300 per week," Dewitt said. "I wish we had more of our friends here to start stores through the mines and carry on business all in one company—for I think there are places within five miles of here where there can be three stores that would pay $10,000 clear of all expenses in one year. That would be making money pretty fast."

Leland agreed and, leaving Jane, now his wife, with her family, went west via Nicaragua, landing at San Francisco in July 1852. He opened just such a branch of the brothers' business as Dewitt described, at Cold Springs, between Coloma and Placerville. The store turned its stock quickly and profitably, although the work was less genteel than lawyer Leland was used to. Thomas recounted a visit to Leland's store:

> When the time came to retire for the night, blankets were brought from under the counters and spread on top of them, with additional blankets elevated by our boots for pillows. These being twin beds to those in my own store, I felt quite at home and soon slept the sleep of a tired man.
>
> In the middle of the night all were awakened by a terrific downpour of rain, and ere long the water came rushing down the valley in which the town was located and began to find its way under the doors and through the cracks in the weather boarding. This was the signal for phenomenal activity. Boots were withdrawn from the blanket pillows, and in record time all were at work elevating the more perishable articles. Leland Stanford, a man of great strength, rendered special service in getting barrels of sugar and other heavy articles upon the counters. When the storm abated the water was knee deep in the store.

Cold Springs proved a false start for Stanford's commercial career, for the gold petered out and the people left. In the spring of 1853 he moved to Michigan Bluff, above the Middle Fork of the American River. The town bestrode some ancient placers; as they were worked, the inhabitants prospered. "There are two banking houses, three express offices, five lawyers, four physicians, one watch maker, ten carpenters, three blacksmith shops, five restaurants, six hotels, four bakeries, ten grocery and provision stores, eleven clothing stores, one drug store, one bookstore, besides four of those unnecessary evils, gambling saloons," reported the *Placer Herald*. Stanford's was one of the grocery and provision stores, and despite the competition, he made good money. He also made good friends, who, learning of his legal background, elected him justice of the peace. As the town lacked a regular courthouse, he delivered his verdicts at the Empire Saloon.

Provisioning the miners required resourcefulness. One winter Stanford ran low on vinegar, which the miners used to flavor their beans. Checking his stocks, he discovered he had plenty of whiskey, which he substituted for the vinegar. The new dish tickled the taste buds of the miners and won Stanford a happy following.

In 1855 he briefly returned east to fetch his wife. Jane had refused to rough it in a mining camp; the ill health of her father afforded a second reason to remain east. But then her father died, and Stanford promised to move his business to Sacramento, and she could no longer say no.

Yet it wasn't just Jane that prompted Stanford's move to Sacramento. The gold-bearing gravel that had brought the miners to Michigan Bluff ran under the town, and in their insatiable quest for gold the hydraulickers turned their water cannons on the town site. Stanford had to leave or be washed away.

In Sacramento he erected the finest structure his profits from Michigan Bluff could buy. He built on the levee, above the floodplain of the Sacramento River. And, to avoid that other scourge of California urban life, fire, he built of concrete. The result was what the *California Times* called a "new and magnificently extensive fire proof store." Doing business as Stanford Brothers, the firm advertised itself as "Importers and Wholesale Dealers in Provisions, Groceries, Wines, Liquors, Cigars, Oils & Camphene, Flour, Grain and Produce, Mining Implements, Miners' Supplies, Etc." It explained, "By Importing our own Merchandise, and one of the Firm being constantly in the Atlantic States, shipping Goods by clipper vessels, expressly for this market, we offer superior inducements to the Country Dealer or Trade in general, and invite an inspection of our stock. Prices will be found as low as those of San Francisco. Orders put up with the utmost care and dispatch."

General stores had long been the crossroads of American communities, and Stanford's placed him in contact with all manner of people. Most supplied merely their patronage, others information, still others new opportunities. More than a few of Stanford's customers came to the counter short of money; in its place they offered stakes in their mines. Stanford accepted the most promising offers and became a miner in spite of himself.

With his mounting success, Stanford gained a higher public profile. As profiles went, it was distinctive but not particularly impressive, at least at first glance. Stanford was a square man with a square head set firmly on square shoulders. (The beard and belly he would grow in later life rounded him a little, but not enough to erase his essential orthogonality.) And Stanford's character seemed to match his appearance: he met life square-on, without pretense or even obvious enthusiasm. He utterly lacked the self-promoting flamboyance of Sam Brannan, for instance; none who knew Stanford could have imagined him engaging in a stunt like Brannan's braying about gold from the plaza of San Francisco. Yet this very lack of flamboyance in Stanford could be reassuring, and that square body and blockish head inspired confidence that here was a man who, once he found his direction, would plow through every obstacle in his way.

As matters happened, he found his direction soon enough. Some of his customers wanted to elevate public literacy by establishing a subscription library; Stanford signed on as a charter member and trustee. The library's membership comprised the most important business figures in Sacramento, including Charles Crocker, a brawny former blacksmith who had failed at mining but was prospering in dry goods; Collis Huntington, an erstwhile peddler who, while stuck on the isthmus in the same crowd as Jessie Frémont, amassed a modest fortune arbitraging between the locals and the emigrants; and Mark Hopkins, a vegetarian with a prematurely white beard who had started around the Horn with a captain even more brutal than Robert Waterman (so brutal he provoked a successful mutiny at Rio de Janeiro), and who completed the journey to become Huntington's partner in hardware.

Beyond books and business, the quartet discovered a common interest in railroads, specifically a railroad connecting California to the rest of the Union. This interest drew them to the nascent Republican party. While opposition to slavery was the primary glue that held together the odd assortment of Whigs, Free-Soilers, Know-Nothings, and northern Democrats who converted to Republicanism, a secondary cement was the old Whig enthusiasm for federally funded improvements to transportation. Foremost of these, now that California was part of the Union, was a railroad to the Pacific. Naturally, a Pacific railroad appealed to California businessmen, who—in addition to sharing the general California sentiment in favor of swifter transport east—favored whatever would spur the growth of the state and thereby its commerce and presumably their profits. Stanford, Crocker, Huntington, and Hopkins found a cause in the railroad to California, and an instrument in the Republican party.

The California Republicans were a cozy group at first. "In Sacramento, where I resided," remembered Cornelius Cole, an original member, "the party at its inception was extremely limited in numbers. No record, I venture to say, can be found of a political organization starting out with fewer adherents. There were C. P. Huntington, Mark Hopkins, Leland Stanford, Edwin B. and Charles Crocker, all personal as well as political friends of mine. There were not for some time, besides these, as many as could be counted on one's fingers."

Being a California Republican wasn't easy. The state was dominated by Democrats with ties to the South, who tarred their new rivals with the brush of abolitionism. "We deprecate the formation of a Republican party in this State," declared the *Sacramento Union*, at that time California's most influential paper. "Its organization will be followed, in our view, by a long train of evils to the people; it will unnecessarily divide the people of the State upon a sectional issue in which they are not directly interested." A competing paper was less diplomatic. "The convention of nigger worshippers assembled yesterday in this city," the Sacramento *State Journal* declared. "This is the first time that this dangerous fanaticism has dared to bare its breast before the people of California. . . . There is dangerous meaning in the spectacle of political degradation now before us. . . . It is high time all national men should unite in saving California from the stain of abolitionism."

WILLIAM SHERMAN DIDN'T like Republicans at this stage of his and their histories, deeming them a disruptive force in national life. And his tightly wound temperament could hardly have contrasted more with that of the phlegmatic Stanford. Yet such was the attraction of gold—or rather, of the opportunities gold created—that Sherman could no more resist throwing over his career as a soldier than Stanford had been able to resist abandoning a career in law. Like Stanford, although less successfully, Sherman during the 1850s became a California businessman—in his case, a banker.

After helping to get the rush to California started by sending Lieutenant Loeser to Washington, Sherman himself went east at the beginning of 1850 with dispatches for the War Department. Already he could see the changes the Gold Rush had wrought: his eastward journey, via steamship and the isthmus, took a mere 30 days, compared to the 196 days his outbound journey around Cape Horn had required in 1846–47.

Sherman had a second, more personal reason for traveling east. He was going to get married. His bride was Ellen Ewing of Ohio, who also happened to be his foster sister. This unusual match was the result, in part, of the death of Sherman's father when the boy was nine; his mother, lacking the resources to feed and clothe her children, farmed the older ones out to neighbors. Red-haired William—until then called Cump, short for Tecumseh, the great Indian chief, whom his father greatly admired—went to the family of Thomas Ewing, a lawyer and aspiring politician. (The early death of his father, and now the effective loss of his mother, doubtless had something to do with Sherman's sober demeanor throughout life. The change of his name—the Ewings insisted on a Christian name in front of his pagan appellation—made the change in his life all the more evident.) Sherman grew up with the Ewings, and fell in love with his foster sister. Meanwhile, Thomas Ewing became a senator, and then secretary of the interior under Zachary Taylor. The Sherman-Ewing wedding consequently attracted various Washington luminaries, including President Taylor and senators Daniel Webster, Henry Clay, and Thomas Benton. The honeymoon journey introduced Ellen to some Sherman relatives in Ohio before returning the newlyweds to Washington in time for the Fourth of July celebration at which the overheated Taylor ingested too many frozen cherries, triggering the stomach troubles that led to his death.

In the East, Sherman gradually realized that California had spoiled him for army life. He had seen men far less capable than himself make far more money than he could ever hope to make in the military. "In these prosperous times, salaried men suffer," he told his brother John. Accordingly he cast about for other opportunities. Through the Ewings he met investors intrigued by the prospects California presented, and impressed by Sherman's intelligence and experience. Two St. Louis bankers, James Lucas and Henry Turner, inquired whether Sherman might be willing to return to San Francisco and head up a new bank. They offered a generous salary, with a partnership interest that was bound to grow. Sherman was tempted, yet didn't wish to abandon his army commission carelessly. He pondered the offer at length, then applied to the War Department for a six-months' leave of absence to travel to San Francisco and test matters on the ground there. "You may depend on it that I will not throw away my present position without a strong probability of decided advantage," he told John.

Arriving back at San Francisco in the spring of 1853, Sherman was amazed at how the city had changed in his absence. The cove—the sheltering place for ships that had provided the original raison d'etre for Yerba Buena—had vanished beneath the advancing streets, which now pressed far out into the bay. New wharves extended even farther, although, without the wind- and wave-breaking effects of the cove, the shelter they offered was inferior to what their predecessors had supplied. The sand hills behind the old village had largely been leveled; even more-stubborn prominences like Telegraph Hill had been severely diminished by continued blasting. The tents and flimsy wooden structures that dominated the city's architecture in the early days had been replaced by imposing edifices of brick and stone—as a consequence of which, Sherman soon learned, fire was far less a threat than previously. Or so, at any rate, judged the insurance companies based in New York and London that now offered fire insurance at rates Sherman discovered to be comparable to those in the East.

The tone of city life had changed almost as much as the city's visual appearance. Gold dust no longer served as money, and the small scales that merchants had used to weigh customers' payments were now mere curiosity pieces. Coins clanked across the counters: American dollars and quarter-dollars, English crowns and shillings, French francs, Mexican dollars and double-reals, Dutch and German florins and guilders, even Indian rupees. The federal assay office in the city stamped gold coins in denominations of ten and twenty dollars, and special "slugs" worth fifty dollars—although San Franciscans anticipated that when the local branch of the United States mint, authorized the previous year by Congress, opened, it would replace the assay office in this regard, besides rendering the foreign coinages unnecessary. Not surprisingly in light of his prospective profession, Sherman paid particular attention to the bank drafts that underwrote larger transactions than the coins allowed: drafts drawn against Page, Bacon & Co., the city's leading bank with deposits of nearly $2 million, in its proud granite building at the corner of California and Montgomery, and against the other financial houses in the same neighborhood.

The city had lost much of its frantic character. By the standards of the East, San Franciscans were still in a hurry, but, in contrast to the early days, they weren't uniformly in a hurry to get somewhere else. The population of the city continued to grow rapidly—this was obvious from all the construction. But a solid core of the population had stabilized. The metal foundries, flour mills, and boatyards of the Happy Valley neighborhood supported a contingent of workers who had discovered that mining wasn't everything they had hoped it would be. The cobblers, upholsterers, harness-makers, jewelers, painters, bakers, printers, and tailors located around the commercial district provided goods and services one might have found in any city—and at prices that, while still often high by eastern standards, were no longer extortionate. A steady market for fruits and vegetables, and the diminishing allure of the mines, had given rise to a truck-farming industry on the city's outskirts and across the bay that furnished San Francisco's tables with everything easterners ate—and more, on account of California's equable climate.

On this visit Sherman might or might not have encountered a Bavarian-born dry-goods merchant named Levi Strauss, who had just arrived from New York and was setting up a business to sell supplies to the miners and their fellows-in-toil. Eventually Strauss's supplies would include distinctive canvas pants first called "waist overalls" but later "jeans"—and finally "levis."

On the other hand, Sherman could hardly have avoided noticing the Pioneer Steam Coffee and Spice Mills on Powell Street, where sails from abandoned whaleships caught the bay breeze and powered a wind-driven grindstone. The company was the brainchild of New Yorker William Bovee, who discovered that miners would pay top dollar for coffee they didn't have to roast and grind themselves; the sails were the work of Bovee's partner, a teenager from Nantucket named James Folger, who would buy the coffee company and rename it for himself.

For all the changes, the city was still recognizably San Francisco. If many of the gambling hells had given way to billiard parlors, that was at least partly because the gambling had moved upscale and downtown: to the banks, which supplied credit for all manner of ambitious mining and commercial ventures, and made fat profits on interest rates of 3 percent per month and more. Sherman, surveying the situation, decided that banking was for him. "My business here," he wrote John, referring to the banking business, "is the best going, provided we have plenty of money."

Returning to St. Louis for consultation, Sherman had no difficulty securing the requisite funds. James Lucas and Henry Turner pledged $200,000 in cash and arranged a credit line of $50,000 with a New York bank in which Lucas was a principal. Sherman resigned his army commission, fetched his family—which now included a daughter, Lizzie—and traveled west once more. They reached San Francisco on October 15, 1853, and set up housekeeping, first at a hotel on Stockton Street near Broadway, then in a rented house on Stockton, and finally in a new brick house on Green Street that Sherman purchased from the builder.

THE BANKING BUSINESS proved more of a challenge than Sherman had anticipated. Costs were greater than he guessed, starting with the cost of constructing an office. He had budgeted $50,000 for acquiring a lot and erecting a building; by the time the new office of Lucas & Turner, located on the corner of Montgomery and Jackson, greeted its first customers, Sherman had spent half again that much.

Yet the hardest part of his new job was distinguishing good risks from bad. Everyone in San Francisco had grand schemes for making money: by subdividing property, developing mines, building streets and hotels and warehouses and homes. Those projects that succeeded paid handsomely, to the entrepreneurs and their lenders alike. But many projects failed, leaving the entrepreneurs illiquid and the noteholders empty-handed.

One of San Francisco's leading entrepreneurs—and one of Sherman's most important customers—was Henry Meiggs, a member of the city council and a businessman with large and varied interests, including a chain of sawmills up the coast near Mendocino. From his mansion on Broadway, Meiggs strode forth each day to tend to his business affairs and the well-being of the city. Like many San Franciscans, he had sizable debts, but these supported his profit-generating activities and appeared hardly out of line.

Yet Sherman developed an uneasy feeling about Meiggs. Some of Sherman's discomfort followed from Meiggs's overrepresentation in the loan portfolio of Lucas & Turner: $80,000 of a loan total of $600,000. Some owed to the circumstance that Meiggs kept his positive balances in other banks, leaving Sherman unclear about the exact state of his liquidity. Finally, certain things about Meiggs just didn't seem right—his promises and explanations were always plausible but never entirely convincing. Consequently, Sherman decided to diminish the bank's exposure in Meiggs's direction. When Meiggs applied for a draft for an additional $20,000, Sherman politely declined. Meiggs indignantly asked whether Sherman distrusted him. No, Sherman said, it was just that the bank had limited resources and as a matter of policy was concentrating them among the customers that did all their business with Lucas & Turner. Thereupon Meiggs invited Sherman to join him on a visit to the local office of a German bank, where Meiggs demonstrated, "as clearly as a proposition in mathematics," in Sherman's ironic characterization, that his business at Mendocino couldn't fail. The new $20,000 would pay for a powerful tugboat to bring his lumber ships into port at San Francisco. The Germans were persuaded; they offered to relieve Sherman of Meiggs's entire debt if he—Sherman—would supply a draft to pay Meiggs's shipbuilder in Philadelphia. Sherman was happy to oblige, as this transaction lightened his load with Meiggs considerably. Moreover, the new note was secured by mortgages on San Francisco real estate and by warrants issued by the city government.

Not much later, Meiggs disappeared. Investigation revealed that he and his family had left on a steamer bound for Chile, well beyond the reach of American law. Additional investigation showed that his debts were far greater than either Sherman or the German bankers knew, totaling more than a million dollars. Sherman took possession of Meiggs's mortgaged properties, redeemed the city warrants, and congratulated himself on following his intuition. The Germans had to admit they'd been humbugged, and were forced to close their doors.

HUMBUGS WERE UBIQUITOUS in California during the Gold Rush era, and the doubts they sowed in the popular mind sprang up to harm everyone. Even in settled circumstances, nearly all banks are failures-in-waiting; the essence of the banking business is to lend out the money depositors bring in, and to receive repayment, including more interest than the depositors get, before the depositors demand their money back. In confident times the arrangement works well, as depositors prefer the interest on their deposits to the security of holding cash. But when confidence is shaken, as by the default of a major bank customer, depositors' preferences shift from interest to security, and they may demand their deposits at once.

Sherman got caught in one such crisis of confidence. The Page, Bacon & Co. bank of San Francisco was part of a larger Page operation that had offices in the East and was engaged in all manner of lending for the nation's booming economy. Most important, both for the bank and for the nation, was the railroad industry; one of the Page's principal customers was the Ohio & Mississippi Railroad. During the winter of 1854–55 the Ohio & Mississippi ran into financial trouble, which spilled over into the affairs of the Page. On February 17, 1855, the Pacific Mail steamer arrived at San Francisco with the news that the Page branch in New York had suspended operations. Despite the best efforts of the Page officers in San Francisco to explain that the difficulty in New York had absolutely no bearing on the finances of the San Francisco house, it *did* have a bearing—for the simple reason that the Page's San Francisco depositors believed it did. Seized by panic, they converged on the Page offices and demanded their deposits. For three days the bank's reserves decreased alarmingly.

The Page bank's director, Henry Haight, approached Sherman for an emergency loan. Despite the jolt the run on the Page caused the San Francisco financial community, Sherman felt confident. Against deposits of some $600,000, his Lucas & Turner bank had cash reserves of nearly $500,000, an usually large fraction. Loans receivable summed to an additional $500,000. In other words, Lucas & Turner was well positioned to withstand a test of its strength.

Sherman was reluctant to weaken that position, and would do so only if given personal assurances that the Page bank would make every endeavor in its own behalf. After the close of business one afternoon he visited the Page bank. To his dismay he discovered that Haight had been drinking, and was now lamenting that "all the banks would break." This was hardly the reassurance Sherman was seeking. On the way out he encountered a group of the city's bankers and leading businessmen, who were preparing a joint statement expressing their faith in the solvency of the Page. They asked Sherman to add his signature to theirs. He inquired whether they had examined the accounts of the Page bank, and pointed out that the proposed statement made them morally, if perhaps not legally, responsible for the Page's fate. This struck them as a novel idea, not entirely germane to the crisis at hand; but they were compelled to reply that they hadn't. Sherman declined to sign, and bade them all good evening.

The run on the Page resumed the next day, and the day after that the bank closed. The financial panic spread across the city, and Sherman, expecting a torrent of frantic depositors at his own doors, prepared for the worst. He opened the Lucas & Turner office at the usual hour, to an anxious crowd. The depositors streamed in, pushing to get to the tellers' windows. "The most noisy and clamorous were men and women who held small certificates," Sherman observed. This was a blessing, as paying them depleted the bank's holdings only slowly. Through the course of the day Sherman managed to satisfy all those who showed up. His reputation for sober diligence kept their number down. "Several gentlemen of my personal acquaintance merely asked my word of honor that their money was safe, and went away." The mood of the crowd was captured in a remark by one of Sherman's depositors, a Frenchman still struggling with English:

"If you got the money, I no want him; but if you no got him, I want it like the devil!"

That evening Sherman began dunning the people who owed him money. Although most of his notes were not callable, he judged that his debtors, who included some of the chief businessmen of the city, ought to share the risk of the city's banks—if only because the ruin of the banks would paralyze the economy of the entire region. Some of the men Sherman approached were themselves paralyzed and unable to act. Of one man who owed $25,000, Sherman wrote, "I found him in great pain and distress, mental and physical. He was sitting in a chair, and bathing his head with a sponge." Nor was he alone. "So great was the shock to public confidence that men slept on their money, and would not loan it for ten per cent a week on any security whatever." Others, fortunately, took a broader view. When Sherman asked the holder of two acceptances, in the amounts of $20,000 and $16,000, to pay one, the man offered to pay both, with a personal check, asking only that Sherman not cash the check unless it proved necessary.

In fact it didn't prove necessary. As word got out that Sherman had the backing of some of San Francisco's most solvent citizens, the pressure on Lucas & Turner eased. Depositors stopped withdrawing money, and began returning funds they had withdrawn the day before.

THE BANK PANIC of 1855 was the most serious calamity to hit San Francisco since the great fire of 1851. Hundreds of businesses went under, erasing millions of dollars of equity. Prices collapsed; workers were idled. A sense of sullen foreboding, of promises broken and golden dreams dashed, pervaded the city.

The ugly mood grew uglier when one of those idled by the panic, a banker named James King of William, took up a new calling. King ("of William" had been added to distinguish this James King from others) turned to journalism and launched a crusade against political corruption in the city. It was an easy target, for in the four years since the Committee of Vigilance had suppressed the Hounds and Ducks, the criminal element had gone into politics. Graft and extortion became a regular part of governance, enforced by thugs on the politicians' payroll and enabled by the same laissez-faire attitude that had allowed the gangs to flourish.

James King, however, refused to let things be. "It's no use trying to dodge the *Bulletin*," he warned the objects of his paper's wrath. Foremost of those objects was James Casey, an erstwhile inmate of New York's Sing Sing Prison who graduated to the San Francisco Board of Supervisors without—in King's plainly stated view—changing his character or much altering his modus operandi. As if to prove King correct, Casey shot him fatally on the street in broad daylight in May 1856.

King's editorials scratched the conscience of those who had allowed the city government to fall into the hands of such as Casey, and his killing remobilized the membership of the dormant Committee of Vigilance. Even as King breathed his last, circulars summoned the city's honest inhabitants to its defense. Casey, the shooter, surrendered himself to the sheriff from fear of the Vigilance crowd—and from hope that the sheriff, who was in league with the criminal element, would allow his escape after things calmed down.

Several hundred, then several thousand, citizens answered the appeal of the revived Vigilance Committee. A subscription almost instantly raised $75,000 for arms and other expenses. An executive committee was chosen, headed by William Coleman, a prominent merchant known for astute judgment and no-nonsense dispatch. Officers were elected to drill the rank and file, who marched about the streets, shouldering bayoneted rifles and pulling cannons commandeered from the armory.

As control of the city slipped to the Vigilance Committee, the mayor, James Van Ness, called on Governor William Johnson for aid. Johnson in turn called on William Sherman, who, in light of the tenuous condition of the banking business, had accepted a part-time commission as major-general of the state militia. Sherman answered Johnson's summons to an emergency meeting. "I found him on the roof of the International [Hotel]," Sherman wrote, "from which we looked down on the whole city, and more especially on the face of Telegraph Hill, which was already covered with a crowd of people, while others were moving toward the jail on Broadway.

Parties of armed men, in good order, were marching by platoons in the same direction, and formed a line along Broadway, facing the jail-door."

An opposition group calling itself the Law and Order Party had gathered in front of the jail to support the sheriff. But on assessing the size and determination of the Vigilance forces, the Law and Order men withdrew, leaving the sheriff to answer the Vigilance demands. The central demand was the surrender of Casey, but while they were there the Vigilance leaders insisted on custody of another prisoner, Charles Cora, who had shot and killed a federal marshal but thus far evaded conviction.

Shortly thereafter the Vigilance Committee conducted a trial of Casey, which yielded the predictable verdict. Cora received a separate trial but the same verdict. On May 22—the day of King's funeral, as it happened—the two men were hanged.

NO TEARS WERE shed for James Casey, but at least a few fell for Charles Cora. Cora had been a professional gambler in New Orleans before coming west, and he continued to ply his craft in San Francisco, with evident success. Yet Cora's luck at cards was nothing next to the luck of his partner, a woman named Belle, at a much older profession.

During the early years of the Gold Rush, California, with far more than its share of single men, had far more than its share of prostitutes. Many came from South America, like Pérez Rosales's shipmate Rosario, who worked her way north before receiving a rousing welcome in San Francisco. Pérez, for the sake of conscience or health, had been one of the few aboard the *Stanguéli* to decline her favors, but as she debarked he felt a certain admiration. "Rosario," he wrote, "like a privateer in her magnificent silk dress, cape and parasol and attended with the utmost eagerness by all who came on board, soon left the vessel and disappeared, surrounded by courtiers, through the heavy fog." Other *filles de joie* were French, driven from Paris by the same combination of economic depression and political upheaval that launched Jean-Nicolas Perlot across two oceans. One Frenchman in California rather proudly described the superiority of his countrywomen: "Americans were irresistibly attracted by their graceful walk, their supple and easy bearing, and charming freedom of manner, qualities, after all, to be found only in France; and they trooped after a French woman whenever she put her nose out of doors, as if they could never see enough of her." Still other prostitutes were Australian and Chinese, the latter including the famously lovely Ah Toy, characterized by one admiring argonaut as "the finest-looking woman I have ever seen."

Life for some of the prostitutes was as hard and hazardous in California as anywhere else. Certain of the Chinese women, for example, were little more than sex slaves for their pimps. (Whether Yee Ah Tye became directly involved in the sex trade is unclear, but in his role as association leader he certainly benefited indirectly.) Yet other women did well, at least financially. At a time when a Paris streetwalker might make the equivalent of two dollars a night, some of the Frenchwomen in San Francisco made $400. Others moved into semipermanent arrangements with men who were willing and able to keep them in style.

And then there were the madams, entrepreneurs like Belle Cora. (Belle wasn't married to Charles Cora but adopted his last name for protection and a semblance of respectability.) How much money Belle made is impossible to know, yet her house on Dupont Street was renowned for the sumptuousness of its furnishings, the quality of its food and wines, the talent of its musicians, and the beauty of its women. Men with lust in their hearts—or merely a desire for the warmth of a woman's touch—and gold in their pockets beat a path through the muddy streets to her door, where she made sure they wiped their feet before entering.

In the early wild days, Belle conducted her business unmolested. Some of the most-distinguished men in San Francisco patronized her establishment, and no one thought the worse of them for it. But as the city settled down, and as mothers and families came to figure more prominently in civic life, Belle encountered increasing disapproval. Sarah Royce lamented the coarsening effect of the general idea that men should pay for feminine favors. Girls from respectable families, performing in school plays or musical recitals, discovered that strange men would throw them money and other gifts. "They commonly accepted them, often with looks of exultation," Sarah explained. "And still worse, there were mothers who not merely countenanced the thing but even boasted of the amount their daughters had thus received. It must indeed be an obtuse moral sense that could not perceive the corrupting tendency of such customs; and I have since seen some sad falls into positive vice of those whose downward course appeared to begin in these and similar practices."

If the women who made a business of accepting men's favors had kept to themselves, they might have suffered less obloquy. Yet this wasn't really an option, for San Francisco had grown so fast, and so haphazardly, that the prostitutes—and their customers—shared neighborhoods and even sidewalks with the most pious members of the community. "Is it not wonderful," declared one indignant matron, "that young men should nightly spend their evenings, like dogs, smelling out all these vile excrescences, peeking through the cracks and crevices of doors, windows and blinds in our crowded thoroughfares, in the full face of ladies and gentlemen going and returning from church?" Another woman complained of the prostitutes: "As I passed up the streets these creatures attracted my attention by giggling, laughing and making impertinent remarks to each other, looking me in the face and passing, and then allowing me to repass them under their licentious stare and meaningless giggle."

Belle was more discreet, but ran into trouble anyway. One evening she and Charles Cora attended a performance at the American Theater. Federal marshal William Richardson and his wife were seated nearby, and Mrs. Richardson complained of the presence of the notorious madam. At his wife's urging, Richardson insisted that the theater manager eject Belle and Cora. The manager refused, causing the Richardsons to leave, although not before they insulted Belle and Cora. The gambler and the madam stayed till the end of the performance, but the next day Cora defended Belle's honor by calling on Richardson and returning the insult. One thing led to another, and Cora shot Richardson dead.

Cora was charged with murder and brought to trial. Belle enlisted the best and most expensive counsel—she reportedly paid $15,000 to lead attorney Edward Baker—on her lover's behalf. Baker cast Cora as a gentleman among gamblers, and Belle as a good-hearted woman merely giving the city what it wanted. Baker's version didn't sufficiently move the jury to acquit, but it did produce a deadlock. Cora was awaiting retrial when the Vigilance Committee stepped in.

Belle realized that neither her money nor her capacity for blackmail—the idea evidently occurred to her—could stay the march of popular justice. (The possibility of being blackmailed, or at least embarrassed by Belle's testimony, may well have influenced the calculations of those who could have kept Cora out of the Vigilance Committee's hands but declined to do so.) Yet she did manage to shame the committee into granting a final request. At the eleventh hour, in the very shadow of the noose, she married Charles Cora. For a moment she was his wife—and then became his widow.

IN A FEW YEARS the world would discover how William Sherman felt about armed resistance to constitutional authority. Those who knew him in San Francisco in 1856 got a preview, as well as a reminder of how close to the frontier the city remained, with everything such proximity implied in terms of lawlessness and lack of stable political institutions.

The hanging of Cora and Casey might have ended the rule of the revived Vigilance Committee if Thomas King, the brother of the murdered reform editor, hadn't taken up the fallen quill. The second King demanded that his brother's mission continue. In an editorial entitled "What the People Expect of the Vigilance Committee," he declared, "The people look to them for reform—a radical reorganization in spirit if not in fact—of our city government." The larger conspiracy behind his brother's murder must be rooted out and the plotters punished, King said. Beyond this, the political corruption that allowed such conspiracies to flourish must be extirpated. "If we would have order hereafter, an example must now be made of the ballot-box stuffers." King minced no words in explaining what he meant. "Let the men who have insulted our community, disgraced our State, and sown the seeds of which we have been lately reaping the fruits, meet their due fate, DEATH BY HANGING. . . . Hang one ballot-box stuffer, and we shall have no more of them."

Not all the Vigilance men considered vote-tampering a capital offense, but most believed that some additional housecleaning was required. A few wanted to extend the forcible reforms beyond the city government to the state. A committee headquarters was established on Stockton Street (called "Fort Gunnybags" after the sandbags that afforded protection from sniper fire; bunkered cannon added an offensive threat). The committee leadership met behind the sandbags, while armed Vigilance squads roamed the city.

Such open sedition compelled Governor Johnson to respond. He summoned Sherman to Benicia, where the local commander of federal troops, General John Wool, was stationed. By Sherman's recollection, Wool agreed to supply Sherman with federal arms and ammunition, which Sherman, as the commander of the California militia, would use to suppress the insurrection at San Francisco.

The governor then prevailed on the chief justice of the California supreme court, David Terry, for a writ of habeas corpus against the Vigilance Committee, to require the committee to hand back another prisoner they had seized from jail. When the committee rejected the writ, the governor issued a proclamation declaring the Vigilance Committee in violation of state law and commanding General Sherman to move against it. Sherman responded by publishing an order to his militiamen, summoning them to service in defense of the state.

Alarmed, several Vigilance leaders visited Sherman. If he carried out his order, they said, blood would flow on San Francisco's streets.

Sherman, perhaps recalling the insubordination of John Frémont and the troubles it caused during the American occupation, had no sympathy for the rebels. Fixing them with his cold blue eyes, he declared that if they wanted to avert bloodshed, they would have to get out of the way. "Remove your fort; cease your midnight councils; and prevent your armed bodies from patrolling the streets," he said.

The rebels asked Sherman where he was going to get arms for his men. He declined to answer, except to say that he would certainly get them. Some while later, a second Vigilance delegation—"a class of the most intelligent and wealthiest men of the city, who earnestly and honestly desired to prevent bloodshed," Sherman thought—approached him. He gave them the same answer he had given the others. "I told them that our men were enrolling very fast, and that, when I deemed the right moment had come, the Vigilance Committee must disperse, else bloodshed and destruction of property would inevitably follow."

Sherman prepared for battle and began to devise his strategy. But suddenly General Wool flinched. The army commander decided not to get involved in a state squabble without express authorization from Washington. Awaiting this, he declined to release the weapons from the federal arsenal to Sherman.

Wool's reversal outraged Sherman. He believed he had Wool's promise to supply the weapons necessary to uphold the law and preserve order; without such a promise Sherman never would have agreed to call out the state troops. But now that Wool refused to cooperate, Sherman was made to appear an impotent fool, a general without arms. He angrily resigned his commission in the militia.

Sherman's resignation marked the beginning of a reign of uncontested power on the part of the Vigilance Committee. For many weeks the committee issued orders from Fort Gunnybags, directing the arrest of prominent malefactors. These were tried, usually in secret, and punished. Besides Casey and Cora, two other men were executed, both for murder. Another man committed suicide while in detention. (Later generations would greet jailhouse "suicides" with rightful skepticism, but considering the readiness of the Vigilance men to conduct executions openly, there is little reason to think they resorted to this ruse.) The committee declined Thomas King's advice to hang vote-tamperers, but it banished those convicted of ballot irregularities, under penalty of death for return.

The illicit authority of the committee met its severest test when Chief Justice Terry, a vicious scrapper besides being a vocal critic of the vigilance movement, got into a fight with one of the committee's constables. In the fight Terry stabbed the constable, who for several days lingered between life and death. The committee arrested Terry and held him at Fort Gunnybags.

Besides revealing the shocking anarchy into which San Francisco and now California were falling—when the Founding Fathers had established the principle of checks and balances between the branches of government, they certainly didn't have daggers in mind—Terry's arrest put the committee in a quandary. To try the judge would be to raise the flag of rebellion even higher, but to let him go would mock the principles for which the committee stood. If the victim died, the committee's dilemma would grow still more acute; consequently the committee leaders prayed for his survival. As it happened, the man did pull through, and Terry was quietly released.

The experience with Terry sobered many of the Vigilance men, and the committee began looking for a graceful way to terminate its business. Sherman wasn't a neutral observer but probably an accurate one when he told his brother, "I think the community is getting sick and disgusted with their secrecy, their street fools, and parades, and mock trials." Anyway, the committee could reasonably claim that its work was done. The example of those brought before the committee had, as anticipated, encouraged many others to leave the city. One tally placed the departures at about 800, in addition to the 25 formally banished.

Accordingly, in August 1856 the Vigilance Committee voted to adjourn. With medals struck for the occasion (showing the All-Seeing Eye on the obverse, the Goddess of Justice on the reverse), the committee authorized a final parade, in which the popular forces of order appeared one last time before marching off—as it turned out, into history.

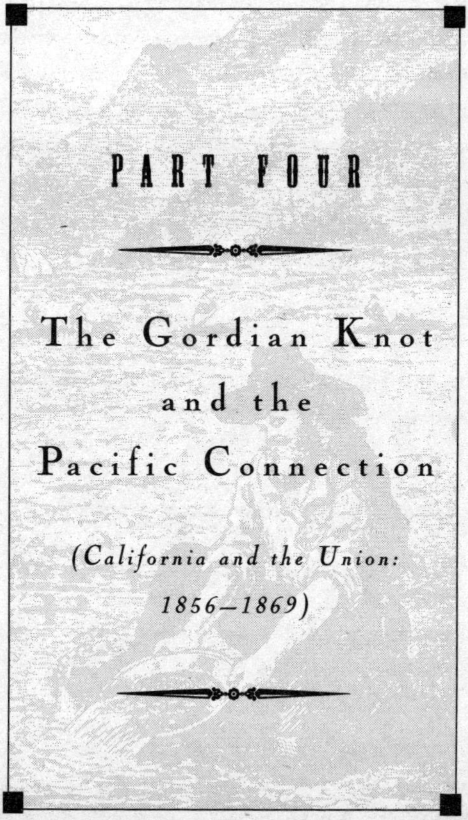

PART FOUR

The Gordian Knot and the Pacific Connection

(California and the Union: 1856–1869)

Home in the gold country

A major river operation

Water cannons at work

Comparing notes, and costumes, after hours

Abandoned ships at San Francisco

Sam Brannan

San Francisco after the great fire of 1851

John Frémont

Jessie Frémont

William Sherman

Leland
Stanford

George Hearst (cleaned-up)

Mariano Vallejo

John Sutter, sadder but wiser

Likewise, James Marshall

The sunburnt immigrant, walking with his wife and little ones beside his gaunt and weary oxen in mid-continent; the sea-traveller pining on shipboard, tortured with mal de mer; the homesick bride whose wedding trip had included a passage of the Isthmus; the merchant whose stock needed replenishing; and the miner fortunate enough to be able to return home—everyone, except of course the men of the Pacific Mail Steamship company, prayed for a Pacific railroad.

—Hubert Howe Bancroft

In conceptualizing America's past, historians often draw a dividing line at 1865, which is accounted a critical moment in the nation's political evolution. And so it was, for in finally settling the dual controversies of slavery and states' rights that had vexed American politics since the founding of the republic, the Confederate defeat finished the work the framers of the Constitution had commenced in 1787.

Yet, from another vantage, the turning point can be detected earlier, in 1848 at Coloma. In political terms, the gold discovery can be seen as the beginning of the end of the antebellum era, as the catalyst for the transforming reactions of the decade that followed. By peopling the West far faster than anyone imagined, the Gold Rush compelled Congress to confront the contradictions it had long preferred to avoid. Had the territory taken from Mexico in 1848 filled up as slowly as the territory acquired from France in 1803, the likelihood of a peaceful resolution of the sectional controversy almost certainly would have been much greater. It is impossible to know whether war might have been averted; history never tells us what would have happened, only what did happen. But the gold discovery collapsed the calendar, demanding an answer to the crucial question of slavery in the territories before the collective wisdom of national politics could devise an answer that didn't fatally antagonize powerful constituencies on both sides of the Mason-Dixon Line. In pounding on the Union's door in 1850, California awakened the dogs of division and set them howling all at once. From the Compromise of 1850 ran a straight, if tortured, path to southern secession and civil war. And Californians, beginning with John Frémont but including such other striking characters as William Walker and Asbury Harpending, did their full part in propelling America down that path.

Beyond politics, the Gold Rush helped initiate the modern era of American economic development. The Industrial Revolution had begun in America before James Marshall struck gold, but the new wealth of the new West accelerated the revolution. The gold of California, and the gold and silver of California's nephew Nevada, poured liquidity east, lubricating the gears of the nation's industrial machinery (and in the process underwriting the Union's victory in the Civil War). More important, California demanded, and received, a transcontinental railroad. The construction of the Pacific railroad was a huge project, the largest construction job of the age; its effects on American capital, commodity, and labor markets were felt from coast to coast (and beyond the coasts to Europe and Asia). But the true significance of the railroad emerged only upon its completion. By tying the coasts together, the Pacific railroad created the largest unified market in the world, the market that allowed the American economy to grow into the colossus it became by the beginning of the twentieth century.

14

The Pathfinder's Return

Had the rest of the country known what William Sherman knew about life in California in 1856, John Frémont might not have won the first Republican nomination for president. But the struggle for order in San Francisco loomed far larger locally than in the affairs of the nation, which had problems aplenty of its own, and Frémont's run of good fortune continued.

That it kept Frémont in politics was rather surprising. By the bad luck of the draw (the other senator selected by California's first legislature, William Gwin, got the longer straw, and hence the longer term) and the slowness of Congress to accept California as a state, Frémont served only a few weeks in the Senate before having to return to California to defend his seat. Although he hadn't been away long, the debate over the Compromise of 1850 so polarized California politics—as it was polarizing politics throughout the country—that an outspoken free-soiler like Frémont could no longer pass muster with the predominantly Democratic and South-leaning California legislature. His candidacy failed (although it took the legislature almost another year to agree on his successor).

The San Francisco fire of 1851 shortly added injury to insult by destroying his and Jessie's home; he responded by taking the family to Europe for an extended holiday. His reputation preceded him and his wealth accompanied him; the family lived and were treated like royalty. In England,

John was most intrigued to meet the Duke of Wellington, now past eighty but still impressive. Jessie preferred her audience with Queen Victoria. In Paris they were entertained by the recovering nobility, who recovered enough before the Frémonts left to put the imperial crown back on the head of a Bonaparte, Napoleon III.

On their return to America, Frémont deposited Jessie and the children in Washington, where she tended to her ailing mother; and he headed west on his fifth exploratory expedition. The plans for a California railroad had by now become thoroughly entangled in the sectional struggle. The secretary of war, Mississippi Democrat Jefferson Davis, aggravated the struggle—in the guise of attempting to resolve it—by commissioning five separate surveys of possible routes. Frémont's previous exploratory work was ignored, as was the explorer himself. Frémont took the snub personally, and politically. The regular army—Davis was a West Pointer—obviously still bore a grudge against the man who had crossed General Kearny; moreover, the Democrats and the South were determined to stall construction of a line that would strengthen the North by linking free California to the other free states. While others besides Frémont complained at the politics of the superfluous surveys, he took matters into his own hands, and his own pocket, by funding a survey of his own.

This final expedition of Frémont's career lacked the grisly drama of some of the previous four. No one ate anyone else, although at one point of low rations Frémont swore everyone to abstinence from human flesh and vowed to shoot the first man who eyed his fellow hungrily. As always, Jessie worried about her husband; she later convinced herself that she knew telepathically the precise moment of the expedition's greatest peril, and, just subsequently, of its deliverance.

The expedition contributed little to public understanding of the West, but it did serve to put Frémont once more in the public eye—which almost certainly was one reason he undertook it. By the time he emerged from the mountains, the sectional controversy had a new twist, in the form of the new party. The Republicans held organizing conventions in 1854; shortly thereafter they began planning for the presidential election of 1856.

They had a cause—antislavery—but they needed a candidate. As a new party, the Republicans had no party stalwarts to call upon, no party regulars to reward, no party debts to repay. The most likely choices from the professional political world carried some heavy baggage. William Seward of New York had stirred antislavery hearts in the debate over California by referring to a "higher law" that transcended federal statutes and even the Constitution. Although few Americans doubted that such a higher law existed, to cite it on the floor of an already divided Congress seemed to many to be dangerously incendiary. ("Wild, reckless and abominable," was Henry Clay's judgment.) Seward, in other words, scared people. A second possibility, Salmon Chase of Ohio, had won his antislavery spurs by defending fugitive slaves ("the attorney general for runaway Negroes," he was often called) and denouncing both the Compromise of 1850 and the Kansas-Nebraska Act. But Chase seemed more comfortable in a courtroom than on the stump. Besides, both Seward and Chase were career politicians with offices and reputations to consider. The chances of a Republican nominee in 1856 weren't so bright as to convince them to jeopardize what they worked for years to gain. Indeed, smart money guessed that the role of the Republican nominee in 1856 would be merely to break trail for the party's candidate four years later.

Frémont had much of what Seward and Chase lacked, and lacked what they had. He was an arresting figure: still young (he turned 43 in 1856), still handsome (a lithograph circulated during the campaign might have made him an idol in the theater), demonstrably brave (in wilderness and war), and wonderfully wealthy (which, besides impressing people, helped with campaign costs). His wife had a reputation of her own as being fearless in the face of physical hardship and unyielding to her husband's political foes. Jessie's Benton heritage added just the right touch of establishment respectability to her husband's outsider appeal. The connection of both John and Jessie to California, whose political troubles paled, in the national mind, beside its still-golden promise, lent an additional aura to a Frémont candidacy. As important as anything else, Frémont possessed no political record, and therefore almost no political enemies.

Frémont's appeal wasn't lost on the Democrats, who were having problems of their own finding an acceptable candidate. By his and others' accounts, he was approached by prominent Democrats and offered the Democratic nomination in exchange for a pledge to accept the Fugitive Slave and Kansas-Nebraska Acts. He was sufficiently interested to present the offer to Jessie, then vacationing on Nantucket.

Jessie's political instincts where sharper than his, and her opposition to slavery more reflexive. She immediately vetoed the offer. Pointing to a lighthouse on the island, she said, "It is the choice between a wreck of dishonor, or a kindly light that will go on its mission of doing good." (This was what she recollected for publication. Almost certainly she was more straightforward in person.) Frémont told the Democrats to keep their nomination.

The Republican nomination came with no conditions. During the spring of 1856 an overwhelming enthusiasm for Frémont arose in the Midwest; one observer likened the surge to a "prairie fire," while the Chicago correspondent of the *New York Tribune* observed, "A sort of intrusive feeling pervades the people that he will be nominated and elected. The same sentiment is extending over Iowa and spreading into Wisconsin. He seems to combine more elements of strength than any man who has yet been named." Frémont's strength continued to increase as the Republican delegates gathered in Philadelphia for their inaugural nominating convention, and it carried him to victory on the first ballot. The platform on which the party placed him opposed the expansion of slavery and endorsed the California railroad.

HER HUSBAND'S NOMINATION thrust Jessie Frémont into the national spotlight as never before. She doubtless knew it would, and by all evidence she relished the experience.

She first emerged as a distinct figure in the campaign during the week after the Republican convention, when a boisterous crowd of well-wishers rallied at New York's Tabernacle in support of the Frémont ticket. One of the speakers recited the candidate's qualifications: explorer of the West, pathfinder through the Rocky Mountains, conqueror of California. The speaker added, "He also won the heart and hand of Thomas H. Benton's daughter!" At this, the crowd erupted into three cheers and many more loud hurrahs, for Jessie Benton Frémont.

The crowd then poured from the Tabernacle up Broadway to Ninth Street, where the Frémonts had purchased a large house. They clambered over the stonework outside the door, shouting to see the candidate and his wife. In the crush, a stone balustrade collapsed, sending scores of bodies sprawling across the pavement. Miraculously, no one was hurt—which seemed to the pious and superstitious among them a sign of God's or some other agency's blessing. Frémont spoke briefly, prompting applause followed by demands that Mrs. Frémont come out. "Jessie! Jessie! Jessie!" the crowd shouted.

In an era when the candidates themselves often held aloof, considering it unseemly to solicit votes on their own behalf, calls upon a candidate's wife to appear in public were essentially unheard-of. Frémont tried to turn the calls aside, but the crowd made plain it would keep shouting for Jessie till she appeared. Finally she did, prompting an explosion of enthusiasm—"as though all their previous cheering were a mere practice to train their voices for this occasion," remembered one participant whose ears were still ringing decades later.

At thirty-two years of age, Jessie had matured into one of the great beauties of American politics. With their wealth, connections, and personal history, she and John made the most glamorous pair in American life. Yet there was more than personal appeal that brought out the crowds for Jessie. The Democratic nominee, Buchanan, was a bachelor, with all the questions bachelorhood raised regarding his masculinity and private life. While Republican posters and cartoons showed him in a dress, Republican orators made the character question a test of Buchanan's capacity for leadership. "I hold that no man who has not had the courage to marry a wife ought to be put up for the president," asserted a typical speaker. More-discreet members of the party simply let the existence of Jessie, and their enthusiasm for her, underscore the point.

Beyond this, the 1856 Republican campaign was the first national campaign that gave substantial voice to women. The American feminist movement grew up with—or rather grew out of—the antislavery movement, most conspicuously after Elizabeth Cady Stanton, Lucretia Mott, and other women delegates to an 1839 antislavery convention in London were forced to sit in a curtained gallery, sequestered from the rest of the convention. Stanton and Mott subsequently organized the first American women's rights conference, at Seneca Falls, New York, in 1848, where they demanded equal rights for women. In the 1850s neither the Republicans nor the Democrats were about to accord women equal rights, but the Republicans, as the more progressive party, seemed far more congenial to the women activists than the Democrats—besides being correct on the crucial issue of slavery. Women's hopes rested with Frémont, wrote Lydia Child. "I would almost lay down my life to have him elected." Few of the feminists, even in demanding a larger role for women, aimed to overturn traditional patterns of family life. Equal partnership between husbands and wives would have been quite satisfactory. In this regard, the partnership between John and Jessie Frémont seemed a model, which made the Frémonts—together—that much worthier of women's support.

Had they known how large a role Jessie actually played in John's campaign, the activists would have been even more impressed. No less a judge of political astuteness than Abraham Lincoln remarked, to her face, that she was "quite a female politician." And so she proved in fighting to get her husband elected. She took control of his correspondence, determining which letters he should see and which not. She covertly coauthored a campaign biography of Frémont that obfuscated his illegitimate birth behind a veil of prevarication. (Democratic reviewers criticized the book—fairly—as reading like a novel, and supplied their own version of the story of Frémont's father. One reviewer remarked, "These incidents in the life of the progenitor of the free-soil candidate for the Presidency show that he was at least a disciple of Free-love, if not of Free-soil.") She wrote numerous letters rebutting allegations that he was a closet Catholic, allegations resting on his French ancestry and the fact that he and Jessie had been married by a priest. (Henry Ward Beecher turned this latter evidence into an opportunity to compliment Jessie. "Had we been in Col. Frémont's place," the famous Congregational minister declared, "we would have been married if it had required us to walk through a row of priests and bishops as long as from Washington to Rome, winding up with the Pope himself.")

Although most of her activities on her husband's behalf remained secret, Jessie became a lightning rod in the campaign. Her supporters recited how at eighteen she had defied the War Department to launch her husband's most famous expedition, and asserted that the same defiant spirit still burned within her. Rallies sprouted signs reading "John and Jessie," "Jessie Bent-on Being Free," and even "Jessie for the White House." Frémont's opponents predictably seized on such outpourings as suggesting that she was the real candidate, the one who wore the pants in the family, the one who would run the country in case of her husband's election.

The Democrats made much of a split in the Benton household. Thomas Benton, having been retired from the Senate for opposing slavery's extension, nonetheless had no use for Republicans, whom, he judged, were harbingers of disunion. Some of the old anger at Frémont for eloping with his daughter seems to have resurfaced, and perhaps resentment at Frémont's having carried her off to California. Whatever the mix of motives, Benton refused to make an exception for his son-in-law in condemning Republicans. "I am above family, and above self when the good of the Union is concerned," he declared. A Republican victory—that is, a Frémont victory—would be lethal to the Union. "We are treading upon a volcano that is liable at any moment to burst forth and overwhelm the nation."

This became the theme of the opposition's campaign. Frémont and the Republicans would wreck the Union, the Democrats said. "The election of Frémont would be the end of the Union, and ought to be," declared Robert Toombs of Georgia. James Mason of Virginia insisted that the only answer to a Frémont victory must be "immediate, absolute, eternal separation." Adding personal invective to the party posturing, Henry Wise of Virginia asked rhetorically, "Tell me, if the hoisting of the Black Republican flag in the hands of an adventurer, born illegitimately in a neighboring state, if not ill-begotten in this very city [Richmond]—tell me, if the hoisting of the black flag over you by a Frenchman's bastard, while the arms of civil war are already clashing, is not to be deemed an overt act and declaration of war?"

Buchanan meanwhile positioned himself as the candidate of compromise and union. He had a point. Unlike Frémont, who didn't even appear on the ballot in most of the South, Buchanan could credibly claim to be a national candidate. (The candidate of the American Party, former president Millard Fillmore, provided Buchanan's chief opposition in the South.) Buchanan self-consciously adopted the mantle of Henry Clay and Daniel Webster, to the point of persuading sons of the two deceased lawmakers to endorse his candidacy.

As the election approached, Buchanan seemed the safe choice, Frémont the risk. And when voters went to the polls, they chose safety—albeit in an ominously sectional fashion. Buchanan carried all the slave states but Maryland, which he lost to Fillmore. Frémont carried all but five free states, which he lost to Buchanan. These last furnished Buchanan's margin of victory.

The result didn't surprise Jessie, who had seen it coming. Indeed, after the Republicans lost a preliminary contest in Pennsylvania, but before the general election, she declared, "I heartily regret the defeat we have met and do not look for things to change for the better." An opportunity had been lost: for the Union, and for her husband—and for herself. She almost certainly was thinking of the two of them in partnership when she wrote, "I wish the cause had triumphed. I do wish Mr. Frémont had been the one to administer the bitter dose of subjection to the South, for he has the coolness and nerve to do it just as it needs to be done, without passion and without sympathy. As coldly as a surgeon over a hospital patient would he have cut off their right hand, Kansas, from the old unhealthy southern body."

NEITHER JOHN NOR Jessie Frémont could know that his 1856 defeat marked a portentous break in the run of their stunning personal good luck since 1849. For the moment it seemed no more than a temporary setback, from which they would soon recover. And in defeat they could congratulate themselves that the simple fact of a Frémont candidacy had advanced the cause of antislavery by drawing the line between slavery and freedom more clearly than ever.

Ironically, even as California gave the nation's new antislavery party its first presidential candidate, California itself was rethinking its opposition to slavery. Or perhaps this wasn't ironic, but merely a measure of how determined and resourceful the advocates of slavery were becoming as their enemies organized against them—and of how California itself was changing, almost a decade after the gold discovery. By the mid-1850s, immigration to California had slowed considerably, as word got out that mining was hard labor, getting harder by the year. Increasingly, new arrivals followed the path of Leland Stanford and William Sherman: into endeavors other than mining. Farmers discovered the virtues of California's climate and soil for growing all manner of crops, and the valleys the argonauts had seen as simply additional distance to be covered en route to the mines attracted populations of their own. The institutions of government and the conventions of society approximated more closely those found in the longer-settled regions of the country; despite renewed outbreaks of vigilantism like that in San Francisco in 1856, lynch law and other extralegal activity was becoming a source of civic embarrassment rather than pride. John Frémont's candidacy for president afforded California a legitimacy that would have been difficult to capture by other means, but it also elevated expectations that California would act like a normal state, with normal law and politics.

"Normal," however, was an ambiguous term during the 1850s, with its meaning largely dependent on which part of the country one inhabited or came from. The South grew more aggressive in its defense of slavery, the North less willing to indulge southern sensitivities. In California, a kind of expatriate politics developed, reflecting the rift in the East. The expatriatism had been implicit since the start of the Gold Rush, but in the early days—for example, at the Monterey convention of 1849—both northerners and southerners had been too distracted by gold to make a big issue of their differing views on slavery and race. As the opportunities in the mines diminished, though—and as the rancor between North and South escalated—California became a battleground over slavery.

Southern Democrats had actually landed the first blow, during the inaugural session of the California legislature. The Monterey constitution barred slavery, but the Democrats won passage of a bill declaring that "no black or mulatto person or Indian shall be permitted to give evidence in favor of or against any white person." This law left African-Americans (and Indians) at the mercy of white-controlled courts, and of white petitioners in those courts.

California's blacks, who constituted between 1 and 2 percent of the state's population during the 1850s, combated this legal discrimination. They repeatedly petitioned the legislature for relief; when their petitions failed, they organized statewide "colored conventions" to publicize the unfairness of their predicament. More than a few whites supported the cause—some from altruism, others from self-interest. The *Sacramento Bee* came out for colored testimony following the 1857 lynching of three white men in Butte County. The lynched were infamous for robbing and abusing Chinese miners, but because the Chinese (who were legally lumped with blacks and Indians) couldn't testify against their tormentors, the thugs ran free. Eventually even whites in the area grew disgusted and hanged the trio. To the *Sacramento Bee* this represented a step backward toward vigilante justice. In the interest of public welfare and due process, the paper's editor declared, colored testimony must be allowed.

The courtroom color bar might have been lifted but for the demoralizing outcome of the *Dred Scott* Supreme Court case. When Chief Justice Roger Taney and the federal high court ruled in 1857 that African-Americans could not be citizens of the United States, the ruling dealt a nationwide blow to hopes for anything approaching black equality. In California it spurred African-Americans to further political and legal efforts. In October 1857 they held another colored convention in San Francisco; more than ever, the delegates deemed their battle the battle of colored people all across the country.

Their battle was also the battle of one black man in particular. Archy Lee was a native of Mississippi, a slave by birth. He came to California in company with a white man named Charles Stovall, whose family had owned Archy (who, like many slaves, went by a single name, only adding

Lee later) in Mississippi. Whether Charles Stovall still owned Archy lay at the heart of one of the more convoluted cases in the history of California jurisprudence.

Archy and Stovall arrived in California in the autumn of 1857. Whether the two had departed Mississippi together or rendezvoused in Missouri after leaving Mississippi separately became a matter of conflicting testimony. Stovall's reason for going west was to improve his health. Archy's reason was either to be Stovall's servant or to flee the wrath of a white man he had wounded in a fight in Mississippi. (The white man definitely had been wounded, and by Archy; the question was whether Archy credibly feared retribution.) In any event, the two young men reached Sacramento in October 1857.

By Stovall's subsequent account, he intended to stay no more than a year or eighteen months, until his health was restored. This became an issue of central importance, for although California barred slave ownership to permanent residents of the state, like several other states it allowed travelers and visitors to retain their slaves during brief stopovers. Unfortunately for Stovall's story, he hadn't been in Sacramento long before he put a notice in a local paper advertising: "Private School for Boys and Girls . . . Terms—$5 per month, in advance." It is uncertain how many pupils accepted his offer, but the notice alone suggested something more than a rest-and-recuperation visit. Meanwhile, Stovall hired Archy out to other employers, taking part of the wages and allowing Archy to keep the remainder.

However long Stovall intended to stay, he decided after two months to send Archy back to Mississippi. Conceivably, Stovall hadn't realized before coming that California barred slavery; he seems to have been a rather oblivious young man. Perhaps he knew about the bar but simply proposed to ignore it; slave-owners in those last years before the Civil War were notorious for what they thought they could get away with. Moreover, despite the antislavery article in California's constitution, the state's pro-South Democrats might be inclined to wink at Stovall's possession of Archy. But by the end of 1857, Stovall was worrying that he wouldn't be able to keep Archy in California. In Mississippi a slave of Archy's age, sex, and robust condition might sell for $1,500; Stovall didn't wish to forfeit such an investment. So he prepared to send Archy to San Francisco to meet a man traveling back to Mississippi, who would escort Archy home.

But Archy didn't want to go home. Not surprisingly, he at first was even less aware than Stovall of the status of slavery under California law; equally unsurprisingly, Stovall declined to share what he learned that might make Archy think he need no longer be a slave. The presence, and activism, of free blacks in California, however, opened Archy's eyes. And as luck would have it, the agitation for black rights after the Dred Scott decision peaked at precisely the moment Archy was to leave Sacramento for San Francisco, Panama, and Mississippi. Some of those engaged in the struggle in California had worked on the Underground Railroad back east, and they saw in Archy a young man who ought not be spirited from the land of the free to the home of the slave. One suggested that Archy take refuge at Hackett House, a rooming establishment run by Negroes in Sacramento. Archy did so, only to be arrested by local authorities serving a warrant initiated by Stovall to have his property—that is, Archy—returned.

Archy thereupon entered the California court system. Charles Parker, a proprietor of Hackett House, arranged for a writ of habeas corpus to have Archy released from jail on grounds that he was being illegally detained. The same laws that prevented blacks from testifying in California prevented their practicing law in the state, and so when the case came before County Judge Robert Robinson, a white attorney named Edwin Crocker led the team representing Archy. Crocker was a prominent antislavery advocate whose defense of radical causes had made him a national celebrity. Stovall's lawyer, James Hardy, was an ardent pro-slavery man (who, as a California judge during the Civil War, would be impeached for Confederate sympathies).

Archy seems to have been nonplussed by the situation in which he found himself. When Judge Robinson inquired whether he really wanted to be free, he was too frightened and confused to answer. Or perhaps he simply desired to let the more eloquent Crocker speak for him. Crocker did, contending that the law in the matter was clear. California did not countenance slavery; therefore Archy could not be a slave under California law. As for federal law (though this was a state court), the sole statute that possibly applied was the Fugitive Slave Act of 1850, but that measure dealt only with slaves fleeing bondage in one state and arriving in another state. Archy had not fled bondage in Mississippi (although he may have fled trouble there, with the man he had wounded; this was where the question of his motive for leaving arose. One version of the story had Archy's Sacramento jailer asking him if white Mississippians didn't kill Negroes who attacked white men, and Archy replying, "Why, Lord bless your soul, master, I didn't give 'em a chance!"). Consequently, Crocker asserted, the federal law did not apply, and Archy must be released.

Stovall's lawyer, Hardy, countered that Archy was Stovall's slave under Mississippi law, and that according to basic principles of comity and the full-faith-and-credit clause of the federal Constitution, California must honor that law. Had Stovall relocated permanently to California, the situation might have been different, but as he was simply a visitor, Archy remained his slave.

Judge Robinson weighed the arguments about Archy at some length; while he did, Hardy decided to take Stovall's case to the federal commissioner in California charged with enforcing the Fugitive Slave Act. A southerner himself, Commissioner George Johnston was thought to be sympathetic to Stovall's side of the argument. Johnston heard Hardy out and pondered the matter for several days, but decided he didn't have jurisdiction. By all evidence, Archy had not commenced his bid for freedom until after reaching California; his flight, such as it was, had not carried him across state lines and consequently had not carried him into the federal system.

Shortly thereafter Judge Robinson rendered his verdict. The Sacramento courtroom was crowded with African-Americans anxious for Archy—and for themselves, in that the verdict in Archy's case promised, or threatened, to be a bellwether for the black community. Again Archy was asked if he wanted to be free; this time he responded forthrightly, "I *don't* want to go back to Mississippi." Archy's fellow blacks burst into cheers when Robinson declared that Archy did not have to go back; he was free.

BUT THE CHEERS gave way to groans almost at once. No sooner had the county bailiff released Archy than a state sheriff rearrested him. Stovall's side, hedging against failure in Robinson's court, had applied to the California Supreme Court for a hearing. The high court consisted of three justices, two of whom were outspokenly antiblack. One of these, Chief Justice David Terry—the knife fighter from San Francisco—agreed to issue the writ Stovall desired, elevating Archy's case to the state supreme court. Till that court convened, Archy remained in jail.

Archy had a new lawyer by the time the supreme court heard the case. For reasons lost to history, Edwin Crocker stepped aside in favor of Joseph Winans, another strong antislavery man and an attorney well versed in fugitive slave cases. James Hardy still spoke for Stovall.

Hardy held that the clause in the California constitution banning slavery required a positive legislative enactment, specifying penalties and the like, to become operative; because the legislature had not so acted, the prohibiting clause had no practical effect. Anyway, Stovall, as a citizen of Mississippi merely visiting California, ought to have security in his property, including Archy. California's ban on slavery did not apply to him.

Joseph Winans replied that a slave-owner passing through a free state, for example on his way to another slave state, might reasonably expect to be secure in his chattel. But as the merest glance at a map showed, California wasn't on the way from any slave state to any other. And Stovall clearly wasn't passing through California. He had opened a school and hired out Archy, and in doing so gave every indication of remaining for some substantial time, if not permanently. He had chosen to live in California, and therefore must submit to California's laws.

Associate Justice Peter Burnett wrote the opinion of the court. Burnett was a politician before a jurist, and a slave-owner (in Missouri) before coming west. While living in Oregon he had taken the lead in persuading the territorial legislature there to bar entrance to blacks, slave or free; as California governor in the early 1850s he had led an unsuccessful fight to keep free Negroes out of the state. Beyond his anti-black prejudices, Burnett was a California booster, eager to attract visitors from every region of the United States. California, he averred, should do nothing to discourage such visitors. "When they come to visit us for health or pleasure, shall they be permitted to bring their domestic servants with them, to attend upon them or their families as waiters? The citizens of the free States can bring their confidential servants with them—why should not the citizens of the slave States be allowed the same privilege?" Honesty and the facts required Burnett to rule that Stovall was not a visitor but a resident. And he rejected the argument of the Stovall side that the California legislature implicitly authorized slavery by not explicitly barring it. Yet having said that Stovall was a resident, and that residents couldn't keep slaves, Burnett nonetheless managed to find for Stovall. "This is the first case; and under these circumstances we are not disposed to rigidly enforce the rule for the first time," he declared. "It is, therefore, ordered that Archy be forthwith released from the custody of the Chief of Police, and given into the custody of the petitioner, Charles A. Stovall."

This remarkable conclusion struck many in California as bizarre. The San Francisco *Argus* expostulated, "It vies with the most despotic decision in the world; and it reflects disgrace upon the spirit of liberty." Another observer cited what was becoming a cynical proverb regarding the slave question: "The law was given to the north and the nigger to the south."

Yet the South was denied Archy. Stovall soon recognized how controversial his victory was, and he took pains to keep Archy out of sight. Opponents of slavery and members of California's black community mobilized to prevent Archy's being taken out of the state; lookouts were posted in Sacramento and around San Francisco Bay. Stovall managed to transport Archy to Stockton, but Archy's supporters heard of the move, and the lookouts began searching every riverboat traveling from Stockton to San Francisco. They scanned the passenger lists of every ship preparing to depart the Golden Gate. At this time the black population of California numbered perhaps four thousand; the watch for Archy gave outsiders the impression that the entire group was involved. In particular, black-owned businesses lent employees to the watch, while the many black dockworkers, ship's stewards, and deckhands were well placed to spot Stovall trying to slip Archy out of the state. Meanwhile, Archy's friends found a sympathetic judge who issued a writ for Archy and a warrant charging Stovall with kidnapping.

In early March 1858 the pro-Archy, antislavery forces received a tip. The source seems to have been the cook on the *Orizaba*, a man married to Mary Ellen Pleasants. Mammy Pleasants was a formidable figure in the African-American community, the owner of a boardinghouse and a principal in the Atheneum saloon, a watering hole and gathering place for San Francisco blacks. The tip suggested that the *Orizaba*, about to depart San Francisco, would receive two unnamed passengers between the wharf and the Golden Gate. Acting on this intelligence, a deputy sheriff and two lieutenants surreptitiously boarded the *Orizaba* and rode with her out into the bay. As the vessel neared Angel Island, one of the passengers waved a white handkerchief from the rail; soon a second handkerchief replied from a rowboat close to the island. The officers, still silent, watched carefully as the rowboat approached the ship. Four men could be seen, one of whom matched the description of Stovall. Only at the last moment did the officers spy Archy, who had been compelled to crouch in the bottom of the boat.

Just as Stovall and Archy were to board, someone on the *Orizaba* recognized the sheriff and called out to Stovall to keep off. But the sheriff leaped from the rail of the ship into the bucking boat. A fight broke out, which spread to the ship as several pro-slavery passengers tried to prevent the sheriff from seizing Archy and arresting Stovall. Luckily for Archy, the ship's captain was a liberty man, and his crew enforced respect for the law.

The sheriff and deputies returned Archy and Stovall to the San Francisco dock. A jubilant crowd of African-Americans and other opponents of slavery greeted them. That night a large rally was held at the Zion African Methodist Episcopal Church on Pacific Street, to raise money for Archy's legal defense fund. (It was characteristic of California that, in contrast to the East, where attorneys in contested slave cases often worked pro bono, those in San Francisco worked only pro auro.) At the end of the meeting the collection basket went around, eliciting $150.

When his case resumed, Archy had yet another new lawyer (doubtless their insistence on pay contributed to the turnover among Archy's attorneys). James Hardy continued to represent Stovall. The kidnapping charge against Stovall was tossed out on a technicality; as this charge had been simply a device to regain custody of Archy, Edward Baker—Charles Cora's defender, and now Archy's new counsel—let it go without a fight. More serious was the charge by Hardy that the basis for the writ to seize Archy was invalid, being based on a complaint by a black man, whose testimony was inadmissible under California law. Baker—a child of English Quakers and an old friend from Illinois of Abraham Lincoln—eloquently ignored the law, including the judgment of the California Supreme Court (which judgment, legally speaking, should have settled the matter), and argued from first principles of natural right and human justice. He concluded with an impassioned plea to the trial judge to honor those principles and set Archy free.

To the astonishment of all present, when the judge solicited a response from Hardy and Stovall, they indicated their willingness to concede Archy's freedom. After a moment to absorb the surprise, the judge slammed his gavel down and ordered the prisoner released.

But Archy's tribulations were not over even yet, for to the still greater astonishment of the crowd, he was immediately arrested again, by a federal marshal acting under the terms of the Fugitive Slave Act. Needless to say, Archy was in despair; his supporters in the courtroom and on the street outside were ready to revolt. Hand-to-hand combat erupted as the marshal and a tight circle of pro-slavery men tried to push their way through the much larger crowd of antislavery partisans. But black leaders pressed restraint on their fellows, and what might have become a really bloody race riot terminated in bruises and abrasions and the arrest of two black men.

Although Federal Commissioner Johnston was unhappy to have to deal with Archy again, the terms of his commission had required him to order the arrest upon Stovall's application. Yet Archy's situation hadn't changed materially in the two months since Johnston had originally declared in Archy's favor. Nor did Stovall help his case by altering his story, saying this time that Archy had actually escaped from bondage in Mississippi and therefore *was* a fugitive slave under the federal law.

The facts of the case again seemed to weigh against Stovall, but he and Hardy were counting on politics to come to their aid. Johnston was a Democrat, and the Democrats were then trying to push a law through the legislature barring blacks from entering the state. Stovall and Hardy hoped Johnston wouldn't wish to keep this particular black, Archy, in California at a time when he and his fellow Democrats were trying to keep all blacks out.

But Stovall's case was too flimsy to stand. When Archy's lawyers brought suit against Stovall alleging assault, battery, and false imprisonment, and when even Johnston began talking about perjury charges, Stovall decided to drop the case. In the middle of the proceeding, without telling anyone, he abruptly fled town.

Yet, unbelievably—except that by now nothing in this case was unbelievable—even Stovall's flight didn't end the strange affair. A brother, William Stovall, mysteriously appeared, determined to carry on in Charles's absence. The second Stovall's testimony managed to provoke a fistfight between Archy's lawyer (another new one) and Hardy. That Hardy was packing a gun rendered the melee even more memorable, and caused Commissioner Johnston himself to step between the two antagonists. Shortly thereafter Hardy, too, disappeared, leaving Stovall's representation to an assistant.

Finally the farce—for such it had become, to all but Archy, anyway—ended. After some additional delay suggesting a reluctance to relinquish the spotlight, Johnston ruled that Archy was not a fugitive slave and therefore was a free man.

In the excitement of the moment, many in the courtroom had failed to notice that Archy himself was not present. Some of those who did notice suspected still another ploy to keep the unfortunate young man in chains. In fact, Johnston, a bit of a publicity hound, hadn't wanted to share his stage, and had ordered that Archy be freed from the jail rather than from the courtroom. The boisterous yet understandably skeptical crowd surged through the city to the Kearny Street jail to make sure Archy finally got his freedom. On their arrival, the jailkeeper went to the cell that had been Archy's home for many weeks, unlocked the door, and declared, "Archy, my boy, you're all right. You're a free man now. Pick up your duds and be off; your friends are waiting for you outside."

15

South by West

Archy's victory was a blow for freedom in California, besides—naturally—being a great relief to Archy himself. Yet it hardly represented a trend, for in the second half of the 1850s, California appeared increasingly sympathetic to the cause of the slave South. Sometimes the sympathy was simply that: a fellow-feeling toward southerners and an emotional sharing in their desires. Sometimes the sympathy was more substantive, as when Californians rejected John Frémont—despite his favorite-son status—in the 1856 election, in favor of James Buchanan. Sometimes the sympathy came armed, as in the astonishing activities of William Walker, who made California the base of operations for an expansion of slavery beyond the borders of the United States, and in so doing gave the South reason to believe that in a parting of the ways, California and California's gold might follow the South out of the Union.

Like Leland Stanford, Walker was a second-generation Gold Rusher. Born in Tennessee, trained as a doctor in Pennsylvania and a lawyer in Louisiana, and practicing as a journalist in New Orleans when he got the itch to move again, Walker arrived in San Francisco amid the corruption and thuggery that provoked the first wave of vigilantism in the city. In his capacity as a journalist he took dead aim at one particularly crooked judge, who hauled him into court and found him guilty of contempt. When

Walker refused to pay the $500 fine, the judge ordered him imprisoned. This sparked a mass meeting against the judge and in support of Walker. A superior court, moved by the popularity of Walker's cause, ordered him released.

Had he desired, Walker could have launched a political career at this point. And so he did—but not the kind of career those who protested in front of his jail cell expected. Although the Gold Rush wasn't three years old, the best placers had played out, forcing many argonauts to work for wages, which wasn't at all what they'd expected on leaving home. More than a few of the frustrated assumed that mines similar to those in California existed south of the border in Mexico—in Sonora especially, long known for its mineral wealth. Why slave for others, or pick through deposits a hundred hands had already sifted, when fresh mines lay ripe for the seizing in Sonora?

Walker initially approached the Mexican government for permission to colonize in Sonora, but was rebuffed. Indeed, President Santa Anna, who after losing Texas in 1836 had no desire to repeat the humiliation, took such offense at Walker that he reportedly put a bounty on his head. Yet Walker didn't discourage easily, and he returned to San Francisco to commence recruiting volunteers for a military expedition against Sonora. Amid the restive placermen, he had no difficulty raising a force.

Most of the appeal of his pitch was the easy wealth the expedition promised, but a not inconsiderable element was his own strange magnetism. "His appearance was that of anything else than a military chieftain," explained a traveler who encountered Walker briefly but unforgettably. "Below the medium height, and very slim, I should hardly imagine him to weigh over a hundred pounds. His hair light and towy, while his almost white eyebrows and lashes concealed a seemingly pupilless, grey, cold eye, and his face was a mass of yellow freckles, the whole expression very heavy. His dress was scarcely less remarkable than his person. His head was surmounted by a huge white fur hat, whose long knap waved with the breeze, which, together with a very ill-made, short-waisted blue coat, with gilt buttons, and a pair of grey, strapless pantaloons, made up the ensemble of as unprepossessing-looking a person as one would meet in a day's walk."

There was more to this man, however. "Any one who estimated Mr. Walker by his personal appearance made a great mistake. Extremely taciturn, he would sit for an hour in company without opening his lips; but once interested, he arrested your attention with the first word he uttered, and as he proceeded, you felt convinced that he was no ordinary person." And when he spoke of his Sonoran project, he seemed "insanely confident of success."

By the tens, then scores, then hundreds, men who thought wealth came too slowly in California signed up with Walker. Unfortunately for his plans, all the interest attracted the attention of federal officials in San Francisco, who felt obliged to enforce American neutrality laws prohibiting private wars launched from American soil. Accordingly, on September 30, 1853, a company of U.S. soldiers boarded the *Arrow*, the brig Walker had hired, and took possession of the ship and its cargo of guns and ammunition. Walker sued for the return of the vessel and its cargo but meanwhile prepared another brig, the *Caroline*, for surreptitious departure. In the dead hours before dawn on October 16, the *Caroline* slipped away from the wharf and out the Golden Gate. Between the needs for haste and stealth, however, Walker took only forty-five men with him.

Such a puny force was far too small to subdue Sonora, especially with the Mexican army awaiting him there. So Walker ordered a landing at La Paz, on the Gulf of California near the southern tip of Baja California. Disguising their approach with a Mexican flag, Walker and his men entered the town before the governor or anyone else realized something was amiss. Walker arrested and jailed the governor, preempting resistance. He proceeded to issue a series of proclamations, starting with: "The Republic of Lower California is hereby declared Free, Sovereign and Independent, and all allegiance to the Republic of Mexico is *forever renounced.*" Walker went on to appoint himself president of the new republic, and adopted the civil code of Louisiana as the law of Lower California.

It wasn't lost on outside observers, especially those in the American South, that the Louisiana code embraced slavery, and that Walker, in adopting it for his putative republic, aimed to restore slavery to this part of

Mexico. Nor was it lost on Walker that many southerners, for this very reason, would applaud his actions.

From his base in Baja, Walker sought to extend his realm. He declared the annexation of Sonora to the Republic of Lower California, which was then rechristened the Republic of Sonora. The laws of Lower California (that is, of Louisiana) were extended to Sonora, including slavery and the rule of President William Walker.

Back in (upper) California, Walker's exploits elicited diverse reactions. The *Alta California* snickered, "He is a veritable Napoleon, of whom it may be said, as of the mighty Corsican, 'he disposes of courts and crowns and camps as mere titulary dignitaries of the chess board.' Santa Anna must feel obliged to the new president that he has not annexed any more of his territory than Sonora. It would have been just as cheap and easy to have annexed the whole of Mexico at once, and would have saved the trouble of making future proclamations." Editorial disdain, however, had little effect on the hundreds of disappointed gold-seekers who preferred plunder in Mexico to wage-work in the mines. Walker bristled at being called a "filibuster," a term descended from "freebooter," or pirate; and indeed it may not have been the best description for one as megalomaniacal as he. But it certainly described those who joined him on his voyage from San Francisco, and the many more who now prepared to follow him south.

Because the U.S. Departments of State, War, and Justice continued to object to private wars of conquest, Walker's reinforcements had to dodge soldiers and sheriffs in making their getaway from San Francisco, literally by the light of the moon. "The scene at the departure was one of the most remarkable on record," wrote William Wells, a Walker supporter.

> About half way down from Front Street a door was thrown open, and, as if by magic, drays and carts made their appearance. Files of men sprung out and passed quantities of powder from the store, besides ammunition of all kinds. A detachment stood guard the while in utter silence, and the movements were made with such celerity that the observer could scarcely perceive where and how

> the articles made their appearance. A heavy squall of rain had just passed over the city, which was succeeded by a clear blue sky, allowing the rays of the moon to light up this singular picture, and giving it the appearance of some smuggling scene in a drama.

The silence held only so long, however. As the conspirators drew near the ship that was to take them away, they were met by friends who wished them favorable weather and happy fighting.

> As the moment of sailing approached, the confusion and noise increased, and all the efforts of the officers to keep silence were unavailing. Several of the men were drunk, and gave vent to the exuberance of their spirits by songs, and denunciations upon the "Greasers" who had made the reported attack upon the party then in the Southern country. . . . When the fasts were cast off, the vessels swung round to the tide, and the expedition was fairly under way. Nothing could now restrain the men, and loud and repeated cheers rose from the vessel, which were heartily responded to from the wharf.

Despite the reinforcements, Walker's first attempt at filibustering failed. He tried to establish a foothold on the Mexican mainland but encountered resistance from his new subjects. (He called them citizens but hardly made them feel that way.) Meanwhile his soldiers discovered that the reality of Sonora fell considerably shy of their imaginings. They began to curse themselves for coming and Walker for enticing them there. Some mutinied, provoking Walker to order their execution. "We had to shoot two men today," wrote one of the troops, "because they so far mistook the object of our coming down here as to attempt to make up an organization, the object of which was to desert and go on a stealing, robbing and murdering expedition."

Between the firing squads and the scant pickings, Walker's army dwindled from three hundred to three dozen. Food ran out, clothing wore out, courage gave out. Walker, reduced to hobbling about on a single boot, led the miserable remnant north to the American border, where he turned himself over to the local American military commander.

He was transported to San Francisco for trial on charges of illegal war-making. The evidence was overwhelmingly with the prosecution, but the jury was with Walker, and after deliberating eight minutes it acquitted him. The failed filibuster and erstwhile *presidente* emerged a popular hero.

The hero lived quietly in California till opportunity again called, as it did soon enough. From independence in the 1820s, Nicaragua had never been a rock of stability, but the Gold Rush, by swamping the Central American isthmus with foreign travelers, unsettled the country unusually. Additional aggravation came from competing American transit companies, which vied for control of the traffic. The leading contender in the mid-1850s was the Accessory Transit Company headed by Cornelius Vanderbilt, the brass-knuckled steamboater who was just discovering railroads. Amid the turmoil, every party angled for any edge it could get. One faction in Nicaragua's chronic civil war sent an emissary to San Francisco to invite Walker to enlist an army and come south. He and his soldiers would receive monthly pay for the duration and grants of land upon victory. Walker agreed, and began recruiting. This time he cleared his expedition with the American authorities, showing them the written invitation from an arguably legitimate regime in Nicaragua (the argument, of course, was the essence of the civil war there). But still he had trouble getting away. The owner of the ship he chartered owed money, and the creditors placed a lien on the vessel, which the sheriff enforced. Yet Walker overpowered the sheriff's deputy (albeit with good humor and hospitality: "There, sir, are cigars and champagne," he said, "and here are handcuffs and irons; pray take your choice") and the ship got away. Again the complications surrounding departure prevented Walker from filling out his ranks; the army of intervention totaled precisely fifty-eight (although a miscount caused the group to be labeled—by themselves more than anyone else—the "Immortal Fifty-six").

Walker's second war went better than his first. He benefited from Indian allies, who may have been persuaded that Walker was the one referred to in their legends about a gray-eyed man who would redeem them from oppression (it was at this time that Walker began to refer to himself as the "gray-eyed man of destiny"). On the other hand, they may simply have reckoned that Walker couldn't be worse than the other whites. He benefited even more from the logistical and financial backing of Vanderbilt's Transit Company, which owed its concession to the faction that invited Walker.

Yet Walker had more in mind than mercenary work. After seizing the enemy stronghold, Granada, he made himself the military master of the country. And following a rigged election in June 1856, he was inaugurated president.

This high-handed action had the historically unprecedented effect of uniting nearly all Nicaraguans in a common purpose: to oust Walker. Moreover, by now Vanderbilt had likewise gone into opposition. Vanderbilt's partners in the Transit Company were as unscrupulous as many in the American transport business (including Vanderbilt himself), and during the first vacation of his life they tried to steal the company out from under him. "Gentlemen," he responded, in a note that entered the annals of boardroom warfare, "you have undertaken to cheat me. I won't sue, for the law is too slow. I'll ruin you." And so he did, in the process blockading steam navigation to Nicaragua and depriving Walker of resupply for his unpopular regime.

Walker appealed to the American South. He rescinded Nicaragua's ban on slavery and prepared to reopen the African slave trade. "A beleaguered force," he explained after the fact, "with no ally outside, must yield to famine at last, unless it can make a sally and burst through the enemy which confines it." His pro-slavery decrees constituted his sally, being calculated, as he put it, "to bind the Southern states to Nicaragua as if she were one of themselves."

Although Walker made plain he did not intend for Nicaragua to be annexed to the United States—his Napoleonic complex was too advanced for that—the prospect of a slave republic in the Caribbean couldn't help winning the approval of American southerners. Unluckily for him, the *dis*approval of Vanderbilt mooted the issue, for the private navy of the Commodore—as Vanderbilt was coming to be called—kept reinforcements away. Walker spoke of attaching the other Central American republics to Nicaragua; those republics immediately banded together against him. As the noose tightened, and hunger and disease exacted their toll, morale plummeted. Walker's aloof style of command contributed to the decline. "Instead of treating us like fellow-soldiers and adventurers in danger . . ." explained one veteran (who deserted), "he bore himself like an Eastern tyrant—reserved and haughty—scarcely saluting when he met us, mixing not at all, but keeping himself close in quarters—some said through fear, lest some of his own men should shoot him, of which indeed there was great danger." The outcome was the same as in Sonora. Unable to hold his army together, Walker abandoned Nicaragua, taking refuge from his enemies with forces of the U.S. military.

Yet though he abandoned Nicaragua, he didn't relinquish the presidency. And after a triumphal tour across the American South, culminating in an audience with President Buchanan in Washington, he recruited a fresh army to help him retake his lost republic. Despite the southern enthusiasm for his cause, however, the federal government, under pressure from Britain—which had its own designs on Nicaragua—ultimately decided it didn't need to encourage unrest in Central America. After Walker's new force landed on Nicaragua's Caribbean coast, American marines followed it in. Walker surrendered and was returned once more to the United States.

Remarkably, this didn't quite end the saga of William Walker. Three years later, in 1860, he went south again, landing in Honduras to evade the fleets of both the United States and Britain. Proceeding carefully along the coast, he nonetheless was spotted and arrested by the British, who turned him over to the Honduran government. On September 12, 1860, he was stood against a wall and executed. As the smoke from the fusillade cleared, the great seal of the Republic of Nicaragua was discovered among his effects.

WHATEVER THEY ACCOMPLISHED for the cause of hemispheric slavery, the exploits of William Walker made life for California's Republicans—Leland Stanford in particular—more difficult during the latter 1850s. Stanford served as a delegate to the 1856 state convention of Republicans, held in Sacramento. The gathering endorsed Frémont and the national Republican platform, resolving "that we inscribe on our banner 'Freedom, Frémont and the Railroad,' and under it we will fight until victory shall crown our efforts." Of the three items on that list, the second and third generated the most excitement—Frémont for his California connection, and the railroad for the connection it would create between California and the rest of the country. Freedom—that is, opposition to slavery—was a harder sell in California, where pro-slavery Democrats controlled politics and pro-slavery filibusters like Walker captured the popular imagination.

Yet Stanford and his comrades looked forward to the election, expecting that their party's support of the railroad would give them an advantage the Democrats would have difficulty countering. As one of Stanford's Republican colleagues explained, "I have strong hopes that the Republican ticket will carry the state. The railroad question will have immense influence. The people of this state have dwelt upon the subject of an Atlantic and Pacific railroad until it has become a kind of mania with them. It is universally understood that nothing whatever is to be hoped from the Democratic party, and that everything is to be feared from it, as far as the railroad is concerned."

Frémont's poor showing in California—he won only 20,000 votes, of more than 100,000 cast—suggested that the mania for the railroad still didn't trump the obsession with slavery. It also suggested that distinction among California Republicans was a dubious honor. Yet Stanford judged that the party was on the right track, and with his customary lack of conspicuous enthusiasm, he climbed the Republican ranks. He was nominated, without opposition, for state treasurer in 1857; he was duly buried in the general election by a margin only slightly less than Frémont's the year before. In the summer of 1859 he was nominated for governor, again without opposition. By all indications another trouncing awaited him in the autumn; accordingly he wasn't being modest when he told the convention that he hadn't sought the nomination, and only accepted it as the responsibility of one who believed in the Republican message. He went on to explain what he—and the California Republican party—stood for. It was antislavery, but also anti-black.

> I feel, Mr. President, that the cause in which we are engaged is one of the greatest in which any one can labor. It is the cause of the white man—the cause of free labor, of justice and of equal rights. I am in favor of free white American citizens. I prefer white citizens to any other class or race. I prefer the white man to the negro as an inhabitant of our country. I believe its greatest good has been derived by having all of the country settled by free white men.

(Whether Stanford had read the speeches of Abraham Lincoln, who took much the same line in his debates with Stephen Douglas in Illinois the previous year, is uncertain.) Stanford disavowed, for himself and the California party, any desire to infringe upon the legitimate rights of slaveholders. "But we do ask that the Federal Government shall be administered equally for all portions of the Confederation alike." Here the convention burst into applause. "We say the Government shall not be administered so as to subserve any one particular interest which shall be considered paramount. We stand up for equal justice for all." More applause. Saying he was "not much of a talker" ("a fact patent to all who heard him," chimed a critic), Stanford briefly reiterated what he and his Republican fellows still saw as their strongest issue. "We are in favor of the Railroad by that natural route which the emigrant in coming to this country has pointed out to us." More applause. "I am in favor of a Railroad, and it is the policy of this State to favor that party which is likely to advance their interests."

The general campaign was an uphill fight, and a lonely one. A rally at Downieville turned out a single Republican, who urged the candidate to cancel the meeting lest it provoke trouble. "There are only two other Republicans here besides myself," he said, "and we hardly dare to show ourselves." The Democrats, nationally and in California, had split over Kansas statehood: one wing (which included Buchanan) backed the admission of Kansas with slavery, under a constitution formulated at the town of

Lecompton; the other wing (including Stephen Douglas) supported a free Kansas. Some of the anti-Lecompton Democrats in California bruited a strategy of fusion with Stanford's Republicans, with the Democrat to head the ticket. Stanford rejected the notion out of hand. "Resistance to the aggressions of slavery is not the only idea of the Republican party," he asserted, rebutting a standard complaint against the Republicans. The railroad was no less central—at least for California Republicans. Besides, for Stanford in 1859, as for Frémont in 1856, the realistic goal was a Republican victory not in the current election but in the presidential race of 1860. For this the party must hold together, rejecting all distractions. "Let them unite with us," Stanford told the fusionists scornfully.

The Republicans remained pure, and heavily outnumbered. Stanford received only 10 percent of the vote. If he had any second thoughts about fusion, he could derive consolation from the fact that the sum of the vote for him and the vote for the anti-Lecompton Democratic candidate fell short of the Lecompton Democrat's total. Stanford took the defeat so placidly that he mentioned the result in a letter to his parents only after reporting that the California state fair had featured pumpkins that weighed over 200 pounds and a single peach ("white clingstone") that tipped the scales at 27 ounces.

YET STANFORD'S 1859 defeat, like Frémont's in 1856, served the purpose of the party, and when the national Republicans gathered in 1860 to choose a presidential candidate, they did so united—in stark contrast to the Democrats. Kansas still split the Democrats, although the violence in that troubled territory had fallen off after the appointment of Governor John Geary, formerly sheriff of San Francisco from the early days of the Gold Rush. To all intents and purposes, the Democrats had become two parties, one of the North and the other of the South. The northerners decried the 1857 Dred Scott decision; the southerners shuddered at John Brown's 1859 raid on Harpers Ferry, which sought to spark a slave rebellion, and shuddered still more at the respect, even reverence, many in the North accorded Brown on his way to the gallows.

Under the circumstances, the Republicans had every hope of picking a winner when their convention met in Chicago. John Frémont had served his purpose, and now was set aside in favor of the professional politicians. William Seward seemed to many the obvious choice after a decade on the front lines of the sectional debate. Yet to many others, that was precisely why Seward should *not* receive the nomination. The Democrats were self-destructing; what the Republicans needed was a figure with a bit more political experience and weight than Frémont, but not much more record. A westerner might do (albeit perhaps not one *so* western as California's Frémont), for although any Republican could probably carry New England and the upper Great Lakes states, a man of the West would have particular pull in the Ohio and Mississippi Valleys, where the contest would be won or lost.

Abraham Lincoln's friends thought the former Illinois congressman fit the description perfectly. And after they recast the railroad lawyer as a rail-splitter, they convinced the convention. Seward led on the first ballot, but Lincoln closed the gap on the second and overtook the New Yorker on the third. Bowing to the inevitable, the Seward forces made the nomination unanimous.

Stanford had intended to represent California at the Republican convention. As the titular leader of the California Republicans, he was chosen by acclamation to be a delegate. And as a New York native, he intended to vote for Seward. But at the last minute, business—to wit, his brothers' sagging end of the fraternal business—prevented his going. "Every dollar I can spare from this business goes to aid them," he told his mother and father. "It would not have been prudent for me to leave." There was an additional business-related reason, which Stanford mentioned only in passing because its importance had yet to be gauged. Various miners from California, frustrated at the diminishing prospects for individuals on the Sierra's western slope, had crossed the mountains into the region that would become Nevada, and made some promising finds. "We are having a good deal of excitement about gold and silver discoveries on the eastern side of the Sierra Nevada mountains," Stanford related. "It will probably prove a rich mineral country. I shall probably make a trip over there about the first of June. I want to see for myself how much of a disturbing element in the business affairs of this state it is likely to be. I may start a store over there."

Like so many others in the Republican party, Stanford didn't know Lincoln personally, but as a loyal Republican he swung into line behind the nominee. He stumped California, starting in Siskiyou County on October 1 and finishing in Amador County on November 3. He spoke every day of the week but Sunday, praising Lincoln and pushing the Pacific railroad—again a part of the Republican platform.

California remained a heavily Democratic state, and the Democrats polled nearly twice as many votes in the presidential election as the Republicans. But the Democratic votes were split, almost evenly, between northerner Douglas and southerner John Breckinridge. As a result, Lincoln narrowly won California's electors. Repeated in key states across the country, this pattern of voting awarded the presidency to Lincoln and the Republicans.

UPON LINCOLN'S VICTORY, the South made good the threat its spokesman had leveled against Frémont in 1856: to leave the Union in the event of a Republican victory. Jessie Frémont had wanted her husband (and herself) to have the opportunity to deal with a rebellious South; instead the task fell to Lincoln, who procrastinated more than the Frémonts likely would have. One can imagine John Frémont saddling up directly after inauguration and leading an army over the Potomac into the rebel states. Lincoln, by contrast, acted deliberately, insisting that the South fire the first shot, at Fort Sumter. Whether Frémont's boldness would have succeeded better than Lincoln's caution is impossible to know. (Lincoln's strategy *did* succeed, of course, which counts in its favor; but it required a long and bloody war, which counts against it.)

Leland Stanford observed Lincoln's strategy at close range. Following the presidential election, Stanford, in his capacity as leader of the California Republicans, sailed east to ensure that his friends and associates receive their share of the offices awarded by the new Republican administration ("having the Federal patronage worthily distributed in California," was how Stanford explained his goal to one of his brothers). He met with Lincoln personally, and developed considerable respect for the new president. Writing home, he expressed "great confidence" that the country had "an Administration equal to the occasion, great as it is." He added, "I look forward through these troublous times with the confident hope that the end will be a broad spirit of Nationality, and Democratic Institutions more firmly than ever planted."

Stanford, accompanied on this trip by his wife, Jane, had hoped to tour the East at leisure, but the outbreak of war forced a return to California. Although Lincoln had carried the state, this was no guarantee the state would support Lincoln against the South. Southern sympathies remained strong in California, and many Californians advocated measures to assist the South, if only indirectly.

Stanford arrived in Sacramento in time to receive a second nomination for governor. He spent the summer of 1861 stumping the state once more; a supporter who saw him at Santa Rosa described the man in his prime:

> His personal appearance was impressive. He was then thirty-seven years of age, large in frame, with a swarthy complexion and something of the plain, rugged features of the frontiersman. He was dignified in manner, with a peculiarly attractive composure. His voice was melodious and pleasant; his language clear and expressive. He was listened to by a large audience with respectful interest.

The party platform again endorsed the Pacific railroad; Stanford again explained how this would benefit California. But the current national crisis elevated another issue—the Union—above the railroad. Privately Stanford was characterizing the contest as pitting opposing visions of government against each other. "Everything confirms the view I long since took that the struggle is one between the Democratic and Aristocratic element of the country," he wrote his brother Philip. "I have ever held that the true end of the Republican party was to maintain the Democratic character of our institutions." In public he simply spoke (and spoke simply, "with the eloquence of an honest conviction," the Santa Rosa admirer explained) of the need to rally to Lincoln and the Union.

As in the recent presidential election, the California Democrats were divided. The Breckinridge wing of the party, headed by gubernatorial candidate John McConnell, openly sympathized with secession; the Douglas wing stood for the Union. Once more calls arose for fusion between the Republicans and the Union Democrats, but this time—with a Republican in the White House—Stanford seemed the more promising bearer of alliance hopes. The heretofore Democratic *San Francisco Bulletin* explained, "The naked truth is that the success of the McConnell ticket next Wednesday week would be tantamount to a declaration of war by California against the general government. Nothing could prevent its being followed by open hostilities in our borders. No man can be so blind to inevitable consequences as not to see it." A group of San Francisco businessmen—including, by their own testimony, several individuals "politically opposed to the Republican party"—circulated a letter decrying "the dreadful consequences that must arise from the division of the Union men of the State, and the possible election of the Secession-McConnell ticket." Dire circumstances compelled distasteful action, the erstwhile Democrats declared. "We have carefully collected the best advices that we could obtain of the relative strength of the Douglas and Republican tickets, and feeling convinced that the latter is the stronger, have unhesitatingly determined to vote for Mr. Stanford, the Republican candidate for Governor—believing that thereby we shall save ourselves from the result of foolish political divisions which now threaten us with ruin and disaster."

Such crossover support carried Stanford to victory in the September 1861 election. He understood the meaning of his victory: that he had been elected as a Unionist rather than a Republican. But that was good enough. As things happened, the first overland telegraph line was completed just weeks after the balloting, and Stanford cabled Lincoln: "Today California is but a second's distance from the national capital. Her patriotism with electric current throbs responsive to that of her sister states and holds civil liberty and union above all price."

THIS WAS AN EXAGGERATION. Notwithstanding Stanford's victory, support for the South persisted in California. Only two years earlier the state legislature had taken the extraordinary step of authorizing secession within the state—that is, of allowing the portion of California lying below the Missouri Compromise line to separate from the rest of the state, with the understanding that this southern region, to be named Colorado, would institute slavery. And in 1860, just months before Lincoln's election, California Democrat Gwin declared, "I believe that the slave-holding states of this confederacy can establish a separate and independent government that will be impregnable to the assaults of all foreign enemies." The senator made clear that he classed the North under the category of "foreign enemies" of a southern confederacy. He went on to predict that in the event of secession, "California would be found with the South."

Yet California stuck with the Union. For some Californians, this decision connoted a genuine attachment to the handiwork of the Founders, and a corresponding reluctance to participate in its undoing. For many others, including a large portion of those with connections to the South, devotion to the Union was more mercenary. After the Republicans took power in Washington, the new congressional leaders made clear that if California remained loyal, it could count on a Pacific railroad, which would do more than anything since the gold discovery itself to enhance the prospects of the state. On the other hand, if California seceded—either to join the Confederacy outright or to establish an independent but effectively pro-South "Pacific republic"—it could forget about the railroad. California collectively required no time at all to make the calculation and affirm its attachment to the Union. The state legislature asserted, "California is ready to maintain the rights and honor of the national government at home and abroad, and at all times to respond to any requisition that may be made upon her to defend the republic against foreign or domestic foes."

A collective decision, however, wasn't the same as a consensus decision, and a substantial part of the state's population abetted the rebellion. Some did so openly and honorably, traveling east to enlist in the Confederate army. Others remained in the West, plotting silent support of the southern cause and hoping to accomplish covertly what the light of the day wouldn't allow.

Of the plotters, none was more fervent in his southern feeling or more audacious in his desire to help the Confederate cause than Asbury Harpending. Another latecomer to California—in his case from Kentucky—Harpending had hoped to join William Walker's "immortals" but was prevented from doing so by those pesky federal agents. Harpending resented their interference, and when the South seceded, he did, too, in spirit. "I was young, hot-headed, and filled with the bitter sectional feeling that was more intense in the border states than in the states farther north or south. It would have been hard to find a more reckless secessionist than myself." Harpending circulated about San Francisco, seeking kindred spirits to join him in opposing the tyrannical Unionism. These weren't hard to discover, and the group began meeting in secret to plot the overthrow of the government of California and its replacement by a pro-southern regime. According to their scheme, each member of the cabal would recruit a small company of soldiers, for whose training, equipment, and pay he would be responsible. As cover, these soldiers would be told that a Walker-like filibustering expedition to Mexico was afoot. The companies would be unknown to one another, for better security against informers. At the appointed moment, all would rise up and overwhelm the small federal garrisons at Fort Point (on the southern shore of the Golden Gate), at Alcatraz Island, at Mare Island (near the property Mariano Vallejo was about to lose), and at Benicia (where the arsenal General Wool had declined to release to Sherman was located). At the same time, the insurgents would assault the militia arsenals in San Francisco and carry off the weapons there.

At first the conspirators hoped for encouragement, if perhaps only tacit, from the federal commander at San Francisco, General Albert Sidney Johnston. Johnston was a Kentuckian like Harpending and had made a name and career in Texas, where he served as commander of the army of the Republic of Texas. He was decorated for valor in the U.S. Army during the Mexican War, and now had charge of the army's Department of the Pacific. A devoted southerner, Johnston was thought to be leaning toward secession. The conspirators decided to sound him out, with Harpending and two others being assigned the delicate task.

"I will never forget that meeting," Harpending wrote. "He was a blond giant of a man with a mass of heavy yellow hair, untouched by age, although he was nearing sixty. He had the nobility of bearing that marks a great leader of men, and it seemed to my youthful imagination that I was looking at some superman of ancient history, like Hannibal or Caesar, come to life again."

The general bade his visitors sit down. As they did so, he said, almost casually, "Before we go further, there is something I want to mention. I have heard foolish talk about an attempt to seize the strongholds of the government under my charge. Knowing this, I have prepared for emergencies, and will defend the property of the United States with every resource at my command, and with the last drop of blood in my body. Tell that to all our southern friends."

Needless to say, this put a crimp in the plotting. But there was something else that, to Harpending's view, was even more important in derailing the conspiracy. Apparently by coincidence, several of the leaders of the cabal had financial interests in the new mines of Nevada, which by now promised to be quite rich. The more they reflected on the logistics of secession, the more they realized that the only defensible eastern frontier of a breakaway California would be the Sierra Nevada, and that their mines would be on the wrong side of that frontier. Harpending explained their thinking:

> When it became apparent that the surface [of the Nevada mines] had been barely scratched and that secession might mean the casting aside of wealth beyond the dreams of avarice, then patriotism and self-interest had a lively tussle. If Nevada could have been car-

> ried out of the Union along with California, I am almost certain that the story of those times would have been widely different. . . . That's the only way I can size up what followed.

What followed was that the plotters abandoned their own plot. A vote was taken on whether to proceed, and a majority chose western wealth over southern patriotism.

Yet Harpending, one of the minority voting to proceed, wasn't so easily deterred. He traveled east to Richmond, where he met with Confederate president Jefferson Davis and proposed a plan to capture the gold being transported east from California to finance the Union war effort. Davis was intrigued. "He fully realized the importance of shutting off the great gold shipments," Harpending wrote. "President Davis said it would be more important than many victories in the field." Davis arranged for Harpending to receive a commission as captain in the Confederate navy, despite Harpending's never having been near a warship in his life. Harpending also received letters of marque, the licenses that under international law made privateers—that is, authorized raiders—of those who would otherwise have been mere pirates. Finally, he was entrusted with a large packet of mail, including highly confidential—because very compromising—letters to Confederate sympathizers in California.

Harpending left Virginia via blockade runner, which carried him to Aspinwall, a town that had grown up on the Caribbean coast of Panama as an alternative to the disease-ridden Chagres. Crossing the isthmus, he boarded the Pacific Mail steamer for San Francisco. The passengers included a niece of John Calhoun, a woman who shared her uncle's fighting spirit and uncompromising southern loyalty. When Harpending informed her of the letters he was carrying, and expressed concern that he might be searched on landing in San Francisco, she insisted that he give the letters to her. And when, indeed, he was frisked and his baggage opened at the dock, she sashayed past the customs men untouched. Shortly she returned the letters, saying that their rumpled appearance resulted from having been hidden in the lining of her dress. "I had to sit up all night sewing those wretched papers in my dress," she explained with a toss of her head. "What was worse, I never dared to change it. Just imagine what the other women thought of me."

Harpending discovered that in his absence the Nevada boom had further diminished the ranks of those willing to promote the separation of California from the Union. He was reduced to going ahead with a single southern partner named Greathouse and an Englishman named Rubery. Harpending earlier had talked Rubery, who happened to be a favorite nephew of the English statesman John Bright, out of a duel in which the young man almost certainly would have been killed; as a result, Rubery became Harpending's bosom friend—and fellow conspirator.

Harpending's plan was to buy and refit a coastal vessel for the privateering work. This ship need serve only temporarily, as its first target would be one of the Pacific Mail steamers that regularly carried the gold south from San Francisco to Panama on its way to New York. The captured craft would be refitted as a privateer to replace the original vessel. Harpending guessed that he could seize at least three gold ships, with cargoes totaling perhaps $12 million, before the news reached the East and the Union navy started pursuing them. "After that we proposed to let events very much take their own course."

Harpending attempted to purchase the *Otter*, a steam vessel registered to an owner in Oregon. But on trial its performance fell short. "She failed to develop a speed much greater than that of a rowboat—not enough either to fight or run away." The three conspirators were lamenting that they'd never find a suitable ship when one pulled into port. The *Chapman* had made a quick passage from New York via Cape Horn, which proved both its speed and its seaworthiness. The owners were willing to sell, and didn't inquire too closely regarding the purchasers' plans.

At this point, local memories of William Walker worked to Harpending's advantage. He hired a Mexican national to present himself around San Francisco as the chief of security for a mine in Mexico beset by filibusters. In this guise the agent purchased a pair of cannons and plenty of shot and shell. He also laid in a supply of smaller arms: rifles, revolvers, cutlasses. As additional cover he bought a variety of trade goods and ordinary provisions.

Harpending meanwhile interviewed and engaged a crew of regular seamen and a separate contingent of twenty men for the raiding and boarding. He vetted the politics of each of this latter group, quietly rejecting all those not in strong sympathy with the South. He didn't inform them of the precise nature of their mission, beyond saying that fighting would be required, and well compensated.

The last man hired was the navigator. Here Harpending had to take a chance, for the South wasn't exactly a school for seamen, especially not experienced navigators who could guide a ship far from land. He settled on a fellow named William Law, who was referred to him by an acquaintance, and who professed to favor the South. Harpending didn't like Law's appearance—"He was the possessor of a sinister, villainous mug, looked capable of any crime, and all in all was the most repulsive reptile in appearance I ever set eyes on"—but none better appeared, and Harpending was impatient to go after the gold.

Departure from San Francisco was set for the night of March 14, 1863. The arms were stowed belowdeck, as were the members of the special fighting force. The crew made the vessel ready. All that was missing was Law, the navigator. Harpending considered sailing without him, but the crew vetoed any such plans. Ten o'clock passed, then midnight, then two o'clock. Harpending's suspicions mounted, yet there seemed nothing to do but get some sleep before daylight, and decide at that point on the next step.

Daylight came, and it revealed that Harpending's suspicions were right. He and the others awoke to find themselves staring into mouths of the guns of the U.S. man-of-war *Cyane*. Law had revealed the plot to the Union commander—not for conscience's sake but for money. As Harpending put it, relating information that came out at the ensuing trial, "It occurred to his sordid mind that a handsome sum of money could be obtained from the government, without any risk at all, by betraying his associates. He made a cold-blooded, mercenary bargain with the authorities through which he realized a small fortune."

All aboard were arrested, and Harpending, Greathouse, and Rubery were tried for treason. The jury convicted them after deliberating four minutes. Each was sentenced to ten years in prison and a fine of $10,000. President Lincoln, however, pardoned Rubery at the request of his influential English uncle, who suggested that the boy hadn't appreciated what he was doing. That the arguments of Uncle John Bright were largely responsible for Britain's decision not to back the Confederacy, despite the long-standing connection between Confederate cotton planters and British cotton spinners, doubtless influenced Lincoln's decision as well.

16

From Sea to Shining Sea

With Harpending in jail, the gold got through. By the beginning of the Civil War, California's mines had produced more than $600 million in gold. During the four years of the war, another $130 million came out of the ground. Not all of the gold went east right away; much was employed to build San Francisco and the other cities and towns of California. But most eventually—during the war, quickly—wound up in the banks of New York or with the Treasury at Washington. (Not a little went to Europe as well.) Before the war, the South received considerably less California gold than the North did, on account of the South's lack of large financial institutions and its relative dearth of goods the miners wished to buy. After the war started, the South was cut off almost completely—which was what drove Harpending to his desperate plot. Some contraband gold penetrated the Union blockade, but in quantities minuscule by comparison with what the North received.

The western mines—including the new mines of Nevada that intrigued Leland Stanford and seduced the sunshine secessionists who abandoned Harpending—weren't what won the war for the North. Union soldiers accomplished that bloody feat. And the fact that there were more of them than Confederate soldiers certainly helped in the task. But the decisive advantage the North had over the South was in economics: in the guns, bullets, boots, bread, bandages, horses, mules, barges, and railroads the Union armies employed to crush the secession. And in an era when precious metals were the bedrock of any economy—and the currency foreign creditors insisted on—control of the western mines gave the Union an advantage the Confederacy had no prayer of offsetting. Or rather, its one prayer went unanswered when Asbury Harpending was arrested.

Yet the transforming effects of gold in American life were only beginning. The project that provoked the fight for Kansas and so contributed centrally to the coming of the war—the California railroad—got under way even while the Federals and Confederates battled on. And four years after the army of Abraham Lincoln and his political allies guaranteed the union of North and South, the railroad of Leland Stanford and his business partners ensured the union of East and West—a feat that was no less crucial than Lincoln's in launching America into the modern era.

AT THE OUTBREAK of the Civil War, William Sherman had no idea what a large role he would play in the terrible conflict; indeed, he had little reason to believe that anything large, or even successful, lay before him. His political humiliation in the affair of the San Francisco Vigilance Committee in 1856 had been followed shortly by financial embarrassment, when another bank panic forced his office of Lucas & Turner to close. His partners sent him to New York to open a branch on Wall Street, but bad luck followed him east. On September 11, 1857, the steamer *Central America* sank in a storm off the Georgia coast. The human cost was great, as more than five hundred passengers went down with the ship. Sherman might easily have been among the dead, having sailed on the vessel before and nearly doing so this time. He informed Ellen from New York, "We are all safe ashore," adding wryly that he guessed he was not doomed to drown, "else I would have been long ago."

But he didn't escape injury altogether. Besides its passengers, the *Central America* was carrying nearly $2 million in California gold bound for the banks of New York. The gold was awaited most anxiously, for the panic that had seized San Francisco was already gripping Wall Street. Shares in

California mines and other enterprises had been soaring; now they plummeted to earth, bringing down banks overextended to the West. The loss of the gold of the *Central America* delivered the coup de grâce to hopes that the situation might be retrieved.

Sherman initially expected to ride out the tempest. He had never been a gambler, and his experience in California had, if anything, rendered him more cautious than ever. The balances of his New York office were solid; his position seemed secure. "Having nothing seemingly at stake," he recalled, regarding the panic around him, "I felt amused."

The joke was on him. Although the Lucas & Turner bank was not directly at risk, one of the principals—Lucas—lost heavily in a separate venture. And his loss compelled the closing of Sherman's New York office. With dark humor Sherman looked back at his recent career. "I suppose I was the Jonah that blew up San Francisco," he told Ellen, "and it took only two months' residence in Wall Street to bust up New York." Shortly after this, Sherman encountered Ulysses S. Grant, whose luck at farming had been no better than Sherman's at banking. They compared notes and spoke of some other former officers they knew; the meeting led Sherman to observe, "West Point and the Regular Army aren't good schools for farmers, bankers, merchants and mechanics."

His latest experience cured Sherman of any residual desire to be a banker. "I would as soon try the faro table as risk the chances of banking," he told Ellen. He attempted law in Kansas, but was not reassured of the high standards of his new profession when he was admitted to the bar simply on grounds of general intelligence. "If I turn lawyer," he predicted, "it will be bungle, bungle, from Monday to Sunday, but if it must be, so be it." In fact, after bungling his way through a couple of cases, he decided he wasn't meant to be a lawyer any more than a banker. He tried to return to the army, but the army wasn't looking for officers.

He finally accepted a position as headmaster of a military academy in Louisiana, a job he found congenial on its merits but increasingly untenable as the country careened toward disunion. Despite the fact that his younger brother had become a Republican stalwart in Congress, he thought the new party pernicious for aggravating the slavery question. "Avoid the subject as a dirty black one," he urged John, to no avail. Sherman's opinion of the Republicans only diminished when they nominated John Frémont for president. Sherman declared of Frémont, "If he is fit for the office of President, then anybody may aspire to that office." All political issues, Sherman complained, were being reduced to "the nigger question." He wanted everyone simply to quiet down and leave things alone. "I would not if I could abolish or modify slavery," he wrote Tom Ewing, his foster brother (and brother-in-law). "I don't know that I would materially change the actual political relation of master and slave. Negroes in the great numbers that exist here must of necessity be slaves." Sherman thought the South had legitimate complaints, and, living among southerners as he did, he was willing to assist his neighbors. "If they design to protect themselves against negroes, or abolitionists, I will help." Yet he would go only so far. "If they propose to leave the Union on account of a supposed fact that the northern people are all abolitionists like [Joshua] Giddings and [John] Brown, then I will stand by Ohio and the North West."

When the South left the Union, Sherman had no choice but to head north. By then, of course, the federal army was looking for trained officers, and he was welcomed back into his original profession. (The Confederate army was looking for officers, too, and unavailingly promised Sherman a high command if he stayed south.) Sherman's experiences during the next four years summarized, in many respects, the wartime experiences of the Union as a whole: defeat followed by disorientation, followed in turn by retrenchment and reorganization, leading only then to the discovery of the secret of victory—namely, the application of overwhelming force against the secessionists.

Sherman saw his first action at Bull Run in July 1861, and he did about as poorly as the rest of the Union army there. Unable to coordinate the actions of his untrained men, he watched with mortification as they broke and ran under the Confederate assault. "I had read of retreats before, have seen the noise and confusion of crowds of men at fires and shipwrecks," he wrote Ellen. "But nothing like this. It was as disgraceful as words can portray."

In the grim weeks that followed, Sherman tried to whip his men into shape. When one volunteer officer from New York asserted that he had served out his term and was heading home, Sherman threatened to shoot him. The officer subsequently complained to President Lincoln, who was visiting Sherman's camp. Lincoln, having seen the determination in Sherman's blue eyes, told the officer he'd better listen when Sherman talked of shooting. "I believe he would do it," Lincoln said.

As the Union forces attempted to regroup, Sherman received charge of the defense of Kentucky. Between the politics that plagued the northern war effort at this point and the special trials of holding a slave state in the Union, Sherman grew increasingly frustrated. He vented his frustration in a meeting overheard by a reporter, who, in an article first published in the *New York Tribune* and widely reprinted around the country, painted Sherman as a defeatist. The negative publicity intensified Sherman's upset and poisoned his feelings toward reporters—who responded by making his life still more miserable, by alleging mental imbalance and even insanity. Sherman gnashed his teeth and lay awake nights; he smoked cigars at a furious rate; he muttered about having to suffer fools and traitors. Finally his superior, Henry W. Halleck—of the Monterey constitutional convention—transferred him west to Missouri, closer to Halleck's headquarters.

It was in the West that Sherman found his footing—at the same time and in the same place as the Union generally. In early 1862, Sherman reconnected with Ulysses Grant, who like Sherman had found his way back to the army, and who was preparing an offensive intended to sever the western wing of the Confederacy from the East. With other Unionists, Sherman took heart from Grant's recent victories in Tennessee; eager to carry the war to the enemy, he volunteered to serve under Grant, despite being Grant's senior. "Command me in any way," he wrote Grant.

Halleck liked the idea and gave Sherman a division in Grant's army. At Shiloh that spring Sherman led his troops bravely into battle, receiving two wounds and having three horses killed beneath him. When Grant reported the—bloody—Union victory, he especially commended Sherman; Halleck, relaying the news to Washington, declared, "Sherman saved the fortune of the day." (Sherman's good fortune was the ill fortune of Albert Sidney Johnston, who, having returned from California to take a commission with the Confederacy, was killed at Shiloh.) Sherman joined Grant in the successful 1863 assault on Vicksburg, which split the Confederacy and recaptured the Mississippi River for the Union. Grant's reward was promotion to command of all Union forces; Sherman was given the western theater.

During the spring of 1864, Sherman laid plans for a campaign that would transform the war (and transform warfare, by setting an example for a subsequent century of generals). He proposed to drive from Tennessee to Atlanta, and from Atlanta to the sea. "If the North can march an army right through the South, it is proof positive that the North can prevail," he told Grant. Skeptics observed that Sherman lacked the men and provisions to hold the territory he captured. That wasn't the point, Sherman answered. He didn't aim to hold territory but to break the enemy's will. "Until we can repopulate Georgia, it is useless to occupy it," he told Grant. "But the utter destruction of its roads, houses and people will cripple their military resources. . . . I can make the march, and make Georgia howl!"

Sherman marched and Georgia howled. From May 1864 to April 1865 he carved a swath of destruction that left Atlanta in cinders and the Carolinas quaking. Along a relentlessly advancing front sixty miles wide, his men burned fields and warehouses, smashed cotton gins and wagons, tore up railroad tracks and loading docks, and generally obliterated everything that might contribute to the Confederate war effort. Many in the North were almost as horrified as everyone in the South by the devastation Sherman wrought. But the rebels got the message. When Grant caught Lee at Appomattox, the Confederate general's capitulation set a precedent for southern surrender; yet equally important in convincing other Confederates to quit was the searing memory of Sherman's march—and the daunting specter of his return.

The war made Sherman a hero (in the North; in the South it made him a second Satan). At the grand victory review on Pennsylvania Avenue in Washington, the crowds applauded him with admiration verging on awe. "The acclamation given Sherman was without precedent," reported the *New York World*. "The whole assemblage raised and waved and shouted as if he had been the personal friend of each and every one of them. . . . Sherman was the idol of the day." His stern demeanor had often frightened the ladies, but now that he was a military conqueror, it was very becoming. Young women planted kisses on his red-bearded cheek; before long he was referred to as "the great American soldier who whipped every foreman who stood before him and kissed every girl that he met." His name and the presidency began frequenting the same sentences.

Yet Sherman—unlike Grant—realized he wasn't cut out for politics. His temper was too short and his tolerance for fools too thin. "At first he was affable," explained an observer of one afternoon's outing. "Then he grew less cordial as the crowds crushed. He pushed down the steps, step by step, and refused proffered hands, finally exclaiming, 'Damn you, get out of the way, damn you!' " When a voice from the crowd called out to know whether he would lead an army to Mexico to drive out the French-imposed emperor Maximilian, Sherman responded, "You can go there if you like, and you can go to hell if you want to!" He understood his limitations in the political arena and explained them to a reporter. "When I speak, I speak to the point; and when I act in earnest, I act to the point. If a man minds his own business I let him alone, but if he crosses my path, he must get out of the way." His politics were simple and didn't require his being president. "I want peace and freedom for every man to go where he pleases, to California or to any other portion of our country without restriction."

SHERMAN'S LISTENERS ON this occasion might have missed it, but California was no idle example for him. As one who had spent a sizable part of his life—cumulatively speaking—getting to and from California, he had long desired a faster route from the East to the Pacific. In San Francisco he had helped organize the Sacramento Valley Railroad, the first railroad west of the Missouri, and served as company vice president. Some of his partners had a grander dream, of a railroad spanning the continent, but Sherman thought their vision premature. "The time for the great national railroad has not yet come," he told brother John in 1856. Much surveying work had to be done, and would require years. Yet a start could be made, and interim benefits secured, by the construction of a highway across the plains and mountains. "A good wagon road is very timely," he said.

"Advocate the wagon road with all the zeal you possess, and you will do a good thing." A well-maintained road would substantially ease the continental crossing, rendering it swifter, cheaper, and more secure. "The great object to be accomplished is to afford convenient resting places, where the emigrant can buy a mule or ox and can have his wagon repaired at moderate cost." The road would also benefit those who traveled lighter and therefore faster. "A stage will use the wagon road as soon as the wants of the people demand."

Others joined Sherman in advocating a road suitable for stages, and in 1858 the horse-powered coaches began operating. Horace Greeley traveled west on one the following year—moralizing, characteristically, the whole way. "There are too many idle, shiftless people in Kansas," he informed the readers of his *New York Tribune*. A dispatch from farther west declared, "The Indians are children. Their arts, wars, treaties, alliances, habitations, crafts, properties, commerce, comforts, all belong to the very lowest and rudest ages of human existence." Indian men were "squalid and conceited, proud and worthless, lazy and lousy," while Indian women were "degraded and filthy." A Mormon sermon overheard in Salt Lake City was "rambling, dogmatic, and ill-digested." The Humboldt River was "the meanest river of its length on earth."

Samuel Clemens had a better time than Greeley. Clemens traveled west in 1861, accompanying his brother Orion, who had just been named assistant secretary of the new Nevada Territory. The appointment rewarded Orion's staunch Unionism, a faith far from universal in his home state of Missouri—or in the Clemens family, which included such secessionist sympathizers as Sam. But Sam preferred sightseeing to fighting, so he and Orion lit out for the territories aboard the overland stage.

The journey provided grist for *Roughing It*, published under the nom de plume—Mark Twain—Clemens adopted while in the West. The distance from St. Joseph, Missouri, to Sacramento was nearly 1,900 miles, and the stage line's mail contract obliged it to complete the journey in nineteen days. To this end the company had established a regular system of relief stations, drivers, and teams. Each stretch of about 250 miles was the responsibility of a division agent, who hired drivers and support staff, purchased horses and mules and provisions, erected the station buildings, dug wells, and generally acted the wilderness autocrat. "He was a very, very great man in his division," Clemens observed, with what would become his trademark combination of irony and respect: "a kind of Grand Mogul, a Sultan of the Indies, in whose presence common men were modest of speech and manner, and in the glare of whose greatness even the dazzling stage-driver dwindled to a penny dip."

Yet the stage-drivers were dazzling enough, at least in their own opinion. Secure in their ability to do what neither the division agents nor the owners—nor anyone else, for that matter—could do, namely cover the requisite hundred miles a day over mountains and deserts, through rain and snow, they scarcely deigned to deal with lesser mortals. Clemens described one of the select fraternity dismounting after a night on the road.

> The driver tossed his gathered reins out on the ground, gaped and stretched complacently, drew off his heavy buckskin gloves with great deliberation and insufferable dignity—taking not the slightest notice of a dozen solicitous inquiries after his health, and humbly facetious flattering accostings, and obsequious tenders of service, from five or six hairy and half-civilized station-keepers and hostlers. . . . In the eyes of the stage-driver of that day, station-keepers and hostlers were a sort of good enough low creatures, useful in their place, and helping to make up a world, but not the kind of beings which a person of distinction could afford to concern himself with.

Clemens and the other paying customers rated hardly better. "The overland driver had but little less contempt for his passengers than he had for his hostlers."

Occasionally the stage would pass a wagon train, an encounter that reminded both parties what an improvement the former was over the latter. "Just beyond the breakfast-station we overtook a Mormon emigrant train of thirty-three wagons," Clemens wrote of a stretch slightly east of South Pass. "And tramping wearily along and driving their herd of loose cows, were dozens of coarse-clad and sad-looking men, women and children, who had walked as they were walking now, day after day for eight lingering weeks, and in that time had compassed the distance our stage had come in *eight days and three hours*—seven hundred and ninety-eight miles!"

Although the stage was the fastest mode of ordinary travel across the plains and mountains, it wasn't the fastest means of communication. That honor went to the year-old Pony Express, whose riders tore past Clemens and the stage like a prairie whirlwind. For many days Clemens and the others strained their eyes eagerly for a glimpse of these intrepid racers, who covered 250 miles a day carrying letters—typically business correspondence—that were literally worth their weight in gold. But somehow the riders all passed the stage in the night, until one day when the stage driver, from his elevated perch, called down, "Here he comes!"

> Every neck is stretched further, and every eye strained wider. Away across the endless dead level of the prairie a black speck appears against the sky, and it is plain that it moves. Well, I should think so!
>
> In a second or two it becomes a horse and rider, rising and falling, rising and falling—sweeping toward us nearer and nearer—growing more and more distinct, more and more sharply defined—nearer and still nearer, and the flutter of the hoofs comes faintly to the ear—another instant a whoop and a hurrah from our upper deck, a wave of the rider's hand, but no reply, and man and horse burst past our excited faces, and go winging away like a belated fragment of a storm!
>
> So sudden is it all, and so like a flash of unreal fancy, that but for the flake of white foam left quivering and perishing on a mail-sack after the vision had flashed by and disappeared, we might have doubted whether we had seen any actual horse and man at all, maybe.

The overland stage relieved the travelers of much of the tedium of crossing the trans-Missouri West, but it couldn't entirely eliminate the hardship. The Great Salt Lake Desert slowed the stagecoach to a painful crawl. "Imagine a vast, waveless ocean stricken dead and turned to ashes," Clemens requested of his readers. "Imagine team, driver, coach and passengers so deeply coated with ashes that they are all one colorless color; imagine ash-drifts roosting above moustaches and eyebrows like snow accumulations on boughs and bushes." The sun beat down with relentless malignity. Not the faintest breath of air eased the heat or lifted the travelers' spirits. "There is not a living creature visible in any direction whither one searches the blank level that stretches its monotonous miles on every hand; there is not a sound—not a sigh—not a whisper—not a buzz, or a whir of wings, or distant pipe of bird—not even a sob from the lost souls that doubtless people that dead air."

The lost souls crowded especially close in the Carson Desert. The barren waste that had nearly consumed Sarah Royce and her family still bore grim evidence of the toll it had claimed.

> From one extremity of this desert to the other, the road was white with the bones of oxen and horses. It would hardly be an exaggeration to say that we could have walked the forty miles and set our feet on a bone at every step! The desert was one prodigious graveyard. And the log-chains, wagon tyres, and rotting wrecks of vehicles were almost as thick as the bones. I think we saw log-chains enough rusting there in the desert, to reach across any State in the Union. Do not these relics suggest something of an idea of the fearful suffering and privation the early emigrants to California endured?

ON THE WESTERN SIDE of the Carson Desert were the towns—which was to say, the mines—of Nevada. There Sam Clemens encountered George Hearst, the greatest miner of the Gold Rush era, and indeed the most successful miner in American history. Hearst looked every inch the rugged man of the earth. His craggy brow and prominent nose appeared to have been rough-chiseled from rock, and his flowing beard always seemed several months from its last appointment with shears or razor. He chewed tobacco religiously, and his juice-streaked beard and spotted shirt betokened his faith.

Hearst and the Clemenses shared Missouri as a home state, although Hearst left it more than a decade earlier, to come out with the overlanders when the trip still took months rather than days. Like Lewis Manly, Hearst had experience of lead mining—in Missouri rather than Wisconsin—and like Manly he guessed that digging gold couldn't be any harder than digging lead and must be more lucrative. As it happened, the mass of miners already in the field (Hearst didn't reach the mines till the autumn of 1850) put him off temporarily. He fell into operating a theater in Nevada City, an establishment that enjoyed a monopoly among the five thousand inhabitants of the town after a March flood in 1852 swept away the dramatic competition. The second floor of the building housed a reading room, where Hearst and his partners set out newspapers delivered from the wider world to Sacramento but left uncalled-for at the post office by their intended recipients. On one of his visits to Sacramento he discovered an opportunity in commerce, and so opened a general store on K Street, not far from where Leland Stanford set up shop.

But Hearst's heart was in the dirt. As a boy he had spent so much time nosing around mines and pits and holes that the remnant Indians in Missouri called him "Boy That Earth Talks To." The earth in California told him that a particular quartz ledge outside Nevada City was deeper and richer than it appeared to the thousands of others who had been over that ground. Naming the mine "Merrimac," after the Missouri river on which he grew up, he dug it out and demonstrated that the earth didn't lie to George Hearst. He did the same with a mine he called the Potosi, after a Missouri mine (itself named after the famous Bolivian district). Before long he owned a pile of money and a reputation for uncanny insight into matters mineral.

It was this reputation that caused him to learn, in 1859, of an unusual load of black dirt sent to an assayer in Nevada City. The sample came from

Washoe, as the district beyond the Sierras was called. The prospectors who sent it were interested in its gold content, which proved considerable. But what amazed the assayer, who shared his amazement with Hearst, was that the part of the sample that was not gold, and which the Washoe miners had apparently been throwing away, was loaded with silver, worth three thousand dollars a ton.

Hearst headed east at once. A hundred miles from Sacramento, on the slopes of a nondescript height named Sun Peak, he found the mine that was the source of the black ore. The mine was called the Ophir, and the owners included a wily prospector named William Comstock, whose stake in the mine owed more to his pushiness than to any priority in discovery. Luck—bad luck—was involved, too; a number of Comstock's partners met untimely deaths, leaving no heirs to dispute his thereby increased portion. As the wealth of the Ophir and the surrounding district became known, Comstock christened the lode underneath it after himself. (One of his partners, a Virginian with a weakness for drink, answered Comstock by accidentally dropping a bottle of whiskey on the ground near the mine; as the booze ran out he salvaged what he could of the situation by declaring the site baptized, as Virginia City. This partner, too, died suddenly, pitched headlong from his horse while drunk. Eventually Comstock himself suffered a violent death, by his own hand, after his wife, who had fled a polygamous Mormon marriage to be with him, then fled him.)

Hearst knew more about the value of the Ophir than its owners, and he arranged to purchase a one-sixth interest for a relative pittance. He proceeded to employ the mining expertise he'd brought from Missouri and sharpened in California, and developed the mine. He imported steam engines, hoists, and pumps, and drove deep into the heart of Sun Peak. When the ore vein proved more extensive than anything in California, requiring more elaborate means of shoring up the roof and walls of the mine, he installed a new modular system of "square set" timbering devised by a German engineer named Philip Deidesheimer. In time the Ophir was yielding millions of dollars per year, making Hearst a very rich man, and making Nevada—as the territory was formally named on being carved from Utah subsequent to the new discoveries—the focus of hopes and dreams much like those that had populated California a decade earlier.

IT WAS THE NEVADA boom that attracted Orion and Sam Clemens, and it was the Nevada boom that got Leland Stanford started building—as opposed to merely advocating—a Pacific railroad. In the early 1860s, Stanford cut a considerable figure in California: wealthy businessman, governor, leader of the newly ascendant Republican party. He was an obvious partner for anyone intending to start a major project in California, especially a project requiring an alliance of public and private resources.

Theodore Judah thought so. Judah was a Connecticut native who developed a monomania for a Pacific railroad. He was an engineer but, more important, a promoter; many judged him a lunatic. He wrote of trains crossing the country in forty hours, traveling a hundred miles an hour, powered by locomotives with driving wheels fourteen feet in diameter. Yet Judah complemented his flights of fancy with hikes of reality. He trudged the ridges and valleys of the Sierras with his surveying instruments, determined to demonstrate the feasibility of a line across that mountain wall. Meanwhile he sought subscriptions for a scheme to raise money to get the construction started. San Francisco spurned his offer, but Sacramento was more receptive. Stanford's friend and fellow Republican, Collis Huntington, listened to Judah's pitch and was intrigued. Huntington shared the idea with Mark Hopkins, with Charles Crocker, and with Stanford. The four sponsored a further survey by Judah, and in the interim drew up articles of incorporation for the Central Pacific Railroad Company of California. On June 28, 1861, they filed the necessary papers. Leland Stanford was listed as president.

Stanford knew no more about railroads than Huntington, Hopkins, or Crocker, and considerably less than Judah. But having been nominated (for the second time) for governor just a week earlier, he lent the project a political heft the others lacked. Judah was frank about the importance of Stanford's political connections. "A good deal depends upon the election of Stanford," Judah informed a friend, "for the prestige of electing a Republican ticket will go a long way toward getting us what we want."

Stanford's election did indeed go far toward getting the Central Pacific what it wanted, although Stanford initially remained more cautious than the obsessed Judah. Stanford wasn't entirely convinced that a railroad clear across the continent was feasible, but he believed that a much shorter line was, and could earn him and his partners a handsome profit. The opening of the Comstock mines had generated a demand for convenient access from the west; Stanford intended for the Central Pacific to provide it. He personally examined the route over the mountains.

> I remember that while we were making our exploration we came to the summit, and at Donner Pass we looked down on Donner Lake, 1200 feet below us, and then looked up at the drifts above us, 2000 feet, and I must confess that it looked very formidable. We there and then discussed the question of the paying qualities of the enterprise and we came to this conclusion: That if there was a way by which a vessel could start from San Francisco or from New York, and sail around Cape Horn in behind those mountains, we could not afford to compete; or if a vessel could start from any of the Atlantic ports and come there around Cape Horn, we could not compete. If this could not be done, however, and if we had only the ox and mule teams to compete with, we saw that we could obtain such a rate for carrying freight and passengers that we could afford to build the road with the prospect of further developments in Nevada. At that time the business of Nevada was very promising, and we had an idea, like everybody else on this side, that most of the mountains in Nevada were filled with mineral wealth.

Stanford and his partners hoped to tap Nevada's mineral wealth even before their railroad crossed the Sierras. The rails would wait on the largest fills, the deepest cuts, the longest tunnels through the most refractory rock; but meanwhile the company could employ its knowledge of the terrain, its initial grading, and its construction crews to build a wagon road to the

Comstock. The tolls on the road would generate a revenue stream that would facilitate work on the railroad. Stanford and the others organized a separate company, the Dutch Flat & Donner Lake Wagon Road Company, for this purpose. By the spring of 1864 it had achieved its goal. "NEW ROAD TO WASHOE," boasted an ad in the *Sacramento Union*. "The Dutch Flat Road is now open for travel, and teamsters can save three days in the round trip to Virginia City, and carry fully one quarter more freight on account of light grades." By this time the railroad had reached Newcastle; as an introductory offer (which revealed the interlocking nature of the rail and road companies) haulers would have their tolls waived on cargoes loaded at the railhead. "Teamsters, try it and see for yourselves," the notice urged.

Not everyone in California was thrilled at the idea of a railroad across the Sierras. The teamsters who benefited from the new Washoe road of Stanford and his partners could see that their benefit had a strict time limit, for the day a railroad reached the Comstock would be their last day in business. (The operators of rival toll roads were already in trouble.) Stage lines and express services over the Sierras faced a similar threat. Even the Sitka Ice Company, which carried the cold stuff from the far Northwest and sold it for five cents a pound at San Francisco, feared being undercut by blocks and cubes carved from the lakes of the high Sierras.

Moreover, everyone realized that the Sierras were the most serious hurdle in the path of a transcontinental railroad. Once through those mountains, construction east would be straightforward—if long, dusty, hot, cold, and sometimes harassed by Indians. Interests akin to those opposing the California-Nevada line disapproved of a transcontinental track. Steamship companies plying the routes between the East Coast and the isthmus, and between the isthmus and San Francisco, feared loss of their passengers. Clipper ship owners would lose the lucrative California leg of their trade. The overland stage would be run out of business, and all the agents, conductors, and drivers who had so impressed Sam Clemens would be thrown out of their jobs. Hoisting a telegraph wire beside a rail line would cost almost nothing; existing telegraphers (who already had killed off the Pony Express) would be deprived of their monopoly on instantaneous communication.

Nor were competitors' complaints the sum of the opposition. Although the Republican victory in the 1860 elections neutralized the southern objections to a federally funded western railroad (the southerners took their objections with them on seceding), it didn't silence eastern opposition. On the contrary, as a western railroad looked more likely, eastern politicians and taxpayers increasingly registered resistance to paying for something that would chiefly benefit the West. Of what use was a California railroad to Massachusetts or New York or Pennsylvania? Easterners argued that they had built their own railroads with private money; let the westerners do likewise.

The answer of Stanford and the Californians was the essence of pragmatism. If the Pacific railroad waited on private funding, it would wait a hundred years. Railroads in the East crossed counties thick with farms and villages and towns and cities—that is, filled with customers who paid the freight that supplied the profits that attracted the investment that built the railroads in the first place. Railroads in the West would cross nothing but emptiness. (Indians didn't count—or if they did, as a cost rather than a benefit.) In time western railroads would spur settlement that would generate traffic, but any strictly private corporation would go broke long before that happened. The only way the present generation would see California tied to the East by rail was for the government to guarantee financing.

Such arguments swayed the broad-minded; for those with a narrower field of vision, other inducements were employed. Stanford and his partners sent Judah to Washington with a suitcase full of Central Pacific shares, to be dispensed among legislators as necessary. How many shares Judah distributed became a matter of subsequent dispute. Stanford conceded to a congressional committee that he and his partners had supplied Judah shares valued at $100,000; he added, with unhelpful vagueness, "I think, however, that he brought back most of it."

At the national capital Judah discovered allies. Stanford and company weren't the only ones hoping to profit from a Pacific railroad; several groups were vying to become the eastern counterpart to the Central Pacific. One such group had the support of Tom Ewing, William Sherman's foster brother and brother-in-law and the son of the former treasury and interior secretary. Another group was headed by Thomas Durant, an ophthalmologist who had forsaken sick eyes for railroad stocks and was currently a principal in the Mississippi & Missouri line. Judah brought California senator James McDougall aboard the transcontinental project, while Ewing gained the backing of Senator James Lane of Kansas, and Durant, whose M&M line was critical to the economy of southern Iowa, secured the support of Iowa senator James Harlan. (Harlan was a close friend of Abraham Lincoln, who had his own connections to the M&M, an offspring of the Rock Island Line, which once employed Lincoln as attorney.)

The lobbyists didn't always pull in the same direction. Ewing and Durant competed with each other for the eastern concession even as they cooperated toward federal funding of the road. But the rail bill finally passed Congress, which pledged loans and land grants in exchange for the construction of a railroad from the Missouri River to the Sacramento Valley. Durant's group, reorganized as the Union Pacific Railroad, won congressional blessing for the eastern end of the line; Stanford's Central Pacific got the nod in the west. "We have drawn the elephant," a jubilant Judah wired Stanford and the other partners on July 1, 1862. "Now let us see if we can harness him up."

NEITHER JUDAH—who died of yellow fever contracted while crossing the isthmus the following year—nor Stanford had any idea how expensive the harnessing would be. The railroad act of 1862 established the principle of federal support for a railroad, but the law's particulars left the builders in a yawning initial lurch. For one thing, they had to lay forty miles of track before they qualified for any federal money. For another, the money they received would be in the form of first-mortgage bonds. The latter condition put private lenders second in line for the assets of the roads, a place few of them wished to be, especially on such a risky venture. The reluctance of the lenders made it difficult for Stanford and Central Pacific, on one hand, and Durant and the Union Pacific, on the other, to raise the money they needed to build the first forty miles.

Yet Stanford's dual identity mitigated the Central Pacific's problem. Although a later generation would consider his presidency of the Central Pacific to pose a patent conflict of interest with his position as California governor, he—and most of his California contemporaries—considered it entirely natural for an able man to pursue the public interest and private interests at the same time. Stanford certainly did both. He employed the powers of the governorship to browbeat the California legislature into putting up $15 million in state bonds for the road; in exchange the Central Pacific promised to transport the state militia gratis during times of domestic distress. In addition the company deeded a granite quarry to the state, with the rocks likewise f.o.b. At the same time, Stanford engineered referendums in San Francisco, Sacramento, and Placer Counties authorizing those counties to invest in the road. On election day, according to multiple reports, Stanford's brother Philip handed out gold coins to encourage a favorable vote, which duly followed. Opponents challenged Stanford's maneuvers, but he shored up his position by appointing Edwin Crocker (Charles Crocker's brother and himself a member of the Central Pacific board of directors, besides being the former defender of Archy Lee) as chief justice of the California Supreme Court.

Before the construction crews of the Central Pacific began moving mountains physically, Stanford accomplished the same feat politically. The federal law specified larger loans for construction through mountains than on the flat ($48,000 per mile versus $16,000 per mile), but applying the law required defining where the mountains started. Needless to say, the closer to Sacramento they started, the more money the Central Pacific would receive. Stanford recalled a statement by an eminent geologist that the eastern base of the Rocky Mountains might, in theory, be defined as the western bank of the Mississippi River. Stanford guessed that the same reasoning could apply to the Sierra Nevada. He dispatched a team of geologists—who happened to work for him, as employees of the state of California—to render an opinion in the matter. Not surprisingly, they determined that the Sierras started well down in the Sacramento Valley. When the federal Interior Department raised its collective eyebrow, Stanford suggested that Aaron Sargent, a California Republican who had ridden into Congress on Stanford's coattails, approach President Lincoln directly. Lincoln had things besides California geology on his mind—the Civil War was going badly at this point—and he accepted the Stanford interpretation in order to rid himself of this annoying congressman. "You see," Sargent reported proudly, "my pertinacity and Abraham's faith moved mountains."

Yet for all the finagles, raising money still proved difficult. After the panic of 1857, investors were wary of speculative schemes, and to most who had been across the Sierras, a railroad to Nevada and beyond seemed speculative in the extreme. Besides, investors in the West were used to higher returns than a railroad could promise. Charles Crocker traveled to the Comstock to prospect for funds among the mining moguls there. "They wanted to know what I expected the road would earn," he recalled. "I said I did not know, though it would earn good interest on the money invested, especially to those who went in at bed rock. 'Well,' they said, 'do you think it will make 2 per cent a month?' 'No,' said I, 'I do not.' 'Well,' they answered, 'we can get 2 per cent a month for our money here,' and they would not think of going into a speculation that would not promise that at once."

Consequently, even as Stanford and his associates (the four principals of the Central Pacific were beginning to call themselves the "Associates") tried to persuade Congress to liberalize the 1862 railroad law, they had to pledge their own private assets as security for the money they borrowed to get the construction started. The four were wealthy as individuals, but building a railroad required fortunes of an entirely different order. At times the burden they took on was downright frightening. Charles Crocker recalled, "I would have been glad, when we had thirty miles of road built, to have got a clean shirt and absolution from my debts. I owed everybody that would trust me, and would have been glad for them to forgive my debts and take everything I had, even the furniture of my family, and to have gone into the world and started anew."

The uncertainty of financing suppressed the desire of the partners to celebrate the start of construction. A locomotive had been ordered from the East and shipped around Cape Horn; on being unloaded at the dock in Sacramento it nearly fell into the river. Christened the *Governor Stanford*, it was hauled to where the first rails were being laid. But beyond this nod to their leader, the partners preferred a quiet start, without ceremony or fanfare. Collis Huntington, looking east, explained, "Those mountains over there look too ugly, and I see too much work ahead of us. We may fail, and if we do, I want to have as few people know it as we can."

The partners divided the decision-making. Crocker and Hopkins headed the construction crews, most often on-site. Huntington handled the financing and purchasing, typically from New York and Washington. Stanford was the political fixer. His partners sometimes accused him of being lazy. "As to work," Crocker complained during one stretch when he and the others were feeling overwhelmed, "he absolutely succeeds in doing nothing as near as a man can. He spends an hour or two per day at the office if we send for him." Yet Stanford could deliver what the others could not, including entrée to the highest levels of the Republican party. "Mr. Huntington is one of our wealthiest and most respected and influential citizens," Stanford wrote Lincoln, by way of introducing his money-hunting partner to the president. "I need hardly add the entire State of California will feel a deep interest in the success of his mission."

Sometimes Stanford had to travel to exercise his political clout. During the summer of 1864 the citizens of Nevada Territory held a constitutional convention; among the clauses considered was an instruction to the inaugural state legislature to award $3 million in state bonds to the first railroad company to reach Nevada from the west. The delegates were sincerely trying to encourage railway construction, but Stanford, having hastened to Carson City from Sacramento, told them bluntly that any such legislation as they proposed would have precisely the opposite effect. Unless Nevada specified the Central Pacific, investors in the East and abroad would suppose that some question existed as to whether the Central Pacific had the best route. "To the extent to which you throw a doubt upon this being the only route," he asserted to the convention, "when we go into the market to negotiate our securities or to sell our stock, to that extent you depreciate their value, and to that extent, of course, you prevent the construction of the road." Stanford's lecture accomplished its purpose: the offending clause was removed.

Stanford also applied his political skills to Brigham Young. No one in America before or since wielded power quite like that exercised by the Mormon leader. Although no longer the governor of Utah Territory, Young still headed the Mormon Church, and in that capacity largely controlled the lives of the Latter Day Saints. He had called back the Mormons from the California goldfields (in part from disgust at the likes of Sam Brannan), but the church needed cash as badly as ever. Young now found himself being wooed by both the Central Pacific and the Union Pacific, each of which coveted the kind of discipline the Mormons brought to their work. The two lines would meet somewhere between the Sierras and the Rockies; the precise place of meeting would determine the size of their federal subsidies. It might also mean the difference between ultimate profitability and ultimate failure, for whichever road first reached the valley of the Great Salt Lake could command the traffic of the Mormons, whose economic activities were beyond all proportion to their numbers.

Stanford journeyed to Salt Lake City five times to talk to Young. On his initial visit—delayed by the birth of the first child of his eighteen-year marriage to Jane, a son they named Leland Jr.—he discovered that the agents of the Union Pacific had got there before him. Young had signed a $2 million contract to do the Union's grading, tunneling, and bridge-building from Ogden east into the Wasatch Mountains. This was big money for the Mormons, and Young was mightily pleased. In addition, the Union's Durant had promised free passes to Mormons traveling over the Union Pacific lines to Salt Lake City, no small consideration for a church that counted on a continuing flow of converts from the East and Europe.

"Brigham was cold and close," Stanford reported to Hopkins, regarding his first audience with the Mormon theocrat. But on this visit and subsequent ones, Stanford thawed Young enough to engage construction crews for the Central Pacific. The Central Saints would work west from Ogden and around the north shore of the Salt Lake.

LABOR WAS A CHRONIC problem, and the most pressing one after an 1864 revision of the federal railroad law put investors *ahead* of the government in claims upon the roads. As the money started coming in, the race between the Central Pacific and the Union Pacific began in earnest. Each side scrambled to find the crews needed to cross the continent. Besides the Mormons in Utah, the Union Pacific relied on Irish immigrants, who had first left Ireland in the potato famine of the 1840s and never stopped coming to America.

The Central Pacific likewise started with Irish laborers. This particularly suited James Strobridge, the superintendent of construction, who had worked with the Irish before. But there weren't enough Irish in the West, and they developed what Stanford and his partners conceived to be an inflated sense of their worth. "Four or five of the Irishmen on pay day got to talking together," Crocker recalled. "And I said to Mr. Strobridge there is some little trouble ahead." The "trouble" materialized in the form of a committee of workmen who requested an increase in wages. "I told Mr. Strobridge then to go over to Auburn and get some Chinamen and put them to work," Crocker continued. This quieted the demand for better pay—so effectively that Crocker wanted to go ahead even after the Irish retreat. Strobridge was reluctant. "I was very much prejudiced against Chinese labor," he conceded. "I did not believe we could make a success of it."

To judge by his earlier comments extolling California as white man's country, Stanford was similarly prejudiced against Chinese labor. Indeed, he had reiterated his anti-Chinese feeling in his inaugural address as governor. "To my mind," he said then, "it is clear that their settlement among us is to be discouraged by every legitimate means. Large numbers are already here, and unless we do something early to check their immigration, the question—which of the two tides of immigration meeting upon the shores of the Pacific [the Caucasian and the Asiatic] shall be turned back—will be forced upon our consideration when far more difficult than now of disposal."

But that had been politics, and this was business. (The distinction became easier when Stanford retired from the governorship after one term to concentrate on the railroad.) Like Strobridge, Stanford modified his views, especially as he discovered how cheaply the Chinese worked. Where white workers received $30 a month plus board, the Chinese got $26 per month and boarded themselves. (Food prices had fallen since the high Gold Rush, but this still represented a major savings.) At first the Chinese were confined to the unskilled jobs. Yet when Irish stonemasons went out on strike, Crocker ordered Chinese replacements. Strobridge objected that he couldn't make masons out of Chinese. Crocker replied that of course he could. "Didn't they build the Chinese Wall?"

The Chinese had built much besides their great wall, and in doing so had mastered techniques they put to spectacular use in the Sierras. On the steepest rock faces they lowered themselves in woven baskets from the cliff tops; swaying in the wind, they drilled holes for blasting powder, then tamped in the charges and lit the fuses before being pulled (usually, but not always) out of harm's way.

The addition of the Chinese to the Central workforce accelerated construction at a critical time for the road. "We swarmed the mountains with men," a satisfied Stanford explained.

WILLIAM SHERMAN'S CONNECTION to the Union Pacific was less direct than Stanford's to the Central Pacific, but it was hardly less significant. Sherman's wartime experience convinced him of the importance of railroads. "The Atlanta campaign would simply have been impossible without the use of the railroads from Louisville to Nashville—one hundred and eighty five miles—and from Chattanooga to Atlanta—one hundred and thirty-seven miles," he wrote. By then he agreed that a railroad across the continent—not a wagon road—was what the nation needed. In fact, he saw the construction of the railroad connecting East and West as no less important than the ongoing efforts to reconnect North and South. "I think this subject as important as Reconstruction," he told brother John, regarding the railroad.

For years John, the lawmaker in the family, had been the one with the power to help or hinder the railroad; now it was William's turn. After the parades and reviews celebrating the Union victory in the Civil War finally ended, Sherman was appointed to command the military division of the Mississippi (a designation later changed to Missouri). His headquarters were at St. Louis, and he had responsibility for a vast stretch of the territory through which the Union Pacific would run. He took a personal interest in the construction. "Every time they build a section," he promised, "I'll be on hand to look at it and see that it is properly built." Making his tours more attractive was the fact that many of the laborers were his former soldiers. As he rode beside the line of work, the men put down their tools and waved their hats for "Uncle Billy." He and they reminisced about the old days in Georgia and the Carolinas, and he laughed to remind them how he had taught them to tear up tracks; now they were doing just the opposite.

Meanwhile the Union Pacific took a special interest in Sherman. His brother Charles was appointed a federal director of the line. (Ostensibly guardians of the public interest, the federal directors in fact were creatures of the companies. "They are not worth an iota to the government," Huntington privately conceded.) An old friend and wartime comrade of Sherman's, Grenville Dodge, became the railroad's chief engineer. Thomas Durant named the Union's first locomotive the *General Sherman*, and he treated the real general to the inaugural ride on the initial stretch of sixteen miles running west from Omaha.

The ride was rough, with the guests seated on nail kegs resting on flatcars. But the rhetoric was appropriately enthusiastic, recalling to Sherman's mind a speech Edward Baker had given on a similar occasion, regarding Sherman's own railroad in California. "Baker had electrified us by his unequalled oratory, painting the glorious things which would result from uniting the Western coast with the East by bands of iron." That had been before the war, which swallowed up Baker (at the Battle of Balls Bluff) and a generation of America's youthful manhood, and forestalled the feat he forecast. Sherman perceived a better chance of success this time, but despite the enthusiasm of Durant and everyone else associated with the Union Pacific, he didn't see success coming easily or soon. "When the orators spoke so confidently of the determination to build two thousand miles of railway across the plains, mountains, and desert, devoid of timber, with no population, but on the contrary raided by the bold and bloody Sioux and Cheyennes, who had almost successfully defied our power for half a century, I was disposed to treat it jocularly." To some of his fellow guests that day, he declared, "This is a great enterprise, but I hardly expect to live to see it completed."

As military commander for the Missouri region, Sherman was responsible for maintaining peace with the Sioux and Cheyennes and other tribes of the plains. He didn't anticipate a great deal of trouble, at least not at first. He wrote Grant in August 1866 that the Indians were "pure beggars and poor devils more to be pitied than dreaded." To be sure, the Indians got into scrapes with white settlers, but the latter were usually to blame. The settlers wanted the army to "kill all the Indians," Sherman told Grant, and they behaved in a manner to force the army's hand. Sherman had scant sympathy for the settlers. There would be no offensive against the Indians if he could help it. "I will not permit them to be warred against as long as they are not banded together in parties large enough to carry on war."

This last part of Sherman's statement was the crux of the difficulty. As the railroad crews pushed out across the plains, the Indians realized that the threat to their way of life posed by the railroad was like nothing they had encountered before. However numerous the overland emigrants had been, clearly they were just passing through, and the less they were molested the sooner they'd be gone. But the railroad altered the landscape—the Indians' home—permanently. Towns were even now springing up beside the rails, and settlers were arriving. Whether or not the Indians—or anyone else, for that matter—fully recognized at this early date what the railroads would do to the buffalo, the chief sustenance of the Indians and of the entire culture of the plains, it was apparent that the Indians' way of life was under mortal assault.

Predictably, the Indians struck back. In an initial statement of purpose, a coalition of Sioux, Cheyennes, and Arapahos surprised a contingent of U.S. cavalry and wiped it out. The attack sent chills across the plains and prompted renewed demands for army action.

Sherman's condition for leaving the Indians alone—that they not threaten white predominance in the West—obviously was not being met. He responded with the same vigor as in the Atlanta campaign. "We must act with vindictive earnestness against the Sioux," he told Grant, "even to their extermination: men, women and children." As events proved, Sherman's temper, and his concern for his troops, had got the better of him in this instance; he never pursued an extermination campaign. But his change of mind from just a few months earlier, when he had seen no cause for an offensive against the Indians, was striking nonetheless. He assured Grenville Dodge that "we can act so energetically that both the Sioux and the Cheyennes must die, or submit to our dictation."

In time the Sioux and Cheyennes did some of both, but meanwhile they terrorized the construction gangs. The spring of 1867 brought a series of attacks along the rail route. An engineering crew was ambushed despite its military escort; a soldier and a surveyor were killed, the latter dying twenty-four hours after being scalped and mutilated. A separate band of Indian raiders killed another surveyor and stole a herd of cattle. A war party attacked a train that had reached the end of the track; three men were killed. A group of Cheyennes pulled up the rails on one stretch of the line; when a locomotive derailed, the Indians killed and scalped the engineer and brakeman. The most shocking attack, albeit not the most violent, occurred against a trainload of dignitaries who came out from Washington to inspect the construction. A hundred Indians ambushed the train; seeing the size of the group, they contented themselves with stealing livestock before disappearing.

The raids on the railroad were part of a broad counteroffensive against the white presence in the West. The famous newsman, Henry Morton Stanley (who hadn't yet discovered David Livingstone in Africa), described the Indians' style of warfare and what it appeared to presage:

> When the opportune moment arrives, from every sandhill and ravine the hawks of the desert swoop down with unrivalled impetuosity, and in a few seconds the post or camp is carried, the tent or ranch burnt, and the emigrants are murdered. It is generally believed here that if the present suicidal policy of the Government is carried on much longer, the plains' settlers must succumb to the unequal conflict, or unite in bands to carry on the war after the manner of the Indians, which means to kill, burn, destroy Indian

villages, innocent papooses and squaws, scalp the warriors, and mutilate the dead; in fact, follow in the same course as the red men, that their name may be rendered a terror to all the Indians.

In the short run the Indian offensive threatened to halt the railroad construction. Grenville Dodge declared, "We've got to clean the damn Indians out or give up building the Union Pacific Railroad. The government may take its choice!" Thomas Durant cabled Grant at the War Department, "Unless some relief can be afforded by your department immediately, I beg leave to assure you that the entire work will be suspended."

Neither Grant nor Sherman was willing to see the construction abandoned. Sherman considered summoning volunteers for a campaign against the Indians, but dropped the idea from fear it would make things seem worse than they were. Instead he authorized the enlistment of four companies of Pawnees, whose knowledge of the plains, combined with their traditional hatred of the Sioux and Cheyennes, made them invaluable allies. The Pawnee companies were assigned to guard the rail crews, and though they had little effect on the larger war, they allowed the work to continue.

At the same time, Sherman addressed the overall question of the future of the Indians on the plains. He communicated to their leaders that if they wanted peace, they would be allowed to live in peace, although not necessarily where they desired. On the other hand, if they chose war, they would get war. In September 1867, Sherman headed a commission delegated by President Andrew Johnson to deliver precisely this ultimatum. The meeting took place at Fort Laramie; hundreds of Indians came, including the principal chiefs of the Sioux and Cheyennes. The chiefs complained that the railroad and the settlers were destroying the Indians' way of life; game was already growing scarce and their women and children were going hungry.

Sherman offered no false hope that the traditional ways could be salvaged. The only answer for the Indians was to accept the land—the reservations—the government was offering them. "If you don't choose your homes now, it will be too late next year," he said. The white men were coming, whether the Indians liked it or not. "You can see for yourselves that travel across the country has increased so much that the slow ox wagons will not answer the white man. We will build iron roads, and you cannot stop the locomotives any more than you can stop the sun or the moon." The one decision left to the Indians was how to accept their defeat. "We now can offer you this: choose your homes and live like white men and we will help you." If the Indians resisted, they would be crushed. "Our people in the East hardly think of what you call war out here, but if they make up their minds to fight, they will come out as thick as the herd of buffaloes, and if you continue fighting you will all be killed."

STANFORD AND THE Central Pacific had fewer Indian problems than Sherman and Union Pacific, but the western builders had troubles the easterners didn't. As John Frémont, the Donner party, and countless other trans-Sierra travelers discovered, those mountains caught snow like no other range in North America. Drifts of twenty, forty, sixty feet weren't uncommon, and in the spring, as warm days and cold nights alternately thawed and refroze the banks, the drifts compacted into iron walls of ice. Stanford later remembered one place where a drift measured at sixty-three feet had been compressed into eighteen feet of ice, which could be removed only by pickax and blasting powder, at enormous expenditure of effort and money and with discouraging loss of time.

The winter of 1866–67 was especially severe. At one point a snowplow driven by five locomotives, one behind the other, bogged down in the drifts. Extrapolating, Stanford calculated that nearly half the year would be lost to the snow and ice. Someone had suggested snowsheds: long, roofed structures to cover the track and keep the snow off. One day at lunch with Crocker, Stanford took out a pencil and began scribbling figures. Before the meal was over, the two men had decided to build the sheds by the time the next snows fell.

The granite of the Sierra batholith was, needless to say, harder than the snow and ice. Ten tunnels had to be blasted and burrowed beneath the ridges that separated the Sacramento Valley from Nevada; the longest of these, the summit tunnel, was surveyed at sixteen hundred feet. Black powder—the same employed in the mines of the Mother Lode—was the explosive of first resort, but as time pressed and the rock resisted, the sappers resorted to nitroglycerine. This new compound was highly unstable. A careless (and uninformed: the precise nature of the cargo was strictly secret) dockhand in Panama blew himself, dozens of his fellows, and most of the wharf to smithereens when he dropped one of seventy crates bound for California. Two weeks later a similar explosion atomized the Wells Fargo freight office in San Francisco.

Stanford and the others realized that some informational efforts were required to prepare the public, and the Central Pacific workforce, for the new explosive. A representative of the manufacturer made a show of splashing the liquid on a stone and smacking it uneventfully with a hammer. An engineering consultant declared the material "free from all danger" if handled properly. The company's engineers pointed out that due to its greater detonating power, nitroglycerine could actually be safer than black powder, since so much less was needed.

In the end, the efficacy of the nitro overrode concerns for safety. Employed in the summit tunnel, where workers blasted inward from both ends and outward from a central shaft dug down to grade level, it sped the burrowing process. "We are getting up pretty near to 2 ft. per day per face," Crocker reported. "*Nitroglycerine tells*."

Eventually the Central Pacific crossed the Sierras, and the Union Pacific crossed the Rockies. Durant needled Stanford about the more rapid pace of his company's construction. "We send you greeting from the highest summit our line crosses between the Atlantic and Pacific Oceans, 8200 feet above tidewater," Durant telegraphed. "Have commenced laying iron on the down grade westward." Stanford responded calmly. "Though you may approach the union of the two roads faster than ourselves you cannot exceed us in earnestness of desire for that great event," he said. "We cheerfully yield you the palm of superior elevation; 7042 feet has been quite sufficient to satisfy our highest ambition. May your descent be easy and rapid."

In November 1868, Stanford journeyed to Utah to sound out Durant regarding the meeting place of the two roads. The two men sidled around the subject, with neither wishing to suggest a junction that might yield ground or profits to the other. "I did not try to do anything with Durant, nor he with me," Stanford informed Hopkins. "We had general talk in the main." Durant preferred the Union Pacific's chances in the field, betting that his crews could grade, lay, and spike faster than those of Stanford's Central. Stanford accepted the challenge. "We parted with the understanding expressed by me in so many words that we had done nothing to commit our respective companies to anything," he said. "To which he assented."

The final race was on. Grading crews of the two companies pushed far ahead of the layers; north of the Great Salt Lake they built competing roadbeds that paralleled and on occasion even crossed each other. (Subsequent stories of violence and sabotage between the Chinese crews of the Central Pacific and the Irish of the Union Pacific were exaggerated, and elided the fact that much of the work for both companies in Utah was done by the Mormons.) As both sides realized, the race would be to the fast, not the fastidious. "Run up and down on the maximum grade instead of making deep cut & fills," Huntington advised Crocker, "and when you can make any time in the construction by using wood instead of stone for culverts &c., use wood, and if we should have now and then a piece of road washed out for the want of a culvert, we could put one in hereafter." Hopkins concurred, summarizing the main objective: "to build road as *fast* as possible of a character acceptable to the commissioners." This last condition posed little problem. The friendliness of the commissioners, who had to approve the construction in order for the railroads to receive their money and land, had been guaranteed by the adroit application of financial enticement and political pressure. "We *know* the commissioners will readily accept as poor a road as we can wish to offer for acceptance," Hopkins told Huntington.

In the end, after much lobbying by both sides, Congress decreed that the meeting place would be Promontory Summit, on the north shore of the Salt Lake. Though this left the Central short of Ogden, the depot for the Salt Lake Valley, Durant and the Union Pacific agreed to sell Stanford and the Central the intervening sixty miles.

The ceremony of meeting was scheduled for May 8, 1869. Stanford set out from Sacramento in a special train bearing assorted invitees. High drifts of snow still covered the Sierras, but the train passed unhindered. One of the guests, Dr. James Stillman, recorded his wonder at the snowsheds that made the passage possible.

> We are cribbed in by timbers, snow-sheds they call them; but how strong! Every timber is a tree trunk, braced and bolted to withstand the snow-slide that starts in mid-winter from the great heights above, and gathering volume as it descends, sweeps desolation in its path; the air is cold around us; snow is on every hand; it looks down upon us from the cliffs, up to us from the ravines, drips from over head and is frozen into stalactites from the rocky wall along which our road is blasted, midway of the granite mountain.

The snowsheds took the train to the summit tunnel. "We are in pitchy darkness in the heart of the mountain," Stillman wrote. Then light again, then more snowsheds, then a breathtaking view of the most heartbreaking scene in all of California: Donner Lake, with all the chilling memories it conjured.

Along the Truckee River the party almost met disaster. ("We came near driving our last spike," Stillman said.) Work crews on the slope above, unaware of the approach of the special train, let a massive log roll down onto the track. A Sacramento editor, riding on the pilot—or "cowcatcher"—in front of the engine for a better view, dove off for his life. The train plowed the log aside, yet sustained substantial damage in the collision. At the first opportunity the cars carrying Stanford and the others were transferred to a fresh engine.

The Carson Desert brought memories of harder days. "Several of our party were among the overland emigrants," Stillman recorded, "and they pointed out where, one by one, their animals perished, where they abandoned their wagons, and where their guns—the last article they could afford to part with—were planted, muzzle downward, into the hillocks in the desperate struggle for water and life." To cross the desert at their current pace almost boggled the mind. But speed was welcome and fully appreciated. "It was a country that one could not travel over too fast."

Stanford's train reached Promontory in good time for the laying of the final tie. Yet Durant, coming from the east, was detained by contractors who hadn't been paid, and who thought this an opportune moment to demand what they were owed, for themselves and their workers. They halted Durant's train and told him he couldn't pass till he handed over $200,000. Durant wired for money while one of his assistants wired for troops. Both messages, carried on the lines along the tracks, were intercepted by the rail workers, who wired back that if troops intervened, the ransom would be taken out of the hostages' hides. Moreover, the Union Pacific could expect a strike all along the road, clear to Omaha. The threat was convincing; the troops remained in their barracks, and $50,000 soon reached kidnap headquarters. The kidnappers called this sufficient and released the hostages.

The delay pushed the celebration back two days. (California couldn't wait, and went ahead with the party that had been scheduled for May 8.) As luck would have it, a wagon train hove into view of the Promontory crowd as the final tie was eased into place; the juxtaposition of old and new struck the celebrants as fittingly dramatic. Stanford swung a silver-plated sledge to drive a spike of California gold into a tie of laurel cut from the slope of Mount Tamalpais. Durant did likewise, and the process was repeated with two other spikes: of Nevada silver, and Arizona iron, silver, and gold. Later tales that the two men had missed their marks weren't borne out by contemporary evidence, and anyway were rendered implausible by the fact Stanford and Durant didn't actually have to drive the spikes, which were too soft and precious to be roughly handled, and so were merely tapped into predrilled holes. (The confusion apparently arose from the fact that after the ceremonial spikes and tie were removed, ordinary substitutes were put in their place. Stanford took a full swing at an iron spike and did miss.)

Telegraphers of the two companies had rigged wires to the spikes, so that the hammer taps closed a circuit and sent the welcome news of completion east and west. California exulted (a second time); Chicago cheered; New York and Philadelphia rang the bells, respectively, of Trinity Church and Independence Hall. In Washington, Ulysses Grant, now president, heard the news at the White House.

William Sherman, who had assumed Grant's old position as commanding general of the army, got the signal at the War Department. "I sat yesterday and heard the mythic taps of the telegraphic battery announce the nailing of the last spike in the great Pacific road," he wired Grenville Dodge, in congratulation. Promising to try the railroad soon, Sherman said his next trip west would be rather faster than his first, "when the only way to California was by sail around Cape Horn, taking our ships 196 days."

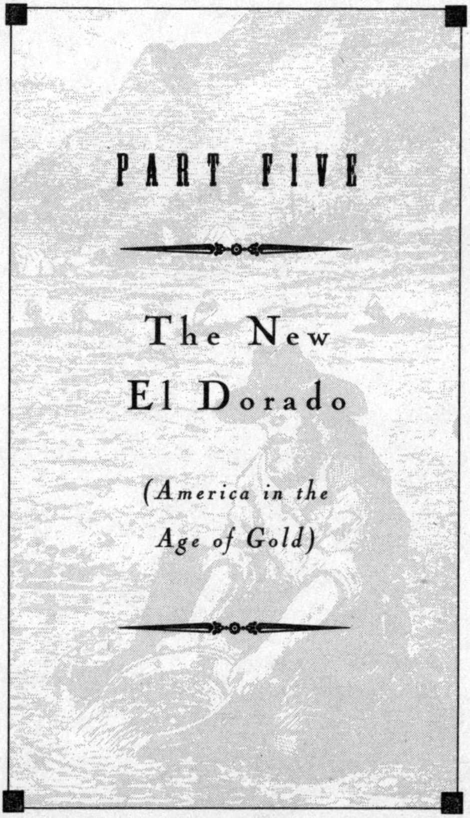

PART FIVE

The New El Dorado

(America in the Age of Gold)

The people who come to California are bold adventurers naturally. We were dissatisfied with life in Europe and the Eastern states, because it was too slow. We came here to enjoy an exciting life and make money rapidly. . . . It is no uncommon thing to see men who have been wealthy on three or four different occasions and then poor again. "A fire," "an unfortunate speculation in merchandise," "a revulsion in real estate," "a crash among the banks," "an unlucky investment in a flume," these are the phrases used every day to explain the fact that this or that man of your familiar acquaintance, though once rich, is now poor. When men fail they do not despair . . . they hope to be rich again.

—John S. Hittell, Forty-Niner and author

One man works hard all his life and ends up a pauper. Another man, no smarter, makes twenty million dollars. Luck has a hell of a lot to do with it.

—Charles Crocker

If the modern era in American history—call it the age of gold—was born at Coloma in 1848, it reached maturity at Promontory in 1869. By then the youthful effervescence of the Gold Rush years—the race from all over the world to California, the frantic assault on the goldfields, the wild times in San Francisco and the mining camps—was fading into memory. The Forty-Niners were growing arthritic; the placermen had long since been muscled aside by the hydraulickers and quartz borers;

many of the camps had closed and fallen into ruin; San Francisco was dully proper compared to the days of the vigilantes and the nights of the wall-to-wall gambling hells. Mining remained the leading industry in California, but ever more it was an *industry* rather than a vehicle for personal hopes and ambitions. Immigrants still flocked to the state, but they did so for the same reasons they flocked to America generally. California, in short, was becoming more like the rest of America.

Yet something else was happening, something of deeper significance: America was becoming more like California. The change commenced the moment the golden news from Coloma reached the East and the visions of the yellow metal littering the ground set imaginations aflame. In that moment a new American dream began to take shape. The old American dream, the dream inherited from ten generations of ancestors, was the dream of the Puritans, of Benjamin Franklin's Poor Richard, of Thomas Jefferson's yeoman farmers: of men and women content to accumulate their modest fortunes a little at a time, year by year by year. The new dream was the dream of instant wealth, won in a twinkling by audacity and good luck. This new dream—the dream of El Dorado—wasn't without precedent in American history. The gentleman-adventurers of the Virginia Company had hoped to strike gold on the James River in the seventeenth century, just as the conquistadors of Spain had struck gold in Mexico and Peru in the sixteenth century. But when no gold appeared in the rivers that ran to the Atlantic, the Virginians and other American colonists adopted a different pattern, more pedestrian and better suited to the virtues of sobriety, thrift, and steady toil that facilitated success in an agricultural society and formed the archetype of the original American character.

The golden dream resurfaced and became a prominent part of the American psyche only after Coloma. James Marshall's discovery electrified the country (and the world), holding forth the promise that wealth could be obtained overnight, that boldness and luck were at least as important as steadiness and frugality—that El Dorado, not some Puritan city on a hill, was the proper abode of the American people.

Under the Puritan aegis of the old American dream, material success required unflagging effort and constant virtue, while failure connoted weakness of will or defect of soul. The California experience provided a persuasive riposte to this received version. Success in the goldfields could come overnight, and signified not virtue but luck. John Frémont was no more virtuous than a thousand other argonauts, but he became a thousand times richer.

Where life was a gamble and success a matter of stumbling on the right stretch of streambed, old standards of risk and reward didn't apply. In the goldfields a person was expected to gamble, and to fail, and to gamble again and again, till success finally came—success likely followed by additional failure, and additional gambling—or energy ran out. Where failure was so common, it lost its stigma. No one in California counted the failures, only the rich strikes that rewarded the tenth or hundredth try. The entrepreneurial spirit had never been absent in American history; every immigrant to America was an entrepreneur of sorts. But in the goldfields the entrepreneurial spirit took flight, freed from the inherited fetters of guilt and blame. And once a-wing in the West—the region to which America had always looked for its future—the spirit soared over all the country.

The no-fault ethos of the new era was hardly an unmitigated blessing. The age of gold was also the age of speculation, corruption, and consolidation on a scale unimaginable before Coloma. Traders in mining shares, in rail stocks, in gold itself colluded to drive prices up or down, and frequently purchased the cooperation of journalists and government officials to abet their schemes. Industrial magnates forged monopolies to extend their power, creating corporate behemoths that intimidated the public and acted as a law unto themselves.

Yet for all its sordid side, the new American dream was an enormously creative force. It unleashed the energies of the American people, and of the many millions of foreigners who, drawn by this compelling dream, chose to become Americans. (It also unleashed the energies of those who stayed in other countries—or in some important cases, returned to other countries from America—and emulated the argonauts of California.) It raised the American standard of living beyond anything ever achieved so broadly. It afforded the most basic freedom—freedom from want—to more people than had ever enjoyed such release. And it gave unprecedented meaning to that really revolutionary idea of Thomas Jefferson: that humans have a right to the pursuit of happiness.

17

Prometheus Unbound

As the construction crews of the transcontinental railroad raced toward their Utah meeting, Jessie and John Frémont traveled to St. Louis for the unveiling of a statue of Thomas Benton. Jessie's father had died some years earlier, still at odds with many Missourians regarding slavery, but now that the Civil War was over his former constituents recalled the unifying aspects of his legacy. "There were more than forty thousand people in the park, hundreds of public school children, both boys and girls, dressed in white and carrying bunches of red roses, father's favorite flower," Jessie told a friend after the ceremony. Speaker after speaker recounted the accomplishments of the distinguished senator. Yet one accomplishment stood out, in Jessie's mind and in the minds of those who commissioned the monument. "Though the sun shone bright, I looked through a mist of tears at the bronze image of my father facing westward with the words carved below: 'There is the East. There lies the road to India.' "

At the golden-spike ceremony, one of the speakers recited Benton's prophecy that California was the way to India. Listening, Leland Stanford certainly hoped it was true. Stanford and his associates intended for their railroad to corner the traffic between the American East and the Asian East, which heretofore had traveled around Cape Horn or the Cape of Good Hope. But they were disappointed, for as important as the Pacific railroad was in the history of transportation, it shared top billing that year with the Suez Canal. The French-sponsored Egyptian canal shortened the water route to the Far East by thousands of miles, undercutting the railroad men. "We were very much disappointed with regard to the business with Asia," Stanford said. "We were very busy building our road, and we had not taken much account of what was going on in the matter of the construction of the Suez Canal. I think the whole country anticipated that when this road was built there would be a great business with Asia, but the opening of the Suez Canal during the very season that we completed our road disappointed us in that anticipated business."

Yet if the Pacific railroad failed to capture the wealth of Asia, it accomplished something far more wonderful. It afforded continental scope to the productive powers of the American people. At once, of course, the railroad linked the mines of the American West to the markets of the American East. No more would the nation's finances be at the mercy of storms like that which sank the *Central America*; the rail line to California became an artery coursing with financial liquidity, the lifeblood of commerce. And the line to California was merely the start of a larger, more elaborate continental network that carried America into the modern age of industry, an age and an arena in which the United States soon outstripped all other nations. The secret of America's ascent to economic primacy was neither the cleverness of its inventors (England's were as smart) nor the richness of its resources (Russia's were richer). Rather, the secret of America's success was its vast domestic market, the largest single market in the world. The Constitution of 1787, by forbidding interstate tariffs, established the legal framework for the American market; the railroad of 1869, and the lines that followed it, by speeding traffic across the length and breadth of the continent, laid the physical framework. Now manufacturers in any part of the country could build plants big enough to serve every part of the country, confident that their wares could be shipped to the farthest districts swiftly and cheaply. The railroads were equally adept at transporting agricultural produce, allowing the different farming districts to specialize and thereby exploit their comparative advantages—the South for cotton and tobacco, the Midwest for corn and wheat, Texas for cattle, California for fruits and vegetables—and further freeing the industrial regions to concentrate on manufacturing.

The results were little short of miraculous. Between 1869 and the end of the nineteenth century, the American economy grew as no economy had ever done before and very few did after. From a laggard in the race to industrialize, trailing Britain, Germany, and France, the United States became the leader of the pack, with a manufacturing output that, by 1900, surpassed the three European powers combined. Iron and steel production multiplied ten times between the commencement of construction of the Pacific railroad and the beginning of the twentieth century. The production of oil—whose discovery in western Pennsylvania in 1859 sparked a rush remarkably akin to the rush for California gold—multiplied more than twenty times during the same period. Agricultural output boomed as well. Cotton and wheat doubled in the two decades after Promontory, and continued to climb through the end of the century. So bountiful was the harvest, and so tremendous the production of America's shops and factories, that although the country's population doubled between 1870 and 1900—which fact itself attested to the power of the American economy, in providing the jobs that attracted the tens of millions of immigrants—American producers fed, clothed, and housed all the new people (fed, housed, and clothed them better, on average, than Americans had ever been supplied before) and dramatically increased American exports besides. The growth wasn't uniform over time: wrenching recessions in the 1870s and 1890s briefly set the economy back. But in each case the hiccup gave way to renewed growth, and the engine of national prosperity roared again to life, hurling the nation ahead faster than before.

WITH THE UNPRECEDENTED economic growth came an unprecedented concentration of economic power. Leland Stanford was hardly the master monopolist of the age—John D. Rockefeller held that dubious distinction—but Stanford's Central Pacific was sufficiently powerful to inspire fear in its competitors and loathing in many of its customers.

After its rocky start—that is, after Congress amended the original railroad law—the Central Pacific became a money machine. The federal, state, and county subsidies of lands and loans, besides underwriting construction, encouraged investors regarding the future of the Central and made the share holdings of Stanford and his partners almost as good as gold. Stanford and the others also benefited directly from the construction of the railroad, having formed a second, closely held corporation, Crocker & Company—subsequently called the Contract and Finance Company—to serve as general contractor. The Central Pacific paid the Contract and Finance Company to build the railroad, funneling profits to Stanford and his associates long before the Central itself began to pay. (In sending Jane some stock certificates of the Contract and Finance Company, Stanford confided, "These shares of stock are very valuable.")

The cozy relationship between the Central and the Contract and Finance Company raised questions among Stanford's critics, a group that grew as the power of the Central Pacific increased. The questions were nowhere near as pointed as those directed at the Union Pacific and its counterpart to the Contract and Finance Company, an entity called the Crédit Mobilier, which became the subject of journalistic exposés, the focus of congressional inquiries, and a watchword for collusion between private corporations and public officials; but the questions did require Stanford to respond. His answers were characteristically unemotional and, for that reason, often effective. During one difficult election in California, a hostile Sacramento paper accused the Central Pacific of interfering in politics; more in sorrow than in anger Stanford denied the accusation. "It is the well settled policy of the company to keep the railroad out of politics," he explained. He went on to say that the railroad had friends enough among fair-minded persons to guarantee fair treatment by government; any effort to ask more would rightly risk a backlash. "The Pacific Railroad [that is, the Central Pacific] seeks to be on good terms with every one. There is no interest in the State whose prosperity can by any possibility be prejudicial to the Pacific Railroad."

On another occasion a reporter queried Stanford regarding his political role, a role that was commonly judged to be uncommonly large. "You have been accredited with controlling state politics and with being deeply interested in political affairs," the reporter said. Did the governor—the title by which Stanford still enjoyed being addressed—care to respond?

Stanford disavowed not only the influence ascribed to him but also any compelling interest in politics. "I suppose you will scarcely credit me when I answer you that I know but little of political matters and that I care less. I am so absorbed in railroad concerns and so entirely employed in business affairs that the details of politics do not interest me, and if they did I have no time to devote to them." Questioned further, Stanford explained that popular perceptions lagged present reality. "When our enterprise was a new one, we had many things to ask and many favors to solicit. We had to demand necessary legislation in order to protect ourselves and carry out our undertaking; we felt the necessity of at least not having our enemies in power to obstruct us by unfriendly laws. This necessity no longer exists, and we now only desire just legislation; we only demand our legal rights, and we do not doubt that they will be accorded to us by any party that shall succeed to power in this state."

This interview took place on California Street in San Francisco, just down the hill from where builders were constructing a magnificent new mansion for the Stanford family. Gesturing toward the unfinished structure, Stanford told the reporter:

> You may assure the readers of the *Chronicle* that I have more important matters on my mind than politics. I have an ambition in altogether a different direction. I know the distrust there is abroad in the community against myself and the management of this great railroad enterprise; but I shall outlive it and all the jealousy such misunderstanding has inspired. I shall hope to live to sit upon yonder balcony and look down upon a city embracing in itself and its suburbs a million of people. I shall see trains of cars laden with merchandise and passengers coming from the East along the present Transcontinental Railroad. I shall see long trains from the line of the 32nd parallel. I shall see cars from the city of Mexico, and trains laden with the gold and silver bullion and grain that comes from Sonora and Chihuahua on the south, and from Washington

> Territory and Oregon on the north. I shall see railroads bearing to and fro the produce and merchandise of each extreme. I shall look out through the Golden Gate and I shall see there fleets of ocean steamers bearing the trade of India, the commerce of Asia, the traffic of the islands of the ocean—steamers from Australia and the southern Pacific. I shall see our thronged and busy streets, our wharves laden with the commerce of the Orient, and I shall say to myself, "I have aided to bring this prosperity and this wealth to the state of my adoption and to the city in which I have chosen my home."

It was an entrancing vision, and one that promised to multiply Stanford's fortune still further, for all those trains and ships would operate under the unified control of Stanford and his associates. From the time Stanford had crossed the Sierras to warn Nevada against encouraging competitors of the Central Pacific, he and the other Central directors had bent every effort of wit, guile, and influence to preserve their monopoly. In 1865 a group of investors in San Francisco incorporated themselves as the Southern Pacific Railroad Company and announced plans to build a line from San Francisco to San Diego. Before long the new company's larger aim appeared: to build east from San Diego and connect with a line coming west from Missouri. In 1866 this project won the approval of Congress, on terms akin to those offered to the Central and Union Pacific railroads.

Stanford immediately understood the threat. As he admitted to a congressional committee afterward, he viewed the new line as "a dangerous rival," one that would compete with the Central Pacific not only in California but across the country. "It was of paramount importance," he added, "that the road should be controlled by the friends of the Central Pacific." Here Stanford was skimping on the truth. The Southern Pacific was shortly snapped up not by friends of the Central Pacific, but by the Central itself, with Stanford et al firmly in charge. "*We must name those directors, and they must be ours and no one's else,*" Stanford insisted to Edwin Crocker, regarding a crucial election to the Southern Pacific board. "There is too much at stake to do otherwise." Stanford and his associates got their directors, and got control of the Southern Pacific. For popular consumption, however, a certain separation between the two lines was allowed to appear to continue, and, when convenient—as in deflecting charges of monopoly—Stanford and his associates spoke of the Central Pacific and the Southern Pacific as distinct entities.

Their monopoly involved more than rail travel. Even after completion of the transcontinental lines (the Southern Pacific linked up with the Santa Fe in 1881 and with the Texas Pacific in 1882), passengers and freight traversing the continent still had the alternative of steamship travel via Central America or Cape Horn. To neutralize this competition, the Central Pacific group organized a steamship line, the Occidental and Oriental Steamship Company. The purpose was not so much to displace the dominant line—the Pacific Mail Steamship Company—as to intimidate it and force it to come to terms favorable to the railroad. Indeed, the Central Pacific ships weren't even sailing before the Pacific Mail struck its flag and sued for peace. The treaty included a provision whereby the Central Pacific set prices on freight carried by the Pacific Mail between New York and San Francisco. The prices, as they were established in practice, allowed the Pacific Mail to continue to exist, but not to threaten the Central's transcontinental traffic.

Meanwhile, Stanford and his partners moved to consolidate their hold on traffic within California. Purchase of the Southern Pacific gave them control of nearly all significant land transport, but river steamers—serving Sacramento and Stockton from San Francisco, most notably—afforded shippers an aquatic alternative. This dried up when the Central purchased the California Steam Navigation Company. A few wildcat shippers remained on the Sacramento and San Joaquin Rivers, but they were no more than a nuisance to the great railroad.

By the 1880s the web of transport Stanford had envisioned was securely in place, and securely in the grip of Stanford and his partners. They set rates as they chose, unimpeded by any concerns of competition, of which there was none, and constrained only by a cool assessment of what the traffic would bear. One instance summarized the line's approach. A new mine in Shasta County began to ship gold ore. The Central Pacific initially charged $50 per carload from Redding to San Francisco. But when the mine thrived, the rate was raised to $73 per car, and then to $95. The mine owner traveled to San Francisco, to the headquarters of the railroad at Fourth and Townsend streets. Why the near-doubling of rates? he demanded. The official in charge of rates on that part of the road replied blandly, "You are sending down ore that would make a prince rich. We can't pull high-grade ore on low-grade rates." The miner declared that the value of the ore had nothing to do with the matter; tonnage was all that should count. Unmoved, the Central official nonetheless offered a compromise. If the miner would submit his account books to the railroad for scrutiny, the road would determine what he could afford to pay, and charge accordingly. The miner rejected the proposal out of hand; years later he was still livid. "For cheek as a business proposition," he said, "I think this stands preeminent."

But behind the cheek was raw power. The Central-Southern combination held the economy of California hostage. At a time when railroads throughout America inspired outrage in farmers and other shippers forced to pay their monopoly tariffs, the California colossus occupied a category all its own. Frank Norris devoted an entire novel to the malign influence of *The Octopus*; a scene from that novel—one of the most striking scenes from the entire genre of American naturalist fiction—summarized the sentiments of those within the monster's grip. In Norris's story, night had fallen over California's Central Valley; Presley, a young poet come west in search of his muse, was soaking up the silence and the peace. Suddenly an apocalyptic presence split the night.

> He had only time to jump back upon the embankment when, with a quivering of all the earth, a locomotive, single, unattached, shot by him with a roar, filling the air with the reek of hot oil, vomiting smoke and sparks; its enormous eye, cyclopean, red, throwing a glare far in advance, shooting by in a sudden crash of confused thunder; filling the night with the terrific clamour of its iron hoofs.

The locomotive raced on, its roar diminishing with distance until, as it entered a declivity in the roadbed, the sound ceased entirely.

But the moment the noise of the engine lapsed, Presley heard another sound: a confusion of heartrending pain. He hurried along the track to investigate, then drew up in shock at what the starlight revealed.

> In some way, the herd of sheep—Vanamee's herd—had found a breach in the wire fence by the right of way and had wandered out upon the tracks. A band had been crossing just at the moment of the engine's passage. The pathos of it was beyond expression. It was a slaughter, a massacre of innocents. The iron monster had charged full into the midst, merciless, inexorable. To the right and left, all the width of the right of way, the little bodies had been flung; backs were snapped against the fence posts; brains knocked out. Caught in the barbs of the wire, wedged in, the bodies hung suspended. Under foot it was terrible. The black blood, winking in the starlight, seeped down into the clinkers between the ties with a prolonged sucking murmur.
>
> Presley turned away, horror-struck, sick at heart, overwhelmed with a quick burst of irresistible compassion for this brute agony he could not relieve. The sweetness was gone from the evening, the sense of peace, of security, and placid contentment was stricken from the landscape. . . .
>
> He hurried on across the Los Muertos ranch, almost running, even putting his hands over his ears till he was out of hearing distance of that all but human distress. Not until he was beyond earshot did he pause, looking back, listening. The night had shut down again. For a moment the silence was profound, unbroken.
>
> Then, faint and prolonged, across the levels of the ranch, he heard the engine whistling for Bonneville. Again and again, at rapid intervals in its flying course, it whistled for road crossings, for sharp curves, for trestles; ominous notes, hoarse, bellowing, ringing with the accents of menace and defiance; and abruptly Presley

saw again, in his imagination, the galloping monster, the terror of steel and steam, with its single eye, cyclopean, red, shooting from horizon to horizon; but saw it now as the symbol of a vast power, huge, terrible, flinging the echo of its thunder over all the reaches of the valley, leaving blood and destruction in its path; the leviathan, with tentacles of steel clutching into the soil, the soulless Force, the iron-hearted Power, the monster, the Colossus, the Octopus.

POWER COULD BE physical in the age of gold; more often it was metaphysical. The metaphysics of gold—the dream of instant wealth—had, in the first instance, caused a quarter million people from all over the planet to abandon their ordinary pursuits and hurry to California, where they scratched and burrowed in the ground in a manner that must have been utterly inexplicable to any observer somehow unfamiliar with the priority humans place on the malleable yellow metal they retrieved from the diggings. Yet the metaphysics of gold extended far beyond those argonauts, to persons and classes who never thought of leaving their comfortable homes and offices, who shuddered at the very idea of the hardships the gold diggers endured.

Jay Gould was the master metaphysician of his day. There were those who suspected that his name had once been "Gold," so cleverly did he manipulate the magic metal in the minds of his contemporaries. (Others reached the same conclusion from a different direction: that no one not named "Gold" or something similarly Jewish could display such a grasp of money.) As a young man, Gould had done some surveying work, but that was as close to a gold mine as he ever got. Yet for a moment in the autumn of 1869, he came within a whisker (of which he had an abundance, grown to conceal his mere thirty-three years) of controlling the gold supply of America, including a large part of what all those argonauts and their corporate successors had been digging out of the ground since 1848.

Gould's partner in conspiracy was James Fisk. "Jubilee Jim" (also known as the "Barnum of Wall Street") had joined Gould in a fight with

Cornelius Vanderbilt for control of the Erie Railroad; having sunk the Commodore, the two now took on the world. Their plan hinged on the historical and psychological fact that while the supply of gold at any given time was limited, the desire of humans for gold was essentially unlimited. Indeed, the desire was so great as to amount to a need: without gold, businesses would fail, governments would fall, men and women and children would be thrown hungry into the streets. In 1869 the need for gold was even greater than usual. Despite the flood of gold and silver from the West during the Civil War (and despite the arrest of Asbury Harpending), the federal government had been compelled to resort to paper money to cover the cost of defeating the rebellion. A dual money supply developed, consisting of paper for domestic commerce and gold for international trade. (American legal tender laws, which mandated acceptance of the greenbacks at home, didn't apply overseas.) In turn a market developed where gold and greenbacks were traded, one for the other.

Gould and Fisk intended to corner the gold market—that is, to gain sufficient control of the gold supply to set its price where they chose. Commodities—cotton, tobacco, pork bellies—had occasionally been cornered before; likewise certain stock issues (including Erie shares, by which Gould and Fisk had defeated Vanderbilt). But to corner gold—the basis for the nation's money supply, the *über* commodity that controlled all else—had never been attempted, perhaps never even contemplated. The sheer audacity of the scheme was what made Gould think it might work.

Gould's plot would unfold in the Gold Room, located near the main stock exchange on Wall Street. Only lately opened, the Gold Room already had a reputation and a distinctive ambience. One regular described it as "a cavern full of dank and noisome vapors" where "the deadly carbonic acid was blended with the fumes of stale smoke and vinous breaths." A journalist employed another metaphor: "Imagine a rat-pit in full blast, with twenty or thirty men ranged around the rat tragedy, each with a canine under his arm, yelling and howling at once." At the center of the room, where the rats would have been, was a marble Cupid spouting water. "The artistic conception is not appropriate," the newsman continued, switching his own metaphor. "Instead of a Cupid throwing a pearly fountain into the air, there should have been a hungry Midas turning everything to gold and starving from sheer inability to eat."

Gould didn't frequent the Gold Room, leaving that to Fisk, whose boyish delight in display and tumult was as great as Gould's aversion to them. Gould also employed a small army of brokers, each kept ignorant of the activities of the others, to buy up gold in many modest lots. By the time the world caught on that a single intelligence was coordinating the purchases and controlled the gold thus acquired, Gould would have accomplished the corner.

Such was the plan, which to Gould's thinking had but one weakness: the largest stock of gold in the country rested in the vaults of the United States Treasury. Ordinarily this gold was kept off the market, as a reserve for the nation's currency and to meet the government's own needs. If it remained off the market, all would be well—for Gould. But if the government determined to intervene, by dumping its gold on the market, it could break any corner, no matter how cleverly conceived, concealed, and executed.

Gould took precautions to keep the government out of the market. He cut President Grant's brother-in-law in on the scheme, paid the assistant federal treasurer in New York to forward information about the intentions of his department, and lobbied Grant himself about the importance of letting gold find its own level, without government intervention.

The gradual rise in price that accompanied the brokers' buying piqued the appetite of gold bears, who didn't know why the price was rising and who now wagered on its fall. Selling short, they did their best—through rumor, intimidation, and all the other techniques of the speculative art—to bring the price down. When they failed, and their financial lives began to pass before their eyes, their wailing and gnashing of teeth filled the Gold Room. Gould, in his office at the Opera House (a setting that suited partner Fisk far better than Gould), smiled behind his beard and unconsciously tore paper into tiny pieces, as he did whenever a complex operation was afoot.

Like a mountain that grows steeper near the summit, this operation grew more treacherous the closer it came to success. Each tick upward of the brass indicator in the center of the Gold Room signaled—to Gould, though not to the hundreds who watched it climb—that he was that much nearer to achieving his coup; but each tick also signaled that the remaining gold would be that much more expensive. And each tick tolled the doom of more of the bears, who clawed desperately to maintain their grip on the steepening slope.

Discretion—common sense, even—counseled a low profile for the purchasers. But Fisk didn't know the meaning of discretion (and probably couldn't spell it either), and he insisted on taking center stage. He waded into the Gold Room, flashing diamonds from his fingers, cuffs, and shirtfront, blowing smoke from his fat cigar, and demanding all the gold anyone would sell, at almost any price they'd sell it. The bears were in agony, and Fisk in his element. "As the roar of battle and the scream of the victims resounded through the New Street," a reporter declared, "it seemed as though human nature were undergoing torments worse than any Dante ever witnessed in hell."

And then, with victory in sight, Gould received the report he had been dreading. Grant's brother-in-law had lost his nerve and was demanding to get out, which told Gould that the government was about to enter the market. Coolly double-crossing Fisk, whom he left to continue to buy, Gould silently began selling. Fisk came back to the Opera House at the close of trading on September 23, more boastful and ebullient than ever, convinced that the corner was at hand, with all the wealth and power control of the gold supply would entail. Gould knew better but kept quiet, the deepening pile of shredded paper about his desk being the only sign of the delicacy of his position.

The next day—September 24, 1869—was the most turbulent in the history of Wall Street till then, and perhaps the most turbulent ever. All morning the price of gold continued to mount; all morning the remaining bears howled in agony. Amid the carnage, Fisk bellowed to buy, gloating in the bears' pain and counting his monopoly profits. But shortly after noon, the telegraph from Washington brought word that the Treasury would sell gold. At once the price collapsed, flabbergasting Fisk and the bulls, and resurrecting those bears that retained a spark of life.

Now it was the bulls that wanted blood—the blood of Fisk and Gould. The two barricaded themselves in the Opera House, shielded by thugs kept in reserve for precisely such emergencies. And it was wise they did, for those who had been betting on gold were now bent on mayhem. One observer asserted that if the conspirators had been caught in public, "the chances were that the lamp-post near by would have very soon been decorated with a breathless body."

The derangement of the gold market spilled over into the broader stock market as banks and brokerages collapsed under the weight of their gold losses; the entire fiasco earned the name "Black Friday" and became a symbol of the corrupt speculation that characterized the new age. Gould survived to speculate anew, albeit never in such spectacular fashion. Fisk, who astonishingly held no grudge against Gould—"It was each man drag out his own corpse," he explained—lived to die at the pistol of a rival in love.

SAM CLEMENS KNEW all about the sordid quest for wealth in the age of gold (although he preferred the label "Gilded Age," a title better suited to his, and coauthor Charles Dudley Warner's, satirical purposes in their novel by that name), for he had caught the fever in Virginia City. George Hearst's Ophir proved but the first of a chain of mines that exploited the Comstock Lode and made their owners fabulously wealthy. The heart of the Comstock was an ore body known as the Big Bonanza. Where the quartz veins of California's Mother Lode measured a few feet wide to perhaps a score, the Big Bonanza was hundreds of feet wide to more than a thousand. And it was rich almost beyond belief, paying up to $10,000 per ton. With thirteen cubic feet of ore to the ton, a cubic yard of ore could fetch $20,000. To be sure, the average yield was lower, but even at a mere hundreds of dollars per yard it made men giddy to think about it.

Yet there was one problem: the great majority of the wealth of the Comstock rested far beneath the surface of the earth. In California, erosion had laid bare large swaths of the ore bodies, washing them down into the valleys for James Marshall and his successors to find. The winds off the Pacific, however, contained only so much moisture, and each gallon that fell as rain or snow on the Sierras was a gallon less for the lands to the east, in the Sierras' rain shadow. The work that nature had done in California, in removing much of the overlying rock and hydraulically sifting the heavy metal from the light sand and gravel, remained for humans to do on the Comstock.

Although the miners on the Comstock applied lessons learned in the quartz mines of California, they soon discovered that the deep ore bodies of Nevada required greater ingenuity and more sophisticated technology than California had ever seen. The miners followed the ore leads down more than two thousand feet into the bowels of Mount Davidson (as Sun Peak was rechristened, in honor of the San Francisco agent of the British House of Rothschild, which invested heavily in the region). There they encountered pressures and strains unlike anything in California. The heat of the rocks at such depth—heat generated by radioactive processes unknown to that generation of geologists, but which the miners were willing to ascribe to the fires of hell—was almost unendurable. "At the depth of from 1,500 to 2,000 feet the rock is so hot that it is painful to the naked hand," reported Dan De Quille of the Virginia City *Territorial Enterprise*. (De Quille's real name was William Wright, but in the West he adopted the fancier nom de plume—at about the same time that Sam Clemens, a friend and colleague on the *Territorial Enterprise*, became Mark Twain.) "In many places," De Quille continued, "from crevices in the rock or from holes drilled into it, streams of boiling water gush out." Men couldn't have survived the heat, let alone worked in it, without a constant supply of cool air forced into the mines by steam-driven blowers. But here "cool" was a relative term; even with the blowers ramming mountain air down the shafts, temperatures at the ore faces could be as high as 130 degrees Fahrenheit.

Needless to say, the equipment required to dig and ventilate these deep mines, and to hoist the ore a vertical quarter-mile to the surface, was hugely expensive. Yet from the start, capital was never lacking. The Comstock benefited not only technologically but financially from California's prior experience. As soon as the initial assays revealed the richness of the Comstock mines—Hearst's secret quickly leaked out—money began pouring into Nevada. Some of the money—Hearst's, for example—consisted of profits from the California mines. A larger portion came from the financial markets of the American East and Europe. Investors slavered over the stories out of Washoe, and they slathered their capital on this newest bonanza. The early rush to California had required profit-seekers to participate directly; the rush to Nevada allowed them to keep a genteel distance, their participation measured not by miles traversed over ocean or isthmus or plains, and by months in the streams or the dry diggings, but by dollars wired from banks in New York or London to banks in San Francisco, and then forwarded to Virginia City.

The primacy of capital on the Comstock might have prevented ordinary folks from cashing in on this new rush, but such was the ingenuity of the miners' moneymen, and such the human capacity for covetous self-delusion, that individuals of the humblest station managed to cut themselves in. Clemens, observing the phenomenon from the city desk of the *Territorial Enterprise*, explained:

> The city and all the great mountain side were riddled with mining shafts. There were more mines than miners. True, not ten of these mines were yielding rock worth hauling to a mill, but everybody said, "Wait till the shaft gets down where the ledge comes in solid, and then you will see!" So nobody was discouraged. These were nearly all "wild cat" mines, and wholly worthless, but nobody believed it then. The "Ophir," the "Gould Curry," the "Mexican," and other great mines on the Comstock lead in Virginia and Gold Hill were turning out huge piles of rich rock every day, and every man believed that his little wild cat claim was as good as any on the "main lead" and would infallibly be worth a thousand dollars a foot when he "got down where it came in solid." Poor fellow, he was blessedly blind to the fact that he never would see that day.
>
> So the thousand wild cat shafts burrowed deeper and deeper into the earth day by day, and all men were beside themselves with hope and happiness. How they labored, prophesied, exulted!

> Surely nothing like it was ever seen before since the world began. Every one of these wild cat mines—not mines, but holes in the ground over imaginary mines—was incorporated and had handsomely engraved "stock" and the stock was salable, too. It was bought and sold with a feverish avidity in the boards every day. You could go up on the mountain side, scratch around and find a ledge (there was no lack of them), put up a "notice" with a grandiloquent name in it, start a shaft, get your stock printed, and with nothing whatever to prove that your mine was worth a straw, you could put your stock on the market and sell out for hundreds and even thousands of dollars. To make money, and make it fast, was as easy as it was to eat your dinner.

Clemens acquired a stake in the Washoe boom by virtue of his access to print. "New claims were taken up daily," he recalled, "and it was the friendly custom to run straight to the newspaper offices, give the reporter forty or fifty 'feet,' and get them to go and examine the mine and publish a notice of it." *What* the reporter wrote mattered less than the mere fact of writing.

> We generally said a word or two to the effect that the "indications" were good, or that the ledge was "six feet wide," or that the rock "resembled the Comstock" (and so it did—but as a general thing the resemblance was not startling enough to knock you down). If the rock was moderately promising, we followed the custom of the country, used strong adjectives and frothed at the mouth as if a very marvel in silver discoveries had transpired. If the mine was a "developed" one, and had no pay ore to show (and of course it hadn't), we praised the tunnel; said it was one of the most infatuating tunnels in the land; driveled and driveled about the tunnel till we ran entirely out of ecstasies—but never said a word about the rock. We would squander half a column of adulation on a shaft, or a new wire rope, or a dressed pine windlass, or a fascinat-

> ing force pump, and close with a burst of admiration of the "gentlemanly and efficient Superintendent" of the mine—but never utter a whisper about the rock.

The reporter's recompense was a tidy supplement to his salary. "We received presents of 'feet' every day. If we needed a hundred dollars or so, we sold some; if not, we hoarded it away, satisfied that it would ultimately be worth a thousand dollars a foot. I had a trunk about half full of 'stock.' When a claim made a stir in the market and went up to a high figure, I searched through my pile to see if I had any of its stock—and generally found it."

Like others on the Comstock, Clemens grew accustomed to his sudden wealth. "I enjoyed what to me was an entirely new phase of existence—a butterfly idleness; nothing to do, nobody to be responsible to, and untroubled with financial uneasiness." He traveled to San Francisco and fell in love with the city. "After the sage-brush and alkali deserts of Washoe, San Francisco was Paradise to me. I lived at the best hotel, exhibited my clothes in the most conspicuous places, infested the opera, and learned to seem enraptured with music which oftener afflicted my ignorant ear than enchanted it, if I had had the vulgar honesty to confess it. . . . I had longed to be a butterfly, and I was one at last. I attended private parties in sumptuous evening dress, simpered and aired my graces like a born beau, and polked and schottisched with a step peculiar to myself—and the kangaroo." In a word, he lived like the king he felt he was about to become. "I kept the due state of a man worth a hundred thousand dollars (prospectively) and likely to reach absolute affluence when that silver-mine sale should be ultimately achieved in the East."

The demand for Comstock shares grew dizzily, then alarmingly. "Stocks went on rising; speculation went mad; bankers, merchants, lawyers, doctors, mechanics, laborers, even the very washerwomen and servant girls, were putting up their earnings on silver stocks, and every sun that rose in the morning went down on paupers enriched and rich men beggared. What a gambling carnival it was! Gould and Curry soared to six thousand three hundred dollars a foot!"

And then . . . "And then—all of a sudden, out went the bottom and everything and everybody went to ruin and destruction! The wreck was complete. The bubble scarcely left a microscopic moisture behind it. I was an early beggar and a thorough one. My hoarded stocks were not worth the paper they were printed on. I threw them all away. I, the cheerful idiot that had been squandering money like water, and thought myself beyond the reach of misfortune, had not now as much as fifty dollars when I gathered together my various debts and paid them."

Clemens's loss was literature's gain. Forced to earn his daily bread once more, he turned to mining in the Mother Lode country. He found little gold, but gathered impressions and experiences. He met Bret Harte, and guessed that if Harte could make money from stories about the gold country, so could he. He proved himself right with a tale about a jumping-frog contest in Calaveras County, which won him a wide and enthusiastic national readership.

THE AGE OF GOLD wasn't confined to America—indeed, had it been so confined, it wouldn't have been much of an age. California taught the world what gold mines looked like, and what they could do for a country.

Edward Hargraves, Tom Archer's shipmate from Sydney, was an apt pupil, which was surprising in that he was an inept miner. Hargraves nearly froze during his first winter in the California goldfields. "Frequently we had to clear the snow from the surface, and break the ice in order to get water to wash the gold with," he wrote. "But our sufferings at night were far more severe. It was scarcely possible to sleep from the intensity of the cold, and often we had to get up at night to shake the snow off the tent, for fear of its breaking through. For my own part I made a bag of my blankets and rug, and slept in that; but even that was insufficient to keep warmth in my body." Nor were the pickings sufficiently rich to pay Hargraves for his suffering. Try as they might, he and his partners couldn't manage to collect more than six dollars in dust a day. "Poor pay indeed for men who had traveled so many thousand miles with the hope of making a rapid fortune!"

Yet amid his troubles, something was occurring to Hargraves. "Far more important thoughts than those of present success or failure were, from the very first, growing up in my mind, and gradually assuming a body and a shape. My attention was naturally drawn to the form and geological structure of the surrounding country, and it soon struck me that I had, some eighteen years before, travelled through a country very similar to one I was now in, in New South Wales. I said to myself, there are the same class of rocks, slates, quartz, granite, red soil, and everything else that appears necessary to constitute a goldfield." Hargraves gradually grew convinced that there must be gold in Australia.

He shared his thoughts with some fellow Aussies. Many laughed; others explained why he had to be wrong, starting with the fact that men far better educated in geology than he was had traveled the outback regions he spoke of and never found gold. Yet Hargraves guessed that geological education was no substitute for practical experience of mining. "It was very possible, nay probable, I thought, that a man deeply read in the science of geology should be ignorant how to wash a pan of earth in search of gold, or where to look for it; just as a great mathematician may be ignorant how to turn an arch, or even lay a brick." Moreover, with no reason to be looking for gold in Australia, geologists would have been especially unlikely to find it.

Hargraves's dream of finding gold down under helped tide him through that difficult winter. (The fact that Australia's goldfields, if any, would certainly be warmer than California's made them all the more enticing.) In the spring of 1850 he wrote a friend in Sydney hinting at an imminent return. "I am very forcibly impressed that I have been in a gold region in New South Wales, within 300 miles of Sydney," he declared. In case this friend got prematurely curious, Hargraves added, "Unless you knew how to find it you might live for a century in the region and know nothing of its existence." Hargraves would have left at once, but he lacked the money. So he worked that summer with a partner on the Yuba River, where they made an average of about two-and-a-half ounces of gold per man per day. "But the greater our success was, the more anxious did I become to put my own persuasion to the test, of the existence of gold in New South Wales." In November he traveled down the Sacramento to San Francisco; exchanging his gold for a ticket back west, he departed for Port Jackson on the bark *Emma*.

In Australia he learned that his views were held in even less regard than in America. "I made known to my friends and companions my confident expectations on the subject; one and all, however, derided me, and treated my views and opinions as those of a madman." Whether mad or not, Hargraves was determined, and he headed off, alone, across the Blue Mountains behind Sydney. At irregular intervals he encountered other humans, including an innkeeper at a lonely crossroads who complained at the lack of business. Hargraves sought to console the fellow by predicting obliquely that soon he would have more business than he wanted. "Of course, he only laughed at me."

Hargraves's fifth day of travel found him near the region of his recollection. The landlady of a local hostel, whose husband he had known years before, offered her son as a guide. Though Hargraves was reluctant to tip his hand, he accepted the offer, not least because the boy seemed utterly guileless, and Hargraves wasn't sure he could find his way unaided to the place he remembered. They set out on the morning of February 12, 1851, under a blazing summer sun. After fifteen miles the terrain began to look reassuringly familiar. "My recollection of it had not deceived me. The resemblance of its formation to that of California could not be doubted or mistaken." Hargraves was hardly able to contain his excitement. "I felt myself surrounded by gold; and with tremulous anxiety panted for the moment of trial, when my magician's wand should transform this trackless wilderness into a region of countless wealth."

While Hargraves panted for gold, his guide and their horses were panting for water. The summer's drought had dried up the creek whose bed they were walking. But the boy said there was water farther along, and Hargraves, knowing he would need water to work his magic, consented to continue till they found it. When they did, the boy assuaged his own thirst and that of the horses while Hargraves prepared the crucial experiment. He employed a pick to knock some gravel and dirt off an outcropping; this he troweled into a pan. He took the pan to the water hole and proceeded to wash it, just as he had washed thousands of pans in California.

The very first trial yielded the telltale flash. "Here it is!" he exclaimed. Hurriedly he washed five more pans of dirt. All but one produced gold.

"This is a memorable day in the history of New South Wales!" he told his guide. "I shall be a baronet, you will be knighted, and my old horse will be stuffed, put into a glass case, and sent to the British Museum!"

Nobility eluded Hargraves and the boy, and the horse escaped taxidermy; but New South Wales experienced everything Hargraves envisioned. Dubbing his find "Ophir," he broadcast the news to the world, and within months a rush to southeastern Australia was under way. The new rush recapitulated the madness experienced on the Pacific's opposite shore. Sydney and Melbourne were drained of their populations before argonauts from overseas arrived (many of them, like Hargraves, Australians returned from California). "Cottages are deserted, houses to let, business is at a stand-still, and even the schools are closed," reported the lieutenant governor of Victoria. As at San Francisco, abandoned ships clogged the harbors; as in the Sierra foothills, towns of two thousand, five thousand, ten thousand souls appeared wherever gold did. The miners of Australia behaved about as the miners of California did. "They are intoxicated with their suddenly-acquired wealth, and run riot in the wildness of their joy," observed an Englishman, John Sherer, who was bent on much the same behavior himself. As in California, the surge of newcomers overwhelmed the aboriginal peoples; as in California, the explosion of wealth made every man the equal—in prospect, at least, and hence in his own mind—of the heretofore most favored. "As riches are now becoming the test of a man's position," remarked Sherer, "it is vain to have any pretensions whatever unless you are supported by that powerful auxiliary."

HARGRAVES'S DISCOVERY IN Australia demonstrated that gold in rush-causing quantities wasn't an American monopoly. California had revealed what gold geology looked like; Australia showed that it could be found in other parts of the world. For centuries before 1848, the search for gold had been a haphazard affair, with lucrative finds so rare as to prevent all but the most desperate or deluded from making a habit of the hunt. But during the second half of the nineteenth century—which was to say, during the first half century of the age of gold—prospectors fanned out across the planet. They found gold (and silver) in Nevada in the late 1850s and 1860s. They found gold along the Fraser River in western Canada during the same period, and along the South Platte near what would become Denver. They found gold in Montana in the 1860s. They found gold (and diamonds) in South Africa in the 1880s and 1890s. They found gold on the Yukon River in Canada and Alaska, and on the beach at Nome, and in western Australia, and in eastern Siberia, during the 1890s.

George Hearst wandered less far, but had hardly less success. The payouts from his (Nevada) Ophir tempted his neighbors, who brought lawsuits regarding the ownership of veins that, while separate at the surface, entwined underground. The litigation was horrendously expensive; one suit involving the Ophir set the litigants back more than a million dollars. (Hearst's head litigator alone received $200,000 per year in fees.) Nor were the lawyers the only ones making money. A story that circulated around Carson City almost certainly embroidered the truth but nonetheless caught the spirit of Nevada justice. In a lawsuit between two mines, according to this tale, a lawyer named Cinc Barnes managed to sell his special expertise—jury-rigging—to one side after the other. He alternately persuaded each party that the fix was in, and that a favorable verdict would follow. He simultaneously leaked the information to stockjobbers, driving up the share price of the one company, then the other, and allowing him to make a killing in each. With some of his loot he paid off the jury, by a fittingly frontier method. The foreman of the jury would lower an empty boot from a window of the room where the jurors were sequestered; Barnes would fill the boot with gold, and attach a note identifying the donor as one party to the suit or the other. The jurors weighed the new evidence, literally, as it came in, until they decided they had enough, when they delivered their verdict. (Precisely how they determined the winner is unclear.)

In time Hearst's Ophir began to play out, prompting him to seek opportunity elsewhere. He dabbled in San Francisco real estate, an occupation that proved mildly profitable—and far more attractive to Hearst's wife, Phoebe, than the rough existence of mining camps—but ultimately unsatisfying to the Boy (now Man) The Earth Talks To. Hearst was never happier than in the field, breaking rocks with his hammer and filling his saddlebags with specimens. One trip took him to the geologically confused region where the Wasatch and Uintah Mountains collide, just southeast of Salt Lake City. A prospector there had grown frustrated trying to develop a claim that had seemed promising at first but now failed to produce. Hearst saw more than the owner did, and bought him out for $30,000. The mine, called the Ontario, yielded mostly silver, and that only with difficulty. Yet Hearst was a master of difficult rock, and although developing the property nearly drained him—he spent a million dollars before making a nickel—in time the Ontario returned $75,000 per month.

Another man—one less confident of his mining acumen, or less addicted to the gamble of mining—might have rested on the stunning success of the Ontario. (Phoebe wished he would, especially as she had no desire to live among the Mormons. Consequently, while George directed the development of the Ontario, she decamped for Europe, where she spent many months enjoying all that George's wealth could purchase in the way of culture for her and education for their ten-year-old son, William Randolph.) But Hearst always had to search farther, to listen to what the earth was telling him.

In the 1870s the earth called him to the Black Hills of Dakota. A reconnaissance expedition under Colonel George Custer had discovered gold in the Black Hills; this set off a rush to the region, which provoked resistance by the Sioux, who considered the Black Hills sacred, and who had been promised the region as part of the settlement William Sherman encouraged by threatening the utter destruction of the Sioux nation. Custer led a contingent against an Indian army headed by Crazy Horse and Sitting Bull; at the Little Bighorn in June 1876, Custer met an annihilating defeat.

Yet the Sioux couldn't keep the miners out of the Black Hills any more than the Yosemite Indians had kept miners out of the Mother Lode; and Hearst joined the rush there. According to family lore, Phoebe was getting terminally tired of his chasing after new discoveries, and particularly of his habit of gambling everything they had on his latest find. "George," she said, while he was packing for Dakota, "if you find a good mine, let's have it as a homestake." "Puss, we will," he agreed. "We'll call it the Homestake mine."

Phoebe was right to worry that the Black Hills would swallow most of Hearst's money, for within months he and a partner had bought some 250 claims, covering an area of 2,600 acres. The ore was very poor by Sierra or Comstock standards, averaging less than four dollars of precious metal per ton. But the veins were hundreds of feet thick, and could be quarried rather than mined. The scale of operations dwarfed anything in California or Nevada; eventually 600 stamps were employed to crush the ore, manned by the workforce of a company town that sprang up to service the Homestake.

The returns were commensurate with the investment. The Homestake turned a profit in 1879; during the next twenty years it yielded $80 million. At the beginning of the twentieth century it was the heaviest producer of gold in the United States, and remained so for several decades. It continued to produce gold until the beginning of the twenty-first century, when it was finally closed.

ALTHOUGH HEARST COULD have been forgiven for forgetting it, especially after the gold of the Homestake made him one of the wealthiest men in America, all that yellow metal wasn't really wealth, but merely a marker for wealth. King Midas knew the difference, but, human nature being what it is, his hard-won insight was often forgotten.

In 1776, the same year that the father of Mariano Vallejo helped Junípero Serra establish the presidio at San Francisco, Scotland's Adam Smith published a book entitled *Inquiry into the Nature and Causes of the Wealth of Nations*. Smith wrote during an era of official amnesia regarding the Midas insight; the conventional wisdom of Smith's day equated national wealth, and the power wealth could purchase, with stockpiles of gold and silver. British imperial policy sought to secure for the mother country as much precious metal as possible, even at the expense of Britain's colonies (*especially* at the expense of Britain's colonies, it seemed to Thomas Jefferson, who penned the other landmark manifesto of that pregnant year: the American Declaration of Independence). Smith contended that this mercantilist thinking was wrong. National wealth, he said, consisted not of gold and silver but of goods and services people could actually use. The wealthiest nation wasn't the one with the fullest coffers, but the one with the most productive people—people busy producing (and consuming) bread and beer and boots and books and bonnets and (the example dearest to Smith's heart) pins. If gold helped a nation become productive—that is, if gold stimulated commerce—then it served a beneficent purpose. If it strangled commerce, it might better be thrown into the sea.

Smith's ideas required time to take hold in Britain. Not till the middle third of the nineteenth century did the British government abandon mercantilism in favor of free trade. (One of those responsible for the conversion was John Bright, the uncle of the frustrated buccaneer who partnered with Asbury Harpending.) Britain's embrace of free trade was an essential element in the ascendancy of its empire during the long Victorian period, a time when the small island attained astonishing sway over a remarkably large patch of the planet. British merchants penetrated nearly every market; British industrialists led the world into the modern era of urban plenty. (Urban poverty existed alongside the plenty, as Charles Dickens and many others noted.)

Yet Britain's new free-trade power rested on gold fully as much as its old mercantilist power had, albeit in a different way. The British hewed to a gold financial standard, largely because in an otherwise uncertain world the solidity and stability of gold offered crucial reassurance to the deep-pocketed investors who were being asked to send their wealth to the far corners of the globe. Britain's initial adherence to the gold standard had been a bit of an accident, the result of one of Isaac Newton's few miscalculations. As master of the royal mint, Newton in 1717 set the price of silver too high, thereby prompting people to hoard their silver coins and pay their debts with gold. Silver gradually disappeared from circulation. Eventually Newton's error came to seem inspired, and in 1821, Britain's de facto gold standard became de jure.

Other countries were less intrinsically enamored of gold, but as British trade expanded, so did the reach of the gold standard. Germany followed Britain's example in embracing gold; as one of the architects of Berlin's new policy explained, "We chose gold not because gold is gold, but because Britain is Britain."

Germany also chose gold because the discoveries in California and elsewhere made such a choice possible. The purpose of money is to lubricate trade: to allow bakers and brewers and chandlers and hostlers to do business with one another without having to resort to barter. For trade to increase, the money supply has to increase. (Otherwise prices fall, discouraging producers from producing.) In modern economies, central banks adjust money supplies to suit the needs of commerce. Under the regime of the gold standard, however, adjustments were essentially fortuitous, dependent on the world supply of gold. The gold strikes in California and Australia and elsewhere greatly augmented the world's available gold supply: credible estimates asserted that in the quarter century after Coloma, more gold was mined around the world than had been mined in the previous 350 years. All this gold amply lubricated world trade and allowed other countries to join Britain on the gold standard.

The United States gravitated toward gold for the same reason Germany did. Much of the money for America's industrial expansion—including the construction of the Pacific railroad and other rail lines—came from Britain. British investors insisted on receiving their payments in gold; this encouraged those American individuals and groups soliciting British investment to insist on receiving *their* payments, from their domestic customers, in gold as well. The only way to guarantee this was to have the government make gold the basis for the American dollar.

But gold wasn't as beloved of the rest of the population as it was among the bankers. Bankers, being creditors, benefit from a strong dollar, one that can purchase at least as much on repayment as at the time of lending. Debtors, by contrast, prefer a weak dollar, one that is worth less at repayment than when borrowed. Farmers are typically debtors, needing loans for land, equipment, seed, and workers' wages; and the large portion of farmers among the American population in the nineteenth century tended to favor a weak dollar. (If a farmer borrowed $100 when a dollar bought one bushel of corn, he had to grow 100 bushels to repay his debt. If the dollar grew stronger, for example to where it bought two bushels, he had to grow 200 bushels to redeem his debt. If the dollar weakened, to where it bought only half a bushel, he had to grow just 50 bushels.)

Much of American politics of the nineteenth century turned on the struggle between debtors and creditors for control of the currency. Creditors acclaimed gold as the only honest money, as the currency God Himself had ordained by making it rare and therefore beyond the manipulation of mere mortals, including that subspecies of mortals so tempted to corruption: politicians. Debtors decried gold as the money of the rich and the chains of the poor. Money was made for the people, they said, and not the people for money. God was no banker, and even if He was, He had also created silver and paper to supplement gold when His children required them.

Whichever side God was on, before 1848 gold was simply too scarce in America to serve as the sole currency. Silver circulated under federal law (as did gold); paper notes were issued by state governments and privately owned banks. The result was a financial hodgepodge, with gold and silver being favored or shunned depending on their comparative availability, and paper being discounted for the distance and unreliability of the issuer.

James Marshall's strike in California, however, marked the beginning of the ascendancy of gold. The boom in the world gold supply eased demands for resort to silver and paper. The Civil War interrupted the trend, as the Union government felt compelled to issue paper currency to cover the cost of the conflict, but within a few years of the end of the war, gold reasserted its centrality. (It was during the period of readjustment that Gould and Fisk launched their raid on the country's gold supply.) The Coinage Act of 1873 neglected to mention silver at all, essentially placing the United States on a gold standard.

But in certain respects, gold did its work too well. Trade and industry expanded during the Civil War and for the next three decades. Production in all sectors increased, outstripping the growth in the (gold) money supply and thereby pushing prices down. Again debtors clamored for relief.

Better organized than before—first in the Farmers' Alliance, then in the Populist party, and finally in the Democratic party—they called for the remonetization of silver. Their rhetoric was often overheated and undercooked. The Coinage Act was dubbed the "Crime of '73." The advocates of gold were said to be the minions of a sinister conspiracy that aimed to rule the world from headquarters in London, a conspiracy controlled by a cabal of Jewish bankers linked to the Rothschilds. William Jennings Bryan climbed to somewhat higher but no less impassioned ground at the Democratic convention of 1896, when he declared defiance to gold and all who served it:

> If they dare to come out in the open field and defend the gold standard as a good thing, we will fight them to the uttermost. Having behind us the producing masses of this nation and the world, supported by the commercial interests, the laboring interests, and the toilers everywhere, we will answer their demand for a gold standard by saying to them: *You shall not press down upon the brow of labor this crown of thorns! You shall not crucify mankind upon a cross of gold!*

Bryan won the Democratic presidential nomination with this speech, but he subsequently lost the country. His inclusive phrases were too generous: most of the commercial and laboring interests of America sided with gold against silver. And why not? Despite a recent depression, the material standard of living of the average American had risen a great deal during the decades the country had been on gold. One didn't have to be a banker to appreciate this, or to desire that the favorable trend continue.

Although Bryan lost to William McKinley, the candidate of gold, in 1896, he didn't discourage easily. He ran again in 1900. By that year, however, his opposition to gold wasn't simply a minority viewpoint but an anachronism. The depression was over and the country was riding another wave of expansion, this one driven by the new discoveries of gold in South Africa and the Yukon, and by new methods of refining gold (which employed cyanide, rather than mercury, to wrest the gold from the surrounding quartz). This latest addition to the gold stream increased the money supply even without silver, setting the United States more firmly on the gold standard than ever. The Gold Standard Act of 1900 made things official.

18

American Dreamers

Jessie Frémont lived long enough to see Republican McKinley elected a half century after her husband John had been the Republican party's first presidential nominee. She doubtless took some satisfaction in the event, although the memory of that earlier contest was bittersweet, for, as things happened, John's nomination for the presidency in 1856 proved to be the high point of his public career, and in certain respects the high point of both of their lives. Several months after the election they encountered serious trouble on the Mariposa, where, among the frustrated placermen forced to take employment in Frémont's quartz mines, there developed great resentment that one man—even one as famous as John C. Frémont—should monopolize so much of the gold. *He* didn't dig the gold; *he* hadn't even discovered it. By right and justice, gold ought to belong to those who brought it out of the earth. Some of the grumblers, emulating Jean-Nicolas Perlot and the other early squatters, began digging on their own behalf on the Mariposa, and defied Frémont to prevent them from keeping what they dug. Others took matters more firmly into their hands, invading one of Frémont's shafts and provoking an armed standoff that threatened to erupt into pitched battle. Although Frémont and the occupiers eventually reached a bloodless settlement, the affair tarnished his reputation among many who had been his staunchest supporters.

The outbreak of the Civil War caught Frémont in France raising money to expand operations on the Mariposa; immediately he turned to purchasing weapons to defeat the Confederates, writing checks for the guns from his own account. Lincoln considered him for minister to Paris, where he retained his popular cachet, but he preferred to return to arms. He received command of the Union army's Department of the West, headquartered near Jessie's family home in St. Louis. His zeal for the antislavery cause—or perhaps it was her zeal, operating through him—outran his authority, and when he issued a proclamation freeing the slaves of Missouri, Lincoln countermanded the order. Frémont rashly allowed himself to be nominated for president in 1864 by Republican radicals vexed with Lincoln; when his candidacy stalled, his star plunged further.

Frémont had never been an astute businessman, and amid the distractions of the Civil War he lost financial control of the Mariposa, which continued to pay, only no longer to him. He tried to recoup his fortune by going into railroads, but found himself competing against Leland Stanford and others who actually knew the business. The money that remained from the Mariposa vanished when his rail venture collapsed in 1870.

All that saved him and Jessie from dire poverty was her pen. As she had come to his literary rescue in the 1840s by drafting his expeditionary reports, now she came to his—and her—financial rescue by contributing dozens of articles to magazines about their lives together and apart. At times the two were compelled to accept the charity of friends. When bronchitis forced Frémont to find a warm climate, Collis Huntington offered his own private car for the trip. Frémont at first resisted the offer, but allowed himself to be persuaded by Huntington's logic: "You forget our road goes over your buried campfires and climbs many a grade you jogged over on a mule. I think we rather owe you this."

Although Congress finally voted Frémont a pension, he didn't live to enjoy it. Seized by a chill while visiting Brooklyn in 1890, during his seventy-eighth year, he weakened quickly. Yet to the end he hoped for a another stroke of good fortune. "If I keep this free of pain," he told his doctor, during a momentary improvement, "I can go home next week."

"Home?" replied the doctor, who was unfamiliar with the full Frémont biography. "What do you call home?"

"Why, California, of course."

Jessie added, in her account of the moment, "And with the name which had been so long his guiding star, he spoke no more."

John's star was Jessie's also. After his death she settled in Los Angeles, the town that had been eclipsed by San Francisco during the Gold Rush but was now coming into its own as the center of activity in southern California. Although she couldn't afford to buy a house, admirers built her a comfortable home of redwood, situated in a grove of orange trees a few miles from the old pueblo. Lily, long since a grown woman, tended to her mother till Jessie died in 1902.

THERE IS NO EVIDENCE that Jessie Frémont ever met Sarah Royce, whose courage and fortitude en route to the goldfields matched her own—the one traveling across the isthmus, the other over the plains and desert. But in Jessie's later years, she did meet Sarah's son, Josiah Royce.

After Weaverville and San Francisco, Sarah and the elder Josiah sampled several locations along the Sierra front and in the Sacramento Valley before settling at Grass Valley, north of Coloma. There Sarah got the house she had been yearning for, and a community more composed than any she had experienced since Iowa. "There were three churches, all very well attended, and each sustaining a Sunday school," she wrote. "There was also a good-sized public school, as well as one or two social and beneficent societies." She and Josiah had two more daughters, a son who died in infancy, and then a second son, named for his father.

The family remained in the gold country till Josiah was ten, when, to improve his educational opportunities—he already was showing signs of brilliance at books—they moved to San Francisco, where he was enrolled in a school recently named for Abraham Lincoln. Though the city's Vigilance Committee had disbanded years before, some of its spirit persisted on the playground. "My comrades very generally found me disagreeably striking in my appearance, by reason of the fact that I was redheaded, freckled, countrified, quaint, and unable to play boys' games," Josiah recalled. "The boys in question gave me my first introduction to the 'majesty of the community.' " He survived to attend high school, and then to cross the bay to Oakland, where the state university specified by the constitution of 1849 had only recently opened (rather than at Vallejo, as Mariano Vallejo had hoped. The university moved to Berkeley midway through Royce's undergraduate years). Royce impressed the president of the university, who, after relocating east, invited Royce to join him at the newly established Johns Hopkins University in Baltimore. There Royce earned a doctorate in philosophy in 1878. Except for a short stint back at Berkeley, he spent the rest of his professional life in the east, mostly at Harvard.

Yet he never forgot his California roots, and when a Boston publisher invited him to write a book about the early days of California, he happily accepted. Research for the book led him to Jessie and John Frémont, whose published version of John's role in the conquest of California struck Royce as entirely too heroic. Royce thought the Mexicans had justice on their side in resisting Frémont, whom Royce castigated as the perpetrator of "purely aggressive" actions against a legitimate government. (To a friend Royce later explained that he might have entitled the pertinent book chapter "Frémont's League with the Devil.") Yet though Royce had nothing good to say about the fiercely protective Jessie, he found John oddly appealing, not least in his convenient lapses of memory. The old soldier displayed, as Royce described it, a "charming and courteous mendacity."

Royce's book was a history of California to 1856; it was also a study of the American character as it evolved under the peculiar conditions of the Gold Rush. Before the Forty-Niners went west, Royce explained, they fairly well represented the national character as it then existed. But amid the pressures of the hunt for wealth, certain traits emerged more clearly in California than elsewhere.

> Nowhere else . . . were we ever before so long forced by circumstances to live at the mercy of a very wayward chance, to give to even our most legitimate business a dangerously speculative char-

> acter. Nowhere else were we driven so hastily to improvise a government for a large body of strangers; and nowhere else did fortune so nearly deprive us for a little time of our natural devotion to the duties of citizenship.

Californians' mistakes were undeniable. "We exhibited a novel degree of carelessness and overhastiness, an extravagant trust in luck, a previously unknown blindness to our social duties, and an indifference to the rights of foreigners." But Californians also showed some of the best American traits, and in doing so set an honorable path for the future. "As a body, our pioneer community in California was persistently cheerful, energetic, courageous, and teachable. In a few years it had repented of its graver faults, it had endured with charming good humor their severest penalties, and it was ready to begin with fresh devotion the work whose true importance it had now at length learned: the work of building a well-organized, permanent, and progressive State on the Pacific Coast."

THAT SARAH ROYCE remained in California after the Gold Rush, making her permanent home there, was no great surprise. That Yee Ah Tye did the same was rather more remarkable. Like most of the argonauts, but especially the Chinese, for whom tending ancestral shrines was a filial duty, Yee aimed to return to his native land once he made his fortune in the goldfields. Yet notwithstanding the rampant prejudice against the Chinese—formalized by the Chinese Exclusion Act of 1882, which banned the immigration of Chinese laborers—Yee chose to stay in California. Perhaps it was the personal freedom of America that appealed to him; perhaps he simply liked the idea of being able to make more money than he could ever imagine making in China. He took what he earned as an association leader in San Francisco and invested in commercial and mining operations on the Feather River. At one point he employed as many as a hundred men. By the time of his 1896 death he was honored among Asian- and Euro-Americans alike. The *Plumas National-Bulletin*, in reporting his passing, described him as "of unusual intelligence and business capacity, and a courteous gentleman." His family ("all of the children being good English scholars, and the girls accomplished musicians") had "many friends among the Americans who will feel sorry to learn of their bereavement." Just before his death, Yee made his strongest statement of attachment to his adopted country, insisting that his bones not be returned to China, as was customary among his countrymen, but remain in America.

OTHER ARGONAUTS DID get home. Vicente Pérez Rosales returned to Chile, where he entered the service of the Chilean government. In recognition of his California experience, he was sent to Europe to promote immigration to the New World—to Chile, naturally, rather than California. Subsequently he became a provincial administrator in Concepción, and then a Chilean senator.

Tom Archer and Edward Hargraves returned to Australia, the former to resume his previous obscurity, the latter to become a national hero (but not a knight).

Jean-Nicolas Perlot made it back to Paris and then Belgium, albeit by a circuitous route. Perlot left California in 1857 for the headwaters of the Columbia River, where gold had been discovered. But he ran out of money in Portland, and opened a vegetable gardening business there. Eventually the call of home drew him east across the United States and the Atlantic. He married a girl from his ancestral town of Herbeumont. He returned with her to Portland, but she missed Belgium and convinced him that the old country was where they belonged. They bought a house in Arlon and raised four children, and vegetables. "I have remained a gardener," Perlot wrote shortly before his death, at the age of seventy-seven. "Only I myself consume the vegetables I grow."

William Swain survived the fevers of Chagres and rejoined Sabrina and Eliza in upstate New York. With the five hundred dollars he brought back from California, he purchased some land and developed an orchard with brother George; before long they were the leading peach growers in Niagara County.

Lewis Manly returned to Wisconsin—only to realize he'd seen too much of the elephant to resume his unexciting former life. He packed up and went west again, this time giving Death Valley a wide berth. He eventually bought a ranch in the Santa Clara Valley, near San Jose.

NOT TILL 1877 did William Sherman make the trip he promised Grenville Dodge: to the Pacific by train. As commanding general of the army, Sherman had his hands full with official duties. He directed continuing efforts to suppress Indian resistance on the plains, employing at times the harsh tactics he warned the Sioux against at Fort Laramie. He stopped short, however, of enlisting civilian volunteers in the wake of Custer's defeat at the Little Bighorn, as many public officials advocated; doubtless his experience with volunteer law enforcement in San Francisco influenced his decision. (In 1881, following the assassination of President James Garfield by Charles Guiteau, Sherman stationed troops around Guiteau's jail cell to forestall any vigilante action.) During this same period he authorized retaliation against the Modoc tribe of northern California after their leader—called Captain Jack by whites—killed General Edward Canby, the head of a truce commission and a comrade of Sherman's from the days at Monterey in the Mexican War. (The defeat of Captain Jack essentially marked the end of Indian resistance in California.)

In 1875, amid the serial scandals that engulfed the presidency of Ulysses Grant, Sherman published his memoirs of the Civil War (and of his time in California before the war). As Grant's stock slipped, Sherman's rose, and he became, in the eyes of many Americans of the North and West, the country's model military hero. That southerners greeted his memoirs with renewed bitterness seemed to leaders of the Republican party all the more cause to sponsor Sherman for the presidency. In 1876, in 1880, and again in 1884, concerted draft-Sherman movements developed; only when he responded to the best-organized of the campaigns, in 1884, with what became the definitive statement of denial—"I will not accept if nominated and will not serve if elected"—did the appeals die down.

For the rest of his life he remained a celebrity and a speaker much in demand. Chauncey Depew, no mean toastmaster himself, called Sherman "the readiest and most original talker in the United States." In Columbus, Ohio, Sherman added another epigram to the American lexicon when he told the younger generation not to get the wrong idea about war. "There is many a boy here today who looks on war as all glory," he said. "But boys, it is all hell."

Having complained during the 1850s at the agitation over slavery, Sherman in the 1880s became an advocate for African-American equality. He recommended against the segregation of black troops within the army, and urged that if the southern states continued to deny the franchise to blacks, they lose seats in Congress or, in the extreme case, face another northern invasion.

With the encouragement of Sam Clemens, he published a revised edition of his memoirs in 1885. He wrote various magazine articles, including one entitled "Old Times in California." He died in New York City in 1891.

ROBERT WATERMAN AND James Douglass were tried in San Francisco for murder and lesser crimes in their brutal treatment of the crew of the *Challenge* on its failed run for the record around Cape Horn. The jury deadlocked over Captain Waterman on the murder charge, convicting him instead of cruel treatment and fining him $400. First Mate Douglass was convicted of murder (in the death of the Italian, Pawpaw) and of assault, but was merely fined $250, the jury evidently accepting Waterman's defiant word—in which Douglass gladly concurred—that the mate was simply following orders.

JOHN SUTTER'S BAD LUCK lasted the rest of his life. Acting on the philosophy he developed by hard experience during the Gold Rush years—"Gold digging is a lottery," he said; "among hundreds, maybe one or two get rich from it. Most people prefer a safe investment; farming is the best of all"—he retired to his farm on the Feather River. He regaled visitors with stories of California before the Gold Rush and sat for portraits by itinerant painters, but drank away what little money he still had. In 1864 the California legislature, embarrassed at the poverty of the man who was widely called the father of California, voted him $15,000, payable over five years at $250 per month. He said he disdained charity but would accept the payment as restitution for the injuries done him.

In 1865 he reprised his earlier role as patron of the tired and hungry, and took in a drifter, who proceeded to rob him. When, reprising his role as law-giver, he had the man apprehended and whipped, the miscreant responded by burning down Sutter's farmhouse. With no place to live, Sutter sailed for the American East, where he hoped to secure compensation from Congress for what he had lost. Various influential people endorsed his petition; William Sherman wrote, "Your hospitality was proverbial. It was the common belief that if not for your fort, and your herds of cattle, sheep, etc., the immigrants arriving in California during the years 1847, 8 and 9 would have suffered for food. It was owing to your efforts to develop the country, more especially in your building the grist mill and the sawmill at Coloma, that the world was indebted for the discovery of the gold mines." After years of dithering, the relevant House committee in 1880 reported favorably on a Sutter relief bill; a joint resolution was introduced in the Senate to grant the old impresario $50,000. The measure got caught in the politics of that election year, yet its sponsors assured Sutter that it would pass first thing the next session.

Sutter died of undetermined but presumably natural causes, before Congress met again.

AMID HIS OWN ill fortune, Sutter could take a certain pleasure from the downfall of the man responsible for much of his grief. Till the end of the 1850s, Sam Brannan maintained his Midas touch. His business operations in Sacramento and San Francisco paid handsomely, allowing him to diversify still further. He bought land in southern California, near Los Angeles, and in Hawaii, at Honolulu. He traded across the Pacific to China, and across the Atlantic to Europe. He imported prime livestock and the best varieties of wine grapes.

He also invested heavily in the Napa Valley, north of San Francisco.

But the valley, which Brannan hoped to develop as a watering spot for the well-to-do, proved deeper than it looked, at least with regard to Brannan's money. Tens of thousands of dollars went in, and very little came out. As one common version of the story explained, the only thing Brannan got from his investment in Napa was the liquor from a distillery there—and he got far too much of that. He began to exhibit the same weakness for drink that afflicted Sutter; this clouded his judgment and limited his ability to deal with such new challenges as the Civil War. Unlike Asbury Harpending and his secessionist friends, Brannan was an outspoken Unionist, although he sometimes spoke too soon, as when he threw a party to celebrate the capture of Charleston—*before* the city fell to Federal forces.

Brannan's wife divorced him and took their children; his payments to her drained him badly. Fair-weather friends fled to others who had better cash flow. He traveled to Mexico to redeem some old bonds and was compensated in land, which he hoped would allow him to turn his affairs around. But the Indians occupying the land had other notions and ran him off. He married again, to a Mexican woman, who cared for him at Escondido, north of San Diego, as his alcoholism deepened and depression set in.

He died at Escondido in 1889. His widow lacked the money to bury him, so the body lay unclaimed in a vault for more than a year. Finally a nephew appeared and arranged an interment.

MARIANO VALLEJO SPENT the last years of his life in poverty of a more genteel sort, on a remnant of his once-vast empire, a small parcel at Sonoma called Lachryma Montis. The name referred to an artesian spring that flowed like tears from a hillside, but it might also have summarized Vallejo's feelings on retreating there.

Yet Vallejo wasn't one to dwell on his losses. Though accustomed to being the bestower of gifts rather than the recipient, he and his wife lived off the generosity of their son-in-law, John Frisbie, until the mid-1870s, when Frisbie lost heavily in a Nevada bubble. The younger man fled his creditors for Mexico, where he ingratiated himself to President Porfirio Díaz by arranging a reduction of American tariffs on Mexican imports.

Díaz rewarded Frisbie with, among other items, a gold mine. Before long he was far richer than he had ever been in the United States, and he resumed support of his parents-in-law.

At times Vallejo waxed nostalgic for the days before the Americans. "If the Californians could all gather together to breathe a lament," he wrote, "it would reach Heaven as a moving sigh which would cause fear and consternation to the Universe. What misery! . . . This country was the true Eden, the land of promise where hunger was never known."

More often, however, he was willing to forgive and forget. To stretch the household budget, he taught himself to do his own maintenance and repair work. He learned to operate the machinery of the Sonoma waterworks. He engaged, in a minor way, in various civic and political activities, accepting appointment to the state horticultural board and addressing audiences on holidays. He wrote his memoirs and gathered the papers and recollections of other native Californians. And he reaffirmed the faith that had been sorely tested during the dark days—for him—of the Gold Rush. "Believe me, Ricardo," he wrote another son-in-law (who happened to be the Mexican consul in California), "American democracy is the best democracy in the world." When one of his sons spoke of pursuing old grievances, Vallejo answered, "No, let it go. What good to keep open an old sore? Let the wound heal."

CONSIDERING THE FATE of Vallejo, Brannan, Sutter, and Frémont, one might easily conclude that, whatever its actual chemical properties, the gold of California was corrosive of personal happiness, and that its coefficient of friction was such that it invariably slipped through the hands of those who acquired it.

Certainly there is something to this observation. Many of those, like Vallejo and Sutter, whose wealth and stature derived from the old regime, did indeed see their positions dissolve as a result of the changes the Gold Rush set in motion. And as for Brannan and Frémont, the proverbial warning about easy come, easy go, doubtless applied.

Yet there were others who managed to hold on to their fortunes, and indeed multiply them. George Hearst was the best example in this regard, with one mining success leading to another and another. But even in Hearst's case, the good example didn't extend to the second generation. William Randolph Hearst proved to be the only child of George and Phoebe, from whom he inherited far more money than was good for him. Like Josiah Royce, Will Hearst found his way to Harvard—as a student who was expelled for a practical joke that involved sending chamber pots to professors. He took up journalism back in San Francisco, importing from New York the obsession with sex scandals, messy murders, and other manifestations of human frailty that gave the yellow press of the 1890s its peculiar hue. He also nominated himself guardian of the people against the monied interests. The incongruity of the millionaire's boy assaulting the citadel of privilege cocked more than a few eyebrows, but when Hearst led a campaign that prevented the Central Pacific from reneging on its debts to American taxpayers, he earned an appreciative, if still somewhat puzzled, following.

Hearst expanded his ambitions east by purchasing the *New York Morning Journal*. Matching Joseph Pulitzer's *New York World* sensation for sensation, Hearst's *Journal* helped provoke the Spanish-American War, and it provided a springboard for its owner's entry into elective politics. He ran for Congress and was twice victorious; in 1904 he sought the Democratic nomination for president. Failing, he ran for governor of New York; when this bid likewise fell shy, he threw himself into the creation of a media empire that spanned the country. He also indulged himself in an openly adulterous and long-running romance, and in the construction of an egregious villa at San Simeon on the California coast, where he dreamed of what could have been had he possessed a little more of the genuine common touch.

THE SON OF LELAND Stanford might have turned out not much different from William Randolph Hearst, had he lived. Like George and Phoebe Hearst, Leland and Jane Stanford had just one child, whom they spoiled no less than the Hearsts spoiled their Will. But Leland Jr. died in his teens, compelling his parents to find something else to do with their money. By the bereaved father's own testimony, he was visited by the ghost of his son, who told him he must devote his fortune to humanity. Reflecting that Leland Jr. would soon have gone off to college, Leland and Jane determined to build a college for other young people. A horse farm they owned at Palo Alto (not far from Lewis Manly's ranch) seemed a suitable site, and within weeks they were interviewing the most distinguished educators in America. The Leland Stanford Junior University was chartered in 1885; construction commenced in 1887; the first students arrived in 1891.

The infant university drew its students primarily from the West Coast. The inaugural class included an orphan from Oregon named Herbert Hoover, who studied mining engineering and went on to make a fortune finding gold and other minerals in Australia, China, Russia, and more exotic locales. His postmining career as American president proved rather less successful, but by the time voters, in the 1932 election, retired Hoover to Palo Alto, Leland Stanford's university was emphasizing engineering of another sort. In the electrical engineering department a professor named Frederick Terman played matchmaker to two former students, encouraging them to commercialize certain promising ideas they'd been talking about; a coin flip determined that William Hewlett's name would precede David Packard's on the masthead of the company they created.

Hewlett-Packard struggled during the late 1930s, along with most of corporate America, but as the Great Depression gave way to World War II, the U.S. government discovered a need for the testing equipment the company produced. By war's end Hewlett-Packard had a hundred employees and sales of more than $1 million per year. Electronics was becoming big business, and Hewlett-Packard led the field.

Soon the neighborhood near Leland Stanford's old farm was full of bright young men (they were nearly all men) with bright new ideas. The brightest idea was the transistor, which multiplied (and miniaturized) into the integrated circuit. Not long after the latter made its market debut, an area booster dubbed the region Silicon Valley, for the humble material that provided the basis for the electronic marvels devised and fabricated there. Yet there was nothing humble about the prices the silicon technology commanded, and the principals of the new companies soon found themselves astonishingly rich.

By then the term "gold rush" had long been applied to any sudden efflorescence of wealth and opportunity. There was a "gold rush" for the oil ("black gold") of Pennsylvania in the 1860s, and of Texas after 1900 and again in the 1930s, and of Alaska in the 1970s. There was a rush for land in Oklahoma in the 1890s and in Florida in the 1920s. The bull market of Wall Street in the 1920s and the defense industry in the 1950s were likened to gold rushes. Any entrepreneur who achieved overnight success, as all dreamed of doing, was described as striking it rich.

But in the case of Silicon Valley in the 1980s and 1990s—the case that epitomized modern American success—the parallels to the original Gold Rush were especially apt. As in the first Gold Rush, people came from all over the world to try their luck in Silicon Valley. The pace of life in the valley was as frenetic as it had been in the diggings—more frenetic, in fact, since neither night nor winter suspended work in the silicon mines. Both settings were permeated by a conviction that tremendous opportunities existed but faded fast. "Time is money," Jean-Nicolas Perlot heard over and over in the gold diggings; his silicon successors constantly sought the grail of "the new new thing." In each case random chance played a large role, and if failure preceded success, the appropriate response was not to blame oneself but one's luck, and try again. A denizen of Silicon Valley described the "vein of gold" that ran through the valley, and declared, "Anybody can reach down into it and strike it rich." But not everybody would. "No matter how big your hand is, if you reach down in the wrong spot, you don't get anything." A Silicon Valley venture capitalist called the phenomenon in which he participated "the largest legal creation of wealth in the history of the planet," which may have been true. But when the high-tech bubble burst in the spring of 2000, the losses were also among the largest in history. It was poetic (or perhaps geologic) justice that silicon was the primary constituent of both the quartz of the Mother Lode and the semiconductors of Silicon Valley; in each case, a lead that looked promising at the surface could attract huge amounts of capital and then play out before yielding a profit.

So striking were the similarities between the Gold Rush and the Silicon Rush that it was tempting to seek a causal connection. Was it blind chance that determined that of all the places in the world where the silicon revolution might have occurred, it happened in the land of the Gold Rush? Silicon is ubiquitous, and smart people are portable; but the highly charged atmosphere in which the two combined to produce Hewlett-Packard and Fairchild and Intel and Xerox PARC and Sun and Cisco and Netscape and Yahoo was peculiar to California; or at least the California atmosphere carried a larger charge—of hell-for-leather entrepreneurship—than the air did elsewhere. California had seen and done it all before. Chambers of commerce in every region of the country envied Silicon Valley's success and tried to reproduce it; Silicon Forest sprang up in the Northwest, Silicon Hills in central Texas, Silicon Alley in New York City. But none of the imitations quite matched the original, perhaps because nowhere else was the new American dream such a fundamental part of the psychic landscape.

"WE ARE ON THE brink of the age of gold," Horace Greeley had said in 1848. The reforming editor wrote better than he knew. The discovery at Coloma commenced a revolution that rumbled across the oceans and continents to the ends of the earth, and echoed down the decades to the dawn of the third millennium. The revolution manifested itself demographically, in drawing hundreds of thousands of people to California; politically, in propelling America along the path to the Civil War; economically, in spurring the construction of the transcontinental railroad. But beyond everything else, the Gold Rush established a new template for the American dream. America had always been the land of promise, but never had the promise been so decidedly—so gloriously—material. The new dream held out the hope that anyone could have what everyone wants: respite from toil, security in old age, a better life for one's children. By no means could all achieve success (fleeting or otherwise) at the level of John Frémont or George Hearst or Sam Brannan or Leland Stanford. But all *could* reasonably hope to emulate Jean-Nicolas Perlot, gardening happily in Herbeumont; or William Swain, in his orchard near Niagara Falls; or Lewis Manly, on his ranch outside San Jose; or Sarah Royce, in her house in Grass Valley; or Yee Ah Tye, on the banks of the Feather River.

To be sure, the new dream had a dark side; it destroyed even as it created. The argonauts dismantled John Sutter's handiwork all at once; the lawyers took longer to dispossess Mariano Vallejo. The Indians of California lost far more. Considering the grim fate of aboriginal peoples almost everywhere the American flag was raised, the destruction of the tribes of California may not have depended on the discovery of gold there, but the gold certainly hastened the process—as it hastened the demise of the plains tribes corralled onto reservations to allow the Pacific railroad to go through. Of a different nature was the damage mining operations did to the ecology of California, from the modest excavations of the placermen to the mountain-moving of the hydraulickers. (Eventually the silting caused by the latter provoked an outcry that compelled the water cannons to cease fire.) The speculative scandals of the post–Civil War era and the emergence of monopolies weren't the work of the California experience alone, but to the extent the Gold Rush mentality migrated east along the route of the Pacific railroad, they too might be fairly charged against the new American dream.

Were the benefits worth the cost? To ask the question is to imply that an alternative existed. Maybe it did, but only if human nature could have resisted the temptation to seek a shortcut to happiness. America's enthronement of individualism magnified the impact of the gold discovery; the gold rushes to Canada and Siberia were more orderly than the rush to California. But they were also less history-shaping, partly because neither the Klondike nor Siberia was anyone's vision of paradise, but also because neither Canada nor Russia elevated the pursuit of happiness to the status of inalienable right. Americans, and those who came to America, cherished that right, and when the gold of California promised a way to find happiness all at once, they couldn't resist.

And in this lay the ultimate meaning of the Gold Rush. The Gold Rush shaped history so profoundly because it harnessed the most basic of human desires, the desire for happiness. None of the gold-seekers went to

California to build a new state, to force a resolution of the sectional conflict, to construct a transcontinental railroad, to reconstruct the American dream. They went to California to seek individual happiness. Some found it; some didn't. But the side effect of their pursuit—the cumulative outcome of their individual quests—was a transformation of American history. The men and women of the Gold Rush hoped to change their lives by going to California; in the bargain they changed their world.

AS FOR THE CARPENTER who set everything in motion, he never reached El Dorado. The sawmill at Coloma cut logs intermittently for three years before river miners diverted the American River and left the mill dry and powerless. Anyway, by then James Marshall had managed to lose the money he made from the cutting, for even less than his partner, Sutter, was the unlucky and unworldly Marshall able to accomplish the transition from the old era to the new. He spent the next thirty-five years trying to win acknowledgment of his role in creating the new California. But his neighbors were in too much of a hurry exploiting his discovery to notice, and he died forgotten and nearly destitute.

Yet he was remembered after his death, and a statue was erected in his honor. The statue stands above the river at Coloma, in a hillside copse of trees. From a stone pedestal Marshall gazes out across the valley. The mill is long gone, and the millrace obliterated. But so is most evidence of the hordes who followed Marshall here, and the general scene isn't much different than it was on that sunny, cold morning in 1848, when the carpenter's eye fell on the glittering yellow flakes that set the heart of the world aquiver.

Sources

The principal sources for this book are the words of the men and women who went to California in search of gold, or whose lives were otherwise touched by the gold discoveries there. In many cases, these words were put to writing contemporaneously, in the form of diaries, journals, and letters. In some cases they were recorded after the fact, as reminiscences or memoirs. A large number of these writings have been published; others remain unpublished, in archives and other depositories. The bibliography below includes all those firsthand accounts that have been quoted in the text as well as many others that have provided important information.

The bibliography also includes secondary works: works authored not by participants or eyewitnesses but by historians and others writing after the fact. In rare cases such secondary studies have been quoted in the text, and are cited, like the primary sources, in the page notes. More often, these works of history, geology, economics, and other disciplines provide background material that broadly informs the text in a way that defies specific citation. A few works are neither quite primary nor exactly secondary, but something in between. J. S. Holliday's *The World Rushed In*, for example, reproduces the diary and letters of William Swain, which have been quoted in several places in the text; the book also provides insightful commentary on Swain's great adventure. Any comprehensive bibliography of secondary works on the Gold Rush and other events related here would run to tens of thousands of entries; consequently, only those works that have been most helpful to the present author have been included.

The notes immediately below provide brief references to collections and works described in full detail in the bibliography.

Prologue: The Baron and the Carpenter

2 "On Christmas morning": Bigler, following p. 66.

2 "Last Sunday": Smith, 108.

5 "Made a contract": Sutter, 72.

6 "decent appearance": Gay, 55.

7 "In May 1847": ibid., 520–23.

11 "Their bones": Smith, 102n.

11 "The provisions": Dillon (1967), 261.

12 "We crossed": Smith, 102.

12–13 "We was . . . chill and fever": ibid., 104–7.

13 "We have had": ibid., 106.

14 "Started 5 wagons": Sutter, 93.

14 "Yesterday . . . ever since": Smith, 106–7.

14 "It raised": Smith, 107.

14 "Clear as a bell": Paul, ed., 61.

16 "I picked up": ibid., 118.

16 "I have found it . . . nothing else": ibid.

17 "odd spells": Smith, 110.

18 "From the unusual agitation": Paul, ed., 122.

18–19 "I declared . . . such a discovery": ibid., 129.

Part One: The Gathering of Peoples

23 "As when some carcass": Bancroft, 6:52.

1. In the Footsteps of Father Serra

28–30 "The hills . . . this might be": Dana, 52, 71, 152–53, 209–10.

33 "band of robbers": Nevins (1928), 1:264–65.

33 "If we are unjustly": Bancroft, 5:14.

34 "Captain, shall I take": Bancroft, 5:171.

36–37 "My acts . . . for duty": Nevins (1928), 2:381–83.

38–39 "Being unfamiliar . . . in the country": Sherman (1875), 43–54.

39 "Two men": Sherman (1875), 64–65.

41 "The Mormon Co.": Larkin, 5:79.
41 "Damn that flag!": Scherer, 12.
42 "We traveled": Bailey, 97.
43–44 "Gold! Gold! . . . per diem": Bancroft, 6:56–60.
44 "I of course": Sherman (1875), 70.
44–45 "The Sacramento . . . frontier town": Sherman and Sherman, 43–44.
45 "on hand . . . to interfere": Sherman (1875), 76–77.
45 "The most moderate": Paul, ed., 95–97.

2. Across the Pacific

48 "The gold nuggets": Pérez Rosales, 271.
49–53 "Four brothers . . . to receive us": ibid., 272–79.
54 "Morals": Archer, 38.
54 "I caught sight": ibid., 45.
55 "We believe": Bateson, 29.
55–56 "Mormons . . . afterwards": Monaghan, 28–29.
57 "my two": Archer, 163.
58 "At least a score": ibid., 167–68.
59 "A more happy": Hargraves, 74.
59 "This was too touching": Archer, 173.
60 "A very queer-looking": ibid., 180–81.
61 "As we entered": Hargraves, 75.
63 "Americans are very rich": McLeod, 23.
64 "Yee Ah Tye": Farkas, 7.
64 "Celestials": ibid.

3. The Peaks of Darien

65 "Miss Jessie": Phillips, 47.
66 "that instinctive sympathy": Herr, 19.
66 "Because I planned": Phillips, 41.
67 "The horseback life": Jessie Frémont memoirs, 54.
68 "I felt the whole situation": ibid., 56–57.
68 "*Only trust me*": Herr, 91.
70 "The accounts": Browning, 36–37.
70 "We are on the brink": Bancroft, 6:119.

70 "The Eldorado": Browning, 45.
71 "Look out": Buck, 27.
71 "The last thing": Browning 43–44.
73 "She was a hard": Jessie Frémont (1878), 12.
73 "I had never been": ibid., 13.
74 "When we reached": ibid., 26.
75 "For three or four days": Borthwick, 21–22.
76 "The eastern shore": Taylor, 9.
77 "We found Chagres": Davis, 7.
77 "negroes in a state": Browning, 174.
77–79 "The town of Chagres . . . die lazily": Marryat, 1–3.
79 "naked, screaming": Jessie Frémont (1878), 27.
79–81 "We were near . . . to the base": ibid., 30–32.
81 "Scrambling up": Taylor, 24.
81 "It was astonishing": Borthwick, 34.
81 "We found the 'road' ": Davis, 7.
81–82 "consisted of frames . . . landed there": Marryat, 5.
82 "There are various reasons": Hanson letter, Dec. 22, 1849.
82–83 "The nights were odious . . . leaving home": Jessie Frémont (1878), 34.
83 "Never were modern": Marryat, 8.
84 "The natives": Borthwick, 39.
84 "is inhabited": Norris letter, Nov. 12, 1851.
84 "Many of the women . . . future occasion": Borthwick, 39.
85 "This morning": Davis, 10.
85 "Keep clear": Bunker letter (from Frederick C. Sanford), Jan. 16, 1849.
86 "I became possessed": Jessie Frémont memoirs, 82.
87 "In starving times": Nevins (1928), 2:410.
87 "The sight was beautiful": ibid., 400.
87–90 "The trail showed . . . bright weather": Jessie Frémont (1878), 44–54.
91 "These two . . . my strength": ibid., 56–60.

4. To the Bottom of the World and Back

95 "There is no French province": Nasatir (1934), 13.
95–103 "The gold fever . . . of the hair": Perlot, 6–21.
105 "a perfect mania": Whipple, 61.

105 "A strutting dude": ibid., 102.
107 "Her bow rises": Howe and Matthews, 1:60–61.
108 "They ate holes": Whipple, 122.
110 "I think it was the worst": ibid., 159.
111–14 "twenty-two days . . . with speed": Perlot, 22–26.
120 "I felt the bones": Whipple, 189. (The account here of the reign of terror aboard the *Challenge* follows Whipple, 178–90.)

5. To See the Elephant

124 "Hugh is making . . . but poetry": Heiskell, xv.
124–26 "I have seen . . . as I have": Durham, 6–12.
127–29 "We are quite sure . . . the spectacle": Holliday (1981), 55–56, 66–74.
130 "We were on board": Bruff, 567.
130 "The slow progress": Holliday, (1981) 78–79.
132 "I felt a change": Manly, 61–62.
133 "Is it not owing": Ingalls, 16.
133 "rattled away": Manly, 66.
133–35 "The morning . . . lovely scene": S. Royce, 3–7.
135 "on nearly as low terms": Ware, 3.
135 "It ought to be": Haskell, xxii–xxiii.
137 "He says": Holliday (1981), 71.
137 "The cholera": Heiskell, xxii.
138–39 "The oldest . . . land of savages?": S. Royce, 14–17.
139 "a treacherous, hostile race": Ingalls, 21.
139–140 "The men . . . sight of them": S. Royce, 13–14.
141 "We are getting": Holliday (1981), 129.
141 "Camp full of Indians": Heiskell, 12.
141 "We found": Manly, 72–73.
142 "It was a revolting sight": Holliday (1981), 162.
142 "This afternoon": ibid., 151–52.
143 "He still kept": Manly, 70.
144 "I presume that not less": Sawyer, May 21, 1850.
145 "We are determined": Heiskell, xxvi.
145 "Over 100 teams": Van Dorn diary, May 13 and August 19, 1849.
145 "At twelve o'clock": Holliday (1981), 167–68.

146 "A flare up": Heiskell, 25.

147 "I did not like this": Manly, 69.

148 "Our Guide Book": S. Royce, 26.

149 "The sun in magnificence": Heiskell, 15–18.

150 "presented the appearance": Holliday (1981), 215.

150 "who he appears . . . cowhiding": Heiskell, 13.

151–52 "It was near sunset . . . western feet": S. Royce, 29–30.

152–61 "This was bad news . . . rough and dangerous": Manly, 76–108.

6. Where Rivers Die

163–64 "The road this evening . . . ride across": Heiskell, 34–36.

163 "The river here": Holliday (1981), 238.

164 "Dent & Crocker": Heiskell, 37.

164 "Range of the Pah Utahs": Bruff, 633.

165 "We no longer see": Heiskell, 51.

166 "Along the edge": Bruff, 147–48.

166–68 "The moon was some . . . miles distant": Holliday (1981), 254–62.

169–74 "After hearing his instructions . . . Carson River": S. Royce, 39–56.

176–85 "I reached the summit . . . bright day": Manly, 146–201.

186–87 "One who has never . . . Death Valley": Manly, 221–41.

188 "We bid a long . . . own hook": Holliday (1981), 276–77.

189 "They brought us": Heiskell, 71–74.

189 "Their rapidity . . . how it was": S. Royce, 63–64.

190 "Rice came in": Heiskell, 72.

190 "I looked down": S. Royce, 72.

Part Two: From Vulcan's Forge

193 "Never, since the Roman legionry": *Hutchings' California Magazine*, May 1859 (p. 167 in Olmsted ed.)

193 "tally of gold-hunters": The best assessment of immigrant numbers is Holliday (1999).

7. With a Washbowl on My Knee

197 "The gold is in fine bright scales": Sherman and Sherman, 45.

198–200 "The system . . . ounces of gold": Pérez Rosales, 44, 51–52.

200 "This new invention": Perlot, 103.

201 "Time is money": Pérez Rosales, 54 and passim.

202 "the astonishment": Jessie Frémont (1878), 80.

204–06 "a long thin young captain . . . greatest wishes": Jessie Frémont (1878), 71–82.

206 "They all appear": John Lambert letter, Nov. 4, 1849.

207 "This they did": Jessie Frémont (1878), 81.

207–09 "The blow was terrible . . . into the trench": Perlot, 32, 41–42, 60–61, 85–86, 102.

210 "I did not see him . . . dreaded hour": Heiskell, 87.

211 "Physicians are all making fortunes": Wyman, 158.

211 "The price of provisions": Archer, 214–15.

212 "a large store": Pérez Rosales, 37–38.

214–16 "All were so absorbed . . . natural prey": S. Royce, 80–87.

216–20 "I soon found myself . . . quarter-ounce nuggets": Archer, 184–85, 192–95, 204–6.

221–22 "I saw many places . . . speedy fortune!": Perlot, 111–12.

222–25 "We judged . . . high hopes": Holliday (1981), 313–15, 331, 337, 358.

8. A Millennium in a Day

226 "Should that sum": *Hutchings' California Magazine*, September 1857 (p. 109 in Olmsted ed.).

229 "A claim at Iowa Hill . . . hundred yards": Paul (1947), 154–55.

230 "The quantity of powder": Browne (1869), 150–51.

231–32 "The Mariposa Estate . . . from the mine": Browne (1869), 21, 28.

235–39 "We descended their shaft . . . several millions of people": *Hutchings' California Magazine*, October 1857 (pp. 170–77 in Olmsted ed.).

239 "I have with me": Holliday (1981), 422–23.

240–42 "But they were ignorant . . . myself alone": Perlot, 118–20.

Part Three: American Athena

245 "Plutus rattled his money bags": Soulé, 507–8.

9. The Miracle of St. Francis

248 "Our fourth ended": Soulé, 171.

248 "God help the city": ibid., 165.
248 "Last Wednesday": Gilman letter, Jan. 22, 1850.
249 "Our type": Soulé, 175.
250 "In the immense crowds": S. Royce, 109.
251 "The usual order": Charles Thompson letter, Sept. 10, 1851.
252 "No place in the world": Soulé, 645–66.
252 "Denison's Exchange": Taylor, 118–19.
254 "California beef": Van Dorn diary, Nov. 13, 1849.
255 "Before eleven": Soulé, 274.
255 "I put into this": John Lambert letter, May 10, 1850.
255 "New buildings": Soulé, 275.
257 "I arrived here": Lotchin, 175.
258 "Her wild fevered gaze": Nevins (1955), 399.
258 "It is more disagreeable": Jessie Frémont (1993), 49.
259 "son of a nigger": Pérez Rosales, 10.
261 "It will be asked": Cary, notebook 1.
261–62 "Compliant . . . making bricks!": Pérez Rosales, 68–69.
263 "The voyage from Sydney": Soulé, 565.
264 "With the families": Cary, notebook 1.
265–68 "the maintenance of the peace . . . the people said *Amen!*": Soulé, 569–81.

10. Sutter's Last Stand

271 "Before the celebration was over": Sherman (1875), 73, 1123.
271 "I was no more": Dillon (1967), 294.
271 "enthusiastic": Sherman (1875), 1123.
271–72 "I went to eat . . . no law": Dillon (1967), 294–98.
273 "where orgies": Vallejo memoirs, 5:160.
274 "Had I not been": Bancroft, 6:447.
275–76 "Hold on . . . by the Lord": Dillon (1967), 303, 306, 314.
277 "As Congress": *Report of Debates*, 3–5.
277 "agriculturist": ibid., 478.
278 "Dr. Gwin": Browne (1969), 121.
278 "I was gravely": Taylor, 158.
279 "Neither slavery": *Report of Debates*, 43.
279 "In a country": Nevins (1928), 2:438.

279 "Nor shall the introduction": *Report of Debates*, 44.

280–81 "No population . . . enlightened principles": ibid., 137–41.

283 "The people of California . . . gambling state": ibid., 91–92.

283 "holy horror": ibid., 327.

283 "associations": ibid., appendix.

283 "I am not wedded": ibid., 259.

284–85 "The hall was cleared . . . from his eyes": Taylor, 159–64.

286 "General . . . prosperity": *Report of Debates*, 476–77.

11. Shaking the Temple

288–89 "gave freedom . . . working forces": Jessie Frémont (1878), 91–94.

289 "All these women": Herr, 208.

289 "Mrs. Frémont": Bosqui, 150.

290 "the better man": Crosby, 35.

290 "One evening": Jessie Frémont (1878), 103.

291 "I had done so many things": ibid., 100–101.

293–95 "But it is impossible . . . heart-rending spectacle": *Congressional Globe* 31:1, app. 116–18, 127.

295–97 "the greatest and the gravest . . . from all responsibility": ibid., 451–55.

297 "He was a black": Peterson, 38.

298 "Liberty and Union": ibid., 178.

298 "That man": Hamilton, 26.

298–301 "I wish to speak . . . certain destiny": *Congressional Globe* 31:1, app. 269–76.

301 "The Government of the United States": John Frémont letters, 3:139.

301 "omnibus speech": Hamilton, 62.

302 "calumniator . . . pistol on me!": ibid., 93.

302–03 "This batch . . . is her cry!": *Congressional Globe* 31:1, 677–84.

303 "The omnibus": Hamilton, 110.

303–04 "I was willing . . . Union stands firm": Peterson, 474–76.

12. Children of the Mother Lode

307 "He is a man": Eccleston, 106–7.

310 "Savage said to them": ibid., 15.

310 "We reached the camp": Bunnell, 22.

311 "He says": Eccleston, 29.
311–12 "From his long acquaintance . . . six mules": Bunnell, 30–33.
313 "We had not the time": ibid., 84.
313 "Burnt over 5000 . . . not long deserted": Eccleston, 49, 67–68.
313 "Their courage": Bunnell, 126.
313–14 "who had been led . . . I am done": ibid., 170–71, 177.
314–15 "We are afraid . . . to the plains": ibid., 43, 60, 62–63.
315 "Where can we now go": ibid., 234.
315 "The whites": ibid., 223.
316 "The white man": Hurtado, 134–35.
317 "high indignation": ibid., 115.
319 "that Swiss adventurer": Vallejo memoirs 5:19.
320 "When we join our fortunes": Rosenus, 90–91.
320 "In spite of the fact": Vallejo memoirs, 5:77.
321 "I left Sacramento": Emparan, 43.
321 "The good ones": Pitt, 52.
321 "the great crowd": Vallejo memoirs, 5:189.
322 "He is better acquainted": Taylor, 157.
322 "it be represented": *Report of Debates*, 323.
323 "I think I will know": Rosenus, 230.
323 "Let me see . . . purest blood of Europe": Pitt, 27.
325 "For some time back": Latta, 36.
326 "The band is led": ibid., 37.
326–27 "We publish today . . . along the road": ibid., 44.
327 "When shot at": Varley, 49–50.
327 "I have been engaged": Boessenecker, 91.
328 "I have arrested": Latta, 479.
328 "Capt. Love": ibid., 474–75.
329 "There is not the least doubt": ibid., 513.
331–32 "We find . . . judicial tribunal": Farkas, 10–11.
333 "all great men . . . do good to them": Cary, notebook 2.

13. Reflections in an All-Seeing Eye

334 "The consummation": McPherson, 76.
334 "another triumph . . . around her": Peterson, 476.

336 "sink in hell": Potter, 155.
336 "raise a hell . . . out & out abolitionist": McPherson, 122–24.
337 "Since there is no escaping . . . the abolitionists": ibid., 145–46.
338–40 "Mining is not . . . care and dispatch": G. Clark, 50–65.
342 "In Sacramento . . . stain of abolitionism": ibid., 73–78.
343 "In these prosperous times": Sherman and Sherman, 51.
346 "My business here": ibid., 53.
347 "as clearly as a proposition": Sherman (1875), 126.
349–50 "all the banks . . . any security whatever": ibid., 130–34.
351 "It's no use": J. Royce, 435.
351 "I found him on the roof": Sherman (1875), 143.
352 "Rosario": Pérez Rosales, 19.
352 "Americans were irresistibly attracted": Levy, 161–62.
353 "the finest-looking woman": ibid., 167.
353 "They commonly accepted": S. Royce, 115–16.
354 "Is it not wonderful . . . meaningless giggle": Lotchin, 257.
355 "What the People Expect": J. Royce, 454.
356 "Remove your fort . . . inevitably follow": Sherman (1875), 146–47.
358 "I think the community": Sherman and Sherman, 58.

Part Four: The Gordian Knot and the Pacific Connection

361 "The sunburnt immigrant": Bancroft, 7:542.

14. The Pathfinder's Return

365 "higher law . . . abominable": McPherson, 73.
366 "It is the choice": Nevins (1928), 2:2:478.
366 "prairie fire . . . yet been named": ibid., 2:481–82.
366–68 "He also won the heart . . . to have him elected": Herr, 254–61.
368 "quite a female politician": Donald, 315.
368 "These incidents": Jessie Frémont (1969), 132.
368 "Had we been": Herr, 265.
369 "John and Jessie . . . Jessie for the White House": ibid., 263; Nevins (1928), 2:496.
369 "I am above": Herr, 268.
369 "We are treading": Nevins (1928), 2:505.

369 "The election . . . eternal separation": Potter, 262.
369 "Tell me": Nevins (1928), 2:509.
370 "I heartily regret": Jessie Frémont (1969), 140.
372 "no black or mulatto": Lapp (1977), 192.
373 "Private School": Lapp (1969), 10.
375 "Why, Lord": ibid., 48.
375 "I *don't* want": ibid., 8.
377 "When they come . . . Charles A. Stovall": Franklin, 149–51.
377 "It vies with the most": ibid., 152.
377 "The law was given": J. Hittell (1878), 271.
381 "Archy, my boy": Lapp (1969), 58.

15. South by West

383 "His appearance": Warren, 212–13.
384 "The Republic": Wells, 24.
385 "He is a veritable": Scroggs, 42.
385 "The scene": Wells, 30–31.
386 "We had to shoot": ibid., 33.
387 "There, sir": Scroggs, 91.
388 "Gentlemen": Brands (1999), 20.
388 "A beleaguered force": Walker, 266.
389 "Instead of treating": Scroggs, 233.
390 "that we inscribe . . . railroad is concerned": G. Clark, 78–79.
391–92 "I feel . . . white clingstone": ibid., 83–91.
393 "Every dollar": ibid., 92.
395–97 "having the Federal . . . above all price": ibid., 99, 108–12.
397 "I believe": Bancroft, 7:258–59.
397 "California is ready": ibid., 7:272.
398 "I was young": Harpending, 17.
399–400 "I will never forget . . . what followed": ibid., 24–26.
400–01 "He fully realized . . . thought of me": ibid., 33–34.
401–02 "After that . . . small fortune": ibid., 49–55.

16. From Sea to Shining Sea

404: $600 million . . . $130 million: Hill (1999), 263.

405 "We are all safe": Sherman (1909), 150–51.
406 "Having nothing": Sherman (1875), 154.
406 "I suppose": L. Lewis, 123.
406 "West Point": ibid., 97.
406 "I would as soon": Sherman (1909), 151.
406 "If I turn": ibid., 153.
406 "Avoid the subject": Sherman and Sherman, 55.
407 "If he is fit . . . nigger question": Marszalek, 109.
407 "I would not": L. Lewis, 119.
407 "If they design": Sherman (1909), 163.
407 "I had read of retreats": Marszalek, 151.
408 "I believe he would do it": Fellman, 91.
408 "Command me in any way": ibid., 102.
408 "Sherman saved": ibid., 115–16.
409 "If the North . . . Georgia howl!": L. Lewis, 429–31.
409–10 "The acclamation . . . every girl that he met": ibid., 575, 585.
410 "At first he was affable . . . without restriction": ibid., 577–78.
410–11 "The time . . . the people demand": Sherman and Sherman, 56–57.
411 "There are too many . . . length on earth": Greeley, 52, 119–21, 186, 229.
412–14 "He was a very . . . California endured?": Twain, *Roughing It*, 39–40, 54–56, 70–72, 97, 143–44, 150.
415 "Boy That Earth Talks To": Older, 29.
417 "A good deal": G. Clark, 175.
418 "I remember": ibid., 173.
419 "NEW ROAD": ibid., 204.
420 "I think": Bain, 109.
421 "We have drawn": ibid., 115.
423 "You see": ibid., 137.
423 "They wanted to know": Daggett, 23–24.
423 "I would have been glad": G. Clark, 208.
424 "Those mountains": Bain, 145.
424 "As to work": ibid., 565.
424 "Mr. Huntington": letter of Nov. 29, 1861, Leland Stanford papers.
424 "To the extent": G. Clark, 210.

425 "Brigham was cold": ibid., 245.
426 "Four or five": ibid., 213–14.
426 "I was very much prejudiced": Bain, 208.
426 "To my mind": G. Clark, 126–27.
427 "Didn't they build": Bain, 221.
427 "We swarmed": ibid., 299–300.
427 "The Atlanta campaign": Sherman (1875), 889.
427 "I think this subject": L. Lewis, 595.
428 "Every time": ibid.
428 "They are not worth": Bancroft, 7:552.
428 "Baker had electrified": Sherman (1875), 901.
429 "This is a great enterprise": Bain, 245.
429 "pure beggars": L. Lewis, 596.
429 "We must act": ibid., 597.
430 "we can act": Bain, 312.
430 "When the opportune moment": ibid., 350.
431 "We've got to clean": ibid., 351.
431 "Unless some relief": ibid.
431 "If you don't choose": L. Lewis, 598.
433 "free from all danger": Bain, 274.
433 "We are getting": ibid., 321.
433 "We send you": G. Clark, 244.
434 "I did not try": ibid., 249–50.
434 "Run up and down": Bain, 447.
434 "to build road": ibid.
435–36 "We are cribbed . . . too fast": ibid., 646–48.
437 "I sat": Dodge, 55.

Part Five: The New El Dorado

441 "The people who come": J. Hittell (1863), 333–34.
441 "One man works hard": O. Lewis, 53.

17. Prometheus Unbound

445 "There were more": Phillips, 284.

446 "We were very much": G. Clark, 231–32.
448 "These shares": letter of May 30, 1868, Leland Stanford papers.
448 "It is the well settled policy": G. Clark, 280.
448–50 "You have been accredited . . . my home": ibid., 309–10.
450 "a dangerous rival": Daggett, 119.
450 "*We must name*": letter of Jan. 3, 1869, Leland Stanford papers.
452 "You are sending": Daggett, 257.
452 "He had only time": Norris, 49–51.
455–58 "a cavern . . . his own corpse": Brands (1999), 41–48.
459 "At the depth": Wright, 386.
460–62 "The city and all . . . generally found it": Twain, *Roughing It*, 306–8.
462–63 "I enjoyed . . . paid them": ibid., 419–20.
463–66 "Frequently we had . . . British Museum": Hargraves, 86–87, 91, 96, 111–16.
466 "Cottages are deserted . . . powerful auxiliary": Hughes, 563–55.
469 "George": Older and Older, 155.
471 "We chose gold": Bernstein, 250.
471 more gold was mined: *Encyclopedia Britannica* (1961), 10:481.
473 "If they dare": Brands (1995), 260–61.

18. American Dreamers

476 "You forget": Nevins (1955), 607.
476 "If I keep this free": Jessie Frémont memoirs, addendum.
477 "There were three churches": S. Royce, 139.
477 "My comrades very generally": J. Royce (1916), 126–27.
478 "purely aggressive": J. Royce (1886), 94.
478 "Frémont's League with the Devil": J. Royce (1970), 170.
478 "charming and courteous mendacity": ibid., 199.
478–79 "Nowhere else . . . on the Pacific Coast": J. Royce (1886), 2.
479 "of unusual intelligence . . . of their bereavement": Farkas, 64.
480 "I have remained": Perlot, 446.
481 "I will not accept . . . it is all hell": L. Lewis, 631–37.
482 "Gold digging is a lottery": Dillon, 332.

483 "Your hospitality": ibid., 345–46.

485 "If the Californians": Emparan, 140–41.

485 "Believe me . . . Let the wound heal": Rosenus, 233.

488 "the new new thing": M. Lewis, *The New New Thing*.

488 "vein of gold": Kaplan, 18.

488 "the largest legal creation": ibid., 16.

489 "We are on the brink": Bancroft, 6:119.

Bibliography

Unpublished manuscripts

Allan, John. Correspondence. Bancroft Library, University of California, Berkeley.

Aram, Joseph. Correspondence. Huntington Library, San Marino, California.

Averett, George Washington Gill. Correspondence. Huntington Library.

Bailey, Mary Stuart. Journal. Huntington Library.

Bishop. Edwin R. Correspondence. Bancroft Library.

Bliss, Seth. Correspondence. Huntington Library.

Brophy, John. Correspondence. Huntington Library.

Browning, Isaac. Correspondence. Bancroft Library.

Bunker, David. Letters. Nantucket Historical Association, Nantucket, Massachusetts.

Cary, Thomas G. Papers. Library of Congress.

Cochran, Charles. Diary. Huntington Library.

Cool, Peter. Journal. Huntington Library.

Copeland, Isaac. Correspondence. Bancroft Library.

Crosby, Elisha O. Correspondence. Huntington Library.

Delano, Ephraim. Correspondence. Huntington Library.

Denniston, William F. Journal. Huntington Library.

Dimon, Theodore. Contract. Huntington Library.

Dinsdale, Matthew. Correspondence. Bancroft Library.

Downie, William. Papers. Beinecke Library, Yale University.

Earl, Robert. Papers. Oregon Historical Society, Portland.

Eckley, Levi. Correspondence. Huntington Library.

Ellis, Charles H. Journal. Huntington Library.

Engle, Jacob H. Correspondence. Huntington Library.

Ewing, Thomas. Family papers. Library of Congress.

Fisher, Jacob. Correspondence. Bancroft Library.

Ford, Norman. Correspondence. Bancroft Library.

Frémont, Jessie Benton. Memoirs. Bancroft Library.

Frémont, John C. Correspondence. Bancroft Library.

Gardner, Daniel B. Papers. Library of Congress.

Gilman, Daniel. Correspondence. Beinecke Library.

Godard, Harlow Bacon. Correspondence. California State Library, Sacramento.

Goff, Selden. Correspondence. California State Library.

Gold Rush Letters. Martha's Vineyard Historical Society, Edgartown, Massachusetts.

Hanson, William. Correspondence. Bancroft Library.

Harvey, Charles Henry. Diary. Library of Congress.

Haun, Catherine Margaret. Papers. Huntington Library, San Marino, California.

Hill, Alonzo. Correspondence. Beinecke Library.

Howard, Barnett Allen. Papers. Library of Congress.

Jackson, Charles P. Correspondence. California State Library.

Jacobs, Enoch. Journal. Huntington Library.

Josselyn, Amos Pratt. Correspondence. California State Library.

Kerr, John M. Correspondence. California State Library.

Kessler, Frederick. Correspondence. California State Library.

Ketcham, Elias S. Diary. Huntington Library.

Lambert, John. Correspondence. Beinecke Library.

Lambert, John S. and John B. Letters. Beinecke Library.

Leonard, Albert. Correspondence. California State Library.

Martin, John L. Correspondence. California State Library.

Masterson, John. Papers. Bancroft Library.

McCulloch, Ben and Henry. Papers. Center for American History, University of Texas, Austin.

Mobley, C. C. Diary. Huntington Library.

Morehouse, Ransom. Correspondence. Bancroft Library.

Mulkey, Cyrenius. Papers. Oregon Historical Society.

Newell, William H. Correspondence. Huntington Library.

Norris, Albert. Correspondence. Bancroft Library.

Parrish, Susan Thompson. Papers. Huntington Library.

Pearl, Frank. Correspondence. Bancroft Library.

Pease, William C. Letters. Nantucket Historical Association.

Perry, James T. Correspondence. Huntington Library.

Pond, Ananias. Journal. Huntington Library.

Pownall, Joseph. Family papers. Huntington Library.

Purdy, J. H. Correspondence. Bancroft Library.

Rose, Preston Robinson. Correspondence. Center for American History, Austin.

Sarah, Bark. Papers. Martha's Vineyard Historical Society.

Sharp, John. Correspondence. Huntington Library.

Sherman, William T. Correspondence. Bancroft Library.

Spiegel, Henry. Correspondence. Bancroft Library.

Stanford, Jane. Papers. Green Library, Stanford University.

Stanford, Leland. Papers. Green Library.

Stone, John N. Journal. Huntington Library.

Thompson, Charles. Correspondence. Bancroft Library.

Townsend, Beeson. Correspondence. California State Library.

Townsend, D. Correspondence. Huntington Library.

Tracy, Frederick P. Correspondence. California State Library.

Vallejo, Mariano G. "Historical and Personal Memoirs Relating to Alta California." Translated by Earl R. Hewitt. Bancroft Library.

Van Dorn, Thomas J. Papers. Beinecke Library.

Walker, John. Correspondence. Bancroft Library.

Walter, W. W. Papers. Oregon Historical Society.

Ward, William. Account book. Huntington Library.

Warner, William. Correspondence. Bancroft Library.

Watson, George W. Bancroft Library.

Wells, William. Correspondence. California State Library.

Winchester, J. Correspondence. Bancroft Library.

Winston, W. G. Correspondence. Huntington Library.

Wood, Joseph. Diary. Huntington Library.

Published works

Adams, Charles F. Jr. "Railroad Inflation." *North American Review*, January 1869.

Adams, Charles F. Jr., and Henry Adams. *Chapters of Erie and Other Essays*. 1871. New York: Augustus M. Kelley, 1967.

Aldrich, Lorenzo D. *A Journal of the Overland Route to California*. 1851. Ann Arbor, Mich.: University Microfilms, 1966.

Ambrose, Stephen E. *Nothing Like It in the World: The Men Who Built the Transcontinental Railroad, 1863–1869*. New York: Simon & Schuster, 2000.

Archer, T. *Recollections of a Rambling Life*. Yokohama: Japan Gazette, 1897; Brisbane: Boolarong Publications, 1988.

Archivo y Biblioteca de la Secretaria de Hacienda. *Las Misiones de la Alta California*. Mexico City: Tipografía de la Oficina Impresora de Estampillas, 1914.

Bailey, Paul. *Sam Brannan and the California Mormons*. 2nd ed. Los Angeles: Westernlore Press, 1953.

Bain, David Haward. *Empire Express: Building the First Transcontinental Railroad*. New York: Viking, 1999.

Bancroft, Hubert Howe. *History of California*. 7 vols. Published as part of *The Works of Hubert Howe Bancroft*. San Francisco: The History Company, 1882–90.

Barry, T. A., and B. A. Patten. *Men and Memories of San Francisco, in the Spring of '50*. San Francisco: A. L. Bancroft, 1873.

Barth, Gunter. *Bitter Strength: A History of the Chinese in the United States, 1850–1870*. Cambridge, Mass.: Harvard University Press, 1964.

Bateson, Charles. *Gold Fleet for California: Forty-Niners from Australia and New Zealand*. Sydney: Ure Smith, 1963.

Beckwourth, James P. *The Life and Adventures of James P. Beckwourth, as told to Thomas D. Bonner*. Edited by Delmont R. Oswald. Lincoln: University of Nebraska Press, 1972.

Beilharz, Edwin A., and Carlos U. López, eds. and translators. *We Were 49ers!: Chilean Accounts of the California Gold Rush*. Pasadena, Calif.: Ward Ritchie Press, 1976.

Beneman, William, ed. *A Year of Mud and Gold: San Francisco in Letters and Diaries, 1849–1850*. Lincoln: University of Nebraska Press, 1999.

Benton, Thomas Hart. *Thirty Years' View, or a History of the Working of the American Government for Thirty Years, from 1820 to 1850*. 2 volumes. New York: D. Appleton & Co., 1854–56.

Bernstein, Peter L. *The Power of Gold: The History of an Obsession*. New York: John Wiley & Sons, 2000.

Bigler, Henry William. *Bigler's Chronicle of the West: The Conquest of California, Discovery of Gold, and Mormon Settlement as Reflected in Henry William Bigler's Diaries*. Edited by Erwin G. Gudde. Berkeley: University of California Press, 1962.

Blodgett, Peter J. *Land of Golden Dreams: California in the Gold Rush Decade, 1848–1858*. San Marino, Calif.: Huntington Library, 1999.

Boessenecker, John. *Gold Dust and Gunsmoke: Tales of Gold Rush Outlaws, Gunfighters, Lawmen, and Vigilantes*. New York: John Wiley & Sons, 1999.

Borthwick, J. D. *The Gold Hunters*. 1857. (Originally published as *Three Years in California*.) New York: Macmillan, 1917.

Bosqui, Edward. *Memoirs*. San Francisco (no publisher given), 1904.

Bowman, J. N. "Driving the Last Spike at Promontory, 1869." *California Historical Quarterly*, June 1957.

Boyle, Robert W. *Gold: History and Genesis of Deposits*. New York: Van Nostrand Reinhold, 1987.

Brands, H. W. *Masters of Enterprise*. New York: Free Press, 1999.

———. *The Reckless Decade: America in the 1890s*. New York: St. Martin's Press, 1995.

Brechin, Gary. *Imperial San Francisco: Urban Power, Earthly Ruin*. Berkeley: University of California Press, 1999.

Brewer, William H. *Up and Down California in 1860–1864*. 1930. Berkeley: University of California Press, 1966.

Brown, John H. *Reminiscences and Incidents of the Early Days of San Francisco*. San Francisco: Mission Journal Publishing Co., 1886.

Browne, J. Ross. *J. Ross Browne: His Letters, Journals and Writings*. Edited by Lina Fergusson Browne. Albuquerque: University of New Mexico Press, 1969.

———. *J. Ross Browne's Illustrated Mining Adventures: California and Nevada, 1863–1865*. Balboa Island, Calif.: Paisano Press, 1961.

———. *Resources of the Pacific Slope*. New York: D. Appleton & Co., 1869.

Browning, Peter, ed. *To the Golden Shore: America Goes to California—1849*. Lafayette, Calif.: Great West Books, 1995.

Bruff, J. Goldsborough. *Gold Rush: The Journals, Drawings, and Other Papers of J. Goldsborough Bruff*. Edited by Georgia Willis Read and Ruth Gaines. New York: Columbia University Press, 1949.

Buck, Franklin A. A *Yankee Trader in the Gold Rush: The Letters of Franklin A. Buck*. Compiled by Katherine A. White. Boston: Houghton Mifflin, 1930.

Buffum, E. Gould. *Six Months in the Gold Mines*. Edited by John W. Caughey. No place given: Ward Ritchie Press, 1959.

Bunnell, Lafayette Houghton. *Discovery of the Yosemite and the Indian War of 1851 Which Led to That Event*. Los Angeles: G. W. Gerlicher, 1911.

Caughey, John Walton. *The California Gold Rush*. Originally published as *Gold is the Cornerstone*, 1948. Berkeley: University of California Press, 1975.

Christman, Enos. *One Man's Gold: The Letters and Journals of a Forty-Niner*. Edited by Florence Morrow Christman. New York: Whittlesey House, 1930.

Clark, George T. *Leland Stanford*. Stanford, Calif.: Stanford University Press, 1931.

Clarke, Dwight L. *William Tecumseh Sherman: Gold Rush Banker*. San Francisco: California Historical Society, 1969.

Clendenning, John. *The Life and Thought of Josiah Royce*. Rev. ed. Nashville, Tenn.: Vanderbilt University Press, 1999.

Cogswell, Moses. *The Gold Rush Diary of Moses Cogswell of New Hampshire*. Edited by Elmer Munson Hunt. Concord: New Hampshire Historical Society, no date given.

Colton, Walter. *Three Years in California*. New York: A. S. Barnes & Co., 1850.

Crampton, Charles Gregory. "The Opening of the Mariposa Mining Region, 1849–1859, with Particular Reference to the Mexican Land Grant of John Charles Frémont." Berkeley: University of California dissertation, 1941.

Crosby, Elisha O. *Memoirs of Elisha Oscar Crosby: Reminiscences of California and Guatemala from 1849 to 1864*. San Marino, Calif.: Huntington Library, 1945.

Cutler, Carl C. *Greyhounds of the Sea: The Story of the American Clipper Ship*. Annapolis, Md.: United States Naval Institute, 1930.

Daggett, Stuart. *Chapters on the History of the Southern Pacific*. New York: Ronald Press, 1922.

Dana, Richard H. Jr. *Two Years Before the Mast*. 1840. New York: Heritage Press, 1941.

Davis, Stephen Chapin. *California Gold Rush Merchant: The Journal of Stephen Chapin Davis*. Edited by Benjamin B. Richards. San Marino, Calif.: Huntington Library, 1956.

Delano, Alonzo. *Alonzo Delano's California Correspondence: Being Letters Hitherto Uncollected from the Ottawa (Illinois) Free Trader and the New Orleans True Delta, 1849–1852*. Edited by Irving McKee. Sacramento: Sacramento Book Collectors' Club, 1952.

Derbec, Etienne. *A French Journalist in the California Gold Rush: The Letters of Etienne Derbec*. Edited by A. P. Nasatir. Georgetown, Calif.: Talisman Press, 1964.

Dillon, Richard H. *J. Ross Browne: Confidential Agent in Old California*. Norman: University of Oklahoma Press, 1965.

———. *Fool's Gold: The Decline and Fall of Captain John Sutter of California*. New York: Coward-McCann, 1967.

Dodge, Grenville M. *How We Built the Union Pacific Railway, and Other Railway Papers and Addresses*. c. 1911. Denver: Sage Books, 1965.

Donald, David Herbert. *Lincoln*. New York: Random House, 1995.

Duane, Dutch Charley. *Against the Vigilantes: The Recollections of Dutch Charley Duane*. Edited by John Boessenecker. Norman: University of Oklahoma Press, 1999.

Durham, Walter T. *Volunteer Forty-Niners: Tennesseeans and the California Gold Rush*. Nashville: Vanderbilt University Press, 1997.

Eccleston, Robert. *The Mariposa Indian War, 1850–1851: Diaries of Robert Eccleston: The California Gold Rush, Yosemite, and the High Sierra*. Edited by C. Gregory Crampton. Salt Lake City: University of Utah Press, 1957.

Egan, Ferol. *The El Dorado Trail: The Story of the Gold Rush Routes across Mexico*. Lincoln: University of Nebraska Press, 1970.

Eichengreen, Barry. *Elusive Stability: Essays in the History of International Finance, 1919–1939*. Cambridge, England: Cambridge University Press, 1990.

———. *Globalizing Capital: A History of the International Monetary System*. Princeton, N.J.: Princeton University Press, 1996.

Ellis, Henry Hiram. *From the Kennebec to California: Reminiscences of a California Pioneer*. Selected by Lucy Ellis Riddell. Edited by Laurence R. Cook. Los Angeles: Warren F. Lewis, 1959.

Emparan, Madie Brown. *The Vallejos of California*. San Francisco: Gleeson Library Associates of the University of San Francisco, 1968.

Fairchild, Lucius. *California Letters of Lucius Fairchild*. Edited by Joseph Schafer. Madison: State Historical Society of Wisconsin, 1931.

Farkas, Lani Ah Tye. *Bury My Bones in America: The Saga of a Chinese Family in California, 1852–1996, from San Francisco to the Sierra Gold Mines*. Nevada City, Calif.: Carl Mautz Publishing, 1998.

Farnham, Eliza W. *California In-Doors and Out: Or How We Farm, Mine, and Live Generally in the Golden State*. New York: Dix, Edwards & Co., 1856.

Farnham, Thomas Jefferson, *Travels in California*. 1855. Oakland: Biobooks, 1947.

Fellman, Michael. *Citizen Sherman: A Life of William Tecumseh Sherman*. New York: Random House, 1995.

Fiero, Bill. *Geology of the Great Basin*. Reno: University of Nevada Press, 1986.

Finkelman, Paul. "The Law of Slavery and Freedom in California, 1848–1860." *California Western Law Review* 17 (1981): 437–64.

Franklin, William E. "The Archy Case: The California Supreme Court Refuses to Free a Slave." *Pacific Historical Review* 32 (1963): 137–54.

Freehling, William W. *The Road to Disunion: Secessionists at Bay, 1776–1854*. New York: Oxford University Press, 1990.

Frémont, Jessie Benton. *A Year of American Travel: Narrative of Personal Experience*. 1878. San Francisco: Book Club of California, 1960.

———. *The Letters of Jessie Benton Frémont*. Edited by Pamela Herr and Mary Lee Spence. Urbana, Ill.: University of Illinois Press, 1993.

Frémont, John Charles. *Memoirs of My Life*. Chicago: Belford, Clarke & Co., 1887.

———. *The Expeditions of John Charles Frémont*. 3 vols. plus maps. Edited by Donald Jackson and Mary Lee Spence. Urbana, Ill.: University of Illinois Press, 1970–84.

Friedman, Milton, and Anna Jacobson Schwartz. *A Monetary History of the United States, 1867–1960*. Princeton, N.J.: Princeton University Press, 1963.

Gasparrini, Claudia. *Gold and Other Precious Metals*. Berlin: Springer-Verlag, 1993.

Gay, Theressa. *James W. Marshall: The Discoverer of California Gold*. Georgetown, Calif.: Talisman Press, 1967.

Gerstäcker, Frederick. *Gerstäcker's Travels: Rio de Janeiro, Buenos Ayres, Ride through the Pampas, Winter Journey across the Cordilleras, Chili, Valparaiso, California and the Gold Fields*. London: T. Nelson & Sons, 1854.

Glasscock, C. B. *Big Bonanza: The Story of the Comstock Lode*. Portland, Ore.: Binfords & Mort, 1931.

Gray, Jack. *Rebellions and Revolutions: China from the 1800s to the 1980s*. Oxford, England: Oxford University Press, 1990.

Greeley, Horace. *An Overland Journey from New York to San Francisco in the Summer of 1859*. 1860. Edited by Charles T. Duncan. New York: Alfred A. Knopf, 1964.

Greer, Richard A. "California Gold: Some Reports to Hawaii." *Hawaiian Journal of History* 4 (1970): 157–73.

Gregson, Eliza Marshall, and James Gregson. *The Gregson Memoirs*. San Francisco: L. R. Kennedy, 1940.

Gudde, Erwin G. *California Gold Camps: A Geographical and Historical Dictionary of Camps, Towns, and Localities Where Gold was Found and Mined; Wayside Stations and Trading Centers*. Edited by Elisabeth K. Gudde. Berkeley: University of California Press, 1975.

Gunn, Lewis C., and Elizabeth Le Breton Gunn. *Records of a California Family: Journals and Letters of Lewis C. Gunn and Elizabeth Le Breton Gunn*. Edited by Ann Lee Marston. San Diego: no publisher given, 1928.

Hamilton, Holman. *Prologue to Conflict: The Crisis and Compromise of 1850*. New York: W. W. Norton, 1966.

Hargraves, Edward Hammond. *Australia and Its Gold Fields*. London: H. Ingram & Co., 1855.

Harpending, Asbury. *The Great Diamond Hoax, and Other Stirring Incidents in the Life of Asbury Harpending*. Edited by James H. Wilkins. Norman: University of Oklahoma Press, 1958.

Harris, Benjamin Butler. *The Gila Trail: The Texas Argonauts and the California Gold Rush*. Edited by Richard H. Dillon. Norman: University of Oklahoma Press, 1960.

Harte, Bret. *Bret Harte's California: Letters to the* Springfield Republican *and* Christian Register, *1866–67*. Edited by Gary Scharnhorst. Albuquerque: University of New Mexico Press, 1990.

Hartford Union Mining and Trading Company. *Around the Horn in '49: Journal of the Hartford Union Mining and Trading Company*. Printed on board the *Henry Lee* by L. J. Hall, 1849.

Heiskell, Hugh Brown. *A Forty-Niner from Tennessee: The Diary of Hugh Brown Heiskell*. Edited by Edward M. Steel. Knoxville: University of Tennessee Press, 1998.

Helper, Hinton R. *The Land of Gold: Reality versus Fiction*. Baltimore: Henry Taylor, 1855.

Herr, Pamela. *Jessie Benton Frémont*. New York: Franklin Watts, 1987.

Hill, Mary. *Geology of the Sierra Nevada*. Berkeley: University of California Press, 1975.

———. *Gold: The California Story*. Berkeley: University of California Press, 1999.

Hittell, John S. *A History of the City of San Francisco, and Incidentally of the State of California*. San Francisco: A. L. Bancroft & Co., 1878.

———. *The Resources of California, Comprising Agriculture, Mining, Geography, Climate, Commerce, etc. etc. and the Past and Future Development of the State*. San Francisco: A. Roman & Co., 1863.

Hittell, Theodore H. *History of California*. 4 volumes. San Francisco: Pacific Press and N. J. Stone & Co., 1885–97.

Hofsommer, Don L. *The Southern Pacific, 1901–1985*. College Station, Tex.: Texas A&M University Press, 1986.

Holliday, J. S. *Rush for Riches: Gold Fever and the Making of California*. Oakland and Berkeley: Oakland Museum of California and University of California Press, 1999.

———. *The World Rushed In: The California Gold Rush Experience*. New York: Simon & Schuster, 1981. (This volume reproduces diaries and some letters of William Swain.)

Hoover, Herbert. *The Memoirs of Herbert Hoover*. 3 volumes. New York: Macmillan, 1951–52.

Howe, Octavius T., and Frederick C. Matthews. *American Clipper Ships, 1833–1858*. 1926–27. New York: Dover, 1986.

Hughes, Robert. *The Fatal Shore: The Epic of Australia's Founding*. New York: Alfred A. Knopf, 1987.

Hunt, Charles B. *Death Valley: Geology, Ecology, Archaeology*. Berkeley: University of California Press, 1975.

Hurtado, Albert L. *Indian Survival on the California Frontier*. New Haven, Conn.: Yale University Press, 1988.

———. *Intimate Frontiers: Sex, Gender, and Culture in Old California*. Albuquerque: University of New Mexico Press, 1999.

Hutchings, James M. *Seeking the Elephant: James M. Hutchings' Journal of His Overland Trek to California, Including His Voyage to America, 1848, and His*

Letters from the Mother Lode. Edited by Shirley Sargent. Glendale, Calif.: Arthur H. Clark Co., 1980.

Hutchings' California Magazine. Reprinted as *Scenes of Wonder & Curiosity from Hutchings' California Magazine, 1856–1861*. Edited by R. R. Olmsted. Berkeley, Calif.: Howell-North, 1962.

Ingalls, Eleazar Stillman. *Journal of a Trip to California by the Overland Route Across the Plains in 1850–51*. Fairfield, Wash.: Galleon Press, 1979.

Jackson, Donald Dale. *Gold Dust*. New York: Alfred A. Knopf, 1980.

Jackson, Joseph Henry, ed. *Gold Rush Album*. New York: Charles Scribner's Sons, 1949.

Jefferson, T. H. *Map of the Emigrant Road from Independence, Mo., to San Francisco, California*. 1849. Edited by George R. Stewart. San Francisco: California Historical Society, 1945.

Johnson, Susan Lee. *Roaring Camp: The Social World of the California Gold Rush*. New York: W. W. Norton, 2000.

Johnson, Theodore T. *Sights in the Gold Region, and Scenes by the Way*. New York: Baker & Scribner, 1849.

Kaplan, David A. *The Silicon Boys and Their Valley of Dreams*. New York: William Morrow, 1999.

Kelley, Robert L. *Gold vs. Grain: The Hydraulic Mining Controversy in California's Sacramento Valley: A Chapter in the Decline of the Concept of Laissez Faire*. Glendale, Calif.: Arthur H. Clark Company, 1959.

Kelly, William. *An Excursion to California over the Prairie, Rocky Mountains, and Great Sierra Nevada, with a Stroll Through the Diggings and Ranches of That Country*. 2 vols. 1851. New York: Arno Press, 1973.

Kemble, John Haskell. *The Panama Route, 1848–1869*. Columbia: University of South Carolina Press, 1990.

Kinder, Gary. *Ship of Gold in the Deep Blue Sea*. New York: Atlantic Monthly Press, 1998.

Kip, Leonard. *California Sketches, with Recollections of the Gold Mines*. Los Angeles: N. A. Kovach, 1946.

Klein, Maury. *Union Pacific: Birth of a Railroad, 1862–1893*. New York: Doubleday, 1987.

Langworthy, Franklin. *Scenery of the Plains, Mountains and Mines*. 1855. Edited by Paul C. Phillips. Princeton, N.J.: Princeton University Press, 1932.

Lapp, Rudolph M. *Archy Lee: A California Fugitive Slave Case*. San Francisco: Book Club of California, 1969.

———. *Blacks in Gold Rush California*. New Haven, Conn.: Yale University Press, 1977.

Larkin, Thomas Oliver. *The Larkin Papers: Personal, Business, and Official Correspondence of Thomas Oliver Larkin, Merchant and United States Consul in California*. Edited by George P. Hammond. 11 volumes. Berkeley: University of California Press, 1951–68.

Latta, Frank F. *Joaquín Murrieta and His Horse Gangs*. Santa Cruz: Bear State Books, 1980.

Lecouvreur, Frank. *From East Prussia to the Golden Gate: Letters and Diary of the California Pioneer*. Edited by Josephine Rosana Lecouvreur. Translated by Julius C. Behnke. New York: Angelina Book Concern, 1906.

Letts, J. M. *California Illustrated: Including a Description of the Panama and Nicaragua Routes*. New York: R. T. Young, 1853.

Levy, Joann. *They Saw the Elephant: Women in the California Gold Rush*. Hamden, Conn.: Archon Books, 1990.

Lewis, Lloyd. *Sherman: Fighting Prophet*. New York: Harcourt, Brace, 1932.

Lewis, Michael. *The New New Thing: A Silicon Valley Story*. New York: W.W. Norton, 2000.

Lewis, Oscar. *Sea Routes to the Gold Fields: The Migration by Water to California in 1849–1852*. New York: Alfred A. Knopf, 1949.

———. *The Big Four: The Story of Huntington, Stanford, Hopkins, and Crocker, and of the Building of the Central Pacific*. New York: Alfred A. Knopf, 1938.

Lienhard, Heinrich. *A Pioneer at Sutter's Fort, 1846–1850: The Adventures of Heinrich Lienhard*. From the 1898 German edition. Translated and edited by Marguerite Eyer Wilbur. Los Angeles: The Calafia Society, 1941.

López Urrutia, Carlos. *Episodios Chilenos en California, 1849–1860*. Valparaiso: Ediciones Universitarias de Valparaiso, 1975.

Lotchin, Roger W. *San Francisco, 1846–1856: From Hamlet to City*. New York: Oxford University Press, 1974.

Manly, William Lewis. *Death Valley in '49*. Edited by Milo Milton Quaife. Chicago: R. R. Donnelley and Sons, 1927.

Marks, Paula Mitchell. *Precious Dust: The American Gold Rush Era, 1848–1900*. New York: William Morrow, 1994.

Marryat, Frank. *Mountains and Molehills, or, Recollections of a Burnt Journal.* 1855. Reprint: Philadelphia: J. B. Lippincott, 1962.

Marszalek, John E. *Sherman: A Soldier's Passion for Order.* New York: Vintage Books, 1994.

Massey, Ernest de. *A Frenchman in the Gold Rush: The Journal of Ernest de Massey, Argonaut of 1849.* Translated by Marguerite Eyer Wilbur. San Francisco: California Historical Society, 1927.

McKittrick, Myrtle M. *Vallejo: Son of California.* Portland: Binford & Mort, 1944.

McLeod, Alexander. *Pigtails and Gold Dust: A Panorama of Chinese Life in Early California.* Caldwell, Idaho: Caxton Printers, 1947.

M'Collum, William. *California as I Saw It: Pencillings by the Way of Its Gold and Gold Diggers, and Incidents of Travel by Land and Water.* Edited by Dale L. Morgan. Los Gatos, Calif.: Talisman Press, 1960.

McGowan, Edward. *Narrative of Edward McGowan, including a Full Account of the Author's Adventures and Perils while Persecuted by the San Francisco Vigilance Committee of 1856.* 1857. San Francisco: Thomas C. Russell, 1917.

McPhee, John. *Assembling California.* New York: Farrar, Straus and Giroux, 1993.

———. *Basin and Range.* New York: Farrar, Straus and Giroux, 1981.

Megquier, Mary Jane. *Apron Full of Gold: The Letters of Mary Jane Megquier from San Francisco, 1849–1856.* Edited by Robert Glass Cleveland. San Marino: Huntington Library, 1949.

Monaghan, Jay. *Australians and the Gold Rush: California and Down Under, 1849–1854.* Berkeley: University of California Press, 1966.

———. *Chile, Peru, and the California Gold Rush of 1849.* Berkeley: University of California Press, 1973.

Moorman, Madison Berryman. *The Journal of Madison Berryman Moorman.* Edited by Irene D. Paden. San Francisco: California Historical Society, 1948.

Morgan, Dale L. *The Humboldt: Highroad of the West.* New York: Farrar & Rinehart, 1943.

Morison, James. *By Sea to San Francisco: The Journal of Dr. James Morison.* Edited by Lonnie J. White and William R. Gillaspie. Memphis: Memphis State University Press, 1977.

Morrell, W. P. *The Gold Rushes.* New York: Macmillan, 1941.

Myers, John Myers. *San Francisco's Reign of Terror.* Garden City, N.Y.: Doubleday, 1966.

Myres, Sandra L., ed. *Ho for California! Women's Overland Diaries from the Huntington Library*. San Marino, Calif.: Huntington Library, 1980.

Nasatir, Abraham P. *The French in the California Gold Rush*. New York: Franco-American Pamphlet Series, 1934.

———. *French Activities in California: An Archival Calendar-Guide*. Stanford, Calif.: Stanford University Press, 1945.

Nasaw, David. *The Chief: The Life of William Randolph Hearst*. Boston: Houghton Mifflin, 2000.

Nash, George H. *The Life of Herbert Hoover*. 3 volumes. New York: W.W. Norton, 1983–96.

Navarro, Ramón Gil. *The Gold Rush Diary of Ramón Gil Navarro*. Edited and translated by María del Carmen Ferreyra and David S. Reher. Lincoln: University of Nebraska Press, 2000.

Nevins, Allan. *Frémont: Pathmarker of the West*. New York: Longman, Green & Co., 1955.

———. *Frémont: The West's Greatest Adventurer*. New York: Harper & Brothers, 1928.

Norris, Frank. *The Octopus: A Story of California*. New York: Doubleday, Page & Co., 1901.

Norris, Robert M., and Robert W. Webb. *Geology of California*. 2nd ed. New York: John Wiley & Sons, 1990.

Older, Mr. and Mrs. Frémont. *George Hearst: California Pioneer*. Los Angeles: Westernlore, 1966.

Osio, Antonio María. *The History of Alta California: A Memoir of Mexican California*. Translated and edited by Rose Marie Beebe and Robert M. Senkewicz. Madison: University of Wisconsin Press, 1996.

Paul, Rodman W. *California Gold: The Beginning of Mining in the Far West*. Cambridge, Mass.: Harvard University Press, 1947.

Paul, Rodman W., ed. *The California Gold Discovery: Sources, Documents, Accounts and Memoirs Relating to the Discovery of Gold at Sutter's Mill*. Georgetown, Calif.: Talisman Press, 1966.

Pérez Rosales, Vicente. *California Adventure*. Translated from the Spanish original—*Recuerdos del Pasado*—by Edwin S. Morby and Arturo Torres-Rioseco. San Francisco: Book Club of California, 1947.

Perlot, Jean-Nicolas. *Gold Seeker: Adventures of a Belgian Argonaut during the Gold Rush Years*. Translated by Helen Harding Bretnor. Edited and introduced by Howard R. Lamar. New Haven, Conn.: Yale University Press, 1985.

Peterson, Merrill D. *The Great Triumvirate: Webster, Clay, and Calhoun*. New York: Oxford University Press, 1987.

Pfeiffer, Ida. *A Lady's Visit to California, 1853*. 1856. Oakland: Biobooks, 1950.

Phillips, Catherine Coffin. *Jessie Benton Frémont: A Woman Who Made History*. San Francisco: John Henry Nash, 1935.

Pitt, Leonard. *The Decline of the Californios: A Social History of the Spanish-Speaking Californians, 1846–1890*. Berkeley: University of California Press, 1970.

Potter, David M. *The Impending Crisis, 1848–1861*. New York: Harper & Row, 1976.

Procter, Ben. *William Randolph Hearst: The Early Years, 1863–1910*. New York: Oxford University Press, 1998.

Report of the Debates in the Convention of California on the Formation of the State Constitution, in September and October, 1849. Edited by J. Ross Browne. Washington: John T. Towers, 1850. Reprinted New York: Arno Press, 1973.

Richman, Irving Berdine. *California under Spain and Mexico, 1535–1847*. Boston: Houghton Mifflin, 1911.

———. *California under Spain and Mexico, 1535–1847*. Boston: Houghton Mifflin, 1911.

Riesenberg, Felix. *Cape Horn*. New York: Dodd, Mead, 1939.

Roberts, Brian. *American Alchemy: The California Gold Rush and Middle-Class Culture*. Chapel Hill: University of North Carolina Press, 2000.

Robinson, Judith. *The Hearsts: An American Dynasty*. Newark: University of Delaware Press, 1981.

Rohrbough, Malcolm J. *Days of Gold: The California Gold Rush and the American Nation*. Berkeley: University of California Press, 1997.

Rosenus, Alan. *General M. G. Vallejo and the Advent of the Americans: A Biography*. Albuquerque: University of New Mexico Press, 1995.

Royce, Josiah. *California: From the Conquest in 1846 to the Second Vigilance Committee in San Francisco: A Study of American Character*. Boston: Houghton Mifflin, 1886, 1914.

———. *The Hope of the Great Community*. New York: Macmillan, 1916.

———. *The Letters of Josiah Royce*. Edited by John Clendenning. Chicago: University of Chicago Press, 1970.

Royce, Sarah. *A Frontier Lady: Recollections of the Gold Rush and Early California*. Edited by Ralph Henry Gabriel. New Haven, Conn.: Yale University Press, 1932.

Sawyer, Lorenzo. *Way Sketches: Containing Incidents of Travel across the Plains from St. Joseph to California*. Selections from the *Wisconsin Family Visitor*. No publisher or date given.

Scherer, James A. B. *The First Forty-Niner, and the Story of the Golden Tea-Caddy*. New York: Minton, Balch & Co., 1925.

Schmidbaur, Hubert, ed. *Gold: Progress in Chemistry, Biochemistry and Technology*. Chichester, England: John Wiley & Sons, 1999.

Schultz, Charles R. *Forty-Niners 'Round the Horn*. Columbia: University of South Carolina Press, 1999.

Scroggs, William O. *Filibusters and Financiers: The Story of William Walker and His Associates*. New York: Russell & Russell, 1916.

Shaw, Pringle. *Ramblings in California: Containing a Description of the Country, Life at the Mines, State of Society, &c.* Toronto: James Bain, no date given.

Shaw, William. *Golden Dreams and Waking Realities; Being the Adventures of a Gold-Seeker in California and the Pacific Islands*. 1851. New York: Arno Press, 1973.

Sherman, William Tecumseh, and John Sherman. *The Sherman Letters: Correspondence Between General and Senator Sherman from 1837 to 1891*. Edited by Rachel Sherman Thorndike. New York: Charles Scribner's Sons, 1894.

Sherman, William Tecumseh. *Home Letters of General Sherman*. Edited by M. A. DeWolfe Howe. New York: Charles Scribner's Sons, 1909.

———. *Memoirs of General W. T. Sherman*. 1875. New York: Library of America, 1990.

Shinn, Charles Howard. *Mining Camps: A Study in American Frontier Government*. New York: Alfred A. Knopf, 1948.

Shirley, Dame (Louise Amelia Knapp). *California in 1851 [–1852]: The Letters of Dame Shirley*. Edited by Carl I. Wheat. San Francisco: Grabhorn Press, 1933.

Sinclair, John. *Geological Aspects of Mining*. London: Sir Isaac Pitman & Sons, 1958.

Smith, Azariah. *The Gold Discovery Journal of Azariah Smith*. Edited by David L. Bigler. Salt Lake City: University of Utah Press, 1990.

Snyder, Eugene E. *Early Portland: Stump-Town Triumphant*. Portland, Ore.: Binfords & Mort, 1970.

Soulé, Frank; John H. Gihon; and James Nisbet. *The Annals of San Francisco, Together with the Continuation, Through 1855*. 1855. Palo Alto, Calif.: Lewis Osborne, 1966. Although this was a joint work, Soulé was the lead author and moving spirit; for the sake of simplicity in the present text, statements made in the *Annals* have been attributed to him.

Spence, Jonathan D. *The Search for Modern China*. New York: W.W. Norton, 1990.

Spoehr, Alexander. "Hawaii and the Gold Rush: George Allan of the Hudson's Bay Company Reports on His 1848 Pursuit of Captain John Sutter." *Hawaiian Journal of History* 26 (1992): 123–32.

Starr, Kevin. *Americans and the California Dream, 1850–1915*. New York: Oxford University Press, 1973.

Starr, Kevin, and Richard J. Orsi, eds. *Rooted in Barbarous Soil: People, Culture, and Community in Gold Rush California*. Berkeley: University of California Press, 2000.

Stellman, Louis J. *Sam Brannan: Builder of San Francisco*. New York: Exposition Press, 1953.

Stephens, L. Dow. *Life Sketches of a Jayhawker of '49*. San Jose, Calif.: Nolta Bros., 1916.

Sutherland, C. H. V. *Gold: Its Beauty, Power and Allure*. New York: McGraw-Hill, 1959.

Sutter, John A. *New Helvetia Diary: A Record of Events Kept by John A. Sutter and His Clerks at New Helvetia, California, from September 9, 1845, to May 25, 1848*. San Francisco: Grabhorn Press, 1939.

Swan, John A. *A Trip to the Gold Mines of California in 1848*. Edited by John A. Hussey. San Francisco: Book Club of California, 1960.

Taylor, Bayard. *Eldorado, or, Adventures in the Path of Empire*. 1850. Glorieta, N.M.: Rio Grande Press, 1967.

Taylor, R. R. *Seeing the Elephant: Letters of R. R. Taylor, Forty-Niner*. Edited by John Walton Caughey. No place given: Ward Ritchie Press, 1951.

Timberlake, Richard H. *Monetary Policy in the United States: An Intellectual and Institutional History*. Chicago: University of Chicago Press, 1993.

Tocqueville, Alexis de. *Democracy in America*. 1835–40. Edited by J. P. Mayer. Translated by George Lawrence. New York: HarperCollins, 1988.

Twain, Mark, and Charles Dudley Warner. *The Gilded Age: A Tale of Today*. 1873. Edited by Ward Just. New York: Oxford University Press, 1996.

Twain, Mark. *Mark Twain's Letters*. 2 vols. Edited by Albert Bigelow Paine. New York: Harper & Bros., 1917.

———. *Mark Twain's San Francisco*. Edited by Bernard Taper. New York: McGraw-Hill, 1963.

———. *Roughing It*. 1871. Hartford, Conn.: American Publishing Co., 1891.

Tyson, James L. *Diary of a Physician in California: Being the Results of Actual Experience, including Notes of the Journey by Land and Water, and Observations on the Climate, Soil, Resources of the Country, etc*. New York: D. Appleton & Co., 1850.

Unruh, John D. Jr. *The Plains Across: The Overland Emigrants and the Trans-Mississippi West, 1840–60*. Urbana: University of Illinois Press, 1978.

Van Dorn, William G. *Oceanography and Seamanship*. New York: Dodd, Mead, 1974.

Van Nostrand, Jeanne, and Edith M. Coulter. *California Pictorial: A History in Contemporary Pictures, 1786 to 1859*. Berkeley: University of California Press, 1948.

Varley, James F. *The Legend of Joaquín Murrieta: California's Gold Rush Bandit*. Twin Falls, Idaho: Big Lost River Press, 1995.

Villiers, Alan. *The War with Cape Horn*. New York: Charles Scribner's Sons, 1971.

Walker, William. *The War in Nicaragua*. Mobile, Ala.: S. H. Goetzel & Co., 1860 (republished by Blaine Ethridge Books, Detroit, 1971).

Ware, Joseph E. *The Emigrants' Guide to California*. 1849. Edited by John Caughey. New York: Da Capo Press, 1972.

Warren, T. Robinson. *Dust and Foam; or, Three Oceans and Two Continents; Being Ten Years' Wanderings in Mexico, South America, Sandwich Islands, the East and West Indies, China, Philippines, Australia and Polynesia*. New York: Charles Scribner, 1859.

Wells, William V. *Walker's Expedition to Nicaragua: A History of the Central American War; and Sonora and Kinney Expeditions.* New York: Stringer & Townsend, 1856.

Whipple, A. B. C. *The Challenge.* New York: William Morrow, 1987.

Wienphal, Robert W., ed. *A Gold Rush Voyage on the Bark Orion from Boston around Cape Horn to San Francisco, 1849–1850.* Glendale, Calif.: Arthur H. Clarke Co., 1978.

Williams, Mary Floyd. *History of the San Francisco Committee of Vigilance of 1851: A Study of Social Control on the California Frontier in the Days of the Gold Rush.* 1921. New York: Da Capo Press, 1969.

Wilson, Elinor. *Jim Beckwourth: Black Mountain Man and War Chief of the Crows.* Norman: University of Oklahoma Press, 1972.

Wilson, Luzena Stanley. *Memories Recalled Years Later for Her Daughter Corennah Wilson Wright.* Mills College, Calif.: Eucalyptus Press, 1937.

Woods, Daniel B. *Sixteen Months at the Gold Diggings.* New York: Harper & Bros., 1851.

Wright, William ("Dan De Quille"). *The Big Bonanza: An Authentic Account of the Discovery, History, and Working of the World-Renowned Comstock Lode of Nevada.* Reprint of the 1876 edition. Introduction by Oscar Lewis. New York: Alfred A. Knopf, 1947.

Wyman, Walker D., ed. *California Emigrant Letters.* New York: Bookman Associates, 1952.

Illustration Credits

Sutter's Fort: Library of Congress
The mill at Coloma: California State Library
North America circa 1852: map by Laura Hartman Maestro
Ready for anything: California State Library
Entering the mountains: Library of Congress
The Challenge: Peabody Essex Museum
Jean-Nicolas Perlot: Bancroft Library
A long tom: California State Library
Chinese miners: California State Library
California in the 1850's: map by Laura Hartman Maestro
Home in the gold country: California State Library
A major river operation: Library of Congress
Water cannons: Bancroft Library
Comparing notes: California State Library
Abandoned ships: San Francisco Maritime Historical Park
Sam Brannan: Bancroft Library
San Francisco after the great fire of 1851: Library of Congress
John Frémont: Library of Congress
Jessie Frémont: Southwest Museum
William Sherman: Library of Congress
Leland Stanford: Bancroft Library
George Hearst: Bancroft Library
Mariano Vallejo: Bancroft Library
John Sutter: California State Library
James Marshall: California State Library

Index

Acknowledgments

The author would like to thank all the archivists and librarians who made the research for this book such a pleasure. The staffs at the Bancroft Library, the Huntington Library, the California State Library, the Beinecke Library, the Library of Congress, the California Historical Society, the Martha's Vineyard Historical Society, the Nantucket Historical Association, the Oregon Historical Society, the Peabody Essex Museum, the San Francisco Maritime National Historical Park, the Southwest Museum, Stanford University's Green Library, the Evans Library at Texas A&M University, and the Center for American History and the Perry-Castaneda Library at the University of Texas at Austin were thoroughly professional and most helpful.

The author would also like to thank Roger Scholl, William Thomas, and Chava Boylan of Doubleday, and Jim Hornfischer of Hornfischer Literary Management.